TWO TREATISES

ON THE ACCENTUATION
OF THE OLD TESTAMENT

THE LIBRARY

OF

BIBLICAL STUDIES

Edited by

Harry M. Orlinsky

TWO TREATISES

ON THE ACCENTUATION
OF THE OLD TESTAMENT

טעמי אמ"ת

ON PSALMS, PROVERBS, AND JOB.

טעמי כ"א ספרים

ON THE TWENTY-ONE PROSE BOOKS

by

WILLIAM WICKES, D.D.

PROLEGOMENON

by

ARON DOTAN

KTAV PUBLISHING HOUSE, INC.
NEW YORK
1970

FIRST PUBLISHED 1881, 1887

NEW MATTER
© COPYRIGHT 1970
KTAV PUBLISHING HOUSE, INC.

SBN 87068-004-8

LIBRARY OF CONGRESS CATALOG CARD NUMBER: 66-26487
MANUFACTURED IN THE UNITED STATES OF AMERICA

טעמי אמ״ת

A

TREATISE ON THE ACCENTUATION

OF THE THREE SO-CALLED

POETICAL BOOKS OF THE OLD TESTAMENT,

PSALMS, PROVERBS, AND JOB.

WITH AN APPENDIX CONTAINING THE TREATISE,

ASSIGNED TO R. JEHUDA BEN-BILʻAM, ON THE SAME SUBJECT,

IN THE ORIGINAL ARABIC.

BY

WILLIAM WICKES, D.D.

FIRST PUBLISHED 1881

CONTENTS.

CONTENTS
VOLUME TWO

PROLEGOMENON

RESEARCH IN BIBLICAL ACCENTUATION

BACKGROUNDS AND TRENDS

Throughout the ages, the Biblical accentuation system has been, and still is, one of the most neglected fields in the study of Hebrew graphemes. For generations, the signs of the accents have meant to the Hebrew reader no more than a kind of musical notation. Anyone who was not concerned with the musical aspect of the recitation of the Hebrew text took no interest in these accents; this is true not only of recent generations but also of important scholars of the Middle Ages, among whom we may find the founders of Hebrew grammar.

The Biblical accents—for the time being only the Tiberian system is being alluded to—originally seem to have had three main functions:

1. The logico-syntactical parsing of verses.
2. The indication of the phonetic accent (stress) of the word.
3. The cantillation.

This order of the functions is arbitrary, and we shall not enter into the question as to which of them was the principal, or first function, a question to which Wickes himself alluded in his introductory chapter to טעמי אמ״ת, pp. 1–3.

It is evident that in any grammatical description of the Hebrew language there has been no need to deal with the *cantillation* of the accents. To be sure, grammarians often referred to the accents when dealing with the position of the *stress* in words, but in such cases the specific identity of the accent played no role; it was only its position that counted, to distinguish the word as מלעיל or מלרע. Only where the vocalization of pausal forms was involved were scholars compelled to distinguish certain accents which might cause the pausal forms. But even for that purpose, a detailed study of the Biblical accents was not necessary.

The aspect of the *logico-syntactical division* was not dealt with by most grammarians. In the main they were content merely to give

VII

the names of all the accents. Sometimes they also mentioned a general division into two groups of accents, conjunctive and disjunctive. Mention of both types of accents, that of the prose books as well as that of the poetical books, was rare. If we do not consider the treatises dealing mainly with the Masora and the Hebrew graphemes (such as טוב טעם,[3] מחברת התיג׳אן,[2] הורית הקורא,[1] etc.), we shall find that allusion to this aspect of the accents, namely the logico-syntactical division, is almost non-existent. Even if we consider all of these treatises, themselves rare for a period of about a thousand years following the introduction of the signs of the accents, we shall not find in any of them a description of the manner in which verses are divided by means of the accents. At most, we might find a few rules as to how some conjunctive accents (*servi*) combine with certain disjunctive accents, but this is still far from a recognition of the hierarchy of the pausal value of the accents.

The work of Elijah Levita (*c.* 1469–1549), who was the master of the Hebrew scholars of his generation, contributed a great deal to the extension of the interest of grammarians in this aspect of the accents, and, since his time, at least the names of the accents and their division into conjunctive and disjunctive accents are to be found in almost every scientific Hebrew grammar (Schultens, Gesenius, Olshausen, Stade, Koenig, and others). It was he, too, who aroused interest in the study and research of the accents among Christian scholars, and so started a line of scholars who devoted specialized treatises to Biblical accents (see below). Still, in the chapter on the accents in grammar books we find only a few innovations—the works of outstanding scholars such as Ewald excepted—their main aim having been to give the student a complete picture of the Hebrew graphemes so that he would not encounter signs foreign to him in the Biblical text being studied.

As the treatises specializing in Biblical accents are relatively scarce and unknown, a short survey of the most outstanding of them would be in place here.

The first is ספר דקדוקי הטעמים by Aharon Ben Asher[4] (of the first half of the tenth century), which is the first definite treatise compiling ancient accent rules, well formulated and defined. Ben Asher's aim was not to teach the Biblical accents, nor to furnish us with exhaustive rules; for him, the accents served as an aid to grammar, namely as directives for the vocalization and correct pronunciation of the Hebrew text.

Another treatise compiling many rules for the accents is an anonymous treatise known to us in many versions and editions. Its Arabic version is known as הדאיה אלקאר, and its translations and Hebrew adaptations go by the names טעמי המקרא, הורית המקרא הקורא,[5] תוכן עזרא,[6] etc.[7] An edition of one of the Arabic adaptations on the poetical accents was published by Wickes himself as an appendix to his טעמי אמ״ת, pp. 102–117. Another anonymous treatise is comprised by the last chapters appended to the two editions of the version of *Kitāb al-Tanqīṭ* by Yehuda Ḥayyūǧ.[8] Some of these chapters were not written by Ḥayyūǧ,[9] and they contain rules for accents by an anonymous author. Ḥayyūǧ himself, like most early Hebrew grammarians, did not deal with the accents.

Rules for the accents are to be found also in the two versions, Arabic and Hebrew, of מחברת התיג׳אן.[10] About one third of this treatise is devoted to these rules, based on the division of the accents into three musical groups. If the Jewish scholars went further than that, it was in order to outline the different possibilities for the sequence of the accents, and especially the rules of the conjunctive accents (the *servi*) preceding each disjunctive accent. Before turning to Christian scholars, Moshe Hanaqdan's דרכי הניקוד והנגינות[11] should be mentioned. Other important treatises, e.g., that of Ye-quti'el Hanaqdan, are mostly still in manuscript.[12]

After a beginning of the study of Biblical accents among Christians by Reuchlin, the impetus for study and research in this field was given by Elijah Levita. Since his time, we encounter names of great Christian scholars who do not cease to contribute to the development of this science, especially the divisional aspect of the accents. At the same time, it must be said that many mistakes were made, mistakes that became deeply intrenched and impeded the progress of the discipline down to the days of Wickes. In the following paragraphs we shall mention, in chronological order, some of the more out-standing of these scholars.

Samuel Bohlius (died 1639), in his books *Scrutinium sensus Scripturae Sacrae ex accentibus* (Rostock, 1636) and *Vera divisio*

Decalogi ex infallibili principio accentuum (Rostock, 1637), discussed especially the text of the Ten Commandments and its accents, as well as general problems of accents and of Biblical exegesis. He is the first of a line of Christian scholars of the seventeenth century. In spite of the fact that he died at the early age of 28, before he could develop into a great authority on this subject, he is worthy of mention because of his proposal to divide the disjunctive accents into four classes, according to their pausal value. This division, although justifiably viewed with reservation today, was accepted by most scholars after him, especially in the seventeenth and eighteenth centuries. It was categorically rejected only by Wickes himself (see טעמי אמ״ת, p. 11), after having been ridiculed by Ewald.[13]

Caspar Ledebuhr took a great stride forward with his book שלשלת המקרא, *Catena Scripturae. Tractatus novus, in quo ratio accentuum, quibus Hebraeus S. Scripturae contextus interpungitur* (Leiden, 1647). This is a systematic and well designed book (544 pages in small format) comprising abundant material. He discusses the prose accents as well as the poetical accents, not separately but in juxtaposition. He is the first scholar to have given thought not only to the interpretation of the sequence of accents actually found in the Biblical text, but also to the theoretical aspects: the different possibilities of accentuating a sentence, any sentence, according to the final disjunctive accent applied; the different syntactical possibilities of the order of words in a sentence, and how a sentence should be accentuated in each case. He also deepened Bohlius' division into classes. For the prose accents he suggested five classes: *Rex* (סילוק), *Dux* (אתנח), *Comites* (זקף, סגול, טפחא), *Dynastae* (שלשלת, רביע, פשטא, זרקא, תביר, [14]מירכא כפולה, יתיב), *Toparchae* (פזר, [15]פסיק, קרני פרה, תלישא גדולה, גרש). The accents in these classes (certainly not in the first two) are divided again, according to their pausal strength, into *maiores* and *minores*, and in the last class (*Toparchae*), they are divided even into four sub-classes: *supremi* (פזר, קרני פרה), *maior* (תלישא גדולה), *minor* (גרש), and *minimus* (פסיק). In the poetical accents, however, he contented himself with four groups, omitting the *Comites*: *Rex* (סילוק), *Duces* (עולה ויורד), *Dynastae* ([16]רביע מוגרש, שלשלת, אתנח), *Dynastae* ([17]רביע פשוט, זרקא, [=] צינור, דחי), and *Toparchae* (פזר, פסיק). Exhaustive and original a study as it is, this book does not cease being what it was intended to be—a textbook. This is true not only because of the abundance of examples for every case and for every rule, but also because of the many exercises and the detailed analysis of the accents (of Joel, Chapters 1–2, and of Psalms, Chapter 68).

Matthias Wasmuth's *Institutio methodica accentuationis Hebraeae* (Rostock, 1664) is more detailed than Ledebuhr's book, but does not add much to it. He, too, divided the disjunctive prose accents into five groups, with a slightly different nomenclature (*Imperatores, Reges, Duces, Comites,* and *Barones*). In the poetical accents he distinguished only three classes, in the first of which are included the *Imperator* (סילוק) as well as the *Reges* (עולה ויורד, אתנח), the two others being *Duces* (parallel to Ledebuhr's *Dynastae*), and *Comites* (parallel to Ledebuhr's *Toparchae*). The detailed tables at the end of the book were an interesting innovation. The clear and precise formulation of the rules made it the generally accepted textbook of the following generations.

The book by Daniel Weimar, תורת טעמי המקרא, *Doctrina accentuationis Hebraeae* (Leipzig), written in 1686,[18] provided in addition an historical survey of the study of Biblical accents among Jews and Christians. This book and Andreas Reinbeck's *Doctrina de accentibus Hebraeorum* (Braunschweig, 1692)[19] offered no essential innovations in the manner of their predecessors, but strove mainly for new ways of presenting the material. In fact, they continued Wasmuth's method, a method that served as the guide for further research in the accents, not only for the above mentioned scholars of the seventeenth century but also for those of the eighteenth, such as Phil. Ouseel, author of *Introductio in accentuationem Hebraeorum metricam* (Leiden, 1714)[19] and *Introductio in accentuationem Hebraeorum prosaicam* (Leiden, 1715),[19] and Ad. Bened. Spitzner, author of *Institutiones ad analyticam sacram textus Hebraici V. T. ex accentibus* (Halle, 1786),[19] who showed more original thinking and was the first scholar to reject the grading of the accents into classes.

The eighteenth century Jewish authority on accents, Salomo Hanau, in his שערי זמרה, first published in 1718,[20] also followed in the footsteps of Christian scholars by accepting the principle of grading; and almost the same classes of accents, with only slight changes, can be discerned through his different set of terms: סילוק) מלכים (זרקא, פשטא, תביר, גרש) פקידים (סגול, זקף, טפחא ,רביע) שרים ,(אתנח

and משוררים (תלישא גדולה, תלישא, פזר). His innovation was—as might be
expected of such an original grammatical thinker as he was—the
study of the relation between the syntactical structure of the verse
and its accentual division. In Chapter V of his book he makes a
first and valuable attempt to formulate a set of rules regulating this
relation.

The methodologist Yehuda Leib Ben-Zeev (end of the eighteenth
century), should be mentioned. He, too, followed the grading of
accents, but did not adopt Hanau's terminology. His four terms
were: משנים, מלכים, קיסרים and שלישים. His grammar, תלמוד לשון
עברי (Breslau, 1796),[21] served, especially in Eastern Europe, as one
of the most convenient Hebrew textbooks for the Biblical accents,
even after Wickes' time.

In the nineteenth century, three Jewish scholars who preceded
Wickes should be mentioned. (We shall not mention here grammarians who devoted chapters to the accents in their grammars;
see above, p. VIII) This century abounded in grammars but, alas!
—as Ewald put it—"Seit Spitzner schienen die christlichen Ge-
lehrten und grammatiker sogar ganz verlernt zu haben dass es
Hebräische accente gäbe, so völlig kindisch war was sie darüber
beibrachten; und jeder schien dies für ein gebiet zu halten von dem
er wünschte es möge lieber garnicht daseyn".[22] Ewald himself is an
exception. His ideas, as stated in the chapter on the accents in his
grammar, are original indeed, but unacceptable. We shall content
ourselves with discussing the accentuologists *par excellence.*

At the beginning of the nineteenth century, the work of Wolf
Heidenheim, one of the most important students of Biblical accentuology, was a turning point in the approach to the study of the
accents. After about two centuries of a discipline that followed
the path paved by Ledebuhr, Wasmuth, and their school, an analytical approach that dealt mainly with the examination of the struc-
tures of Biblical verses according to different sequences of accents
and was based on a principle of hierarchical classes of disjunctive
accents, Héidenheim introduced a decisive change. In fact, his
approach could be considered somewhat reactionary *vis-à-vis* that
of his predecessors, Jews and Christians alike. It was not because
he did not know their methods that he condemned them, but, on the
contrary, because of his thorough knowledge of them.

In his book ספר משפטי הטעמים הוסד ע"פ גאוני הלשון הקדמונים

ה״ה בעלי המסרת ובן אשר ובן בלעם וחיוג ושארי זקני לה״ק נ״ע (Rödelheim, 1808), Heidenheim expressly declared his attitude (at the
beginning of his preface): דברי האחרונים במשפטי הטעמים ואם הם
One. מעטים רובם המצאות חקריות, וסברות בדויות, על אדני הדמיון בנויות...
of the reasons for the failure of these אחרונים was that they depended
on unreliable Biblical printed editions, and not on carefully transmitted manuscripts. He preached the importance of going back to
the teaching of the Ancients. He called, in fact, for a Renaissance
in the study of the accents, according to the Jewish scholars of the
Middle Ages. That was the aim of his book, which is nothing but
a compilation of the teachings of the Ancients, especially דקדוקי
הטעמים of Aharon Ben Asher, ספר טעמי המקרא (which he mistakenly
attributed, as was generally till the end of the last century,
to Yehuda Ibn Bal'am), שער הניקוד והנגינות by Moshe Hanaqdan,
and another anonymous treatise. This compilation by Heidenheim
is all quotations, illuminated, sometimes extensively, and accompanied by important remarks by him. In most cases there is also a
typographical distinction between the quotations and the author's
own remarks. Only the fourth part (שער ד׳) of the treatise—on the
rules of the געיה and the מקף—is, according to the evidence of his
preface, from the author's own hand.[23]

Seligman Baer might be regarded as the direct follower of Heidenheim, though it seems the two never met.[24] He followed his method
and continued his work, since Heidenheim never had the opportunity to write a comprehensive book on the poetical accents.[25]
Such a book was written by Baer:

תורת אמת, ספר כולל תורת טעמי תהלים ומשלי ואיוב לכל דרכיהם ומשפטיהם
על פי המסרת ועל פי הכללים אשר הניחו לנו הגאונים בן אשר ובן בלעם ושאר
שרי הלשון הקדמונים, חובר על ידי יצחק בן אריה יוסף דוב, ונספחה אליו
אגרת נחמדה על אודות הטעמים שלוחה על ידי החכם המהולל שמואל דוד לוצאטו
פראפעסאר בקאללעגיום ראביניקום בעיר פאדובה (Rödelheim, 1852).

The German adaptation of this book, *Das Accentuationssystem
der drei biblischen Bücher Psalmen, Sprüche Salomo's und Iob
überlieferungsgemäss dargestellt von Dr. S. Baer*, was published as
an appendix to Franz Delitzsch's *Biblischer Kommentar über die
Psalmen*[5] (Leipzig, 1894). This version is less known than the
Hebrew original; it is also shorter and less detailed. On the other
hand, it has some additional chapters (Chapters XVI–XIX) that are
not present in the Hebrew original and that were written, to the best

of the present author's judgment, under the influence of Wickes'
book on the poetical accents, although this is not stated and Wickes'
name is not mentioned even once there.[26] A Latin epitome of the
rules was published in ספר תהלות *Liber Psalmorum*, ed. S. Baer and
F. Delitzsch (Leipzig, 1880), pp. IX–XII (and in previous editions,
as well).

תורת אמת generally follows the structure and order of subjects of
Heidenheim's משפטי הטעמים; unlike the latter, however, it is not a
compilation from ancient authors, but an original work containing
a well-arranged and forthright discussion, and rules of the utmost
clarity.

Heidenheim and Baer have a common approach to our subject—
the approach of Masoretes; in fact, they both continue the work
of the ancient Masoretes who edited Biblical manuscripts and who
labored with the subtleties of the vocalization, the accentuation,
and the Masora of the Bible. This line of Masoretes never ceased
to exist even after the printing of "the Masora," that random
compilation published by Ya'aqov ben Ḥayyim ibn Adonijah in
the Second Rabbinic Bible (Venice, 1524–1525), a compilation
which today, unfortunately, represents to many the Masora in
general. On the face of it, it might have been expected that after
this "codification" of the Masora there would be no further
Masoretes. But this is not the case, as testify, for instance,
Menaḥem di Lonzano, אור תורה (first published in 1618),[27]
Solomon Jedidiah of Norzi, מנחת שי,[28] and other important
works of the same kind. Heidenheim and Baer should be
regarded as additional links in this chain of Masoretes, their
main interest also being the exact transmission of the Bible
text. Their many Bible editions are well known. Heidenheim
published an edition of the Pentateuch entitled מאור עינים (Rödelheim, 1818–1821) with Yequti'el Hanaqdan's masoretic notes
עין הקורא as well as Heidenheim's own extensive masoretic commentary; and an edition of Psalms (Rödelheim, 1825). Baer, in turn,
edited (jointly with Franz Delitzsch) almost all the books of the
Bible (Genesis, the Prophets, and Hagiographa) annotated with
critical remarks, especially as regards the vocalization and the
accentuation.

Baer's entire work is characterized by a strong drive to arrive
at the "correct" and "original" text of the Bible.[29] Nevertheless, we

find at the end of Baer's תורת אמת one chapter that shows a deviation from this masoretic approach toward the analytical approach of scholarship during the preceding centuries, although in quite an original manner. He does not content himself with the study of the accentuation of the Biblical text, but he gives rules for the active application of the accents to any free text. In fact, this is an exercise in the free use of accents. Instead of specific rules he gives, in an almost modern structural method, a list of 32 patterns of sentences representing some of the various possibilities of analysis of Hebrew sentences: sentences of 4 words (6 patterns), of 5 words (6 patterns), and of 6 words (21 patterns). Every pattern is furnished with its appropriate accents, and some Biblical verses are cited as evidence.

The appendix to this book by Seligman Baer brings us to the third Jewish scholar of the nineteenth century, Samuel David Luzzatto, whose letter of criticism on Baer's book, with Baer's answers to these critical remarks, were published at the end of this book (pp. 54–71). In fact, Luzzatto anticipated Baer, and had already in 1836 published an appendix on the accents (*Appendice V. Degli Accenti*), in his book *Prolegomeni ad una grammatica ragionata della lingua ebraica* (Padova, 1836),[30] pp. 177–191. Here Luzzatto proposed a grading of the accents into *three* classes: מלכים (פשטא, זרקא) פקידים (סגול, זקף, טפחא, רביע) שרים, (סילוק, אתנח) and תביר, גרש.[31] But in addition to this, he paid much attention to difficulties in the analysis of certain Biblical verses, difficulties already noted by the Talmud and medieval Biblical commentators. The student of the accents will find in this book a very useful list of medieval references, grammarians, and commentators in connection with the accents or the interpretation of Biblical verses according to the accentuation.

In his grammar, *Grammatica della lingua ebraica* (Padova, 1853), pp. 47–75, Luzzatto offered a systematic discussion of the rules of the accents. Since he did not know when he would succeed in publishing his grammar, Luzzatto extracted some of his innovations in the field of Biblical accentuation from the manuscript of this grammar, and added them to his letter to Baer, in addition to his critical remarks on תורת אמת. These innovations do not concern the poetical accents, but only the prose accents (תורת אמת, pp. 61–71).

Although Luzzatto , strictly speaking, does not belong to the group of Hebrew Masoretes like Heidenheim and Baer, but rather to the group of the grammarians, it must be admitted, nevertheless, that, as opposed to most of the authors of grammars, he had an original mode of thought and made important contributions to the clarification of some rules in the field of Biblical accentuation.

*   *
*

Wickes' greatness arises from the creative synthesis of the approaches of the Jewish scholars of the nineteenth century with the approach of the seventeenth century Christian scholars, a synthesis which, while reconciling and perfecting its constituents, in itself constitutes a new approach.

Wickes accepted from Christian scholars the principle of continuous dichotomy—a principle laid down by C. Florinus in his *Doctrina de Accentuatione divina* in 1667,[32] and which was later, in the eighteenth century, further developed, but, as Wickes puts it (טעמי אמ״ת, p. 38, n. 1): "A satisfactory result is certainly not worked out." Wickes developed this principle to a very great extent both for the poetical and for the prose accents, and tried to apply it systematically to a syntactical analysis of the Biblical text. Here again, in the study of the relation between syntax and accentual division, he found some beginnings in Ewald's *Ausführliches Lehrbuch der Hebräischen Sprache des Alten Bundes* (7th edition, Göttingen, 1863), *Anhang*: "Uebereinstimmung der Accentuation mit der Syntax," pp. 855–858. However, Wickes was unable to accept Ewald's approach, for the latter had not followed the principle of the continuous dichotomy. Following all these predecessors, Wickes was able to show the relation of the continuous dichotomy to the logico-syntactical division.[33]

On the other hand, Wickes abandoned altogether the idea of class hierarchy of three, four, or five groups of accents—first introduced by Christian accentuologists and later accepted by some Hebrew grammarians as well—and returned to the idea of individual hierarchy held, for instance, by Heidenheim and Baer, following the lead of their Jewish predecessors from the Masoretes' school. But again, unlike the latter, Wickes does not devote the same amount of space and attention to all the accents, conjunctive and disjunctive alike. His approach to the accents, as a means of logico-syntactical division

of the verse, makes him devote a major portion of his discussions to
the disjunctive accents, which alone have a divisional significance.
From the standpoint of the divisional power, there is no difference
whatever between the different conjunctive accents. They all join
words to the same degree, the difference between them being merely
musical. Therefore, the rules pertaining to the conjuctive accents
are brought as an appendix to every chapter, and are relatively short.

If we compare Wickes' two books with Baer's תורת אמת, we shall
see immediately the outstanding difference between the approaches
of the two authors in this respect. The main part of Baer's book
comprises rules on the conjunctive accents—and this indeed is also
the main subject of the Masoretes—while the main part of Wickes'
books is the laws of the disjunctive accents. Whereas Baer, following
his predecessors, determines merely the possibilities of sequence
of the disjunctive accents, Wickes enters into minute details of the
rules of the various disjunctive accents, rules depending on the length
of the verse, the clause, etc., and of the distance of the dichotomy
from the end of the verse, the clause, etc. These rules, the perfection
and elaboration of which are Wickes' main innovation, have raised
his books to a first class scientific level.

The structure of the books serves a dual end, thanks to its scientific approach on the one hand, and its methodologically aimed
arrangement on the other. Each of the two books has an historical
introduction; an etymologico-semantic survey of the names of the
accents; two chapters on the general dichotomy (dependent on the
recitative demands of the reading of the text in public, on the
prosody, etc.), and on the syntactical dichotomy; and finally a
series of chapters, each dealing with a single disjunctive accent,
the different possibilities of the internal division of its clause, and
the ways of marking this division. Only at the end of each of these
chapters do the rules of the conjunctive accents, combining with the
particular disjunctive accent, appear, sometimes followed by "Corrigenda" where Wickes proposed his corrections to false accentuations in current editions of the Bible.

From the methodological standpoint, Wickes succeeded in
composing an ideal treatise with regard to the manner of presenting
the theory of the accents and its rules, as well as the method of
learning this theory for beginners and advanced students alike.
It seems that there remains very little to add to the work of Wickes

from the standpoint of methodology, and this indeed seems to be the main reason for the fact that his books have remained standard to this day.

Of the three nineteenth century Jewish scholars who paved the way for Wickes and influenced him to a great extent, it was Baer whom Wickes himself recognized most pronouncedly, repeatedly underlining the importance of Baer's work and his treatises (טעמי אמ״ת, pp. v, vi, x). He cited Heidenheim to a a lesser degree (e.g., טעמי כ״א ספרים, p. xiv), while Luzzatto is not even mentioned in Wickes' bibliographical lists. Yet he was influenced by all three of them. From Heidenheim and Baer he learned to maintain a close link with the Hebrew sources and to search incessantly for ancient Biblical manuscripts. As against this, it may be said that he was more than once misled by Baer—be it by accepting Baer's readings without checking them, or by adopting Baer's method of choosing from manuscripts a reading which seemed to him most felicitously to support his thesis, or by the arbitrary and deliberate correction of readings.

For example, Wickes' rejection of the Aleppo Codex and his denial of its Ben Asheric authenticity is based solely on his examination of its readings in the light of criteria fixed by Baer (we shall return to this later). Wickes often attacked Ben Asher for his "wrong" readings, all because he had been misled by Baer, who had attributed to Ben Asher readings that were not his.[34]

Neither can one deny Luzzatto's influence on Wickes. To give one example, it was Luzzatto who discovered and formulated (in his letter to Baer, תורת אמת, pp. 62–69) the rule determining the cases where, in a sequence of two or more *Revia*'s, the second is transformed into a *Pashṭa*, a rule that had been sought for some hundred years since Ledebuhr and Wasmuth. Luzzatto showed that the cause of this transformation was connected with the interval between the words involved, that is to say, the number of words separating the *Revia*'s. The principle of this rule was accepted by Wickes, too, who, after an extensive examination of the material, adapted it to a certain degree (טעמי כ״א ספרים, p. 78). But only in a note (p. 78, n. 10) does Wickes dispute with Luzzatto over the *details of this rule*, without mentioning the fact that the whole rule was first formulated by Luzzatto himself.

Wickes' debt to his predecessors of the nineteenth century as well

as of the preceding centuries, to whatever extent he did or did not
acknowledge it, does not in the least detract from his own achievement and his new approach. While his interest in the accents was
aroused by the general awakening of interest in them during the
nineteenth century, which began with Heidenheim and reached its
peak with Wickes' contemporary, Baer, his dependence on the
theories of the seventeenth century Christian scholars cannot be
overestimated, especially in matters concerning the dichotomy and
the continuous dichotomy. However, just as Wickes was not always
aware of the extent of the influence exerted on him by some of his
contemporaries, so too he sometimes tended to minimize the contribution of his predecessors to his theory, e.g.: "Even from Christian
accentuologists, as Wasmuth, Ouseel, Spitzner, and Ewald, I have
derived little or no help" (טעמי כ״א ספרים, p. xiv), although he did
cite Wasmuth, Ouseel and Spitzner in the bibliography of his
previous book (טעמי אמ״ת, p. x). He does not, however, completely
deny their contribution in this field, and he acknowledges elsewhere
(טעמי כ״א ספרים, p. 29, n. 1) that "Its discovery [viz., the law of
continuous dichotomy] is due to the unwearied diligence, with
which the study of the accents was pursued by Christian scholars
of the seventeenth century." This somewhat mitigates the dis-
paraging remarks in טעמי אמ״ת, p. 38, n. 1, and p. 39, n. 2.

As to the details, Wickes' own work admits of criticism and
requires correction of specific errors. Following the Jewish scholars,
Wickes invested a great deal of effort in the examination of Biblical
manuscripts. It seems that he was deeply impressed by Baer's
procedure in this respect. There is no debate as to the vital role the
collation of manuscripts must play in the determination of the
accentuation rules. However, balanced evaluation of the manuscripts
themselves, as well as extreme caution in the application of the
results of the collation, must be employed. The chief flaw in Wickes'
work may be said to be the manner in which he utilized the manuscript material, in which respect, too, he seems to have followed Baer.

It has already been noted by various scholars[35] that Baer did not
regard manuscripts as sources that have to be accepted as they are
and that have to be studied in order to determine the information
they can yield, but as an auxiliary means to his main purpose,
namely to establish the "masoretic" and "correct" Biblical text.
In his own mind, he knew what this text should be, and to him the

role of the manuscripts was only to confirm this text of his. When there was a contradiction between the manuscripts and his opinion, he simply "adjusted" the information of the manuscripts to fit his opinion, in spite of the fact that he himself attacked Luzzatto on his tendency to rationalize the rules and determine them according to learned speculation while sometimes disregarding the Masora (Baer's notes to Luzzatto's letter to him, תורת אמת, p. 69, n. 24). Baer himself did not *disregard* the Masora, but he adjusted it to his ends.

I have not encountered a single case in which Wickes tampered with the Masora for his own ends or cited it inaccurately (though I have not conducted a comprehensive check); but it is clear that he drew from it only that evidence that he needed in support of the rules he thought to be correct, and on the grounds of which he permitted himself to propose corrections to current accentuation readings. To his credit, one must state that he did not conceal this fact but, out of a critical sense and scholarly responsibility, he always noted the fact of the correction and its manuscript evidence. He did not content himself, however, with extracting from the Masora the material that served his purposes. He also directed his criticism against the Masora: "Even the Massoretes have not always been as correct as we should have expected" (טעמי כ״א ספרים, p. 81, n. 18).

But were the Masoretes really expected to furnish us with material for smoothly applicable rules? Anyone who expects this of them misses a true understanding of the Masora. This is neither a normative discipline nor a set of rules, the application of which results in the Biblical text. The concept of Masora is in frank opposition to grammar and to everything that is represented by normative grammar.

Wickes' criterion for the acceptance of the Masora's evidence —and he always meant that artificial Masora collated and published by Yaʻaqov ben Ḥayyim ibn Adonijah in the Second Rabbinic Bible (Venice, 1524–1525) — was the extent of its agreement with the rules he thought to be correct.

In the event of disagreement or deviation, there had to be found a satisfying explanation to qualify these cases to be regarded as

exceptions; otherwise they would be stamped as mistakes. Sometimes Wickes was prepared to accept exceptions as they were, as
for instance in טעמי כ״א ספרים, p. 118: "The accentuators must have
designed by this exceptional accentuation to signalize these passages as deserving of special notice or special emphasis. The reader
may be left to trace for himself these Massoretic fancies, which
(it so happens) are for the most part sufficiently obvious." At other
times, he supplied an explanation for an exceptional accentuation,
as for instance in טעמי כ״א ספרים, pp. 133–134, where he explains
the irregular *Legarmeh* in the *Geresh* clause in II Kings 18:17. Here,
as in many other places, one gets the impression that he was trying
to "save" the masoretic accentuation at all costs, thus sometimes
arriving at explanations completely unacceptable to an objective
critic. In the above-mentioned example, there was no logical need
for an irregular accentuation. The same effect, to stress that Tartan
and Rab-saris were not sent from Lachish, could have been achieved
by employing a *Great Telisha*, the regular accent in this position,
instead of the *Legarmeh*. Besides, the same accentual irregularity,
namely *Legarmeh* in the *Geresh* clause, occurs elsewhere no less
than eleven times (see, e.g., the masoretic note to Genesis 28:9).
Wickes proposed no explanation for the other ten cases.

On the other hand, he sometimes displays a complete lack of
regard for masoretic lists, as for instance טעמי כ״א ספרים, p. 107,
n. 24: "So far the list answers a certain purpose. But in itself it is a
poor one . . . " Or he may take pains to clarify the correct list of
exceptions and, after enumerating all the items of the amended
list, deny its value altogether, as he does in טעמי כ״א ספרים, p. 108,
n. 29: "It is clear to my mind that we have in these exceptions
(and those which follow) merely the errors of some model Codex,
for *the same words in the same connection* are at one time pointed
according to rule, at another against it." But what *is* an exception
at all? Why should *these* exceptions be labeled errors? Another
example of a superficial solution of a masoretic difficulty may be
found in טעמי אמ״ת, p. 82, n. 8, where Wickes terms "fanciful" an
accentuation which can be explained very well.[36]

There is therefore a great internal conflict in his approach. On the
one hand, he accepts the lists of the Masora, i.e., the lists of exceptions, sometimes endeavoring to cloak them with a logical explanation; on the other hand, he frequently expresses his dissatisfaction

with the inconsistencies, for exceptions *are* inconsistencies. Thus in
טעמי אמ״ת, p. 89, n. 6, he remarks: " . . . But at least consistency
should have been observed . . . Such irregularity of itself points to
mistakes made. The original accentuators could hardly have been
so inconsistent."

In Wickes' opinion, it is perfectly legitimate and valid to make
corrections in the Biblical text, and in his preface to טעמי אמ״ת,
p. v, he says: "I may draw attention to one respect in which the
present Work differs from any of those which have preceded it.
It is founded, in a great measure, on an extensive examination
of MSS. I soon saw that even our best texts need correction, as far
as the accents are concerned; and that, without a correct text,
I could not hope to establish any rules on a satisfactory basis."

But what is the criterion for a "correct" text? On the one hand,
Wickes labeled as correct, readings that conformed to his rules,
and on the other, formulated his rules on the basis of his correct
readings. It is a vicious circle that this method cannot break out of.

In fact, Wickes added lists of Corrigenda to almost every chapter
of his two books, corrigenda which are "in accordance with the
rules laid down in this chapter," as he remarked in a sub-heading
to the first list of טעמי כ״א ספרים (p. 59). To understand Wickes'
attitude, one should note, e.g., his concluding remark to this list
(p. 60): "In these *trifling* [italics mine] matters, I have been often
satisfied, when I have found *two* Codd. supporting the obviously
necessary correction. The instances shew how even the best editors
have failed to master, or at least to observe, the simplest rules of
the accentuation." And elsewhere (טעמי אמ״ת, p. 88): "If we make
the corrections, suggested at the end of this chapter, the rules for
the dichotomy will be found carefully carried out."

Wickes grants anyone the right to make such corrections according
to his rules, e.g.: "Zaqeph fails, or has been wrongly introduced, in
the following passages (which must be corrected, as we should
correct cases of false interpunction in a modern text)" (טעמי כ״א
ספרים, p. 67), or "Other similar instances will doubtless be found,
which have escaped my notice, and which will all have to be corrected
in the same way, unless (as is sometimes the case) they should admit
of explanation, from the application of some special rule" (p. 60).
But how should anyone know if there existed at the time an explanation other than that known to us? Not even Wickes claimed

to know all the "special" rules. Does not every grammar and every normative ruling admit of exceptions?

This is the only point at which Wickes' systematic approach falters, and it constitutes, in the opinion of the present writer, the main defect of his work. Correcting a text can be all too easy. Codices can be found to support almost any imaginable reading (whether false or correct). Wickes seems to have taken insufficient consideration of the relative value and importance of the codices he consulted, and of their authenticity. While he does realize the shortcomings of copyists and of punctuators, he stresses the point only when he is interested in contradicting them, not when he cites them to support his views. The idea that these punctuators might have attempted to "correct" the text, just as he himself was doing, never seemed to occur to him. It is astonishing how such a critical scholar as he, could altogether abandon the principle of *lectio difficilior*, investing a great deal of work in research and collation of codices in order to iron out Biblical accentuated texts, and concomitantly, his rules.

The outcome is a set of rules which does not represent any one particular extant text. It is a set of rules based on a series of main texts, principally the *textus receptus* (Venice, 1524–1525), arbitrarily corrected according to readings found in other manuscripts, however few or relatively recent.

Wickes went even further, condemning texts and readings without even bothering about evidence, e.g., statements like: "Hence such careless mistakes as occur in ... must at once be corrected" (טעמי כ״א ספרים, p. 79, n. 11); "Our texts, of course, need constant correction..."(טעמי כ״א ספרים, p. 81, n. 18); and "Of the many examples that come under this head, fully a third are falsely pointed in our texts. See Corrigenda" (טעמי כ״א ספרים, p. 80, n. 13). Of one of these examples he stated that "none of our modern editors has thought of correcting." Sometimes he introduced a correction against all evidence, when *"not a single one"* of the existing codices supported him (טעמי כ״א ספרים, p. 88).

In view of the above, Wickes' statement in his preface to טעמי כ״א ספרים (pp. v–vi) can now be properly evaluated. For what seemed to be a highly scientific and methodical striving for perfectionism has in fact proved to be the chief flaw in Wickes' method. He states that he has

"... not intentionally allowed difficulties in the accentuation to pass unnoticed. My plan has been, either, by a process of induction, to bring such instances under a general rule; or to furnish a special explanation of them, partly in the course of the Work, and more particularly in the Notes collected in Appendix I. Of course, I have not been concerned to *defend* the accentuation in all cases. It is enough if we can trace the principles on which the accentuators proceeded, or the interpretation which in particular instances led to the accentuation employed.

"I have found it necessary often to propose a correction of the *textus receptus;* but have very rarely done so without manuscript authority."

The term "authority" used here and elsewhere by Wickes should be well understood. On the one hand, for him, *any* manuscript written or copied by *anyone* is an "authority" when its evidence supports Wickes' theory. On the other hand, the authority of manuscripts is questioned when not in conformity with Wickes' ideas. In this respect, Baer's authority carries great weight for Wickes. On this ground Wickes condemned the authority of the Aleppo Codex. His "conclusive proof is to be found in the fact that the punctuation is, in many instances, *at variance with Ben-Asher's known practice* and the rules laid down by the Palestinian Massoretes" (טעמי כ״א ספרים, p. viii). To illustrate "Ben-Asher's known practice" he cites *Baer's* publications, and he rejects the Ben Asheric authority of the Codex because its readings are either in contradiction to Baer's *Meteg* rules, which he, following Baer, believed to be Ben Asher's, or in contradiction to Baer's Lists of Variations between Ben Asher and Ben Naftali,[37] or, finally, in contradiction to Baer's edition of דקדוקי הטעמים.[38] While Wickes' proofs in this respect are altogether false, it is the present author's belief that, although the punctuation of the Aleppo Codex is very close to Ben Asher's theories, Ben Asher's actual *authorship* of it cannot be proved beyond reasonable doubt. In fact, there is considerable evidence to the contrary.[39] It happens that Wickes' conclusions were not altogether wrong, though his method cannot be admitted.

Yet Wickes did not always accept Baer's theories. Sometimes he attempted to improve upon him (טעמי כ״א ספרים, p. 121) and even opposed him, as for instance in the question of the quality of a single *Shewa* in medial position following a long vowel (טעמי כ״א

ספרים, p. 108, n. 30), a question in which Wickes' view cannot be accepted, and anyway the grammatical aspect was not his strongest side.

A word should be added here on Wickes' concept of the "Masora," a concept which, although generally accepted in his time, proves to be wrong, and is thus one of the things that misled him. One gets the impression, although it is nowhere expressly stated, that to him the Masora is one distinct entity. In recent years it is becoming more and more clear that the term "Masora" has several different meanings. It signifies first of all the literary *genre* of notes accompanying the Biblical text, but it also signifies the specific notes attached to a definite Biblical text. The adjective of this noun, "masoretic," also has several meanings, one of which is: pertaining to the Biblical text accepted by the Jews—that is, a meaning which does not derive its definition directly from any one of the nominal meanings of the term. Hence a Biblical text which is "non-masoretic" may be accompanied by "Masora," i.e., by notes to the text, as for example the Biblical text of the Babylonian tradition, or the Biblical text with unconventional Tiberian punctuation.[40]

On the other hand, a "masoretic" text is not necessarily identical with the *textus receptus* collated by Ya'aqov ben Ḥayyim ibn Adonijah, and therefore its Masora is not and cannot be THE Masora, the only Masora. In fact, within the *genre* "Masora" many types of Masora (second meaning) could exist, nay, had to exist. Theoretically, every different Biblical text, differing in the most minute matters of punctuation, had to have its own Masora, and all this within the scope of what is called the *masoretic text*[40a].

The situation deteriorated, however, because of copyists who did not understand the high level of interdependence between a certain text and its Masora, and therefore copied the notes of the Masora alongside a Biblical text they did not belong to. Ya'aqov ben Ḥayyim wished to correct this situation, and he compiled from manuscripts a new Masora that was to conform, to the best of his knowledge, to his Biblical text, the text he thought to be correct. Since then, the impression became general that there was one Masora and one masoretic text, namely the *textus receptus* of Ya'aqov ben Ḥayyim. But in fact there is no single, specific "masoretic" text. Even the attribution to Ben Asher of the *textus receptus* is unfounded. Ben Asher was *one* of the Masoretes who enjoyed wide prestige, which became even wider because of Maimonides' reference to him in the matter of the open and closed *Parashas* (פרשיות פתוחות וסתומות). The recently enunciated opinion[41] that the masoretic text was fixed by Ben Asher is therefore likewise completely unfounded.

With regard to the subject at hand, the conclusion to be drawn from the above stated facts is that every text must be considered to stand by itself. Masoras should not be mixed, nor should one text be corrected according to Masoras intended for other texts. Grammatical rules, and accentuation rules, as well, should be based on one particular text, possibly a text of authority, and on its particular Masora notes. The approach should be descriptive, not normative. Thus would we formulate the corrective for Wickes' work.

The above applies even more to the accentuation of the three poetical books. Through the ages, these have been more neglected than have the prose accents, with the result that the transmission of the text in the poetical books is, from the standpoint of the accents, more lax and unstable, and the differences of readings between various manuscripts or printed editions are vast. Consequently Wickes' corrections in the readings of the poetical accentuation are relatively more numerous than his corrections of the prose accents.[42]

At the end of טעמי כ״א ספרים (pp. 142 ff.), we find as Appendix II the study "On the superlinear [so-called Babylonian] system of accentuation." This study is mentioned here for the sake of comprehensiveness, though it contains no real contribution to the knowledge accumulated by his predecessors in this field.[43] While attempting to show the differences between the two accentuation systems, the Babylonian and the Tiberian (which he called "Palestinian"), Wickes did not succeed in solving the basic problem concerning the place of the Babylonian system within the various Hebrew traditions. Although he had seen Babylonian manuscripts other than Codex Babylonicus of the year 916, of the Petersburg Library,[44] he did not realize the mixed character of this codex. From his analysis of this manuscript he arrived at certain conclusions concerning Babylonian punctuation in general, and it is no wonder that these conclusions are quite mistaken. We can hardly view as more than an historical curiosity his statement, on pages 149–150: "We may conclude, with absolute certainty, from the instances cited, that the Palestinian[45] punctuation was before the originators of this

superlinear system. Their attempt, however, to modify and improve
upon it must, as far at least as the accents are concerned, be pronounced a failure, and for us quite worthless. Inconsequent and
contradictory, this new system is a mere travesty of the Palestinian."[45]

Of lasting importance, however, is Wickes' Appendix to טעמי
אמ״ת (pp. 102–117), for in it he published one of the Arabic versions,
probably a compendium, of *Hidāyat al-Qāri* (הדאיה אלקאר), containing the poetical accents. In his brief introduction to this treatise,
he rightly rejected the opinion that the author was Yehuda Ibn
Bal'am, an opinion no longer held by anyone today.

The reader should, however, be warned of a grave mistake that
led Wickes to suggest (on p. 104)—with all due reserve, it is true—
another author for this treatise, by the name of Sa'îd 'Alî, on the basis
of a remark found in the oldest of the four manuscripts consulted
(MS. A). It is not surprising that he observes that this name is
"otherwise (I believe) unknown" (p. 104), since it is based on a
misreading and misinterpretation of the Arabic text in this manuscript (p. 108, n. 15): זיאדה ללמעלם סעיד עלי צאחב אלכתאב. Wickes
must have translated: "an addition by the master Sa'îd 'Alî the
author of the book." This is erroneous, and the translation should
read: "an addition by the master Sa'îd *to* (what was written by)
the author of the book," עלי being the preposition *'ala*, not the name
" 'Alî". Sa'îd (and not Sa'îd 'Alî) was, then, not the author, but
another master who wrote additional remarks to our treatise. Who,
indeed, might this Sa'îd have been? Could it not conceivably have
been *Abu* Sa'îd (the Arabic appellation of Aharon Ben Asher)?
We have not enough ground for any conclusion.

Whatever flaws we may have found in Wickes' work do not in the
least detract from the fundamental value of his enormous achievement. As fate would have it, his work was not properly appreciated,
neither in his own time nor in the years following, in large part
because of the small number of specialists in this field. The present
author does not know of a single serious review of his books.[46]
Certainly an evaluation like Kahle's[47]: "Das Buch ist eine zuver-
lässige Materialsammlung, wenn auch seine These von der
'Dichotomy' und 'continuous Dichotomy' in der Weise, wie er
sie in dem Buch durchzuführen sucht, sicher nicht richtig ist" is
most unjust to Wickes, while it betrays the limitations of its

utterer.[48] Wickes was and remains unique, head and shoulders
above everyone else in the study of Biblical accents, and to this
day his is a basic standard work and an excellent textbook for the
student as well.

*   *

*

We shall now proceed to review, in chronological order, other
treatises in the domain of Biblical accentuation, published after
Wickes, in order to follow the progress of research to the present
time. Let it be said immediately that within the Tiberian tradition
it is difficult to point out essential progress and real achievements
since Wickes. The main development and innovations have been
within the domain of the Babylonian tradition, in which, as we
have seen, Wickes' knowledge was not extensive, and in the domain
of the Palestinian tradition, which was still unknown to Wickes
when he published his books (see below).

In 1891, Adolf Büchler published his *Untersuchungen zur Ent-
stehung und Entwickelung der hebräischen Accente. I. Theil: Die
Ursprünge der verticalen Bestandtheile in der Accentuation des
hebräischen Bibeltextes und ihre masoretische Bedeutung* as volume
CXXIV of the *Sitzungsberichte der kaiserlichen Akademie der Wissen-
schaften in Wien.* The aim of this book was, according to the testimony of its author (p. 4): "die Ursprünge der verticalen Bestandtheile
der Accentuation an der Hand masoretischer Angaben nachzu-
weisen und aus der Entwicklung derselben die aufgeworfenen
Fragen, wie auch andere Ausnahmen und eigenthümlichen Erschei-
nungen zu erklären und zu lösen." Büchler attempted to solve
problems that did not exist, by a fantastic method of analyzing the
graphic shape of the signs of the accents. He derived most of the
signs from a prototypical vertical line (this derivation group is
called "Verticalaccenten") and, on the supposition of an imaginary
development of the graphical signs, he attempted to arrive at an
explanation of some of the accentuation rules, particularly of several
exceptional cases. He aspired to explain phenomena that were not
explained by Wickes because there was no need for explanation,
or phenomena for which Wickes had proposed causes which Büchler
considered unsatisfactory, as for instance the cause of "musical
variation" which is unsatisfactory in his opinion "da uns der mu-

allusion to the beginning of the Biblical verse this whole final Hebrew phrase would seem completely out of place.[57] It is not an uncommon practice to quote a part of a Biblical verse or of another well-known passage in order to hint at the other part which in fact contains the essential information but which, for various reasons, cannot be expressly stated. Whether this oblique reference to his plagiarism was in the nature of a private joke, or the result of some psychological quirk by which he was attempting to justify himself, or even deny what he had done, remains a matter of speculation. What seems clear is that he did not intend thereby to draw anyone's attention to his offense; and in fact it has, till now, gone unnoticed.

In the following two years, Franz Praetorius published two books, not dealing with the study of the accents themselves, but intended to solve the problems of the origins and formation of the accents: *Über die Herkunft der hebräischen Accente* (Berlin, 1901) and *Die Übernahme der früh-mittelgriechischen Neumen durch den Juden* (Berlin, 1902). As the second title shows, Praetorius' aim was to prove the Greek origin of the Hebrew signs. This was not the first attempt to prove that the accents were of foreign origin. In 1889, Adalbert Merx, in his *Historia artis grammaticae apud Syros* (Leipzig, 1889—reprinted 1966), pp. 62–75, tried to prove the Syrian origin of the Hebrew signs, and this following his opinion, which is in any case more probable, that the Syriac accents in their turn were of Greek origin.[58] This last view has already been refuted, and it is in place to cite here the relatively recent publication of J. B. Segal, *The Diacritical Point and the Accents in Syriac* (1953), who says of the attribution of the fruits of Syriac creativity to the Greeks, sometimes already suggested by the Syrians themselves (p. 63): "although the influence of Greek rhetoric on the Syriac accents was very great in later times, these statements should be treated with caution. So high was the regard for Greek science that systems, whether of logic or philosophy, were held to be above dispute only if they were assigned a Greek parentage, and much that was of pure Syrian origin was Graecized ... From internal evidence we may assume a native Syrian origin for the accents." And he concludes, "The resemblance between the Syriac accents and the Greek *neuma* system is no greater than might be expected from their common *raison d'être* and their application to the same work, the Bible." To this he adds (in n. 6) an instructive citation from Nöldeke:

sikalische Werth der Accente völlig unbekannt ist" (p. 2). Büchler's book derived almost all its information from Wickes, who is referred to on almost every page, and it contains no contribution whatever to the advancement of the study of accentuation.

Quite different is A. Ackermann's book, *Das hermeneutische Element der biblischen Accentuation—Ein Beitrag zur Geschichte der hebräischen Sprache* (Berlin, 1893). He intended to prove that the accents were introduced originally for hermeneutical purposes, that is to say, that the exegetical, and not the musical division was the main purpose of the signs. The book includes an interesting historical survey of the theories of the formation of the accents and their essential nature, at the end of which the author arrives at a rather convincing conclusion (p. 88): "bei Erfindung der Accentuation selbständig, unabhängig, ohne alle Rücksicht auf den musikalischen Vortrag, die Absicht thätig war, einen Kommentar zur heiligen schrift zu schaffen." As to the music, he concludes: "die Entwickelung und Ausbildung des Accentsystems nahm gewiss einen grossen Zeitraum in Anspruch, und jedenfalls hat die Anlehnung der Melodien an dasselbe auf seine weitere Ausgestaltung bedeutenden Einfluss geübt, woher es kommt, dass manche Accentverbindungen nur durch musikalische Momente erklärt werden können." In his discussion he includes four chapters surveying Biblical exegesis by means of the accents: in the Talmud and Midrash[49] (Chapter II), by Saadia Gaon (Chapter III), Rashi and his school (Chapter IV), and Abraham Ibn Ezra (Chapter V); and in the last chapter (Chapter VI) he surveys briefly the more recent accentual exegesis, stressing S. Hanau and S. D. Luzzatto.

Ackerman had done a great deal of reading about the accents, but he displayed a lack of elementary knowledge concerning their rules. He stumbled, for instance, in an extremely elementary matter when he mentioned (p. 3) among the postpositive accents the *Great Telisha* and *Deḥi* (which are both prepositive) and *Revia' Mugrash* (which is neither); and among the prepositive accents the *Little Telisha* (which is postpositive). He sometimes argues with Wickes about principles, but only very rarely, and one gets the impression that he did not bother to read him attentively. It is not impossible that he had difficulty in reading English—otherwise it would be difficult to understand why he did not refer more than five or six times to Wickes' basic and important books, where most of the relevant problems are discussed, Wickes' second book having been published only six years earlier. This suspicion is reinforced by the fact that he referred (on p. 39) to the chapters on the accents from ספר הנקוד as being by Ḥayyuǧ, also according to Nutt's edition of 1870,[50] whereas Nutt explicitly stressed in the English introduction to his edition (p. XII) that these chapters were definitely not written by Ḥayyuǧ (an opinion that has been generally accepted ever since).

J. M. Japhet's book, מורה הקורא, *Die Accente der heiligen Schrift* (Frankfurt a.M., 1896), is a good textbook for Biblical accentuation without pretensions to scientific research, intended especially for ritual purposes. It teaches the elements of division of the prose accents according to the four-grade terminology of Ben-Zeev, as well as their exegetical ramifications. It is, in fact, the only semi-popular German textbook for the prose accents,[51] opening the closed gates of this domain for the German reader who had access neither to the English of Wickes nor to the Hebrew תלמוד לשון עברי of Ben-Zeev.[52] In accordance with its purpose, the book is furnished with many examples, but owing to the custom of synagogal rite most of them are taken from the Pentateuch or the Book of Esther. The final pages of musical notations for some Pentateuch passages also serve the author's purpose, namely to guide cantors.

In 1900 there appeared in London a textbook of the accents in English by Arthur Davis, למנצח בנגינות משכיל, *The Hebrew Accents of the Twenty-one Books of the Bible* (כ״א ספרים)... *with a New Introduction*. The justification for publishing this book a few years after the appearance of Wickes' books is not apparent. Is it possible that the author intended to furnish the reader with a more popular treatise? It is, in fact, full of mistakes, and only makes things harder for the reader, confusing him. It is a considerable regression from Wickes' work.

Even more, the present author wishes to draw attention to a fact which, to the best of his knowledge, has not yet been commented upon. Davis' book is in the main a *literal translation*, sometimes a bad one, of the chapters relevant to the accents in Ben-Zeev's תלמוד לשון עברי. Thus, the tables of accents in Davis pp. 4–5[53] are copied from Ben-Zeev §מה, pp. 46–47[54]; the list of the disjunctive accents in Davis, p. 8 (there called "distinctive" accents), is copied from Ben-Zeev §שפח, p. 305; the table on p. 9 is similar to that found in Ben-Zeev §שפז, p. 305; the large "Table of the connective and

distinctive accents in order of consecution" (Davis, p. exact copy, almost photographic, of the same table in §שצד, p. 315. Thereafter, on pp. 11–54, Davis offered a literal translation of each and every rule of Ben-Zeev §§ת— pp. 306–323, with some enlargements and paraphrases ne for the English reader, as well as a few omissions. He adhered original to such an extent that he copied most of the examples same order as in the original, and even with the same mist A single illustration will suffice. On p. 22 he refers to "seven instances" of *Double Merkha* found in the Biblical text, an e copied from Ben-Zeev §(3)שצ, p. 310: פעמים יבוא מרכא כפולה ת׳ התביר;[55] it is well known that this accent appears only *fourte* times in the Bible. At the end of his book (pp. 54–69), Davis presente some grammatical rules necessary for the comprehension of the ac cents. These, too, are verbatim translations of Ben-Zeev's chapters on the Intonation (נגינה), the Regression (נסוג אחור), the *Meteg* (מתג), and the *Maqqef* (מקף), in §§מט — עה, pp. 48–59. The remaining few pages on the *Shewa* (pp. 1–3) and on double accentuated passages (pp. 69–70) do not seem to be original either, but it did not seem worthwhile looking for their source.

It is worthy of note that Davis did not mention Ben-Zeev's name even once in his book. Even in his introduction (p. 11 of the first pagination),[53] where he mentioned the names of writers on the accents,[56] up to and including Baer and Wickes, he carefully refrained from mentioning Ben-Zeev. Only one who is aware of the fact of the plagiarism will properly understand the significance of the book's subtitle: "with a *new* introduction." None of the rest is new, and it is doubtful whether there is much of his own even in the introduction. In view of the above, one should pay attention also to the Hebrew words printed at the end of the book (p. 70): על כן עמד טעמו בו וריחו לא נמר, which is the second half of Jeremiah 48:11: "therefore his taste remained in him and his scent is not changed," an expression which would be meaningful only to someone who was aware of this offense. The choice of this half-verse becomes even more significant with reference to the first half of the Biblical verse, where we find the expression: ולא הורק מכלי אל כלי, "and hath not been emptied from vessel to vessel." Now the metaphor הריק מכלי אל כלי just happens to be a common Hebrew idiom for "translation"! It even seems justified to assume that without this distinctive accents in order of consecution" (Davis, p. 10) is an exact copy, almost photographic, of the same table in Ben-Zeev § שצד, p. 315. Thereafter, on pp. 11–54, Davis offered an almost literal translation of each and every rule of Ben-Zeev § §שפח(1)—ח, pp. 306–323, with some enlargements and paraphrases necessary for the English reader, as well as a few omissions. He adhered to the original to such an extent that he copied most of the examples in the same order as in the original, and even with the same mistakes. A single illustration will suffice. On p. 22 he refers to "seventeen instances" of *Double Merkha* found in the Biblical text, an error copied from Ben-Zeev §(3)שצ, p. 310: וי״ז פעמים יבוא מרכָא כפולה ;התביר ת' ;[55] it is well known that this accent appears only *fourteen* times in the Bible. At the end of his book (pp. 54–69), Davis presented some grammatical rules necessary for the comprehension of the accents. These, too, are verbatim translations of Ben-Zeev's chapters on the Intonation (נגינה), the Regression (נסוג אחור), the *Meteg* (מתג), and the *Maqqef* (מקף), in § §מט — עה, pp. 48–59. The remaining few pages on the *Shewa* (pp. 1–3) and on double accentuated passages (pp. 69–70) do not seem to be original either, but it did not seem worthwhile looking for their source.

It is worthy of note that Davis did not mention Ben-Zeev's name even once in his book. Even in his introduction (p. 11 of the first pagination),[53] where he mentioned the names of writers on the accents,[56] up to and including Baer and Wickes, he carefully refrained from mentioning Ben-Zeev. Only one who is aware of the fact of the plagiarism will properly understand the significance of the book's subtitle: "with a *new* introduction." None of the rest is new, and it is doubtful whether there is much of his own even in the introduction. In view of the above, one should pay attention also to the Hebrew words printed at the end of the book (p. 70): על כן עמד טעמו בו וריחו לא נמר, which is the second half of Jeremiah 48:11: "therefore his taste remained in him and his scent is not changed," an expression which would be meaningful only to someone who was aware of this offense. The choice of this half-verse becomes even more significant with reference to the first half of the Biblical verse, where we find the expression: ולא הורק מכלי אל כלי, "and hath not been emptied from vessel to vessel." Now the metaphor הריק מכלי אל כלי just happens to be a common Hebrew idiom for "translation"! It even seems justified to assume that without this allusion to the beginning of the Biblical verse this whole final Hebrew phrase would seem completely out of place.[57] It is not an uncommon practice to quote a part of a Biblical verse or of another well-known passage in order to hint at the other part which in fact contains the essential information but which, for various reasons, cannot be expressly stated. Whether this oblique reference to his plagiarism was in the nature of a private joke, or the result of some psychological quirk by which he was attempting to justify himself, or even deny what he had done, remains a matter of speculation. What seems clear is that he did not intend thereby to draw anyone's attention to his offense; and in fact it has, till now, gone unnoticed.

In the following two years, Franz Praetorius published two books, not dealing with the study of the accents themselves, but intended to solve the problems of the origins and formation of the accents: *Über die Herkunft der hebräischen Accente* (Berlin, 1901) and *Die Übernahme der früh-mittelgriechischen Neumen durch den Juden* (Berlin, 1902). As the second title shows, Praetorius' aim was to prove the Greek origin of the Hebrew signs. This was not the first attempt to prove that the accents were of foreign origin. In 1889, Adalbert Merx, in his *Historia artis grammaticae apud Syros* (Leipzig, 1889—reprinted 1966), pp. 62–75, tried to prove the Syrian origin of the Hebrew signs, and this following his opinion, which is in any case more probable, that the Syriac accents in their turn were of Greek origin.[58] This last view has already been refuted, and it is in place to cite here the relatively recent publication of J. B. Segal, *The Diacritical Point and the Accents in Syriac* (1953), who says of the attribution of the fruits of Syriac creativity to the Greeks, sometimes already suggested by the Syrians themselves (p. 63): "although the influence of Greek rhetoric on the Syriac accents was very great in later times, these statements should be treated with caution. So high was the regard for Greek science that systems, whether of logic or philosophy, were held to be above dispute only if they were assigned a Greek parentage, and much that was of pure Syrian origin was Graecized . . . From internal evidence we may assume a native Syrian origin for the accents." And he concludes, "The resemblance between the Syriac accents and the Greek *neuma* system is no greater than might be expected from their common *raison d'être* and their application to the same work, the Bible." To this he adds (in n. 6) an instructive citation from Nöldeke:

sikalische Werth der Accente völlig unbekannt ist" (p. 2). Büchler's
book derived almost all its information from Wickes, who is referred
to on almost every page, and it contains no contribution whatever
to the advancement of the study of accentuation.

Quite different is A. Ackermann's book, *Das hermeneutische
Element der biblischen Accentuation—Ein Beitrag zur Geschichte
der hebräischen Sprache* (Berlin, 1893). He intended to prove that
the accents were introduced originally for hermeneutical purposes,
that is to say, that the exegetical, and not the musical division
was the main purpose of the signs. The book includes an interesting
historical survey of the theories of the formation of the accents
and their essential nature, at the end of which the author arrives at
a rather convincing conclusion (p. 88): "bei Erfindung der Accentuation selbständig, unabhängig, ohne alle Rücksicht auf den musikalischen Vortrag, die Absicht thätig war, einen Kommentar zur
heiligen schrift zu schaffen." As to the music, he concludes: "die
Entwickelung und Ausbildung des Accentsystems nahm gewiss
einen grossen Zeitraum in Anspruch, und jedenfalls hat die Anlehnung der Melodien an dasselbe auf seine weitere Ausgestaltung
bedeutenden Einfluss geübt, woher es kommt, dass manche Accentverbindungen nur durch musikalische Momente erklärt werden
können." In his discussion he includes four chapters surveying
Biblical exegesis by means of the accents: in the Talmud and
Midrash[49] (Chapter II), by Saadia Gaon (Chapter III), Rashi and his
school (Chapter IV), and Abraham Ibn Ezra (Chapter V); and in the
last chapter (Chapter VI) he surveys briefly the more recent accentual
exegesis, stressing S. Hanau and S. D. Luzzatto.

Ackerman had done a great deal of reading about the accents, but
he displayed a lack of elementary knowledge concerning their rules.
He stumbled, for instance, in an extremely elementary matter when
he mentioned (p. 3) among the postpositive accents the *Great Telisha*
and *Deḥi* (which are both prepositive) and *Revia' Mugrash* (which
is neither); and among the prepositive accents the *Little Telisha*
(which is postpositive). He sometimes argues with Wickes about
principles, but only very rarely, and one gets the impression that
he did not bother to read him attentively. It is not impossible that
he had difficulty in reading English—otherwise it would be difficult
to understand why he did not refer more than five or six times to
Wickes' basic and important books, where most of the relevant

problems are discussed, Wickes' second book having been published
only six years earlier. This suspicion is reinforced by the fact that he
referred (on p. 39) to the chapters on the accents from ספר הנקוד as
being by Ḥayyuǧ, also according to Nutt's edition of 1870,[50] whereas
Nutt explicitly stressed in the English introduction to his edition
(p. XII) that these chapters were definitely not written by Ḥayyuǧ
(an opinion that has been generally accepted ever since).

J. M. Japhet's book, מורה הקורא, *Die Accente der heiligen Schrift*
(Frankfurt a.M., 1896), is a good textbook for Biblical accentuation
without pretensions to scientific research, intended especially for
ritual purposes. It teaches the elements of division of the prose
accents according to the four-grade terminology of Ben-Zeev, as
well as their exegetical ramifications. It is, in fact, the only semi-
popular German textbook for the prose accents,[51] opening the
closed gates of this domain for the German reader who had access
neither to the English of Wickes nor to the Hebrew תלמוד לשון עברי
of Ben-Zeev.[52] In accordance with its purpose, the book is furnished
with many examples, but owing to the custom of synagogal rite
most of them are taken from the Pentateuch or the Book of Esther.
The final pages of musical notations for some Pentateuch passages
also serve the author's purpose, namely to guide cantors.

In 1900 there appeared in London a textbook of the accents in
English by Arthur Davis, למנצח בנגינות משכיל, *The Hebrew Accents
of the Twenty-one Books of the Bible* (כ״א ספרים)... *with a New Introduction*. The justification for publishing this book a few years after
the appearance of Wickes' books is not apparent. Is it possible
that the author intended to furnish the reader with a more popular
treatise? It is, in fact, full of mistakes, and only makes things harder
for the reader, confusing him. It is a considerable regression from
Wickes' work.

Even more, the present author wishes to draw attention to a fact
which, to the best of his knowledge, has not yet been commented
upon. Davis' book is in the main a *literal translation*, sometimes a
bad one, of the chapters relevant to the accents in Ben-Zeev's
תלמוד לשון עברי. Thus, the tables of accents in Davis pp. 4–5[53] are
copied from Ben-Zeev §מה, pp. 46–47[54]; the list of the disjunctive
accents in Davis, p. 8 (there called "distinctive" accents), is copied
from Ben-Zeev §שפ, p. 305; the table on p. 9 is similar to that found
in Ben-Zeev §שפז, p. 305; the large "Table of the connective and

"Everything is not immediately to be regarded as a Graecism which looks like one."

To return to Praetorius and to his supposition of the Greek-Hebrew parentage of the accents, it must be said that his attempt was doomed to failure. Among other things, he did not take into consideration the other accentuation systems, the Babylonian and the Palestinian, which are undoubtedly older than the Tiberian. Although this had already been pointed out by Bergsträsser (*Hebräische Grammatik*, §12q, p. 81), it did not prevent Kahle (*apud* Bauer-Leander, *Historische Grammatik der Hebräischen Sprache des Alten Testamentes*, §9u, pp. 141–142, §9x, pp. 143–145), with all his knowledge of the other punctuation systems, from supporting Praetorius' theory nonetheless. But this brings us to the question of the other punctuation systems, a question to which we shall return immediately. Suffice it to say that the whole problem of the origin and formation of the accents deserves nowadays a new study and evaluation.[59]

The book of Eberhard Homel, *Untersuchungen zur hebräischen Lautlehre, Erster Teil: Der Akzent des Hebräischen nach Zeugnissen der Dialekte und der alten Grammatiker mit Beiträgen zur Geschichte der Phonetik* (Leipzig, 1917), made no substantial contribution to the advancement of this study, and it is amazing that this book was included in such an important series as Rudolf Kittel's *Beiträge zur Wissenschaft vom Alten Testament* (*Heft* 23). The author devoted his book to the "*Untersuchungen*" of everything that the term "*Akzent*" comprises, especially the phonetic stress on the one hand, and the Biblical accent on the other. In order to cover such a wide field, he gathered vast material from the domain of Hebrew and Semitic phonetics as compared to Greek and Latin sources, and Roman and Slavic languages, as well as from the domain of Hebrew and Aramaic dialectology, musicology, metaphysics, and Kabbala, and Biblical accentuation and the Masora according to its various traditions (Babylonian, Palestinian). This was drawn from all the sources at his disposal, be it written medieval sources or living pronunciation of various contemporary communities. All this material is arranged in great disorder. It is self-evident that he could bring but very superficial information from all these domains, and one seeks in vain for any real method and achievement in his research.

We come now, in our survey, to the most important work on accents after Wickes, and the most recent one. This is the book of Arthur Spanier, *Die massoretischen Akzente—Eine Darlegung ihres Systems nebst Beiträgen zum Verständnis ihrer Entwicklung* (Berlin, 1927). He, too, made it the crux of his study to determine the original objective of the Biblical accents. Unlike some of his predecessors, Ackermann, for instance, he did not content himself with "external" considerations deriving from the evidence of various sources, literary and historical, outside the accents, but based his entire research on an internal historical study of the accentuation system itself. He understood that there is no possibility of coming to decisive conclusions in the questions of the origin and the development of the accents solely on the basis of the Tiberian system, and therefore he invested no little effort in the study of the other accentuation systems, especially the Babylonian.

In 1901 Kahle had already pointed out[60] Wickes' fundamental error in the evaluation of the Babylonian accents in the Petersburg manuscript of the Prophets, an error that deprived him of a true understanding of the Babylonian system, and of a reasonable estimate of its date.[61] Kahle published many texts in Babylonian punctuation, primarily MS. Berlin or. qu. 680 of the Hagiographa, which served as the basis for his book *Der masoretische Text des Alten Testaments, nach der Überlieferung der babylonischen Juden* (Leiden, 1902—reprinted 1966). The overall method of the Babylonian accentuation in these texts is quite different from that of the Petersburg manuscript, and with regard to the conjuctive accents they are totally different. Thus the ground was cut from under Wickes' hypothesis as regards the Babylonian accentuation, but there was no new one to take its place. Kahle contented himself with accepting, with some adaptations, Praetorius' opinion on the origin of the accents. But this opinion was based on the facts of the Tiberian system, and Kahle did not go as far in his comparative study with regard to the other systems as was to be expected, especially since, in his opinion, the two other systems, the Babylonian and the Palestinian, were older than the Tiberian system. It is more than evident that a discussion of the origin of all the systems has to rely principally on the more ancient ones.

This was done by Spanier. He rightly put the stress on what he called the *Satzakzent*, and examined the internal structure of the division and the function of the graphemes in every one of the systems. These aspects interested him more than the observation of the graphic shapes of the signs and their nomenclature, as studied by Kahle.[62] Spanier compared the most current *Akzentkonstellationen* of the Tiberian system with those of the Babylonian. This brought him to quite a detailed analysis of the structure of the sentence (*Satzstruktur*) and its various types, verbal clauses (*Verbalsätze*), nominal clauses (*Nominalsätze*), and even some definite sentence members (*Satzteile*), first of all in the Tiberian system, but also quite thoroughly in the Babylonian system. Although he devoted an entire chapter to the examination of the Petersburg manuscript (Codex Babylonicus), he dealt no less thoroughly, in another chapter, with the methods of the Babylonian accentuation as current in other manuscripts, especially in fragments of the Geniza. These methods he summed up and classified in three groups (a, b, c) also exhibiting more "primitive" traits than the complicated (*Kompliziert*) method of the Petersburg manuscript.

He dealt with the Palestinian system to a lesser degree, for he had only a few texts at his disposal. On the basis of these few texts he was able to arrive at a conclusion different from Kahle's as to the ages of the various systems. In his opinion (p. 106), the Babylonian is the oldest system; from it derived the Palestinian system, and finally the Tiberian—as against Kahle, who thought the Palestinian system to be the first one, followed later by the Babylonian.[63] Only when Spanier's book was coming off the press did Kahle's *Masoreten des Westens*, Vol. I (1927) appear, with its abundance of Palestinian texts. Spanier remarked in the *Nachtrag* to his book (p. 143) that in the light of this new material, although it does not comprise many accentuated Biblical texts, the relation between the various accentuation systems seems much more complicated than he had thought, and in any case the Palestinian system cannot be a development of the Babylonian system.

The minute examination of the accentuation systems brought Spanier to some important conclusions in basic questions of the accentuation. Although attempts had been made before him, to solve these questions, it was never on the basis of a comparative historical study. Regarding the question of the primary objective of the accents, Spanier categorically ruled out the possibility of the musical theory which claims that the accents were fixed primarily as musical notes (p. 110). Of the two other theories, the hermeneutic and the rhetoric, Spanier gave preference to the second, being of the opinion that the correct reading of the text was essentially the main objective of the accents. He adduced evidence for his view, especially from the mutual influences between the accentuation and the vocalization, an influence that is due to naught but the natural interrelation between the *Satzakzent* and the *Wortakzent*. Were the masoretic rules of the correct reading, as expressed by the accents, norms for the reader, fixed by the Masoretes? Or were these accents nothing but a form of notation of the reading transmitted for generations? According to Spanier (p. 112), "lässt sich das eine vom anderen gar nicht trennen; insbesondere ist nicht einzusehen, wie man Normen der Vortragsweise schaffen konnte, ohne dabei die Überlieferung aufs weitgehendste zu berücksichtigen. Die Vortragsweise, die aus der akzentuatorischen Gliederung resultiert, ist daher im ganzen als die Überlieferung anzusehen, die die Akzentuatoren vorfanden."

And from here he comes to questions of influence by foreign cultural spheres like Greek, according to Praetorius,[64] and Syrian, according to Merx.[64] Spanier disagrees with both scholars because they did not take into consideration the other, older accentuation systems. Besides, the Hebrew accents are essentially different from the foreign ones, especially the Greek, as he states (p. 114): "die hebräischen Akzente—soviel darf jetzt wohl als erwiesen gelten—beziehen sich unmittelbar nur auf ein quantitatives Element des rednerischen Vortrages, nämlich auf die verschiedenen Masse der Pausenlängen; dass dabei auch das Auf- und Absteigen der Stimme sowie andere qualitative Momente zur Geltung kommen, ist gewissermassen nur zufällig. Das war im Griechischen bei der ganz anders gearteten Struktur der Sprache kaum möglich, und die von Praetorius behandelten Neumen sind denn auch nach seiner eigenen Darstellung von vornherein auf qualitative Momente des Ausdrucks basiert."

Spanier also disagreed, and rightly so, with the idea of Syrian provenance, and here he had an additional reason—the chronology. According to Merx,[65] the Hebrew accentuation system was borrowed from the Syrians not before the sixth century. According to Spanier, the *terminus a quo* of the accentuation is earlier, as the accentuation was already known among the Jews around the year

400.[66] According to the present author, one might consider an earlier date, even one century before.[67] In any case, at such an early date the Syrian accentuation system was not yet developed.[68] His conclusion is, then, (p. 115): "Äusserliche Zeichen der Akzentuation mögen um 400 noch gefehlt haben—obgleich auch das keineswegs wahrscheinlich ist; aber man besass doch jedenfalls schon das klare Bewusstsein, dass die Akzentuation durch die Syntax bedingt sei. Das aber ist das Entscheidende."

Spanier's attitude was severely criticized in P. Kahle's review of his book in *OLZ*, 31 (1928), cols. 581–584, Kahle manifesting as little tolerance toward Spanier as he did toward Wickes.[69] Spanier responded in a self-edited 16-leaf booklet, *Der Satzakzent im Hebräischen. Eine Erwiederung auf eine Rezension meines Buches "Die massoretischen Akzente"* (Berlin, 1928). This was reviewed by G. Bergsträsser in *OLZ*, 33 (1930), cols. 528–530, who utilized the opportunity to intervene in the dispute. While he did not take exception to Spanier's book as categorically as did Kahle, he quite rightly was not prepared to accept Spanier's view that the accents as known to us represent the ancient *Satzakzent* dating from the time Hebrew was a living language. On the other hand, Bergsträsser definitely preferred Spanier's approach. In his opinion, Spanier's studies in the rules of accentuation, their application, and their significance had led him much further in the attempt to solve such basic problems as he had set forth. He thought Kahle less qualified for this and did not hesitate to say so (col. 528): "In seinen eigenen umfassenden, vor allem auf die Geschichte der Akzentzeichen und Akzentnamen gerichteten Forschungen befangen ist Kahle anderen Betrachtungsweisen der hebräischen Akzentuation vielleicht zu wenig zugänglich."

*   *

*

Spanier's study is indeed the first extensive comparative work in the various accentuation systems, and almost the only one to this day. Study of the accents since then has, in fact, shown but small progress. The chief interest has been in the publication of new texts, especially of the other punctuation systems. This material is not rich in accents; nevertheless, some material has been accumuluated during these years, material that makes a more fundamental and thorough study both possible and necessary.

The great stimulus to the publication of texts in other punctuation systems after Wickes was given by Paul Kahle in his book, *Der masoretische Text des Alten Testaments, nach der Überlieferung der babylonischen Juden* (Leipzig, 1902—reprinted 1966), where he published portions of Ms. or. qu. 680 of the Royal Library of Berlin, containing parts of the Hagiographa with Babylonian vocalization and accentuation. After some years appeared his *Masoreten den Ostens* (Leipzig, 1913—reprinted 1966), in which he published the largest collection—approximately 100 pages—of Babylonian texts with vocalization and accentuation. J. Weerts also published a text of some chapters of Job, with a detailed analysis, in his article, "Über die babylonisch punktierte Handschrift No. 1546 der II. Firkowitschschen Sammlung (Codex Tschufutkale No. 3)," *ZAW*, 26 (1906), pp. 49–84.

More recently, Alejandro Díez Macho published an additional text, "Fragmento del texto hebreo y arameo del libro de Númerus escrito en una muy antigua megil.lá en el sistema babilónico," *Sefarad*, 17 (1957), pp. 386–388.[70] An important fragment with Babylonian accents in a text of abbreviations was published by I. Yeivin, "A Babylonian Fragment of the Bible in the Abbreviated System," *Textus*, 2 (1962), pp. 120–139. He also described and published photographs of a Yemenite manuscript with Babylonian punctuation in *Kirjath Sepher*, 39 (1963–1964), pp. 563–572.

In the domain of the Palestinian punctuation, the material is even more scarce. The first publication of this system appeared only after the publication of Wickes' books. A. Neubauer, in "The Hebrew Bible in Shorthand Writing," *JQR* O.S., 7 (1895), pp. 361–364, published for the first time a fragment written in abbreviations and furnished—this he did not realize—with Palestinian vocalization and accentuation. The deciphering of this system was done by M. Friedländer, "A Third System of Symbols for the Hebrew Vowels and Accents," in the same year and journal, pp. 564–568, as well as in his paper, "Some Fragments of the Hebrew Bible with Peculiar Abbreviations and Peculiar Signs for Vowels and Accents," *Proceedings of the Society of Biblical Archaeology*, 18 (1896), pp. 86–98.[71] After them, Kahle published a long article "Beiträge zur Geschichte der hebräischen Punktation, " *ZAW*, 21

(1901), pp. 273–317, in which there is a long text written in abbreviations with Palestinian vocalization and accentuation. And a few years later appeared Kahle's *Masoreten des Westens*, in which he discussed, among other subjects, the Palestinian punctuation, and where he published quite a number of texts: liturgical texts in Vol. I (1927), and, what is more pertinent to our subject, texts of the Bible and the (Palestinian) Aramaic version with Palestinian vocalization and accentuation in Vol. II (1930). (Both volumes were reissued in 1967.)

In recent years Alejandro Díez Macho published some new fragments with Palestinian accentuation: "Tres nuevos manuscritos bíblicos 'palestinenses'," *Estudios Bíblicos*, 13 (1954), pp. 247–265; "Un manuscrito 'palestinense' en la Biblioteca Nacional de Estrasburgo," *Sefarad*, 17 (1957), pp. 11–17; and, together with N. Allony, "Dos Manuscritos 'palestinenses' más de la Geniza del Cairo," *Estudios Bíblicos*, 17 (1958), pp. 83–100; "Otros dos manuscritos 'Palestinenses' de Salmos," *Sefarad*, 18 (1958), pp. 254–271.

A little material on the accents is to be found also in the important contribution to the study of the Palestinian vocalization by A. Murtonen, *Materials for a non-Masoretic Hebrew Grammar, I. Liturgical Texts and Psalm Fragments Provided with the So-Called Palestinian Punctuation* (Helsinki, 1958). The Biblical material in this publication is identical with the texts published in the same year by Allony and Díez Macho in *Estudios Bíblicos* and in *Sefarad* (see above) . These texts are very poor in accents and were not published with great accuracy; see the corrections to these texts by N. Allony and A. Díez Macho, "Lista de variantes en la edición de los Mss. 'Palestinenses' T–S 20/58 y 20/52," *Estudios Bíblicos*, 18 (1959), pp. 293–298.

An important contribution to accentuology was made by Díez Macho in "La cantilación protomasorética del Pentateuco," *Estudios Bíblicos*, 18 (1959), pp. 223–251, where he published and discussed a photocopy of a manuscript with unconventional Tiberian[72] punctuation and paid special attention to its accentuation, which, although using the graphemes and the conventions of the Tiberian system, displays a different way of dividing verses. Díez Macho had already published a text of this kind in "Un manuscrito hebreo protomasorético y nueva teoría acerca de los llamados MSS. Ben Naftalí," *Estudios Bíblicos*, 15 (1956), pp. 187–222; but the thorough examination of this accentuation system was done some years later in the above-mentioned paper. Through a comparative study with the conventional Tiberian system and the other accentuation systems he arrives at interesting conclusions regarding the formation of the recitational tradition of the Biblical text, a tradition which, in his opinion, had been rather unstable for some time. In this he takes Kahle's side as against Spanier.

Lately some mixed texts simultaneously showing different punctuation signs have been published, and they can shed new light on the problems of the origin and formation of the vocalization and accentuation systems. Here again A. Díez Macho exhibited primacy, for already in 1954 he drew attention to this in his above-mentioned paper in *Estudios Biblicos* 13, where he discussed a Palestinian manuscript with additional Tiberian vocalization and accentuation, and published a Babylonian manuscript with additional Palestinian vocalization and accentuation. The text of the Palestinian-Tiberian manuscript mentioned was later published by Paul Kahle, *The Cairo Geniza*[2] (Oxford, 1959), Appendix III, pp. 336–344, and Plates 5–6, and by Díez Macho himself in the above-mentioned paper in *Estudios Biblicos*, 18 (1959), pp. 223–251 (the deciphering of the two is not identical). Another Palestinian-Tiberian text with the deciphering of Manfried Dietrich was published by Kahle, *Der Hebräische Bibeltext seit Franz Delitzsch* (Stuttgart, 1961), Plates 19–20. Still another fragment of this type was published by Israel Yeivin, "A Palestinian Fragment of Haftaroth and Other MSS with Mixed Pointing (with two plates)," *Textus*, 3 (1963), pp. 121–127.

It seems that this aspect of mixed punctuation had not been dwelt upon in the earlier years of the publication of non-Tiberian texts. Only a very sharp and knowing eye, looking constantly for additional signs, can detect traces of other systems in a manuscript. The chances diminish when it is photocopies rather than the original manuscripts that are being checked. Insofar as nobody had been looking for such signs prior to the appearance of Díez Macho's above-mentioned paper, it stands to reason that many specimens have been overlooked and the additional signs passed unnoticed. To give one instance which the present author has encountered: he believes that he has detected some definitely clear Tiberian accents, and only accents, in an Oxford Geniza fragment with Babylonian vocalization and accentuation, published by Kahle in

Masoreten des Ostens (pp. 30–32) under No. 24 b, of which one page
was photographically reproduced in *Tafel* 5 there. These are not
conjunctive accents occasionally found in complementary distribu-
tion in systematically contaminated texts, e.g., Codex Babylonicus,[73]
but regular disjunctive accents such as *Pashṭa*, *Tevir*, *Geresh*, and
Revia' in their regular places according to our Tiberian Text, side
by side with their Babylonian counterparts. This is, then, still
another mixed text, Babylonian-Tiberian—and had gone unnoticed
by Kahle. It goes without saying that the original manuscript may
yield more than the photograph. It seems that this aspect of mixed
punctuation—vocalization and accentuation alike—should be re-
investigated and all manuscripts, both published and unpublished,
should undergo a thorough checking.

Most of the articles on other accentuation systems have as their
main objective the mere publication of the material, and only
infrequently its analysis for the determination of its accentuation
rules. Research into the laws of accentuation according to the
different systems—the Babylonian and especially the Palestinian—
has been scanty since Spanier. Scholars have contented themselves
with pointing out the Babylonian or Palestinian equivalents of the
Tiberian accents in any examined context. Each accentuation system
has been examined very little *per se*, without reference to the Tiberian
system. The question of whether there is in another system, or at
least in some manuscripts, a principle of division different from the
principle underlying the Tiberian division has, to the best of the
present author's knowledge, not yet been presented; and it is time
to do so and to attempt an answer. All the new material which has
been published lately certainly deserves and justifies a new study.

In recent years, since Spanier, only a few studies merit special
attention, such as the posthumous article of Akiba E. Schlesinger
טעמי אמ״ת וטעמי כ״א ספרים (= "The Accent Systems of Psalms,
Proverbs, and Job, and those of the Other Books of the Bible"),
Eretz-Israel: Archeological, Historical and Geographical Studies,
3 (1954), pp. 194–198.[74] This article touched on some questions
of the interrelation of the Tiberian and Babylonian accentuation
systems. Another interesting study is the paper of I. Yeivin, השפעה
תחבירית והשפעה מוסיקאלית על דרכי הקפת תיבות זעירות) = Syntactical
and musical influence on the *Maqqef* of small words), *Leshonenu*,
23 (1959), pp. 35–48. More important is another article by Yeivin,

dealing with a neglected aspect of the accents, namely the accentuation of non-Biblical texts: הטעמת תורה שבעל פה בטעמים (= The accentuation of texts of the Oral Law), *Leshonenu*, 24 (1960), pp. 47–69, 167–178, 207–231. This is a comprehensive article reviewing a large part of the texts, mostly Geniza, of Mishna and Midrash (and in an Appendix, also some פיוטים), with Tiberian and Palestinian (not Babylonian) accentuation, whether similar to the Biblical accentuation or methodically different from it.

While it has been possible to point out some new texts and a few recently published articles in the domain of research, almost nothing has been done in the domain of instructional textbooks in this subject. The only book that may be mentioned is that by M. Breuer, פיסוק טעמים שבמקרא (Jerusalem, 1958), a book with no scientific pretensions, into which a great deal of good will has been invested, but whose declared major aim, i.e., didactic, does not seem to have been successfully achieved, for the student, especially the beginner, is sometimes rather confused by this textbook. The final chapter on the hermeneutic application of the accents is quite useful.

It seems to the present author that in the field of instruction, too, as a method for learning the accentuation, no less than in the domain of research, Wickes' work was, and still remains, the basic standard work with no substitute. The republication of his books, which ran out of print long ago, is therefore timely, and the publisher should be congratulated for his initiative and the editor of the series for his felicitous choice. It is to be hoped that this new edition will enable wider circles to enter into this neglected domain. and thus arouse public interest in Biblical accentuation and advance its study.

Aron Dotan,
Head of Dept. of Hebrew Language,
Tel Aviv University

December 1968

NOTES

1. An ancient treatise known to us through many versions, adaptations, and compendia. For a detailed survey of the extant manuscripts and printed editions, see A. Bendavid, in *Beth Mikra*, 3 (1958), p. 8.

2. On the two versions of this treatise, see below, note 10.

3. Elijah Levita's treatise on the accents, first published in Venice in 1538, with many subsequent editions.

4. See now the present author's edition of this book, *The Diqduqé Haṭṭe'amim of Aharon ben Moše ben Ašer, with a Critical Edition of the Original Text from New Manuscripts*, published by the Academy of the Hebrew Language, Jerusalem, 1967. (Hereafter: Dotan, *DQHT*.)

5. Attributed erroneously to Yehuda Ibn Bal'am. Published by J. Mercerus, ספר טעמי המקרא *Liber de accentibus scripturae autore R. Juda filio Balaam* (Paris, 1565).

6. Manuscript in the Ambrosian Library, Milan, No. A. 186. Wickes made use of this manuscript and discussed it (טעמי כ״א ספרים, pp. X–XI). A detailed description was given by C. Bernheimer, *Codices hebraici Bybliothecae Ambrosianae* (Florence, 1933), pp. 112–114 (Ms. No. 88).

7. One of the adaptations of the treatise is included also in the book '*Adat Devorim*, which is a compilation and also includes some additional works, such as the *Kitāb al-Khulaf* by Mishael ben 'Uzziel (Hebrew version), and some material of *Diqduqé Haṭṭeamim*, etc. See A. Bendavid's paper mentioned in note 1 above, on the different manuscripts of this treatise and their names.

8. Leopold Dukes, *Grammatische Werke des R. Jehuda Chajjug aus Fess* (Stuttgart, 1844), pp. 191 ff.; John W. Nutt, *Two Treatises on Verbs Containing Feeble and Double Letters by R. Jehuda Ḥayug of Fez . . . to which was added the Treatise on Punctuation . . .* (London and Berlin, 1870), Hebrew text, pp. 126 ff.

9. As was already pointed out by Nutt in the English introduction to his edition (see previous note), p. XII.

10. The Arabic version published by A. Neubauer, *Petite grammaire hébraïque provenant de Yemen, texte arabe publié d'après les manuscrits connus* (Leipzig, 1891). The Hebrew version was published by J. Derenbourg, *Manuel du lecteur, d'un auteur inconnu, publié d'après un manuscrit venu du Yémen et accompagné de notes* (Paris, 1871; = *JA*, 16 (1870), pp. 309–550).

11. Published first by Ya'aqov ben Ḥayyim ibn Adonijah in the Second Rabbinic Bible (Venice, 1524–25), and many times since, sometimes under the name שער הניקוד והנגינות.

12. One chapter of his treatise was published by Y. F. Gumpertz, *Leshonenu*, 22 (1958), pp. 36–47, 137–146.

13. *Ausführliches Lehrbuch der Hebräischen Sprache des Alten Bundes*, 7. Ausgabe (Göttingen, 1863), p. 251.

14. *Double Merkha* was regarded as a disjunctive accent, although from the pausal standpoint it is no doubt a conjunctive accent. See also Dotan, *DQHT*, pp. 157, 337.

15. Especially as a part of the disjunctive accent מונח לגרמיה.

16. There it is named rather מורכב (in the original: "*compl.*").

17. This is my rendering of "*simpl.*" (= *simplex*). The term should then include both *Great Revia'* and *Little Revia'*.

18. This date is given at the end of the introduction.

19. I have not seen this publication.

20. As an appendix to his grammatical compendium שערי תורה (Hamburg, 1718). This edition is now very rare. The first independent edition of שערי זמרה is probably the 1762 Fürth edition.

21. This first, and now rare, edition was followed by many editions from all over Europe.

22. H. Ewald, *op. cit.* (see n. 13 above), p. 251.

23. In fact, it is chiefly the verbal formulation that is the author's work. But as to the contents, Heidenheim drew much, as we know today, from the work of Yequti'el Hanaqdan (יהב״י), which he had before him in manuscript form, see Y. F. Gumpertz, *op. cit.* (see n. 12 above), pp. 36 ff.

24. Baer was 7 years old when Heidenheim died, so it is astonishing that Kahle could say: "Seligman Baer (1825–97) in his early youth seems to have been in contact with Wolf Heidenheim (1757–1832)" (*The Cairo Geniza*[2], Oxford, 1959, p. 113).

25. Heidenheim only gave some isolated rules on the accents of the poetical books in the introduction of his Psalms edition (Rödelheim, 1825). He had, however, intended to publish such a book (ספר משפטי טעמי אמת), as he himself stated at the end of this introduction (p. יב).

26. For instance, we find a whole discussion of the transformation of accents (the title of Chapter XVIII being "Transformation der Accente"), a concept and a term borrowed wholly from Wickes. I have not seen the first edition of this German work, which is appended to the first edition of Delitzsch's Commentary on Psalms, Vol. II (Leipzig, 1860), but I suppose that these additional chapters are not to be found there. (Wickes' book on the poetical accents was published only in 1881.)

27. As the first part of his work שתי ידות (Venice, 1618).

28. First published posthumously in the Mantua Bible, 1740–1742.

29. We find the same tendency in the way he edited the *Dikduke Ha-Teamim* (Leipzig, 1879).

30. There also appeared an English translation of this book: *Prolegomena to a Grammar of the Hebrew Language by Samuel David Luzzatto, translated from Italian by Sabato Morais* (New York, 5656–1896). This was published as an appendix to *Proceedings of the Fifth Biennial Convention of the Jewish Theological Seminary Association;* however, the English version does not include the appendices, nor the most important appendix on the accents.

31. The minor accents, תלישא גדולה and פזר, and sometimes also מונח לגרמיה, are generally regarded as forming another class, but here they are considered as substitutes for other accents rather than as independent accents.

32. According to Wickes, טעמי אמ״ת, p. 38, n. 1, who quotes Spitzner. The present author has had no opportunity to consult the book directly.

33. One has to wonder that Wickes did not make use of the valuable first steps taken by S. Hanau in this regard (see above, p. xi), nor did he even mention him in the bibliographical lists of his books.

34. See, e.g., Dotan, *DQHT*, Part III, p. 358, n. 19.

35. Lazar Lipschütz, *Der Bibeltext der tiberischen Masoretenschulen, Ben Ašer – Ben Naftali. Eine Abhandlung des Mischael ben 'Uzziel, nach Leningrader Handschriften veröffentlicht* (Mukačevo, 1935), pp. 15–18; Paul Kahle, *The Cairo Geniza*[2] (Oxford, 1959), pp. 114–116; A. Dotan, *Beth Mikra*, 23–24 (1965), pp. 105–106.

36. See Dotan, *DQHT*, Part II, pp. 194–195.

37. See טעמי כ״א ספרים, p. viii, nn. 6, 7; p. ix, nn. 8, 9. That Baer's lists were a fabrication has already been proved, first by L. Lipschütz (see above, n. 35), pp. 14 ff.

38. טעמי כ״א ספרים, p. viii. But see now Dotan, *DQHT*, Part II, p. 237, where Baer's false interpretation is rectified.

39. This view was advanced by the present author in his paper, "Was the Aleppo Codex Actually Vocalized by Aharon Ben Asher?", *Tarbiz*, 34 (1965), pp. 136–155, and was favorably received in scholarly circles; see, e.g., H. M. Orlinsky in his Prolegomenon *The Masoretic Text: A Critical Evaluation* to C. D. Ginsburg, *Introduction to the Massoretico-Critical Edition of the Hebrew Bible* (KTAV Publishing House, 1966), pp. XVI–XVII, XXX–XXXI, XXXIV. The present author had in mind mainly to call attention to the fact that not every single reading in the Codex, however characteristically divergent from

our concept of Ben Asher's reading, need really be regarded as Ben Asher's authentic reading only because it appears in the Codex. And in consequence, the Codex should not be our sole documentation for Ben Asher's readings, as it has indeed been held to be by some scholars. However, it seems that a statement of the situation such as that given by M. H. Goshen-Gottstein, *The Book of Isaiah, Sample Edition with Introduction* (Jerusalem, 1965), p. 20, §30, already takes into account the difficulties pointed out in the above-mentioned paper, and proposes a new attitude which seems a considerable departure from his former one, and takes into reasonable consideration the possibility that the Codex was not produced by Ben Asher *prima manus*.

40. As found, for instance, in the Codex Reuchlinianus and the like. Various names have been proposed for this system, like "pseudo-Palestinian," "Palestinian-Tiberian," "proto-masoretic," or even "non-masoretic." Kahle's term, "Ben Naftali," for this system is, as is now generally accepted, wrong. The term "unconventional Tiberian" herewith proposed for the first time, seems to the present author most adequate, for it says nothing about the chronology of the system ("proto"), or about its relation to the other systems (Palestinian?), but simply indicates that while using Tiberian signs this system does not follow the conventional Tiberian manner of punctuation. Since unconventional Tiberian texts do have Masora, it is evident that any appellation like "proto-masoretic" or "non-masoretic" proves to be misleading.

40a. See also H. M. Orlinsky's enlightening discussion of the concept "*the* masoretic text" in his Prolegomenon (mentioned above in n. 39), pp. XXXV–XXXVI, where he rightly claims: "While it is impossible *a priori* to achieve '*the* masoretic text' when none ever obtained, it would seem possible in theory to produce a Hebrew text of the Bible with the claim that it is derived from '*a* masoretic text'."

41. For instance, by P. Kahle, *Der hebräische Bibeltext seit Franz Delitzsch* (Stuttgart, 1961), pp. 67–69. See now H. M. Orlinsky, op. cit. (cf. n. 39, above), pp. XXIX ff.

42. As an example of the present author's idea about the method that should be applied in formulating accentuation rules, see Dotan, *DQHT*, pp. 203–205, where he attempted a new rendering of the rules of the disjunctive *Şinnor* in the poetical books, based solely on the description of the situation in one manuscript, namely Leningrad B19a (= *Biblia Hebraica*[3]).

43. S. Pinsker, *Einleitung in das babylonisch-hebräische Punktationssystem* (Wien, 1863); and also (as mentioned in טעמי כ״א ספרים, p. 147, note 15) H. L. Strack in *Zeitschrift für Lutheranische Theologie*, 1877, pp. 31–32, and in *Herzog's Encyclopaedie*, IX, p. 393, "Masora."

44. The manuscript was published in 1876, in a photo-lithographic edition, by H. L. Strack, *Prophetarum posteriorum Codex Babylonicus Petropolitanus.*

45. I.e., Tiberian.

46. See "*Extracts from notices and reviews*" on his טעמי אמ״ת (with quotations from S. R. Driver, A. Neubauer, C. Siegfried, F. Delitzsch, and Prof. Guidi), printed on the reverse side of the last page (p. 155) of טעמי כ״א ספרים.

47. P. Kahle *apud* Bauer-Leander, *Historische Grammatik der Hebräischen Sprache des Alten Testamentes*, p. 147, note 1.

48. And see below (p. xxxvii) Bergsträsser's low opinion of Kahle's qualifications.

49. In this chapter he does not, in fact, deal with the accentual exegesis but with the question of whether the accents are mentioned at all in the Talmud. His conclusion is the current negative one.

50. Mentioned in note 8 above.

51. For the poetical accents there existed Baer's German version of תורת אמת, see p. xiii above.

52. See p. xii above.

53. Davis has a double pagination, one for the introduction, pp. 1–28, and another for the rest of the book, starting again from p. 1. Hereafter, unless

otherwise indicated, reference will be made only to the second pagination, not to that of the introduction.

54. References are according to the Königsberg edition of 1859.

55. Rendered by Davis: "and there are seventeen instances where מֶרְכָּא כְפוּלָה is employed in the place of תְּבִיר."

56. And in what sequence: Elias Levita before David Kimchi!

57. There is another oddity about this final phrase. Over some of its letters there are asterisks: עַל כֵּן עָמַד טַעְמוּ בּוֹ וְרֵיחוֹ לֹא נָמָר. The sum total of the numerical values of all the asterisked letters (עמעמבררלר) is 652; and if this number should refer to the Hebrew calendar year (תרנ״ב), then it corresponds to the year 1892. But the book was published in 1900, as printed on the title page. Perhaps 1892 was the year when Davis finished his manuscript. Curiously enough, G. Bergsträsser, in his *Hebräische Grammatik* (Leipzig, 1918), when referring to this book (§12a, p. 73) indicated 1892 as the year of publication! Where does this date come from? It might be an interesting, highly coincidental printer's error in Bergsträsser's work. It seems hardly possible that he intentionally abandoned the date formally indicated on Davis' title page, preferring this hinted date.

58. In this particular supposition he was preceded already by Rubens Duval, *Traité de grammaire Syriaque* (Paris, 1881), pp. 137 ff.

59. Chronologically speaking, I. Adams, *Sermons in Accents* (London, 1906) should have been discussed here, but unfortunately this book was not accessible to the present author.

60. "Zur Geschichte der hebräischen Accente," *ZDMG*, 55 (1901), pp. 184–186.

61. See p. xxvi above.

62. See p. xxxvii below for Bergsträsser's pertinent criticism of Kahle in this respect.

63. See Kahle, *apud* Bauer-Leander, *op. cit.*, §9s p. 140, §9w p. 143.

64. See p. xxxii above.

65. A Merx, *Historia artis grammaticae apud Syros* (Leipzig, 1889—reprinted 1966), pp. 75–76.

66. Spanier, p. 115. He is not far from Wickes' opinion, who suggested as *terminus a quo* the early part of the 5th century (טעמי אמ״ת, p. 9).

67. He intends to discuss this question in another paper.

68. J. B. Segal, *The Diacritical Point and the Accents in Syriac*, p. 58, maintains that the real development of the Syriac accents took place in the course of the 5th century.

69. See p. xxvii above.

70. In what follows, mention will be made only of publications of new material, not of announcements of discovered manuscripts, or mere descriptions. We shall deal only with texts of all kinds containing accents, therefore excluding publications like those of A. Díez Macho in *Estudios Bíblicos*, 16 (1957) and 18 (1959), *et al.*

71. The other discoverer of the Palestinian punctuation was Caspar Levias, who published a slightly different text in his paper, "The Palestinian Vocalization," *AJSL*, 15 (1898/99), pp. 156–164 (the present author has not seen this paper). But his texts do not concern us, because they are liturgical texts without accents.

72. On this term, see note 40 above.

73. See above: pp. xxvi, xxxiv and note 44.

74. This was reprinted in his memorial volume, *Researches in the Exegesis and Language of the Bible by Akiba Schlesinger* (Publications of the Israel Society for Biblical Research, Vol. 9; Jerusalem, 1962), pp. 79–89.

PREFACE.

In preparing the following treatise I have had to depend almost entirely on my own investigations. The Christian accentuologists of the 17th and 18th centuries, to whom we owe the discovery of the leading principles that underlie the Hebrew accentuation, were not successful (as, I presume, all who have consulted their Works will allow) in dealing with the peculiar system of the three so-called Poetical Books. I have gained therefore but little help from them. In the present century, only two scholars, Ewald and Baer, have ventured on an independent examination of the subject. Ewald's speculations[1] I have not been able to accept. Baer's treatises[2]—which shew very careful preparation, and are valuable, as containing (like Heidenheim's משפטי הטעמים for the twenty-one Books) the traditional views handed down by Rabbinical authorities—I did not find reach far enough for my purpose.

I may draw attention to one respect in which the present Work differs from any of those which have preceded it. It is founded, in a great measure, on an extensive examination of MSS. I soon saw that even our best texts need correction, as far as the accents are concerned; and that, without a correct text, I could not hope to establish any rules on a satisfactory basis. I therefore visited the leading Libraries of Europe, and collated, as far as seemed necessary, most of the known MSS. The main results are given in the course of the following pages. I venture to hope that this part of my Work will be particularly acceptable to scholars.

---

[1] Lehrbuch der Heb. Sprache, p. 227 ff.

[2] תורת אמת (Rödelheim, 1852), and Das Accentuationssystem der Psalmen, des Buches Iob und der Sprüche, überlieferungsgemäss seinen Gesetzen nach dargestellt, in an Appendix to Delitzsch's Commentary on the Psalms (Leipzig, 1860).

I have given, as an Appendix, the treatise assigned to Ben-Bil'am, in the original Arabic. This treatise is so far interesting as it contains the first known attempt to furnish a systematic account of the accentuation of the three Books, and as it remained, through the Middle Ages, the chief authority on the subject. The reader must, however, be prepared to find the rules given quite elementary.

In conclusion, I have to acknowledge my obligations to Dr. Baer, as a personal friend. The assistance he has willingly rendered me, whenever his extensive Masoretic and Rabbinical learning could be of service to me, has been very valuable. I am also indebted to Dr. A. Neubauer for much kind interest and advice.

W. WICKES.

11, Woodstock Road, Oxford,
August, 1881.

MSS. CONSULTED FOR THE PRESENT WORK.

I. Bible MSS.

B. M. MSS. in the British Museum. For the sake of brevity, I have given my own numbers to these MSS.[1] 1 stands for Add. 21161[2]; 2 for Add. 15250; 3 for King's 1, 271 E; 4, 5, 6, 7, 8, 9, and 10 for Harl. 1528, 5498, 5506, 5711, 5715, 5775, and 7622 respectively; and 11, 12, 13, 14, 15, 16, 17, and 18 for Add. 9398, 9399, 9402, 9406, 15251, 15252, 15451, and 18830.

Ber. MSS. in the Royal Library, Berlin. The numbers given are those of the printed catalogue.

Cam. MSS. in the University Library, Cambridge. See printed catalogue.

Cop. MSS. in the Royal Library, Copenhagen. See printed catalogue.

De R. De Rossi's MSS., now in the Royal Library, Parma. See De Rossi's printed catalogue.

Erf. The well-known Erfurt MSS. 1–4, described by Lagarde in his Symmicta, p. 133 ff. (These MSS. are now in the Royal Library, Berlin.)[3]

Fr. A MS. at Frankfurt on the Main, written A.D. 1294 by the grandson of the punctator Simson (now in the possession of Herr S. M. Goldschmidt).

Ghet. Three MSS. in the Ghetto, Rome—No. 1 in the *Scuola del Tempio*, Nos. 2 and 3 in the Castilian Synagogue.

---

[1] It is a disgrace to our great national Library that there is no printed catalogue of the Hebrew MSS. Nor are steps being taken, as far as I can ascertain, to have one made. One has to hunt now, with loss of time and patience, through poorly prepared written catalogues—in one of which Heb. MSS. are mixed up with Sanskrit, Persian, &c. (and no Index)—to find what one wants.

[2] A very interesting and original MS. I have been able to identify it, as the one described by Kennicott, Cod. 201. (It was formerly at Nürnberg, whither I went some years ago to examine it, but to my great disappointment it had disappeared; nor could any one tell me what had become of it.) Kennicott is quite right in his estimate of it: *Codex antiquissimis præstantissimisque accensendus.* I believe that this and Erf. 3 are two of the oldest (perhaps the two oldest) MSS. we have, containing the three Books.

[3] Erf. 5, often quoted by Michaelis in the notes to his ed. of the Heb. Bible, is now in the Library of the Graf von Schönborn, at Pommersfelden, near Bamberg. I walked over in 1877 to see it, but was not able to gain admission to the Library.

Hm. MSS. in the Town Library, Hamburg. The numbers are those of the printed catalogue.

K. Where I had no printed catalogue to refer to, as in the case of the smaller Libraries, I have given the numbers according to Kennicott's list.

Ox. MSS. in the Bodleian Library, Oxford. See printed catalogue.

Par. MSS. in the National Library, Paris. See printed catalogue.

Pet. Refers to the MS. B. 19ª (A. D. 1009) in the Imperial Library at St. Petersburg. One or two other MSS. of this Library have been quoted by the numbers in the catalogue.

Vat. MSS. in the Vatican, according to Assemani's and Card. Mai's catalogues.

Vi. MSS. in the Imperial Library, Vienna, according to printed catalogue.

II. MSS. ON THE ACCENTS OF THE THREE BOOKS.

1. The Arab. and Heb. MSS., which contain, in whole or part, the treatise assigned to Ben-Bil'am on the accentuation of these Books. On these MSS. see p. 102 ff.

2. A MS. recently acquired by the British Museum (Or. 2375), containing a fragment of the Work הדאיה אלקאר (הורית הקורא). It was from this Work that the compendium was prepared, of which the above treatise, No. 1, is part. For a further description of this MS., see p. 103.

3. That part of חבור הקונים—written by Simson the punctator (circa 1230)—which refers to our subject. Simson does little else than copy the above treatise. Of this Work—sometimes called Simsonî, from its author—there are three copies known, one in the Br. Mus. (Or. 1016), one in the University Library, Leipzig (Or. 102ª), and one in De Rossi's Library, Parma (389). Having examined them all I am able to say that they agree almost *verbatim et literatim*[4].

4. Two treatises on the accents of the three Books—the second quite fragmentary—in the Royal Library, Berlin (Heb. Cat. 118, p. 123 ff.). The writers had evidently No. 1 before them, but handle it much more freely than Simson. They not only curtail it much, but add views of their own. What little is to be gleaned from them I

---

[4] Any one who is curious to know something more of this work may consult Hupfeld, *Commentatio de antiquioribus apud Judæos accentuum scriptoribus*, Partic. II, p. 11 ff. (Halle, 1846).

have quoted in the course of the present Work. I find, however, that I have made a slight mistake in saying here and there in the notes that the first of these treatises is assigned to Samuel the grammarian. It may indeed, with great probability, be attributed to him, for it is a necessary supplement to the part on the *prose* accentuation, which is distinctly assigned to him. Still there is no statement in the MS. to that effect[5].

III. MS. ON THE MASORA.

Erf. Mas. A MS. formerly at Erfurt (now in the Royal Library, Berlin), which contains the *Mas. parva*, with additions not found in the printed text. It is briefly described by Lagarde, Symmicta, p. 142.

THE PRINCIPAL PRINTED TEXTS
QUOTED IN THE PRESENT WORK.

Sonc. First ed. of the entire Heb. Bible, printed at Soncino, 1488.

Bomb. 1. 1st Rabbinical Bible, printed by Bomberg, Venice, 1518.

Bomb. 2. 2nd Rabbinical Bible, printed by Bomberg, Venice, 1525.

Jabl. Heb. Bible edited by D. E. Jablonski, Berlin, 1699.

Opit. Heb. Bible edited by H. Opitius, Kiel, 1709.

Mich. Heb. Bible edited by J. H. Michaelis, Halle, 1720. This ed. is valuable to the student because of the various accentual readings, taken from the Erfurt MSS.

The three last-named edd. are all much more correct, as far as the accents are concerned, than our common edd. Modern editors (excepting of course Heidenheim and Baer) have one and all gone on perpetuating the errors of the Van der Hooght text, without taking the trouble of enquiring whether more correct texts were not available.

Norzi. מנחת שי. A text of the Heb. Bible (Mantua, 1744), with critical notes (according to Jewish ideas). Norzi did not, however, understand much about the accents.

---

[5] The date of this Samuel, who is no doubt the same as the well-known punctator, I am able to fix from an epigraph, which I found in Kenn. Cod. 95 (in the Library of St. John's College, Cambridge), a copy of which I sent to Dr. Steinschneider, who published it in the Heb. Bibliographie, No. 109. This epigraph states that the Cod. in question was pointed by him in the year 1260.

Heid. Heidenheim's ed. of the Psalms (Rödelheim, 1825).

Baer. Edd. of the Psalms (Leipzig, 1880), Proverbs (1880), and Job
(1875). In these edd. Baer aims at giving the correct Masoretic
text, and at establishing the same by means of critical notes. I
strongly recommend my readers to procure them for themselves.
The price is very trifling.

Ben-Bil. My references are to Polak's ed. (Amsterdam, 1858) of Ben-
Bil'am's treatise on the accents of the three Books, entitled שער
טעמי ג׳ ספרים אמ״ת חברו ר׳ יהודה בן בלעם ספרדי. This is a mere
reprint of the original ed. by Mercerus[6], from the Paris MS. (Paris,
1556). Polak's task has been poorly performed. The text is full
of mistakes, most of which might have been corrected by a collation of the Ox. MS. A copy of this MS. was, to my knowledge,
offered to him ; but he did not care to accept the offer !

Wasmuth. *Institutio methodica accentuationis Hebraeae* (Rostock, 1664).

Ouseel. *Introductio in accentuationem Hebraeorum metricam* (Leyden,
1714).

Spitzner. *Institutiones ad Analyticam sacram textus Hebraici V. T. ex
accentibus* (Halle, 1786).

Tor. em. תורת אמת. See Pref. p. v.

Man. du Lect. Manuel du Lecteur,— a name given by J. Derenbourg
to a compendium of grammar and masora, published by him
(Paris, 1871), taken from Ox. 1505. Fragments of what seems
to be the original Arabic of this treatise are in the Bodleian and
Cambridge University Libraries, and will, I am informed, be also
edited by M. Derenbourg.

Dikd. hat. ספר דקדוקי הטעמים לרבי אהרן בן משה בן אשר עם מסורות
עתיקות אחרות, edited by S. Baer and H. L. Strack (Leipzig, 1879).
This Work contains, with other matter, the rules assigned to Ben-
Asher on the accents.

N. B. I beg my readers to notice that when referring to any part
of the present Work, I have generally given page and line : thus
80. 14 is p. 80, l. 14.

---

[6] Of this ed. only two copies are known, one in the Library of the Dutch Jews'
Seminary, Amsterdam, and the other in that of the Jewish Theological Seminary,
Breslau. (This latter copy belonged formerly to Dr. Beer, of Dresden.)

CHAPTER I.

INTRODUCTORY.

FROM time immemorial the reading of the sacred books in the synagogue has been a kind of *cantillation, or musical declamation*[1]. This mode of recitation was propagated at first, and through many generations, by oral instruction and manual signs[2] alone. At length—probably towards the close of the seventh century of our era—the attempt was made to represent it by *written* signs, introduced into the text. The Greek and Syriac Churches had both by this time nearly perfected their systems of musical notation and interpunction[3]; and it was doubtless their examples—and particularly that of the Syriac Church—which stirred up the Jews in Palestine and in the farther East to make the attempt named. The introduction of these musical signs was, in all probability, simultaneous with that of the vowel-signs—an improvement in which, too, the Syrians had led the

---

[1] The earliest intimation of this cantillation is found in the Talmud, and it is there named נְעִימָה, 'melody:' כל הקורא בלא נעימה . . . עליו הכתוב אומר וגם אני נתתי להם חקים לא טובים (Megilla 32, end).

[2] These signs were made by the teacher, when giving instruction in the recitation. They are referred to by the Talmud, Berachoth 62ᵃ: מראה בימין טעמי תורה; and continued in use long after the written signs were introduced. Thus Rashi, in his comment on the above passage, says that he had seen them used by Readers who came from the land of Israel. Comp. Dikd. hat. 18. 1, and Man. du Lect. 108. 2, where examples are given. According to Sappir (אבן ספיר, I. 56ᵇ) this method of instruction is still practised by the Jews of Yemen. We may suppose that these signs, sketched in the air, were more or less reproduced in the *written* accentuation.

In the Greek Church, too, this mode of directing the singing was observed long before musical signs were noted in the text, and had the particular name of χειρονομία (Christ et Paranikas, Anthologia Græca carminum Christianorum, p. cxiv: *Manuum variis motibus, altitudinem, depressionem, flexus vocis significabant*).

[3] Tzetzes, Die altgriechische Musik in der Griechischen Kirche, pp. 19 and 20; and Martin, Histoire de la Ponctuation chez les Syriens, p. 103 seq.

way. The one notation fixed the traditional *pronunciation*
of each word, the other its traditional *modulation*. The two
together furnished the needful directions to the Reader for the
correct recitation of the sacred text.

These musical signs, or accents (as we term them)[4], are
marked, according to the Palestinian system,[5] in our printed
texts. We find there two sets of signs,—representing, of course,
different modes of recitation,—the one employed for the twenty-
one (so-called) Prose Books, the other for the three Poetical
Books, Job, Psalms, and Proverbs[6]. It is the accentuation of
these three books that I propose to examine in the present
treatise.

But what interest, it may be asked, have these musical signs
for *us?* And it must be allowed that, regarded simply as
musical signs, they have no interest or importance at all; for
the Jews themselves allow that the musical value of the accents
of the three Poetical Books is altogether lost[7]. Happily, however, they have *another* value. Those who arranged this system
of musical recitation must have felt that they had something
more important to do than merely to produce a melody pleasing

---

[4] They no doubt received this name from their indicating (which they do by their
position) the *tone-syllable* of the word. But as musical signs they mean much more
than this. Each Hebrew accent denotes an entire musical phrase, and, as such,
embraces several notes. (The German Jews assign, in the present day, to the
prose Athnach, three notes; to Pazer, seven; to M'huppakh, three; to Mer'kha,
two; and so on.) And this must have been the case with the Syriac accents, from
the small number of signs which we often find in a verse; and so the signs in use in
the Greek Church, and the *neumes* (musical signs) of the Latin Church represented
often two or more notes (Gevaert, Histoire et Théorie de la Musique de l'Anti-
quité, p. 394). To avoid the introduction of a new term, I shall use the word
'accent,' not only for the 'musical sign,' but for the 'modulation,' which the sign
represents, and which was in use before the signs were invented.

[5] In the Babylonian system many of the signs are different.

[6] Often termed by Rabbinical writers אמ״ת, a *vox memorialis* formed from the
initial letters of their names : איוב, משלי, and תהלים. Of Job, however, the pro-
logue to iii. 2, and the epilogue from xlii. 7, are accented like the Prose Books.

[7] Such is the testimony of the European Jews. But according to Eben Sappir,
55ª, the Jews of Yemen have still a particular melody for the three books.

to the ear. The text was to be so recited *as to be understood.*
Above all things it was necessary to draw out its *meaning,* and
impress it on the minds of the hearers. The music itself was to
be made subsidiary to this end[8]. Hence the *logical* pauses
were duly represented—and that according to their gradation—
by *musical* pauses; and when no logical pause occurred in a
sentence, then the *syntactical* relation of the words to one
another and to the whole sentence decided which of them were
to be sung together, and which were to be separated by a
musical pause. In this way the music was made to mark not
only the broad lines, but the finest shades, of distinction in the
sense; and when its signs were introduced into the text, they
were also the signs of *interpunction;* no others were needed.
The value and importance of the accents from this point of view
is at once apparent. They help us, in the most effective way
possible, to the understanding of the text; they give us,
that is, the meaning which tradition among the Jews assigned
to it. On this account they have from the very earliest times
been held in high esteem. The Talmud informs us that
teachers were paid for giving instruction in the 'pausal system
of the accents[9].' Indeed their very name, טְעָמִים, points to

---

[8] I think we may see a manifest advantage in the employment of a *musical
system* at a time when written signs were not admitted into the text. The absence
of vowel as well as interpunctional signs from the text necessitated careful and long-
continued instruction on the part of the teacher. This instruction commenced in
early years. Now if the teaching had been merely that of plain reading, it would
have been hard for the teacher to make his pupils, in difficult and doubtful passages,
remember the proper logical pauses. With a musical recitation it was much easier.
The musical form was of itself a help to the memory. And what was learned in
youth was retained, by constant repetition, in after years. The melody thus became
a valuable help for preserving the meaning of the text; and probably not a verse
was ever quoted *vivâ voce* without it.

[9] Nedarim 37[a], שכר פיסוק טעמים. It is to be observed that it is not for instruction in their *melody,* נעימה, but in their *divisional value* that the teacher is said to
have been paid. The two went together; but the latter appeared to the Talmudic
authorities the more important. Comp. Chagiga 6[b], where the פיסקי טעמים, 'the
divisions made by the accents,' are referred to, as determining the sense. Later
Rabbinical writers fully recognise this function of the accents. See Rashi, e.g. on
Deut. xi. 30 and Ezek. i. 11. So in Kuzari ii. 72 the accents are said to be specially

the importance attached to them in this respect : they were so
called because they were considered really to indicate the
'*meanings*[10].' And so, in the present day, there is not a work
which touches on the subject of the accents but lays special stress
on this their *interpunctional* value.

If, now, this system had been only regularly carried out in
practice, the Hebrew accentuation would be simple enough.
But here, at the very outset, our difficulties begin. We find,
when we come to examine the text for ourselves, words *united*,
which ought from the sense or construction to be *separated*, and
separated, where we should have expected them to be *united*.
Nor do such instances turn up only here and there ; they are, on
the contrary, of very frequent occurrence. And such discredit
have these and similar irregularities brought upon the whole
system, that few scholars in the present day trouble themselves
about the Hebrew accents, or give them more than a general and
superficial consideration. Yet what if it be possible to find a
fair and sufficient explanation of these irregularities ? What if
in some cases we can correct and remove them ? What if in
others (and those the great majority) we can trace laws which
cross and modify the laws of logic and grammar, and co-operate
in forming the system as it lies before us ? In these latter cases
we shall not indeed be able to restore the missing interpunction,

---

designed להבין העינינים, 'to make the meanings intelligible;' and in Man. du Lect.
14, 71. לא יתבארו עניני הפיסוק אלא בטעמים. Hence, too, Aben-Ezra's well-
known rule (מאזנים 4^b): כל פירוש שאיננו על פירוש הטעמים לא תאבה לו ולא
תשמע אליו.

[10] Another explanation of the origin of the name is indeed possible ; but, when we
consider the marked importance which so old an authority as the Talmud assigns to
the logical value of the accents, hardly probable. We may take, that is, the primary
meaning of the word טַעַם, 'taste, flavour,' and consider that they were so called
because the whole 'flavour' (as it were) of the recitation, in regard both to melody
and meaning, depended on them. Comp. a note of Moscato's to Kuzari ii. 80
(quoted by Buxtorf, De Punctorum Antiq. p. 258), הטעמים לתיבות כתבלין לקדרה
הן ליופי הקריאה הן לתועלת העינינים, *accentus sunt dictionibus, quod condimenta
ollæ* (i.e. *cibis*), *cum ad pulchritudinem lectionis, tum ad commodum sensuum.*
But even on this supposition there is an ultimate reference, in part at least, to their
logical value.

but shall, at least, account for the accentuation as it stands; order will take the place of confusion; and, with due allowance for disturbing causes, we shall still be able to accept the accents as reliable helps for the exegesis of the text. The prospect of finding the needful explanations is not indeed very encouraging. It may almost seem like courting failure to renew an attempt which has met with so little success in the hands of the diligent and careful scholars who have preceded me. Still I venture to think that the difficulties are not insurmountable, and to hope that results which have satisfied my own mind will prove not less satisfactory to the minds of others. Of course a detailed examination of the anomalies in question will be necessary, for which the following general remarks are intended to prepare the way[11].

In the first place, it is clear that we must secure, as far as possible, *a correct text*. One fruitful source of perplexity has been the corrupt state of even our best and most carefully edited texts. Exceptions arising from this cause I have sought to eliminate by an extensive collation of MSS.[12]

Secondly, I take it for granted that we are willing to remove the unmeaning additions which the accentuators made to the original text, to their own perplexity as well as ours. I refer particularly to the superscriptions of many Psalms, not put apart by themselves—we might then have left the accentuators

---

[11] My readers will understand my dwelling upon this part of my subject; for all else that has to be established—the rules of sequence of the accents, &c.—is of very minor importance compared with it. It is only as guides to the meaning of the text that the accents have any value for us.

[12] But it is vain to hope to eliminate them all. Our oldest MS. does not come within three hundred years of the time when we suppose the accents were first marked. And most MSS. are far younger. Here then was ample time for many errors to have crept in. And when an eminent authority like Ben-Asher gave a false accentuation the sanction of his name, it became the recognised reading in a large class of MSS. for all time. It is most unfortunate for us that we have no Hebrew MSS. of any considerable age, as we have Syriac MSS. that reach up to the fifth century, and enable us to trace the Syriac punctuation back to its very first beginnings, and to watch its gradual development.

to their own devices—but made an integral part of the first verses; and to סֶלָה attached to the end of a verse. In such cases we may claim to have the text as it came from the poet's hands, and accentuate for ourselves accordingly[13].

The other cases, that occasion us difficulty, are mostly of quite another kind. We shall find in them an accentuation, which we have no reason to suppose is false, and for which an adequate explanation has (if possible) to be found. The following considerations will have here to be borne in mind:

A. The essentially *musical* character of the accentual system.

If, then, it *generally* adapts itself (as we have supposed above) to the logical and grammatical laws of the verse and its clauses, we may expect that at other times its purely *musical* character will make itself felt. And this we shall find to be often the case. Indeed, *most of the exceptional cases that occur are due to this cause.* But then they are referable to certain *definite laws,* so that we know beforehand *when* they will take place. Given certain conditions, the exception will follow.

B. The *rhetorical* character of the declamation.

A good public reader does not despise oratorical effect, as his main object is to *impress* what he reads on the minds of his hearers. Hence he may hurry over some words, to come to what he counts the pith and marrow of the sentence, to the part which appears to him most weighty and important; hence too he will introduce a pause here and an emphasis there. This liberty we must grant to the Hebrew Reader.

C. The peculiar *form* of composition, as exhibited in the *parallelismus membrorum.*

For not unfrequently the logical or grammatical division is passed over, that prominence may be given to this *form.*

---

[13] Take, for example, Ps. xi. 1, which, as it stands in the text, is so pointed: לַמְנַצֵּחַ לְדָוִד בַּיהֹוָה ׀ חָסִיתִי אֵיךְ תֹּאמְרוּ לְנַפְשִׁי נוּדִי הַרְכֶם צִפּוֹר׃ But here we require Olév'yored on חָסִיתִי, where the main division in the sense occurs. We put the superscription on one side, and point: בַּיהֹוָה חָסִיתִי אֵיךְ תֹּאמְרוּ לְנַפְשִׁי נוּדִי הַרְכֶם צִפּוֹר׃ In De R. 1244 I actually found the words so accented.

By the application of these rules and principles, it is believed that most of the apparent irregularities of our texts will be either corrected or explained. A few cases will yet remain, which may perhaps be put under the heads of (1) *clerical errors*, which our MSS. do not enable us to correct; and (2) *accentual licenses*, which find their parallel in the metrical licenses, which poets of all ages have indulged in. In regard to these last—certainly not the most important—exceptions, my readers will probably agree with me, when we come to them: *De minimis non curat lex.*

One remark in conclusion. We must not attempt to force the accents to yield a meaning which they were not intended to represent. The meaning they give is that which had become traditional among the Jews. It may seem to us incorrect. But, when explaining the accents, we have nothing to do with the correctness or incorrectness of the sense they indicate. Let me cite an example. Ps. i. 3 admits of two interpretations[14], one which refers the last clause of the verse to the flourishing *tree*, and the other to the prosperous *man*. The accentuators chose the former, and the accents are to be explained accordingly. And so, in many other passages, the accentuation may be perfectly correct, though founded on a false conception of the meaning. In some cases, we find a double accentuation in the MSS. Of course, we are then at liberty to choose the one which seems to us the more suitable.

In the next chapter I shall give the names and signs of the accents; and I shall then proceed to examine the construction of the verse, and to analyse its several parts. In the course of the examination thus pursued, the exceptional cases, to which I have referred, will come under review.

Obs. The questions have often been asked, Why the three (so-called) Poetical Books—Psalms, Proverbs, and Job—have a different accentuation from the twenty-one Prose Books;

---

[14] See Targ. and Aben-Ezra's note.

and again, why—if there was to be a distinction—the poetical
accentuation should have been *confined* to the three books
above-named, when there are other books which, if their poetical
character be regarded, seem equally to claim it[15]. There was
clearly no *necessity* for any distinction at all, for we find the
same portions, Pss. xviii and cv. 1–15, at one time marked with
the poetical, and at another (see 2 Sam. xxii and 1 Chron. xvi.
8–22) with the prose, accents; and in the Babylonian system
of punctuation, Psalms, Proverbs, and Job were accented in the
same way as the other books[16]. We have then to do with a
refinement peculiar to the Palestinian synagogues and schools,—
a refinement (as it would seem) of a purely *musical* character.
At least, we find the melody much more frequently interfering
with the rules of the accentuation, as fixed by the logical or
grammatical construction of the verse, than in the other books.
The idea seems to have been to compensate for *the shortness of
the verses* (which is a marked characteristic[17] of the greater

---

[15] We have ourselves added unnecessarily to the difficulty of the question by this
distinction (as far as I have observed, quite a modern one) of *prose* and *poetical*
books. That of *prose* and *metrical* (though older) is equally objectionable, for we
have no *metre* here, in any true sense of the term. Rabbinical writers know nothing
of such distinctions. They speak simply, and rightly, of the accentuation of the
three books and that of the twenty-one books. If I might venture to propose terms
which should indicate the difference in question, I would suggest 'plain' and
'musical' accentuation,—the former as designating the simpler cantillation of the
twenty-one books, the latter the more finished melody of the three books. The
accentuation of the twenty-one books was indeed also musical, but in *a less marked
degree* than that of the three books. The latter might be termed 'musical,' κατ'
ἐξοχήν.

It is interesting to notice that, in the Greek Church also, there were two systems
of notation—the one for the rhythmical reading, e. g. of the Gospels; the other, of a
more distinctly musical character, for the singing of Psalms, &c. (Tzetzes, ib., p. 130);
and that, similarly, there was in the Latin Church the recitative (*Tonus prophetiarum,
Tonus evangelii et epistolarum*), and the chant, of which the *neumes* were the
notation.

[16] See a specimen, prefixed to Baer's edition of Job.

[17] Ben-Bil., I. 3, mentions it as a distinguishing mark of the three books,
שהפסוקים שלהן קטנים; and R. Isaac (grandson of Rashi), in the Tosaphoth to
Baba B. 14[b], names, in the same way, as one of their characteristics, מקראות קצרים
(quoted by Baer, Torath emeth, p. 55 note).

part of these books) by a finer and fuller, more artificial and impressive, melody[18]. For the Psalms a peculiar melody was suitable enough, and it may not have been inappropriate when applied to the brief and pregnant verses of Job and Proverbs.

When and by whom this improvement in the cantillation of the synagogue was introduced, we are unable to say. By the help of the Talmud we can trace the accents to the first centuries of the Christian era; but the Talmud (Palestinian as well as Babylonian) gives no hint as to any variation in the accentuation of the several books. The *argumentum e silentio* may perhaps be allowed its weight here, particularly as Jerome also does not allude to having heard from his Jewish teacher a particular mode of reading for the three books, although he draws special attention to their other peculiarities,—metre (as it seemed to him) and stichical division in the writing[19]. Moreover, if this accentuation had been due to an *early* tradition, we should expect to find it represented in the Babylonian system of punctuation. I venture therefore to think that it had its origin in a comparatively recent period, the *terminus a quo* being the early part of the fifth century, at which time the Palestinian Talmud had been closed, and Jerome was dead; and that *ad quem*, the close of the seventh century, when, in all probability, written signs were first employed for the accents. It would not, on account of this its later origin, lose its interest for us, because it would still represent the traditional division and interpretation of the text.

---

[18] Moreover, it is a melody that suits *only* these short verses. When applied to longer (prose) verses, as Ps. xviii. 1, it is in danger of breaking down. Of course *every accent* will be affected by it. We must not suppose, because the accentual arrangement of a verse is short and simple, that the melody is not there.

[19] See his prefaces to Job and Isaiah.

CHAPTER II.

ON THE DIVISION, NAMES, SIGNS, ETC. OF THE ACCENTS.

THE meaning of the word טְעָמִים, the original name of the accents, has been already explained. The Arabic-speaking Jews introduced a name that had exclusive reference to their musical value, أَلْكَان, 'melodies, modulations[1];' and to this name corresponds the Hebrew נְגִינוֹת, as used by later Rabbinical writers[2].

The melody of the three books is, as has been stated, unknown in the present day. We observe only that even for the melody *pauses* were necessary, and that the accents admit of being divided into two classes, according to their *pausal* or *non-pausal* character[3]. By most writers on the accents the *pausal* accent is termed *disjunctive*, as separating by its pause its own word from the word following; and the *non-pausal* accent *conjunctive*, as connecting without a pause its word with the following. But if we employ these terms we must bear in mind (which is not always done) that they hold only for the *melody*. If applied to the accents as signs of *interpunction*, they are only *partially* true. The musical separation and connection do not always agree with the logical or syntactical.

The above-named distinction, which is obvious enough, has been adopted, as the basis of the accentual system, by most modern scholars. It did not, however, commend itself, as such, to Rabbinical writers on the accents, though, of course, they were aware of its existence. Ben-Asher[4] tells us of *conjunctive* accents (מחברים) and their opposites. In Man. du Lect. 71. 15, we read of an accent that

---

[1] This is the name used e. g. in the Arabic text of Ben-Bil'am.

[2] The word properly meant the notes produced by *striking* the lyre or other stringed instrument, and then came to be used for musical notes generally.

[3] It is to be noted that *every word* in the text has its accent, either pausal or non-pausal. The only exception is, that two or more words united by the hyphen, called Maqqeph, were regarded for the purposes of accentuation as constituting a *single* word. Thus כָּל־אַפְסֵי־אָרֶץ, Ps. xxii. 28, has only one accent, not three.

[4] Dikd. hat. 16. 7. Comp. מפסיק 28. 13.

makes a pause (פוסק), and of another that *joins* word to word (מחביר זו לזו). Whilst Moses Qimchi[5] gives us the lists of the *pausal* (ט' מפסיקים) and *non-pausal* accents (ט' שאינם מפסיקים)[6]. But such notices are few and far between. Ben-Bil., in his formal treatise on the poetical accents, alludes only once, and that incidentally (8. 11), to this distinction. On the other hand, the principle, which lay at the foundation of the Rabbinical division of the accents, was the *weakness or strength, the dependence or independence,* of the modulations. Those accents, which could not stand alone, but only prepared the way for, and found their complete expression in, a final and fuller modulation, were called מְשָׁרְתִים, *servi.* Whilst the accents in which they merged, and on which they were clearly dependent, were regarded as the leading, ruling accents. These latter had not only a fuller and stronger modulation, which gave the tone to the melody of the verse, but they could occupy an independent position, could stand alone, with their modulation complete in itself. Hence the high-sounding title, by which they were distinguished, of מְלָכִים, Kings, or שָׂרִים, Princes[7]. This distinction is, however, insufficient, because it furnishes no indication of—what is to us the most important matter—the relation of the מְלָכִים to one another. Hence many modern writers have adopted the division of these accents into the several grades of Emperors, Kings, Dukes, Counts, etc.[8], to represent their relative pausal value and dependence one on the other. But this fanciful division we may also dispense with. I shall give hereafter the classification I suggest instead. The only title of those named above which I propose to retain is that of מְשָׁרְתִים, *servi,* a useful *terminus technicus,* as marking the *subordinate* position of the conjunctive accents.

Divided into the two classes above-named, the accents, with their usual names[9] and signs, are as follows :—

---

[5] מהלך 11ᵃ, ed. Hamb. 1785.

[6] Comp. Michlol 89ᵃ, ed. Fürth.

[7] The term מְצָמִים properly belongs to both these classes, but is often applied, κατ' ἐξοχήν, to the latter, as playing the more important part in the verse. In Greek Church music we have ἦχοι κύριοι, and τόνοι δεσπόζοντες, even ἡ διαφορὰ κατὰ διάζευξιν καὶ συναφήν (Tzetzes, ib. p. 56), but all in quite a different sense.

[8] First proposed by Sam. Bohlius, in his Scrutinium S. S. ex accentibus, 1636.

[9] The *names* of the accents, as handed down to us by the Jews of the Middle Ages, vary considerably, apparently according to the schools (of Tiberias, Jerusalem, etc.) in which they originated. Some of those given above are of more recent date. I have retained them, as they have become current amongst us, and it seemed better to avoid the confusion which would be caused by reverting to the older names. The *form* of the names is in some cases Aramaic, in others Hebrew. The *meanings* may be traced (see below) to their figure, position, or musical or pausal value.

I. Pausal, or Disjunctive Accents.

1. ⸺ Silluq (סִלּוּק), as in . . . . . דָּבָר

2. ⸺ Olév'yored (עוֹלֶה וְיוֹרֵד), as in . . . דָּבָר

3. ⸺ Athnach (אַתְנָח), as in . . . . . דָּבָר

4. *a* ⸺ Great R'bhia (רְבִיעַ גָּדוֹל), as in . . . דִּבָּר

  β ⸺ Little R'bhia (רְבִיעַ קָטוֹן)[10], as in . . דִּבָּר

5. ⸺ R'bhia mugrash (רְבִיעַ מֻגְרָשׁ), as in . . דִּבָּר

6. ⸺ Ṣinnor (צִנּוֹר), *postpositive*, as in . . . דָּבָר

7. ⸺ D'chî (דְּחִי), *prepositive*, as in . . . . דָּבָר

8. ⸺ Pazer (פָּזֵר), as in . . . . . . דָּבָר

9. ⸺ Great Shalshéleth (שַׁלְשֶׁלֶת גְדוֹלָה), as in . דָּבָר׀

10. *a* ⸺ Azla l'garmeh (אַזְלָא לְגַרְמֵהּ), as in . . דָּבָר׀

  β ⸺ M'huppakh l'garmeh (מְהֻפָּךְ לְגַרְמֵהּ) . . דָּבָר׀

II. Non-pausal, or Conjunctive Accents (*Servi*).

1. ⸺ Mer'kha (מֵירְכָא), as in . . . . . דָּבָר

2. ⸺ Ṭarcha (טַרְחָא) . . . . . . דָּבָר

3. ⸺ Azla (אַזְלָא), as in . . . . . דִּבָּר

4. ⸺ Munach (מוּנַח) . . . . . . דָּבָר

5. ⸺ Illuy (עִלּוּי) . . . . דִּבָּר

6. ⸺ M'huppakh (מְהֻפָּךְ), as in . . . . דָּבָר

7. ⸺ Galgal (גַּלְגַּל), as in . . . . . דָּבָר

8. ⸺ Little Shalshéleth (שַׁלְשֶׁלֶת קְטַנָּה), as in . דָּבָר

9. ⸺ Ṣinnorîth (צִנּוֹרִית), *pretonic*, as in . . . דָּבָר

The signs fall generally on the tone-syllable. The only exceptions are D'chî, Ṣinnor, and Ṣinnorîth, on which see below. Where there are two signs, the *second* marks the tone.

---

[10] Little R'bhia is distinguished by its *position*, which is always immediately before Olév'yored. Anywhere else in the verse the accent will be Great R'bhia.

The semantik, represented above, must strike one as being of a very simple character. And it becomes still more simple when we revert to the earliest and original forms. The elements into which it then readily resolves itself are the *point*, the *straight line*, and (in one case) the *curved line*.

From these elements the Greek grammarians derived their system of accentuation and interpunction; and to the same elements may be referred the musical notation of both the Greek and Latin Churches of the Middle Ages[12].

REMARKS ON THE SEVERAL ACCENTS[13].

I. 1. סִלּוּק signifies 'cessation, close,' i. e. of the melody. Its sign is a perpendicular stroke[14] below the tone-syllable of the word. Ben-Asher's name is חֵזֶר[15].

The term סוֹף פָּסוּק, which is often used for Silluq, refers properly to the two points which mark the 'end of the verse,' but which have nothing to do (as their position alone shews) with the present system of accentuation[16]. As they always however immediately follow Silluq they became identified with it.

---

[12] For the former, see Tzetzes, ib., p. 129; for the latter, Coussemaker, Histoire de l'Harmonie au Moyen Age, p. 158.

[13] In these remarks, I have occasion to refer to lists of the accents found in the following MSS. :

Vat. 25.—In the Vatican Library (? 14th century).

Cas.—H. III. 13 in the Casanatensian Library, Rome (A. D. 1466).

De R. 333 and 1016.—Two of De Rossi's MSS., now in the Royal Library at Parma (A. D. 1392 and ? 14th century).

Ox. 125.—In the Bodleian Library, Oxford (? 14th century).

Pet. 123.—In the St. Petersburg Imperial Library (? 16th century).

(This last is the list referred to by Pinsker, Einleitung etc., p. 44.)

Ben-Asher's names of the accents I have taken from Dikduke ha-teʿamim, p. 20 ; Chayyug's, from Nutt's edition of הנקוד 'ס, p. 129 (this part of the work is not, however, by Chayyug himself ; see Nutt's remarks, p. xii) ; Eliezer Provenzale's, from a list, printed by him at the end of בשם קדמון, A. D. 1596 (a copy of this rare book is in the British Museum) ; and Lombroso's, from his edition of the Bible, A. D. 1639, p. 348.

Cod. Bab. is the famous MS. of the Prophets with the Babylonian accentuation (A. D. 916), photo-lithographed 1875.

[14] This stroke is often used (as we shall see) to indicate a pause.

[15] Apparently חָזַר, 'returning,' 'recurring.' Whatever other accent fails (and they all fail in their turn) Silluq never does.

[16] These two points (or strokes, Dikd. hat. 18. 5) seem to be the relics of an earlier and simpler notation, in which a single point (or stroke) marked the cæsura at Athnach, and *two* the close of the verse. (So in Armenian, a sentence is divided by a single point, and closed by a double point ; and in Sanskrit the half-verse is marked by a single stroke, the end of the verse by a double stroke.) When the

2. עוֹלֶה וְיוֹרֵר, so named from its 'ascending and descending' modulation (see chapter on Olév'yored). It is represented (in our texts) by
a sign, like M'huppakh, *above*[17], and *before* the tone-syllable, and by a
second, like Mer'kha, *below, with* the tone-syllable. The name I found
in Vat. 25, Cas., and De R. 333, 1016. It is also used by El. Prov., Lombroso, and later writers on the accents. Ben-Asher's name is סָלֵק,
'ascending.'

Rabbinical writers generally regard this accent as dependent on,
because it always follows, R'bhia or Zarqa, and have no other name
for it than רודפי הרביע and רודפי הזרקא[18]! The name used by most
Christian writers, *Merca Mahpachatum*, is altogether false. Ben-Bil.
(8. 11) has long ago warned us that we have nothing to do here with
Mer'kha. The lower sign in MSS. is just like the Silluq-sign, and
designates Olév'yored as a pausal accent.

3. אַתְנָח, אֲתַנְחְתָּא, אֲתַנְחָא, or אַתְנָה[19].

The name (Aram.) is derived from the inf. Aphel of תְּנַח[20], secondary
form of נוּחַ, Properly it would mean 'the causing to rest;' then
abstr. for concr. (comp. אַזְכָּרָה in Heb.), 'what causes to rest or
pause[21].' Ben-Asher has טָרֵף, 'breaking off;' Vat. 25, Cas., De R.
333, 1016, and El. Prov. חוֹנֶה, 'encamping,'=resting.

The form, as it occurs in Cod. Bab. (our oldest Cod.), is ⎯̭⎯, which,
by rounding off the angle, became ⎯̯⎯, and then ⎯̬⎯, as we find it in
our printed texts.

---

present accent-signs were introduced, the two points were retained, as serving to
mark clearly the limit between two consecutive verses, and then the simple stroke
below was deemed sufficient for Silluq. Otherwise (as it seems to me) we should
certainly have had a more prominent sign for this, the chief accent of the verse.

[17] Sometimes I have found, as in Ox. 15 and in Br. Mus. 1, a sign like Ṣinnorith
for M'huppakh.

[18] According to them, it belongs neither to the מְלָכִים nor to the מְשָׁרְתִים,—not
to the former because it is a *dependent* accent, and not to the latter because its
word *stands apart* from the word following (as is seen by the Dagesh after a vowel).
And so it is left out in the cold! They treated S'golta in the same way, in the prose
accentuation.

[19] The vocalization, with Pathach in the first syllable, is unquestionably the
traditional one. I have found it in Vat. 25, Cas., and Pet. 123, and in the
Spanish and Italian Zarqa-lists. The German Jews alone, I believe, pronounce
אֶתְנַחְתָּא.

[20] This form occurs (as my friend Dr. Baer has pointed out to me) in the Talmud,
Erubin 53ª: נתקיימא (or סימני) בני יהודה דדייקי לישנא ומתנדֵי להו סימנא
תורתם בידם, 'the Jews, who are accurate in their speech, and set signs for themselves, their Law is established in their hand.'

[21] A similar *nom. verb.* is אַתְחַלְתָּא, 'beginning,' from תחל (Root, הלל). Müller,
in his recent edition of Masechet Sopherim, p. 173, explains אתנח as meaning 'sign
of rest' (אות=את). But such a form is, I believe, without analogy; and certainly
one would expect, instead of נח, נחת or נוח.

The original form was (as it seems to me) $\underset{\scriptscriptstyle\wedge}{\underline{}}$, a compound sign made up of Silluq and Ṭiphcha. This composition (like the mixing of wine with water) represents Athnach as an intermediate accent, neither so strong as the former, nor so weak as the latter (comp. 7 end). An exact parallel is furnished by the Syriac accentuation, where Tachtaya (= Athnach) $\bullet\underset{\scriptscriptstyle\bullet}{\underline{}}$ is derived from the union of Pasûqa (= Silluq) and Samka (= Ṭiphcha). The origin of the sign was after a time forgotten, and the perpendicular stroke became inclined to the left, just as is often the case (in MSS.) with Silluq itself.

4. רְבִיעַ is represented by a point placed over the tone-syllable of the word. It is also called מְיוּשָׁב [22]. This latter name, ('settled, fixed,') is used technically to indicate a 'sustained' note [23]. The name R'bhîa therefore, 'resting,' (from Aram. רְבַע = Heb. רָבַץ,) refers probably not to the *pause*, but to the *modulation* of the voice, as 'resting, dwelling' on one and the same note [24], neither ascending nor descending in the scale [25]. Ben-Asher's name is תְּקֵף, 'strong, firm,' = מְיוּשָׁב.

The R'bhîa-sign represents two accents— בִּשְׁנֵי דְרָכִים מְתַקֵּף (Ben-Asher),—which, however, are readily distinguished by their *position*. The ancients, and most modern writers on the accents, make no distinction (as far as name is concerned) between the two R'bhîas. Lombroso was the first to propose the title רְבִיעַ גָּדוֹל. That of רְבִיעַ קָטֹן was added by the author of שערי נעימה (1765), whom Heidenheim and Baer have followed. This simple and necessary distinction I have also adopted.

So the Eastern Syrians, who had the same sign (a point above the word) for two different accents, distinguished between them, as ܡܕܢܚܐ ܪܒܐ and ܪܚܘܦܐ ('Great' and 'Little' M'zi'ana) [26].

5. There is a third accent, marked by the same sign as R'bhîa, but distinguished from it by a stroke (in MSS. a straight line) over the first letter and on its right hand, thus דָּבָר. As this stroke resembles the Géresh-sign of the prose accentuation, the accent has been called רְבִיעַ מֻגְרָשׁ, *R'bhîa Gereshatum*. This is, however, quite a modern name (first employed by Lombroso), and quite inappropriate, for

---

[22] This name I found in Vat. 25, Cas., and De R. 333, 1016. It is also used by El. Prov.

[23] See Man. du Lect. 87. 6, ולשון מיושב שהמלה תצא בו בנעימה מיושבת לא למעלה ולא למטה.

[24] That this note was a *high* note, we learn from Chayyug, p. 129. 1.

[25] The name רביע is sometimes explained as *punctum quadratum*. But this form is not found in MSS., and where it occurs in printed texts is simply due to the fancy of editors.

[26] See Bar-Hebræus on Syriac Accents (Phillips' edition), p. 50, and Bar-Zu'bî (Martin's edition), p. 18.

Géresh is altogether unknown in the accentuation of the three books [27]. Rabbinical writers term our accent טִפְחָא, because it occupies the same position before Silluq, as Tiphcha does in the prose accentuation. Nay more, the stroke over the first letter is, no doubt, *the Tiphcha-sign itself*, transferred from below [28] (where there is no longer any place for it, as this sign *below* is, in the three books, used for quite a different accent). The placing of the two signs *apart* seems to indicate that each had its own modulation, although the intonation of the word was always with the second sign [29].

This accent appears only before Silluq. Ben-Asher calls it גֶּ֫זֶר, 'cutting off;' and certainly no accent 'cuts off,' so often and so abruptly, the word on which it falls from the following word (e. g. חֹשְׁבֵ֣י רָעָתִ֑י Ps. xxxv. 4) ; and *that,* because there is a musical necessity for its presence before Silluq.

6. צִנּוֹר, צִנּוֹרִי, or זַרְקָא. The form of this accent seems to point to a winding, meandering note; *circumflexione vocis gaudebat* (as an old writer says) [30]. Its *name* was taken from its *form*, which was likened to the meandering of a 'canal,' or 'water-channel [31],' such as were common in the East. Ben-Asher calls it מְתַח, 'drawing out,' because of its long-drawn form or tone. The former is very conspicuous in many MSS.

As regards *position*, it is (what is called) a *postpositive* accent (made so, to distinguish it from Ṣinnorîth, which has the same form, but occurs at the beginning, or in the middle of the word, see p. 22). In correct MSS., when the tone falls on the penultimate, it is (at least, in all doubtful cases) *repeated*, to mark the tone and prevent the possibility of a mistake in the chanting, thus : בְּטֶ֫חְתִּי֮, בָּאָרֶץ֮.

7. דְּחִי is the Tiphcha which precedes Athnach in the prose accentuation, transferred to the first letter, and made *prepositive*. (It was made so, to distinguish it from the conjunctive Tarcha, which has the same form, but is placed under the *tone-syllable* of the word ; see

---

[27] It has, however, become established among us, and I do not propose to change it. A suitable name (as it seems to me) would be רְבִיעַ מְרֻכָּב, 'compound R.'

[28] Just as R'bhîa is transferred from *above*, in the prose accentuation, to form with Mer'kha the accent T'bhîr.

[29] Where the tone falls on the first letter, the two signs come together, as מִ֫י, תָּ֫מּוּ. But this would not prevent the double modulation, as the Masora to Gen. v. 29 shews. Where two words are united by Maqqeph, both signs fall on the second word, as עַל־צִּיּ֫וֹן. In practice, the one or other of these signs is often dropped, through the carelessness of punctators and editors.

[30] Like the *Sinuosum* of the Latin neumes. (See Helmore, Plain-song, p. 6.)

[31] צִנּוֹר is used in this sense in the Talmud, and probably זַרְקָא had the same meaning. I do not find it (as Heidenheim, Mishp. hat. p. 6, states) in Chaldee; but in Arabic زُقَاق signifies 'rigole, saignée.' (See Dozy, Supplément aux Dictionnaires Arabes.)

p. 20)[32]. It is represented by a straight line, inclining to the right, and is, in many MSS., *repeated* when the tone falls elsewhere than on the first syllable, and there might be a doubt as to its position, thus, עוּרָה, גְּמַלְתִּי[33].

There are few accents that can boast of so many names. As representative of the prose Ṭiphcha, it is still, by some writers, named Tiphcha, or *Tiphcha præpositivum*. טַרְחָא and דְּחִי are synonyms of the prose Ṭiphcha[34]; hence Moses Qimchi and others have named it טַרְחָא[35]; Lombroso and those who follow him, דְּחִי. By Rabbinical writers generally it is known as יְתִיב, 'stationary, pausal[36],' in contradistinction to the *conjunctive* accent of the same form. Vat. 25, De R. 333, 1016, and El. Prov. name it יְמָנִית, from its position on the *right hand* of the word. In many MSS. I have found it, to my surprise, marked like the prose accent תְּבִיר, and Cas. *names* it so. This sign—as made up of R'bhia and Mer'kha—would represent it as an intermediate accent, neither so strong as the former, nor so weak as the latter[37] (all three, as we shall see, appear regularly before Athnach). With this form it ceases to be *prepositive*.

8. פָּזֵר derives its name from its modulation, הוּא הַקּוֹל יְפַזֵּר (Man. du Lect. 73. 23). It was a 'shake' or 'trill.' Hence it is named in Cas., De R. 333, 1016, and by El. Prov. מַרְעִיד, 'making to tremble.' Similarly, in Greek church music the trill was designated τρομικόν. Ben-Asher calls it נִצָּח, 'conspicuous,' 'clear,' in reference, no doubt, to its sharply-defined tone.

---

[32] When two words are united by Maqqeph, D'chî is placed before the first letter of the *second* word, thus: שֶׁבְּמֵרֵיהָ, וּבְכָל־לַיְלָה.

[33] Baer (following Ben-Bil. 6, below) makes the second sign here Métheg. MSS. vary. The Métheg-sign has the advantage of preventing confusion with Ṭarcha, see the ex. p. 32.

[34] For Ṭarcha this is well known. For D'chî see Chayyug̒ 127. 1, and a list at the end of the first Bomberg Bible. דְּחִי properly signifies 'thrust back,' in reference to the backward inclination of the sign. In Pinsker, p. 43, this accent is called in Arabic وَاجِل, 'thrusting back,' viz. its sign. The name דְּחִי is appropriate enough for us, seeing that the sign is 'thrust back' from its proper position on the tone-syllable to the first letter of the word.

[35] The name is found first so used in Dikd. hat. 26. 5. But in his list of the accents of the three books, Ben-Asher calls this accent חֶרֶץ, apparently because of its *straight, undeviating* course. It is always the forerunner of Athnach (or of Athnach's representative), whereas the other pausal accents *vary* in their sequence.

[36] So in the prose accentuation Y'thîbh is 'stationary, pausal,' in opposition to the conjunctive M'huppakh, and so also Pashṭa is often (e. g. in Man. du Lect. 76. 9) called יְתִיב, in opposition to אַזְלָא, 'going on,' not pausing.

[37] The same explanation applies to תְּבִיר in the Prose Books. See Derenbourg's note, Man. du Lect. 219.

To explain the *form,* we must go back to the prose system, where it occurs constantly as a somewhat greater pause, in the same clause with Géresh. Luzzatto[39] regards it as a mere substitute for Géresh. However that may be, I do not doubt that its *form* is derived from Géresh, viz. by the addition of the pausal stroke, thus, ⟋[40], which, with the sharp angle rounded off, becomes the Pazer, ⌐, of our texts[41].

9. I שַׁלְשֶׁ֓לֶת. This zigzag line represents the musical character of the accent. (Comp. the similar sign sometimes used in modern music for a trill.) Shalshéleth was an *ascending shake* or trill. It belonged to the same class as Pazer. Hence the two are often confounded in MSS., and where Ben-Asher has the one, as in Ps. cxxv. 3, לְמֹ֓עַ, Ben-Naphtali has the other, I לְמֹ֓עַ. Hence, too, Shalshéleth is described in Cas., De R. 333, 1016, and by El. Prov. as מַרְעִישׁ, a term of the same meaning as that used by them for Pazer above. There must, of course, have been a difference between the two ; and, no doubt, Shalshéleth was the more extended and emphatic trill[42]. It occurs far less frequently than Pazer.

Ben-Asher's name for this accent is רָתֵק, which has the same meaning as שַׁלְשֶׁלֶת, 'chain' (comp. Heb. רַתּוֹק and רְתֻקוֹת)[43]. The name 'chain' has by some been referred to the succession of tones, 'in linked sweetness long drawn out,' which characterized this accent,—making it perhaps like the *trillo di catena* of the present day ; but see note.

The stroke on the left hand is the pausal sign, Paseq, which distinguishes it as a pausal accent from the conjunctive of the same form and name. Lombroso was the first to apply to these two accents the distinctive titles of גְּדוֹלָה and קְטַנָּה.

10 and 11. I לְגַרְמֵהּ, 'by itself,' 'independent,'= Heb. לְנַפְשׁוֹ. Like Shalshéleth, M'huppakh and Azla become independent pausal accents,

---

[39] In Torath emeth, p. 61.

[40] A form still found in some MSS. It must be remembered that the sign for Géresh is properly a *straight line* inclined to the right.

[41] So Zaqeph gadôl ⌐ is from Zaqeph qatôn ⸫, by the addition of the pausal stroke.

[42] Ben-Asher says of it : לֹא בִמְהֵרָה יִנָּתֵק, 'it is not quickly broken off.'

[43] In Cod. Bab. Amos i. 2, we find the original form of the accent ⫶. Here the points one above another were taken to represent the several rings of a pendent 'chain,' whence the name Shalshéleth. They were probably originally meant to symbolize the several ascending notes of the trill. It is observable that the *Quilisma,* or trill of the Latin neumes, has also ' the form of several dots hanging one on the other' (Helmore, Plain-song, p. 10). With this form of Shalshéleth may be also compared the Syriac accent ܠܡܐܚ, ' chain,' with two points, one above the other, ܠ⫶ (Zeitschrift für die Kunde des Morgenlandes, i. p. 206), and the vowel-sign R'bhaṣa, with its two points, called also ܠܡܐܚ, 'chain' (Merx, Gram. Syr. p. 30).

by the addition of Paseq. Ben-Asher names the former שׁוֹפָר הָרַב, and Cas. פּוֹנֶה נַרְמִי. Neither mentions the latter; nor do other Rabbinical writers distinguish between the two. It is convenient, however, to do so (as Heidenheim and Baer have done) by the names of the accents (M'huppakh and Azla) from which they are derived.

II. 1. The usual names of this accent, מַאֲרִיךְ, מַאֲרְכָא, and מֵירְכָא, or מֵרְכָא, are all from the same root (מֵירְכָא like מֵימְרָא and מֵיכְלָא), and indicate it, as *prolonging* the modulation. Comp. the Arabic name in Pinsker, p. 42 مَدّ, 'lengthening out,' 'prolonging.' By Ben-Asher it is termed יוֹרֵד, from its *descending* tone: לְמַטָּה טַעֲמוֹ (Dikd. hat. 24. 12). Hence the further Arabic name in Pinsker, p. 43 خَاطَة, 'descending.' In MSS. it is generally represented by a straight line, turning more or less to the left hand.

2. טַרְחָה or טַרְחָא [44], a name first used by M. Qimchi (in Mahᵃlakh 11ᵇ). By the older grammarians (with the exception of Ben-Asher), it is divided into three accents—each, of course, with its own modulation [45]— a sign that it is one of the most important of the conjunctives :

a. מָאיְלָה or מָאיְלָא when it occurs before Silluq. Unquestionably the Arabic مَآيَّلَ, 'inclined [46],' and so written in Pet. 123, מַאיְלֶה *maylé* (modern Arabic pronunciation), not as it is usually pronounced מָאיְלָה. This derivation is confirmed by the name נְטוּיָה [47], 'inclined,' given to this accent in Man. du Lect. 74. 6.

β. דְּחוּיָה when it occurs before Athnach [48]. For the meaning of the term, see D'chî, note 34 : (דְּחוּי and נָטוּי are used as synonyms, Ps. lxii. 4.)

γ. שׁוֹכֵב when it occurs before R'bhîa mugrash. שׁוֹכֵב is *recumbens*, *se inclinans* = נְטוּיָה above [49].

---

[44] A synonym of the pausal Ṭiphcha in the prose accentuation (derived from טָרַח, *laboravit*, 'labouring, heavy, slow'), but here applied to a *conjunctive* accent. Yet the name is perhaps not so inappropriate, for the employment of the *sign* seems to imply a similar *slow* modulation.

[45] So in the prose system, Munach, Illuy, and M'kharbel have all the same sign, but different modulations. Ben-Bil. (Oxford MS.) has the following remark on the intonation of two of the above accents : הדחויה יציאתה בכובד ושוכב יוצא רפה בלא כובד, i. e. the enunciation of D. was *pesante*, that of Sh. *leggiero*. But if the intonation before Athnach was *pesante*, much more (we may be sure) must it have been so before Silluq.

[46] See Man. du Lect. 96, Derenbourg's note. Even in the old MS., Cod. Bab., I find a form derived from the Arabic, מסלסלין, Masora to Amos i. 2.

[47] נטויה refers to the *sign*, not to the *tone*, as is clear from the expression נטויה לאחור, 'inclined backwards,' 77. 19.

[48] Or before R'bhîa mugrash, when it takes the place of Athnach.

[49] Derenbourg, in Man. du Lect. 74. 6, has made the sign of שׁוֹכֵב like Galgal, but in the original MS. it is שׁוּכָב, i. e. שׁוֹכָב; the double accentuation, with Mer'kha

The sign of these accents is (in MSS.) a straight line, inclined to the right, and *under the tone-syllable*. D'chî has the same form, but is distinguished from them by being always placed outside the word before the first consonant. Ben-Asher, like ourselves, has only one name for the three accents, בֵּין, which points to the position *between* the letters of the word, as דָּבָר. El. Prov. and other moderns employ the name Tiphcha, since the form and position is the same as that of Tiphcha, in the prose accentuation.

3. אַזְלָא, a name taken from the prose accentuation, and first employed by Lombroso. (On its meaning see note 36.) The older writers call it simply מַקֵּל (Ox. 125 עצא, i. e. عَصَا), 'rod, stroke[50];' Ben-Asher מְעַלָּה, from its ascending tone[51].

Its sign is a straight line, inclined to the left, over the tone-syllable.

The next three accents belong to the Shophar-class, so called because of their fancied resemblance to the שׁוֹפָר, 'trumpet,' used by the Jews on certain festival days[52].

4. שׁוֹפָר מוּנָח. The form is two lines, inclined at a right (in MSS. often an acute) angle to one another, and placed *under* the tone-syllable. The name here given is that adopted by most writers. Chayyug has שׁוֹפָר נָחַת [53], 'Shophar of rest' (=מוּנָח). Lombroso, and others since his time, make it שׁ׳ הוֹלֵךְ, the name of the prose Munach in the Spanish Zarqa-list. Often it is מוּנָח מִלְּמַטָּה, *Munach inferius*, to distinguish it from the following sign. Sometimes, as the leading representative of the Shophar-class, it is called simply שׁוֹפָר [54].

---

and Tarcha, pointing to the *variations in MSS.*; some, with Ben-Naphtali, having Mer'kha, and others, with Ben-Asher, Tarcha. In Chayyug's list, and in Ox. 125, we meet with the strange names תלישא רבה and תלישא זעירה ('Great and Little T'lisha') for α and γ (β and γ), a lame attempt (as it would seem) to introduce the prose nomenclature into our accentuation.

[50] Comp. ῥάβδος, *virgula*, as used by Greek grammarians (Osann, Anecdotum Romanum, p. 133), and the *virga* or *virgula* of the Latin neumes (Helmore, Plainsong, p. 4). In the musical notation of the Greek Church this sign was called κέντημα, 'goad' (Christ and Paranikas, Anthologia Græca, p. cxxv), the דָּרְבָן of Man. du Lect. 90. 1.

[51] Dikd. hat. 22. 9.

[52] This trumpet (as I have seen it) is made of a straight (flattened) horn, somewhat more than a foot in length, turned up a few inches at the end. A good representation may be seen in Stainer's Music of the Bible, fig. 75, p. 127.

[53] For so, no doubt, we must point, not with Hupfeld, נוֹחַ, 'descending.' In Ox. 125 we have the Arabic name שׁוֹפַר וצֵ, where وَضْع, *positio, depositio*, is evidently the rendering of נַחַת.

[54] In Cas. and De R. 333 occurs the name קַלְקֵל; according to Chayyug 128. 15 a synonym of מְכַרְבֵּל. But there is no reason for the introduction of מְכַרְבֵּל here! El.

But the correct designation of this accent is, no doubt, that used by Ben-Bil. and those who follow him, שׁוֹפַר עִלּוּי [55], a name given it because of its *ascending* tone [56], answering to that of the accent of the same name in the prose system [57]; whereas מוּנָח implies an *equal*, *sustained* tone (לֹא לְמַעֲלָה וְלֹא לְמַטָּה) [58]. Ben-Asher has a similar name, עוֹלֶה, 'ascending.' These fine musical distinctions have, however, no meaning for us. I have therefore retained the common name Munach, and then the name עִלּוּי will be employed for the following accent.

5. שׁוֹפַר עִלּוּי. This name is convenient enough for us, as descriptive of the position of the accent, *above* the tone-syllable of the word. It was first used (I believe) by Lombroso. Ben-Asher has a similar name, תּוֹלָה, 'suspended.' Others use the term מוּנָח מִלְמַעְלָה, *Munach superius.*

But the best authorities introduce us here to a *new* accent (the counterpart of which is not found in the prose system), שׁוֹפַר שָׁבוּר, an accent, the modulation of which (from its name) must have been of a broken character, and was probably a plain shake—shake on one note [59]—the Greek πεττεία. It is easy to see how it might thence get the name (which is found in Man. du Lect. 74. 5) of מְפַזֵּז 'שׁ, 'the tripping Shophar' (2 Sam. vi. 16). In this note we have one of the musical refinements of the three books [60].

Prov. (whom Norzi follows) has made confusion worse confounded by changing (as it would seem) this name into גַּלְגַּל !!

[55] In the original Arabic, and in Pet. 123, רפע 'שׁ, i. e. رُفْع, 'Sh. of elevation.'

[56] See Dikd. hat. 24. 12, and Baer's note there.

[57] See Man. du Lect. 87. 5. The name used for עִלּוּי there is מוּרָם.

[58] See Man. du Lect. 87. 5. For מוּנָח we have there מְיוּשָּׁב (a name used also by Chayyuǵ, 128. 24). We thus ascertain the meaning of the term מוּנָח. It is the same as מְיוּשָּׁב, 'settled,' unvarying, in its tone (see above, under R'bhia).

[59] In Man. du Lect. 102. 4, the term שָׁבוּר is opposed to מְיוּשָּׁב, just as, in any dictionary of music, the *vibrato*, or plain shake, is opposed to a pure sustained tone. So Ben-Asher, Dikd. hat. 19. 7, tells us of מוּנָח 'שׁ, that its modulation is *not broken* (נעימתו בל תופר), in accordance with the preceding note.

[60] In the printed text of Ben-Bil. (taken from the Paris Cod.) we find מוּנח instead of שׁבור. So that the strange phenomenon presents itself, of Ben-Bil.'s calling our Munach by the name of Illuy, and *vice versâ*. With regard to Illuy, I have already explained above; and as to Munach, it is simply, in the case before us, a correction of some early copyist, who missed an accent with which he was familiar in the prose accentuation. I say 'an early copyist,' because the correction is already found in Hadassi (A. D. 1148). It is also in the De Rossi Cod. (evidently from the same original as the Par. Cod.) and in the grammatical work of Samuel hanaqdan, Berlin Cat. No. 118. But in the original Arabic of Ben-Bil., and in Ox. 125,

6. שׁוֹפָר מְהֻפָּךְ, שׁ׳ מַהְפָּךְ, or שׁ׳ הָפוּךְ. This is the שׁוֹפָר, 'turned round[61],' properly (as in some texts) ‒͜. Ben-Asher, Vat. 25, Cas., and others term it פּוֹנֶה, which has the same meaning. Ben-Asher's description of the prose M'huppakh shews us that the modulations of the conjunctive accents played no unimportant part in the melody of the verse: 'It first descends, then mounts up, and keeps itself mounted up' (יוֹרֵד וְעוֹלֶה וּמִתְעַלֶּה).

7. גַּלְגַּל, 'wheel[62];' Ox. 125 הליל כבירה[63], i. e. هلال كبيرة, 'great new moon,' from its semicircular form. (In the prose list this accent is יָרֵחַ בֶּן־יוֹמוֹ, 'the moon a day old.') In Cas. and De R. 333, 1016, it is named מְנַדְנֵד, 'making to tremble,' a designation which must refer to the modulation, similar to that of Pazer, which it immediately precedes.

8. See Shalshéleth among the pausal accents. Little Sh. is of very rare occurrence.

9. צִנּוֹרִית—in Ox. 125 צִנּוֹרָה—has the same sign as צִנּוֹר, but צִנּוֹר is *postpositive*, whereas it is *pretonic*. It occurs only in an open

---

and Pet. 123, we have שׁופר תכסיר (i. e. تكسير), *Sh. fractionis* = *Sh. fractus*; and in the Ox. and Vat. texts of Ben-Bil., and in Simsoni, שׁבור שׁ׳. In Cas., De R. 333, 1016, and by El. Prov. the accent is not named. By Chayyug̣ it is called simply שׁופר (שׁבור has probably fallen out).

[61] In the Arabic text of Ben-Bil., Ox. 125, and Pet. 123, שׁופר מקלוב, i.e. مَقْلُوب, 'turned about.' In the same sense, Greek and Latin grammarians used the terms ἀπεστραμμένος and *aversus*. Thus כ is Σίγμα ἀπεστραμμένον. We even find a sign just like ours, and called by the same name, < *aversa* (C. Suetoni Tranquilli Reliquiæ, p. 140).

[62] But this name and the form do not agree. Here we must once more recur to the prose accentuation. Galgal is there the servus of Pazer gadôl, usually represented by two T'lishas, ꝗꝗ the original form of which was ꝯꝯ (for so T'lisha appears in our oldest MS., Cod. Bab.) One of these T'lishas was then taken for the servus, ‒͡, as is clear from the name given to the servus in Man. du Lect. 89. 14, *T'lisha q'ṭanna*. The usual name is Galgal. We now understand why Galgal and Pazer, coming together, are described in the Masora as אופן ועגלה, 'wheel and waggon,' the single circle representing the wheel, and the double the waggon. By putting the part for the whole, we get the form usual in MSS., ‒͡, and with the ornamentation of printed texts, ‒͞ᵥ. But it is questionable whether this particular *form* does not come from ‒͞ᵥ, a form of the servus common enough in MSS., and corresponding to the form ⌐ for Pazer gadôl, which latter is also frequent enough, e. g. all through Man. du Lect. Ben-Asher's name for Galgal is שׁכל, of which nothing can be made. Baer proposes עגול, 'round.' I would suggest שׁכלל=משׁכלל, 'completing.' The wheel *completes* the waggon. The root of this form is used by Ben-Asher, in describing the prose Galgal, 19. 4: 'A waggon with wheel *complete*' (כלולה).

[63] According to the pronunciation in most parts of Syria. See Wallin, Zeitschrift der Deutschen Morgenländischen Gesellschaft, xii. p. 669.

syllable *before* Mer'kha or M'huppakh, e. g. דָּבָר, דְּבַר[64]. Ben-Asher names it מְמַלֵּא, because it serves as a *complement* to these accents. Yet it had its own modulation, which must, to some extent, have resembled that of Ṣinnor. The form צִנּוֹרִית seems to be the fem. of a *nom. rel.*, like יְמָנִית, p. 17.

On the pausal sign Paseq, which is no accent, for it has no modulation attaching to it, see special chapter.

In the above remarks, I have aimed at bringing together the various names used for the accents, and at explaining them and the corresponding signs. At the same time I have collected the scattered notices, as far as they seemed of an authentic character, relating to the musical character of the accents. The information submitted, although not of much practical value, has a certain literary and historical interest. The investigation could not have been passed over altogether, and having undertaken it, I have sought to make it,—even at the risk of some wearisomeness of detail,—as complete as possible.

The first step towards the accentuation was the arranging of the text in a number of small divisions, called פְּסוּקִים, 'sections[65],' or מִקְרָאוֹת, 'lections.' These are what we call 'verses.' Each of these sections or verses was recited separately, and each is to be regarded in tracing the laws of accentuation as an *independent whole*. Logically, a verse may be closely connected with the one preceding or following it; but musically and accentually no such connection exists. The individual verse is to be taken, and the relation of its accents to one another to be alone considered.

The fundamental tone ('key-note' perhaps we may call it) of the verse was furnished by the end-accent, Silluq. This was the only *constant* musical element; in other words, Silluq is the only accent that never fails. The other accents vary in character and number, according to musical laws which we have to determine. This is the task that lies before us in the following chapters.

---

[64] Two words joined by Maqqeph are regarded for the purposes of accentuation as *one* word. If, now, Ṣinnorîth falls on the first of two such words, the Maqqeph is dropped; thus, הוּא כִּי for כִּי־הוּא. Ṣinnorîth joins the words so closely together, that Maqqeph is no longer needed.

[65] פָּסוּק, 'cut off,' 'a segment, section.' These sections are mentioned in both the Mishna and Talmud, and in Kiddushin 30[a], the number of them is given for certain books.

CHAPTER III.

THE DICHOTOMY.

ONE of the distinguishing characteristics of the Hebrew verse is what has been termed its DICHOTOMY.

As I use the term in the present chapter, I would be understood to mean that every verse in the three books is divided by a cæsura into *two* parts.

The lengths of these parts, and the accents that mark the cæsura, vary in different verses, but *the cæsura itself cannot fail.*

In the present chapter we have to determine—

First, the *position* of this cæsura, or chief musical division of the verse ; and secondly, the *notation* that is employed to mark it.

I. Our main guide to the dichotomy of the verse will be the *parallelismus membrorum*, the characteristic of poetry, and of the higher style generally, in Hebrew composition.

1. In such simple cases as the following, it will be seen at once that the dichotomy can come nowhere else than between the members of the parallelism.

    a. Synonymous parallelism :

> Jehovah, rebuke me not in thine anger, |
>   Neither chasten me in thy hot displeasure (Ps. vi. 1).
> If thine enemy hunger, give him bread to eat, |
>   And if he thirst, give him water to drink (Prov. xxv. 21).

    b. Antithetic parallelism :

> There is that giveth himself out as rich, with nothing at all, |
>   There is that giveth himself out as poor, with much wealth (Prov. xiii. 7).
> A soft answer turneth away wrath, |
>   But a grievous word bringeth up anger (Prov. xv. 1).

2. But the parallelism is far from being always so exact as in these examples. Indeed, such verses would soon become wearisome by their monotony. The poets therefore allow themselves the utmost liberty in varying the form of the parallelism[1].

---

[1] I confine myself in what follows to examples of synonymous parallelism. The *principle* is all that it is necessary to establish.

The perpendicular line used above is, I need hardly say, meant to indicate the *position* of the dichotomy.

1. Sometimes it is *loose* and *general:*

> But in Jehovah's law is his delight, |
> And in His law doth he meditate day and night (Ps. i. 2).

> The precepts of Jehovah are right, rejoicing the heart ; |
> The commandment of Jehovah is pure, enlightening the eyes (Ps. xix. 9).

2. Still more frequently it is *limited* and *partial:*

a. So an accessory part may appear in the *second* member, e.g.

> And Jehovah helpeth them, and rescueth them ; |
> He rescueth them from the wicked and saveth them, because they trust in
> Him (Ps. xxxvii. 40).

Comp. Ps. xviii. 51; xxi. 12 ; xxvii. 11; cxli. 8.

β. But it is much more common in the *first.* Indeed, the *main idea* of the verse (and this it is important to notice) is often given in the first member, and the second member merely echoes *a part* —a word only, it may be—of the first, which it may, or may not, expand or add to :

> Ask of me, and I will give thee the heathen as thine inheritance, |
> And as thy possession the ends of the earth (Ps. ii. 8).

> Life he asked of thee ; thou hast given it to him, |
> Length of days for ever and ever (Ps. xxi. 5).

> Cast it on Jehovah; let Him deliver him, |
> Let Him rescue him, seeing He hath pleasure in him (Ps. xxii. 9).

Comp. Ps. ix. 18; xviii. 8 and 12 (הוֹשִׁיעֵ); xxviii. 2; xxxi. 20; cxv. 14; cxxxv. 12; cxl. 13; Prov. i. 33; Job xx. 4; xxxvi. 5.

Such cases often come (as the examples given above shew) under C, p. 6. The verse is divided to exhibit the parallelism, and the logical division has to give way.

Some peculiar cases of partial parallelism must be here noticed.

γ. When two parallel expressions follow one another in the course of a continuous construction (*progressive parallelism* this has been termed) they are often separated by the cæsura, so as to produce *parallelismus membrorum.* Such cases come also under C, p. 6; but here it is the *syntactical*, more frequently than the logical division, which is passed over.

> The splendour of the glory of thy majesty, |
> And thy wondrous works,—will I consider (Ps. cxlv. 5).

> As I have seen, those who plough iniquity, |
> And sow trouble,—reap it (Job iv. 8).
>
> Therefore I came out, to meet thee, |
> To seek thy face,—and have found thee (Prov. vii. 15).
>
> There is no wisdom, and no understanding, |
> And no counsel,—against Jehovah (Prov. xxi. 30).

The other passages that come under this head are (as far as I have noted): Ps. xvi. 3; l. 4; lxvi. 14; lxxv. 7[2]; xc. 2; cvi. 37[3]; cvii. 17; cxxxix. 20; Prov. iii. 2; vii. 6, 12; viii. 2, 3, 25; xvi. 30; xxv. 3; xxx. 32; Job iv. 10; v. 15; xi. 10; xx. 17; xxxii. 8; xxxvii. 13.

δ. In a few instances, words occurring in the first part of the verse are *repeated,* for the sake of effect, before the grammatical construction is completed. Here there is necessarily a pause before the repetition, and so a suitable place is found for the dichotomy:

> How long shall the wicked, O Jehovah, |
> How long shall the wicked—triumph? (Ps. xciv. 3).

And so in Ps. xxix. 1[4]; lxxxix. 52; xciv. 1; xcvi. 7; cxiii. 1; and Job xviii. 13. Ps. lxx. 2 is similar.

3. Where the verse consists of three members, two of which exhibit parallelism, but the third contains a different idea, we should expect the dichotomy to come either after or before the parallelism, and this we find to be generally the case, e. g.

a. When the parallelism *precedes*:

> On thee have I stayed myself from the womb,
> From my mother's bowels, thou art my sufficiency; |
> Of thee is my praise continually (Ps. lxxi. 6).
>
> Hear, O my people, and I will speak;
> O Israel, and I will testify against thee: |
> God, thy God, am I (Ps. l. 7).

Comp. Ps. xxiv. 7; xxxix. 6; xl. 10; liv. 5; lv. 16; &c.

But here a certain amount of liberty is claimed. Sometimes the division comes *between* the members of the parallelism:

---

[2] Correcting the last part of the verse, thus : וְלֹא מִמְּדְבַּר הָרִים: with the following Codd., B. M. 2; Cam. 13; De R. 732; Par. 80; Ber. 17, 51; &c.

[3] Pointing אֶת־בְּנֵיהֶם with Ox. 15, 17, 72; Erf. 1, 3; &c.

[4] Leaving out the superscription.

> For he shall hide me in his tabernacle, in the day of evil, |
> He shall conceal me in the concealment of his tent,
> > On a rock shall he exalt me (Ps. xxvii. 5).
> Jehovah reigneth, hath robed himself with majesty, |
> Jehovah hath robed, hath girt himself with strength,
> > The world also standeth fast, doth not move (Ps. xciii. 1).

Comp. Ps. xxxvii. 5; lxix. 5; cxvi. 16; and cxliii. 12[5].

In such instances, attention seems to be drawn to the close connection between the idea contained in the parallelism, and the new idea introduced by the third member. Thus, in Ps. xxvii. 5, 'He shall hide me in his tent, where I shall be safe as on a rock above the reach of mine enemies;' and in xciii. 1, 'Jehovah hath put on his might and majesty, and order is, in consequence, once more established in the world[6].' We have here merely instances of what we have already seen in a simpler form above, viz. of parallelism, *with addition in the second member*. This is a recognised principle in Hebrew verse, and need not occasion any difficulty. Such an addition often comes in, with marked effect, at the close of the verse.

b. Again, when the parallelism *follows*, it is generally marked off by the dichotomy, e. g.

> I will exult and rejoice in thy mercy, |
> > That thou hast seen my affliction,
> > Hast regarded the distresses of my soul (Ps. xxxi. 8).

> Thou wilt make me know the path of life; |
> > Fulness of joys is with thy presence,
> > Pleasures in thy right hand for evermore (Ps. xvi. 11).

Comp. Ps. xxiv. 8; xxxv. 10; lxvii. 5; lxxviii. 21, 50; &c.

But here, as before, and apparently for the same reason, *mutatis mutandis*, the dichotomy sometimes appears *between* the members of the parallelism :

> Yea! though I walk through the valley of the shadow of death, I will fear no evil,
> For thou art with me, |
> Thy rod and thy staff—they comfort me (Ps. xxiii. 4).
> > Cause me to go in thy truth, and teach me,
> > For thou art the God of my salvation, |
> > In thee have I hoped all the day long (Ps. xxv. 5).

Comp. Ps. iii. 8; iv. 3; vi. 7; vii. 6; xiii. 6; xxvii. 6; xxxviii. 13; xcv. 10; cxlviii. 13; Job ix. 21.

It is unnecessary therefore to propose—as commentators, who have failed to notice this peculiarity in the division of the verse, sometimes do propose[7]—to shift back the cæsura to the early part of the verse, so

---

[5] So also Is. liv. 1.

[6] That such is the connection of ideas may be seen by comparing xcvi. 10.

[7] E. g. Hupf. and Hitz. in Ps. xiii. 6, and Hupf. in xxv. 5. But, to be consistent, we must make the same change in cases like Ps. xii. 2; xxx. 2; lxviii. 2; and xcvii. 1; where, however, neither Hupf. nor Hitz. have thought of suggesting it.

as to make the musical agree with the logical pause. In reality, we have here merely instances of that *partial* parallelism, which we noticed on a smaller scale, under 2, 2 β. The sentiment of the verse is first given, and then comes an echo (as it were) of the *concluding words* of that sentiment. This too is an established principle of the Hebrew versification.

4. The verse may admit of division into *three* members, more or less parallel. Here the dichotomy will be found at the close of the first member, and rightly; for this is evidently the leading clause. It gives the sense of the verse, which the other two members merely echo and emphasize:

> Blessed the man, who hath not walked in the counsel of the wicked, |
> Nor stood in the way of sinners,
> Nor sat in the seat of scorners! (Ps. i. 1).

And so in Ps. vii. 15; xxviii. 4; lii. 7; cxv. 12; cxxxix. 12; cxl. 6[8]; and Job xxxi. 7.

5. Where the verse consists of two parts, *each* of which contains a parallelism, the dichotomy will of course come at the close of the first part:

> For my life is spent with grief,
> And my years with sighing; |
> My strength faileth, because of mine iniquity,
> And my bones are consumed (Ps. xxxi. 11).

Comp. Ps. ii. 2; xi. 4; xviii. 16; xxx. 6; li. 6; &c.

II. But often *parallelismus membrorum* fails altogether, as a guide to the division of the verse.

1. The main *musical* will then correspond with the main *logical* pause:

> I will not be afraid of ten thousands of the people, |
> Who set themselves against me round about (Ps. iii. 7).
>
> And I had said in my confusion:
> 'I am cut off away from thine eyes.' |
> Yet thou didst hear the voice of my supplications,
> When I cried unto thee (Ps. xxxi. 23).

Such instances abound in every page[9]. Of course where there

---

[8] See *corrigenda*, at the end of this chapter.

[9] Scholars generally, following Bishop Lowth, classify them as instances of *synthetic* parallelism. This classification does not, however, seem to be very suitable: nor could I use it without an explanation and examples, which, for the purpose of the

are two or more logical divisions, of equal strength, in a verse, e. g. in Prov. xxiii. 29, the accentuators exercised their own judgment as to the position of the dichotomy.

2. Where no logical pause exists, the position of the dichotomy will be fixed by what we may call the *syntactical* pause, i. e. the words will be formed into two groups, according to their connection in sense and construction, and the dichotomy will come between[10]:

Yet have I set my King |
On Zion, my holy mountain (Ps. ii. 6).

And give back to our neighbours sevenfold into their bosom |
Their reproach wherewith they have reproached thee, O Lord (Ps. lxxix. 12).

And so in Ps. xxv. 22; xxxiii. 14; xlviii. 3, 8; lxx. 4; lxxiv. 6; cxvi. 15; cxxi. 4; cxxiv. 5.

Exceptional cases, where the dichotomy is not found at the logical (or syntactical) pause, may be brought under the two following heads:

(1) In the more *musical* accentuation of the three books, there is an apparent reluctance to place the main dividing accent after the *first*, or before the *last* word of the verse. In cases where, according to the logical (or syntactical) division, it would come there, it is generally[11] moved forwards or backwards to where a convenient resting-place is found for it. The musical equilibrium is thus better preserved.

שָׁקַדְתִּי וָאֶהְיֶה כְּצִפּוֹר בּוֹדֵד עַל־גָּג׃ (Ps. cii. 8)[12].

אָהַבְתִּי כִּי־יִשְׁמַע ׀ יְהוָה אֶת־קוֹלִי תַּחֲנוּנָי׃ (Ps. cxvi. 1).

And so in Ps. xlviii. 4; lxxii. 20; lxxiv. 5; cxix. 18; and cxxii. 3.

The instances of Athnach drawn *backwards* are:

גָּרְסָה נַפְשִׁי לְתַאֲבָה אֶל־מִשְׁפָּטֶיךָ בְכָל־עֵת׃ (Ps. cxix. 20).

אֶל־יְהוָה בַּצָּרָתָה לִּי קָרָאתִי וַיַּעֲנֵנִי׃ (Ps. cxx. 1)[13].

וְאַתָּה מָרוֹם לְעֹלָם יְהוָה׃ (Ps. xcii. 9).

רוּם־עֵינַיִם וּרְחַב־לֵב נִר רְשָׁעִים חַטָּאת׃ (Prov. xxi. 4).

---

present investigation, are quite unnecessary. Those who choose to employ it can do so. The result will be the same.

[10] On the principles which regulate the division in these cases, see chapter IV.

[11] In a few cases, however, where it was considered that the removal would do too great violence to the logical construction, it does not take place, see p. 33 below.

[12] Properly Athnach should be on שָׁקַדְתִּי. Hupfeld is completely puzzled by its removal to וָאֶהְיֶה.

[13] Leaving out the superscription.

יָדֶיךָ עִצְּבוּנִי וַיַּעֲשׂוּנִי יַחַד סָבִיב וַתְּבַלְּעֵנִי׃ (Job x. 8).

Further, some of the examples given in 2, 2 γ, e.g. Ps. cxlv. 5; Job iv. 8, might be brought under this head.

(2) The verb אָמַר and cognate expressions—with more or less of addition—are not unfrequently found at the commencement of the verse, without at all affecting the division of the same. It is the *speech itself*, which the melody aims at marking and emphasizing. Such cases will come under B, p. 6.

> He hath said in his heart: God hath forgotten, |
> Hath hidden his face, hath never seen it (Ps. x. 11).

> Jehovah hath sworn (and will not repent): Thou art a priest for ever, |
> After the order of Melchisedek (Ps. cx. 4).

He will sing before men, and say: I had sinned and perverted what was right, |
And it was not requited to me (Job xxxiii. 27).

These cases are common enough. See Ps. xii. 5; xvi. 2; lx. 8; lxxxiii. 13; lxxxix. 20; Job xxxiii. 24; xxxiv. 9 [14].

Such are the rules for the dichotomy of the verse in the three books. The principles here laid down suffice (I believe) to meet all requirements, and to remove the difficulties that have suggested themselves to scholars. The rules are simple enough, and a beginner will soon learn to apply them to the various cases, as they arise.

The *position* of the dichotomy fixed, we have next to enquire *what accent* is employed to mark it.

As the accentuators have fixed their rules,—

i. Olév'yored will occur in the *sixth* word [15] from Silluq, or further;

ii. Olév'yored or Athnach in the *fourth* or *fifth* word; and

iii. Athnach in the *first, second,* or *third* word:—

i.e. near to Silluq, Athnach will be employed; at a distance from Silluq, Olév'yored; and in an intermediate position, sometimes Athnach and sometimes Olév'yored.

We have clearly here to do with *musical* reasons. Athnach is, under any circumstances, bound to appear as a preparatory note to

---

[14] The same tendency is very common in the Prose Books, see Gen. iii. 16; iv. 23; xx. 6; &c.

[15] I observe again, that when two or more words are united by Maqqeph, e.g. כָּל־אַפְסֵי־אָרֶץ, אֵס־בְּתוֹרַת, they are counted, for the purposes of melody, as *one* word.

Silluq. But owing to the limited number of accents which the laws of melody allow (so different, in this respect, from those of the Prose Books), between Athnach and Silluq, the former cannot be removed further back than the *fifth* word. Hence the necessity for another dividing accent. That Olév'yored trespasses on the *fourth* and *fifth* word, which we should have expected to be reserved for Athnach, is due (as we shall immediately see) to the same cause.

I may observe, in passing, that owing to the *shortness of the verses* in the three books, Athnach divides the verse more than ten times as often as Olév'yored[16].

i. This rule is strictly carried out. There is not a single exception.

ii *a*. With the dichotomy on the *fifth* word, Olév'yored is usually—i. e. in about four cases out of five—employed.

I must here assume, what will be hereafter proved, that between the dichotomy and Silluq a musical pause must be introduced. This pause might fall on any of the intermediate words, but is almost always found (that so the rhythmical equilibrium might be better preserved) on the *second* or *third* word[17]. Now, with it on the *third* word, the only practically available accent for marking it was Athnach[18], and then of course Olév'yored had to be used for the dichotomy. Comp. Ps. vi. 3; vii. 9; viii. 3; ix. 7; &c.

But it might fall on the *second* word. Here the accentuators had their choice of two notations. They might mark the pause with R'bhîa mugrash, and then Athnach would mark the dichotomy, as in Ps. xix. 8, 9; xxiii. 5; xxvii. 12; &c. Or they might prefer Athnach, for the sake both of the *melody*, and of the more effective division of the verse, according to the *sense*,—for Athnach in this position implies R'bhîa mugrash following, and D'chî preceding. In three cases out of four they made the latter choice, and then, necessarily, Olév'yored preceded in the fifth place. See Ps. xiv. 2; xxvii. 5, 11, 14; xxviii. 3; and cxxv. 2.

---

[16] The proportion in the Books of Proverbs and Job is still greater. There, whole chapters occur in succession, without a single instance of Olév'yored. See chapters xi–xxii in Proverbs, iv–vi in Job, &c.

[17] There are, I believe, only three cases, Ps. xlii. 2; lxvi. 20; and cxxv. 3, where it falls on the *first* word; and two where it falls on the *fourth* word, viz. Ps. lxxix. 6 and Job xi. 6. And these five cases will admit, on the testimony of Codd. (as we shall see hereafter), of being reduced to *two*, with Olév'yored, as usual, on the fifth word. I take no notice of Ps. iii. 3; xxxii. 5; xlvii. 5; and liv. 5; which have סֶלָה for their last word, see p. 6.

[18] In four cases only does a different accent appear, viz. R'bhîa mugrash in Ps. xviii. 31; lxviii. 19 (a doubtful instance); and Prov. xxv. 1; and Shalshéleth in Ps. lxxxix. 2. These accents properly follow immediately after Athnach. Here they occur with a servus between them and Athnach.

to. In the next chapter, I shall lay down the laws for *syntactical* division.

I. We often see a tendency to delay the dichotomy, till the main statement of the verse or clause has been set before the reader,— what follows the dichotomy serving to supplement, explain, qualify, &c. the *last part* of what precedes it. Looked at from the rhetorical point of view, such a division is often effective enough, although it may come in the middle of a subordinate clause, or may cut in two the apodosis. There is nothing peculiar in it, for we often adopt it in our own interpunction. (In the examples given, the vertical line marks the position of the dichotomy):

'For God doth know that, in the day ye eat thereof, then your eyes shall be opened, | and ye shall be as gods, knowing good and evil' (Gen. iii. 5).

'And Jehovah God said unto the serpent, Because thou hast done this, cursed art thou above all cattle and above every beast of the field; | upon thy belly shalt thou go, and dust shalt thou eat all the days of thy life' (iii. 14).

'Are we not counted of him strangers? for he hath sold us, | and hath also quite devoured our money' (xxxi. 15).

'When thou comest into thy neighbour's vineyard, then thou mayest eat grapes thy fill at thine own pleasure; | but thou shalt not put any in thy vessel' (Deut. xxiii. 25).

'Jehoshaphat made ships of Tarshish to go to Ophir for gold. But none went; | for the ships were broken at Ezion-geber' (1 Ki. xxii. 49).

Further examples are unnecessary.

II. *Emphasis* is distinctly marked:

'In the beginning *God created* | the heavens and the earth' (Gen. i. 1. Comp. Ex. xx. 11).

'Thy sons and thy daughters shall be given unto another people, *and thine eyes shall see it* | and fail with longing for them all the day' (Deut. xxviii. 32).

'And the king of Israel said unto Jehoshaphat, There is yet one man by whom we may enquire of Jehovah; *but I hate him,* | for he doth not prophesy good concerning me, but evil' (1 Ki. xxii. 8).

'Who gave Jacob for a spoil, and Israel to the robbers? *Did not Jehovah?*' | [emphatic pause[3]]; 'He against whom we have sinned, &c.' (Is. xlii. 24).

'If any stir up strife, it is *not* | *of me*' (liv. 15)[4].

'*No peace,* | saith Jehovah, for the wicked' (xlviii. 22; lvii. 21).

---

[3] I cannot agree with Delitzsch's remark: *Das Athnach ist an unrechter Stelle.* Comp. Athnach before אשר, Jer. xli. 2[b].

[4] Luzzatto is completely puzzled by the accentuation, as other commentators would no doubt have been, if they had noticed it.

Such examples are common enough. Had they been wanting, we might well have questioned the taste of the accentuators. What calls for remark is the lengths to which they went in carrying out this principle of division. In their desire to mark the emphasis, they did not scruple to pass over the most prominent logical pauses. (These pauses were indeed marked by musical pauses, but the *main musical pause* was reserved for the emphasis.) In no other way can we explain the division in such cases as the following :

'And it came to pass at the end of two months that she returned to her father, *who did with her according to his vow which he had vowed;*' | [pause for effect at these solemn words [5], on which the whole narrative hinges]; 'and she had not known a man. So it became a custom in Israel' (Judg. xi. 39) [6].

'Therefore thus saith the Lord Jehovah, Behold, I have founded in Zion a *stone,*' | [the Messiah] [7], 'a tried stone, a precious corner-stone of sure foundation : he that believeth shall not make haste' (Is. xxviii. 16).

'Then said Jehovah unto me, What seest thou, Jeremiah? and I said, *Figs;* | the good figs, very good; and the bad, very bad, &c.' (Jer. xxiv. 3).

'Then this Daniel *distinguished himself above the presidents and satraps,*' | [an emphasis not altogether unsuitable in view of the narrative following], 'because an excellent spirit was in him; and the king thought to set him over the whole realm' (Dan. vi. 4).

Other examples will occur in the sequel.

Occasionally (it must be allowed) the accentuators have been led into fanciful extremes by the Midrash-teaching of the Schools. Thus in Gen. i. 21 the Athnach is with הַתַּנִּינִם הַגְּדֹלִים, instead of at its proper place before וַיַּרְא אֱלֹהִים כִּי־טוֹב. And why? Because these wonderful creatures, about which Jewish fable has so much to relate [8], were counted to have nothing in common with the other creatures named. They were beings *per se,* and are put *by themselves* at the beginning of the verse! In Gen. xxxv. 10 the Athnach rests on

---

[5] Josephus, Targum, and Rabb. Comm. generally, suppose that Jephthah really offered up his daughter, in fulfilment of his vow.

[6] Comp. Judg. iv. 21, where Athnach is properly due at וְהוּא־נִרְדָּם, but has been transposed for the sake of emphasis and effect. The attention was to be fixed on the details of Jael's heroic act, culminating in the words וַתִּצְנַח בָּאָרֶץ.

[7] So Rashi explains. Raymund Martini, in Pugio Fidei, ii. 5. 2, quotes the Targum as also rendering אבן by מלך המשיח. So far he is right that the מלך תקיף of the Targum evidently points to the Messiah (comp. 1 Pet. ii. 6).

[8] See e. g. Rashi, *ad loc.,* and Levy, Neuhebr. W. B. s. v. לויתן.

made for the dichotomy occurring there. *It was contrary to the rules of melody of the three Books that either Olév'yored or Athnach should be admitted on the first word*[26]. And we have seen, p. 29, that the main musical pause, when due there, was moved forward to where a suitable resting-place could be found for it.

What then was to be done, when, by the accentuation of the superscriptions and other additions prefixed to the original text, the main pause came on the *first word* ? The accentuators had to make shift, as best they could, with substitutes for Olév'yored and Athnach. For the former they chose Azla l'garmeh, for the latter Pazer ! Thus,

a. לְדָוִד׀ the first word of Pss. xxvi, xxvii, xxxv, xxxvii, ciii, cxxxviii, and cxliv[27]; לִשְׁלֹמֹה׀ of lxxii; and הַלְלוּיָהּ׀ of cvi, cxi–cxiii, cxxxv, and cxlviii–cl. And

b. וַיֹּאמֶר Ps. xviii. 2 (comp. וַיֹּאמַר 2 Sam. xxii. 2); לְדָוִד xxv. 1[28]; מִזְמוֹר xxx. 1[28]; and הַלְלוּיָהּ cxlvi. 1[29].

(We could wish that they had confined this anomalous accentuation to the instances given, but in three cases they have introduced it into the original text, viz. in Ps. xlv. 13 וּבַת־צֹר׀[30]; cxlvii. 1 הַלְלוּיָהּ׀[31]; and Prov. i. 10 בְּנִי[32]. Otherwise, they kept to the traditional division, as laid down in p. 29.)

---

[26] It is otherwise in the prose accentuation, see Gen. xv. 8; xxxiv. 31; &c. Ordinary edd. indeed have Athnach sometimes on the first word, as in Ps. cxix. 84; Prov. vii. 9; but correct texts avoid such mistakes.

[27] Fixed by the *Masora magna* to Ps. xxvi. 1.

[28]   ,,   ,,   to this verse.

[29] In Ps. xxviii. 1 and xcviii. 1, Pazer is used to mark the dichotomy on the first word, *although Athnach follows* in the verse! (It is fixed by the *Masora* to Ps. xxv. 1 and xxx. 1.) L'garmeh ought to have been employed here, and the accents following in xxviii. 1 to have been modified accordingly. Other instances of inaccurate accentuation are to be found in xviii, xxxiv, xlv, lxv, and lxviii. I believe that in the pointing of the superscriptions generally,—both in Psalms and Job,—we may trace not only a later but a less careful hand than that which fixed the accentuation of the text. Such mistakes are, however, of the very smallest moment to us.

[30] That we have not L'garmeh proper here will be seen when we come to the chapter on D'chî. The original accent was probably R'bhîa.

[31] Here undoubtedly this word belongs to the original text. Olév'yored is chosen (instead of R'bhîa) for the sake of agreement with Pss. preceding and following. (See *a* above.)

[32] Here Codd., B. M. 4, Ox. 5, Erf. 1, Hm. 7, K. 198, 599 have R'bhîa. Comp. xxiii. 15 with D'chî.

We must here notice, that where the verse containing the superscription consists of only *three* words, Pazer is dropped, and R'bhia
mugrash[33] employed instead. This suits better the proximity of the
pause to Silluq, which always claims (if possible) this latter accent
before it, e. g. : לְדָוִד מִזְמוֹר לַמְנַצֵּחַ (Ps. xiii. 1), and so in the superscriptions of Pss. xix, xx, xxi, &c.[34]

N. B. In the superscriptions of eight Pss., viz. xxxvi, xliv, xlvii,
xlix, lxi, lxix, lxxxi, and lxxxv, we have the strange accentuation
of Silluq, preceded *by two Illuys*, e. g. : מִזְמוֹר לִבְנֵי־קֹרַח לַמְנַצֵּחַ (xlvii. 1).
And this accentuation has the support of most Codd.[35] Yet I have
noted many which point regularly[36], as Ox. 1, 5, 71, 72, 98, &c., for
the example just given : מִזְמוֹר לִבְנֵי־קֹרַח לַמְנַצֵּחַ. And so I have found
ample authority for R'bhia mugrash on the first word, in Pss. xxxvi,
xliv, xlix, and lxxxv. For the remaining three examples, we require
R'bhia mugrash (transformed) on the word before Silluq, thus לַמְנַצֵּחַ
לְדָוִד עַל־נְגִינַת : (lxi. 1), with Codd. Ox. 5, 72 ; Ber. 32 ; K. 157, 246 ;
De R. 304 ; &c. For lxix and lxxxi there is like testimony.

In conclusion I would correct some passages in which the
dichotomy has been falsely made, or in which it might have been
better made. In all, the Codd. enable us to make the change
which is necessary, or which seems advisable. The corrections
(I venture to think) speak for themselves, and need no comment
on my part.

---

[33] In Codd. and edd. mostly *R'bhia simplex* (see note 25). In one instance, Ps.
xcii. 1, it occurs in a verse of *four* words, where Athnach might have stood.

[34] So ordinary texts are quite right in xl. 1 and lxx. 1, and the accentuation with
two servi, introduced by Heidenheim and Baer, must be rejected. The *Masora
magna* to lxx. 1, למנצח ב' בטעם, indicates R'bhia mugrash (and *not R'bhia simplex*,
as Codd. generally point in other similar passages, see note above) as required here.
And this is just what Ben-Bil. 10. 7 expressly lays down for these two passages,
and Codd. and edd. generally exhibit. Comp. xli. 1.

[35] Not, however, of Ben-Asher, who without doubt pointed, although quite irregularly, מִזְמוֹר לִבְנֵי־קֹרַח l לַמְנַצֵּחַ, &c. On the other hand, Ben-Naphtali has no
Paseq, and seems to have given the accentuation, which has crept into our texts.
Both accentuations probably originated in the fanciful notion of setting a peculiar
mark on a number of superscriptions, that have the common characteristic of למנצח
for their *first* word, and of a double word formed by Maqqeph for their *second!*
Baer assigns the two Illuys to Ben-Asher. But in all the lists of the Varr., which
I have been able to consult, I have found the first word pointed as above, with
L'garmeh, and then the second will, according to rule, have Illuy.

[36] Just as Codd. and edd. do, in the similar case, xlii. 1.

Corrigenda.

Ps. xi. 6.   Divide at גָּפְרִית with B. M. 3; Ox. 13; Ber. 2; K. 240,
246, 250, 251; De R. 2; &c.

יַמְטֵר עַל־רְשָׁעִים ׀ פַּחִים אֵשׁ וְגָפְרִית וְרוּחַ זִלְעָפוֹת מְנָת כּוֹסָם׃

Ps. xix. 14.   Divide at בִי with B. M. 1, 2; Ox. 71; K. 240; De R.
3, 34, 193; &c.[37]

גַּם מִזֵּדִים ׀ חֲשֹׂךְ עַבְדֶּךָ אַל־יִמְשְׁלוּ בִי אָז אֵיתָם וְנִקֵּיתִי מִפֶּשַׁע רָב׃

Ps. xlii. 5.   This verse has been a *crux* to accentuologists. Ouseel,
p. 46, says of it: *locus singularissimus, codicum fide et collatione dijudi-
candus*. The main division of the verse is clearly at נַפְשִׁי, which ought
therefore to be marked (as B. M. 2, 4; Ox. 2332; Par. 4, 30; Ghet. 1;
and De R. 2, 304, do mark it) with Olév'yored. אֱלֹהִים following
will then necessarily have Athnach (with Ox. 2332; Par. 4). So that
the pointing will be:

אֵלֶּה אֶזְכְּרָה וְאֶשְׁפְּכָה עָלַי ׀ נַפְשִׁי כִּי אֶעֱבֹר ׀ בַּסָּךְ אֶדַּדֵּם עַד־בֵּית אֱלֹהִים
בְּקוֹל־רִנָּה וְתוֹדָה הָמוֹן חוֹגֵג׃

Ps. xlii. 9.   It is better to divide this verse, with Par. 30; Ber. 2, 32;
Vat. 468; Ghet. 1; De R. 304, 350, at the end of the first clause (comp.
xl. 4[a]), thus:

יוֹמָם ׀ יְצַוֶּה יְהֹוָה חַסְדּוֹ וּבַלַּיְלָה שִׁירֹה עִמִּי תְּפִלָּה לְאֵל חַיָּי׃

Ps. lxvi. 12.   Clearly the last clause here will come in with much better effect if it stand by itself, and if we point with B. M. 2, 4; Ox. 17,
2332; Ber. 17; De R. 372;

הִרְכַּבְתָּ אֱנוֹשׁ ׀ לְרֹאשֵׁנוּ בָּאנוּ בָאֵשׁ וּבַמַּיִם [38] וַתּוֹצִיאֵנוּ לָרְוָיָה׃

Ps. lxxi. 3.   Divide at תָּמִיד with B. M. 7, 8; Par. 111; Erf. 3;
Fr.; De R. 732; &c.

הֱיֵה לִי ׀ לְצוּר מָעוֹן לָבוֹא תָּמִיד צִוִּיתָ לְהוֹשִׁיעֵנִי כִּי־סַלְעִי וּמְצוּדָתִי אָתָּה׃

Ps. lxxvi. 8.   Divide as follows with Par. 9, 30; Erf. 1, 2; Ber. 2;
De R. 304; &c.

אַתָּה נוֹרָא אַתָּה וּמִי־יַעֲמֹד לְפָנֶיךָ מֵאָז אַפֶּךָ׃

Ps. xciii. 5.   Falsely divided in all texts. The correct division is
found in B. M. 5; Vat. 27; K. 192; De R. 35;

עֵדֹתֶיךָ נֶאֶמְנוּ מְאֹד לְבֵיתְךָ נַאֲוָה־קֹדֶשׁ יְהֹוָה לְאֹרֶךְ יָמִים׃

---

[37] Most of these Codd. indeed exhibit only the *lower* sign of Olév'yored. But the
omission of the *upper* sign is very common.

[38] We must then deviate from the *Masora* here (פתח באתנח) and point with
Qames, as our common edd. do.

Job x. 15.   Divide at לֹ֑ with Ox. 19 ; Ber. 2 ; K. 166 ; De R. 380,
589, 847 ;

אִם־רָשַׁ֗עְתִּי֮ אַלְלַ֪י לִ֥י וְ֭צָדַקְתִּי לֹא־אֶשָּׂ֣א רֹאשִׁ֑י שְׂבַ֥ע קָ֝ל֗וֹן וּרְאֵ֥ה עָנְיִֽי׃

Job xx. 25.   Divide at יַהֲלֹ֑ךְ with Ox. 19 ; Par. 6, 9, 36 ; Vat. Urb.
1 ; De R. 368, 380 ; &c.

שָׁלַ֤ף ׀ וַיֵּצֵ֬א מִגֵּוָ֗ה וּ֭בָרָק מִֽמְּרֹרָת֥וֹ יַהֲלֹ֗ךְ עָלָ֥יו אֵמִֽים׃

(Other texts, as B. M. 13 ; Ox. 100, 127 ; Erf. 2 ; Hm. 8 ; &c., point
מִֽמְּרֹרָת֥וֹ יַהֲלֹ֗ךְ עָלָ֥יו אֵמִֽים׃.)

Job xxviii. 3.   Divide at לַחֹ֗שֶׁךְ with K. 246, 251, 531 ; De R. 349,
847 ; Ghet. 3 ;

קֵ֤ץ ׀ שָׂ֤ם לַחֹ֗שֶׁךְ וּֽלְכָל־תַּ֭כְלִית ה֣וּא חוֹקֵ֑ר אֶ֖בֶן אֹ֣פֶל וְצַלְמָֽוֶת׃

Job xxxiv. 20.   Divide at יָמֻ֗תוּ, though I have found only two Codd.,
De R. 349, 715, that do so.   (The subject of יָמֻ֗תוּ is שָׂרִים, v. 19.)

רֶ֤גַע ׀ יָמֻתוּ֮ וַחֲצ֪וֹת לָ֥יְלָה יְגֹעֲשׁ֣וּ עָ֑ם וְיַעֲבֹ֗רוּ וְיָסִ֥ירוּ אַ֝בִּ֗יר לֹ֣א בְיָֽד׃

Job xxxvii. 12.   Divide at בְּתַחְבּוּלֹתָ֗ו with Ox. 19 ; Cam. 25 ; Par.
9 ; K. 251, 403, 531 ; De R. 847 ;

וְה֤וּא מְסִבּ֨וֹת ׀ מִתְהַפֵּ֬ךְ בְּתַחְבּוּלֹתָ֗ו לְפָעֳלָ֥ם כֹּ֛ל אֲשֶׁר־יְצַוֵּ֖ם ׀ עַל־פְּנֵ֖י תֵבֵ֣ל אָֽרְצָה׃

Job xxxix. 25.   Divide at הֶאָ֗ח with Ox. 18 ; Ber. 2 ; K. 528, 531 ;
De R. 32, 587, 847 ; &c.

בְּדֵ֤י שֹׁפָ֨ר ׀ יֹ֘אמַ֤ר הֶאָ֗ח וּֽ֭מֵרָחוֹק יָרִ֣יחַ מִלְחָמָ֑ה רַ֥עַם שָׂ֝רִ֗ים וּתְרוּעָֽה׃

Baer has already corrected Ps. xxii. 26 ; lxviii. 18 ; xcv. 7 ; cxl. 6 ;
and Prov. xxx. 8 ; with full support (as I have found) from the Codd.
On the other hand, his division of cxix. 57 is quite without MS.
authority (he names indeed Fr., but by a *lapsus calami*) ; and in lxxxvi.
11 his correction must be rejected,—ordinary edd. are quite right.

The above are the only passages I have noted, as seeming to me to
call for correction, in the matter of the dichotomy.   There are a few
cases besides—as Ps. i. 3 ; xvii. 7 ; xxii. 30 ; Job xxvii. 8—where the
sense has been misunderstood (as may be seen from the Rabbinical commentaries on these passages), and the division is, in consequence, false.
Generally speaking, however, the punctators have shewn correct taste
and a due apprehension of the meaning of the text, in the bisection of
the verses.   Considering that they had to deal with several thousands
of cases, a few mistakes on their part are excusable.

The importance of the law laid down in this chapter cannot be
over-estimated.   It furnishes the principle on which the whole
system of the accentuation is constructed.

CHAPTER IV.

CONTINUOUS DICHOTOMY.

THE two halves of the verse having been constituted by the main dichotomy, we have next to enquire how *they*, in their turn, are prepared for musical recitation.

And the answer is, that the same principle is further applied in detail. Each half of the verse—*supposing it to contain three or more words*—is treated in just the same way as the verse itself. Should there be in it a parallelism of parts, the dichotomy—in this its second stage—will come between. Failing that, it will be fixed by the logical or syntactical pause.

Nor does the musical subdivision stop even here. It proceeds to bisect each minor clause, into which the half of the verse has been divided, *supposing three words, at least, remain in it;* and so on continuously, with every new clause that is formed, so long as the condition just named be fulfilled.

This is what has been termed the CONTINUOUS DICHOTOMY[1]. In the following chapters it will be our duty to trace the application of this law,—with the modifications to which it is subjected,—in the clauses governed by the various accents.

When the dichotomy is fixed by parallelism, or a logical pause, there is no difficulty in accounting for its presence; but in almost every verse—owing to the minute subdivisions which the continuous dichotomy introduces—we have to deal with cases, where the *syntactical* relation of the words to one another and to the whole clause of which they form a part, alone decides its position.

---

[1] The first to start the hypothesis of a continuous dichotomy was (according to Spitzner) C. Florinus, in his Doctrina de accent. divina, 1667. The two writers to whom is assigned the credit of having done most to establish the principle are J. Francke, in his Diacritica Sacra, 1710, and A. B. Spitzner, in his Institutiones ad analyticam sacram textus Hebr. V. T. ex accentibus, 1786. The former of these works I have not been able to consult. The latter I have read carefully through. It relates chiefly to the prose accents, and contains some good hints, but nothing more. A satisfactory result is certainly not worked out.

And it is not always easy to see on what principle the dichotomy, in such cases, is made. It is, therefore, necessary to consider what *the relation is between syntax and the accentual division*[2].

With clauses consisting of only *two* words we have (as I have stated) no concern. Music, logic, emphasis may occasionally introduce a separation here, but it is clear that rhythm must have been destroyed altogether, if such separation had been made at all general. Concepts therefore—as subject and predicate, adverb and verb,—which are generally kept apart in longer clauses, are here constantly brought together, thus: יְהֹוָה מָלָךְ (Ps. xcvii. 1); נַפְשִׁי לַאדֹנָי (cxxx. 6); כְּחַסְדְּךָ חַיֵּנִי (cxix. 88). And, as words united by Maqqeph are regarded as constituting a single word, we meet with such combinations as: אֲבוֹתֵינוּ תִּדְרוֹשׁ (xliv. 2); אִם־עֲוֹנוֹת תִּשְׁמָר־יָהּ (cxxx. 3); סְפְּרוּ־לָנוּ רְשָׁעוּ בַל־תִּמְצָא: (x. 15).

But in sentences, consisting of three or more words, the dichotomy is, with certain recognised exceptions, regularly introduced. Here the first step is to notice which of the component parts of a grammatical clause—subject, object, verb, &c.—*precedes*.

I. The SUBJECT may precede, and—from its independent position[3]—is almost always followed by the dichotomy, e. g. הָאֵל | תָּמִים דַּרְכּוֹ (xviii. 31), 'God — perfect is His way;' הַשָּׁמַיִם | מְסַפְּרִים כְּבוֹד־אֵל (xix. 2), 'The heavens—they declare the glory of God;' רוּחֲךָ טוֹבָה | תַּנְחֵנִי בְּאֶרֶץ מִישׁוֹר (cxliii. 10).

The variations that occur come under the following heads:

(1) The *personal pronoun* is not always accounted of sufficient importance to stand by itself: אֲנִי שָׁמַרְתִּי | אָרְחוֹת פָּרִיץ (xvii. 4); אַתָּה רִצַּצְתָּ | רָאשֵׁי לִוְיָתָן (lxxiv. 14); הוּא (xxv. 15; Job xxxvii. 12);

---

[2] The only scholar (as far as I am aware) who has treated this subject, has been Ewald, in an Appendix to his Lehrbuch der Hebräischen Sprache, pp. 869–873, but I cannot say that I have found his remarks of any service; as my readers will understand, when I mention, that he altogether discards the dichotomical principle.

[3] See Ges. Gr. § 144.

הֵמָּה (cvii. 24)[4]. And so the *interrogative* מִי (iv. 7), and מָה (Job xvi. 6); and the *relative* אֲשֶׁר (Ps. i. 3; iii. 7).

(2) The dichotomy is sometimes found after the *second* member of the clause, when the subject with that member admits of being taken to form a proposition *complete in itself*, capable of standing alone, *without* the member that closes the clause, e. g. יְהוָֹה יִשְׁמַע | בְּקָרְאִי אֵלָיו (iv. 4); עוֹלָם וָעֶד | יְהוָֹה מֶלֶךְ (x. 16); עֵינִי דָאֲבָה | מִנִּי־עֹנִי (lxxxviii. 10)[5]. (As for the closing member in such cases, it is necessarily merely *supplemental*,—a *Zusatz*,—most commonly an adverb, or preposition with its government.) On like conditions, the main dichotomy may come even after the *third* member, but then the subject must be marked off by a *minor* dichotomy, e. g. וַאֲנִי נָסַכְתִּי מַלְכִּי^{d 1}|^{d 2} עַל־צִיּוֹן הַר־קָדְשִׁי (ii. 6)[6]. Only, when the second and third members are *united by Maqqeph*, this minor dichotomy is not required, as in חֲבָלִים נָפְלוּ־לִי | בַּנְּעִמִים (xvi. 6).

(3) The dichotomy is also transposed to the second member, when that member is the *vocative*, in such expressions as וְאַתָּה יְהוָֹה | מָגֵן בַּעֲדִי (iii. 4); כִּסְאֲךָ אֱלֹהִים | עוֹלָם וָעֶד (xlv. 7); and often[7].

(4) In a few instances *assonance* has decided: יוֹם לְיוֹם | יַבִּיעַ אֹמֶר (xix. 3). So also in xlii. 8; cxlv. 4; Prov. xxvii. 17; Job xli. 8.

I have noticed no other variations, save such as are open to correction (see *Corrigenda*).

II. The OBJECT may precede; and as a certain emphasis is implied by its position at the commencement of the sentence[8], it is marked off by the dichotomy: פִּתְּחוּ רְשָׁעִים | חֶרֶב (Ps. xxxvii. 14); מַטֵּה עֻזְּךָ | יִשְׁלַח יְהוָֹה מִצִּיּוֹן (cx. 2).

The variations follow closely the lines laid down for the *subject*.

(1) Examples of the *pronoun* are indeed confined to מָה and אֲשֶׁר, as אֲשֶׁר אֲנִי | אֶחֱזֶה־לִּי (Job xix. 27); מַה־יִּתֶּן לָךְ (cxx. 3). The pers. pron. appears mostly as a *suffix*, and, in the few cases in which it occurs under the independent forms אֹתִי, אֹתוֹ &c., does not call for any remark. מִי too is rare in the accusative.

---

[4] Or, where it must be marked off, we find an *inferior*, instead of the *main*, dichotomy employed, e. g. וַאֲנִי | for וַאֲנִי[ׂ] (lxxiii. 28).

[5] Such cases are not, however, numerous; and where this division is adopted in one text, other texts often point regularly; comp. common edd. and Baer's text in xlviii. 15^b; li. 5^b; lxxxix. 37^b; cxix. 142^a. In Job xxx. 30 the position of the dichotomy varies in the *two halves* of the verse.

[6] The main and minor dichotomy I indicate by *d* 1 and *d* 2 respectively.

[7] The vocative also naturally takes the dichotomy at the *beginning* of a sentence, see iii. 2; v. 4; viii. 2; lxxxviii. 2.

[8] See Ges. Gr. § 145.

(2) If we substitute 'object' for 'subject' in I. 2, we have the explanation of such instances as, שְׁמָם מָחִיתָ | לְעוֹלָם וָעֶד (Ps. ix. 6); and נִדְרַי אֲשַׁלֵּם | נֶגֶד יְרֵאָיו (xxii. 26)[9]. It is very rarely that the *Zusatz* consists of *two* members, as in cxix. 65; Job xxxiii. 29.

A peculiar class of variations is possible, under this head. A clause, syntactically complete, may be formed by the object, verb, and pronominal subject (latent in the verb); and then the real subject may follow supplementally. Thus in (Prov. v. 3) כִּי נֹפֶת תִּטֹּפְנָה | שִׂפְתֵי זָרָה, 'For honey do they drop—the lips of the harlot;' Ps. lxxv. 9b (where Hupf. alone translates according to the accents) and Job xxxi. 35b. This accentual arrangement brings with it a slowness and emphasis in the expression, which is not without effect. But it is quite uncommon.

(3) The *vocative* occurs, as in I. 3, e. g. דְּרָכֶיךָ יְהוָה | הוֹדִיעֵנִי (Ps. xxv. 4); and חַסְדְּךָ יְהוָה | מָלְאָה הָאָרֶץ (cxix. 64).
Other variations I have not observed.

III. ADVERBS, adverbial expressions, and PREPOSITIONS with their government, when at the beginning of a clause, derive (like the *object*) a measure of emphasis from their position, and are generally marked off by the dichotomy, e. g. יוֹמָם יְצַוֶּה יְהוָה חַסְדּוֹ (Ps. xlii. 9); מְאֹד | עָמְקוּ מַחְשְׁבֹתֶיךָ (xcii. 6); בְּתוֹכָחוֹת עַל־עָוֹן | יִסַּרְתָּ | עָלֶיךָ | הָשְׁלַכְתִּי מֵרָחֶם (xxii. 11); בְּרוּחַ קָדִים | תְּשַׁבֵּר אֳנִיּוֹת תַּרְשִׁישׁ (xlviii. 8). אִישׁ (xxxix. 12);

The variations run parallel for the most part to those given above:

(1) Thus a preposition with *pronominal suffix*, or with the *pronoun* מָה or אֲשֶׁר, attaches itself readily to the word following, e. g. מִמֶּנּוּ בַּמֶּה יָזְכֶּה־ (xli. 8); עָלַי יִתְלַחֲשׁוּ | כָּל־שֹׂנְאָי | כָּל־יֹשְׁבֵי תֵבֵל יָגוּרוּ (xxxiii. 8); לַאֲשֶׁר (xliii. 2); לְמַה־תֹּדֵר אֶתְהַלֵּךְ | בְּלַחַץ אוֹיֵב | נַעַר | אֶת־אָרְחוֹ (cxix. 9); הֵבִיא אֱלוֹהַּ | בְּיָדוֹ (Job xii. 6).

(2) We have cases corresponding to those given in I. 2 and II. 2, e. g. מְאֹד נַעֲלֵיתָ | עַל־כָּל־אֱלֹהִים | וּבְתוֹרָתוֹ יֶהְגֶּה | יוֹמָם וָלַיְלָה (Ps. i. 2); (xcvii. 9)[10]. In xxv. 7b and xciii. 5b, the *Zusatz* consists of *two* members.

---

[9] Here also Codd. often vary; thus some point הַאֲזִינָה יְהוָה | אֲמָרַי (v. 2), but our edd. with a better emphasis אֲמָרַי הַאֲזִינָה | יְהוָה. So common edd. and Baer's text differ in x. 17; lvii. 7; cxix. 133, 149.

[10] As before, Codd. vary; thus some have תְּהִלָּתִי בְּקָהָל רָב | מֵאִתְּךָ (xxii. 26), ' Of Thee | shall be my praise, in the great congregation;' others place the dichotomy after תְּהִלָּתִי, 'Of Thee shall be *my praise* | in the great congregation.' Common edd. and Baer's text differ in xxi. 13b; lxxviii. 40; cxxxix. 7; Job xxiii. 14b.

(3) The *vocative* occurs as before, e. g. אֶקְרָא | יְהֹוָה אֵלֶיךָ (xxviii. 1);
לְמַעַן־שִׁמְךָ יְהֹוָה | תְּחַיֵּנִי (cxliii. 11).

We notice that the vocative also sometimes claims the pause, even
when no suffix of the second person precedes, e. g. | עַד־אָנָה יְהֹוָה
(xiii. 2); | וְעַתָּה בָנִים (cxix. 89); | עַד־מָתַי עָצֵל (Prov. vi. 9); | לְעוֹלָם יְהֹוָה
(v. 7). (The vocative in such cases comes in *parenthetically*, and the
pointing is according to rule with a parenthesis[11].)

(4) Lastly, the rule is, as might have been expected, *relaxed*, in the
case of the *common and less important* adverbs, which are often
(*a*) joined to the word following, as אָז (Ps. li. 21); אַף (lxii. 2, 5); אַיֵּה
(lxxiii. 19); כֵּן (cxxiii. 2); שָׁם (xxxvi. 13); מָתַי (cxix. 84); עוֹד (Job
xxxvi. 2); מָה (Ps. xlii. 12); הִנֵּה (xxxix. 6)[12]; or (*β*) marked by a *minor*
pausal accent, instead of the main dichotomy of the clause, e. g.
עַל־מֶה for עַל־מֶה (x. 13); עַל־זֹאת for עַל־זֹאת (xxxii. 6); | לָכֵן for לָכֵן
(lxxiii. 10); | שָׁם for שָׁם (cxxxii. 17); | וְעַתָּה for וְעַתָּה (Job xxx. 1).
In these minor matters the punctators claimed full liberty, and in
consequence often differ among themselves: in Ps. i. 5 some have
עַל־כֵּן |, others עַל־כֵּן; in ii. 5 some אָז, others אָז; and so on. Such
variations were allowable, the only difference for us being that the
stronger accent implies a fuller emphasis of the word on which it falls.

Other variations than those named are hardly to be found.
In | עַתָּה יָדַעְתִּי (xx. 7) and | קֶדֶם יָדַעְתִּי (cxix. 152) the emphasis rests
mainly on the *second* word, and therefore the dichotomy is rightly
assigned to it. And similarly in Job xxviii. 3[b]; only there the
adverbial expression has the *minor* dichotomy.

[If it be asked how, in the cases already considered, when we
have marked off the first member, we are to proceed with the
further division of the clause, the answer is very simple. We
start *de novo* with the members remaining. Thus in an example
like יָתוֹם |[d2] אַתָּה |[d1] הָיִיתָ עוֹזֵר (Ps. x. 14[b]) we first of all mark off
the object יָתוֹם, next the subject אַתָּה, and then, as there are
only two words remaining, the division of the clause is complete.

---

[11] Comp. for instance the parenthesis in Ps. xii. 6[b]; xl. 6[a]; cxxxii. 11[a].

[12] So יוֹם (Ps. lxxxviii. 2), in the sense of 'when,' is not counted of sufficient importance to be marked off by the dichotomy. And so I would account for the
accentuation of מֵעֵת in Ps. iv. 8[b]. The clause must have been construed (as the
old Verss. and comm. shew), 'From the time (i. e. *since*) their corn and their wine |
they increased,'—an unusual construction (it must be allowed), and altered in consequence by Ben-Bil. into מֵעֵת רַבּוּ דְגָנָם וְתִירוֹשָׁם,—yet not quite without parallel.
Comp. בְּטֶרֶם הָרִים | הָטְבָּעוּ (Prov. viii. 25), 'Before the mountains | they were sunk
down.'

To take another instance : הָרִים ‖ᵈ¹ כַּדּוֹנַג ‖ᵈ² נָמַסּוּ ‖ᵈ² מִלִּפְנֵי יְהֹוָה ‖
(xcvii. 5), first the subject הָרִים is marked off, next the adverbial
expression כַּדּוֹנַג, and lastly the verb נָמַסּוּ, according to rule IV,
immediately following. And so in other cases.]

IV. When the VERB [13] precedes, we are introduced to quite
a different system of division. Then, supposing subject, object,
&c. follow, the first dichotomy will be *before the last member,*
the second before the last but one, and so on. Thus : שִׁיתָה

יְבָרֵךְ כָּל־בָּשָׂר ‖ᵈ² שֵׁם ‖ᵈ² קָדְשׁוֹ ‖ᵈ¹ יְהֹוָה ‖ᵈ² מוֹרָה ‖ᵈ² לָהֶם ‖ᵈ² (ix. 21) :
אִם־תִּכְתּוֹשׁ אֶת־הָאֱוִיל ‖ᵈ³ בַּמַּכְתֵּשׁ ‖ᵈ² בְּתוֹךְ ‖ᵈ¹ (cxlv.21); לְעוֹלָם וָעֶד
הָרִפוֹת ‖ᵈ¹ בֶּעֱלִי ‖ (Prov. xxvii. 22).

The principle involved is a sound one. The first members of the
clause, which are already closely connected in grammatical construction, are kept together by the first dichotomy, and referred—for determination of their meaning—to the last member. Thus : 'Put, O Jehovah,
fear | in them;' and, 'Let all flesh bless His holy name | for ever and
ever.' These members are then taken *by themselves,* and—if they
contain three or more words—are again divided in the same way, and
on the same principle, 'Put, O Jehovah | fear;' 'Let all flesh bless |
His holy name.' It is very rarely that a *third* dichotomy, as in the
ex. given above from Prov., is necessary. In such a case as לֹא־יָקֻמוּ
רְשָׁעִים | בַּמִּשְׁפָּט (Ps. i. 5), a *single* dichotomy suffices. And in the still
simpler case, where there are only *two* members in the clause, the
dichotomy simply separates the one from the other, as תְּרֹעֵם | בְּשֵׁבֶט
בַּרְזֶל (ii. 9) [14].

The rule is most carefully observed. Such a case as תִּצְרֶנּוּ | מִן־הַדּוֹר זוּ
לְעוֹלָם (xii. 8),—a double *Zusatz* after the verbal predicate,—stands
(as far as I have observed) quite *per se.* יִגְמָר־נָא רַע | רְשָׁעִים (vii. 10)
is no exception, but must be rendered (with Aben-Ezra and Qimchi),
i. e. if we keep to the accents, 'Let evil make an end of the wicked'
(comp. xxxiv. 22). זְכָר־אֲנִי מֶה־חָלֶד (lxxxix. 48) is one of the very few
passages, which I propose to correct, without the authority of Codd.,

---

[13] It need hardly be mentioned that participles, infinitives, and verbal adjectives
follow, so far as they have verbal government, the same rule as the verb itself.

[14] It may be stated that the vocative is generally treated as a separate member
in this division, e. g. אֲמֶרָה שִׁמְךָ | עָלְיוֹן (ix. 3); but sometimes not, when the suffix,
which refers to it, immediately precedes. Thus בְּתוֹנֲכִי מִצְרָיִם (cxxxv. 9) are kept
together by the accents.

thus זְכֹר | אֲנִי מֶה־חָלֶד [15]. In lxi. 6[b] and Job xxxi. 31[b], the sense was misunderstood (as the Targ., LXX., and Vulg. shew); hence the (for us) false accentuation. We find one exception, Ps. xxxiv. 8, due to the presence of the anomalous accent, Little Shalshéleth.

V. In nominal sentences, *when the predicate precedes*, the division will follow the same rule (and on the same principle) as in verbal sentences, e. g. מָרוֹם מִשְׁפָּטֶיךָ | מִנֶּגְדּוֹ (x. 5); זֶה[d2] | אֱלֹהִים אֱלֹהֵינוּ[d1] | הוּא | לְכֹל הַחוֹסִים בּוֹ (xviii. 31); עוֹלָם וָעֶד (xlviii. 15, 'Such a one is God, our God, for ever').

This rule is strictly carried out. Only when הָיָה follows, the dichotomy falls not on *it*, but on the predicate[16], e. g. בְּהֵמוֹת | הָיִיתִי אָח | הָיִיתִי לְתַנִּים (lxxiii. 22); עִמָּךְ זְמִרוֹת | הָיוּ־לִי חֻקֶּיךָ (cxix. 54); עֲמָדוֹת | הָיוּ רַגְלֵינוּ (Ps. cxxii. 2). (Job xxx. 29);

In Prov. xxv. 7, כִּי טוֹב אֲמָר־לְךָ | עֲלֵה־הֵנָּה, there is a slight license—the division should properly have been at טוֹב, as in xxi. 19—for the purpose of bringing out with effect *the words spoken*. Just so in our modern punctuation.

VI. Lastly, the CONJUNCTIONS, as אֲשֶׁר, אוֹ, אִם, אַף, גַּם, יַעַן, כִּי, לוֹ, לְמַעַן, פֶּן, עַד, the NEGATIVES לֹא, בַּל, אֵין, בְּלִי, and forms compounded from them, as אִם לֹא, כִּי לֹא, עַל כִּי, כִּי אִם, &c., need not detain us. They are, from their character, generally *joined*, either by a conjunctive accent or Maqqeph, to the word following. It is unnecessary to give examples, as they may be found in every page. It may however be noted that these particles often affect the division of the clause, thus כִּי שֶׁמֶשׁ | וּמָגֵן (Ps. lxxxiv. 12), where, without the כִּי, there would be no dichotomy; and so אֲשֶׁר רָאִיתָ | אֶת־עָנְיִי (xxxi. 8); וְלֹא אָמְרוּ | הָעֹבְרִים (cxxix. 8), &c.

But, sometimes on musical grounds, sometimes with a view to

---

[15] K. 156 has זכר מה־חלד אני, a very good correction (comp. xxxix. 5[b]), but more violent than is necessary.

[16] In reality this word is, as we learn from the Arabic, in the *adverbial accusative*. The passage from Job is rendered in the Polyglot Vers. أَخَا كُنْتُ لِأَوْلَادِ ٱلْوُحُوشِ. And عَمָדَוֹת הָיוּ רַגְלֵינוּ answers to قَآئِمًا كَانَ زَيْدٌ (Wright, Arab. Gr. ii. p. 109). We see then in the accentuation a fine appreciation of the grammatical construction.

emphasis[17], even these unimportant words, which have so little claim
to an independent position, are found marked with a pausal accent,
thus : אַף (cxix. 3) ; ו אֲשֶׁר (cix. 16) ; בַּאֲשֶׁר (xxxiii. 22) ; גַּם (cxxix. 2) ;
יַעַן (cix. 16) ; ו כִּי (xvi. 10) ;. לְמַעַן (lx. 7) ; לוֹ (lxxxi. 14) ; בְּלֹא (xvii. 1) ;
בְּלִי (xix. 4) ; בַּל (xxxii. 9) ; עַל (Job xvi. 17) ; אַל־נָא (xxxii. 21) ; תַּחַת
(Prov. i. 29), &c.

Thus far, we have had to do with the division of the *clause* into its
several members, but there is a further point that requires consideration,
and that is, the division, in certain cases, of the *members themselves*.
Every member of a clause—subject, object, &c.—will be either *simple*,
consisting of one word, or *compound*, consisting of two or more words.
And such compound members introduce a new element into the dichotomy of the verse, about which it is necessary to say a few words.

(α) Two nouns in *apposition* are almost always kept together by the
accentuation : דָּוִד עַבְדּוֹ (Ps. xvii. 8) ; אַתָּה שִׁמְךָ (lxxxiii. 19) ; כְּאִישׁוֹן בַּת־עָיִן
(cxliv. 10) ; כֶּסֶף מְחִירָהּ (Job xxviii. 15).

The punctators did not, however, tie themselves to rule. Sometimes
the dichotomy comes, with a certain emphasis, *between* the two nouns,
e. g. אֶרְחׇמְךָ יְהוָה | חִזְקִי (Ps. xviii. 2).

But, if *three* nouns occur in apposition, the dichotomy becomes
necessary, as יְהוָה | אֵל אֱלֹהִים (l. 1) ; or if one of the members of appo-
sition consists of two words, as יְהוָה | אֱלֹהֵי יִשְׂרָאֵל . In particular cases
we may even require a *second* dichotomy, as in the compound subject :
הַר־צִיּוֹן |ᵈ¹ יַרְכְּתֵי צָפוֹן |ᵈ² קִרְיַת מֶלֶךְ רָב (xlviii. 3).

(β) Two nouns in the same construction, and united by the conjunction *and*, are joined by the accentuation : מִשְׁפָּטִי וְדִינִי (ix. 5) ;
לְדֹר וָדֹר (x. 6) ; שָׁמַיִם וָאָרֶץ (lxix. 35) ; גָּדוֹל וְנוֹרָא (xcix. 3)[18].
Yet not unfrequently the punctators emphasize two such words,
particularly when they shew parallelism, by placing the dichotomy
between, e. g. וְשֵׂיבָה | עַד־זִקְנָה וְנַם (lxxi. 18) ; וּלְבָבִי | כָּלָה שְׁאֵרִי (lxxiii.
26) ; וְאָדָם | בְּעֵינֵי אֱלֹהִים (Prov. iii. 4). That they held themselves quite
free in this respect is shewn by the different grouping of the words in
the *same* verse, וּמְתַנְקֵם | מַחֲרֵף וּמְנַדֵּף מִפְּנֵי אוֹיֵב | מִקּוֹל (Ps. xliv. 17).

But when *three* nouns come together the dichotomy cannot fail :
וּכְלִמָּתִי | חֶרְפָּתִי וּבָשְׁתִּי (lxix. 20). And so, if for one of the nouns, we
have a nominal expression containing two words, as רָשָׁע | וְאֹהֵב חָמָס
(xi. 5).

---

[17] It was left to the taste of the Reader to *discriminate* between these two cases,
and to give emphasis, where emphasis was due.

[18] Occasionally the two nouns stand ἀσυνδέτως, as צִנִּים פַּחִים (Prov. xxii. 5) ;
and עֶלְיוֹן נוֹרָא (Ps. xlvii. 3).

(γ) The *substantive* and its qualifying *adjective* are necessarily taken together: מֶלֶךְ גָּדוֹל (xcv. 3); רוּחַ טוֹבָה (cxliii. 10). The *participle* also is generally joined to its substantive, as עַם נִבְרָא (cii. 19)[19].

Instead of the adjective, we may have an adverb, a preposition with its government, or a verb (with the relative understood), e.g. מָגֵן בַּעֲדִי (iii. 4); צוֹרְרֵי רֵיקָם (vii. 5); שֹׁחֵד עַל־נָקִי (xv. 5); אֹיְבַי בְּנֶפֶשׁ (xvii. 9); מַלְכֵי מִקֶּדֶם (lxxiv. 12); אָדָם בִּיקָר (xlix. 21); מֶלֶךְ לְעוֹלָם (xxix. 10); עַם לֹא־יְדַעְתִּי (Ps. xviii. 44)[20]. שְׁאוֹל מָטָּה (ib. 24); דָּבָר בְּעִתּוֹ (Prov. xv. 23); But the connection in such expressions is not so close as that between substantive and adjective, and the punctators were quite at liberty to bring in the dichotomy *between* the words, if the constitution of the clause allowed, and they meant an emphasis (more or less) to rest on the words. So we meet with בַּל־אַפִּיךְ נִסְפֶּחֶם | מָדָם זָכַרְתִּי יָמִים | (xvi. 4); מִקֶּדֶם (cxliii. 5). Comp. l. 4[a]; lxxx. 14[a]; lxxxv. 5[b]; Job xxxi. 28[b] [21].

When however *two* adjectives or participles follow, the dichotomy must appear, e.g. עֹז וְגִבּוֹר | יְהֹוָה טֹרֵף וְשֹׁאֵג | אַרְיֵה (Ps. xxiv. 8); (xxii. 14). (Sometimes *between* the adjectives, as וְרָעוֹת | צָרוֹת רַבּוֹת (lxxi. 20); וְנָעִים | כָּל־הוֹן יָקָר (Prov. xxiv. 4).) And so, when in any other way, the qualifying expression consists of two or more words, as נַם ; (xviii. 48) הָאֵל | הַנּוֹתֵן נְקָמוֹת לִי | שָׁתוּל עַל־פַּלְגֵי־מָיִם | בְּעֵץ (Ps. i. 3); נָגִיד | חֲסַר תְּבוּנוֹת וְרַב מַעֲשַׁקּוֹת ; (xli. 10) אִישׁ־שְׁלוֹמִי | אֲשֶׁר־בָּטַחְתִּי בוֹ (Prov. xxviii. 16).

Exceptions are exceedingly uncommon. In the difficult passage כֶּסֶף צָרוּף | בַּעֲלִיל לָאָרֶץ (Ps. xii. 7), the sense was misunderstood (as we may gather from the old Verss. and Rabb. comm.) In עֹבֵר מִתְעַבֵּר (Prov. xxvi. 17), the two words have probably been kept together, for the sake of the *assonance*. A slight laxity, perhaps due to emphasis, has crept into Prov. vi. 18: 'Feet that are *eager* | to run to evil;' and in אִישׁ־עָנָה (xxv. 18) and אִישׁ־שָׁתָה (Job xv. 16) the compound expressions seem loosely treated as the simple participles עָנָה and שָׁתָה. For Job iii. 3[b] see the explanation p. 44, l. 16.

(δ) The union by means of the *status constructus* is of the very closest description; but here also, if *two* words with this construction follow one another, the first is marked off by the dichotomy, as referring

---

[19] Yet sometimes it stands with good effect *apart*, as in Ps. lxviii. 26: 'In the midst of damsels | (who are) playing the timbrel,' and Prov. xxx. 20, 'So is the way of a woman | (who has been) committing adultery.' Such cases come under η below.

[20] The preposition with its noun may even *precede*, as in בְּדִמְעוֹת שָׁלִישׁ (lxxx. 6; where Hitzig is, no doubt, right in translating: *Ein Becher, in Thränen bestehend*) and בַּצִּיּוֹת נָהָר (cv. 41), 'a river in the desert.'

[21] Of course the punctators often differ, as in Ps. xviii. 19[b] (comp. 2 Sam. xxii. 19); cviii. 13[a]; cxix. 142[a]; Job vi. 25[b]; xxxi. 28[b] (above); xxxiii. 10[b]; &c.

to the *compound idea* expressed by the second and third words, thus:
עֵת | לֶדֶת יַעֲלִי־סָלַע | אַשְׁרֵי | כָּל־חוֹסֵי בוֹ (Ps. ii. 12); שֵׁם | אֱלֹהֵי יַעֲקֹב (xx. 2); אֶת | יוֹם יְרוּשָׁלָ͏ִם (Ps. xcvii. 5); even מִלִּפְנֵי | אֲדוֹן כָּל־הָאָרֶץ (Job xxxix. 1); בָּל | יְמֵי חַיָּיִךְ (cxxviii. 5)[22]. And עַל | אַדְמַת נֵכָר (ib. 4); (cxxxvii. 7); so, when the words following contain a compound idea, formed in some other way, the dichotomy will be equally due, e. g. עֵט | סוֹפֵר מָהִיר (xlv. 2); וְאַשְׁרֵי | דְּרָכַי יִשְׁמֹרוּ (Prov. viii. 32). בַּעֲבוּר | דָּוִד עַבְדֶּךָ (cxxxii. 10); Sometimes it comes *between*, מִפִּי | עוֹלְלִים וְיֹנְקִים (Ps. viii. 3); comp. β.

Exceptions I have not noticed, save cxxxvii. 8[b], 9[a]; in the former of which verses, a slight license has been admitted, for the sake of rhythm; and in the latter the clause has been thrown out of gear by the introduction of Little Shalshéleth.

(ε) *Adverbial expressions* like עוֹלָם וָעֶד (x. 16); יוֹמָם וָלַיְלָה (lv. 11); מִבְקֹר לָעֶרֶב (lxxiv. 8); מֵחַיִל אֶל־חָיִל (lxxxiv. 8); מַיִם עַד־יָם (lxxii. 8); (Job iv. 20) are properly held together by the accents. And so, generally, the punctators are careful to keep the several parts of one and the same adverbial phrase together, e.g. בְּתוֹכָחוֹת עַל־עָוֹן (Ps. xxxix. 12); בַּחֲלוֹם מֵהָקִיץ (lxxiii. 20); although of course, where there are three or more words, the minor dichotomy must appear, as בְּהִתְעַטֵּף עָלַי [d2] רוּחִי [d1] (cxlii. 4); בִּקְרֹב עָלַי [d3] מְרֵעִים [d2] לֶאֱכֹל אֶת־בְּשָׂרִי [d1] (xxvii. 2)[23].

(ζ) With regard to the *Verb*, we have to notice—

(1) That the *infin. absol.* is united with the corresponding *verb. fin.*, as קַוֹּה קִוִּיתִי (xl. 2); הָלוֹךְ יֵלֵךְ (cxxvi. 6); שִׁמְעוּ שָׁמוֹעַ (Job xxi. 2).

(2) That two verbs, joined in the same construction, are generally also united accentually, as וִישִׂישִׂים | אֱלֹהִים יְחָנֵּנוּ וִיבָרְכֵנוּ (Ps. lxvii. 2); אָכְלוּ וַיִּשְׁתַּחֲווּ | כָּל־דִּשְׁנֵי־אָרֶץ (Ps. xxii. 30); קָמוּ עָמָדוּ (Job xxix. 8); מַהֵר עֲנֵנִי | יְהֹוָה (cxliii. 7).

But sometimes the dichotomy appears *between:* יָדֶיךָ עִצְּבוּנִי | וַיַּעֲשׂוּנִי (Job x. 8); חָדַל לְהַשְׂכִּיל | לְהֵיטִיב (Ps. xxxvi. 4); אֶרֶץ יָרְאָה | וְשָׁקָטָה (lxxvi. 9). We find variation, even in the *same* verse: הֵמָּה | כָּרְעוּ וְנָפָלוּ וַאֲנַחְנוּ קַמְנוּ | וַנִּתְעוֹדָד: (xx. 9).

If, however, either of the verbs receives an *addition* of any kind, a minor dichotomy must be introduced: יִזְכְּרוּ [d2] וְיָשֻׁבוּ אֶל־יְהֹוָה [d1] כָּל־ אַפְסֵי־אָרֶץ (xxii. 28); לֹא יָדְעוּ | וְלֹא יָבִינוּ (lxxii. 5). And so when *three* verbs occur in sequence, פִּצְחוּ וְרַנְּנוּ | וְזַמֵּרוּ (xcviii. 4).

(This is all analogous to what we saw with the noun, β.)

---

[22] But these small words, which are so used to Maqqeph, constantly appear with it, in this construction. See עַל־ (cvi. 17); עִם־ (cxx. 5, comp. 4); כָּל־ (vi. 9); אֶת־ (lx. 2).

[23] As these adverbial expressions begin with an infinitive, they are divided as *verbal* clauses.

(3) In a few cases, two verbs are brought together, which a strict regard to syntax would have kept apart : לְכוּ חֲזוּ | מִפְעֲלוֹת יְהֹוָה (xlvi. 9) ; הַרְפּוּ וּדְעוּ | כִּי־אָנֹכִי אֱלֹהִים (ib. 11) ; comp. lxvi. 5, 16 ; lxxxvi. 9. The punctators were here quite right in deciding that the first verb has not sufficient importance to claim the dichotomy. It is merely introductory to the second, on which the main stress and emphasis lies. Syntax therefore has to give way. On the other hand, they rightly separate לְכוּ | נְרַנְּנָה לַיהֹוָה (xcv. 1) ; and כַּבְּסֵנִי מֵעֲוֺנִי | הֶרֶב (li. 4).

(η) The *relative* clause, in whatever form it appears,—with or without אֲשֶׁר, or as a participle or verbal adjective,—is constantly treated as a separate and independent member, even when the substantive precedes, to which it properly belongs. (It is so in our own punctuation.) Thus אַשְׁרֵי הָאִישׁ | אֲשֶׁר יָגֹרְתִּי | הֶעָבֵר חֶרְפָּתִי (cxix. 39) ; יִמָּאֲסוּ כְמוֹ־מַיִם | יִתְהַלְּכוּ־לָמוֹ | אֲשֶׁר לֹא הָלַךְ בַּעֲצַת רְשָׁעִים (lviii. 8) ; (i. 1) ; כֵּן יְבֹרַךְ גָּבֶר | יְרֵא יְהֹוָה (lxix. 32) ; וְתִיטַב לַיהֹוָה מִשּׁוֹר פָּר | מַקְרִן מַפְרִיס (cxxviii. 4). On the other hand, זִכְרוּ | נִפְלְאוֹתָיו אֲשֶׁר עָשָׂה (cv. 5). Baer's text and ordinary edd. differ in ix. 12 ; xvi. 7 ; lxxix. 6 ; cxli. 9 ; Job xxiii. 5.

Such are the laws for the accentual division of a syntactical clause,—laws of no little importance, for they enable us to decide, in many a doubtful case,—where Codd. differ,—what the true accentuation is [24]. In applying them however we have to make allowance for other musical rules,—particularly that of transformation,—which will be given in due course. The student will understand that, till he is familiar with these additional rules, he must not attempt to apply for himself the laws laid down above. But these rules mastered, he will be surprised to find how strictly the laws (so modified) are carried out, and how simple and easy the accentual analysis becomes, under their guidance.

We must now for a moment retrace our steps. It has already been noticed that the principle of *parallelism*—which is our chief guide for the main dichotomy of the verse—shews itself also in the minor divisions. Here also it may be *complete*

---

[24] These laws may, for the most part, be traced in the prose accentuation as well, but undergo such very different modifications, that it is impossible to consider the two systems together. The accentuation of the three Books seems to me much the simpler, so that the study of it may well serve as an introduction to that of the other.

(e. g. Ps. lxiii. 2[b]), *general* (v. 11[a]), or *partial* (xviii. 7[a]); and under
the last-named head, *progressive* (xi. 4[b]), or simply *repetitive*
(xciii. 3[a])[25]. It may occur at the beginning (lxiii. 2[b]), the middle
(xxxi. 3[b]), or the end (ib. 11[a]) of a clause, and is particularly
common at the *end.* It is marked in the finest detail, being often
confined to the smallest possible limits of *two words* (lxxi. 18[a]).
Of course, we have to make allowance for it, when dividing
according to our rules; and in most cases an *additional
dichotomy* will be necessary, to separate the members of the
parallelism from one another; for instance in Ps. xxxi. 3[b]:

$$\text{הָיָה לִי} \mid \text{לְצוּר} \mid \text{מָעוֹז} \mid \text{לְבֵית} \mid \text{מְצוּדוֹת} \mid \text{לְהוֹשִׁיעֵנִי} :$$

where, without the parallelism, we should have had

$$\text{הָיָה לִי} \mid \text{לְצוּר} \mid \text{מָעוֹז} \mid \text{לְהוֹשִׁיעֵנִי} :$$

This additional dichotomy is the only modification of our rules which
parallelism introduces. We may indeed notice a distinct tendency to
emphasize the parallelism, as though the punctators felt that the poet,
in introducing it, did not do so without a meaning, but had intended,
by the repetition of the idea, that a certain *stress* should be laid upon
it. When therefore there was a choice, we find them constantly
selecting the stronger and more important accent for the parallelism.
Thus, in the ex. given above, הָיָה לִי is not marked (as it might properly
have been) with *d* 2, but this division was reserved for the members of
the parallelism. Hence too such cases as

$$\text{כִּי לֹא יָבִינוּ} \mid \text{אֶל־פְּעֻלֹּת יְהֹוָה} \mid \text{וְאֶל־מַעֲשֵׂה יָדָיו} \quad \text{(xxviii. 5)};$$

$$\text{הֵן הִכָּה־צוּר} \mid \text{וַיָּזוּבוּ מַיִם} \mid \text{וּנְחָלִים יִשְׁטֹפוּ} \quad \text{(lxxviii. 20)};$$

$$\text{תֹּסֵף רוּחָם} \mid \text{יִגְוָעוּן} \mid \text{וְאֶל־עֲפָרָם יְשׁוּבוּן} : \quad \text{(civ. 29)}.$$

I draw attention to these cases, because, had not the punctators
decided to mark and intone the parallelism, *d* 1 would, in accordance
with the syntactical or logical division, have come where *d* 2 now
stands, and *vice versa*[26]. We have here, on a smaller scale, the same
principle which we noticed (25. 14) under the main dichotomy,
viz. the main idea first given, and then an echo following of a *part* of
the same,—the part to which attention was to be specially drawn.

---

[25] Comp. pp. 24–26.

[26] Baer has indeed (following Heid.) adopted this division for the second of the
examples given above; but with very slight MS. authority.

Lastly, there is another principle of division, which we have already noticed in I. 2; II. 2, &c. The part of the clause, which follows the dichotomy, is often not parallel, but *supplemental*. The main idea is given, in the first part of the clause,—in a form, syntactically complete,—and then comes what is explanatory, qualifying, amplifying, &c. Of course the division is here often according to our rules, but not always. Thus, instead of 'How long | shall I be forming plans in my soul?' (xiii. 3), we find 'How long shall I be forming plans | in my soul?' instead of 'When I was silent, | my bones wasted away through my roaring all the day' (xxxii. 3), we have 'When I was silent, my bones wasted away | through my roaring all the day.' And so,

> If I did not believe to look on the goodness of Jehovah | in the land of the living! (xxvii. 13).
>
> Hope thou in God, for I shall yet praise Him | the help of my countenance and my God (xlii. 12).
>
> El, Elohim, Jehovah hath spoken, and called the earth | from the rising of the sun to the going down thereof (l. 1).
>
> And they shall know that God ruleth in Jacob | to the ends of the earth (lix. 14).
>
> By the rivers of Babylon, there we sat, and wept too | as we remembered Zion (cxxxvii. 1).

In such cases the supplemental part belongs properly to the *latter* part of the clause preceding. Here also the division may be regarded as more or less *emphatic*.

If now it be asked, What is the *meaning* of the continuous dichotomy, the rules of which have been investigated in the present chapter? What *principle* underlies it? I can only give the answer, which I have given before, with regard to the general objects of the accentuation. The principle was clearly twofold—primarily *melody*, and secondarily (as far as the laws of melody allowed) *development of the sense*. Whatever the melody may have been, the succession of pauses, which the continuous dichotomy introduced, afforded ample opportunity for the production of *musical effect*, e. g. with the trills, of which Eastern music is so fond; whilst all *monotony* was avoided by the change of accentuation, which the varying lengths of successive verses and their divisions rendered necessary. (The accents

themselves, I presume, see p. 2, note 4, supplied in full measure
that rising and falling of the voice—the *arsis* and *thesis* of the
Greeks—on which the melody of public recitation so largely
depends.)[27] With regard to the second object of the accentuation,
we have seen that the continuous dichotomy not only takes note
of the *logical* divisions, but aims at keeping apart for distinct
enunciation the several members of a *syntactical* clause—i. e.
whenever the length of the clause seems to make such separation
necessary—at the same time giving *emphasis*, where emphasis is
due. The accentuators thus did their best to assist both reader
and hearers in apprehending what seemed to them the true meaning of the Sacred Text. And this is for us the recommendation
of their system.

Some corrections of the *textus receptus* are necessary, in
accordance with the rules laid down in this chapter. I shall
then proceed to apply these rules to the clauses governed by the
several disjunctive accents.

Corrigenda[28]

(arranged according to the order of the rules, pp. 39–44).

SUBJECT. Ps. xxix. 7. :שֵׁאׁ תוֹבָהֲלַ בֵצֹח הָוׁהְי לוֹק with B. M. 2, 6, 8,
13; Erf. 2.

Ps. xcv. 7. וׁדָי ןאֹצְו וׁתיָעְרַמ םַע ׀ וּנְחַנֲאַֽו with Ox. 109; Par. 9, 30;
Ber. 32; De R. 304; Ghet. 1.

Prov. xiv. 6. :לָקֵנ ןוֹבָנְל תַעַֽדְו with Ox. 5, 17, 72; Erf. 1; Par. 4;
K. 157.

Prov. xiv. 13. :הָגׁוּת [29] הָתיִרֲחַֽאְו הָחְמִש with B. M. 1; Ox. 15, 17,
111, 2322; Pet. Comp. v. 22ª.

Prov. xv. 31. םיִיַח תַחַכוֹתּ תַעַמֹשֽ ןֶזֹא with Ox. 5, 6, 15, 17, 96;
Pet.

---

[27] On these points of detail I desire to speak with all diffidence, as I have no
knowledge of music.

[28] Some instances I have, for special reasons, reserved for the chapters following.
It was not necessary to give them there and here too.

[29] Munach stands here, by transformation (as will be hereafter shewn), for R'bhia
mugrash.

Prov. xxii. 3. Better עָרוּם רָאָה רָעָה וְנִסְתָּר with Par. 30; Ber. 1, 32; De R. 304, 518; Vat. 3. Comp. *b.* So also in xxvii. 12.

Job xxii. 18. וְהוּא מִלֵּא בָתֵּיהֶם טוֹב with B. M. 5, 8, 14; Ox. 1, 19, 2323.

Job xxxvii. 23. Better שַׁדַּי לֹא מְצָאנֻהוּ שַׂגִּיא־כֹחַ with Ox. 19; Erf. 2; Fr.; K. 157; De R. 593, 737.

Job xxxix. 13. אִם־אֶבְרָה חֲסִידָה [30]וְנֹצָה: with B. M. 1; Par. 17, 30; Erf. 1, 4; Fr.

OBJECT. Job xxxviii. 32. וְעַיִשׁ עַל־בָּנֶיהָ [30]תַנְחֵם: with B. M. 14; Ox. 18; Vi. 4, 8, 11. Comp. Hos. x. 14[b].

ADVERB, &c. Ps. iv. 9. בְּשָׁלוֹם יַחְדָּו אֶשְׁכְּבָה וְאִישָׁן, though I have found only two Codd., Erf. 1 and K. 538, that point so. The punctators generally seem to have adopted the rendering, which we find in Aben-Ezra and Qimchi, that יַחְדָּו=עמהם, 'with them,' my enemies!

Ps. xxxv. 7. כִּי־חִנָּם טָמְנוּ־לִי שַׁחַת רִשְׁתָּם with Ox. 71, 2332; Erf. 2.

Ps. xliv. 25. לָמָה פָנֶיךָ תַסְתִּיר with B. M. 4, 8, 13; Ox. 5, 71; &c. So also correct Job xiii. 24.

Prov. xiv. 14. מִדְּרָכָיו יִשְׂבַּע סוּג־לֵב with Ox. 1; or מִדְּרָכָיו יִשְׂבַּע סוּג לֵב with B. M. 5, 7, 8, 12, 13; Ox. 5. Comp. xviii. 20.

Job vi. 14. לַמָּס מֵרֵעֵהוּ חָסֶד with B. M. 4; Ox. 1, 17, 71; Erf. 2, 3.

Job xvii. 15. וְאַיֵּה אֵפוֹ[31] תִקְוָתִי with B. M. 3; Ox. 19; Fr.; K. 445; De R. 2, 589.

Job xvii. 16. אִם־יַחַד עַל־עָפָר נָחַת: with B. M. 3, 4; Ox. 13, 72, 101; Fr. Comp. xxi. 26.

Job xxix. 25. כַּאֲשֶׁר אֲבֵלִים יְנַחֵם: with Ox. 19, 72; Ber. 2; Fr.; De R. 349, 368. Comp. Ps. lvi. 7[b].

VERB. Ps. v. 3. הַקְשִׁיבָה ׀ לְקוֹל שַׁוְעִי. See Norzi's note: בספרים מדוייקים כן הוא בטעם גרמיה.

Ps. xi. 1. If we take the reading of the K'thîbh, we have necessarily the pointing

אֵיךְ תֹּאמְרוּ לְנַפְשִׁי נוּדוּ הַרְכֶם[30] צִפּוֹר:

The Q'rî (as it seems to me) can only be rendered:

'Flee thou! Off to your mountain, ye birds[32]!'

---

[30] See p. 51, note 29.

[31] אֵפוֹ, as is well known, attaches itself to the word preceding.

[32] It must be borne in mind that the accentuation is always *according to the Q'rî.*

Ps. xxxii. 5. אוֹדֶה ׀ עֲלֵי פְשָׁעַי לַיהֹוָה with Par. 9 ; Fr. ; K. 188, 403 ;
De R. 350; or אוֹדֶה עֲלֵי־פֶּשַׁע with Par. 21, 24, 30 ; K. 157, 246 ; &c.

Ps. lxxxix. 6. [33]וְיוֹדוּ שָׁמַיִם פִּלְאֲךָ יְהֹוָה with B. M. 1; Ox. 13, 15, 2323;
Erf. 3 ; Bomb. 2.

Ps. cxix. 138. צִוִּיתָ צֶדֶק עֵדֹתֶיךָ with Ox. 1, 6 ; Par. 4, 30 ; Erf. 2 ; Fr.

Job ix. 30. וַהֲזִכּוֹתִי בְּבֹר[34] כַּפָּי : with Ox. 96 ; Par. 17, 36 ; Ber. 52 ;
De R. 2, 596. Comp. Ps. lxxiii. 13.

Job xv. 22. לֹא־יַאֲמִין שׁוּב מִנִּי־חֹשֶׁךְ with B. M. 3, 4 ; Ox. 1, 7, 19, 96.

Job xix. 21. חָנֻּנִי חָנֻּנִי אַתֶּם רֵעָי with Ox. 1, 5 ; Erf. 3, 4 ; K. 157,
606 ; Sonc.

Job xxiv. 9. יִגְזְלוּ מִשֹּׁד[33] יָתוֹם with Ox. 1, 72 ; Cam. 28; Fr. ;
K. 224; De R. 380.

Job xxxi. 15. וַיְכֻנֶּנּוּ בָרֶחֶם[34] אֶחָד : with B. M. 14, 16; Ox. 101;
Ber. 32 ; Hm. 8, 21.

Job xxxi. 16. אִם־אֶמְנַע מֵחֵפֶץ[33] דַּלִּים with B. M. 6 ; Ox. 18 ; Erf. 2 ;
Hm. 15, 32; Vi. 8. Comp. xxxviii. 15.

Job xxxix. 10. הֲתִקְשָׁר־רֵים בְּתֶלֶם[33] עֲבֹתוֹ (taking עֲבֹתוֹ as accus.
instrumenti) with B. M. 11 ; Ox. 9, 2437; Erf. 1 ; Hm. 8 ; Cop. 4.

Job xl. 2. הֲרֹב עִם־שַׁדַּי[33] יִסּוֹר with B. M. 12 ; Ox. 1, 5, 19, 100, 101.

NOM. PREDICATE. Ps. xc. 1. The simplest correction of our texts
would be מָעוֹן אַתָּה הָיִיתָ לָּנוּ בְּדֹר וָדֹר :אֲדֹנָי, but no Cod. points מָעוֹן
with R'bhîa, whereas many—B. M. 4, 8 ; Ox. 4, 13, 72, 97, &c.—
have מָעוֹן אַתָּה, which removes all difficulty, as far as the accents are
concerned : 'O Lord, a refuge art THOU ; Thou hast been for us
(comp. הָיָה לָּנוּ cxxiv. 1) in generation and generation.'

Job xxix. 15. עֵינַיִם הָיִיתִי לַעִוֵּר with B. M. 7, 8 ; Ox. 5, 7, 15, 19.

Many other similar corrections have been made in the text by
Heidenheim and Baer, which I shall have occasion to refer to hereafter.

---

[33] Munach stands here, by transformation, for D'chi.
[34] See p. 51, note 29.

CHAPTER V.

WE saw, in chapter III, that every verse is divided into two parts by either Olév'yored or Athnach. These parts have now to be taken *separately*. Each has its own musical arrangement, which makes it so far independent of the other. In this chapter and the next I purpose considering the *first* part, as closed by Olév'-yored and Athnach. I shall then proceed to the examination of the *second* part, lying between the one or other of these accents and Silluq.

OLÉV'YORED [1].

We have already noticed (34. 2) that this accent cannot come at the *beginning* of the verse; in other words, Olév'yored's clause cannot consist of a *single word*.

I. When it contains *two* words, Little R'bhîa is always required in the first, e. g. אֲסַפְּרָה אֶל חֹק (Ps. ii. 7); רִגְזוּ וְאַל־תֶּחֱטָאוּ (iv. 5).

---

[1] The name of this accent was doubtless chosen to indicate its twofold melody, in the chanting of which the voice first *ascended* (עלה) and then *descended* (ירד) in the scale. In support of this derivation, it may be mentioned that Ben-Asher (Dikd. hat. 20. 16) employs these same terms עולה and יורד for the accents Munach and Mer'kha, of which he distinctly states (24. 12), that the former has an *ascending*, and the latter a *descending* melody; and that in the *Mas. magna* to Num. xxxvi. 3, we find the terms סלק ונחת (=עולה ויורד) used of the *ascending* melody of Azla, followed by the *descending* melody of Mer'kha. Did we know more of the accentual melodies, we might perhaps find that the commencing melody of Olév'yored *resembled* the melody of M'huppakh, and that *that* was the reason why M'huppakh was chosen to represent it. The lower sign is (as has been stated) in MSS. like Silluq,—קו זקוף El. Levita calls it,—and designates Olév'yored as a *pausal* accent. (The same stroke is also used, to indicate a *pause*, for Paseq and Métheg.)
' With regard to the *position* of the first sign, I have found in the Codd. that—
a. If the tone be on any other than the first syllable, it is placed over the preceding syllable, as רְשָׁעִים (i. 1); הֲפָצוּ (i. 2). Similarly, if the tone be on the first syllable, and Sh'va precede, as מֹצָא (xxxii. 6); שְׁמוֹ (lxviii. 5). It will be remembered that two words joined by Maqqeph are counted as one word; we might then expect that עַל־פַּלְגֵי־מָיִם (i. 3), אֶל־חֹק (ii. 7) would be so pointed, but the Maqqeph is in such cases dropped, as no longer necessary. β. If the tone be on the first syllable—and Sh'va do not precede—the M'huppakh-sign is transferred to the last syllable of the preceding word, supposing that syllable is unac-

Such verses are not, however, numerous,—if we except the superscriptions, hardly 20 in the whole of the three Books,—and when we
examine them, we find that the poet, in dividing his verse so near
to its beginning, has taken care that the words should be *emphatic*
in their character; so that the accentuators decided rightly in
insisting on a *pausal*, instead of a conjunctive accent, here[2]. The
additional pause gives a weight to this short half of the verse.

II. When the clause contains three or more words, the position of the dichotomy will be fixed by the rules laid down in the
preceding chapter, and the accents employed to mark it will be
as follows[3]:

1. Little R'bhîa, if the dichotomy fall on the *first* word before
Olév'yored, e. g. וָאִישָׁנָה שָׁכַבְתִּי אֲנִי (iii. 6), p. 47. l. 28[4];
חַטָּאוֹת אֶהֱבוּ אֶת־יְהוָֹה כָּל־חֲסִידָיו (xxxi. 24), 43. 22;
אִם־אֵלֵךְ ׀ בְּקֶרֶב נְעוּרַי ׀ וּפְשָׁעַי אַל־תִּזְכֹּר (xxv. 7), 40. 23;
צָרָה תְחַיֵּנִי (cxxxviii. 7), 38. 11.

2. Ṣinnor, on the *second* word[5]: יְהוָֹה יָדִין עַמִּים (vii. 9),
39. 20; חֶרֶב ׀ בְּיוֹם צָרַתִי אֲדֹנָי דְּרַשְׁתִּי (lxxvii. 3), 41. 17;
תְּשִׁיתֵמוֹ ׀ פָּתְחוּ רְשָׁעִים וְדָרְכוּ קַשְׁתָּם (xxxvii. 14), 38. 9;
כְּתַנּוּר אֵשׁ לְעֵת פָּנֶיךָ (xxi. 10), 43. 5.

In such cases, the first word will almost always have the *servus*
Galgal. But Little R'bhîa is musically admissible, and we find it

---

cented, as מִי־יִרְאֶנּוּ טוֹב (iv. 7); פָּעֳלֵי אָוֶן (xiv. 4). But if it is accented, then the
sign remains on the first syllable, as שָׁוּב נָא אֵתָּה (lxxx. 15); וְיָשָּׁר אַתָּה (Job viii. 6).
Some Codd. adopt this pointing even in the former case, thus מִי־יִרְאֵנוּ טוֹב,
פָּעֳלֵי אָוֶן. (Comp. R'bhîa mugrash, p. 16, note 29.)

[2] Not unfrequently the one or other of these signs is dropped in Codd. In particular, the upper sign often falls away, when the tone is on the first syllable, as
יוֹם ׀ יוֹם (Ps. lxviii. 20). So too R'bhîa mugrash often loses one of its signs.

[2] They have, however, in one case, hardly caught the division intended by the
poet. The first two words of cxliv. 14 belong clearly (see Hupf.) to the previous
verse, which must then, in its turn, be otherwise divided. On Job xxxii. 12 see
Delitzsch's remark.

[3] The three accents, named in 1, 2, and 3, furnish a sufficient musical variety before
Olév'yored.

[4] Here, at the beginning, I refer in each case to the page and line, where the rule
is to be found.

[5] This is by far the most common division of Olév'yored's clause.

introduced, apparently for the sake of emphasis, in a few passages of the *textus receptus*, viz. Ps. xxii. 15; xxxv. 10; xxxix. 13; Prov. xxiii. 35; xxx. 9. Perhaps in the Codd. other examples might be found; but the matter is not of any moment.

3. Great R'bhia, on the *third* word or further, e. g. אַשְׁרֵי וְהָיָה כְּעֵץ (i. 1), 48. 14; הָאִישׁ אֲשֶׁר ׀ לֹא הָלַךְ בַּעֲצַת רְשָׁעִים יְהֹוָה מִשָּׁמַיִם הִשְׁקִיף עַל־ (i. 3), 43. 23; שָׁתוּל עַל־פַּלְגֵי מָיִם עַתָּה יָדַעְתִּי כִּי הוֹשִׁיעַ ׀ יְהֹוָה מְשִׁיחוֹ בְּנֵי־אָדָם (xiv. 2), 39. 20; (xx. 7), 42. 22.

In such cases, we have to notice that there are three or more words left between Great R'bhia and the end of the clause. These words then will claim a minor dichotomy. And the same accents will be employed (i. e. the same musical notes will be required) before Olév'yored, as above under 1 and 2. If this minor dichotomy fall on the *first* word, it will be marked by Little R'bhia; if on the *second*, by Ṣinnor[6].

The above rules are simple enough. One class of exceptions alone has to be noted. The two R'bhias cannot, from musical reasons, occur in too close proximity. At least, *two* words, with their respective accents, must intervene[7]. Where this is not the case, Ṣinnor is employed instead of Great R'bhia[8], as in the following examples:

---

[6] Further back than the second word this minor dichotomy does not come, save in one passage, where Olév'yored's clause is of unusual length, and an additional dichotomy becomes necessary, which is made by the *repetition* of Ṣinnor: מְבַחֲתִים יָדְךָ ׀ יְהֹוָה מְבָחֲתִים מֵחֶלֶד חֶלְקָם בַּחַיִּים וּצְפוּנְךָ תְּמַלֵּא בִטְנָם (xvii. 14).

[7] Similarly, in the prose Books, a certain interval must occur between two consecutive R'bhias; otherwise one of them is changed into Pashṭa. The rule is modified in the three Books, for here two Great R'bhias (as we shall see under Athnach) can stand together, but a suitable interval must separate the two *different kinds* of R'bhias. No writer on the accents has (as far as I am aware) noticed this peculiarity.

[8] I have observed only one passage, cxxxiii. 2, in our texts, at variance with this rule. But here Codd. vary much. Some, as Ox. 13, Par. 4, K. 192, De R. 593, have בַּשֶּׁמֶן הַטּוֹב ׀ עַל־הָרֹאשׁ יֹרֵד עַל־הַזָּקָן; whilst many—B. M.: 2; Ox. 6, 111; Fr.; K. 155, 598; &c.—drop Olév'yored, and have D'chî instead, יֹרֵד עַל־הַזָּקָן. Either of these pointings does away with all difficulty. In xxviii. 7 we have a solitary ex. of *Ṣinnor* with *two* words between it and Little R'bhia, but these words may be joined by Maqqeph, with B. M. 4, 7; Par. 20, 21, 25, 30; &c. The punctuation of common edd., and not that of the Heid.-Baer text, must be taken for xv. 5; xxxii. 4; li. 6; and lii. 9.

כִּי הַצַּלְתָּ נַפְשִׁי מִמָּוֶת (xv. 5); בֵּסְפּוּ ׀ לֹא־נָתַן בְּנֶשֶׁךְ וְשֹׁחַד עַל־נָקִי לֹא־לָקַח הֲלֹא רַגְלֵי מֵדֶחִי (lvi. 14). Comp. xiii. 6; xxvii. 9; xxxii. 4; xxxv. 10; xl. 6, 15. On the other hand Great R'bhîa. can remain in xx. 7; lii. 9; cxxvii. 5; cxxxix. 14.

When the dichotomy of Olév'yored's clause is thus completed, Great and Little R'bhîa, and Ṣinnor will often be left with clauses of their own, containing three or more words. For the accentuation of such subordinate clauses I must refer to the chapters reserved for these accents.

SERVUS OF OLÉV'YORED.

The servus of Olév'yored is (as we have seen) Galgal. In two passages it comes, instead of Métheg, in the same word with Olév'yored, מִמּוֹעֲצוֹתֵיהֶם (v. 11) and יָבֵהֵלוּן (civ. 29)[8].

EXCEPTIONS: (1) In three passages, where Paseq intervenes, Galgal is changed into M'huppakh, thus בָּרוּךְ אֲדֹנָי יוֹם ׀ יוֹם (lxviii. 20); and so in lxxxv. 9 and Prov. xxx. 15. (Paseq fails here in common edd.)[9]

(2) In two passages Mer'kha comes as servus between Little R'bhîa and Olév'yored: יְהֹוָה מִי כָמוֹךָ (Ps. xxxv. 10) and וְאָמַרְתִּי מִי יְהֹוָה (Prov. xxx. 9)[10].

Olév'yored has never more than *one* servus.

---

[8] In lv. 22; lxxviii. 38; civ. 29; cvi. 47; cxl. 4; Prov. i. 22; and Job xxiv. 13, Galgal is wanting in our texts. For lv. 22 point וּקְרָב (see Norzi's note). In cvi. 47 I would propose to make R'bhîa and Ṣinnor change places. The other instances have been already corrected by Heid. and Baer.

[9] Some Codd. and Ben-Bil. (8. 9) make this change, when the tone is on *the first letter* of the word, e.g. מִי זֶה מֶלֶךְ הַכָּבוֹד (xxiv. 8). Common edd., with their usual inconsistency, point sometimes with Galgal (xii. 3; xvi. 11), sometimes with M'huppakh (vi. 3; xxiv. 8). The former was Ben-Asher's punctuation, the latter Ben-Naphtali's. Of course, Codd. generally follow Ben-Asher.

[10] We shall see elsewhere, in the Masoretic text, Mer'kha taking (exceptionally) the place of Maqqeph, which is here (at least for the passage in Prov.) retained by Ben-Naphtali (see Ginsburg's Masora, vol. i. p. 588). In this use of Mer'kha, I believe that we have simply an instance of Masoretic trifling. Thus there are just these two cases of מִי before Olév'yored, and so they are made to pair off, with an abnormal accentuation! (Comp. p. 63, notes 23 and 24.) Mer'kha in Ps. xlii. 5 I have already corrected, p. 36. In xv. 5 introduce Maqqeph with Heid. and Baer.

CHAPTER VI.

ATHNACH.

Athnach, like Olév'yored, is never found in the *first word* of
the verse (34. 3).

I. When Athnach's clause consists of *two* words (and such
cases are very common), the first has generally the servus
Mer'kha[1], as לֹא־כֵן הָרְשָׁעִים (i. 4), but sometimes D'chî, as
נִנְתְּקָה אֶת־מוֹסְרוֹתֵימוֹ (ii. 3).

We may suppose that the original intention was to reserve D'chî for
cases of *pause* or *emphasis*, like כִּי־אָמַרְתִּי פֶּן־יִשְׂמְחוּ־לִי (xxxviii. 17);
שִׁמְעוּ־זֹאת כָּל־הָעַמִּים (xlix. 2). But this rule is far from being always
observed in our printed texts. For a matter of so little consequence,
I have not thought it worth while to examine the Codd.[2], with the
view of correcting exceptional cases.

II. When Athnach's clause consists of *three or more* words,
the rules for the dichotomy are applied, just as in the case of
Olév'yored, and the accents employed to mark it are:

1. D'chî, when the dichotomy falls on the word immediately
preceding Athnach, e. g. שָׁמַע יְהֹוָה תְּחִנָּתִי (vi. 10); אָמַר בְּלִבּוֹ
בַּל־אֶמּוֹט (x. 6).

2. D'chî also, when it falls on the *second* word before Athnach
(for here we have no accent answering to Ṣinnor before Olév'-
yored), e. g. שׁוּבָה (v. 3); הַקְשִׁיבָה ׀ לְקוֹל שַׁוְעִי מַלְכִּי וֵאלֹהָי
יְהֹוָה חָלְצָה נַפְשִׁי (vi. 5)[3].

But not unfrequently Great R'bhîa appears instead, e. g.
הוֹשִׁיעָה אֶת־עַמֶּךָ וּבָרֵךְ (xix. 2); הַשָּׁמַיִם מְסַפְּרִים כְּבוֹד־אֵל
אֶת־נַחֲלָתֶךָ (xxviii. 9).

---

[1] *After Olév'yored* Mer'kha is always employed, as in vii. 1; xviii. 36; xxv. 7. I
have observed only three exceptions, lxii. 11; Prov. xxx. 17; and Job xxxiii. 9,
which are corrected in Codd.

[2] I have noticed, however, incidentally that they often vary, as in viii. 5; xxvi. 4;
xxxvii. 13, 24, 29; Job xxi. 15, 22; xxxvii. 13.

[3] This is by far the most frequent division of Athnach's clause.

R'bhîa, when contrasted with D'chî, marks a *greater pause* (logical or syntactical). This principle is however—for such clauses as those before us—only partially carried out in our texts. D'chî occurs where we should have expected R'bhîa and *vice versa*. The point is not of any importance to us, for the *sense* is not appreciably affected, which-ever accent be employed [4].

Generally, when R'bhîa occupies this position, the first word has Mer'kha (as above), but in a few instances D'chî. The examples are Ps. xlv. 5; l. 1; lix. 8; lxxviii. 31; lxxxii. 1; cxliv. 3; Job xiii. 4; xxxii. 11; xxxiv. 25. The appearance of D'chî in these cases is parallel to that of Little R'bhîa between Ṣinnor and Olév'yored (55. 22).

3. Great R'bhîa, when the dichotomy falls on the *third* word or further, e. g. שָׁאַל מִמֶּנִּי וְאֶתְּנָה גוֹיִם נַחֲלָתֶךָ (ii. 8); אַל־תֹּאמַר כַּאֲשֶׁר עָשָׂה־לִי כֵּן אֶעֱשֶׂה־לוֹ (Prov. xxiv. 29); הֲיָדַעְתָּ עֵת לֶדֶת יַעֲלֵי־סָלַע (Job xxxix. 1). Great R'bhîa divides in the same way (as we have seen) Olév'yored's clause.

But here we notice that, with R'bhîa on the third word (or further), three words (or more) remain between it and the end of the clause. These words then will require a second dichotomy, which, in the examples given (as falling on the first or second word, see 1 and 2), is marked by D'chî. But, what if this second dichotomy itself fall on the third word (or further), where D'chî cannot be employed to mark it [5]? Then, *R'bhîa is repeated* [6], and D'chî comes in for the third dichotomy, which has now become necessary. Thus חַטָּאתִי ׀ אוֹדִיעֲךָ וַעֲוֺנִי לֹא־כִסִּיתִי אָמַרְתִּי אוֹדֶה ׀ עֲלֵי פְשָׁעַי לַיהוָה (Ps. xxxii. 5). The other examples (as far as I have noted) are l. 21; lxxviii. 4; lxxxix. 20; xcv. 10; xcvii. 5; cii. 25; Prov. xxvii. 10; and Job vii. 4 [7].

---

[4] On this point the Codd. themselves exhibit no little variation. Thus שֻׁוּעִי and שֶׁוְעִי (v. 3); יְהֹוָה and יְהוָה (vi. 2); סָבִיב and סָבִיב (xii. 9); רַבָּתִי and רַבָּתִי (xvii. 1); &c.

[5] It is a fixed rule that D'chî *cannot occur further back than the second word from Athnach*. Hence such mistakes, as in Ps. cxxxv. 4, Prov. xx. 4, Job xvi. 19, in common edd., must be at once corrected.

[6] Just as, under similar circumstances, R'bhîa is repeated in the prose Books. It is clear, from the nature of the case, that the second R'bhîa has a *less pausal value* than the first.

[7] In Ps. xvii. 1, xli. 7, xlvi. 5, lix. 6, Prov. iv. 4, Job xxiv. 24, xxxiii. 23, a second R'bhîa appears, but merely as a substitute for D'chî (see II. 2 above).

(R'bhîa is not repeated more than once; in other words, the division of Athnach's clause does not proceed beyond the third dichotomy, and only in the few passages just named, beyond the second.)

Such are the simple rules for the analysis of Athnach's clause. Of course, the clauses closed by R'bhîa and D'chî may have (as in the last ex.) their own subordinate pausal accents, the rules for which will be considered in the chapters on Great R'bhîa and D'chî. One point only remains to be noticed, and that is the frequent change of D'chî—when due, from the dichotomy, in the first word before Athnach—into a *servus*. This change is, of course, simply musical, and is occasioned by the *shortness* of that part of Athnach's word which precedes the tone. When it contains two (or more) syllables, or one long syllable, followed by vocal Sh'va, D'chî can stand. Otherwise, a servus must come instead. Thus we have לְךָ ־ אֲנִי הוֹשִׁיעֵנִי (cxix. 94); but עַבְדְּךָ ־ אָנִי הֲבִינֵנִי (ib. 125); and אֲבַדּוֹן וָמָוֶת אָמְרוּ (Job xxviii. 22); but אֲמוּנָתְךָ וּתְשׁוּעָתְךָ אָמָרְתִּי (Ps. xl. 11). This law of *transformation* (as it has been termed) mars, in no slight degree, for us, here and elsewhere, the order and symmetry of the accentual system.

In connection with this transformation, I explain such cases as כִּי אֵלֶיךָ ׀ יְהֹוִה (lxxiii. 28) and שַׁתִּי ׀ בַּאדֹנָי יְהֹוִה מַחְסִי אֲדֹנָי עֵינָי (cxli. 8), where L'garmeh comes in the third word before Athnach[8]. At first sight, it often appears as if we had

---

[8] In Ps. v. 5 L'garmeh appears on the *fourth* word; but the explanation is the same. On the other hand, in Ps. lxii. 11, where it comes *immediately before* Athnach, it must be dropped (with B. M. 3; Ox. 13, 17, 27; Erf. 2; Fr. &c.). And so in Prov. xvi. 10 (see Baer's note). Further, I would correct Ps. xiv. 5,—where our edd. place it in the *second* word,—thus שָׁם פַּחֲדוּ פָחַד with B. M. 2; Par. 4, 9, 29, 30; Ber. 32; &c. And in Job xxxviii. 2, if we divide with Athnach, as various Codd. and Baer do, we must point either מִי זֶה מַחְשִׁיךְ עֵצָה with B. M. 3; Hm. 8; De R. 349; or מִי זֶה מַחְשִׁיךְ עֵצָה with B. M. 14; Ox. 18; K. 403. (In xxxvii. 1, cvi. 1, cxxxviii. 1, cl. 1, L'garmeh stands for Olév'yored (34. 12) and does not come into consideration here.)

here a substitute of R'bhîa, but such a substitution would be quite inexplicable; whereas, if we take L'garmeh as the pausal accent in D'chî's clause, *which remains, when D'chî is transformed*, all is clear. A comparison of Job xxvii. 13 with xx. 29 shews, beyond all possibility of doubt, that this is really the case. Other examples are Ps. xviii. 50 (compared with 2 Sam. xxii. 50); xxxi. 15; xliv. 24; cxxii. 5; Job iv. 5; xxxi. 2. Once, Ps. xix. 15, Pazer—the other pausal accent in D'chî's clause—is employed in the same way[9]. (But some Codd. point here with R'bhîa.)

This L'garmeh is very rarely wanting in its proper place. That the distinguishing Paseq now and then fails, will surprise no one who has any acquaintance with the Codd. Thus it must be supplied to הִנֵּה ׀ in Ps. lxxxvii. 4; cxxvii. 3; Prov. i. 23; Job xxxii. 12 (as I have found in various Codd.); and so Prov. xvii. 12 must be corrected פָּנוֹשׁ ׀ דֹּב, שַׂכִּיל בְּאִישׁ; and xxi. 29 הֵעֵז ׀ אִישׁ רָשָׁע בְּפָנָיו[10]. I have noticed no other exceptions.

Servi of Athnach[11].

Athnach has often one, two, and three servi, rarely more than three.

1. One servus. This is (a) Munach, after D'chî, e. g. תִּרְעֵם בְּשֵׁבֶט בַּרְזֶל (Ps. ii. 9); יְהוָֹה מָלָךְ יִרְגְּזוּ עַמִּים (xcix. 1); (β) Mer'kha in all other cases, i. e. after Olév'yored[12] or R'bhîa, or at the beginning of the verse, e. g. אֲפָפוּנִי חֶבְלֵי־מָוֶת (xviii. 13); יַצִּילֵנִי מֵאֹיְבִי עָז (ib. 18); מִמֶּנָּה נֶגְדּוֹ עָבָיו עָבְרוּ (ib. 5)[13].

Exceptions. Munach (under a) is changed into Mer'kha, *when Paseq follows*, thus אָמְרוּ הֶאָח ׀ הֶאָח (xxxv. 21). This change is sup-

---

[9] The passages, Ps. xlv. 8, lxviii. 5, cix. 16, where Pazer appears in the *second* word before Athnach, are manifest mistakes, which are already corrected in the Heid.-Baer text.

[10] No Cod., however, in these two passages, gives Paseq, though many have M'huppakh. If, therefore, we wish to keep to the testimony of Codd., we must point פָּנוֹשׁ דֹּב־שַׂכִּיל (with De R. 2; K. 166; Vat. 468), and הֵעֵז אִישׁ־רָשָׁע (with B. M. 12; Par. 30; Ber. 32; Vi. 2; K. 250). This accentuation is equally correct.

[11] I take no notice of the endless mistakes of common edd., as they are corrected in Baer's texts.

[12] In xxxvii. 1, cxxxviii. 1, cl. 1, Mer'kha comes after L'garmeh, but L'garmeh is here the representative of Olév'yored (34. 12).

[13] A strange exception occurs in Prov. vi. 3, where Ben-Asher has וְהִנָּצֵל כִּי בָאתָ בְכַף־רֵעֶךָ. Here we must take Ben-Naphtali's pointing, which is regular, כִּי־בָאתָ.

ported by the analogy of Paseq with two servi (below), and by the testimony, more or less regular, of Codd.[14]

2. Two servi. These are both Munachs, as: עָבְדוּ אֶת־יְהוָה בְּיִרְאָה (ii. 11),—properly עָבְדוּ אֶת־יְהוָה (see p. 60). Indeed, in *all* cases, where Athnach has two or more servi, the servus adjoining Athnach stands, by transformation, for D'chî. It is important (with a view to the sense) to bear this in mind. Without the operation of the law of transformation, Athnach, like Olév'yored, *would never have more than one servus.*

EXCEPTIONS. When Paseq comes after the second servus, it is changed into Mer'kha, and the preceding Munach into Ṭarcha, e. g. ׀ נָאָץ רָשָׁע אֱלֹהִים (x. 13). Comp. xliv. 24; lxvi. 8; lxvii. 4. This rule is laid down by Ben-Bil. (5. 5) and is fully borne out by the Codd.[15]

3. Three servi. The two adjoining Athnach are, as before, Munachs, —or, with Paseq, Ṭarcha and Mer'kha[16]. The first servus will be M'huppakh or Illuy, according to the following rules[17]:

a. M'huppakh, when the tone is on the *first* syllable, e. g. אָז יְדַבֵּר יְהִי כְּבוֹד יְהוָה לְעוֹלָם (civ. 31). In one instance, the first and second servi come in the same word, שָׁאַל (cxlvi. 5, comp. 3).

β. M'huppakh also, when the tone is on the *second* syllable, supposing vocal Sh'va does not precede, e. g. אַתָּה פוֹרַרְתָּ בְעָזְּךָ יָם (lxxiv. 13). The other examples are: שִׁוִּיתִי (xvi. 8); הַפֵּה (lxxxvi. 1); אַתָּה (lxxxix. 11); תִּקְרַב (cxix. 169); תִּכּוֹן (cxli. 2); בִּקֵּשׁ (Prov. xiv. 6); זַרְעָם (Job xxi. 8).

---

[14] Ben-Bil. (4. 30) lays down a further class of exceptions, by pointing Mer'kha, instead of Munach, after D'chî, when the servus falls on the *first letter* of the word, e. g. רְשָׁעִים זוּ שַׁדּוּנִי (xvii. 9). But Ben-Asher does not agree. Ps. lxxxiii. 13 furnishes a test-passage. There all the lists of the Varr. I have seen assign to him the regular pointing: אָמְרוּ נִירֲשָׁה לָּנוּ. And it need hardly be added that Codd. generally follow him, there and elsewhere. (Of course, an occasional variation may occur. Thus, in Ps. i. 1, Bomb. 2,—followed by subsequent edd.,—has brought in Mer'kha, לֹא עָמָד; but the older edd. and Codd. have לֹא עָמָד. And elsewhere Bomb. 2 has regularly Munach.) It is therefore to be regretted that Baer has adopted Ben-Bil.'s pointing, all through his texts. We have already seen (p. 57, note 9) that Ben-Bil. is wrong in a similar change before Olév'yored; and certainly, the fewer exceptions we have to our rules, the better.

[15] Ben-Bil. (5. 8) gives two passages, Job v. 27, xxxiii. 31, as marked by these accents, *although Paseq is wanting,* and Codd. are found, which agree with him. But many point regularly, and we may well follow their example.

[16] There are only two cases of these accents, Ps. v. 5 and lxxxix. 52.

[17] This servus is, in reality, the first servus of D'chî, which remains, when D'chî is transformed. In fact, when transformation takes place, Athnach takes over all D'chî's accents, conjunctive and disjunctive.

γ. Illuy, when the tone is on the second syllable, vocal Sh'va preceding[18],—or when it is on the *third* syllable, e. g. נָתְנוּ רְשָׁעִים פַּח לִי (cxix. 110); הֲנִפָּה דְבָר אֵלֶיךָ תִּלְאֶה (Job iv. 2); וַיַּמְטֵר עֲלֵיהֶם מָן לֶאֱכֹל (Ps. lxxviii. 24, comp. 27). The other examples are: לַעֲשׂוֹת (xl. 9); וַיְהִי[19] (xciv. 22); מָפְּלוּ (cxix. 69); הַפַּכְפָּךְ (Prov. xxi. 8); and לֹא־יַחְשֹׁב (Ps. xxxii. 2); כִּי־אַתָּה (lxxxiii. 19); וְאַל־תֵּצֵל (cxix. 43).

δ. M'huppakh with Ṣinnorith, when an open syllable directly precedes the tone, e. g. לֹא נֵין לוֹ וְלֹא־נֶכֶד אוֹדֶה יְהֹוָה מְאֹד בְּפִי (cix. 30); בְּעַמּוֹ (Job xviii. 19, where Ṣinnoríth, as usual, displaces the Maqqeph). The other examples are: וַיְהִי[20] (Ps. ix. 10); גָּדוֹל (xlviii. 2; cxlv. 3); יְהֹוָה (lxxx. 20); עָנִי (lxxxviii. 16); וְיֹודוּ (lxxxix. 6); זָכַרְתִּי (cxix. 55); לְעֹשֵׂה (cxxxvi. 4); וְנָעַר (ib. 15); אָכֹל (Prov. xxv. 27); הַאִם[21] (Job vi. 13); נֹדֵד (xv. 23); הַאַף[22] (xxxiv. 17).

EXCEPTIONS. The servi are irregular in יִשְׂאוּ הָרִים שָׁלוֹם לָעָם (Ps. lxxii. 3); לִוְיַת חֵן הֵם לְרֹאשֶׁךָ (Prov. i. 9); הֲיַחְתֶּה אִישׁ אֵשׁ בְּחֵיקוֹ (vi. 27); all (it will be observed) with Shalshéleth, the melody of which naturally affected the accents adjoining.

4. The following are the only examples in which Athnach has more than three servi: כִּי[23] אֶת אֲשֶׁר גָּדוֹל יְהֹוָה וּמְהֻלָּל מְאֹד (Ps. xcvi. 4); יֶאֱהַב יְהֹוָה יוֹכִיחַ[24] (Prov. iii. 12); and one with Shalshéleth, לְךָ דֻמִיָּה תְהִלָּה אֱלֹהִים בְּצִיּוֹן (Ps. lxv. 2).

---

[18] Vocal Sh'va is here, for the purposes of accentuation, counted as a syllable, so that the tone is really on the *third* syllable.

[19] On the vocal Sh'va here, see Olsh., § 82 a. (Common edd. have, as often, *Munach inferius* for *superius;* but the more correct edd. of Opit., Jabl., and Mich. are right.)

[20] No Cod. (as far as I have observed) has Baer's accentuation וַיְהִי.

[21] So I point with Ox. 15, Par. 3, K. 446, De R. 1261 (other Codd. have הַאִם, Ṣinnoríth, as often, failing). The pointing of edd. הַאִם cannot stand. Better הַאִם, with Par. 6, Cop. 16, Vi. 12, which emphasizes the question with good effect.

[22] So B. M. 1; Ox. 15; Par. 42; De R. 1022, 1261. Edd. have here also Illuy. B. M. 4; Par. 80; Hm. 19; De R. 349, 596; Bomb. 1, point הַאַף. Comp. 40. 8.

[23] Common edd. have כִּי with Maqqeph, which is the regular pointing. But the Masora to Ps. cxliii. 3 has fixed Mer'kha. There are just two cases (here and in Job xxxiv. 37) of כִּי before Ṣinnoríth and M'huppakh in Athnach's clause; so they are made to pair off, marked with an anomalous accentuation! The Masora joins with them two similar cases of כִּי in L'garmeh's clause!

We may note that מְאֹד in this verse is made by the accents to refer to גָּדוֹל, as well as to מְהֻלָּל. Otherwise, we must have had D'chi with יְהֹוָה. The same clause is accented in the same way in 1 Chron. xvi. 25.

[24] On this verse see Baer's note (p. 55 of his ed. of Prov.). Yet surely, we must

Corrigenda.

Ps. ix. 14. חָנְנֵנִי יְהֹוָה רְאֵה עָנְיִי מִשֹּׂנְאָי, with B. M. 1; Par. 3; De R. 350, 661, 865, 1261. Comp. Norzi's note.

Ps. lxii. 12. Better שְׁתַּיִם זוּ שָׁמָעְתִּי with B. M. 4, 5; Ox. 1, 5, 7, 109.

Ps. lxxiii. 8. יָמִיקוּ וִידַבְּרוּ בְרָע עֹשֶׁק with Par. 30; Ber. 32; De R. 304; Ghet. 1.

Ps. xciv. 12. Better אַשְׁרֵי הַגֶּבֶר אֲשֶׁר־תְּיַסְּרֶנּוּ יָּהּ with Ox. 1, 7, 111; Par. 4, 20, 30.

Prov. xxviii. 23. מוֹכִיחַ אָדָם אַחֲרַי חֵן יִמְצָא with B. M. 8; Ox. 71; K. 170; De R. 304, 308, 518. 'He that reproveth a man shall afterwards find favour' (as Vulg., Ewald, Hitz., &c.)[25].

Other corrections have been made by Heid. and Baer, which generally have the full support of Codd.[26] But in xlviii. 5, xlix. 13, liv. 9, lxxix. 12, lxxxviii. 1, their emendations must be cancelled. Common edd. are right.

---

at least point אֶת אֲשֶׁר (comp. אֶת גְּאוֹן xlvii. 5 before Silluq), *Munach superius* having been confounded, as is often the case, with *Munach inferius*. אֶת is fixed by the Masora to this passage. This is the only instance in which אֶת precedes the third servus in Athnach's clause. It pairs off with a similar אֶת before Silluq (Ps. xlvii. 5)! The true accentuation is indicated, in part at least, by Ben-Naphtali כִּי ׀ אֶת־אֲשֶׁר.

[25] The accentuation of *text. rec.* represents the view of the Talmud, Aben-Ezra, and others, that אַחֲרַי means '*after me*,' God or Solomon being supposed to be the speaker (see Delitzsch's Comm.). Some Jewish commentators (whom Delitzsch himself follows) render: 'He that reproveth a man *who is going backwards*,' &c.; but that would require מוֹכִיחַ ׀ אָדָם אַחֲרָיו, which no Cod. exhibits.

[26] It may interest some of my readers to examine these corrections for themselves. They refer, first (this arrangement of them is my own), to cases in which the (main or minor) dichotomy has been falsely introduced in common edd., Ps. ix. 9, lxxiii. 7, lxxviii. 66, cii. 23, Prov. xxiii. 26, xxxi. 17, Job xiv. 19, xxiii. 8, xxiv. 8, xxxi. 27, xxxiii. 12, 17, xxxv. 9, xxxviii. 36, xl. 9, xli. 26; and secondly, to cases in which the dichotomy fails, Ps. xviii. 42, xxxv. 19, lxxx. 9, lxxxvi. 6, ci. 6, cv. 11, cxix. 142, 150, Prov. ii. 7, 13, iii. 4, xiv. 10, xvii. 11, xxi. 19, xxix. 14, Job x. 17, xxi. 18, xxiv. 15, xxxi. 37, xxxviii. 38. (The corrections are by Heid. and Baer for the Pss., by Baer alone for Prov. and Job.)

CHAPTER VII.

SILLUQ.

HAVING completed (as far as is necessary for the present) our examination of the *first* half of the verse,—whether closed by Olév'yored or Athnach,—we proceed next to consider the *second* half, lying between the one or other of these accents and Silluq, the part of the verse, which may be regarded as specially under Silluq's control.

I. We take first the case when Olév'yored divides the verse.

The most important point to notice here is, that Athnach is still due between Olév'yored and Silluq. It marks the chief dichotomy in Silluq's clause; and its position is fixed, by the rules with which we are now familiar. Thus it may separate the members of a *parallelism :* וּבְדֶרֶךְ חַטָּאִים לֹא עָמָד וּבְמוֹשַׁב לֵצִים לֹא יָשָׁב : (Ps. i. 1). Or it may mark any other kind of *logical* pause, as in : רְפָאֵנִי יְהוָה כִּי נִבְהֲלוּ עֲצָמָי (vi. 3). Or (less frequently) it may simply note a *syntactical* division, e. g. בַּל־יוֹסִיף עוֹד לַעֲרֹץ אֱנוֹשׁ מִן־הָאָרֶץ : (x. 18).

The position of Athnach determined, we have only to consider the clause lying between it and Silluq. But this is just the consideration before us, *when Athnach divides the verse.* For our further investigation then the two cases merge into *one* [1].

II. To arrive at the various forms that the clause lying between Athnach and Silluq may assume, the simplest course will be to take *seriatim* the various possible positions of Athnach. Here, at every step, we shall find that we have to deal with a *musical* system.

---

[1] As for Athnach's own clause, the rules for the pausal accents and servi (ch. VI) hold equally good, whether Athnach marks the main dichotomy of the verse, or only the dichotomy of the second half, after Olév'yored. There is just one point that may be mentioned. Athnach cannot stand in the first word of the *verse*, but it may stand in the word immediately following Olév'yored. The instances are : Ps. iii. 6; iv. 7; v. 13; xxix. 9; lviii. 3; lxxvi. 12; lxxix. 6; Job xxvii. 5; xxxvii. 12 (p. 37).

1. Athnach may be due on the *first* word before Silluq. In this case, the clause vanishes altogether. But such instances are rare. A regard for rhythm prevented their frequent occurrence. With Olév'yored preceding, I have noticed only iii. 3 ; xviii. 51 ; xxxi. 3 ; xlv. 8 ; lv. 23 ; lxviii. 20 ; cix. 16 ; cxxv. 3 ; Prov. viii. 13. The few cases without Olév'yored have been already given, p. 33.

Moreover the melody does not allow Athnach to *remain* here, but changes it into R'bhîa mugrash, e. g. וְעֹ֣שֶׂה חֶ֗סֶד ׀ לִמְשִׁיחֹו֮ שְׁפְטֵ֥נִי כְצִדְקְךָ֖ יְהוָ֑ה (Ps. xviii. 51)*[2] ; לְדָוִ֣ד וּלְזַרְעֹ֖ו עַד־עֹולָֽם ׃ אֱלֹהָ֑י וְאַל־יִשְׂמְחוּ־לִֽי ׃ (xxxv. 24).

2. Athnach may come on the *second* word. Then R'bhîa mugrash is due, as Foretone to Silluq, in the first word, e. g. לָ֤מָּה רָגְשׁ֣וּ גֹויִ֑ם ; (xl. 15)* ; יִסֹּ֣גוּ אָחֹור֮ וְיִכָּלְמ֗וּ חֲפֵצֵ֥י רָעָתִֽי ׃ וּלְאֻמִּ֗ים יֶהְגּוּ־רִֽיק ׃ (ii. 1) ; and so often. Of course the pause made by R'bhîa mugrash in such cases is simply and purely *musical.*

3. Athnach may come on the *third* word. Three words will then remain between it and the end of the clause ; and the rules for the dichotomy must be applied. The accent employed to mark it,—whether it fall on the first or second word,—is as above R'bhîa mugrash (the accent whose melody is best suited for Silluq following), e. g. יִשְׂבְּע֣וּ בָנִ֑ים וְהִנִּ֥יחוּ יִתְרָ֗ם לְעֹֽולְלֵיהֶֽם ׃ (xvii. 14)* and יְהוָ֗ה מָֽה־רַבּ֥וּ צָרָ֑י רַבִּ֗ים קָמִ֥ים עָלָֽי ׃ (iii. 2). Examples are found in every page.

4. Athnach may come on the *fourth* word. R'bhîa mugrash will still in most cases mark the dichotomy, as (a) when it falls on the *first* word, אָבֹ֣וא בֵיתְךָ֮ אֶשְׁתַּחֲוֶ֢ה אֶל־הֵיכַ֖ל קָדְשְׁךָ֣ בְּיִרְאָתֶֽךָ ׃ (v. 8) ; or (β) on the *second* word,—and this is by far its most frequent position,—וּבְדֶ֣רֶךְ חַ֭טָּאִים לֹ֥א עָמָ֑ד וּבְמֹושַׁ֥ב לֵ֝צִ֗ים לֹ֣א יָשָֽׁב ׃ (i. 1)* ; or (γ) on the *third* word, as עָלֶ֗יךָ

_____

[2] In the cases where an asterisk is marked, *Olév'yored precedes.*

(x. 14)* and מֶלֶךְ יַעֲקֹב חֲלָכָה נָתוֹם אַתָּה ׀ הָיִיתָ עוֹזֵר:
(xlvii. 9). אֱלֹהִים עַל־גּוֹיִם אֱלֹהִים יָשַׁב ׀ עַל־כִּסֵּא קָדְשׁוֹ:

But, when this is the case, three words are left between R'bhîa
mugrash and the end of the verse, and *a further dichotomy becomes
necessary*. In the instances given, this dichotomy falls on the
second word from Silluq, and is marked by L'garmeh. (And such
is the constant rule in all like cases[3].) But how, if it fall on the
first word[4]? Will the same accents be possible? For instance, can
we so point : יְהֹוָה עֹז לְעַמּוֹ יִתֵּן ׀ יְהֹוָה יְבָרֵךְ אֶת־עַמּוֹ ׀ בַשָּׁלוֹם
(xxix. 11)? This is the accentuation we should have expected.
But we do not find it. And we can only suppose that such a
juxtaposition of Silluq and L'garmeh was against the rules of
melody, and that L'garmeh had, in consequence, to be changed
into a servus. But this change necessitated another; for R'bhîa
mugrash cannot (again we must suppose, on musical grounds)
stand in the third place, with Tarcha following[5]. Nothing
remained then but to provide a substitute for it; and the accent
chosen was Great Shalshéleth. So that finally the melody, in the
ex. before us, found rest in the form יְהֹוָה ׀ יְבָרֵךְ אֶת־עַמּוֹ
בַשָּׁלוֹם:. Such also is the accentuation in the other passages,
where the same division of Silluq's clause is found[6].

---

[3] I give a list of these passages, as some of my readers may like to compare them:
iii. 1; x. 14; xviii. 31; xx. 2; xlv. 2 ; xlvii. 9; lvi. 8; lxviii. 19; lxxii. 20; lxxiv.
2; lxxxviii. 11 (so most Codd.); xcviii. 6; xcix. 4; cii. 20; civ. 8, 26; cv. 3; cxix.
69, 104; cxxvii. 1; cxlviii. 4; Prov. xix. 10; xxi. 29; xxv. 1, 28; Job iii. 13; xv. 24;
xviii. 21; xxi. 28; xxxvi. 28; xxxvii. 14. Total 31. I have left out Ps. xviii. 7 (see
Corrigenda). Heid. and Baer have brought in wrongly xix. 5, and unnecessarily
xxx. 11.

[4] See the contrast between Job xv. 23 and 24. And note the true rendering of
xxxvii. 12. Verss. and Comm. all explain as if we had R'bhîa mugrash and L'garmeh.

[5] Common edd. have indeed a few instances, iii. 5; iv. 7; xxxviii. 21; &c. And
even Baer leaves xlvi. 8 (12). But all these exceptions are corrected in Codd., if
not already in the better edd.

[6] The following is a list of these passages: vii. 6; x. 2; xii. 8; xiii. 2, 3; xx. 8;
xxix. 11; xxxiii. 12; xli. 8; xliv. 9; xlix. 14; l. 6; lii. 5; lxvi. 7; lxvii. 5; lxxvii. 4;
lxxxix. 2, 3; xciv. 17; cxxxi. 1; cxliii. 6, 11; cxlvi. 3; Prov. vi. 10 (xxiv. 33); Job
xi. 6 (see *Corrigenda*); xv. 23; xvi. 9; xxxii. 6; xxxvii. 12; xl. 23. Again (if we
reckon the repetition in Prov. as *one*, and add xlii. 2, see note 7) a total of 31. Is

5. Athnach may come on the *fifth* word.　Here we have nothing that is new.　All the cases come under the several categories of 4, the great majority,—e. g. xiv. 1; xix. 8, 9; xxiii. 5,—with R'bhîa mugrash on the *second* word.　With it on the *first* word, there are only two doubtful examples, xlii. 2 and lxvi. 20[7] (if we drop xxxii. 5; xlvii. 5; liv. 5; all with סֶ֖לָה at the end).　With it or Shalshéleth, on the *third* word (a *servus* coming between them and Athnach), we have xviii. 31; lxxxix. 2 ; xcix. 4; cxxvii. 1; Prov. xxv. 1; and Job xxxvii. 12 (p. 37).　Of the dichotomy on the *fourth* word there is no example.

6. Further back than the *fifth* word Athnach does not occur, save in the prose verse, Ps. xviii. 1 (on which see p. 76, note 8), and the hybrid verse,—half prose and half poetry,—Job xxxii. 6, in which Shalshéleth appears with two servi, but which does not otherwise present any difficulty.

The result then of the above investigation is to shew, that whenever the dichotomy is by rule required between Athnach and Silluq, R'bhîa mugrash is employed to mark it,—excepting only the few (clearly defined) cases, in which Great Shalshéleth appears as its substitute ;—and that, when further a minor dichotomy is due between R'bhîa mugrash and Silluq, M'huppakh L'garmeh marks it.　For the laws regulating R'bhîa mugrash's own clause, I must refer to the chapter next following.

The accentual division of Silluq's clause completed, it remains only to mention that, here as elsewhere, the law of transformation often comes in, and obliterates or changes the pausal accent,

---

this coincidence accidental?　We should be glad to see Shalshéleth here and there, e. g. in Ps. lxviii. 32, Job xv. 16, where it fails.　On the other hand, it will disappear from nine of the above passages, e. g. Ps. vii. 6, xliv. 9, and R'bhîa mugrash come instead, if we leave out סֶלָה at the end of the verse.

It is to be observed that this Great Shalshéleth appears only in the position above assigned to it.　It comes therefore under quite different circumstances, and with a very different value, from Shalshéleth in the prose accentuation.

[7] Some Codd.—B. M. 3, 4, 7 ; Ox. 6, 71; K. 155—pointing xlii. 2 with Shalshéleth, and some introducing (with Ben-Bil. I. 11) Maqqeph after אֲשֶׁר in lxvi. 20.

which the above rules have fixed. Were it not for the operation
of this law, we should find R'bhîa mugrash introduced in every
verse (except in the few cases where Athnach would come on
the first word), as a subsidiary tone and necessary precursor to
Silluq,—just as Ṭiphcha is in the prose Books. But owing to this
law, it is more frequently *absent* than present. The conditions
for its presence are the same as those already laid down for D'chî
before Athnach (p. 60). Thus, it remains in : כְּאִמְרָתְךָ֫ הַצִּילֵ֫נִי
(cxix. 170), but is transformed in : כִּדְבָרְךָ֫ הֲבִינֵ֫נִי (ib. 169); it
remains in : וּמַלְאַ֫ךְ יְהֹוָה֫ רֹדְפָ֫ם (xxxv. 6), but not in וּמַלְאַ֫ךְ
: יְהֹוָה דֹּחֶ֫ה (ib. 5).

Athnach too, as well as R'bhîa mugrash, is affected by this
law. We have seen that it is always transformed, when it falls
on the *first* word before Silluq[8]; and it is not unfrequently so,
even on the *second* word. When, namely, R'bhîa mugrash has
been transformed in the first word, and this word is like Silluq's
word (without two syllables, &c., before the tone), then Athnach
must give way to R'bhîa mugrash, e. g. הַדְּבָרוֹת עַל־צַדִּיק עָתָ֫ק
עֹרָה הַנֵּ֫בֶל וְכִנּ֫וֹר אָעִ֫ירָה שָּׁ֫חַר : (xxxi. 19); בִּגְאַוָ֫ה וָבֽוּז :
(lvii. 9). Comp. i. 2, iv. 5, v. 7, vii. 10.

SERVI OF SILLUQ[9].

Silluq, like Athnach, has often one, two, and three servi, rarely four.

1. One servus. This is (*a*) Munach, when the tone is on the *first*
syllable, e. g. : לֹא יָשָׁ֫ב (Ps. i. 1), : לְמַ֫עַן חַסְדֶּ֫ךָ (vi. 5); (*β*) Mer'kha, when
on any other syllable, e. g. : הַיּ֫וֹם יְלִדְתִּ֫יךָ (ii. 7), : אֲשֶׁר־תִּדְּפֶ֫נּוּ ר֫וּחַ (i. 4).
Here, if an open syllable precede the tone, it is marked in some Codd.
with Ṣinnorith, e. g. : יוֹמָ֫ם וָלַ֫יְלָה (i. 2); : יֹּפִ֫יחַ בָּהֶ֫ם (x. 5)[10].

---

[8] In lxviii. 20, cix. 16, Prov. viii. 13, the R'bhîa mugrash, which should have
represented Athnach in the first word, has been itself changed into a servus, but
has left its pausal accents behind it unchanged. So that Silluq appears with Great
R'bhîa or D'chî dividing its clause! Some Codd. point in the same way Ps. iv. 7,
but see Baer's note.

[9] I need not say that I cannot undertake to notice the many inexcusable mistakes
of our ordinary edd. Nor is it necessary, as Baer has already corrected them in his
carefully prepared texts.

[10] The Codd. in which I have noticed this Ṣinnorith are B. M. 1; Ox. 15; Par. 3.

EXCEPTIONS. (a) When L'garmeh precedes (67.6), the servus is always Illuy, e. g. :אֲנִי בְּכָל־לֵב ׀ אֱצֹּר פִּקּוּדֶיךָ (cxix. 69). (β) In two passages, :נְתִיץ ׀ יְהֹוָה (lviii. 7) and :יוֹם ׀ יוֹם (lxi. 9), Munach is changed into Mer'kha, because of Paseq following[11].

2. Two servi. The first is Ṭarcha and the second Munach, e. g. :וְכֹל׀ אֲשֶׁר־יַעֲשֶׂה יַצְלִיחַ (i. 3). The two servi have here a closer affinity to one another than the second one has to Silluq; and *that*, for the simple reason that this latter stands for R'bhîa mugrash. Indeed, in *all* cases, in which Silluq has two or more servi, the servus adjoining Silluq stands, by transformation, for R'bhîa mugrash. It is important (with a view to the sense) to bear this in mind. Without the operation of the law of transformation, Silluq would—as in the prose system— *never have more than one servus.*

Tarcha may take the place of Métheg in the *same word* with Munach (supposing always that R'bhîa mugrash does not precede[12]), e. g. :רְעוֹתֶיהָ מוּבָאוֹת לָךְ (xlv. 15); :יַאחֲזוּנִי יְמֵי־עֹנִי (Job xxx. 16)[13]. This is, of course, a mere musical embellishment.

108; Erf. 3; K. 446; De R. 331, 350, 1261. It appears also in a few instances— Ps. x. 3, 5; xviii. 20; xli. 14; &c.—in common edd. Baer has therefore authority for marking it (as he has done) regularly in his texts. But it is questionable whether it was worth while to revive a sign, which had fallen into all but general disuse, and which for us has no meaning. Moreover there seems never to have been any general agreement as to its employment. Ben-Bil. found in the MSS. which he used, a *different* sign, which he terms מתיגה (in the original Arabic המזה), and which was like an upper Métheg, thus :יָפִיחַ בָּהֶם. The musical value and meaning of this sign he discusses at length (6. 5 ff.), and it is plain that it was to him something quite distinct from Ṣinnorîth. We have then here another instance of the חלופים that prevailed among the punctators. Some employed Ṣinnorîth, others M'thiga, and others again no sign at all beside the Mer'kha. As to Ben-Bil.'s M'thiga, it is still more rare in Codd. than the Ṣinnorîth, I have found it only in the old Cod. Erf. 3, and occasionally in Cam. 15. It appears indeed in the prose accentuation (see משפטי הטעמים 13b), but under quite different conditions.

[11] Three strange exceptions are claimed by Ben-Bil. (7. 21) and the Erf. Mas. (MS.), are found also in some Codd., and are introduced by Baer into the text, viz. :וּמִמַּעֲמַקֵּי מָיִם (lxix. 15); :יַעַמְדוּ מָיִם (civ. 6); and :וַיֵּהָפְכוּ אָרֶץ (Job xii. 15). All with Ṭarcha! But there can be no doubt that common edd. are right in pointing with Métheg and Maqqeph. The Maqqeph (we may suppose) was dropped in some early and model copy, and the Métheg taken for Ṭarcha. (These signs are often alike in MSS. See note 13 and Man. du Lect. 90. 2.) Ben-Asher knows nothing of these exceptions; for he was bound to notice them Dikd. hat. § 25 (סימן סופי הפסוקים), had he recognised them.

[12] Because R'bhîa mugrash cannot have Ṭarcha after it (67. 16).

[13] Common edd. have constantly such false punctuation as אָרְחוֹתֶיךָ (xxv. 4), וּשְׁבֻעָתִי (cv. 9), Ṭarcha having been mistaken for Métheg.

EXCEPTIONS. (*a*) Munach is changed into Mer'kha in לֹא יִשְׁמַע ׀ אֲדֹנָי (Ps. lxvi. 18), because of Paseq following. (β) In three passages, the servi are irregular, because of the irregularity of the pausal accent preceding אִישׁ־עָנִי וְאֶבְיוֹן (Ps. lxviii. 20); יַעֲמָס־לָנוּ הָאֵל יְשׁוּעָתֵנוּ סֶלָה; וְנִכְאֶה לֵבָב לְמוֹתֵת (cix.16); וְדֶרֶךְ רָע וּפִי תַהְפֻּכוֹת שָׂנֵאתִי (Prov. viii. 13)[14]. (γ) For the two Illuys, which are found in the superscriptions of certain Psalms, see p. 35[15].

3. Three servi. The second and third remain unchanged; the first is M'huppakh or Azla, according to the following rules[16]:

a. M'huppakh, when the tone is on the *first* syllable, e. g. כִּי לֹא־עֲזַבְתָּ לְכֹל אֲשֶׁר יִקְרָאֻהוּ בֶאֱמֶת (cxlv. 18). In cxlvi. 3, the first and second servi occur in the same word, שֶׁאַיִן (comp. *v.* 5).

β. M'huppakh[17] also, when the tone is on the *second* syllable, and vocal Sh'va does not precede, e. g. עַל־כֵּן יוֹרֶה חַטָּאִים בַּדָּרֶךְ (xxv. 8; xlv. 3). I have found only two other exx., הֵגֶּה (lxxiii. 15) and מִנִּי (Job xx. iv).

γ. Azla, when the tone is on the second syllable, *vocal Sh'va preceding,*—or when the tone is on the *third* syllable, e. g. יְמַלֵּט נַפְשׁוֹ אֶבְחָנֶךָ (lvi. 1); בֶּאֱחֹז אוֹתוֹ פְלִשְׁתִּים בְּגַת (lxxxix. 49); מִיַּד־שָׁאוּל סֶלָה; מְבַקְשֵׁי עַל־מֵי מְרִיבָה סֶלָה (lxxxi. 8). The other exx. are, וַיַּעֲנֵנִי (iii. 5); כִּי־רָאִיתִי (xxiv. 6); יִרְעֲשׁוּ (xlvi. 4); מִשְׁגָּב־לָנוּ (ib. 8, 12); וְשַׁרְשֵׁךְ (lii. 7); כִּי־אַתָּה (lxii. 13); אֲחֶסֶה (lxi. 5); אַל־תָּחֹן (lix. 6); כִּי־רַבִּים (lvi. 3); וְאַל־תְּאַמַּר (lxix. 16); אָנֹכִי (lxxv. 4); אִם־קָפַץ (lxxvii. 10); אֶעֱשֶׂה (lxvi. 15); הֶעֱטִית (ib. 46); וְאַתָּה (cxlv. 15); הַאֲזִינָה (lxxxiv. 9); וּבָנִיתִי (lxxxix. 5); בִּהְיוֹת[18] (Prov. iii. 27); לַאֲשֶׁר (Job xii. 6); וּרְאֵה (xxii. 12)[19].

---

[14] On these examples see note 8.

[15] Baer would establish a still further class of exceptions, by the rule that, when the two tone-syllables come together, Mer'kha takes the place of Munach, e. g. בִּמְזִמּוֹת זוּ חָשָׁבוּ (x. 2). Ben-Bil. does indeed say (7. 26) that, *according to some* (מקצתם), this is the case. But Ben-Asher expresses himself (Dikd. hat. 25. 30) as decidedly opposed to such a change (אם בראש התיבה או באמצע התיבה כולם בשופר), pointing the ex. just given בִּמְזִמּוֹת זוּ חָשָׁבוּ. I need hardly add that Codd. (with rare exceptions) agree with him. See too Norzi's note to Ps. cxxii. 9.

[16] Observe, that if we substitute Azla for Illuy, the rules here are the same as for the corresponding servus before *Athnach* (pp. 62, 63).

[17] Ben-Bil. (8. 2) points with *Azla;* but the unvarying testimony of Codd. is in favour of M'huppakh. He is equally wrong in giving the first servus of Athnach (5. 29).

[18] On the vocal Sh'va here, see Olshausen, § 85 b.

[19] I may mention that I have, in every doubtful instance, found ample MS. authority for the pointing with Azla given in the above list.

δ. M'huppakh with Ṣinnorîth, when an open syllable directly pre-
cedes the tone, e. g. חֻרְבֹּתַם אֲשֶׁר חֲרֵפוּ (liv. 8); אוֹדֶה יְהוָה שִׁמְךָ כִּי־טוֹב
אֲדֹנָי (lxxix. 12). The other exx. are, [20] מֵעֵת (iv. 8); כִּי הוּא (xxv. 15);
וּמֵעָוֹן (xxviii. 8); מֵאִישׁ (xliii. 1); אֱלֹהִים (xlviii. 9); מוֹצְאֵי (lxv. 9);
יָאֵר (lxvii. 2); תָּכִין (lxviii. 11); הֲלִיכוֹת (ib. 25); יֵנָאֵץ (lxxiv. 10); מֵעֵן
(lxxvi. 4); צִירָה (lxxviii. 25); מָתַי (cxix. 84); מֵאִיר (Prov. xxix. 13);
וְאֹתִי (Job xiv. 3); תָּשִׁית (ib. 13)[21].

With the tone on the *third* syllable, the punctators were at
liberty to follow either this rule or the previous one. Thus, we have
חֻרְבֹּתַם above, and on the other hand אָנֹכִי. Generally, as the examples
given shew, they took the latter course.

4. Four servi. The following are the only examples : אֵין יְשׁוּעָתָה לּוֹ
בֵּן נַפְשִׁי (xxxii. 5); וְאַתָּה נָשָׂאתָ עֲוֹן חַטָּאתִי סֶלָה (iii. 3); בֵּאלֹהִים סֶלָה:
אֶת [22] גְּאוֹן יַעֲקֹב אֲשֶׁר־אָהֵב סֶלָה (xlvii. 5); תַּעֲרֹג אֵלֶיךָ אֱלֹהִים:
לֹא שָׂמוּ אֱלֹהִים לְנֶגְדָּם סֶלָה (liv. 5). It will be observed that four of
the above passages end with סֶלָה. If then we reject it (as the poet,
if he were living, would require us to do), and point xlii. 2 with Great
Shalshéleth (note 7), we do away with these examples altogether.
The accentuation will then be as follows : אֵין יְשׁוּעָתָה לּוֹ בֵּאלֹהִים: (iii. 3);
בֵּן נַפְשִׁי ׀ תַּעֲרֹג אֵלֶיךָ אֱלֹהִים: (xlii. 2); וְאַתָּה נָשָׂאתָ עֲוֹן חַטָּאתִי:
אֶת־גְּאוֹן יַעֲקֹב אֲשֶׁר אָהֵב: (xlvii. 5); לֹא שָׂמוּ אֱלֹהִים לְנֶגְדָּם: (liv. 5).

---

[20] So I point with B. M. 1; Par. 3. 6; Vat. 475; De R. 1261. All edd. have
Illuy, which is the third servus of Athnach, not of Silluq. Ben-Bil.'s authority
(8. 1) may indeed be quoted in its favour, but his rules here are otherwise false, as
we have already seen, note 17. (Of course, I do not accept Baer's rule, Accentuationssystem, § 4, note 2, '*Die Präfixa* בוכלם *erhalten kein Zinnorith.*' The
testimony of Codd. is against it.) מֵעֵן (lxxvi. 4), צִירָה (lxxviii. 25), and מָתַי
(cxix. 84) are pointed in the same way, but must be corrected, with various Codd.

[21] Our texts exhibit an exceptional accentuation for several of the examples given
above, thus, תָּשִׁית, מֵאִיר, תָּכִין, יָאֵר, מֵאִישׁ,—an accentuation against all rule, and
(as it seems to me) unmeaning, except as indicating a *diversity of practice*, viz. that
some punctators employ Mer'kha, others M'huppakh,—as is really the case, for nothing is more common in the Codd. than to find Mer'kha, as servus to Silluq, instead
of M'huppakh (or Azla). The latter was Ben-Asher's punctuation, and the former
seems (as far as I can gather from the lists of Varr.) to have been Ben-Naphtali's.
But many Codd. point these words with M'huppakh in the *ultima*, and some few add
Ṣinnorith. I have therefore not hesitated to accent them regularly.

[22] אֶת (Mer'kha for Maqqeph) is fixed by the Masora to this passage. See p. 63,
note 24.

Corrigenda.

Ps. xviii. 7. וְשַׁוְעָתִי לְפָנָיו תָּבוֹא בְאָזְנָיו׃ with Ox. 17; Par. 17; Ber. 2; K. 170; De R. 1244, 1252. Comp. the old Verss.; and see Delitzsch's note, who, however, has quite misapprehended the meaning of the ordinary punctuation.

Ps. xlix. 15. וַיִּרְדּוּ־בָם יְשָׁרִים לַבֹּקֶר וְצוּרָם לְבַלּוֹת שְׁאוֹל מִזְּבֻל לוֹ׃ Athnach with B. M. 8; Par. 4, 19; Ber. 2; K. 157, 224.

Ps. cxxv. 3. The accentuation with L'garmeh is against all rule. If there had been no transformation, the clause would have stood לְמַעַן לֹא־יִשְׁלְחוּ הַצַּדִּיקִים בְּעַוְלָתָה יְדֵיהֶם׃; and making allowance for the same, we may point regularly לְמַעַן [23] לֹא־יִשְׁלְחוּ הַצַּדִּיקִים בְּעַוְלָתָה יְדֵיהֶם׃ with B. M. 1; Par. 28; Vat. 12, 468, 482; K. 598. But the clause is long and heavy, and *that* no doubt was the reason why many punctators divided it with L'garmeh. If, however, we have a division at all, it ought to be made (as the melody requires) with R'bhia mugrash, לְמַעַן לֹא־יִשְׁלְחוּ הַצַּדִּיקִים. B. M. 2, 3, 4; Ox. 15; Fr.; K. 157, point so.

Job xi. 6. Here too the accentuation of our texts is altogether anomalous[24]. I would point regularly thus: וְיַגֶּד־לְךָ ׀ תַּעֲלֻמוֹת חָכְמָה כִּי־כִפְלַיִם לְתוּשִׁיָּה וְדַע ׀ כִּי־יַשֶּׁה־לְךָ אֱלוֹהַּ מֵעֲוֺנֶךָ׃. Many Codd.—B. M. 6; Ox. 19, 100; Hm. 1; De R. 847, 874; &c.—have Athnach; and Ox. 100, Par. 6, K. 155, 246, give the above pointing for the last words.

As before, I should have had many more corrections to propose, had not Heid. and Baer preceded me. Their corrections are for the most part necessary and made on good authority. Few, however, will agree with them in cxviii. 5 (see Baer's note); even Delitzsch does not. And in xxiv. 6 (with the substitution of Azla for Mer'kha), and xcvii. 3, the pointing of common edd. is to be retained.

---

[23] We shall then have a second instance of Pazer before D'chî (transformed). The other is xix. 15 (common edd.)

[24] There is no place for Athnach, Shalshéleth follows Olév'yored, and R'bhia mugrash Shalshéleth,—three violations of ordinary rules, not one of which is to be found elsewhere. The simplest correction would be וְדַע, leaving Olév'yored in its place; the anomalies would then all vanish together. But this I have not found in any Cod. Probably Athnach and Olév'yored would then have been brought too close together for the chanting,—with only Sh'va between them.

CHAPTER VIII.

R'BHÎA MUGRASH.

I TAKE this accent next, because of its intimate connection with
those last considered — Athnach and Silluq.

In this chapter we regard it, — as we have regarded the preceding accents, — in its *independent* character, as set over a clause
of its own, and determining other accents in that clause. Here
all will depend on whether Athnach be present in the verse or not.

I. If Athnach be present, R'bhîa mugrash divides the clause
between it and Silluq, and can have one, two, or three words in
its own clause (pp. 66–68). The first two cases call for no remark.
But when there are *three* words, as in הַצִּילֵנוּ וְכַפֵּר עַל־חַטֹּאתֵינוּ
(Ps. lxxix. 9), the clause becomes subject to the rule for the dichotomy, and should be divided by a subordinate pausal accent, — in
the ex. given, at הַצִּילֵנוּ (as the sense requires). This division,
however, never takes place. Probably the musical relation between Athnach and R'bhîa mugrash was such that a break, or
pause, in the melody between them would have produced an
unmusical effect. For this or some other reason connected with
the melody, *the dichotomy always fails in R'bhîa mugrash's
clause, when Athnach precedes.* (The consequence is that, when
R'bhîa mugrash is transformed, we have *three* servi between
Athnach and Silluq (71. 8).)

II. If Athnach be *not* present, it is because R'bhîa mugrash
has, by the law of transformation (69. 12), taken its place in the
first or second word before Silluq. Athnach's clause has in consequence become transferred to R'bhîa mugrash. This transfer,
however, does not in any way affect the *division* of the same.
Great R'bhîa and D'chî appear, just as if Athnach were present.
Take for instance, [1] וָאֶשָּׂא כַפַּי אֶל־מִצְוֹתֶיךָ אֲשֶׁר אָהָבְתִּי

---

[1] R'bhîa mugrash retains also (as this ex. shews) the *long vowel* due with Athnach.
Sometimes, however, a *short* vowel is found. A list of these exceptional cases is

וְאָשִׂיחָה בְחֻקֶּיךָ׃ (cxix. 48); and comp. xxxi. 23; xxxv. 24;
lvii. 9; lxxix. 3; cxv. 18; Job xxxiii. 24, 27 (where R'bhîa is
repeated). So D'chî, if it would be changed into a servus before
Athnach (60. 15), is equally changed before R'bhîa mugrash, e. g.
גְּמֹל עַל־עַבְדְּךָ אֶחְיֶה (Ps. cxix. 17); and so too, subject to this
change of D'chî, L'garmeh appears in the *third* word before
R'bhîa mugrash (60. 24), e. g. הוּא נֹתֵן ׀ עֹז וְתַעֲצֻמוֹת לָעָם
(lxviii. 36)[2]. In short, R'bhîa mugrash is the complete representative of the Athnach it has displaced. *The rules for the
dichotomy of its clause are,* in consequence — in direct contrast
to the practice under § I — *strictly carried out.*

OBS. So striking are the changes which the accent has here under-
gone in its pausal value, its functions, and (doubtless also) its melody,
that the early punctators were misled to the notion that it could no
longer be regarded as R'bhîa mugrash (proper). The distinguishing
sign therefore of R'bhîa mugrash was dropped, and the R'bhîa-sign
alone left to represent it, — an accentuation, which is found in the
oldest MSS., and is sanctioned by the Masora itself (see p. 35, note 34)[3].
We must not, however, assign it to the original accentuators, for it is
impossible to suppose that, when they were selecting the accentual
symbols, they should have designedly represented — in the short verses
of the three Books — *three different accents by one and the same sign.*
The awkward and confusing nature of such a notation is evident, and

---

quite as necessary as that of the פתחין באתנח וסוף פסוק, and is given (at least
for the Pss.) in Ginsburg's Masora, vol. i, p. 653 (taken from the old Cod. B. M. 1).
There is, however, one mistake in this list. For lvi. 14, (query) xlvii. 10 must be
substituted. We shall no doubt some day find corresponding lists for Prov. and Job.

[2] But it cannot come in the word *immediately before* R'bhîa mugrash, as our texts
have it in lxxi. 21 and cix. 28. The former passage I point גְּדֻלָּתִי חֶרֶב with B. M. 4;
Ox. 17; Par. 4, 30; Erf. 2; &c.; and the latter קָמוּ וַיֵּבֹשׁוּ with B. M. 9; Ox. 17;
Par. 4, 30; Fr.; &c. L'garmeh in the *second* word, Job iii. 26, must be also corrected, thus: לֹא שָׁלַוְתִּי ׀ וְלֹא שָׁקַטְתִּי וְלֹא־נָחְתִּי with Ox. 5, 15, 98, 125, 2322, 2323,
&c. *Pazer* in the second word, Ps. lviii. 3 (common edd.), has been already corrected by Baer. (Comp. Athnach, notes 8 and 9.)

[3] Ben-Bil. too, all through his treatise, uses this R'bhîa, when Athnach fails. Of
course common edd. do the same, — retaining, however, often R'bhîa mugrash *after*
Olév'yored, as in i. 2, contrary to the practice of Codd.

This R'bhîa has a *name of its own* — shewing that it was counted quite distinct from
the two other R'bhîas — in Cod. B. M. 1, viz. פור. (See, beside the list referred to in
note 1, another list, ib. p. 652.) We must suppose that the punctator, who prepared
this Cod., had, like Ben-Asher, another name for *our* Pazer.

has been felt by many writers on the accents[4], indeed by some of the punctators themselves, for I have found R'bhîa mugrash regularly marked in the following Codd.: B. M. 2, Ox. 1, Hm. 8, 12, 19, and De R. 2. Jablonski and Baer have introduced it into their texts. No doubt we have a *different kind* of R'bhîa mugrash from that under § I (just as we have two different kinds of *R'bhîa simplex*); but the essential (musical) character of the accent may well have been retained in the changes it underwent. As foretone to Silluq, it cannot be dispensed with.

Servi of R'bhîa mugrash[5].

R'bhîa mugrash has often one and two servi, less frequently three.

1. One servus. This is always Mer'kha, e. g. כִּי אִם־כַּמֹּץ (i. 4); קַשְׁתּוֹ דָרַךְ (vii. 13). If an open syllable precede the tone, it is marked in some Codd. with Ṣinnorîth[6], as וּבְמוֹשַׁב לֵצִים (i. 1); וּבְתוֹרָתוֹ יֶהְגֶּה (i. 2).

2. Two servi. The first is Ṭarcha, the second (as above) Mer'kha, e. g. עֵדוּת יְהוָֹה נֶאֱמָנָה (xix. 8); פָּדִיתָ אוֹתִי יְהוָֹה (xxxi. 6)[7].

3. Three servi. The second and third remain unchanged; the first is M'huppakh on the first or second syllable,—M'huppakh with Ṣinnorîth, if an open syllable precede the tone. The following are the only exx.: זָכַרְתִּי מִשְׁפָּטֶיךָ מֵעוֹלָם ׀ יְהוָֹה (lxxiii. 1); אַךְ טוֹב לְיִשְׂרָאֵל אֱלֹהִים (cxix. 52); and[8] בְּיוֹם (xviii. 1); כִּי (xlvii. 8); אֲשֶׁר (lxvi. 20); שֶׁלֹּא (cxxix. 7).

---

[4] Eliezer Provenzale (Tor. em. p. 1), Wasmuth (Tab. ii, nota β), Ouseel (p. 6), the author of שערי נעימה (p. 1), Spitzner (p. 210), and Baer (Tor. em. p. 58) all advocate the restoration of R'bhîa mugrash to its proper place in the verse.

[5] As before, I refer to Baer's texts for correction of the mistakes of common edd. The most notable of those mistakes occur in Ps. xxxi. 22; lxvi. 20; lxxix. 3; cxvi. 19; Prov. vii. 7; in all which cases there is abundant MS. authority for the necessary corrections.

[6] On this Ṣinnorîth see Silluq, p. 69, note 10. The remarks made there apply *mutatis mutandis* here.

[7] A curious distinction is observed in some of the best Codd., and has passed into our printed texts, that *when Athnach precedes* (as in xix. 8 above), *the servi are both Mer'khas*. But this is Ben-Naphtali's punctuation (as the lists of Varr. clearly shew). Ben-Asher has always Ṭarcha and Mer'kha. And the Masoretic text is bound to conform (as we have often had occasion to observe) to *his* rules. Heid. and Baer therefore have been quite right in discarding the punctuation with two Mer'khas. The old Cod. B. M. 1 does the same. No doubt the punctators who adopted it *imagined* that they were following Ben-Asher. Erf. 3, in a marginal note to xcvi. 2, expressly assigns it to him. *Humanum est errare.*

[8] I point the clause, which has given so much trouble to punctators and accentuologists, thus: בְּיוֹם הִצִּיל־יְהוָֹה אוֹתוֹ מִכַּף־כָּל־אֹיְבָיו. B. M. 12, Ox. 96, and Fr. join מִכַּף with Maqqeph. All is then regular. But the case does not really concern us at all.

EXCEPTIONS. The three passages הִנֵּה מַלְאַךְ־יְהֹוָה סָבִיב לִירֵאָיו (xxxiv.
8); בְּפָרֵשׂ שַׁדַּי מְלָכִים בָּהּ (lxviii. 15); and אַשְׁרֵי שֶׁיֹּאחֵז וְנִפֵּץ אֶת־עֹלָלַיִךְ
(cxxxvii. 9); where the first servus indeed is regular, but the intro-
duction of Little Shalshéleth has necessitated a change in the servus
immediately preceding R'bhîa mugrash.

CHAPTER IX.

GREAT R'BHÎA[1].

GREAT R'BHÎA may stand alone—as indeed may all the accents
we have yet to consider—or have two or more words in its clause.

I. If the clause contain only *two* words, the first has generally
a *servus*, e. g. שְׁאַל מִמֶּ֫נִּי (Ps. ii. 8); but sometimes—when a slight
pause or emphasis is to be marked—the pausal accent, L'garmeh,
e. g. אַךְ־בְּצֶלֶם ׀ יִתְהַלֶּךְ־אִישׁ (xci. 15); יִקְרָאֵנִי ׀ וְאֶעֱנֵהוּ
(xxxix. 7). Comp. the similar use of D'chî before Athnach (58. 7).

Such cases are not, however, numerous. I have noticed hardly
more than a dozen in the whole of the Pss. And even where they
occur, we are not bound by them. For Codd. often vary. And this
is no more than we should have expected,—some punctators assigning
an emphasis or pause to a particular word, which others drop[2].

II. When there are *three or more* words in the clause, the
rules for the dichotomy are strictly carried out; and as there
is no transformation before Great R'bhîa, the division of the
clause is always clear and distinct. The accents employed to
mark it are L'garmeh and Pazer, the latter with a (relatively)

---

[1] The distinction between Great and Little R'bhîa has been already alluded to,
p. 12, note. We name them 'Great' and 'Little,' because, where they come together
in the same verse (as in xx. 7, cxxxix. 14), we notice that the former has the *greater*
pausal value,—the reason being that it marks the *main* dichotomy, whereas the
latter marks only a *minor* dichotomy.

[2] In Ps. xv. 3 I would point with various Codd. לֹא רָגַל ׀ עַל־לְשֹׁנוֹ, and in xxxix. 4
חַם לִבִּי ׀ בְּקִרְבִּי. For the false accentuation יֵסֶר ׀ לֵץ (Prov. ix. 7) in common edd.,
point יֹסֵר לֵץ with Codd. and Baer.

greater disjunctive value than the former. The rules for their employment are as follows:

1. L'garmeh, when only *one* dichotomy is required, e. g. כִּי יְהוָֹה ׀ אֹהֵב מִשְׁפָּט (vii. 7); קוּמָה יְהוָֹה ׀ בְּאַפֶּךָ (xxxvii. 28); עָלֶיךָ ׀ נִסְמַכְתִּי מִבֶּטֶן (lxxi. 6). And so, very often, for this is by far the most frequent division of R'bhîa's clause[3].

EXCEPTIONS. (*a*) In a few instances, Pazer comes, with the second word, where we should have expected L'garmeh, as in יְפִיפִיתָ מִבְּנֵי אָדָם (xlv. 3); and in lxxix. 2; xcix. 5 (9); cvi. 23; Job x. 15; xxiv. 14. (The employment of Pazer here is parallel to that of Great R'bhîa for D'chî, before Athnach, p. 58 below.)

(*β*) Again, Pazer *necessarily* takes the place of L'garmeh, when the melody introduces *two servi*[4] before the word on which the dichotomy rests, as in לוּ יֵשׁ נַפְשְׁכֶם תַּחַת נַפְשִׁי (Ps. xi. 2); כִּי הִנֵּה הָרְשָׁעִים יִדְרְכוּן קֶשֶׁת (Job xvi. 4); and in Ps. xliv. 4; lix. 4; lxxxix. 20; xc. 4; xcii. 10; cxxv. 3; Prov. vii. 23; xxx. 33; Job vi. 4. (Here L'garmeh could not have been used, because it admits of only *one* servus.)

2. When a minor dichotomy is required, either before or after the main dichotomy, Pazer marks the latter, and L'garmeh the former, e. g. מִמְתִים יָדְךָ ׀ יְהוָֹה מִמְתִים מֵחֶלֶד (Ps. xvii. 14); נַשְּׁקוּ־בַר פֶּן־יֶאֱנַף ׀ וְתֹאבְדוּ דֶרֶךְ (ii. 12); and so in iv. 2; vii. 6; cxxvii. 2; Prov. xxii. 29; xxiv. 31; &c.[5] The case is similar in Ps. xxxv. 13 and l. 1. Of course a minor dichotomy may *both* precede and follow, as in יִתַּמּוּ חַטָּאִים ׀ מִן־הָאָרֶץ וּרְשָׁעִים ׀ עוֹד אֵינָם (civ. 35), and so in xc. 10, cvi. 48, cxli. 4.

EXCEPTIONS. In xxxv. 13 (some texts), xlii. 9, and lxviii. 7, *two* L'garmehs are used, instead of Pazer and L'garmeh, on the principle that when an accent is *repeated*, it has the second time a less disjunctive value than the first[6].

---

[3] Cases like נְרַנְּנָה ׀ בִּישׁוּעָתֶךָ ׀ בְּגֹל (xx. 6), עַל־נַהֲרוֹת ׀ בָּבֶל (cxxxvii. 1), come under this head, because two accents in one word produce the same musical effect as if they stood in different words.

[4] For this use of two servi, see chapter on Pazer. It might always have been avoided (as the first word is small) by the employment of Maqqeph.

[5] In Prov. xxiv. 31 Pazer is wanting in common edd.

[6] Pazer itself is repeated, with L'garmeh preceding and following, in an unusually long sentence in Prov. xxx. 4, and I venture to think rightly (comp. the similar repetition of Ṣinnor, p. 56, note 6), although Ben-Bil. does not allude to it (I. 7). Some Codd., however, and Baer point with R'bhîa.

SERVUS OF GREAT R'BHÎA.

Great R'bhîa has only *one* servus, which is Illuy or M'huppakh,— rarely Mer'kha,—according to the following rules:

1. When L'garmeh or Pazer precedes, the servus is,

a. In most cases, Illuy, e. g. יְהֹוָה ׀ נְחֵנִי בְצִדְקָתֶךָ (Ps. v. 9); יְפֵיפִיתָ
מִבְּנֵי אָדָם (xlv. 3); and so in i. 3; ii. 12; x. 9; xi. 2; xviii. 16; xxii. 25; and often[7].

β. But M'huppakh with Ṣinnorîth, if an open syllable directly[8] precedes the tone, e. g. אֱלֹהַי ׀ צִדְקִי עֲנֵנִי (iv. 2); יָקוּם רוֹצֵחַ לָאוֹר (Job xxiv. 14); comp. Ps. iii. 8; xi. 4; xv. 4; xvii. 3; xix. 5; xcix. 5. In two passages, בִּישׁוּעָתֶךָ (xx. 6) and נֶחֱמָתִי (Job vi. 10), these accents appear in the *same word* with Great R'bhîa, M'huppakh taking the place of Métheg.

2. When neither L'garmeh nor Pazer precedes, the servus is

a. Almost always M'huppakh, as שָׁאַל מִמֶּנִּי (Ps. ii. 8); יְהֹוָה אֲדֹנֵינוּ (viii. 2); and so in x. 12; xx. 7; xl. 12; lii. 9; &c.[9]
EXCEPTIONS. אַשְׁרֵי (i. 1; xxxii. 2; xl. 5); יַחְפְּשׂוּ (lxiv. 7, see Norzi); לְפָנָי (xcviii. 9, see do.); and נִבְהָל (Prov. xxviii. 22). One loses patience at having to quote such trivialities, which are paraded—at least the first three—in the Masora[10], and supported by Codd. An anomalous accentuation is associated with an anomalous pronunciation! (That both are merely fanciful may be seen from comparing cxxvii. 5; Prov. ii. 4; Ps. xcvi. 13; xxx. 8; where the same forms are given, without any irregularity.)

β. Mer'kha, in the few instances in which another R'bhîa precedes, e. g.

---

[7] Most of the mistakes in our texts have been already corrected by Baer. The following remain: בְּאָזְנֵינוּ (xliv. 2); קָמוּ (liv. 5); שֹׁכְבֵי (lxxxviii. 6); מַיִם (xciii. 4); שָׁבֶט (cxxv. 3); מֶלֶךְ (cxxxv. 11); תַּחַת (Job xvi. 4); שָׁמְרָה (xxiv. 15); יֵצֵא (xxxi. 40). For all of these I have found Illuy in many Codd. For lxxvi. 8 and Job xxviii. 3, see pp. 36, 37. In xci. 4 the best texts have D'chî.

[8] I say 'directly,' because, if vocal Sh'va (simple or composite) comes between, as in אֹיְבָ֑י (xxvii. 6) and מְחָתִים (xvii. 14), few Codd. point with Ṣinnorîth. In וּמִי (Job xxxiv. 29), the ו is too weak for Ṣinnorîth. For lxxi. 3, see p. 36.

[9] The few mistakes in common edd. have been corrected by Baer; but he has himself wrongly introduced Mer'kha in lxxxv. 9; xcvii. 9 (see Norzi's note); and cxxv. 5. In xcv. 7 we must point כִּי־הוּא אֱלֹהֵינוּ, with Ox. 1, 109; Cam. 12; Erf. 3; K. 599, 606.

[10] See Ginsburg's Masora, vol. i, p. 113, אשרי ד' רא' פסו' במע' מארכין וסימ'
'וכו. (The term מארכין applies both to Gaya and Mer'kha, see Frensdorff, *Die Masora magna*, p. 7. The fourth ex. is Prov. viii. 34.) The *Mas. fin.* 11[b] gives these exceptions in a form which has completely puzzled Rabbinical scholars, אשרי ד' במעם זרקא! Has not a line fallen out, and may not the original reading have been זרקא [מארכין ר"פ ג' ברביע וחד] ד' במעם, or something similar?

וַיֹּרֵנִי וַיֹּאמֶר לִי (Prov. iv. 4). I
have noticed besides only Ps. lxxviii. 4; Prov. xxvii. 10; and Job
xxxii. 5[11].

In Ps. lv. 24 and lxxxvi. 14 R'bhía appears in our texts with *two*
servi. I correct the former תּוֹרִדֵם לִבְאֵר־שַׁחַת, with Erf. 1, 2; Fr.;
K. 80, 155; De R. 350; and the latter זֵדִים קָמוּ־עָלַי, with Ox. 2323;
Par. 30; Ber. 32; K. 80, 94; De R. 412.

CHAPTER X.

ṢINNOR.

THE rules for the division of Ṣinnor's clause are the same as
those we have just laid down for Great R'bhîa.

I. If the clause consist of only *two* words, the first has generally a servus, e. g. חָנֵּנִי יְהוָה (Ps. vi. 3)[1]; but in a few instances,
—where a slight emphasis is to be marked,—L'garmeh, e. g.
הֵמָּה יֹאבֵדוּ (cii. 27); לָמָּה תְּרַצְּדוּן (lxviii. 17).

II. 1. When there are *three or more* words in the clause, and
only one dichotomy is necessary, L'garmeh is employed to mark it,
e. g. גַּם־אֲנִי אוֹדְךָ בִכְלִי־נֶבֶל (xviii. 7); בַּצַּר־לִי אֶקְרָא יְהוָה
(lxxi. 22); אִם־יִשְׁמְרוּ בָנֶיךָ בְּרִיתִי (cxxxii. 12)[2].

---

[11] This accentuation seems to have been adopted for the sake of conformity
with cases like לִמְשִׁיחוֹ לְדָוִד וּלְזַרְעוֹ (xviii. 51), which (as we have seen, p. 75) are so
pointed in Codd. Of the exx. given above, the last is wrongly accented in all
texts. Point פִּי־אֵין with B. M. 7; Par. 6; K. 599; De R. 368, 1014, 1252.

[1] So Prov. xxiv. 24 is better pointed אֹמֵר לְרָשָׁע with B. M. 4; Ox. 17; Ber. 2;
De R. 380, 518; and Jabl.

[2] This is the usual division of Ṣinnor's clause,—a single dichotomy, represented by
L'garmeh. And here I would observe that this rule for the dichotomy is *most strictly
carried out* in Codd., even where we should hardly expect it, as in אֲשֶׁר לֹא הָלַךְ
(i. 1). Hence, the instances of laxity, which are found in the Heid.-Baer text, in
i. 1, xxx. 6, xxxi. 21, xxxii. 7, liii. 6, lxii. 10, lxxxiv. 4, cix. 16, cxv. 1, must be
all corrected. (In these cases common edd. are generally right.) In his last ed-
of the Pss., Baer has introduced another exceptional case, xxvii. 4. But I cannot
say that I have been convinced by the reasons adduced in his note.

But when the melody introduces *two servi* before the word, on which the dichotomy falls, as in כִּי כָלוּ בְיָגוֹן חַיַּי (xxxi. 11), Pazer must be employed, as L'garmeh has never more than *one* servus. The other examples are v. 10; lvi. 14; cxxvi. 2.

2. When a minor dichotomy precedes or follows the main dichotomy, Pazer marks the latter, and L'garmeh the former, e. g. עַל־זֹאת יִתְפַּלֵּל (cxxxii. 11); נִשְׁבַּע יְהֹוָה׀ לְדָוִד׀ אֱמֶת כָּל־חָסִיד׀ אֵלֶיךָ (xxxii. 6). The other examples are x. 14; xxxi. 12; xxxix. 13; lxxv. 9; lxxxiv. 4; Job vii. 20.

EXCEPTIONS. In one instance L'garmeh is *repeated :* רַבּוֹת עָשִׂיתָ׀ אַתָּה׀ יְהֹוָה אֱלֹהַי (xl. 6)[3]. Comp. the repetition of L'garmeh *after* Pazer in x. 14. The principle has been already explained.

SERVUS OF ṢINNOR.

Ṣinnor, like Great R'bhîa, has only *one* servus, which is

1. Mer'kha, when the tone is on the *first* syllable, e. g. לֹא הָלַךְ (i. 1); הֲלֹא יָדְעוּ (xiv. 4); מָלֵא מֶסֶךְ (lxxv. 9).

2. Munach, when on any other syllable, e. g. אָהַבְתָּ צֶּדֶק (xlv. 8); בְּחַסְדְּךָ בָטַחְתִּי (xiii. 6)[4].

EXCEPTIONS. (*a*) Munach is changed into Mer'kha, if the letter on which it is due is pointed with *Dagesh* (*forte* or *lene*), e. g. רַבִּים אֹמְרִים (iv. 7); מִי־יִתֵּן מִצִּיּוֹן (xiv. 7); יַרְבּוּ עַצְּבוֹתָם (xvi. 4)[5]. (β) In two pas-

---

[3] So pointed in all the Codd. I have examined. In common edd. the second Paseq is out of its place, in the Heid.-Baer text omitted.

[4] *Mer'kha* has taken the place of Munach—according to Ben-Bil. (2. 20), the Erf. Mas. (MS.), and *textus receptus*—in חֶלְקָם בַּֽחַיִּים וּצְפוּנְךָ (xvii. 14), where we have the unique accentuation of *two consecutive Ṣinnors*. The irregularity is reflected in the servus preceding! [Since writing the above, I have found the same view expressed in a marginal note on the passage in Simson hanaqdan's חבור הקונים (Br. Mus. Or. 1016, p. 75ᵇ). ואני המגיה ראיתי טעם שנשתנה בעבור הב' זרקות רצופות.] Many Codd., however, point regularly with Munach. On a second exception, fixed by the Masora, אַשְׁרֵי אָדָם (Prov. viii. 34), see Great R'bhîa (p. 79, note 10).

[5] According to Ben-Asher (Dikd. hat. 24. 22), Ben-Bil. (Arab. text), and *textus receptus*, the Munach is retained in three instances, לַֽמְנַצֵּחַ אַל־תַּשְׁחֵת (lix. 1); אָנָּה יְהֹוָה (cxvi. 16); and לֹא־תִשָּׂא פְשָׁעִי (Job vii. 21). One only wonders that it has not been oftener retained. For on what principle Dagesh is made to affect the servus, before Ṣinnor alone of all the accents, it is impossible to understand. There are between twenty and thirty such passages.

sages, where Paseq follows, Munach is changed into M'huppakh,
הָאֵל ⁶ ׀ לָנוּ (lxviii. 21); עַד־מָתַי ׀ פְּתָיִם (Prov. i. 22).

Ṣinnor is found with *two* servi in מִי הוּא זֶה (Ps. xxiv. 10); מַה רַב טוּבְךָ
(xxxi. 20); and אֱלִיהוּא בֶן־בַּרַכְאֵל הַבּוּזִי (Job xxxii. 2)[7]. But in the two
first instances, many Codd. have Maqqeph; and the last does not
concern us, the irregularity being due to an attempt to force the poetic
accentuation on a *prose* passage not at all suited to bear it. There is
further the strange accentuation אֶת אֲרַם נַהֲרַיִם וְאֶת־אֲרַם צוֹבָה (Ps. lx.
2), where the first Mer'kha takes the place of Maqqeph[8].

CHAPTER XI.

D'CHÎ.

The division of D'chî's clause would follow precisely the same
rules as those given for Great R'bhîa and Ṣinnor, were it not that
the law of transformation often interferes with their application.
Those rules—to repeat them once more and apply them to D'chî's
clause—are as follows:

I. When there are only *two* words in the clause, the first has
always a *servus,* e. g. עַד־אָנָה יְהוָה (v. 6); לֹא־יִתְיַצְּבוּ הוֹלְלִים
(xiii. 2). L'garmeh never appears, as in Great R'bhîa's and Ṣinnor's clauses, see next page.

II. 1. When there are *three or more* words in the clause and
only *one* dichotomy is necessary, L'garmeh is employed to mark
it, e. g. אֲשֶׁר אָמְרוּ ׀ לִלְשֹׁנֵנוּ נַגְבִּיר (Ps. x. 7); אֵלֶּה ׀ פִּיהוּ מָלֵא
(xii. 5). This is the most common division of D'chî's clause[1].

----

[6] Wrongly pointed in most Codd. and in common edd., thus הָאֵל ׀. But the
Masora parva to B. M. 12, 16, expressly notes ד'במ' to הָאֵל ׀ in the text, (see also
Baer, Accentuationssystem, p. 494, note 2.) A Concordance shews the three other
passages to be Jer. xxxii. 18, Ps. lxxxv. 9, and Dan. ix. 4.

[7] In a treatise on the accents, assigned to Samuel the grammarian, in the Royal
Library at Berlin (No. 118, p. 124), the above three instances are allowed, and no
more. After quoting them, the writer adds ולא מצאתי יותר בשנים.

[8] It is fixed by the same Masora as the cases named, p. 63, note 24. Here we
have *two* instances of את־ארם in the same clause. The one is by this fanciful
accentuation *distinguished* from the other, as though the regular accents were not
enough for that purpose!

[1] Some mistakes in our texts—Ps. v. 3, xxxii. 5, xcv. 7, Prov. xxviii. 23—I have

EXCEPTIONS. (*a*) In three passages Pazer appears, with the second word, where we should have expected L'garmeh, יִגְאָלֻהוּ חֹשֶׁךְ וְצַלְמָוֶת (Job iii. 5), and Ps. lxviii. 5, and cix. 16.

(β) In two passages Pazer *necessarily* appears, because *two servi* precede the word on which the dichotomy falls, כִּי לֹא יָבִינוּ אֶל־פְּעֻלֹּת יְהֹוָה (xxviii. 5) and מִרְמָה כִּי פִי רָשָׁע וּפִי (cix. 2).

2. When a *second* dichotomy is necessary, both Pazer and L'garmeh appear, כִּי שָׁם ׀ שְׁאֵלוּנוּ שׁוֹבֵינוּ דִּבְרֵי־שִׁיר (cxxxvii. 3); אִם־תִּכְתּוֹשׁ אֶת־הָאֱוִיל ׀ בַּמַּכְתֵּשׁ בְּתוֹךְ הָרִפוֹת (Prov. xxvii. 22). The other exx. are Ps. v. 12 (corrected p. 89) and cxxii. 4 (ditto). xliv. 3 and xlv. 8 are similar. D'chî's clause is seldom of sufficient length to require more than *one* dichotomy.

The cases in which the above rules are affected by the law of transformation are the following:

First, L'garmeh when due by emphasis or the dichotomy *in the word immediately preceding D'chî*, cannot stand there[2]. It must have been contrary to the laws of melody to bring these two accents together. A servus therefore takes the place of L'garmeh. Thus the emphasis is not marked in עַד־אָנָה ׀ יְהֹוָה (xiii. 2); and instead of תּוֹרַת יְהֹוָה ׀ תְּמִימָה (xix. 8),—as the dichotomy requires, comp. יִרְאַת יְהֹוָה ׀ טְהוֹרָה, ib. 10,—we have תּוֹרַת יְהֹוָה תְּמִימָה בְּנֵי־אִישׁ עַד־מֶה כְבוֹדִי. So also instead of עַד־מֶה כְבוֹדִי לִכְלִמָּה (iv. 3) we find עַד־מֶה כְבוֹדִי לִכְלִמָּה לִכְלִמָּה. This rule of transformation is strictly carried out[3]. For other exx. see xiv. 1, xxxv. 15, lv. 19, lvii. 8, lxiii. 2. In xxiii. 6 and lvi. 1, 10, L'garmeh

---

already corrected pp. 51–53, 64. הִנֵּה must have L'garmeh in Ps. xxxiii. 18, Job iii. 7, v. 17, with various Codd. The Heid.-Baer text has wrongly dropped the dichotomy in Ps. lxix. 3, cxxi. 4, cxxxiv. 1, and cxlv. 12.

Observe that in xxxv. 1, ciii. 1, cxi. 1, cxii. 1, cxlviii. 1, and cxlix. 1, the L'garmeh *does not mark the dichotomy* in D'chî's clause, but is the representative of Olév'yored (34. 13). The same remark applies to the first L'garmeh in xxvii. 1.

[2] This peculiarity has been observed by Christian writers on the accents, as Wasmuth (p. 183) and Spitzner (p. 227). I believe that we have a parallel in the transformation of L'garmeh before Silluq, when Great Shalshéleth precedes (67. 13).

[3] Norzi, Baer, and perhaps Ben-Asher are therefore wrong in xxxi. 3. Other texts are right; comp. lxxi. 3.

would have been *repeated* (comp. 78. 26 and 81. 10), if there had
been no transformation[4].

That transformation has really taken place is clear not only
from the requirements of the dichotomy, but from the circumstance
that the servus preceding is always that which would have come, *had
L'garmeh remained in its place.* (See the exx. given above.)

Secondly, although the dichotomy is generally marked, when
it falls on the *second* word before D'chî (comp. the exx. under
§ II), *small words*, standing at the beginning of the clause and
accented on the *first* syllable, reject it and take a *servus* (or
Maqqeph) instead, thus : שְׁמַ֖ע ק֥וֹל תַּחֲנוּנַ֑י (xxviii. 2); ט֥וֹב
אִישׁ־אֹהֵ֣ב (xvi. 4); כָּל־פֹּ֖עַל יְהוָ֑ה (Prov. xv. 17); אֲרֻחַ֣ת יָרָ֗ק
הָכְמָ֑ה (xxix. 3). (It is only when an *emphasis* is made to rest
on them that the sign of the dichotomy remains. The few instances are: סֹ֣לּוּ (Ps. lxviii. 5); זֹ֣את ' (cix. 20); and זֶ֣ה ' (Job
xx. 29).) This peculiarity is shared with D'chî by Pazer and
Little R'bhîa—minor pausal accents like itself—but not by
Great R'bhîa and Ṣinnor. The comparative slightness of the
musical pause following was doubtless the cause that the melody
did not *dwell* on the small words in question.

It is important to notice that, even in the cases where D'chî
undergoes transformation (60. 11), the above rules remain unchanged. L'garmeh appears in the *second* word, when due there,
just as if D'chî were present (see 60. 24; 75. 6)[5]. On the other

---

[4] Again, we must be careful to distinguish the cases, in which L'garmeh precedes
D'chî, *as the representative of Olév'yored*, for instance, cxiii. 1, cxxxv. 1, cxlvii.
1. To this class belongs also וּבַת־צֹ֖ר ' בְּמִנְחָ֑ה (xlv. 13). L'garmeh proper, even
if it were admissible, would give no sense here, and must have been marked with
M'huppakh, not Azla, as וּבָרְכֵ֣ךְ ' (lxxii. 19). The translation usually adopted would
require the accentuation וּבַת־צֹ֖ר בְּמִנְחָ֑ה. With the accents of the text, וּבַת־צֹ֖ר
can only be taken as the *vocative* (with Jerome, Hupf., and Hitz.)—comp. Olév'yored
with the voc., cxxxvii. 8 ;—or, which is far less natural, as *nom. absol.* (with Delitzsch).
Whether the punctators were right is another question. (No doubt, the L'garmeh in
these cases was chanted with a special pause, and the melody began anew with D'chî.)

[5] My readers must not imagine that these are trifling matters, which might be
passed over without notice ; for, unless we observe them, we shall be in danger of

hand, it is always absent from the *first* word, e. g. לַעֲשׂוֹת רְצוֹנְךָ

[6].(לַעֲשׂוֹת רְצוֹנְךָ ׀ אֱלֹהַי חָפַצְתִּי (xl. 9; properly אֱלֹהַי חָפַצְתִּי
And small words, like those named above, are not marked by the
dichotomy, unless, as before, an *emphasis* is laid upon them, e. g.
עוּרָה ׀ לָמָּה תִישַׁן ׀ אֲדֹנָי (cxix. 66), but טוֹב טַעַם וָדַעַת לַמְּדֵנִי
(xliv. 24)[7]. It is but rarely that even ordinary edd. exhibit any
deviation[8].

---

falling into such mistakes as Delitzsch has made, in his explanation of the passage :
עַד־אָנָה ׀ תְּשִׂימוּן קִנְצֵי לְמִלִּין (Job xviii. 2) : 'Die Accentuation nimmt עַד־אָנָה (mit
Legarmeh) für sich : Wie lange noch ? Macht ein Ende den Worten !' But had
this been the meaning designed by the accentuation, עַד־אָנָה *must have been marked
with R'bhia*. As it is, it is just like עַל־מָה ׀ (xiii. 14).

[6] The double transformation thus introduced completely obscures the division
(logical and syntactical) of Athnach's clause. Still, from the rules laid down, we
need never be at a loss to know what the true division is, and what the sense
designed by the accentuation. Thus in the difficult passage הֲפַכְפַּךְ דֶּרֶךְ אִישׁ וָזָר
(Prov. xxi. 8) we may be sure, from the pointing of the first word, that L'garmeh
has fallen out, and that, if there had been no transformation, the accentuation would
have been הֲפַכְפַּךְ ׀ דֶּרֶךְ ׀ אִישׁ וָזָר,—the meaning of which can only be : *Perversus
viæ est vir, et deflectens* (scil. *a recta via*), 'a man' (i. e. one man and another) 'is
perverse in his way, and goes wrong.' My friend Professor Delitzsch will, I am sure,
excuse my again pointing out that his explanation of the accents cannot stand. If,
as he supposes, דֶּרֶךְ אִישׁ was meant to be taken as *subject*, and הֲפַכְפַּךְ as *predicate*,
the pointing must have been הֲפַכְפַּךְ ׀ דֶּרֶךְ אִישׁ וָזָר.

[7] The other similar exx. are כֵּן ׀ (lxi. 9); שָׁוְא ׀ (cxxvii. 1, in some Codd.); שָׁם ׀
(cxxxii. 17); and זֶה ׀ (Job xxvii. 13). We have also a slight (emphatic) pause after
כִּי in a few passages, as Ps. xvi. 10, 'For—Thou wilt not leave my soul to Hades ;'
and in li. 18; xciv. 14; xcvi. 5; Prov. xxiv. 20; Job v. 6; xx. 20. The כִּי ׀ in these
cases is fixed by the Masora (see Ginsburg, vol. ii, p. 29). In trifling matters of
this kind we may or may not agree with the Masoretes.

[8] There is, however, one passage, Ps. v. 5, in which both printed texts and
Codd. exhibit an extraordinary confusion. The regular pointing would have been
כִּי לֹא־אֵל ׀ חָפֵץ רֶשַׁע ׀ אָתָּה, but we may be satisfied that the original accentuators
shrank from such an accentuation, as suggesting an idea which was nothing short of
blasphemy (comp. Deut. xxxii. 21). To avoid the possibility of such a rendering,
they joined אֵל by Maqqeph to the word following. (Here common edd. are right.)
כִּי לֹא ׀ was then left for the dichotomy. But לֹא is never so separated from its
clause. The dichotomy was therefore moved back (a case certainly without parallel)
to the *third* word from D'chî (transformed), and the accentuation fixed in the form
כִּי ׀ לֹא אֵל־חָפֵץ רֶשַׁע ׀ אָתָּה. If any one wishes for authority for the Ṭarcha and
Mer'kha, according to rule (62. 10), it is found in B. M. 1; Ox. 15, 17, 71, 96; Par. 3.
כִּי ׀ is fixed by the Masora quoted in note 7.

SERVI OF D'CHÎ.

D'chî may have one or two servi.

1. **One servus.** This is always Munach, e. g. וּבְדֶרֶךְ חַטָּאִים (i. 1);
בְּרֹב חַסְדֶּךָ (v. 8).

This servus may appear, instead of Métheg, in the *same word* with
D'chî, e. g. וְהִנָּשְׂאוּ (xxiv. 7); וַיֹּאמְרוּ (xciv. 7)[9]. The substitution is,
however, subject to certain conditions. Ben-Bil. (4. 14) restricts it to
such cases, as those just given, in which Qámeṣ or Chôlem, followed by
vocal Sh'va, immediately precedes the tone-syllable. And Codd. agree
with him[10]. Other exx. may be seen, in Baer's text, in xxxvii. 38;
lxxvi. 7; xcviii. 6; cvi. 28; cvii. 32. (Common edd. generally retain
the Métheg.)

2. **Two servi.** The servus adjoining D'chî remains Munach; the
first servus is M'huppakh or Illuy, according to the rules already laid
down (pp. 62, 63) for the first of three servi before Athnach.

The presence of *two* servi is—as in the cases of Athnach and Silluq—
entirely due to *transformation*. The difference in the case of D'chî
is, that the transformation may take place not only in the *first* but in
the *second* word: (a) in the *first* word (83. 16), in which case L'garmeh leaves its servus behind it, which becomes the first servus of
D'chî[11]; (b) in the *second* word, if that word has the tone on the *first*
syllable (84. 8). The first servus is then

a. M'huppakh, when the tone is on the *first* syllable, e. g. זֶה עָנִי קָרָא
(xxxiv. 7); שְׁמַע קוֹל תַּחֲנוּנַי (xxviii. 2); and often.

β. M'huppakh, when the tone is on the *second* syllable, and vocal
Sh'va does not precede, e. g. עֶרְמָה כְבוֹדִי לְכִלְמָּה (iv. 3). The other
exx. are [12]אַנְשֵׁי (lv. 24); [13]עַל־יוֹנַת (lvi. 1); יִשְׂמַח (lxiv. 11); and יַרְעֵם
(Job xxxvii. 5).

---

[9] Of course, in the chanting, the Munach was first given, and then the D'chî on
the tone-syllable of the word.

[10] Many Codd. and common edd. have, however, two instances with *Chîreq*,
לְהַצִּילְךָ (Prov. ii. 12, 16) and מֵהַשְׁפִּילְךָ (xxv. 7). Comp. the exceptional case,
בְּבִירְתָא, under a similar rule in the prose accentuation (משפטי הטעמים, 26ᵇ).
Three manifest blunders (query, in some model Cod.?), הַעֲזֻבִים (Prov. ii. 13),
הֲמִירָאֲתְךָ (Job xxii. 4), and הֲתַמְבִּינְתָך (xxxix. 26), have been magnified by Ben-
Asher (Dikd. hat. 26. 20) into *exceptions!* But Ben-Bil. does not accept these exceptions, for he makes the second ex. a case of *regular pointing*, הֲמִירָאֲתְךָ.

[11] And as Athnach takes over all D'chî's accents, without any change, when D'chî
is transformed, we now understand how it is that the servus of L'garmeh, the first
of two servi of D'chî, and the first of three servi of Athnach, *are all fixed by
precisely the same rules* (the transformation under (b) not making any difference in
those rules).

[12] The vocal Sh'va is here so slight, that it is not taken into account.

[13] So I point with Ox. 15, 72, 98; K. 538; De R. 331, 1261.

γ. Illuy, when the tone is on the second syllable, *vocal Sh'va pre-ceding*,—or when it is on the *third* syllable, e. g. בָּהֶם עֹרֵב יְשַׁלַּח (Ps. lxxviii. 45); נֶאֶסְפוּ עָלַי נֵכִים (xxxv. 15); הָיְתָה־לִּי דִמְעָתִי לֶחֶם (xlii. 4). There are only two other examples[14], שִׂמְחוּ (xxxii. 11); מַלְכֵי (lxxii. 10).

δ. M'huppakh with Ṣinnorith, when an open syllable comes directly before the tone, e. g. אָמַר נָבָל בְּלִבּוֹ (xiv. 1; liii. 2). The other exx. are, יָבֵשׁוּ (vi. 11); תּוֹרַת פִּקּוּדֵי (xix. 9); וְהָרֵק (xxxv. 3); פְּדֵה (lv. 19); יֵשׁוּבוּ (lvi. 10); נָבַוָן (lvii. 8); נָתַתָּה (lx. 6); עֹלוֹת (lxvi. 15); וְהָשֵׁב (lxxix. 12); יֶהֱוֶה (lxxxiv. 9); וַיָּשִׂימוּ (cix. 5); זָרַח (cxii. 4); טָמַן (Prov. xix. 24; xxvi. 15); לָבַשׁ (Job vii. 5); גֵּרֵי (xix. 15); and צָעִיר (xxxii. 6).

3. Of three servi there is only one example[15], כִּי יֹסִיף עַל־חַטָּאתוֹ פֶשַׁע (Job xxxiv. 37), where כִּי (Mer'kha instead of Maqqeph) is fixed by the Masora; see Athnach, p. 63, note 23.

CHAPTER XII.

PAZER.

PAZER's proper office is (as we have seen) to mark the major dichotomy in the clauses of Great R'bhîa, Ṣinnor, and D'chî. It is particularly common before Great R'bhîa.

Its own clause is always short, never exceeding four words. One disjunctive therefore—L'garmeh—generally suffices.

I. This disjunctive may appear, when there is a slight empha-sis, in a clause consisting of only *two* words, as in עַל־כֵּן ׀ מְשָׁחֲךָ (Ps. xlv. 8); [1]אֶל ׀ אֱלֹהִים (l. 1); and xxxv. 13 (some Texts) and xliv. 3 (ditto). These are the only examples.

II. Instances of the dichotomy with *three* or *four* words are: יִתַּמּוּ חַטָּאִים ׀ מִן־הָאָרֶץ גַּם־צִפּוֹר ׀ מָצְאָה בַיִת (lxxxiv. 4);

---

[14] And these some Codd. point with M'huppakh, מַלְכֵי, שִׂמְחוּ,—owing to the slightness of the vocal Sh'va.

[15] The Heid.-Baer text has indeed two other exx. in Ps. xxiii. 6 and lvi. 1; but common edd. have there rightly L'garmeh.

[1] Most edd. have here a stupid mistake, אֱלֹהִים (like וְהִנֵּה Prov. xxiv. 31). But Pazer appears in the more correct texts of Opit., Jabl., Mich., and Heid.-Baer.

(civ. 35); בָּרוּךְ יְהוָֹה ׀ אֱלֹהֵי יִשְׂרָאֵל (cvi. 48). If we make the corrections, suggested at the end of this chapter, the rules for the dichotomy will be found carefully carried out[2].

The only exceptions will then be,—as in the cases of D'chî and Little R'bhîa,—when the word on which it should fall (at the beginning of the clause) is a *monosyllable*, viz. כִּי (v. 10, and often); גְּעַר (lxviii. 31); אָז (cxxvi. 2); עַד (Prov. vii. 23); and לוּ (Job xvi. 4).

SERVI OF PAZER.

1. When there is *one*, it is Galgal, e. g. מָצְאָה בַּיִת (Ps. lxxxiv. 4); אֱלֹהֵי יִשְׂרָאֵל (cvi. 48). In אוֹדִיעֲךָ (xxxii. 5) and וַתִּשְׁקְקֶהָ (lxv. 10) Galgal appears, instead of Métheg, in the same word with Pazer.

EXCEPTIONS. Galgal is changed into M'huppakh, in the two passages לְדָבָר ׀ רָע (cxli. 4) and אֵפוֹא ׀ בְּנִי (Prov. vi. 3, see below), because of Paseq following.

2. When there are *two* servi, the second remains Galgal; the first is (a) M'huppakh, when it falls on the *first letter* of the word, as כִּי אֵין בְּפִיהוּ (Ps. v. 10); (β) Azla on the *second letter* and further. Most of the passages, in which Azla occurs in our texts, I have ventured to correct (see *Corrigenda*, next page). But we may retain it, with Ben-Asher, in גְּעַר[3] חַיַּת קָנֶה (lxviii. 31), and in עֹשֵׂה־זֹּאת[4] אֵפוֹא ׀ בְּנִי (Prov. vi. 3), where the slight pause made by Paseq may be taken to mark the dichotomy[5].

---

[2] Ordinary texts must be further corrected in lxv. 10; cxxvii. 2; Prov. xxiii. 29; and the Heid.-Baer text in xl. 13 and cxxxvii. 3, where the former are right.

[3] This is the only instance—even if we retain all Ben-Asher's examples—of Azla on the second *letter* (as opposed to the second *syllable*); but the rule is found in the prose accentuation for the corresponding servus of Pashṭa and T'bhir (see משפטי המטעמים, 25ᵃ and 29ᵃ), and may be accepted here.

[4] So I point with B. M. 9, Ox. 96, Cam. 25, Par. 10, De R. 413, 941, &c. See also chapter on Paseq, § IV.

[5] Galgal is strangely interchanged in ordinary texts with M'huppakh (comp. v. 12 with xiii. 3; xxviii. 5 with xliv. 4; lvi. 14 with lix. 4),—a source of great perplexity to Christian writers on the accents. I have already drawn attention (p. 57, note 9) to the confusion between these accents before Olév'yored. The explanation is the same here. Ben-Naphtali's pointing (M'huppakh) has found its way (more or less) into some Codd. and printed texts. But Bomb. 1, and of course Heid. and Baer,—to say nothing of Codd., as B. M. 4, 5, 7; Ox. 1; Cam. 13, &c.,—have regularly Ben-Asher's accentuation, Galgal.

Corrigenda.

Most texts, following Ben-Asher[6], have excluded the dichotomy from the following passages. But as no reason can be assigned for its omission, and it is actually found in many Codd., I do not hesitate to propose its insertion:

Ps. v. 12. וְיִשְׂמְחוּ ׀ כָל־חוֹסֵי בָךְ (Vat. 468, K. 155, De R. 2, &c.);

Ps. xiii. 3. עַד־אָנָה ׀ אָשִׁית עֵצוֹת (Vat. 468, K. 155, De R. 2, &c.);

Ps. xxii. 25. כִּי לְא־בָזָה ׀ וְלָא שִׁקַּץ (Ox. 98, Par. 4, Fr., &c.);

Ps. xxiii. 4. גַּם כִּי־אֵלֵךְ ׀ בְּגֵיא צַלְמָוֶת (Ox. 98, Par. 4, Fr., &c.);

Ps. xxvii. 6. וְעַתָּה ׀ יָרוּם רֹאשִׁי (Ox. 79, 111; Bomb. 1, &c.);

Ps. xxxi. 12. מִכָּל־צֹרְרַי ׀ הָיִיתִי חֶרְפָּה (B. M. 1, 8, K. 525, &c.);

Ps. xxxii. 5. חַטָּאתִי ׀ אוֹדִיעֲךָ (Ox. 98, De R. 2, K. 525, &c.);

Ps. cvi. 38. וַיִּשְׁפְּכוּ ׀ דָם נָקִי (Par. 4, Erf. 2, K. 246, &c.);

Ps. cxxii. 4. שֶׁשָּׁם ׀ עָלוּ שְׁבָטִים (Ox. 93, 111, K. 246, &c.);

Ps. cxxiii. 2. הִנֵּה ׀ כְּעֵינֵי עֲבָדִים (B. M. 8, Par. 4, K. 246, &c.);

Ps. cxxxviii. 2. אֶשְׁתַּחֲוֶה ׀ אֶל־הֵיכַל קָדְשְׁךָ (B. M. 13, Ox. 13, 93, &c.);

Prov. xxvii. 10. רֵעֲךָ ׀ וְרֵעֵה אָבִיךָ (B. M. 8, Erf. 2, Bomb. 1, &c.)

N. B. Writers on the accents have quietly adopted the above corrections as necessary, see Ouseel, p. 94, and Spitzner, p. 231. The former simply remarks *Psiq nonnunquam excidit!*

Beside the above, I propose to correct:

Ps. lix. 6. וְאַתָּה ׀ יְהֹוָה אֱלֹהִים ׀ צְבָאוֹת. (The first dichotomy at וְאַתָּה[7] with B. M. 7, Ox. 12, Par. 30, Fr., De R. 350, &c.; for the second, see p. 96. 18.)

And Ps. xc. 10. יְמֵי־שְׁנוֹתֵינוּ ׀ בָהֶם ׀ שִׁבְעִים שָׁנָה. Here a second dichotomy is needed at בָּהֶם, and is indicated by Codd.,—as Vi. 3, De R. 2,

---

[6] We have already seen that Ben-Asher is no infallible authority. Such variations, as those here pointed out—which he of course merely copied from texts before him—may have originated in the desire to make the *melody* more easy and flowing, a result which was perhaps attained by the substitution of Azla for L'garmeh. But at least consistency should have been observed. If the change was made in xxxi. 12, why not in lxxxiv. 4? If in xxii. 25 and xxiii. 4, why not also in lxxi. 3 and cxxvii. 2? Such irregularity of itself points to mistakes made. The original accentuators could hardly have been so inconsistent.

[7] Not as in the Heid.-Baer text at יְהֹוָה ׀. The two words יְהֹוָה אֱלֹהִים must be kept together,—either by Maqqeph or by a conjunctive accent,—as in lxxx. 5, 20; lxxxiv. 9.

K. 246,—which point בָּהֶם שִׁבְעִים שָׁנָה; but no Cod. has a second
L'garmeh. Some Codd. have L'garmeh after ׀ בָּהֶם, but then it fails
before. We need it *both* before and after. Comp. the division in Job
xxviii. 5, אֶרֶץ מִמֶּנָּה יֵצֵא לָחֶם (Baer's text). For the two L'garmehs,
comp. Ps. xl. 6 (81. 10).

CHAPTER XIII.

LITTLE R'BHîA.

THE division of Little R'bhîa's clause is of the simplest character.
We have never more than a single dichotomy, represented by
L'garmeh[1]: וּבָרוּךְ ׀ שֵׁם כְּבוֹדוֹ אֱלֹהִים ׀ אֵלִי אַתָּה (lxiii. 2);
(lxxii. 19); הֲתָעִיף עֵינֶיךָ ׀ בּוֹ (Prov. xxiii. 5); מִי זֶה ׀ מַעְלִים
עֵצָה (Job xlii. 3); לֹא לָנוּ ׀ יְהֹוָה (Ps. cxv. 1 with Codd.)[2]

The dichotomy fails—as with D'chî and Pazer—in the case
of small words, standing at the beginning of the clause[3] and
accented on the first syllable, as כִּי in כִּי אִם־בְּתוֹרַת יְהֹוָה
(i. 2); לֹא (lii. 9); אֲשֶׁר (cxxvii. 5); כָּל (cxxxv. 6); עַל (cxxxix.
14); מִי (Job xxxviii. 41). Still, if the punctators wished to lay
an emphasis on these small words, they were at liberty to retain
the dichotomy, as in ׀ לְמַעַן (Ps. lxviii. 24); ׀ כִּי (Prov. xxiii. 7);
and ׀ כֵּן (xxiv. 14; xxx. 20).

Twice L'garmeh comes, with a certain emphasis, in a clause
of only *two* words: אָוֶן ׀ יַחְשֹׁב (Ps. xxxvi. 5, comp. xii. 3) and
נַעַר ׀ הָיִיתִי (xxxvii. 25).

---

[1] Little R'bhîa's clause rarely contains more than *three* words. Only in lxxi. 20,
xc. 17, Job xxxii. 6 (prose), and xlii. 3 are there *four*. The clause being small, one
disjunctive is all that is required.

[2] The rules for the dichotomy are strictly observed. I have no corrections
to propose, except that in Ps. lv. 13 I would introduce it for the sake of emphasis,
כִּי לֹא־אוֹיֵב ׀ יְחָרְפֵנִי, with Ox. 71, 118; Hm. 7; Cop. 2; Vi. 2. It must be
replaced in Baer's text, in cxxxviii. 7 and Prov. xxiii. 5.

[3] In one case, וִיהִי ׀ נֹעַם אֲדֹנָי אֱלֹהֵינוּ (xc. 17), it is the *second* dichotomy that
fails.

Servi of Little R'bhîa.

Little R'bhîa may have one or two servi.

a. If there is one servus, it is Mer'kha, as אֲנִי שָׁכַבְתִּי (iii. 6);
אֱלֹהִים ׀ דִּבֶּר בְּקָדְשׁוֹ (lx. 8); and often.

β. If there are two servi, the first is M'huppakh, the second as
before Mer'kha, e. g. כִּי אִם־בְּתוֹרַת יְהֹוָה חֶפְצוֹ (i. 2). This additional
servus occurs properly only in the case of the small words named
above, כִּי, אֲשֶׁר, כָּל, &c.[4]

The two servi appear, however, occasionally in the *same word*, when
the syllable immediately preceding the tone is an open one, e. g.
יָגֵל לִבִּי (xiii. 6); וַיֵּשֶׁב קֶדֶם (lv. 20). And so in xxvii. 11; l. 3, 23;
lxviii. 36; lxxix. 13; Prov. vii. 22. This rule—which reminds one
of the introduction of Ṣinnorîth before the servus (Mer'kha) of R'bhîa
mugrash (76. 14)—was perhaps observed by Ben-Asher[5], but is only
very partially regarded by the punctators; nor does Ben-Bil. or any
other early authority on the accents allude to it. Even Baer, who
recognises it, seems to count it more honoured in the breach than the
observance. But a rule that is only half observed, is no rule at all.
We may then dispense with it (as some Codd. do), even in the case of
the few words (not more than nine or ten) to which it has been applied.

CHAPTER XIV.

L'garmeh

marks, where it occurs, the last division (sometimes the last *two*
divisions) in a clause. With it the continuous dichotomy comes
to an end. L'garmeh has, in consequence, no disjunctive accent
in its own clause[1].

---

[4] Exceptions in our texts are the two prose passages, Ps. xviii. 1 and Job xxxii. 6.
In the former, however, we must, no doubt, point לְעֶבֶד ׀ לַמְנַצֵּחַ יְהֹוָה, with Ox. 9;
K. 164, 224; De R. 940. (Many other Codd. have *M'huppakh* L'garmeh.) The
latter ought properly to be divided (as many Codd. do divide it) into *two* verses.
Little R'bhîa would then be changed into R'bhîa mugrash.

[5] See the חלופי נקוד to Ps. l. 23 and Job xviii. 4.

[1] One is sometimes in doubt—as in דּוּם ׀ לַיהֹוָה (xxxvii. 7); אֶל ׀ אֱלֹהִים (l. 1)—
whether Paseq or L'garmeh is intended by the accentuation. A correct list of the
Paseqs would therefore be of service. This some Codd. (as B. M. 1, 15; Pet.; K. 542)
undertake to furnish. Many more (as B. M. 1; Ox. 15, 71; Par. 107; Erf. 3; Vat.

The two forms of this accent are one and the same in disjunctive value. They differ only musically. The laws for the selection of the one or the other are as follows:

1. When a servus precedes, Azla L'garmeh is always used, e. g. ' יְהוָֹה יְצַוֶּה (Ps. xlii. 9); ' לֹא עָשָׂה כֵן (cxlvii. 20).

2. When there is no servus,—if the tone fall on the *first* or *second* syllable, M'huppakh L'garmeh is employed; if on the *third or further*, Azla L'garmeh.

  a. On the *first* syllable, e. g. ' כִּי (v. 5); ' עֲנֵנִי (iv. 2); ' חֶרֶב (xxxvii. 14)[2].

  β. On the *second* syllable, as: ' יֵשֵׁב (x. 8); [3] ' יְהוָֹה (v. 9); [3] ' אֱלֹהִים (xliv. 2); ' נְרַנְּנָה (xx. 6); ' גַּם־אֲנִי (lxxi. 22); ' אוֹדְךָ (lxxxvi. 12); ' לַמְדֵנִי (cxliii. 10)[4].

  γ. On the *third* syllable and further, as: ' יִתְיַצְּבוּ (ii. 2); ' מִן־הָעוֹלָם (cvi. 48); ' בְּהִתְהַלֶּכְךָ (Prov. vi. 22).

EXCEPTIONS. The L'garmeh between R'bhîa mugrash and Silluq (p. 67) is always M'huppakh L'garmeh. Hence we have ' מִשָּׁמַיִם (Ps. cii. 20) and ' וְהִתְבּוֹנֵן (Job xxxvii. 14).

SERVUS OF L'GARMEH.

L'garmeh has only *one* servus, which is M'huppakh or Illuy, according to rules, which we are already familiar with (see pp. 62 and 86):

  a. M'huppakh, when the tone is on the *first* syllable, e. g. אֲשֶׁר ' יִתֵּן ' פִּרְיוֹ בְּעִתּוֹ (Ps. i. 3); ' יֵשֶׁת חֹשֶׁךְ ' סִתְרוֹ (xviii. 12); and very often.

EXCEPTIONS. The two parallel passages, כָּל עַצְמוֹתַי ' תֹּאמַרְנָה (xxxv.

6; K. 94, 446; De R. 2, 319, 331, 775, 1261) seek to smooth matters for the Reader by marking in the margin לֹג for L'garmeh, and פס for Paseq. But as ἀκρίβεια is not the forte of Jewish punctators, neither this notation nor the lists they give us are by any means trustworthy. The most correct Paseq-list I have seen is in Bomb. 2 (see p. 96).

[2] ' אַזּוּ (lvi. 10) furnishes a curious instance of the way in which a trifling error perpetuates itself. It is found so pointed in almost all Codd. But B. M. 8, Ox. 96, Cam. 25, K. 434, 525, De R. 350 are right, ' אֵזּוּ.

[3] So Texts and Codd., almost without exception. Yet Baer points always with Azla L'garmeh.

[4] Recognised exceptions are ' לְדָוִד, the first word in certain Pss.,—where Azla L'garmeh stands for Olév'yored, see p. 34 a.

10) and בָּל אֲחֵי־רָשׁ ׀ שְׂנֵאֻהוּ (Prov. xix. 7), in which Mer'kha has
taken the place of Maqqeph[5].

β. M'huppakh also, when the tone is on the *second* syllable and vocal
Sh'va does not precede, e. g. ׀ מִפִּי עוֹלֲלִים (Ps. viii. 3); ׀ יִשְׁלַח מִשָּׁמַיִם
(lvii. 4); and often[6].

In the following cases the punctators found the vocal Sh'va so
slight, that they took no account of it: שִׁמְעָה (xvii. 1; l. 7); מִקְצֵה
(xix. 7); יְרֵאתָ (ib. 10); יְרֵאֵי (xxii. 24); שְׁפָטֵנִי (xliii. 1); וַיִּגְרֶשׁ (lxxviii.
55); בִּפְרֹחַ (xcii. 8); אִמְרוּ (xcvi. 10); לִפְנֵי (ib. 13); שְׁמֵרֵנִי (cxl. 5). It
is not necessary to add any of these cases to the mistakes enumerated
in note 7 below.

γ. Illuy, when the tone is on the second syllable, *vocal Sh'va preceding*,— or when it is on the *third* syllable, e. g. ׀ יָאֹרֵב בַּמִּסְתָּר (x. 9);
צָמְאָה נַפְשִׁי ׀ (xlii. 3); יְצַוֶּה יְהוָה ׀ (ib. 9); נִכְסְפָה וְגַם־כָּלְתָה ׀ (lxxxiv. 3);
and ׀ יִנְמָר־נָא רַע (vii. 10); ׀ וַיַּרְעֵם בַּשָּׁמַיִם (xviii. 14). The exx. are far
too numerous to quote in full[7].

EXCEPTIONS. יְרַדֹּף (vii. 6) and שִׁמְעָה (xxxix. 13),—an anomalous
accentuation joined to an anomalous *vocalization!* (comp. similar
cases before R'bhîa, p. 79. 17.) No doubt מְמֵתִים (xvii. 14) would
have been accented regularly, but that another מְמֵתִים immediately
follows, and the fancy was to *distinguish* one from the other by their
accents! We have had a parallel instance, p. 82, note 8[8].

δ. M'huppakh with Ṣinnôrîth, when an open syllable directly pre-

---

[5] Fixed by the *Masora magna* to Ps. xxxv. 10. L'garmeh is often followed immediately by another pausal accent, but these are the only instances, in which כֹּל
precedes. And it really seems as if, on this account, they were made to pair off,
attention being drawn to them by an anomalous accentuation! It is impossible to
hold the original accentuators responsible for such trifling.

[6] So Codd. point rightly ׀ יְהִיוּ לְרָצוֹן (xix. 15), the Sh'va not being pronounced.
(See Baer, *Die Metheg-setzung*, in Merx's Archiv, vol. i, p. 65.)

[7] The mistakes of common edd.—in xxxii. 6; lv. 24; lxv. 14; lxxix. 13; xciii. 3;
cvi. 1 (and elsewhere); cxli. 5; cxlvii. 8; Prov. xxvii. 22; Job x. 17—have been
corrected by Heid. and Baer, with more or less support from Codd. וְאִם־בָּא
(Ps. xli. 7) must be also corrected with Erf. 3 (other Codd. have *Munach inf.*)
But for בְּקֹרֵב (xxvii. 2); כַּאֲשֶׁר (xlviii. 9); וַאֲנִי (lxix. 14); בְּרֵדוּ (ciii. 22, comp. פָּעֳרוּ
Job xvi. 10); and לַעֲשׂוֹת (cxlix. 9), the testimony of Codd. fails altogether. In fact,
the punctators never rightly apprehended the rules for the servus of L'garmeh.
Ben-Bil. does not venture to give them. Simson (Br. Mus. Or. 1016, p. 76[b]) con-
fesses the general ignorance: ולא נתברר לנו טעם משרתיו למה זה ככה ולמה
זה ככה. Only Samuel the grammarian (Berl. 118, p. 126) makes a feeble attempt
to supply the deficiency. No wonder then that Codd. are full of blunders.

[8] On the still more extraordinary pointing with Ṭarcha, cxxv. 3, see p. 73.

cedes the tone, e. g. ׳ קוּמָה יְהֹוָה (iii. 8); ׳ בְּתוֹבְׇחֹת עַל־עָוֹן (xxxix. 12); ׳ וַיִּרְדּוּ בָם יְשָׁרִים (xlix. 15); and very often[9].

The servus may appear in the *same word* with L'garmeh, instead of Métheg, e. g. ׳ וְלָרָשָׁע (l. 16); ׳ וַיֵּירָאוּ (lxv. 9); ׳ מַה־תִּשְׁתּוֹחֲחִי (xlii. 6). The cases are not, however, numerous in which the change can take place; and in several of these it is lacking in Codd. The one pointing was simply more musical than the other.

In only two passages has L'garmeh more than *one* servus: כִּי נָבֵר עָלֵינוּ ׳ חַסְדּוֹ (cxvii. 2); כִּי רָדַף אוֹיֵב ׳ נַפְשִׁי ׳ (cxliii. 3); where Mer'kha has taken the place of Maqqeph (comp. כָּל above). These passages are fixed by the Masora to cxliii. 3; see p. 63, note 23.

CHAPTER XV.

SHALSHÉLETH.

I. ALL that it is necessary to say about Great Shalshéleth has been already given, pp. 67, 68. Its presence in the latter half of the verse was there accounted for. It is distinguished from Little Shalshéleth by the Paseq-sign attached to it, which constitutes it a disjunctive accent[1].

II. But what reason led to the introduction of Little Shalshéleth, as a conjunctive accent, we can only conjecture. It occurs eight times[2]; once before Silluq—virtually before Athnach (transformed) —(p. 72); four times before Athnach (p. 63); and three times

---

[9] It is only very rarely that this accentuation is adopted, when vocal Sh'va intervenes, as יֶאֱרֹב (Ps. x. 9) in B. M. 1, Ox. 6, Par. 3; תֶּאֱרָךְ (xxiii. 5) in B. M. 1, Par. 3, De R. 1261; פֶּאֱרֵנִי (Job xvi. 10) in B. M. 1, K. 446, De R. 1261.

One strange mistake occurs in common edd. הֶתָעִיף for הֲתָעִיף (Prov. xxiii. 5).

[1] Common edd. are, however, quite indifferent to this distinction, see Ps. x. 2; xiii. 2, 3; lxv. 2; lxviii. 15; &c.

[2] These eight passages are fixed by Ben-Bil. (3. 2), the Erf. Mas. (MS.), and the *Masora parva* to Ox. 96 (פסקן דלא שלשלן ח׳). Seven of them are found in the *first half* of the verse; and it has sometimes seemed to me that they were intended as a kind of counterpart to the seven Shalshéleths that appear in the *first half* of the verse in the prose Books. The 8th ex., which comes in the *latter half* of the verse (Ps. iii. 3), would then stand *per se*.

before R'bhîa mugrash — where again Athnach has been transformed — (p. 77)[3]. In Ps. xxxiv. 8 and cxxxvii. 9 it interferes
with the introduction of the dichotomy, and perhaps this circumstance marks it as of *later date* than the other accents. The
later date is, as it seems to me, further indicated by the absence of
a list of the passages in which it occurs from the *Masora magna.*

It is unnecessary to say anything about its servi, as it occurs so
seldom. The servi of Great Shalshéleth, in the few instances in which
it has them, — Ps. xlii. 2 (see p. 72), lxxxix. 2; Job xxxii. 6, xxxvii.
12, — are the same as those of R'bhîa mugrash, for which it stands.

CHAPTER XVI.

Paseq.

The form of Paseq is a short perpendicular line between two
words. (In Codd. it is just like Métheg and Silluq.) The name
פְּסֵק, 'cutting off,' i. e. separating, the one word from the other, —
used e. g. by Ben-Asher and Ben-Bil'am, — is more suitable than
that commonly employed, פָּסִיק, ' cut off,' separated.

Placed after Shalshéleth, Azla, and M'huppakh, it transforms
them into disjunctive accents, with new and distinctive melodies.

It might have been well perhaps (I speak, of course, only of
the three Books) if it had been confined to this use. There was
no necessity for employing it elsewhere; and much confusion
would have been avoided.

But the accentuators thought otherwise, and they have introduced it into some 57 other passages, for reasons that are not
always clear and have not, as yet, been satisfactorily explained[1].
In these passages Paseq marks a slight pause between two words

---

[3] Little Shalshéleth then *precedes* Athnach (proper or transformed), whereas Great
Shalshéleth always *follows* it.

[1] Ben-Asher's rules (Dikd. hat. § 28) do not meet all the cases that occur; and
Norzi, who explains where all is clear, passes over, *sicco pede*, most of the passages
in which there is any difficulty.

that would, without it, be joined by the accents[2]. Properly speaking, therefore, it changes every conjunctive accent, with which it is associated, into a disjunctive. But as it has no modulation of its own, it is not counted among the accents.

The most correct (printed) list of the Paseqs is that given in the 2nd ed. of Bomberg's Rabbinical Bible (*Mas. fin.* letter 'פ), and copied thence into Buxtorf's Rabbinical Bible (ditto, p. 61).

This list I have been able to compare with four MS. lists, found in the following Codd., B. M. 1, 15; Pet.; and K. 542. B. M. 1 and Pet. are two of the *oldest*, B. M. 15 and K. 542 two of the *youngest*, MSS. Together, therefore, they may be taken to cover the whole ground. And as they nearly agree, it is possible to ascertain with approximate accuracy what the Paseqs were, which the early Masoretes appointed. After careful comparison, the only change I find it necessary to propose in the Bomb. list (which is identical with B. M. 15[3]) is the omission of Ps. lix. 6, lxviii. 36,—which do not appear in the two older Codd.,—and lxxxiv. 4, which appears only in B. M. 15. (Ps. lix. 6 is pointed with L'garmeh in many Codd., as B. M. 2, 11, 13, Ox. 6, 15, 71; lxviii. 36 is evidently false; and for lxxxiv. 4 Paseq fails in Codd. generally.)[4] Having deducted these three, I give the other examples under the heads that follow.

Various reasons led to the introduction of Paseq.

I. Most frequent in the three Books, is the use of what we may call *Paseq euphemisticum*, which occurs before or after the Divine Name, to prevent its being joined, in the reading, to a

---

[2] Of course, it is not needed after a *pausal* accent (comp. e. g. Ps. xviii. 50 with 2 Sam. xxii. 50, or Job xx. 29 with xxvii. 13), although common edd. often place it there, as in Ps. v. 13; x. 14; lv. 20; lxxvi. 1; ciii. 20; &c. Even Olshausen, § 43, has been misled by this false pointing. But common edd., like many Codd., go all wrong in the matter of Paseq, placing it where it should not occur, and omitting it — e.g. in v. 2, 5; xviii. 50; lxvi. 18; lxxxv. 9 — where it should occur. As Paseq marks a pause, it is followed by *Dagesh lene*, in בְּנִי ׀ אִם־תִּקַּח (Prov. vi. 3).

[3] This identity led me to suspect that the Bomb. list was derived from this very Cod. And on examination I found that the Cod. *came from Venice*, where the Bomberg press was established. It is the one briefly described by Kennicott, No. 572. When one takes into account the rarity of the Paseq-lists in MSS., the circumstantial evidence may suffice, I think, to establish my point.

[4] Baer's additions of xxii. 2, xxxvi. 7, xxxvii. 7, l. 1, lv. 20, lxix. 34, lxxxvi. 1, cxviii. 27, Job vii. 20 are not found in any of the lists, and must therefore be rejected. Unfortunately, the list printed in Ginsburg's Masora, vol. i, p. 650, is of no value.

word, which—in the opinion of the accentuators—it was not seemly, מִשּׁוּם כְּבוֹד הַשֵּׁם, to bring into contact with it, e. g. נָאֵץ רָשָׁע ׀ אֱלֹהִים (x. 13); מְשַׂנְאֶיךָ יְהֹוָה ׀ אֶשְׂנָא (cxxxix. 21).

Thus it was counted unbecoming to speak of 'the heathen' (xviii. 50; lvii. 10; lxvi. 8; lxvii. 4, 6; cviii. 4; cxiii. 4); of 'the wicked' (xciv. 3; cxxxix. 19; Job xxvii. 13); of 'God's enemies' (Ps. lxxxix. 52) or 'the Psalmist's enemies' (lix. 2; cxliii. 9), who were one and the same; of 'other gods' (lxxxvi. 8), or 'a plurality,' רַבִּים (cxix. 156),—in the same breath with the Divine Name. (In one instance, v. 5, the personal pronoun takes the place of the Divine Name.) So also verbs signifying 'to abominate' (v. 7), 'to despise' (x. 3), 'to destroy, overthrow' (lviii. 7, Prov. xv. 25), 'to abuse' (Ps. lxxiv. 18), 'to reject' (lxxvii. 8),—even when the Divine Being Himself is the subject,—are separated by a pause from the Divine Name following. The verb 'to sleep' (xliv. 24) and the adj. 'sleeping' (lxxviii. 65),— as conveying a strongly anthropomorphic idea,—are treated in the same way. For the fanciful reasons that commended themselves to the punctators for the employment of Paseq in lxxxix. 9, 50, cxix. 52, I must refer to Norzi's notes.

Paseq is otherwise very loosely employed. Thus we have,

II. *Paseq euphonicum*, introduced in a few cases, to insure distinct pronunciation, when one word ends, and the next begins, with the *same letter*, הָאֵל ׀ לָנוּ כָּאֵל ׀ לָךְ (lxviii. 21); (Job xl. 9); לְדַבֵּר ׀ רָע (Ps. cxli. 4); אֹהֲבַי ׀ יֵשׁ (Prov. viii. 21). But this rule is more frequently neglected than observed, see exx. in Ps. xxx. 12; xxxvii. 7, 24; xlix. 15; lxiv. 6; cvii. 35; Job xxi. 17; &c.[5]

III. *Paseq emphaticum.* Such, in my opinion, is the explanation of its use in אִמְרַי הַאֲזִינָה ׀ יְהֹוָה הוֹשִׁיעַ ׀ יְהֹוָה (Ps. v. 2); מְשִׁיחוֹ (xx. 7); [6] לֹא יִשְׁמַע ׀ אֲדֹנָי (lxvi. 18; cxvi. 1; comp. Job xxvii. 9; xxxv. 13); הָאֵל ׀ יְהֹוָה (lxxxv. 9); עַד־מָתַי ׀ פְּתָיִם (Prov. i. 22); עַד־מָתַי עָצֵל ׀ תִּשְׁכָּב (vi. 9). We have seen, again

---

[5] In Job xxxviii. 1, xl. 6, Paseq comes, for distinctness of reading, to mark the Q'rî. Comp. Neh. ii. 13.

[6] Delitzsch (see his note on cxvi. 1) explains these two cases thus: 'Das Paseq hinter יִשְׁמַע will die Verflösung des Auslauts a‘ mit dem Anlaut ’a von אדני verhüten;' but he says nothing of the numberless instances in which his rule fails, e. g. i. 6; vi. 9, 10; xxvii. 7; lxxviii. 21; cx. 4; &c.

and again, that the punctators claim the liberty of marking the emphasis wherever they please. And in most of the above cases they could only do so by the employment of Paseq. In the others, they had the choice of Paseq or L'garmeh.

Perhaps under this head we may place the instances in which Paseq marks the *repetition* of a word, viz. יוֹם ' יוֹם (Ps. lxi. 9; lxviii. 20; Prov. viii. 30, 34); עָרוּ ' עָרוּ (Ps. cxxxvii. 7); הֲבַ ' הַב (Prov. xxx. 15); הֶאָח ' הֶאָח (Ps. xxxv. 21; xl. 16; lxx. 4); אָמֵן ' וְאָמֵן (xli. 14; lxxii. 19; lxxxix. 53). But this rule is not carried out in xxii. 2; lxviii. 13; Prov. xx. 14.

IV. I believe that in only one passage, Prov. vi. 3, is Paseq used simply to mark the *dichotomy*, see p. 88. In the prose accentuation it seems not unfrequently so employed. Comp., for instance, Gen. i. 27; ii. 21; xviii. 15; xxi. 14; xxvi. 28.

CHAPTER XVII.

TRANSFORMATION.

I BRING together in this chapter the various instances of transformation to which I have already drawn attention in the chapters preceding, as some additional remarks are necessary.

Transformation is, as we have seen, of two kinds, that of a disjunctive into a conjunctive accent; and that of one disjunctive into another. It is always due to *musical* considerations alone. Its advantage, in the most important instances of its occurrence, was, that it gave *variety to the melody*, and did away with much of the stiffness and sameness, that characterises the prose accentuation.

I. Of the class first named above are—

1. The transformation of R'bhîa mugrash, when it falls on the word immediately preceding Silluq. For, that R'bhîa mugrash may occupy this position, Silluq's word must have *two or more* syllables before the tone, e. g. וְגִילוּ בִּרְעָדָה׃ (Ps. ii. 11),

הוֹדְךָ֣ עַל־הַשָּׁמָֽיִם׃ (viii. 2); or, if but *one* syllable, that syllable must have a long vowel[1], followed by vocal Sh'va, e. g.
בַּל־תַּנִּיחֵ֣נִי לְעָשְׁקָ֑י׃ (ci. 6); ה֤וּא יְשָׁרְתֵֽנִי׃ (cxix. 121). If these
conditions are not fulfilled, a servus takes the place of R'bhia
mugrash. Comp. וּמַלְאַ֤ךְ יְהֹוָ֣ה רֹדֵֽפָם׃ (xxxv. 6) with וּמַלְאָ֣ךְ
וְתוֹרָֽתְךָ֣ (ib. 5); וְתוֹרָֽתְךָ֣ שַׁעֲשֻׁעָ֑י׃ (cxix. 174) with יְהֹוָ֣ה דְּחָֽה׃
(ib. 142); and וּבְפִ֣י רְשָׁעִ֣ים תֵּהָרֵֽס׃ (Prov. xi. 11) with אֱמֶ֑ת׃
וּבַאֲבֹ֥ד רְשָׁעִ֣ים רִנָּֽה׃ (ib. 10). The *sense* may very clearly
require a disjunctive accent, as in שֶׁ֣קֶר רְדָפ֑וּנִי עָזְרֵֽנִי׃ (Ps.
cxix. 86), but the melody does not allow it.

Exceptions to the rule are the verses in Job, which introduce the
speeches, e. g. וַיַּ֥עַן אֱלִיפַ֖ז הַתֵּֽימָנִ֣י וַיֹּאמַֽר׃ (iv. 1); וַיַּ֥עַן אִיּ֖וֹב וַיֹּאמַֽר׃ (iii. 2);
and וַיֹּ֣סֶף אִיּ֗וֹב שְׂאֵ֥ת מְשָׁל֣וֹ וַיֹּאמַֽר׃ (xxvii. 1). But these are prose passages, which do not concern us.

In ordinary texts the rule is not always carried out,—see Ps. xix.
10; xxxiv. 3; xxxv. 15,—but such cases, not many in number, are
corrected in Codd. and better edd.[2]

2. The transformation of D'chî in the word immediately before
Athnach, which is subject to precisely the same conditions as
that of R'bhia mugrash before Silluq. Thus it is required in
יִסֹּ֤גוּ אָח֣וֹר וְיִבָּלְמ֑וּ (Ps. xxxv. 4), but not in יִסֹּ֙גוּ֙ אָח֣וֹר וְיַחְפְּר֖וּ
יְהַלֵּֽלוּ׃ (xl. 15); in יִרְא֣וּ אֶת־יְהֹוָ֣ה קְדֹשָׁ֑יו (xxxiv. 10), but not in
יְהֹוָ֣ה דִּרְשָׁ֑יו (xxii. 27); in חֵֽלֶק־אָדָ֣ם רָשָׁ֤ע ׀ עִם־אֵ֗ל (Job xxvii.
13), but not in חֵ֤לֶק־אָדָ֣ם רָשָׁ֥ע מֵאֱלֹהִ֑ים (xx. 29). As before,
the transformation often interferes with the *logical* division of
the clause, e. g. in הֲלֹא־מְעַ֣ט יָמַ֣י יַחְדָּ֑ל (Job x. 20)[3].

---

[1] In practice this long vowel is Qámeṣ or Chôlem. Of Ṣere (for this rule and
those following) I have found only two exx., Ps. lxix. 24ᵃ and Job xxxiii. 12ᵇ; of
Shûreq and long Chîreq I have not noticed a single example.

[2] On the other hand, transformation is sometimes introduced, where it is not
required, e. g. עַ֤ם לֹֽא־יָדַ֥עְתִּי יַֽעַבְד֥וּנִי׃ (xviii. 44), as though the last word had been
pointed יַֽעַבְד֑וּנִי. Similar instances occur in xxvii. 10; cxix. 175; Prov. xxix. 4;
Job vi. 4; xxx. 18.

[3] It is interesting to compare (as far as they admit of comparison) the passages
in Ps. xviii, in which transformation has taken place according to rules 1 and 2,
with the prose accentuation of 2 Sam. xxii. Here we find, *in every instance, the*

The few mistakes in common edd. have been mostly corrected by
Baer, but in Prov. xxvii. 22, if we retain D'chî, we must point
בְּתוֹךְ הָרִפוֹת בַּעֲלִי, with Erf. 1, 2; K. 198, 599, 606; Sonc.—Erf. 1 has
in margin to בָּעֲלִי, ל וכן נקוד.

3. The *transformatio perpetua* in the word before Silluq, when
Great Shalshéleth precedes, see p. 67.

4. The *transformatio perpetua*, when L'garmeh is due in the
word immediately preceding D'chî, see p. 83.

5. The *transformatio perpetua*, when R'bhîa mugrash's clause
consists of three words, Athnach preceding, see p. 74.

6. The transformation in monosyllables, and other small words
with the tone on the first syllable, coming in the second place
before D'chî, Pazer, and Little R'bhîa. See the chapters on
those accents.

II. To the second kind of transformation belongs—

1. That of Athnach into R'bhîa mugrash, which must always
take place, when Athnach would come on the word *immediately
preceding* Silluq, see p. 66[4].

2. The same change in the *second* word before Silluq, when
R'bhîa mugrash has been transformed in the first word, and that
word—like Silluq's word—has not two syllables before the tone,
nor one syllable with a long vowel and vocal Sh'va. Thus Athnach
will stand in such cases as : יוֹשֵׁב בַּשָּׁמַיִם יִשְׂחָק אֲדֹנָי יִלְעַג־לָמוֹ
(ii. 4); דֶּרֶךְ־אֱמוּנָה בָחָרְתִּי מִשְׁפָּטֶיךָ שִׁוִּיתִי: (cxix. 30);
יְהוָה בְּאַפּוֹ: מִשְׁפְּטֵי־יְהוָה אֱמֶת צָדְקוּ יַחְדָּו: (xix. 10);
יְבַלְעֵם וַתֹּאכְלֵם אֵשׁ: (xxi. 10). But it must be transformed
in עוּרָה הַנֵּבֶל (lv. 22); רַכּוּ דְבָרָיו מִשֶּׁמֶן וְהֵמָּה פְתִחוֹת:
וְכִנּוֹר אָעִירָה שָּׁחַר: (lvii. 9)[5].

---

disjunctive accent (Ṭiphcha) introduced,—a further proof of the reality of our rules.
See *vv.* 5[b], 6[a], 23[a], 33[b], 36[b], 41[a], &c.

[4] Here a double transformation may take place,—but is very rare,—that of
Athnach into R'bhîa mugrash, and then of R'bhîa mugrash into a servus. See
p. 69, note 8, and p. 33 (3).

[5] The short *vv.* of Ps. cxix furnish many exx. of this transformation, e. g. 2, 4, 5,
12, 14, 17, 24. In *vv.* 3, 6, 8, 9, 10, 13, &c., on the other hand, Athnach remains
unchanged.

Common edd. have, of course, their mistakes, which however all yield to the collation of Codd., save Prov. iv. 6 (where I have found De R. 874 alone right) and Job xxxix. 12 (where all Codd. are wrong). These may be regarded as the exceptions that prove the rule. Even Baer's text is wrong in Ps. v. 2 (where we must point יְהֹוָה בִּינָה הֲגִיגִי׃, with Codd., see Norzi's note בס״ם בטעם מיושב בשם) and cxix. 165 (where common edd. are right).

3. The transformation of R'bhîa mugrash into Great Shalshéleth, as explained p. 67.

4. The transformation of Great R'bhîa—when it would come in close proximity to Little R'bhîa—into Ṣinnor, see p. 56 below.

Such are the laws of transformation. Perhaps some of my readers may think that no little confusion must be the result of their application, and that it will be often difficult to trace the true logical (or syntactical) division, underlying this purely musical accentuation. But, in reality, there need be no confusion or difficulty at all. The main point to bear in mind is that, wherever two or more servi precede Athnach or Silluq, a pause is due from the dichotomy, and *should be made in the reading, on the last servus.* Cases I. 1–3 are thus disposed of.—In a few instances under I. 4, it will be necessary to allow for the transformation which has taken place in the word immediately preceding D'chî (proper or transformed). Prov. xxi. 8, as explained p. 85, note 6, is an example in point.—Under I. 5 and 6, I have not noticed a single instance in which the sense is in the slightest degree obscured by the transformation. And as for II. 1–4, no confusion or difficulty is possible, for we have merely a *change* in the disjunctive accent. The logical (or syntactical) division remains as clearly marked as if no transformation had taken place.

For the discovery of these remarkable laws of transformation we are mainly indebted to Christian accentuologists of the seventeenth century. They are almost all found in Wasmuth's *Institutio methodica accentuationis Hebrææ* (Rostock, 1664). Rabbinical writers on the accents had not the slightest idea of them.

APPENDIX

CONTAINING THE ORIGINAL ARABIC OF THE TREATISE, ASSIGNED TO
R. JEHUDA BEN-BIL'AM, ON THE ACCENTS OF THE THREE BOOKS.

Two years ago, Dr. Bytschkow, Vice-director of the Imperial Library
at St. Petersburg, was good enough to send me a MS., containing
a portion of the following text[1]. And last year, when I visited
St. Petersburg, Dr. Harkavy, Sub-librarian of the Imperial Library,
handed me a bundle of fragments of MSS. (on Hebrew grammar, &c.),
—which had been collected by Firkowitsch in various parts of the
East,—and left me to see if I could find anything for my purpose
among them. After no little trouble, I succeeded in arranging the
disjecta membra, so as to produce portions of three several copies of
the text. Fortunately, the fragments supplement one another, so that
the Treatise is now submitted *complete* to scholars. The four MSS. I
name A, B, C, and D. The first is decidedly the oldest, and D perhaps
older than B and C, which have epigraphs assigning them to the years
1337 and 1339 respectively. All four are written on paper (small
size) and in Rabbinical characters[2].

That the Hebrew text, often quoted in the previous pages, is a
translation from the Arabic, has been long known to scholars from
the superscriptions to the Ox. and Vat. MSS.[3] But up to the present
time the original Arabic was not known to be in existence. That the
following text supplies it will be clear to any one who will take the

---

[1] I am indebted to Dr. Neubauer for having drawn my attention to this MS., and
to the Marquis of Salisbury, then Secretary of State for Foreign Affairs, for having
condescended to use his influence to procure me the loan of it.

[2] They all come under the same No. 634 of the second Firkowitsch Collection.
I noticed only one MS., B, to contain a part of the treatise on the accentuation of
the twenty-one Books.

[3] The Ox. MS. is No. 1465 in the Bodleian Catal., and belonged formerly to Oppen-
heim. The Vat. MS. is No. 402 in Assemani's Catal. The superscription in these
MSS. is as follows: זה ספר הורית [.Vat הוריית] הקורא אשר הובא מירושלים לבאר
[.Vat נבאר] בדרך קצרה והביאו יוסף בן חייא הסופר משם מתורגם בלשון ערבי
כאשר העתיקו לשם וلّ נתנאל בّ משלם [.Vat ר' משלם בن נתנאל] הפכו מלשון
ערבי ללשון הקודש בעיר מיינצא. (Having collated the Vat. MS. I am able to state
that Assemani's transcript of these words is far from correct.) For לבאר בדרך קצרה
I propose to read נשלם בדרך קצרה (the mistakes in the Heb. text are often
perfectly astounding, see p. 103, note 1), 'complete in a compendious form,' answering
to the words at the close of the Vat. MS.: תם ספר הוריית הקורא ונשלם בדרך קצרה.
The statement מתורגם בלשון ערבי, '*translated* in the Arabic tongue,' may be set
down as a *conjecture* on the part of the writer, like many other unfounded conjectures, that have been since made, on the subject of the Work. The city מיינצא is
no doubt Mainz. It may be mentioned that our treatise forms the last part of this
compendium of הורית הקורא. It is preceded by rules for the נקודים (Dagesh, the
vowels, and Sh'va), and for the accentuation of the twenty-one Books.

trouble of comparing it with the Hebrew. Its publication is not without importance, as it enables us to correct the serious mistakes which so often interfere with the sense in the Hebrew translation[4].

That this treatise is abridged from a larger Work is stated in the epigraphs to B and C, which both begin תם אלמכתצר, 'the *Compendium* is finished.' The name also of this larger Work is given (see p. 110, l. 19),[5] הדראיה אלקאר, i. e. هِدَايَة اَلْقَارِ, 'Direction for the Reader.' We thus recover the long-lost original title, of which הוֹרָיַת הַקּוֹרֵא (see note 3) is the translation. But I have a still more interesting announcement to make, and that is that a portion of the larger Work itself has been at length discovered. M. Shapira of Jerusalem acquired, during a recent visit to Yemen, a MS. on the טעמי אמ״ת, from which he kindly sent me some extracts, and which he has just brought to England and disposed of to the British Museum. I have delayed putting the finishing stroke to my Work, that I might examine this MS. The result of my examination has been to satisfy me that it contains a part of הדראיה אלקאר, in the original Arabic. The reasons for my conclusion are the following: First, the general plan and arrangement is the same as in the Compendium. Secondly, as was bound to be the case, the subject is treated more fully and completely. Thirdly, the examples, even the false ones (e. g. p. 110, note 30), given in the Compendium are almost all (100 out of 105) found in the larger Work. Fourthly, in p. 110, l. 19, we read: 'Thou wilt find in הדראיה אלקאר a *sixth* reason,' i. e. for Mer'kha before Athnach; and on turning to the larger Work we find this additional reason given[6]. Against these grounds for the identification, there is only one point to be mentioned, that two of the *servi* (כדאם) have different names; נלגל is called שופר מקלוב,—תלשה צנירה (M'huppakh) שופר מקלוב and תלשה כבירה being the name given to the upper sign of Olév'yored[7]. We may suppose that the author himself, when he prepared the Compendium[8] (perhaps after an interval of some years), changed these names into others, which he found more generally in use.

---

[4] I have before me a long list of these mistakes. The following may serve, by way of specimen : p. 3, l. 18, סוף for ראש ; p. 4, l. 12, שבסוף for שבפסוק ; p. 6, l. 18, עלוי for עליו , אז for או , and מנוע for מניע ; ib., l. 29, דלת for ריש ; p. 7, l. 15, ימצא for ויצא ; ib., l. 26, מאיילא for דיבור ; p. 8, l. 24, הם for ח׳ ; p. 9, l. 22, שלא omitted.

[5] This form is used all through the text for קארי , قَارِئ.

[6] It refers to cases that do not come under the previous heads, and is thus expressed : אלא ליס בין אלאתנחה ובין מרקבהא לא נגמה ולא שוא פאנהא איצא במארכה כקו׳ ומפֵּז רָב (Ps. xix. 11) אַף־לֶךְ לֵילָה (lxxiv. 16) לעשות רָע (Prov. ii. 14) ואמתאל דאלך.

[7] We now understand Chayyug's list (Nutt's ed., p. 129, l. 3), which has hitherto baffled all attempts at explanation. The list at the end of Ox. 125 (Hunt 511) is similar. My own note p. 20 must be cancelled.

[8] That both Works were written by the same author, we learn from a statement in the first section of the prose accents : וככבר זכרתי בס׳ הורית הקורא וכו .

The MS. is not complete. The part of the Compendium to which it corresponds is from p. 108, l. 9 to p. 115, l. 3, and again p. 117, ll. 6–15. It is clearly written in Yemenite characters, on paper (? fifteenth century). The following pages were already in type when I examined it. But, had I seen it earlier, I should not have decided to print it in preference. The author's later Work is the better of the two. It is better arranged and more clearly expressed; and, as it is complete, is in every way more fitted to give the student an idea of the rules that commended themselves to Rabbinical scholars in the Middle Ages. I have given one extract from the larger Work, and that may suffice. Indeed, I have found nothing else of sufficient importance to copy[9].

As to the *authorship* of our treatise, it is assigned in A (see p. 108, note 15) to Sa'îd 'Alî,—a name otherwise (I believe) unknown. An isolated notice of this kind—although occurring in what is probably the oldest MS.—cannot, however, be taken to settle the question. On the other hand, modern authorities agree in regarding Ben-Bil'am as the author; but, as it seems to me, on quite insufficient grounds.

The *only* authority for attributing the Work to him has been the title prefixed to the Paris MS. (1221), ספר טעמי המקרא המתייחס לר׳ יהודה בן בלעם ספרדי נע[10]. On the ground of this title, Mercerus, when he published the text from the Paris MS., announced Ben-Bil'am as the author, and scholars since have, one and all, accepted his statement. Yet what is the value of this title? The very name, כ׳ טעמי המקרא, with which it begins, betrays its later origin[11]. There is nothing answering to this name in the original Arabic, or in the superscription to the translation made from the Arabic (see note 3). The 'assignment' of the Work to Ben-Bil'am has, in the same way, no support from the earlier texts. Nor can testimony be cited in its favour from any other source. Not a single one of those who borrow from the Work or quote it,—as Hadassi, Simson, Jequtiel,—associates Ben-Bil'am's name with it. And no other Rabbinical author can be named who makes mention of it, as written by him[12]. Indeed, so far from a

---

[9] Should any of my readers be curious to see what is preserved of the הראיה אלקאר proper, their curiosity will soon be gratified, for Dr. Ginsburg purposes printing it in the Appendix to the 2nd volume of his ed. of the Masora, which will appear shortly.

[10] The De R. MS. (488) has the same title; but these two MSS. agree so exactly, *verbatim et literatim*, that their testimony can only be counted as that of one MS. Either the one was copied from the other, or both must have been copied from the same MS.

[11] The name is also a *misnomer*, for the greater part of the Work is *not* taken up with the טעמים, but with the נקודים.

[12] Dr. Steinschneider has suggested (*Catal. libr. hebr. bibl. Bodl.* col. 1295) that our Work, הורית הקורא, 'Direction for the Reader,' is identical with Ben-Bil'am's כתאב אלארשאד, 'Book of *Direction*,' described by Moses ben-Ezra. (Perhaps the same idea may have led, in the Middle Ages, to the 'assigning' of it to him.) But now that we have the Arabic title of our Work we know that there is nothing in the suggestion. Were it necessary, it might be shewn that the two Works differed in *contents* as well.

Western writer, like Ben-Bilʻam (who belonged to Toledo, in Spain), having been the author, the evidence, both external and internal, points to an *Eastern origin* of the Work. (*a*) The known MSS. can be traced directly or indirectly to the East[13]; and now too a part of the original הדראיה אלקאר has been brought from a remote corner of the East. (*β*) The Work was known and used in the East—as by Hadassi in אשכל 'ס, p. 61 (A.D. 1148)—long before any Western writer made use of it[14]. (*γ*) The acquaintance the author shews with the *melody* of the three Books may suit an Eastern (see p. 2, note 7), but is irreconcilable with a Western, origin. Lastly, the rules about המזה (p. 112) could not have been drawn up from Western MSS., for Western punctators do not employ this sign. (The old Cod. Erf. 3 which has this sign is doubtless of Eastern origin[15].)

If, on these grounds, we reject the authorship of Ben-Bilʻam[16], we have no *data* for fixing the age of our treatise. We know only that it is older than Hadassi (early part of twelfth century).

In the following text, the words in brackets have been added and a few obvious faults have been corrected. I am also responsible for the interpunction, and for the vocalization and accentuation of the examples cited. Otherwise I have printed the text as I found it. The few grammatical irregularities and orthographical inconsistencies will not cause the reader any trouble. Of course he will be prepared to meet with modern Arabic forms.

---

[13] Eight MSS. are known. Four of these were brought by Firkowitsch from the East. Two, Ox. 1465 and Vat. 402, carry on their forefront (see note 3) that they are derived from an Eastern MS. The remaining two, Par. 1221 and De R. 488, are undoubtedly copies of this same translation. I have collated them carefully (as far as our treatise is concerned), and find that they have *common mistakes with Ox. and Vat., not found in the Arabic*, whilst the variations admit of ready explanation.

[14] The first Western writers (as far as it is at present known) to make use of it were the Naqdanîm, Simson, Moses, and Jequtiel, all of whom belong to the following century, and are a hundred years (more or less) later than Hadassi.

[15] Comp. Baer's statement, made on other grounds, in the pref. to his ed. of the Minor Prophets, p. vii : *Cod. Erf. 3 sine dubitatione ab homine Orientali scriptus est.*

[16] That I have always cited the treatise as by Ben-Bilʻam was unavoidable. I had to adopt a name, and could of course only employ that by which it is generally known.

אלכלאם פי אלחאן אלתלתה אספאר
תהלות ואיוב ומשלי.

אעלם אן הדה אלתלתה אספאר מתגﹼירה מן אלואחד ועשרין ספר בתלתה
וגוה. אלואחד נפס כתאבתהא ונטﹼר תסטירהא פי תורﹼיק אלצחף פאן דלך
תשריג אלכתאב בתרך בעﹾ אלאסטר כאליה עלי בניה אלשירה פי אלכתאבה׳
ואלתאני אן פואסיקהא צגאר׳ ואלתאלת גﹼיר אלחאנהא[1]:

פצל. אלחאן הדה אלתלתה אספאר תמאניה והי פזר וזרקה ורביע ולגרמיה.
ויתיב וטפחה ואתנחה וסלוק. וכדאמהא שופר רפע וגלגל ושופר מקלוב ושופר
תכסיר ומאילה ומארכה וסלסלה ומקל וצנורית ושוכב ודחויה:

פצל. אעלם אן אלחאן הדה אלתלתה אספאר פיהא מא יגוז תראדפה
ואחד בעד אלאכר ופיהא מא ימתנע פיה אלתראדף׳ פאלדי ימכן פיה
אלתראדף רביע וזרקה ולגרמיה ומא סואהם פממתנע אלתראדף:

פצל פי מואצע אלכדאם. אעלם אן הדה אלתמאניה אלחאן תנקסם פי
תרתיב אלכדאם ארבעה אקסאם. אלאול מא אמכן אן יכן לה כאדמין ולא
אכתר והמא אלזרקה ואלטפחה נחו הָאֵל ׀ לָנוּ[2] ואמתאלה ונחו עֵדוּת יְהֹוָה
נֶאֱמָנָה[3] גﹼיר אן תם ואחד ליס מתלה לה ארבעה כדאם והו בְּיוֹם הִצִּיל־יְהֹוָה
אוֹתוֹ מִכַּף כָּל־אֹיְבָיו[4]. ואלתאני הו מא יכן לה תלתה כדאם ולא אזיד והמא

---

[1] Three points are mentioned in which the three Books differ from the others:
1st, their writing; 2nd, the shortness of their verses; and 3rd, their accents. The
first point of difference is expressed thus: 'Their writing itself, with the observing
of their lineation in the copying (see Dozy) of the pages, and that arrangement of
the writing consists in leaving a part of the lines blank (خالية), according to the
build of the שירה in the writing.' The 'lineation' or ruling named may be seen in
any Cod. (It is the same for the three, as for the twenty-one, Books; hence in the
Heb. we have תיקון שירטוטם כתיקון ספר.) The other directions are taken from
Sopherim, xiii. 1, where פתיחות באתנחייתא ובסוף פסוק (open spaces at Athnach
and at Sôph Pasûq) are enjoined for the three Books, together with the form of the
שירה (as in Ex. xv and Judg. v). But in practice, this calligraphical arrangement is
confined to Ps. xviii, and even for that is rare in Codd.

[2] Ps. lxviii. 21.   [3] xix. 8.   [4] xviii. 1.

אתנאן לגרמיה ופזר נחו כִּי נָבַר עָלֵינוּ ׀ חַסְדּוֹ[1] גַּם כִּי־אֵלֵךְ בְּגֵיא צַלְמָוֶת[2].
ואלתאלת מא אמכן אן יכון לה ארבעה כדאם ולא אזיד והמא אתנאן רביע
ויתיב נחו זָכַרְתִּי מִשְׁפָּטֶיךָ מֵעוֹלָם ׀ יְהֹוָה[3] כִּי יֹסִיף עַל־חַטָּאתוֹ פֶּשַׁע[4]. ואלראבע
מא אמכן אן יכון לה כמסה כדאם ולא אזיד והמא אתנאן אתנחה וסוף פסוק
נחו כִּי אֶת אֲשֶׁר יֶאֱהַב יְהֹוָה יוֹכִיחַ[5] וְאַתָּה נָשָׂאתָ עֲוֹן חַטָּאתִי סֶלָה[6]:

פצל פי שרח עלל אלאלחאן.

אלפזר ‾‾ קד יכון שכלין צורה טית[ט] וצורה צדי[ץ] ואלדי אונב לה צורה
אלטית אלגלגל[7] ומא ערפת פרק בין תנגים אלצורתין פי הדה אלתלתה
אספאר. אלפזר אדא כדמה כאדמין קד יכון אלאול מארכה וקד יכון
שופר מקלוב ואלתאני קד יכון שופר מקלוב וקד יכון גלגל· ואלשרט פי דלך
אנה אן כאן אלאול מע אול חרף מן כלמתה כאן שופר מקלוב ואדא כאן
איצא אלתאני מע אול כלמתה כאן גלגל מתל כִּי כוֹס בְּיַד־יְהֹוָה[8] כִּי לֹא
בְחַרְבָּם[9]. פאן זאל אלכאדם אלאול ען אול חרף צאר במארכה או מקל לאנה
כלף מתל וַיִּשְׂמְחוּ כָל־חֹסֵי בָךְ[10] ואדא זאל איצא אלכאדם אלתאני ען אול
אלכלמה צאר בשופר מקלוב· ואכלאף אלקרא פי הדא אלמוצע כתיר ודאך
אן פיהם מן אדא זאל אלכאדם אלתאני ען אול אלחרף געלה גלגל מתל
וְעַתָּה יָרוּם רֹאשִׁי[11] ופיהם מן יקרא וְעַתָּה יָרוּם רֹאשִׁי ופיהם מן לא ידכל פי
כדמה אלפזר גלגל פי אלתלתה אספאר בתה· פמתי ראית פי אלמצאחף הדה
אלתגיירַאת לא תטן אנהא אנגלאט:

אלורקה ‾‾ אדא כדמהא כאדם ואחד אן כאן מע אול חרף כאן מארכה
מתל אַתָּה ׀ סֵתֶר לִי[12] לֹא הָלָךְ[13] ואן כאן אלכאדם עלי אלחרף אלתאני מן
כלמתה וכאן תחת אלחרף אלאול שוא כאן אלכאדם מארכה איצא מתל

---

[1] Ps. cxvii. 2.   [2] xxiii. 4.   [3] cxix. 52.   [4] Job xxxiv. 37.

[5] Prov. iii. 12.   [6] Ps. xxxii. 5.

[7] In the twenty-one Books the Pazer *with Galgal* is known as גדול‎ פ' or פרה קרני‎ (the form of which is likened to טית‎), and that *without,* as קטן‎ פ' (like final צדי‎). But for the three Books no such distinction is observed in Codd., the sign of קטן‎ פ' being that almost always employed, whether Galgal precedes or not.

[8] lxxv. 9.   [9] xliv. 4.

[10] v. 12. Ben-Asher and Ben-Naphtali differ in the way mentioned, the former pointing וישמחו‎, the latter וישמחו‎.

[11] xxvii. 6.   [12] xxxii. 7.   [13] i. 1.

אַל־תִּהְיוּ ׀ כְּסוּס כְּפֶרֶד֑ ¹ בְּקֶרֶב בֵּיתִי ²• ואן כאן תחת אלחרף אלאול מלך כאן
אלכאדם שופר רפע מתל וַאֲנִי ׀ אָשִׁיר עֻזְּךָ֑ ³ אָהַבְתָּ צֶּדֶק֮ ⁴• ואן צאר אלכאדם
עלי אלחרף אלתאלת ואלראבע ומא זאד כאן אלכאדם שופר רפע מתל
בִּשְׁלוֹם יַחְדָּו֮ ⁵ אֱלֹהִים צְבָאוֹת֒ ⁶ אלא מוצע ואחד והו חֶלְקָם בַּחַיִּים֒ ⁷ פאנה מע
אלתאלת והו במארכה. ואדא כאן אלכאדם מע חרף ולדלך אלחרף דגש פהו
אבדא מארכה שא ⁷ᵃ אן יכון מע אלתאני או מע אלתאלת או מא זאד ען דלך
מתל מִשֶּׁד עֲנִיִּים֮ ⁸ רַבִּים אֹמְרִים֮ ⁹ מא סוי לַמְנַצֵּחַ אַל־תַּשְׁחֵת֮ בשלח שאול ¹⁰
אָנָּה יְהֹוָה֮ ¹¹ כִּי אֲנִי לֹא־תִשָּׂא פְשָׁעִי֒ ¹²• וקאלו אן אדא כאנת אלזורקה פי כלמתין
לא תכון אלאולה במקף בל בכאדם אלא כִּי־יְהֹוָה הוּא־אֱלֹהִים֒ ¹³ יְקַלְלוּ־הֵמָּה֮ ¹⁴•
ואן כאן קד קאלו אן יְקַלְלוּ כלף יְקַלְלוּ הֵמָּה֮• וקד וגדת גיר הדין אלמוצעין ¹⁵:

אלסלסלה. משהור אלסלסלה פי אלתלתה אספאר כונהא קאימה בנפסהא
ולא יכדמהא אבדא כאדם ואחד בל קד יכדמהא כאדמין פי מוצעין והמא
עַל־כֵּן זָחַלְתִּי וָאִירָא ׀ ¹⁶ כָּל אֲשֶׁר יְצֻוֶּם ¹⁷• ומתי כאן קבל אלסלסלה אתנחה
כאנת קאימה בנפסהא אעני תכון לחן מתל וַיִּרְמֹם לָאָרֶץ חַיָּי וּכְבוֹדִי ׀ ¹⁸
תִּשְׁכָּחֵנִי נֶצַח עַד־אָנָה ׀ ¹⁹• ואדא לם יכן קבלהא אתנחה כאנת כאדם מתל
אֵין יְשׁוּעָתָה לּוֹ בֵאלֹהִים סֶלָה ²⁰ והי תמאניה כדאם פי אלתלתה אספאר
יְשׁוּעָתָה ²⁰ דּוּמִיָּה [תְהִלָּה] ²¹ מַלְאַךְ־יְהֹוָה ²² בְּפָרֵשׂ שַׁדַּי ²³ יִשְׂאוּ [הָרִים] ²⁴ שֶׁיֹּאחֵז ²⁵
לִוְיַת חֵן ²⁶ הַיְחִתָּה [אִישׁ] ²⁷• ויגעלו מתל אלפסק עלאמה ללחן מנהא:

אלרביע ²⁸ אדא כדמה כאדם ואחד קד יכון שופר מקלוב וקד יכון מארכה
וקד יכון שופר תכסיר• אלשרט פי הדא אלאבתלאפאת הו אן תנטר אן
כאן בער אלרביע תאבעתה פאלכאדם מארכה מתל אֲנִי שָׁכַבְתִּי וָאִישָׁנָה ²⁹
כָּלָה שְׁאֵרִי וּלְבָבִי ³⁰• וכדלך אן כאן בעדה סוף פסוק כאן איצא אלכאדם
מארכה מתל מִצִּיּוֹן מִכְלַל־יֹפִי אֱלֹהִים הוֹפִיעַ ³¹• וכדלך אן כאן קבלה לגרמיה

---

¹ Ps. xxxii. 9.   ² ci. 7.   ³ lix. 17.   ⁴ xlv. 8.   ⁵ iv. 9.
⁶ lxxx. 15.   ⁷ xvii. 14.   ⁷ᵃ Query סוא 'equally.'   ⁸ xii. 6.   ⁹ iv. 7.
¹⁰ lix. 1.   ¹¹ cxvi. 16.   ¹² Job vii. 21. In B and C this ex. is wanting.
¹³ Ps. c. 3.   ¹⁴ cix. 28.   ¹⁵ A. adds זיאדה ללמעלם סעיד עלי צאחב אלכתאב.
¹⁶ Job xxxii. 6.   ¹⁷ xxxvii. 12.   ¹⁸ Ps. vii. 6.   ¹⁹ xiii. 2.
²⁰ iii. 3.   ²¹ lxv. 2.   ²² xxxiv. 8.   ²³ lxviii. 15.   ²⁴ lxxii. 3.
²⁵ cxxxvii. 9.   ²⁶ Prov. i. 9.   ²⁷ vi. 27.
²⁸ The rules that follow are very defective. Those given in אלקאר הדאיה are fuller
and more complete, but so far from correct, that I have not thought it worth while
to copy them. The Heb. (3. 12 ff.) supplies one omission.
²⁹ Ps. iii. 6.   ³⁰ lxxiii. 26.   ³¹ l. 2. For the R'bhia here, see p. 75, note 3.

כאן אלכאדם איצֿא מארכה ולאנה יכון בעדה תאבעתה מתֿל אַזְכִּיר ׳ רַהַב
וּבָבֶל לְיֹדְעָי ׳. ואלשרט פי ו נוב אלשופר אלמקלוב הו אן אלרביע אדא כאן
הו אול אלפסוק וליס בעדה תאבעתה כאן אלכאדם שופר מקלוב מתֿל
שָׁאַל מִפֶּנִי ² רֶכֶב אֱלֹהִים ³.   אלרביע אדא כדמה כאדמין וכאן בעדה אכר
אפסוק ⁴ כאן אלכאדם אלאול דחויה ואלתאני מארכה מתֿל בְּדֶרֶךְ עֵדְוֹתֶיךָ
שָׂשְׂתִּי ⁵ גְּמֹל עַל־עַבְדְּךָ אֶחְיֶה וְאֶשְׁמְרָה דְבָרֶךְ ⁶ ׳ והדֿא אלנגם לא יכתלף אדא
צאר לה תֿלתֿה כדאם ואנמא יכתלף אלאול מן אלתֿלתֿה כדאם יכון שופר
מקלוב מתֿל כִּי מֶלֶךְ כָּל־הָאָרֶץ אֱלֹהִים ⁷ ׳ וכדֿא אן כדמה ארבעה כדאם מא
אכתלף אלדחויה ואלמארכה ואנמא יכתלפאן אלאולין אלאול ׳ יכון צנורית
ואלתאני שופר [מקלוב] מתֿל זָכַרְתִּי מִשְׁפָּטֶיךָ מֵעוֹלָם ׀ יְהֹוָה ⁸ מא סוי ואחד
תכתלף פיה אלדחויה ואלמארכה והו בְּפָרֶשׂ שַׁדַּי מְלָכִים בָּהּ ⁹ ׳

אללגרמיה.   אללגרמיה הו מן אלאלחאן אלדֿי יתגייר כדאמה פי אלואחד
ועשרין ספרא פקד יכדמה שופר מקלוב מתֿל אֲשֶׁר פָּרִיוֹ ¹⁰ ומארכה יְתְיַצְבוּ ¹¹
ושופר תכסיר וַתִּגְעַשׁ וַתִּרְעַשׁ ¹² וצנורית הַדְרִיכֵנִי בַאֲמִתֶּךָ ¹³. ומא צח ענדי
פיה עלה אדֿכרהא. וכתֿיר ממא יגעל אלנאס אללגרמיה פסק ואלדֿי יפצל בין
אללגרמיה ואלפסק וגהין ׳ אלואחד הו אן בעץֿ אלמצֿאחף אלגיאד תרי מן
ברא ¹⁴ מכתוב קדאם אללגרמיה לגרמיה וקדאם אלפסק פסק וקד יכון דלך
רמז וגד רמז גיר אן ליס גמיע אלמצֿאחף תפעל דלך׳ ואלוגה אלאכר אן
אלפאסקאת פי כל ספר מעדודה פלו כאן כל מא כאן פי אלתֿלתֿה אספאר
הו פסק למא אחתאגו אן יעדוהא קט ואנמא יעדוהא פי כל ספר לתתמיז
מן אללגרמיה לאן שכל אלפסק ואללגרמיה ואחד והו אלעצֿאה אלתֿי בין
אלכלמתין :

אליתיב הו מן אלאלחאן אלדֿי יתגייר שכלה מן שכל אליתיב אלדֿי פי
אלואחד ועשרין ספרא. אליתיב יכון בגיר כאדם ויכון לה כאדם פכאדמה
אלשופר אדא כאן בין אלחרף אלדֿי עליה אליתיב ובין אלחרף אלמתוהם
עליה שופר מלכין ומא זאד והו אלחרף אלאול מן אלכלמה יגב לה אלשופר

---

¹ Ps. lxxxvii. 4.   ² ii. 8.   ³ lxviii. 18.   ⁴ I.e. סוֹף פסוק.   ⁵ cxix. 14.
⁶ cxix. 17. Samuel (p. 125) rightly adds here: ואם אין אחריו סלוק ויש רודפין
אחריו הראשון מהפך והשני מרכא בּוֹ בָּמֶה לִבִּי וְנֶעֱזָרְתִּי (xxviii. 7).
⁷ xlvii. 8.   ⁸ cxix. 52.   ⁹ lxviii. 15.   ¹⁰ i. 3.
¹¹ ii. 2. The Gaya here is made Mer'kha!   ¹² xviii. 8.   ¹³ xxv. 5.
¹⁴ تَرَى مِن بَرّا, 'thou wilt see on the outside (the margin),' see p. 92, note 1.

בקו׳ מִי הִקְדִּימַנִי וַאֲשַׁלֵּם 1 כִּי מְבֹרָכָיו 2 כִּי עֲוֹנֹתַי 3 כִּי לָחֲמוּ 4 עַיִן שְׁזָפַתּוּ 5 הֵמָּה
רָאוּ 6 שֶׁקֶר הַסּוּס 7 ואמתאלה. ואדא כאן כאדמה מעה פי אלכלמה פינטר אן
כאן וסטהא פיה אחד מלכין אלואחד חלֵם ואלאחר קָמֵץ ובין אלחלֵם או
אלקָמֵץ ובין חרף אליתיב שוא פאן אחד אלמלכין ירפע בשופר כקו׳ יִלָּפְתוּ 8
הֲמִירְאָתֶךָ 9 בְּהִשָּׁפְטוֹ 10 ואמתאל דלי׳ וממא פי וסט אלכלמה אלחלֵם קולה
וַיֹּאמְרוּ לֹא יִרְאֶה יָּהּ 11 וְיָרֹמִמְךָ לְרִשֶׁת 12 ואמתאלהמא׳ פאן כאן פי וסט
אלכלמה גיר הדין אלמלכין לם תרפע בשופר כקו׳ לְתַאֲוָה 13 בְּמַקְהֵלוֹת 14 וכדלך
אן תגיר שרט אלשוא ועלי אחד אלמלכין חאצר לם תרפע בשופר כקו׳
מֵהֵיכָלֶךָ 15 ואמתאלה 16 :

אלאתנחה. אלאתנחה אדא כדמהא כאדם ואחד קד יכון מדה שופר
ויכון מדה מאריכה׳ פאלדי יוגב אלמאריכה אשיא ה׳ [אלואחד] אן תכון
אלאתנחה הי אול לחן פי אלפסוק 17 כקו׳ נָבוֹאָה לְמִשְׁכְּנוֹתָיו 18 שָׁקַדְתִּי וָאֶהְיֶה 19
ואמתאלהמא׳ ואלתאני אן תכון אלאתנחה בעד רביע מתל הַשָּׁמַיִם מְסַפְּרִים
כְּבוֹד־אֵל 20 וָאֶשְׁחָקֵם כְּעָפָר עַל־פְּנֵי־רוּחַ 21 אֲדֹנָי נֶגְדְּךָ כָל־תַּאֲוָתִי 22 ואמתאל
דלי׳ ואלתאלת תכון אלאתנחה [בעד] תאבעה אלרביע מתל שִׁיר הַמַּעֲלוֹת
זְכוֹר־יְהֹוָה לְדָוִד 23 יָבֹא אֱלֹהֵינוּ וְאַל־יֶחֱרַשׁ אֵשׁ־לְפָנָיו תֹּאכֵל 24 ואמתאלהמא׳
ואלראבע תכון אלאתנחה בעד תאבעה אלזרקה מתל וּצְפוּנְךָ תְּמַלֵּא בִטְנָם
יִשְׂבְּעוּ בָנִים 25 ואמתאלה׳ ואלכאמס אן יכון מוצע אלכאדם עלי אול חרף מן
כלמתה מתל זֶה שַׁדַּוְני 26 לֹא עָמָד 27 ואנת תציב פי הדאיה אלקאר 28 וגהא
סאדם 29 גיר אן אלכארג ענה כתיר. וממא לם תתבת לה הדה אלשרוט כאן
אלכאדם שופר מתל וְצֹאן יָדְךָ 30 מוּסַר אָבִיךָ 31 הֵקִים כָּל־אַפְסֵי־אָרֶץ 32 ואמתאל
דלך. אלאתנחה אדא כדמהא כאדמין יכונא אלכאדמין תארה שופרין ותארה
דחויה ומאריכה׳ אלשרט פי דלך אן כאן בין כלמה אלאתנחה ובין כלמה

---

1 Job xli. 3.　　　2 Ps. xxxvii. 22.　　　3 xxxviii. 5.　　　4 Prov. iv. 17.

5 Job xx. 9.　　6 Ps. cvii. 24.　　7 xxxiii. 17.　　8 Job vi. 18.　　9 xxii. 4.

10 Ps. cix. 7.　　11 xciv. 7.　　12 xxxvii. 34.　　13 Prov. xviii. 1.

14 Ps. lxviii. 27.　　15 ib. 30.

16 הדאיה אלקאר gives the rules for D'chî with two and three servi, but incorrectly.

17 אפסוק occurs elsewhere in the text for פסוק.

18 Ps. cxxxii. 7.　　19 cii. 8.　　20 xix. 2.　　21 xviii. 43.　　22 xxxviii. 10.

23 cxxxii. 1.　　24 l. 3.　　25 xvii. 14.　　26 ib. 9.　　27 i. 1.

28 See p. 103.　　　　　29 MS. has כאדם!! Of course, the Heb. has שׁשׂי.

30 xcv. 7. I substitute this for the false ex. וְצֹאן מַרְעִיתוֹ (c. 3), which is given in
both the Arab. and Heb. texts.　　31 Prov. i. 8.　　32 xxx. 4.

אלכאדם אלקריב אליה פאסקה כאן אלכאדם אבדא דחויה ואלתאני מארכה

מתל בָּרֲכוּ עַמִּים ׀ אֱלֹהֵינוּ¹ הֲלוֹא־מְשַׂנְאֶיךָ יְהוָה ׀ אֶשְׂנָא² מא סוי מוצעין בדחויה

ומארכה וליס ביונהמא פסק והמא הֵנֵּה־זֹאת חֲקַרְנוּהָ כֶּן־הִיא³ הַקְשֵׁב אִיוֹב

שְׁמַע־לִי⁴ פאן לם תכן פאסקה צאר אלכאדמין שופרין מתל שָׁמֵוֹ אָדוֹן

לְבֵיתוֹ⁵ בְּרֹב שַׂרְעַפַּי בְּקִרְבִּי⁶. ואעלם אן אלדחויה לא תכדם אלא אלרביע

ואלאתנחה ואלשוכב פי אלטפחה מתל נִצְּבָה שֵׁגַל לִימִינֶךָ⁷ ומעני קולי

שוכב הו אן אן תחטّה בגיר חרכה⁸ מתל נִצְּבָה ומעני דחויה הו אנך תרפעהא

אלי ורא נחו נחו אלכמס נגמאת⁹ נחו קולך אָמְרֵי הַאֲזִינָה ׀ יְהוָה¹⁰. פאלשוכב

אבדא לאלטפחה ואלדחויה אבדא לאלרביע ואלאתנחה פאחפטה לאנה משכל¹¹ :

─────────────────

אלטפחה מן אלאלחאן אלתי יתגיר שכלהא. פאדא כאן קבלהא לא ולא

וכאנת אלטפחה עלי אלחרף אלאול או אלתאני או אלתאלת כאנת לא במקף

מתל וְלֹא־בָטַחְתִּי¹² ואמתאלהא· ואדא כאנת עלי אלחרף אלראבע ומא זאד

כאן לא במארכה מתל וְלֹא נֶאֱמְנוּ¹³· ואדא ראית לָא שָׁמֵעוּ¹⁴ וְלֹא כְחַדֹו¹⁵

פליס הו עלי אלחרף אלתאלת בל עלי אלראבע לאן שָׁמְעוּ אלקאמצה פי

צמנהא אלף וכדלך כְחַדֹו פי צמן אלנקטה יוד. אלטפחה אדא כדמתהא

אלמארכה וכאן קבל חרף אלמארכה נקטה אָ או אֶ או אֹ או אֹ כאן דלך אלחרף

ירפע רפעא יסירא כפיפא לתעתדל אלנגמה¹⁶· לאן אלאן כתיר ממן ינגם

עלי חרף ליס עליה תנגים ויחרך אמא אלי אספל ואמא אלי פוק או תרגיח¹⁷

לא יכון דלך אלחרף יסתחק מנה שי בתה· ואלקאר יגב אן יסוק חרוף

אלכלמה מן גיר חרכה בתה חרף אלי חרף אלתנגים והו אלחרף אלדי

עליה אלטעם אמא כאדם אמא לחן פינגמה וסואה לא ידכלה תנגים בתה·

─────────────────

¹ Ps. lxvi. 8. ² cxxxix. 21. ³ Job v. 27. ⁴ xxxiii. 31.

⁵ Ps. cv. 21. ⁶ xciv. 19. ⁷ xlv. 10.

⁸ 'That thou bring it down, without a movement, or impulse,' הנעה Heb.

⁹ 'That thou bring it up behind, like the five tones,' perhaps referring to some
ascending scale in use. ¹⁰ v. 2.

¹¹ The omission here of the rules for three or more משרתים is partially supplied
in the Heb., and more fully in הדאיה אלקאר, but in neither case correctly.

¹² Again a false ex. Perhaps the author was thinking of כִּי־בָטַחְתִּי (cxix. 42),
which would have been quite right, for the rule applies to all small words resem-
bling לא. ¹³ Ps. lxxviii. 37. ¹⁴ Job iii. 18. ¹⁵ xv. 18.

¹⁶ It may be noticed that the melody of Mer'kha was *below*. There was a rising
and falling inflection, producing the equilibrium spoken of.

¹⁷ A word seems left out here, Heb. יכריע הכרעה, 'he makes a preponderance,
lays a stress.' This passage is wanting in הדאיה אלקאר.

וילוח לי אן הדה אלהמזה[1] אלתי געלוהא פי מוצע לא יתם ללקאר[2] פיה
פסאד אלנגמה בתחריכה חרף לא יגב אן יחרך לאן אדא רפע אלחרף בהא
אלי פוק קלילא תעדלת אלנגמה[3]. והדה אלהמזה יחלו אלשיל בהא פי לחנין
פי אלטפחה ואלסלוק מתל קֶרֶץ שְׂפָתָיו[4] שָׂמֵחַ לְאֵיד[5] וּבְרָקִים רָב[6] ופי
אלסלוק חָכְמָה תוֹדִיעֵנִי[7]. וקד יעמלהא בעץ אלסופרים פי גיר הדא אלחנין
ומע גיר אלתלתה מלוך אלמדכורה. וילוח לי אנהם געלוהא לאסקאט
אלשופר מן כלמתהא ולגוב אלמארכה לאן כל כלמה יכון עליהא הדה
אלהמזה לא יכון פיהא שופר ולא בד להא מן מארכה. ואעלם אן
אלטפחה הי אלנקטה מן פוק אלבלמה וילוח לי אנהם געלו אלעצאה עלי
אלחרף אלאול לילא יטן אן אלנקטה רביע פאלקאר מא יגעל באלה אלא
אלי אלעצאה אלתי מע אול חרף מתל וְחַטָּאִים בעדת[8] גיר אן מתי אשכל
עליה אימא הו חרף אלתנגים רגע אלי אלנקטה נגם[9] חרפהא.   אליתיב
איצא לא יכתב אלא מע אול חרף וקד יכון חרף אלתנגים וקד לא יכון
חרף אלתנגים· וכתיר ממא ישכל עלי אלקאר דלך פינגם אלחרף אלאול אלדי
עליה אליתיב ולא יכון הו אלחרף אלדי יסתחק אלתנגים פמא ירגע פיה אלא
אלי[10] אלתלקין· גיר אן בעץ אלסופרים יגעל תחת חרף אלתנגים פי אלמואצע
אלמשבלה עצאה שכל אלמארכה וליסת הי מארכה בל ליעלם אנה אלחרף

---

[1] On this המזה, or מתיגה, see p. 70, note 10. One is surprised to find هَمْز
employed to designate what must have been a kind of *secondary tone*. I am glad
therefore to be able to give an explanation of the term from the point of view of
Jewish grammarians. The following passage occurs in a MS. recently acquired by
the Bodleian Library, very similar, in its contents, to the 'Manuel du Lecteur'
(Opp. Add. Quo. 158, p. 12): ואיצא שכל אבר יסמי המזה ויסמי דרבן מענאה
מהמאז והו הו לא לחן ולא באדם ואנמא יעמל ליהז אלחרף אלדי הו עליה והו צד
אלגעיה לאן אלגעיה תמד אלחרף ואלהמזה תהמז (? תהמזה) ותכון מן פוק אלחרף
וצורתה מתל אלאזלה. We are here told that, whilst Gaya *prolongs* the letter,
Hamza *gives a movement*, or *impulse*, to it. (Rt. هَمَز, *impulit, trusit*.) This agrees
with what is said in the text above, l. 2, where we also learn that the movement, or
impulse, was *upwards*. It was, however, clearly a mistake to borrow a *terminus
technicus* from Arabic grammarians, and employ it in a sense so different from that
which properly belongs to it.   [2] Heb. לא יתכן לקרוא בה.

[3] تَعَدَّلَتِ النَّغْمَة. So Par. נשתוותה הנעימה. But this could not have been
the author's meaning. . Read rather عَدَّلَت עדלת, 'deviates,' 'goes wrong;' similarly Ox. and Vat. נשחתה, 'is spoilt.'

[4] Prov. xvi. 30.   [5] xvii. 5.   [6] Ps. xviii. 15.
[7] li. 8. Hardly a correct ex., for we require Qámes, not Qámes-chatûph.
[8] i. 5.   [9] Query ונגם.
[10] Query עלי, 'he does not retract it, except on instruction.' Heb. על דרך הלימוד.

אלמנגם מתל עֻוּרָה הנבל וכנור[1] בְּיוֹם צָרָתִי[2] לאן לא יצח אן יקרא אליתיב
עלי אלרֵיש ואלתֵו גמיעא פגעלו אלעצאה תפצל. אלטפחה אדא כדמהא
כאדמין קד יכונאן מארבתין וקד יכון אלאול ואלתאני מארכה·
פאלשרט פי וגוב אלמארכה פי אלאול קיל אן תכון מע אול חרף או מע
אלתאני ויכון אלאול תחתה שוא מתל כִּי אֵלֶיךָ[3] זְכֹר חֶרְפָּתְךָ מִנִּי־נָבָל כל
היום[4] ואמתאלהמא· פאן זאל אלכאדם ען אול חרף וכאן תחת אלאול מלך
צאר אלכאדם אלאול שוכב מתל עֵדוּת יְהֹוָה נֶאֱמָנָה[5] מִצְוַת יְהֹוָה בָּרָה[6] והדא
ילוח לי אנה כלף בינהם[7] :

אלסלוק. אלסלוק אדא לם יכן לה כאדם פלא כלאם עליה מתל
מִצְוֹתֶיךָ[8]. פאדא כדמה כאדם ואחד קד יכון שופר רפע וקד יכון מארכה
וקד יכון שופר תכסיר. אלשרט פי וגוב אלשופר אלרפע כונה מע אול חרף
מתל שְׁפְטֵי אֶרֶץ[9] בִּינָה הַגִּינִי[10] ואמתאלהמא· ואן צאר מע אלחרף אלתאני
וכאן תחת אלאול שוא וגב אלשופר איצֹא מתל וְדֻמּוּ סֶלָה[11] בְּצֹאן מַרְעִיתֶךָ[12]
ואמתאל דלך. ואלשרט פי וגוב אלמארכה כונהא מע אלחרף אלתאני אדא
כאן תחת אלאול מלך מתל וְאַחַר כָּבוֹד תִּקָּחֵנִי[13] תָּרגֻם יְמִינֶךָ[14] ואמתאלהמא·
ואדא צאר מע אלתאלת ומא זאד לא תתגיר אלמארכה מתל אֲשֶׁר־תִּדְּפֶנּוּ
רוּחַ[15] בַּעֲדַת צַדִּיקִים[16] ואמתאלהמא וקד יכרג ען הדא שואד. ואלשרט פי וגוב
אלשופר אלתכסיר הו אן יכון קבלה לגרמיה מתל מִפְּנֵי ׀ אַבְשָׁלוֹם בְּנוֹ[17]
שֵׁם ׀ אֱלֹהֵי יַעֲקֹב[18] ואמתאלהמא. וקד אבתלף פי אלכלמה אלתי פיהא אחד
חרוף אהֹהֹע ויכון פי אלכלמה חרף דגש פאן אלבעץֹ יבאלף אלשרט ויקראה
אלי פוק[19] מתל כָּל־פֹּעֲלֵי אָוֶן[20] אַתָּה תְשַׁבְּחֵם[21] ואמתאלהמא· ואמתאלהמא ואדא כאן
בלמה צגירה מתל כָּל וְעַל וְאֵת וכאנת במקף פהם יגרוהא מגרי בעץֹ אלכלמה
מתל כָּל־פֹּעֲלֵי אָוֶן[20]. וקד יכדם אלסלוק שוכב פי תלתה מואצע והי יַעַמְדוּ
מָיִם[22] וּמִמַּעֲמַקֵּי מָיִם[23] וַיַּהַפְכוּ אָרֶץ[24]. אלסלוק אדא כדמה כאדמין פאלאול
אבדא במאילה ואלתאני שופר רפע מתל וְכֹל אֲשֶׁר־יַעֲשֶׂה יַצְלִיחַ[25] אֲשֶׁר
התעתְּדוּ לְגַלִּים[26] וקד כרג ען דלך שואד מתל וְנִכְאָה לֵבָב לְמוֹתֵת[27]· וקד

---

[1] Ps. lvii. 9.   [2] lxxxvi. 7.   [3] ib. 4.   [4] lxxiv. 22.   [5] xix. 8.   [6] ib. 9.
[7] So for the last three exx., Ben-Asher and Ben-Naphtali differ. See p. 76, note 7.
[8] cxix. 10.   [9] ii. 10.   [10] v. 2.   [11] iv. 5.   [12] lxxiv. 1.   [13] lxxiii. 24.
[14] lxxxix. 14.   [15] i. 4.   [16] ib. 5.   [17] iii. 1.   [18] xx. 2.
[19] I. e. with שופר רפע.   [20] Ps. v. 6.   [21] lxxxix. 10.   [22] civ. 6.
[23] lxix. 15.   [24] Job xii. 15.   [25] Ps. i. 3.   [26] Job xv. 28.   [27] Ps. cix. 16.

אכתלף פי אלכאדם אלתאני והו אן בעצהם אדא לם יכן בין חרף אלמאילה

ובין חרף אלשופר מלך אצלא נער אלשופר מארכה מתל מְדַבֵּר צֶדֶק סֶלָה[1]

וְצִפְוֹנִי הוּא אֱלֵי־חָרֶב[2].   אלסלוק אדא כדמה תלתה כדאם מא תתגיר

אלכאדמין ואנמא יתגיר אלכאדם אלאול והו אן כאן מע אול חרף כאן

שופר מקלוב מתל כִּי לֹא־עָזַבְתָּ דֹרְשֶׁיךָ יְהוָה[3] ואן צאר מע אלחרף אלתאני

צאר שופר תכסיר מן פוק מתל מָגֵן וְחֶרֶב וּמִלְחָמָה סֶלָה[4] ואן צאר מע

אלתאלת ומא זאד צאר מקל מתל אֶבְחָנְךָ עַל־מֵי מְרִיבָה סֶלָה[5] והדא עלי

אלאשהר. ואלשופר אדא כאן קבל אלסלוק אן כאן אלסלוק מע אבר מלך

כאן רפעה אלשופר חפיפה מתל לֹא יָשֵׁב[6] ואדא כאן אלסלוק בעדה מלך

כאן רפעה אלשופר בהמזה[7] אלי פוק ליואזי תקל אלסלוק פיגו כפיף מע

כפיף ותקיל מע תקיל פיעתדל אלתנגים:

_____

תאבעה אלזורקה.   תאבעה אלזורקה מא חסבוהא לא מע אלאלחאן ולא

מע אלכדאם.   והי תגי עלי ותלתה צרוב אלואחד מתל מֶרְכְּבֵי אִישׁ[8] ואלתאני

מתל בַּעֲצַת רְשָׁעִים[9] ואלתאלת אדא כאן מע אול חרף כאן שופר מקלוב

מתל יִמְחַץ רֹאשׁ אֹיְבָיו[10] מִי זֶה מֶלֶךְ הַכָּבוֹד[11]. וליס הדה אלעצאה אלתי

תחת אֹיְבָיו וְהַכָּבוֹד מארכה לאנהא ליס מתצל במא בעדהא[12] ואנמא הי

עלאמה ללחרף אלדי ינגם לאנה ישבל מתל זִבְחֵי אֱלֹהִים רוּחַ נִשְׁבָּרָה[13] לולם

יגעל מע אלרֵישׁ עלאמה אנה חרף אלתנגים לקרית עלי אלבָּא[14]:

_____

פצל פי חצץ אלכדאם[15].   חצה אלגלגל פי אלפזר.   חצה אלמקל פי

אלסלוק.   חצה אלשופר אלמקלוב פי סבעה מואצע פי אלפזר ואלזורקה

ואללגרמיה ואלרביע ואליתיב ואלאתנחה ואלסלוק.   חצה אלצנארה[16] פי

---

[1] Ps. lii. 5.   [2] Job xv. 22.   [3] Ps. ix. 11.   [4] lxxvi. 4.   [5] lxxxi. 8.   [6] i. 1.

[7] I question whether המזה is right here, although Par. has also מתיגה.   There is nothing corresponding in אלקאר הדאיה.

[8] xxxi. 21.   [9] i. 1.   [10] lxviii. 22.   [11] xxiv. 8.

[12] Simson (p. 75^b) adds: כי הרודף מעמיד התיבה כמו אתנחתא ומקמיץ התיבה הפתוחה כאתנחתא גם לפעמים מתש כה האתנחתא.

[13] li. 19.   [14] 'Then it would have been read on the ב,' נִשְׁבְּרָה (as in Ps. xxxiv. 21).   Samuel (p. 126) concludes this section with רודפי רביע הם שנים האחרונים של זרקא כגון הוכֵרְנִי יהוה דרכך (xxvii. 11).

[15] This list is so full of mistakes that I do not think it worth while to particularize them.

[16] צנארה is another name for צנורית, regularly used in אלקאר הדאיה.

כמסה מואצֹע מכצוצה פי אללגרמיה פי מכאן מכצוץ ואלרביע ואליתיב
ואלאתנחה ואלסלוק פי אמכנה מכצוצה והי תכון מעינה ללשופר אלמקלוב·
ומא צח לי פי אלתצניר שרט פאדכרה¹.　חצה אלשופר אלרפע
פי אלזרקה ואלאתנחה פי מואצֹע מכצוצה.　חצה שופר אלתכסיר פי
אלרביע ואללגרמיה ואליתיב ואלאתנחה ואכר אלפסוק פי מואצֹע מכצוצה.
חצה אלמארכה פי אלאלחאן כלהא פי מואצֹע מכצוצה.　חצה אלדחויה פי
אלרביע ואלאתנחה פי מואצֹע מכצוצה.　חצה אלמאילה פי אכר אלפסוק
פי מואצֹע מכצוצה.　חצה אלשוכב פי אלטפחה ופי אלסלוק פי תלתה
מואצֹע יַֽעֲמֹדוּ כַֽיִם ואבויה.　אלסלסלה אדא כאנת כאדם כדמת אתנחה
ורביע וסלוק:

פצֹל פי מגֹאורה אלאלחאן. הדה אלתמאניה אלחאן ליס פיהא ואגֹב אלואחד
בעד אלאכר אלא אלסלסלה פאנהא אדא כאנת לחן לא בד מן אן יכון
קבלהא אתנחה.　אלפזר ימכן בעדה זרקה כִּי כָל־בֵּינֹו חַיָּֽ² ורביע פֵּח לִי³
ולגרמיה וַיֵּרֶד מַי אֲסַף־רוּחַ ׀ בְּחָפְנָיו⁴ ויתיב יִגְאָלֵהוּ חֹשֶׁךְ וְצַלְמָוֶת⁵ וטפחה לְדָוִד
אֵלֶיךָ יְהֹוָה⁶ וסלוק וַיֹּאמַר אֶרְחָמְךָ יְהֹוָה חִזְקִי⁷.　אלזרקה אדא תבעתהא
תאבעתהא ארבעה אלחאן· אלפזר חָכְמָה כִּֽי־כִפְלַיִם לְתוּשִׁיָּה וְדַע⁸ ואלרביע
בָּרוּךְ אֲדֹנָי ׀ יוֹם יוֹם יַֽעֲמָס־לָנוּ⁹ ואמתאל דלך ואליתיב אֲבָחַר דַּרְכָּם וְאֵשֵׁב
רֹאש וְאֶשְׁכּוֹן¹⁰ ואמתאל דלך ואלאתנחה גַּם־אֲנִי ׀ אוֹדְךָ בִכְלִי־נֶבֶל אֲמִתְּךָ אֱלֹהָי
אֲזַמְּרָה לְּךָ בְכִנּוֹר¹¹ ואמתאלה· ואן לם יכן בעדהא תאבעתהא לם ימכן
בעדהא אלה אלרביע פקט בכו' הַאֲזִינָה אֶל־דִּמְעָתִי¹² בַּשָּׁמַיִם דֶּרֶךְ נָחָשׁ¹³.
אלרביע ימכן בעדה כמסה· אלזרקה מְמַתִים מֵחֶלֶד חֶלְקָם בַּֽחַיִּים¹⁴ ואמתאלה
ואליתיב חַסְדּו וּבַלַּיְלָה¹⁵ ואמתאלה ואלאתנחה כְּמוֹבֶם לֹא־נֹפֶל אָנֹכִי מִכֶּם¹⁶
ואמתאלה ואללגרמיה אַשְׁרֵי הָאִישׁ אֲשֶׁר ׀ לֹא הָלַךְ¹⁷ ואמתאלה ואלסלוק פֶּתַח
דְּבָרֶיךָ יָאִיר [מֵבִין פְּתָיִם]¹⁸ ואמתאלה.　אללגרמיה ימכן בעדה אלפזר טָמְנוּ

---

¹ The word תצניר is a denominative from צנארה and *Nom. Verbi* of the second
Form, the sense apparently being: 'And what is clear to me, there is a condition
in regard to the making (placing) of Ṣinnorith, and so I mention it.' The condition
has been named in the words immediately preceding.

² Ps. xxxi. 11.　　³ cxl. 6.　　⁴ Prov. xxx. 4.　　⁵ Job iii. 5.
⁶ Ps. xxv. 1.　　⁷ xviii. 2.　　⁸ Job xi. 6.　　⁹ Ps. lxviii. 20.
¹⁰ Job xxix. 25.　　¹¹ Ps. lxxi. 22.　　¹² xxxix. 13.　　¹³ Prov. xxx. 19.
¹⁴ Ps. xvii. 14.　　¹⁵ xlii. 9.　　¹⁶ Job xii. 3.　　¹⁷ Ps. i. 1.
¹⁸ cxix. 130.

גְּאִים ׀ פֵּחַ ׀ לִי 1 וזרקה וַיַּגֶּד־לָךְ ׀ תַּעֲלֻמוֹת חָכְמָה 2 ואלרביע אָכְלוּ וַיִּשְׁתַּחֲוּוּ ׀ כָּל־
דִּשְׁנֵי־אֶרֶץ 3 ואליתיב עַל־כֵּן ׀ לֹא־יָקֻמוּ רְשָׁעִים 4 ואתנחה כִּי שָׁמָּה ׀ יָשְׁבוּ כִסְאוֹת
לְמִשְׁפָּט 5 ואלסלוק שָׁם ׀ אֱלֹהֵי יַעֲקֹב 6.   ואליתיב ימכן בעדה תלתה אלחאן ·
אתנחה יְהֹוָה עֹז לְעַמּוֹ יִתֵּן 7 ואמתאלה ואלרביע בְּפִי שְׁלֹשֶׁת הָאֲנָשִׁים 8
ואלסלוק מוֹצְאֵי וְדֶרֶךְ רָע וּפִי תַהְפֻּכוֹת [שָׂנֵאתִי] 9 אִישׁ־עָנִי וְאֶבְיוֹן וְנִכְאֵה לֵבָב
לְמוֹתֵת 10.   אלאתנחה ימכן בעדהא לחנין · טפחה וְעַתָּה מְלָכִים הַשְׂכִּילוּ
[הִוָּסְרוּ] 11 וסלוק לְמֹצְאֵיהֶם וּלְכָל־בְּשָׂרוֹ מַרְפֵּא 12.   אלטפחה ימכן בעדהא
לגרמיה [שָׂנֵאתִי] אָז ׀ יָנוּחַ לִי 13 וסלוק מְאֹד עָמְקוּ מַחְשְׁבֹתֶיךָ 14 כל טפחה יכון
בעדהא לגרמיה לא בד ממא אן יכון בעד אללגרמיה סלוק ויכון קבל
אלטפחה אתנחה :

פצל פי אחצא 15 כדאם הדה כם יכון לכל לחן מן כאדם.   כדאם אלפזר
תלתה מארכה ושופר מקלוב ונלגל.   כדאם אלזורקה תלתה שופר מקלוב
ומארכה ושופר רפע.   כדאם אלרביע [סתה] מארכה ושופר מקלוב וצנאארה
ושופר תכסיר ודחויה וסלסלה.   כדאם אללגרמיה ארבעה מארכה ושופר
תכסיר ושופר מקלוב וצנאארה.   כדאם אליתיב כמסה אלשופר ושופר תכסיר
ושופר מקלוב וצנאארה ומארכה.   כדאם אלאתנחה סבעה שופר ודחויה
ומארכה ושופר תכסיר ושופר מקלוב וצנארה וסלסלה.   כדאם אלטפחה
אתנאן שוכב ומארכה.   כדאם אלסלוק תמאניה שופר ומארכה ומאילה
ושופר תכסיר ומקל ושופר מקלוב וצנורית וסלסלה :

ואליק מא תתבת הדה אלחאן הכדא 16 · בעד אלפזר [לגרמיה בעד]
אללגרמיה זרקה בעד אלזורקה רביע בעד אלרביע יתיב ואתנחה בעד אליתיב
אתנחה בעד אלאתנחה טפחה בעד אלטפחה סלוק :

והדה אלתמאניה אלחאן אלחאן תצלח אן תכון כלהא רום פואסיק עלי אלאשהר
אלא אליתיב 17 ואלסלוק פאנהמא שואד · ודאך אן אלטפחה לא תכון פי

---

1 Ps. cxl. 6.   2 Job xi. 6.   3 Ps. xxii. 30.   4 i. 5.   5 cxxii. 5.
6 xx. 2.   7 xxix. 11.   8 Job xxxii. 5.   9 Prov. viii. 13.
10 Ps. cix. 16.   11 ii. 10.   12 Prov. iv. 22.   13 Job iii. 13.
14 Ps. xcii. 6.   15 I.e. אחצא, احصاء, 'the numbering.'
16 'And these accents are most suitably fixed as follows.' We should have expected תרתיב, אכתר מא תרתבת, 'are most frequently arranged.' תרתיב is the technical
term for this sequence. The list here given corresponds to the Zarqa-table in the
prose accentuation.   17 It is clear that for יתיב we must read טפחה.

אלתלתה אספאר אלא פי נצף אלפסוק אלתאני ולא תכון פי נצפה אלאול

כמא תכון אלטפחה פי אול אלפסוק פי אלואחד ועשרין ספר מתל בְּרֵאשִׁית ¹

פלדלך ביّנת אלטפחה לא תוגד האהנא פי אלנצף אלאול אלא שאד פי

תלתה מואצע פאתנין מנהם בגיר כאדם והמא לַמְנַצֵּחַ לְדָוִד מִזְמוֹר: קוה קויתי

יהוה ² לַמְנַצֵּחַ לְדָוִד לְהַזְכִּיר: אלהים להצילני ³ ואלדי בכאדם שִׁיר מִזְמוֹר

לִבְנֵי־קֹרַח: גדול יהוה ומהלל מאד ⁴. ואמא אלסלוק פלא יוגד פי אלואחד

ועשרין ספרא פי אול פסוק ⁵ לאן לא יכדמה אלא כאדם ואחד ופסוק מן

כלמתין לא יוגד ופי הדה אלתלתה אלאספאר יכדמה אזיד מן כאדם פלדלך נא

האהנא אול פסוק וביאן דלך אן לים פי אלפסוק לחן סואה · ודאך אנך תגדה

פי עשרה ⁶ מואצע תלתה מנהא להא כאדמין והי [שִׁיר מִזְמוֹר לְדָוִד ⁷] שִׁיר

מִזְמוֹר לְאָסָף ⁸ מִזְמוֹר לְדָוִד לְהַזְכִּיר: יהוה אל בקצפך ⁹ ומנהא סבעה בשופרות

תכסיר והי למנצח לבני־קרח משכיל: אלהים באזנינו שמענו ¹⁰ למנצח לבני־

קרח מזמור: רצית יהוה ארצך ¹¹ למנצח על־נגינת לדוד ¹²: למנצח על־שושנים

לדוד: הושיעני אלהים ¹³ למנצח על־הגתית לאסף ¹⁴: למנצח לבני־קרח מזמור:

כל העמים תקעו כף ¹⁵ למנצח לעבד־יהוה לדוד: נאם פשע ¹⁶:

ואגתמאע הדה אלתמאניה אלחאן וגד פי פסוק על זאת יתפלל כל חסיד

אליך ¹⁷ ומא יגמע סבעה אלחאן פהו פסוק אשרי האיש ¹⁸ לדוד אליך יהוה

אקרא ¹⁹ ראיתה כי אתה עמל וכעס תביט ²⁰:

תם אלמכתצר בחמד אללה ׃

---

¹ Gen. i. 1.   ² Ps. xl. 1.   ³ lxx. 1.   ⁴ xlviii. 1.
⁵ Here and in the lines following there is in the text אסםוק for פסוק.
⁶ תמאניה for סבעה, and in the next line הדאיה אלקאר has אחד עשר for עשרה,
adding xlix. 1.
⁷ cviii. 1. This ex. fails in the text, but is in the Heb.   ⁸ lxxxiii. 1.
⁹ xxxviii. 1.   ¹⁰ xliv. 1.   ¹¹ lxxxv. 1.   ¹² lxi. 1.   ¹³ lxix. 1.   ¹⁴ lxxxi. 1.
¹⁵ xlvii. 1.   ¹⁶ xxxvi. 1.   ¹⁷ xxxii. 6.   ¹⁸ i. 1.   ¹⁹ xxviii. 1.   ²⁰ x. 14.

INDEX

ERRATA.

Page 20, note 53, *for* נוֹחַת *read* נָחַת

  „   31, note 18, *for* 'four' *read* 'three,' *and delete* 'Ps. xviii. 31'

  „   33, l. 17 from bottom, *for* 'lx' *read* 'lxi'

  „   33, note 25, *for* 'at end' *read* 'p. 75'

  „   40, l. 14 from bottom, *point* אֲחֻזָּה

  „   82, note 6, *for* 'B. M. 16' *read* 'B. M. 17'

טעמי כ״א ספרים

A

TREATISE ON THE ACCENTUATION

OF THE TWENTY-ONE SO-CALLED

PROSE BOOKS OF THE OLD TESTAMENT

WITH A FACSIMILE OF A PAGE OF THE CODEX ASSIGNED TO

BEN-ASHER IN ALEPPO

BY

WILLIAM WICKES, D.D.

FIRST PUBLISHED 1887

PREFACE.

THE present Treatise aims at explaining the accentuation of
the so-called Prose Books—twenty-one in number, according to
Jewish reckoning[1]—of the Hebrew Bible. The favourable re-
ception given to my Work ‏ט‏״מ אמי טעמי‏, on the accentuation of
the three Poetical Books (Psalms, Proverbs, and Job), has en-
couraged me to proceed further, and complete the investigation
which I then commenced.

I have been asked why, contrary to the usual practice, I *began*
with the accentuation of the three Books. My answer is that
the subject seemed to me to stand in special need of careful
examination[2]. There was besides this advantage in taking the
three Books first, that owing to their comparatively small com-
pass, it was more easy to examine them exhaustively and so to
arrive at the general principles underlying their accentuation.
Those principles once established had then only to be applied,
with the necessary modifications, to the twenty-one Books.

I have endeavoured to carry out with thoroughness the task
I had undertaken, and have not intentionally allowed difficulties
in the accentuation to pass unnoticed. My plan has been, either,
by a process of induction, to bring such instances under a general
rule; or to furnish a special explanation of them, partly in the
course of the Work, and more particularly in the Notes collected
in Appendix I. Of course, I have not been concerned to *defend*

---

[1] The two Books of 1 and 2 Samuel, 1 and 2 Kings, and 1 and 2 Chronicles are
counted respectively as one. The same is the case with Ezra and Nehemiah.
The ten Minor Prophets are also taken together to make one book. In this
calculation the beginning and the end of Job (i. 1–iii. 1 and xlii. 7–17) are not
taken into account, which however are pointed according to the same system.—
It is to be observed that Jewish writers know nothing of the distinction between
Prose and Poetical Books; they speak simply of the twenty-one and three Books.

[2] I hope that it is no breach of confidence on my part, when I state that the late
Prof. Ewald told me that, whilst he had no doubt that he had furnished the true explanation of the prose accentuation, he was not so satisfied in regard to the poetical.

the accentuation in all cases. It is enough if we can trace the principles on which the accentuators proceeded, or the interpretation which in particular instances led to the accentuation employed.

I have found it necessary often to propose a correction of the *textus receptus;* but have very rarely done so without manuscript authority. The labour of collating MSS. in our great English collections and the Libraries of the Continent, for a text of such extent as that of the Old Testament, has been very considerable, and one which no previous writer on the accents has thought of undertaking. Yet, without a correct text, what hope can there be of establishing any rules on a satisfactory basis?

One Codex, which is in the Synagogue at Aleppo, and which I have been able to consult, although only indirectly, has the reputation of having come from the hand of Ben-Asher himself, and of having been, on that account, always regarded as a model copy for fixing the readings of the Sacred Text. Its claim to the exceptional importance thus assigned to it I have considered in the pages immediately following.

I have once more to express my obligations to my friend Dr. Baer, for the valuable assistance he has willingly rendered me. His familiar acquaintance with the Massora—a department of study in which he ranks *facile princeps* [1]—has been of special service to me.

W. WICKES.

81, WOODSTOCK ROAD, OXFORD,
May, 1887.

---

[1] I have the pleasure of informing scholars, that there is at length a prospect of a complete and correct edition of the Massora. The firm Romm in Wilna (already favourably known through a splendid edition of the Babylonian Talmud lately brought out by them) have in hand a new edition of the so-called Great Rabbinical Bible (מקרא גדול), to which Dr. Baer has undertaken to furnish the Massora. The arrangement adopted will be the same as in Jacob ben-Chayyim's edition, with this exception, that wherever a word occurs *for the first time,* there all that is Massoretic in regard to it will be given; so that, by the help of a Concordance, any particular rubric will be readily traced. I may add that the first part of Dr. Baer's manuscript is already in the printers' hands.

MSS. CONSULTED FOR THE PRESENT WORK.

I. BIBLE MSS.

Codex in the Synagogue at Aleppo—containing the whole text, the punctuation of which is assigned in an epigraph [1] to the famous Aaron ben-Asher (beginning of the 10th century). M. Isidore Loeb, Secretary of L'Alliance Israélite, well known from his learned contributions to the Revue des Études Juives, was good enough to procure for me, through his correspondent at Aleppo, some of the accentual readings of this Codex.

As it is of no little importance for us to know whether such a model codex [2] really exists, to which we might refer for the correction of the *textus receptus* [3], I think it necessary to say a few words on the subject of the epigraph above referred to.—Jacob Sappir, who (in his Work, אבן ספיר, vol. i. p. 12[b]) was the first to furnish a copy of this epigraph, which he obtained through a friend at Aleppo, accepted it as genuine, and was followed by Graetz (Monatsch. für Gesch. und Wiss. des Judenthums, 1871, p. 6, 1887, p. 30), and by Strack (Prol. crit., pp. 44–46). My reasons for arriving at an opposite conclusion are briefly the following :—

1. *The character of writing* of the Codex. M. Loeb succeeded in obtaining for me a photograph of a page of the same (Gen. xxvi. 34–xxvii. 30),—a copy of which serves as Frontispiece to the present Work [4]. Although this copy has not been quite so successfully executed as I could have wished, it is sufficiently clear to enable adepts to form a judgment as to the approximate date of the writing. I venture to give my own opinion, which is that the MS. presents a specimen of

---

[1] Copied Dikd. hat., p. xxii. inf.

[2] Ben-Asher was (as is well known) the normative authority for fixing the text as we now have it.

[3] For fixing the *accentuation* such a Codex would be invaluable. My remarks on it therefore will be seen not to be out of place.

[4] The photograph and the copy are both much reduced in size. The height of each column of writing (without the Massora) is in the original 23 cm., and average breadth 6 cm. The size of each page is therefore somewhat smaller than that of Codex Babylonicus. The MS. is of parchment equally smooth (*très poli*, I am told) on both sides.

calligraphy, not in keeping with the early period to which it is assigned. Really old MSS., provided with Massora—as Codex Baby- lonicus (of the date of Ben-Asher, A. D. 916) and Erfurt 3 (a facsimile of which will appear in Stade's Geschichte Israel's, vol. i)—have a plainer and less finished appearance, and the characters are of a coarser type. I would draw attention, in particular, to the artificial arrange- ment by which a separate Massoretic rubric of two lines and no more is introduced above and below each column.—It is not, however, on the graphical peculiarities that I lay the main stress.

2. The conclusive proof is to be found in the fact that the punc- tuation is, in many instances, *at variance with Ben-Asher's known practice* and the rules laid down by the Palestinian Massoretes.

It will be observed that *Métheg generally fails*, e. g. יַעֲקֹב (often; only once, col. 3, l. 7, יַ֖עֲקֹב); אָנֹכִי (col. 2, l. 3, although אָנֹ֫כִי, col. 2, l. 6 from below); קִלְלָתְךָ (col. 2, l. 8); הַאַתָּה (col. 3, l. 3); וָאֹבְרֲכֶה (col. 1, l. 21); &c. Now although this is constantly the case in Spanish and even Oriental MSS.,[5] we should not expect such an irregularity in a model text marked by the careful hand of the Master himself (המלמד הגדול, as he is termed), particularly when we bear in mind that it is just on the use of Métheg that his controversy with his rival, Ben-Naphtali, mainly turns. Still less should we be prepared for the *false introduction of Métheg*, as in קַח־לִי (col. 1, l. 5 from below) and וַיִּשְׁתַּחוּ (col. 3, l. 6 from below),—the latter Ben- Naphtali's pointing[6], and expressly condemned in Dikd. hat. § 30, אִם הַקֵּיף תָּפוּל הַנַּעְיָא. Moreover, קִלְלָתְךָ (col. 2, l. 8) is Ben-Naphtali's vocalization, whereas Ben-Asher would have pointed קִלֲלָתְךָ[7].

---

[5] It is the *light* Métheg that generally fails; *heavy* Métheg is as generally in- troduced, and so in this page, אֶת־יַעֲקֹב, וְיִתֶּן־לְךָ, וַיְבָרֲכֵהוּ. On the failure of Métheg, comp. Man. du Lect., p. 98, ובמקצת ספרים כותבין הגעיה ובמקצת אין כותבין אלא סומכין על דעת הקורא.

[6] Cf. the examples brought together by Baer, Gen., p. 82, note 1.

[7] See the list of Variations between Ben-Asher and Ben-Naphtali in Baer's Gen., p. 84.

We may also be surprised at not finding the Parasha (col. 1, l. 3) marked in the margin, for it was expressly to note these divisions that Maimonides (see ספר תורה, יד החזקה, c. viii, § 4) consulted a text written and pointed by Ben- Asher.—N. B. The ס (col. 1, l. 3, margin) does not stand for סתומה, as the same sign (col. 3, l. 20) shews, but for סדר. Many punctators, who took no notice of the Parashas, were in the habit of marking in this way the Palestinian Sidras, as may be seen in Ox. 10, 2326; Br. Mus. Or. 2201.

So much from the page before us. Other proofs are not wanting. Sappir informs us (ibid., p. 12) that he sent from Jerusalem a list of words, which he had found variously written in texts (as to punctuation, *scriptio plena* and *def.*, &c.), to a distinguished Jewish scholar in Aleppo, with the request that he would examine the Codex and note for him how these words were written in it. This was done, and subsequently Sappir published in the Jewish periodical, לבנון (I. pp. 31, 32), some of these various readings, from which I select the following: יְהִי אוֹר (Gen. i. 3)[8]; הָאָזְנָה (iv. 23)[9]; בֵּית אֵל (xii. 8, two words)[10]; כְּסְיָה (Ex. xvii. 16, one word)[11]; all contrary to Ben-Asher's rules or the Palestinian Massora, and which therefore could not have been so written by Ben-Asher himself. I also sent a list of passages, which I wished compared on account of the accentuation, and M. Loeb's correspondent volunteered the information that וְאֵינֶנּוּ (Qoh. vi. 2) is so pointed with Gaya, and יִבְחַר (ix. 4) so vocalized, for יָבַחַר; both mistakes which we may be sure would never have been made by Ben-Asher.

From these few test-passages we may conclude that the statement, assigning this Codex to Ben-Asher, is a *fabrication*,—merely introduced to enhance the value of the same,—and that the whole long epigraph, with its list of Qaraite names (shewing it to be of Qaraite origin), &c., is untrustworthy and undeserving of serious notice. How many other epigraphs to Jewish texts would, when carefully tested, have to be rejected, notably that of the Cambridge Codex 12, which makes a Spanish MS., unquestionably younger than the one we have been considering, written in the year 856[12]!

Attached to the Aleppo Codex is what the Jews call a קונטרס (a copy of which M. Loeb also procured for me). This farrago of grammatical and Massoretic rules has been sufficiently described in Dikd. hat., Pref., pp. xxi–xxiii, from a copy obtained by the Qaraite,

---

[8] So Ben-Naphtali. Cf. Baer, Gen., p. 74; Ginsb. Mas. ח, § 589.

[9] So Ben-Naphtali. Cf. Baer, Gen., p. 82, note 7; Pss. 1880, p. 138, note 6.

[10] So the Orientals. See Cod. Bab. passim. Comp. also Baer, Gen., p. 76, where the Palestinian Massora is quoted.

[11] So the Orientals. See Cod. Bab., Massora magna to Is. xxxvi. 12; and comp. the Palestinian Massora,—as given by Norzi, ad loc., or Ginsb. Mas. א, § 238,—which requires כֵּס יָה to be written as *two words*.

[12] I have myself no doubt, from personal inspection, that the Codex B. 19ᵃ, in the Imperial Library at St. Petersburg, dated 1009, is much younger, although the editors of the Catalogue accept the date.

A. Firkowitsch, when at Aleppo [13]. It contains the list of Paseqs, to which I refer, p. 121 note.

Bab. Codex prophetarum posteriorum Petropolitanus Babylonicus (A. D. 916), the text marked with the so-called Babylonian punctuation, photo-lithographed, under the editorship of Dr. Strack, 1875.

Ber. MSS. in the Royal Library, Berlin. The numbers given are those of the printed catalogue.

MSS. in the British Museum,—cited according to the press-marks Add., Harl., and Or., e.g. Add. 21161; Harl. 1528; Or. 4709. The reader will please notice that I have not thought it necessary to prefix *Br. Mus.* to these marks.

De R. De Rossi's MSS., now in the Royal Library, Parma. See De Rossi's printed catalogue.

Erf. The Erfurt MSS. 1–4, described by Lagarde in his Symmicta, p. 133 ff. (These MSS. are now in the Royal Library, Berlin.)

Hm. MSS. in the Town Library, Hamburg. The numbers are those of the printed catalogue.

K. When I had no printed catalogue to refer to, as in the case of the smaller Libraries, I have given the numbers according to Kennicott's list.

Ox. MSS. in the Bodleian Library, Oxford. See printed catalogue.

Par. MSS. in the National Library, Paris. See printed catalogue.

Vi. MSS. in the Imperial Library, Vienna.

II. MSS. ON THE ACCENTS OF THE TWENTY-ONE BOOKS.

1. Ambrosian Library, Milan, A. 186. This MS. consists of two quite distinct parts : *a.* The first and larger part (18 pp.) is headed זה הוא תוכן עזרא, a name which occurs again just before the list of the accents, וזה מן העתק תוכן עזרא. A cursory examination shewed me that this part is (as far as it goes) identical with the epitome of הורית הקורא, edited by Mercerus (Paris, 1565) under the title of ספר טעמי המקרא [14], and

---

[13] In this copy, however, a section has been dropped at the end of both Parts of the קונטרס, and three others introduced (§§ 22, 23, 24, ibid., p. xxiii) which are not in the original. That Firkowitsch was in the habit of falsifying texts that passed through his hands is well known. Were the Qaraites ἀεὶ ψεῦσται ?

[14] How far the two texts agree I am not able to state, for I had not Mercerus' edition with me when examining this MS.

assigned by him (on the authority of the Paris MS.) and by all scholars since,—falsely, as I believe I have shewn, טעמי אמ״ת, pp. 104–5,—to R. Jehuda ben-Bil'am. This conclusion of mine seems to receive the fullest confirmation from the title above given. For I would ask Jewish scholars whether it may not be taken for certain that the *name of the author* is given in the double-entendre which it conveys? Ezra was the name not only of the great סופר, but of a distinguished scribe whose copy of the Tora is constantly quoted, under the name of ספר עזרא, as of authority [15]. Such an experienced scribe we may well suppose to have been competent to treat of דקדוק המקרא בנקודיה ובטעמיה (as the subject of the Work is described in the introductory words). Another discovery we make is that the proper title of the epitome of הורית הקורא is תּוֹכֶן עֶזְרָא, 'Ezra's arrangement' [16]. But it would seem that it was only a fragment of this Work that lay before the copyist, for at the section on the accent יתיב he suddenly breaks off, and adds matter of his own. β. At this point we read in the margin: מכאן והלאן היא העתק דייקות מת׳ מנחם ברבי [שלמה] דרך קצרה העלה על אבן בחן [17]. Unfortunately what follows (6½ pp.), mostly about the accents, is marked by blunders, and of no value. Whatever Menachem's other acquirements he was evidently no accentuologist.

2. That part of חִבּוּר הַקּוֹנִים—written by Simson the punctator (circa 1230)—which refers to our subject. Simson does little else

---

[15] See e. g. Lonzano, Ôr Tora, on Gen. iv. 13; vii. 11; ix. 29; etc.; Ox. Cat. 2543; Ginsb. Mas. i. p. 611 (*bis*), iii. p. 25. Meïri (קרית ספר, Part I, 8ᵇ) states that in his time (end of the 13th century) ספר עזרא was in Toledo, and was consulted, as a standard authority, for its readings.

[16] I beg my readers to observe that this is the *earliest* notice we have of the Work assigned to Ben-Bil'am, and as being nearer to the source, is more likely to be correct. Moreover as the copyist, himself a grammarian by profession (see note following), lived within a few years of Ben-Bil'am, we may take it for granted that he would have known, and would have stated, the fact, if the author had been really Ben-Bil'am.

[17] With this agrees the statement at the end of the Part about the accents: ותשלם מערכתם העתק ספר אבן בחן, אך אני מנחם אצלתי לי עיקר חנותם דרך קצרה וישרה. Menachem, therefore, himself condensed and copied this Part from his larger Work, אבן בחן,—'ein grammatisch-lexicalisch-hermeneutisches Werk' (not a mere Lexicon, as is generally supposed), as Dr. Perles, who has examined the unique MS. of it in the Munich Library, informs me. (Comp. Steinschneider, Hebr. Bibliographie, pp. 38 ff. and 131–4.) In this MS. the sections (שערים) about the accents are wanting.—It may be added that the treatise in the Ambrosian Library was originally attached (as the epigraph states) to a copy of the twenty-four Books, made also by Menachem, in the year 1145.

than copy the treatise assigned to Ben-Bil'am. Of this Work—sometimes called Simsonî, from its author—there are three copies known, one in the Br. Mus. (Or. 1016), one in the University Library, Leipzig (Or. 102[a]), and one in De Rossi's Library, Parma (389)[18].

3. Ber. 118 (Heb. Cat.) contains (a) some rules for the accents, more or less fragmentary—in part by Samuel, the grammarian and punctator[19]—full of mistakes and quite worthless. (β) A poem (otherwise known[20]) in forty-five verses on the accents of the twenty-one Books, by R. Tam. Written in a crabbed fantastic style, it merely gives in a condensed form Ben-Bil'am's well-known rules for the *servi*, and is altogether undeserving of notice. (γ) A poem in ninety verses by Joseph ben-Qalonymos (circa 1240), on the same subject, to which the same remarks apply[21].

4. Prefixed to the Bible-text, Par. 5, is a treatise on the accents of the twenty-one Books, by Zalman the punctator[22]. He twice quotes הוריות הקורא by name, and gives the same title to his own treatise. It contains nothing of consequence.

5. Ox. 2512, a grammatical treatise in Arabic (brought from Yemen), containing at the end rules for the accents, the most interesting part of which I give, pp. 13, 14.

---

[18] Any one who is curious to know something more of this work may consult Hupfeld, *Commentatio de antiquioribus apud Judæos accentuum scriptoribus*, Partic. II, p. 11 ff. (Halle, 1846).

[19] How little he understood of the rudiments of his craft I found out when examining a MS. pointed by him (A. D. 1260), in the Library of St. John's College, Cambridge.

[20] Brought out in Kobak's Jeshurun, v. p. 126 ff.

[21] A poem on the accents of the three Books by the same author has been recently edited by Dr. Berliner (Berlin, 1886). But it is lost labour to publish such a work. Moreover, the editor's part has been very negligently performed. Both text and commentary are made in his hands to express arrant nonsense. And yet the publication is intended 'die jüdische Literatur zu bereichern!' (Pref. p. 5.)

[22] Not to be confounded with Jequthiel (Zunz, Zur Geschichte und Literatur, p. 115), for I found that his rule about Paseq after Shalshéleth is opposed to Jequthiel's remarks, Gen. xix. 16. He is doubtless the punctator (not named by Zunz), who is quoted in Br. Mus. Add. 9403 (section on ש), יסוד ר' זלמן הנקדן מרוטנבורק.—The Paris MS., to which this treatise is prefixed, is dated 1298; and Zalman may have lived about this time, for as he is not named in other works on the accents, he would seem to have been a late punctator.

THE PRINCIPAL PRINTED TEXTS

QUOTED IN THE PRESENT WORK.

Bomb. 1. 1st Rabbinical Bible, printed by Bomberg, Venice, 1518.

Bomb. 2. 2nd Rabbinical Bible, printed by Bomberg, Venice, 1525.

Jabl. Heb. Bible edited by D. E. Jablonski, Berlin, 1699.

Mich. Heb. Bible edited by J. H. Michaelis, Halle, 1720. This ed. is valuable to the student because of the various accentual readings, taken from the Erfurt MSS.

Baer. Edd. of Genesis (Leipzig, 1869), Isaiah (1872), Ezekiel (1884), Minor Prophets (1878), Five Megillôth (1886), and Daniel, Ezra, and Nehemiah (1882), by this distinguished Massoretic scholar. I strongly recommend my readers to procure these carefully prepared texts for themselves, as I have rarely thought it necessary to take notice of errors, which Baer had already corrected.

Dikd. hat. ספר דקדוקי הטעמים לרבי אהרן בן משה בן אשר עם מסורות עתיקות אחרות, edited by S. Baer and H. L. Strack (Leipzig, 1879). This Work contains, with other matter, the rules assigned to Ben-Asher on the accents, the oldest notices that we have on the subject.

Ben-Bil. The epitome of הוֹרָיַת הַקּוֹרֵא, 'Instruction for the reader,' edited by Mercerus (see p. vi), and assigned by him to R. Jehuda ben-Bil'am. My references are to the copious extracts in Heidenheim's משפטי הטעמים (see below). Occasionally I have quoted the Ox. MS. (1465)[23]. The proper title of this Work I have given above, p. xi.

Chayyuǵ. I quote from Nutt's ed. of ספר הנקוד, pp. 126–9. This part of the Work is not, however, by Chayyuǵ himself (see Nutt's remarks, p. xii).

עֵט סוֹפֵר, 'Pen of the Scribe,' by David Qimchi. The text has been

---

[23] The original הורית הקורא is not known to exist, with the exception of a fragment on the accentuation of the three Books printed in Ginsb. Mas. iii. p. 43 ff., § 246*, from a MS. (Or. 2375) in the British Museum. (The second section, however, with the same no. 246* has nothing to do with it, but comes from quite a different source.) Comp. my remarks in טעמי אמ"ת, pp. 103–5.

carelessly copied and carelessly edited by B. Goldberg [24] (Lyck, 1864). The part relating to the accents is fragmentary and of little importance.

Moses the punctator [25], reputed author of דַּרְכֵי הַנִּקּוּד וְהַנְּגִינוֹת. I quote Frensdorff's edition (Hannover, 1847). The שער הנגינות in this Work is almost entirely from Ben-Bil'am.

Jequthiel, author of עֵין הַקּוֹרֵא [26], an orthographical commentary,— mostly in regard to vowels and accents,—on the Pentateuch ; published by Heidenheim, in his edition of the Pentateuch entitled מאור עינים (Rödelheim, 1818).

Man. du Lect. Manuel du Lecteur,—a name given by J. Derenbourg to a compendium of grammar and massora, edited by him (Paris, 1871), from a Yemen MS. now in the Bodleian Library (1505). The proper title is מחברת התיגאן [27], 'The Bible-treatise.' (It is strange that Derenbourg has neither used nor explained this name.) This or some similar Work constantly appears as a Preface or Introduction in Yemen Bible Codd.

Mishp. hat. מִשְׁפְּטֵי הטעמים, a useful compilation from the works of early Jewish writers on the accents of the twenty-one Books, by Wolf Heidenheim (Rödelheim, 1808), with his own comments.

(Other known Works, such as Norzi's מנחת שי, the Massoretic compilation אכלה ואכלה, and Die Massora magna (the two latter edited by Frensdorff), do not need particular notice. Nothing is to be learned from El. Levita's טוב טעם, Arqivolti's ערונת הבושם, and the Works of Jewish writers on the Accents, other than those named above. Even from Christian accentuologists, as Wasmuth, Ouseel, Spitzner, and Ewald, I have derived little or no help.)

---

[24] Thus, the very first words, הא לך, are given as המלך, and in p. לב, שופר נשוא, 'the elevated Sh.,' is made שופר בשוא, 'Sh. with Sh'va.'

[25] The fullest notice about this writer will be found in Histoire Littéraire de la France, xxvii. p. 484 ff.

[26] On the work and its author, see Zunz, Zur Geschichte und Literatur, p. 115.

[27] تِيجَان is pl. of تَاج, 'crown,' a name given to the Tora or Bible (תנ"ך) as the 'crown' of Books. See אבן ספיר, p. 12^b, note.

CONTENTS.

ERRATA AND ADDENDA.

Page 16, note 25, *add* a third example of סיחפא, from Cod. Bab. p. 181[a]

„   23, l. 7, *point* מְנַעֲנַע

„   41, note 22, *for* Is. ix. 8 *read* Is. ix. 6[b]

„   51, l. 1, *point* אֲרוֹן

„   70, l. 21, אֶת־הָאָרֶץ, *dele* Métheg

„   88, l. 21, *dele* 'Even Ben-Asher's famous Codex &c.'

„   129, note 28, *for* 2 Ki. xxv. 2 *read* 2 Ki. xxv. 4

CHAPTER I.

INTRODUCTION [1].

THE Hebrew accentuation is essentially a musical system. The accents are *musical signs*—originally designed to represent and preserve a particular mode of cantillation or musical declamation, which was in use for the public reading of the Old Testament text at the time of their introduction, and which had been handed down by tradition from much earlier times [2]. That the signs introduced failed to answer their purpose, and that

---

[1] I may be permitted to refer to my previous treatise, chap. I, for some general remarks, which I do not think it necessary to repeat here.

[2] From the testimony of the Talmud, we are able to trace the practice of such a system to the first centuries of the Christian era, and it may have been much older. Thus the statements on the subject in Megilla 32ᵃ and Nedarim 37ᵇ are given in the names of R. Jochanan and Rab (who lived towards the middle of the third century), and that in Berakhoth 62ᵃ on R. ʿAqiba's authority (which brings us close to the beginning of the second century). Besides these, which may be regarded as historical notices, we have the tradition (Megilla 3ᵃ) that the system was in use even in Ezra's time. Nor is this tradition (as it seems to me) to be altogether rejected. It requires only to be rightly interpreted. The method of musical recitation may well have been one of the institutions established under the second temple, *and soon after Ezra's time,* for the more formal and solemn conduct of public worship. Originally introduced by the Sopherim, Ezra's immediate successors, as a kind of סְיָג לַתּוֹרָה — distinguishing the public reading of the Law, fixing its sense, and serving as a help to the memory in retaining its precepts—it may afterwards have been applied to the other Sacred Books. From the Temple it would pass into the Synagogue. And perhaps Christ Himself made use of it, when reading from the prophet Isaiah (Luke iv. 17 ff.).

(On the activity of these early סופרים, and the influence their *dicta* and the rules they laid down exercised, see Graetz, Geschichte, ii. 2, p. 180 ff. That they regulated the arrangements for public worship seems certain, ibid., p. 190. Their work was creative, and left its mark behind it.)

it is quite uncertain how far the modern chanting of the Jews—
whether Oriental, Ashkenazic, or Sephardic [3]—represents the
original melodies, is on various accounts to be regretted. For
—independently of the interest attaching to the earliest development of sacred music—if these melodies had been preserved, we
should be able to understand the reasons of various musical
changes, of which we have to take account, but for the introduction of which we can at present only offer conjectures.

One marked peculiarity of the system could not, however,
so long as the signs were accurately preserved, be lost. From
the first, the aim had been so to arrange the musical declamation,
as to give suitable expression to the *meaning* of the Sacred Text.
For this purpose, the *logical* pauses of the verse were duly
marked—and that according to their gradation—by pausal
melodies [4], later by the accentual signs that represented those
melodies; and where no logical pause occurred in a clause, the
syntactical relation of the words to one another and to the whole
clause was indicated by suitable melodies—partly pausal, partly
conjunctive—and their corresponding signs. In this way, the
originators of the system, and the accentuators who aimed at
stereotyping their work, sought to draw out the sense and
impress it on the minds of both reader and hearers. It need
hardly be added that it is this, their *interpunctional* character,
which constitutes for us the chief value of the accents.

Generally speaking, the logical and syntactical division has
been carefully carried out, in the way just indicated. And so
far we have before us a system of interpunction, which, for

---

[3] For the differences between these several modes, comp. Fétis, Histoire
Générale de la Musique, i. p. 445 ff. The character of the cantillation seems to
have been influenced by the style of music of the particular nation in which the
Jews were settled.

[4] These are the פסקי טעמים or פיסוק ט' of the Talmud (e. g. Megilla 3ᵃ,
Nedarim 37ᵃ), which, before the introduction of the *signs*, could only be learned
from oral instruction and continued practice. Hence we read of professional
teachers, who received their fee (שכר פסקי טעמים, Nedarim, l. c.) for giving
instruction in this branch.

minuteness and accuracy, leaves nothing to be desired,—a system whose only fault is that it errs on the side of excessive minuteness and apparent striving after accuracy. But it is not always so. When we come to examine the text carefully, we meet with many exceptions. We find words joined by the accents, which ought, according to rule, to be separated; and separated, which ought to be joined; moreover, pausal accents out of their place, a greater where a less is due and *vice versa*.

Such irregularities (if we are so to term them) cannot be ignored. What then are we to say to them? Are we, on account of them, to reject the whole system, as unreliable for the discrimination of the sense? or are we to try and find some explanation of them, so that we may make due allowance, in every case, for disturbances as they occur? Unquestionably, the latter is the true scientific course; nor till we have failed in discovering the necessary explanation, have we any right to condemn what it may turn out we did not understand.

One main object of the present work is to attempt to remove these stumbling-blocks in the way of accepting the accentual system of the twenty-one Books—the same task which I took in hand for the three Books. And the explanation proposed will be virtually the same.

I. In many instances, the accentuation of our texts is *false*, and has to be corrected by the testimony of MSS. Yet I do not know a single writer on the accents, who has been at the pains of seeking to remove this source of error.

II. The *predominance* of the *musical element* must be recognised. This was plainly evident in the examination of the three Books, and must be accepted, though it does not shew itself in so marked a manner, for the twenty-one Books. But then all such exceptional cases come under rule, and need occasion no difficulty. Given certain conditions, the exception must, or at least may, follow. Cases of *transformation* come under this head; and where the musical division ceases, as it often does before the minor pausal accents, there the logical or (what is more common in such cases) the syntactical division necessarily ceases also [5].

III. The well-known law of *parallelismus membrorum*—by no means confined to the poetical, or even the prophetical parts—frequently leads to an irregular division of the text.

IV. The accentuators did not hesitate to make the strict rules for logical (or syntactical) division give way, when they wished to express *emphasis*, or otherwise give effect to the reading. Undoubtedly they were right in principle; although, as we have here to do with questions of taste, we may not always agree with them.

The irregularities here briefly alluded to will of course come fully under review in the sequel.

We start then on the supposition that the accentuation does *not* furnish a perfect system of interpunction. Still, if (as I hope to be able to shew) we can trace and make allowance for disturbing causes, we shall be able to accept it as a reliable guide to the exegesis of the text. Even with what may seem to us its short-comings [6] and superfluities, it fixes the sense in a far more effective and satisfactory way than our modern system of punctuation [7].

I conclude this chapter with a few remarks on a subject of some interest, about which much has been written, viz. the *date* of the introduction of the accentual signs [8].

---

[5] I do not find in the accentual division of the twenty-one Books that *musical equilibrium* was much regarded. Rhythmical effect was much more studied.

[6] Among which may be mentioned that owing to the purely musical character of the signs employed, it was not possible to mark the interrogation, exclamation, parenthesis, &c.

[7] This has often struck me in comparing the Hebrew text with modern translations, even those few that are careful and accurate in their punctuation.

[8] The student must be warned against statements to be found in the works of some modern scholars, Graetz, Delitzsch, and others, assigning the invention of the Babylonian signs to a certain Moses the punctator, in the sixth century, and that of the Palestinian to two Qaraites, Mocha and his son Moses, at the end of the eighth century. These scholars were misled by certain forgeries and pretended discoveries of the well-known literary impostor, Abraham Firkowitsch, which have been since exposed by Harkavy (Mem. de l'Acad. Imp. des Sciences de St. Pet., xxiv. 8 ff.) and Strack (Luth. Zeitsch., 1875, p. 619).

The silence of the Talmud on the subject of the punctuation, and Jerome's express testimony [9] that it was not found in the texts of his day, have long since satisfied scholars that it cannot have been *earlier* than the fifth century [10]. The following considerations will (I think) shew that it could not have been *later* than the seventh century. (We have thus a sufficient interval for any stages of development, through which it may have passed.) Direct historical notices on the subject fail, as is well known, altogether.

1. We find that in the latter half of the ninth century as little was known about the origin of the punctuation as in the present day. All that Mar Natronaï II, Gaon (A.D. 859–869), can say about it is : לא נתן נקוד בסיני כי החכמים ציינוהו לסימן [11] ; whilst Ben-Asher (who completed the Massoretic Work on which his father had been engaged at the close of the same century [12], and who may be considered to give his father's views) more distinctly, but erroneously, assigns it to the Prophets, Sopherim, and wise men, who, with Ezra at their head, were supposed to have constituted the Great Synagogue [13]. It is clear that a system, the origin of which was lost in obscurity at the end of the ninth century, was of *much older date*.

---

[9] Jerome's testimony refers indeed to the vowel-signs (see his Comm. on Is. xxvi. 14; Jer. ix. 21; Hos. xi. 10, &c.). As to the accents (in our sense of the term) he is significantly silent; so in his Preface to Isaiah he states that he has introduced divisions of *his own* into the text (*interpretationem novam novo scribendi genere distinximus*), but makes no reference to division by the accents, Athnach &c., shewing that they were not before him. Indeed, the vocalization and accentuation were no doubt introduced at the same time. Where the one failed, so did the other.

[10] See Bleek's Einleitung, 3rd ed., § 330.

[11] Graetz, Geschichte, 2nd ed., v. p. 502.

[12] Dikd. hat., p. xvi, 1.

[13] Ibid., § 16 and passim. The notion that Ezra was the author and inventor of the signs for the vowels and accents, due to a false interpretation of a passage in the Talmud, Megilla 3ª (see Man. du Lect., p. 53), was generally accepted by the Jews in the middle ages (Buxtorf, De punctorum origine, p. 313). Some Rabbinical authorities indeed maintained that the punctuation was revealed to Moses on Sinai (ibid., p. 312); whilst others went so far as to make it coeval with the language itself, and communicated to Adam in Paradise (ibid., p. 305).

To these testimonies may be added those of Nissi ben-Noach (A.D. 840) and Mar Ṣemach ben-Chayyim, Gaon (889–896), who both refer to well-known differences in the matter of punctuation between the two great Schools of the East and West [14]. Now who does not see that a considerable space of time must have elapsed for those differences to have developed themselves and to have become formally tabulated? We are thus brought to the same conclusion that the punctuation was *much older than the ninth century*.

2. The above-named famous Aaron ben-Asher, who has the credit of having finally fixed the punctuation as we have it in our texts, was the last of a distinguished family of Massoretes and punctators, whose genealogy we are able to trace through several members up to the latter half of the eighth century [15]. There seems no reason to question the correctness of this genealogical table, when we bear in mind the care which the Jews

---

Elias Levita, himself a Jew, in his Massoreth ha-massoreth (1538), was the first to refute systematically these false notions, and to lay down correct views on the subject. (On the controversy to which this epoch-making work gave rise, and which lasted, off and on, for a century and a half,—the chief disputants being the Buxtorfs, father and son, as the assailants, and Ludovicus Cappellus as the defender, of El. Levita's views,—see an interesting pamphlet by Dr. Schneidermann, Die Controverse des L. Cappellus mit den Buxtorfen, Leipzig, 1879, or Bleek's Einleitung, 3rd ed., § 329.)

[14] The former recommends the student to make himself acquainted with the peculiarities of the Babylonian system: לאלף נקודות ומשרתות ופסוק טעמים וחסרות ויתרות לאנשי שנער (quoted in Pinsker's Liqqute Qadmonioth, p. מא). The latter alludes to the variations which the written texts of his time exhibited: במקראות שהם כתובים וקבועים יש שנוי בהם בין בבל לארץ ישראל בחסרות ויתרות ובפתוחות וסתומות ובפסקי הטעמים ובמסורות ובחתוך הפסוקים (end of ספר אלדר).

[15] See Dikd. hat., p. 79 above: (1) his father, Moses, who wrote in the year 895 a Cod. of the Prophets, still preserved in the Qaraite Synagogue in Cairo; (2) Asher ben-Moses; (3) Moses ben-Nehemiah; (4) Nehemiah; (5) Asher הזקן הגדול.—From Nos. 1 to 5 we may well allow a period of 120 years, which will bring us to A.D. 775.

From about 750 to 920 must have been a time of special activity in elaborating rules and fixing all the details of the vocalization and accentuation, for we have two lists (in which many of the names are *the same*, and which therefore confirm one another) of distinguished punctators, who flourished in this period. (Dikd. hat., pp. 78, 79.)

have always exercised in such matters. It follows that the punctuation must have been *older than the middle of the eighth century*.

3. A difficulty has indeed been started, which, however, when examined, only confirms the view above expressed as to the date of the first introduction of the punctuation. It has been argued that because a book like Sepher Jeṣîra, assigned to the eighth century, contains no allusion to the vowel-signs or accents,— although from the subjects of which it treats, such allusion was to be expected,—therefore they were not known at that time [16]. But the *argumentum ex silentio* will not apply here. The silence may be explained from the simple circumstance that pointed texts were at the time in question regarded as an *innovation*. They had still to overcome the prejudices of learned doctors and scribes who, when compiling works that dealt with early tradition, ignored them altogether. We know that the pointing of the text of the Qorân had to encounter, in the same way, at the first, objections and opposition (see Nöldeke, Geschichte des Qorân's, p. 309). Among peoples imbued with such conservative tendencies as those of the East, changes which affected their Sacred Books could be only gradually introduced. Let us suppose the eighth century to have been such a period of transition, and the difficulties broached by scholars disappear. If, however, the punctuation was at this time regarded with

---

[16] See, e. g. Derenbourg in Revue Critique, 1879, p. 455. When, however, he asserts that in the post-talmudic Tract Sopherim no trace can be found of graphical signs, for the indication of the vowels or accents, few scholars will agree with him. The best printed texts and most MSS. name *Athnach* and *Soph Pasuq* in xiii. § 1; and in iii. § 7, שבו פסוקים ראשי שניקר או שפסקו ספר אל יקרא בו, the term פסקו most naturally refers to the 'accentual divisions.' (Comp. the parallel passage in M. Sepharim, i. § 4, בו יקרא לא המנוקד ספר, where מנוקד indicates both the vocalization and accentuation.) Zunz, in his Gottesdienstliche Vorträge, p. 264, draws attention to the absence of all allusion to the punctuation in the Midrash on Canticles, at the word נקדות, chap. i. 11, and in the Hagada of the Gaonic period generally, and finds therein a proof of the late origin of the same. But such conclusions prove too much. We *know* (see above) that it was in use in the Gaonic period.

suspicion as an *innovation*, the seventh century and most probably the latter part of that century must have been the date of its introduction [17]. I pointed out in my former treatise, p. 1, that this date suits otherwise well, as it was that at which the Syriac and Greek Churches had perfected (or nearly so) their systems of interpunction and musical notation. The Arabs copied somewhat later for the Qorân the examples thus set them.

By whom and under what circumstances these graphical signs were introduced into the Hebrew text, we have no evidence to assist us in deciding. It may have been that the leading signs were first employed for the instruction of children in school. Even in the time of the Talmud, the case of children was considered, and the reading of the text made more easy for them [18]. And among the Arabs, pointed texts of the Qorân were allowed for school-teaching by authorities who forbad the use of them for public reading [19]. But on such points we are never likely to advance beyond mere conjecture.

---

[17] I mean in anything like a *complete* form. Up to this time, it would have been following a course of gradual development.

[18] In Megilla 22[a] R. Chananya says: לא התיר לי לפסוק אלא לתינוקות של בית רבן, i.e. 'I was not allowed to break up a Bible-verse, except in the instruction of school-children.'

[19] Nöldeke, l.c. p. 310.

CHAPTER II.

ON THE DIVISION, NAMES, SIGNS, ETC. OF THE ACCENTS.

THE name טְעָמִים, 'meanings' commonly given to the accents (and κατ᾽ ἐξοχήν to the *pausal* accents), refers to their function as indicators of the *sense* of the text [1]. The Arabic-speaking Jews employed another name, having reference to their *musical value*, أَلْـكَـان, 'melodies, modulations.' A corresponding Hebrew name נְגִינוֹת is used by later Rabbinical writers.

The accents may be divided into two classes, according to their *pausal* (disjunctive), or *non-pausal* (conjunctive) character [2]. In using these terms, however, we must be careful to remember that they apply, strictly speaking, only to the *melody*. (It has been already pointed out that the musical division does not always correspond to the interpunctional.) Jewish grammarians indeed generally distinguish otherwise. By what was with them a favourite figure of speech, they commonly term the pausal accents מְלָכִים or שָׂרִים, as dominating the verse, in regard to both the melody and the sense; whilst the other accents as subordinated to them, and only able to stand when a pausal accent follows, are called מְשָׁרְתִים, *servi* [3]. The latter is a useful *terminus technicus*, and may be retained.

---

[1] This name is first found in the Talmud, which more than once draws special attention to the *logical* importance of the accents. It must be remembered, however, that the Talmud knew nothing of the *signs* (which had not, at the time of its composition, been introduced into the text). If, therefore, we render the term טעמים, as used in the Talmud, by 'accents,' we must understand the melodies, and specially the *pausal melodies*, which determined the meaning. These melodies were afterwards represented by the *signs*. (Some scholars seem to forget that the *system* was precisely the same, before and after the introduction of the signs.)

[2] Comp. the terms מפסיקים, מחברים, &c., occasionally used by Rabb. writers for these two classes, טעמי אמ״ת, p. 10 inf.

[3] So the seven Vowels, which were regarded as dominating the pronunciation,

The following list gives the signs and names of the accents in common use, according to the Palestinian (or Tiberian) system [4] :—

I. Pausal or Disjunctive Accents (מְלָכִים) [5].

1.	— Silluq (סִלּוּק), as in	. . . .	דָּבָר
2.	— Athnach (אַתְנָח), as in .	. .	דָּבָר
3.	— S'gôlta (סְגוֹלְתָּא), *postpositive*, as in	.	דָּבָר
	— Shalshéleth (שַׁלְשֶׁלֶת), as in . . .		דָּבָר
4.	— Great Zaqeph (זָקֵף גָּדוֹל), as in . .		דָּבָר
	— Little Zaqeph (זָקֵף קָטוֹן), as in . .		דָּבָר
5.	— Ṭiphcha (טִפְחָא), as in		דָּבָר
6.	— R'bhîa (רְבִיעַ), as in		דָּבָר
7.	— Zarqa (זַרְקָא), *postpositive*, as in . .		דָּבָר
8.	— Pashṭa (פַּשְׁטָא), *postpositive*, as in . .		דָּבָר
	— Y'thîbh (יְתִיב), *prepositive*, as in . . .		מֶלֶךְ
9.	— T'bhîr (תְּבִיר), as in		דָּבָר

are often called מלכים, the משרתים in this case being the half-vowels, which can only stand when a full vowel follows (עט סופר, p. 4). We may also compare the אותיות משרתות, 'servile letters,' each of which has its נגיד ושר (Dikd. hat., p. 4 inf.) in the stem-word.

[4] There is another system of accentuation—the so-called Babylonian—agreeing in some respects with, but differing in others from, the Palestinian, and known to us chiefly by a MS. of the Prophets in the Imperial Library at St. Petersburg. In my opinion, this system is not only younger than, but completely dependent on, the Palestinian. I propose therefore to confine our attention, for the present, to the latter, and to give, in an Appendix, the particulars in which the other differs from it.

[5] The orthodox number of the מלכים is twelve—(S'gôlta and Shalshéleth were not counted, as we shall see further on)—answering, according to Rabbinical fancy, to the twelve signs of the Zodiac. So even Aben-Ezra, Ṣachoth 2[b], המעמים שנים עשר כנגד חלקי גלגל המזלות. On the other hand, the seven vowels were the seven planets (ibid.). Vowels and accents together were supposed to lighten up, like the heavenly bodies, what would have been otherwise dark and perplexing.

10. ﹉ Géresh (גֶּרֶשׁ), as in .   .   .   .   . דָּבָר

   ﹉ Gersháyim, or Double Géresh (גֵּרְשַׁיִם)[6], as in . דָּבָר

11. ﹉ Pazer (פָּזֶר), as in .   .   .   .   . דָּבָר

   ﹉ Great Pazer (קַרְנֵי פָרָה or פָּזֵר גָּדוֹל), as in . דָּבָר

12. ﹉ Great T'lîsha (תְּלִישָׁא גְדוֹלָה), prepositive, as in דָּבָר

13. ׀ ﹉ L'garmeh (לְגַרְמֵיהּ), as in .   .   .   . דָּבָר׀

II. Non-pausal or Conjunctive Accents (מְשָׁרְתִים).

1. ﹍ Munach (מוּנַח), as in .   .   .   .   . דָּבָר

2. ﹍ M'huppakh (מְהֻפָּךְ), as in .   .   .   . דָּבָר

3. ﹍ Mer'kha (מֵירְכָא), as in .   .   .   . דָּבָר

   ﹍ Double Mer'kha (מֵירְכָא כְפוּלָה), as in .   . דָּבָר

4. ﹍ Darga (דַּרְגָּא), as in .   .   .   .   . דָּבָר

5. ﹍ Azla (אַזְלָא), as in .   .   .   .   . דָּבָר

6. ﹍ Little T'lîsha (תְּלִישָׁא קְטַנָּה), postpositive, as in דָּבָר

7. ﹍ Galgal (גַּלְגַּל), as in .   .   .   .   . דָּבָר

[8. ﹍ Mây'la (מָאיְלָא), as in .   .   .   . לְהַחֲלוֹ]

The *notation* (signs) given in the above list may be regarded
as original[7]. The *names* are in some cases Aramaic, in others

(The Jews were not alone in indulging in such fancies. The Greeks compared
the seven notes of the lyre to the seven planets, the twenty-eight sounds to
the twenty-eight days of the month, &c. See Chappell's History of Music,
pp. 30, 52.)

[6] So written and pronounced. The regular form would of course be גֵּרָשִׁים,
like קְרָנַיִם, &c.

[7] Certainly not derived from the Syriac, as Ewald (Abhandlungen, p. 130)
seems to assert. If in one or two minor points a resemblance can be traced, it
is purely accidental.

In some leather Tora-rolls, brought from Yemen, and now in the British
Museum (Or. 1451, 1452, 1453, 1457), there is indeed what seems at first sight
an approximation to the *Syriac system*. A point (not in ink, but marked by an

Hebrew. The meanings of the same may be traced (see below) to their figure, their position, their pausal and above all their musical value.

The signs fall generally on the *tone-syllable*. This (as is well-known) is a subsidiary purpose served by the accentuation. When therefore, in the case of a prepositive or postpositive accent, the tone does not fall on the first or last syllable respectively, the accent is bound to be *repeated* on the tone-syllable. With Pashṭa the rule is carried out, e. g. תֹּהוּ הַמֶּלֶךְ [8]; but with S'gôlta, Zarqa, and the two T'lishas, it is very irregularly observed, in both Codd. [9] and printed Texts. Jequthiel, indeed, in his carefully prepared text (עֵין הקורא) and Baer in his editions repeat the accent, e. g. הַמֶּלֶךְ, הַמֶּלֶךְ, הַמֶּלֶךְ, and הַמֶּלֶךְ. A Codex, like Par. 1, that regularly does so, is very rare indeed.—For the reasons which led to the omission of the second sign, see the remarks on the several accents.

It is to be observed that every word in the text has its proper melody assigned to it, and is provided with either a disjunctive or conjunctive accent. The only exception is in the case of two or more words, joined by the hyphen, called Maqqeph, which are treated as a single word. Thus כָּל־אַפְסֵי־אָרֶץ (Is. lii. 10) has only one accent, not three.

The character of the accentuation is (as has been stated) pre-eminently musical. We should expect therefore a classification of the accents based on their *musical* value. And this has been

---

instrument, that left a small circular indentation) to the *left hand* of the word, marks the close of the verse, and one *under* the word the position of Athnach. Moreover, a diacritic point is placed *over* the word, to ensure the proper pronunciation, in the cases of אֵת (אֶת), בֹּל (כֹּל), and הוּא (הִיא). Thus

בְּרֵאשִׁית בָּרָא אֱלֹהִים אֵת הַשָּׁמַיִם וְאֵת הָאָרֶץ ֫ (Gen. i. 1).

But these points are apparently of *modern* date (later than the writing), and can hardly be due to the influence of the old Syriac notation. (In Or. 1453, 1457 the attempt has been made, more or less, to erase them.)

[8] Many Codd. omit the second Pashṭa (found in Baer's and other texts) in forms like נֹחַ (Gen. viii. 13); שֹׁמֵעַ (Judg. xi. 10); וַיִּבְךְּ (2 Sam. iii. 32); אָמַרְתְּ (Is. xlvii. 10). So too it is unnecessary to point, with Heidenheim and Baer, כֹּל־בָּ, אֹשֶּׁר (Gen. vi. 22; vii. 2).

[9] Even those which lay claim to exceptional correctness, as De R. 413, which professes to have been copied from the famous Cod. Hillell. Comp. Man. du Lect., p. 92, l. 13, where it is taken for granted that S'gôlta, Zarqa, &c. are *not* repeated.

attempted in some earlier treatises [10], but in terms so brief and enigmatical that no one has yet succeeded in deciphering and explaining them. The difficulty has in a great measure arisen from scholars not having had before them the original Arabic *termini technici,* which the Hebrew terms but imperfectly represent. This deficiency I am able to supply from an Arabic treatise on the accents in the Bodleian Library [11], by the help of which we can arrive at a sufficiently clear idea of what the old grammarians meant. They divided then the מלכים under three heads :—

I. Those which were chanted with the *highest* tone [12], Pazer, T'lîsha, and Géresh. As these accents often *lead off* the melody, the highest notes were suitably enough assigned to them. In this class we must further include Shalshéleth [13], a very rare accent, which (as we shall see further on) belonged to the same musical category as Pazer.

II. Those which were chanted *high* [14], viz. Zarqa [S'gôlta],

---

[10] See Ben-Bil. in Mishp. hat., p. 8, and Chayyúǵ, p. 128.

[11] Ox. 2512. The same treatise is found in Or. 2349 and Par. 1327. These MSS. are all from Yemen.

[12] Of this division, Ben-Bil., p. 8, says simply ירים הקול ויעלהו. The author of Man. du Lect., p. 90, who styles it דרך גובה, describes it in the same way, and adds, by way of illustration, that when two or three Pazers occur in the same verse 'the voice of the reader is elevated, so as to be heard afar off' (יגבה קול הקוראים וישמע עד למרחוק). In Ox. 2512, p. 13, we have the original Arabic *terminus technicus,* الإِعْلَان, which is thus explained : معنى الاعلان هو انك ترفع الصوت وتعلنه [sic] الى فوق بقوّة. The proper meaning of اعلان is 'a making (or being) known.' (Hence Chayyúǵ, p. 128, has derived his strange name of ידיעה for this division.) It came then to signify 'a publishing abroad, making (the voice) heard aloud,' and in this latter sense was used as synonymous with رفع الصوت, 'lifting up of the voice' (comp. Sa'adia's rendering of Is. xlii. 2, 11, and Abu'l-walîd s.v. נשא). We have therefore no proper distinction between the terms used for the first and second divisions. Only *conventionally* can الاعلان have signified a higher and more powerful elevation of the voice than الرفع.

[13] As Ox. 2512 also distinctly states : سلسلة من هذا القسم.

[14] Ben-Bil. and Chayyúǵ call this division עלוי, Man. du Lect., p. 75, דרך רום. The Arabic name agrees, الرَفَع. All that Ox. 2512 says of it is that it is intermediate between I and III : معنى الرفع ان يكون متوسّط بين الاعلان والوضع.

R'bhîa, L'garmeh, T'bhîr. These accents constantly occupy in practice an intermediate position between those of I and III, and so had an intermediate melody (comp. note 14). Even T'bhîr was made a *high* note, in antithesis to the fall of the voice with Ṭiphcha, which always follows.

III. We pass on, in natural order, to the *low*, which were at the same time *sustained*, tones [15], represented by Pashṭa, Zaqeph, Ṭiphcha, Athnach, and Silluq. The voice dropped and proceeded in measured tones, on approaching the two great pauses in the middle and at the end of the verse, and also the pauses next in magnitude to them marked by Zaqeph. (This last rule is indeed contrary to what we should have expected, for Zaqeph and its foretone Pashṭa seem from form and position *high* notes [16].) When however the word, on which any of these accents falls, is Mil'el, we are told [17] that the melody changed and that they were chanted with a *high* note (the voice dropping however again, I presume, with the last syllable). The *arsis* in such cases explains the change in the melody.

The author of Man. du Lect. (p. 75) informs us that the משרתים, *servi*, admit of being divided in the same way, but no particulars are given.

One error Jewish grammarians avoided. They did not attempt to classify the מלכים according to their supposed *interpunctional*

---

[15] Ben-Bil. calls this division מוֹנַח, Chayyug הַעֲמָדָה, Man. du Lect., pp. 75 and 93, דרך נצב and דרך שחייה. The Arabic name is الوَضع. The term שחייה shews that the tones were '*low*.' The other names are synonymous, and indicate steady '*sustained*' tones. Comp. Man. du Lect., p. 96: עניָן נצב שׁיְיַשֵׁב את הנעימה לא יִנְבִּיהֶנָה בקוֹלוֹ, ולא ירימֶנָה בגרוֹנוֹ, ולא ישפילֶנָה בהגיוֹנוֹ, אלא ומعنى الوَضع هو ان تَحطّ. ישׁבֶנָה במתק לשוֹנוֹ (*dolce*). Ox. 2512 agrees: الذى هم عليها ولا تعلن الصوت بها ولا ترفعه بل تضعه وضعا ساكنا.

[16] If we were to transfer these accents to Class II, and bring T'bhîr into Class III, we might suppose that all was in order. But we know too little of the musical value of the accents to be able to dogmatize.

[17] See Ben-Bil., and more fully Man. du Lect., p. 97 sup. In the latter passage, however, two of the quotations are falsely accented. For Gen. i. 1, take 2 Chr. ii. 11; and for Ex. i. 2, Gen. xxxv. 23.

value. On the other hand, early Christian writers on the accents aimed at establishing on this basis a kind of hierarchy, consisting of *Imperatores, Reges, Duces, Comites*, &c. Strange indeed is it to find this fanciful and misleading distinction (long ago rejected by Spitzner) still retained in so standard a Work as Gesenius' Heb. Gr., p. 52. Athnach and Silluq are both made *Imperatores*, although (as will be seen hereafter) the former is as much subordinated to the latter, as Zaqeph is to Athnach. Nor can Ṭiphcha (as in the early editions) be properly placed in the same class with Zaqeph, &c. (The present editor has indeed avoided the last-named error, but only to fall into a more serious one. He has actually reckoned R'bhia among the *Reges*, whilst Ṭiphcha follows only as a *Dux!* And this mistake has already begun to circulate as current coin, see Curtiss, Outlines of Heb. Gr., p. 20, and König, Lehrgebäude der Hebr. Sprache, p. 76.) The few pages devoted to the accentuation in this otherwise correct and useful Work sadly need revision.

REMARKS ON THE SEVERAL ACCENTS [18].

The variety of names assigned to some of the accents will perhaps appear surprising to the student. They are doubtless to be mainly accounted for, as having originated in different schools, or under the influence of this or that distinguished teacher. Occasionally, perhaps, we may trace the fancy of some unimportant punctator,—the names he proposed not being found elsewhere than in the list he drew up. It is with the least important accents that the greatest liberties have been taken. The names of the leading accents, Silluq, Athnach, Zaqeph, &c. were left for the most part undisturbed. After all, any modern Dictionary of Music will shew almost as great a variety

---

[18] In these remarks, I quote not only printed lists, but lists found in the following MSS.: Ox. 2512 (already described); Vat. 475 (? 14th century); De R. 333 (dated 1392), 1016 (? 14th century), and 1262 (dated 1454). The Arabic list, Pet. 123 (? 16th century), has been printed in Pinsker's Einleitung &c., pp. 42–43.

I also refer occasionally to the *Zarqa-lists*, so named from the accent with which they all commence. Three such lists are current, differing slightly from one another, and named after the communities in which they are in use,—ספרד'י (Spanish), אימליאני (Italian), and אשכנזי (German). The date of their introduction is uncertain, but they can hardly be older than the 14th century, for no writer on the accents alludes to them, and they are very rare in manuscript. Perhaps they were originally intended for popular use, for giving instruction to children in school,—a purpose which they still serve,—&c. Accurate they are not. Any one who is curious to see them will find them in Norzi's Bible, i. p. 135[b], after the Megilloth. As given in Bartolocci's Biblioth. magna rabbin., iv. 441–442, they are full of mistakes.

of names for many notes, particularly for musical figures, graces, &c.,
such as were more or less in use in the Hebrew cantillation [19].

I have quoted several times Villoteau's description of the musical
value of the accents [20]. A distinguished musician, he took great
pains to ascertain and reproduce correctly the melodies in use in the
synagogues of Egypt. These Oriental melodies seem to me sometimes
really to represent the true character of the accents.

DISJUNCTIVES. I. 1. The terms סִלּוּק and סוֹף פָּסוּק׃ are indiffer-
ently used for the final accent of the verse. The former, which means
'cessation,' 'close,' i.e. of the melody, is the name of the stroke
(inclining often in Codd. slightly to the left [21]) placed under the tone-
syllable of the word. The latter term indicates properly the two
points (or small strokes) which separate the verses from one another [22].
Evidently, these points served as the main guide for the reader.
In Yemen Codd. the stroke under the tone-syllable is often wanting
altogether [23].

2. אֶתְנַחְתָּא, אַתְנָחָה, or אַתְנָח. An Aramaic name, derived from
the Aphel of תְּנַח, secondary form of נוּחַ [24], and properly signifying
'a causing to rest' (comp. אַפְטָרָה, אַזְכָּרָה, &c.). Another name of
very rare occurrence is סַחְפָּא (so written in Codd.), which means
'a turning over.' This name properly belongs, as it seems to me, to
the Babylonian system, in which Tiphcha is represented by ⌄, and
Athnach following by the same sign *turned over*, ⌃ [25]. For an
explanation of the form see טעמי אמ״ת, p. 15.

3. סְגוֹלְתָּא, סְגוּלָה, or סְגוֹל, so named from its similarity to the
vowel-sign S'gôl [26]. The three points have, however, a meaning of

---

[19] Heidenheim (Mishp. hat., p. 5[b]) has given various names of the accents, but
has mixed together those of the three and twenty-one Books, and copied, without
scruple, blunders of Qalonymos and El. Levita.

[20] In the great Work, Description de l'Egypte, État moderne, vol. i. p. 838 ff.

[21] As the Arabic treatise, Ox. 2512, says, in describing Silluq : هو شكل عصا
واقف يميل الى اليسار قليلا.

[22] Sometimes, as in Or. 1467, 1477, 2363, and Ox. 2484 (all Yemen Codd.), a
single point (or stroke) is used, as in Syriac.

[23] As in Or. 1469, 1473, 1477, 2366; Ox. 2484; Par. 1325, &c.

[24] The part. of this form, מתנח, occurs in the Talmud, Erubin 53[a].

[25] Full as our Massora is, the name occurs but *once*, in the mas. parva to Lev.
xviii. 15; whereas, in the scanty remains that have come down to us of the
Oriental Massora, it has already been found twice, in Cod. Bab. mas. parva to
Hos. xiii. 12, and in a rubric given in Ginsb. Mas., iii. p. 246. (In the list at the
end of Bomb. 1, the word is misprinted סטפא.) The very name Sichpha (a
strange form) may have been intended as a play on the word Tiphcha.

[26] Hence called by Hadassi (Sepher ha-eshkol, p. 61) סגול העליון.

their own, being intended to indicate that S'gôlta was (relatively) a greater pausal accent than Zaqeph with its *two* points, as Zaqeph, in its turn, was greater than R'bhîa with only *one* point. A probably older name, which is intimated in Cod. Bab. and is used by Chayyúg (p. 127) and retained in the Italian Zarqa-list, is שָׁרֵי, 'encamping,' 'halting for rest [27],' by which the greater pause made by S'gôlta was indicated. Rabbinical writers have also another name, הָרוֹדֵף לְזַרְקָא, due to their fanciful notion that, as S'gôlta always 'follows Zarqa,' it was not entitled to rank as a separate and independent accent [28]. Ben-Asher's strange name קַבְלָה, meaning 'What is over-against' (Zarqa), conveys the same idea (Dikd. hat., p. 18).

This accent was made *postpositive* (according to the grammarians [29]) for clearness' sake, that its points might not be mixed up with the others that appear above the word, as they would have been, e. g. in שְׁלֹמֹה, יְהוֹשֻׁעַ. For the same reason doubtless it was but seldom *repeated*, when the word is Mil'el.

4. שַׁלְשֶׁלֶת', 'Chain [30].' A very rare accent, occurring only seven times in the twenty-one Books [31]. The sign (which was supposed to represent a hanging chain [32]) and the name both point to the melody, which is described as a double-trill [33], with its *chain* of notes; or as two notes connected by an *ascending chain* of sounds [34]. The former melody suits better the descriptive terms applied to this accent in the Massora and elsewhere [35].—The Paseq, which accompanies it (Mas. to

---

[27] Comp. חוֹנֶה used for Athnach, טעמי אמ"ח, p. 14. Or שָׁרֵי may mean *dissolvens, separans*, like the Syriac accent, ܠܒ (Duval, Gr. Syr., p. 154).

[28] See Mishp. hat., p. 36ᵃ below. 'Olev'yored in the three Books is treated in the same way.

[29] Comp. Mishp. hat., p. 38ᵇ.

[30] Sometimes the form סלסלה is used (e. g. in Pet. 123) = سِلْسِلَة. In Dikd. hat., § 16ᵃ, the name is רָתָק, in Vat. 475 רתוק, comp. Is. xl. 19.

[31] As it occurs so seldom it was not counted entitled to a place among the מלכים (see Mishp. hat., p. 7).

[32] צורתו כשלשלת ברול (Zalman the punctator in Par. 5).

[33] Comp. El. Levita's description of it as sung by the Ashkenazim of his day: § 4). (טוב טעם) יש לו קול יותר גבוה מכל המלכים עד שמנגנים אותו כשני פזורים (For Pazer as a trill, see p. 21.)

[34] According to the Oriental mode, see Villoteau, p. 838.

[35] מַרְעִים, 'reverberating' (Mas. to Lev. viii. 23; Dikd. hat., p. 18 below); מַרְעִיד, 'making to tremble' (Ox. 41; Par. 4; St. Pet. Cat., p. 85); מַרְפָא, 'agitating, shaking' the voice (De R. 861; comp. Ginsb. Mas. מ, § 235),—terms all suiting its character as a *tremolo* or trill.

Lev. viii. 23), was introduced for the sake of conformity with the pausal Shalshéleth of the three Books [36].

5. זָקֵף‎, זַקְפָא‎. Doubtless derived its name from the 'upright' finger employed, in the teaching of the cantillation, to mark it. Comp. Ben-Asher (Dikd. hat., p. 18), מיוחד באצבע זקף‎. Why *two points*—instead of an upright line, as we should have expected—were chosen as its sign, has been explained under S'gôlta. But the upright line was not lost sight of, as we shall see immediately.

Zaqeph is an accent of very frequent occurrence,—four or more often appearing in one verse,—and probably on this account was subjected (more than any other accent) to various musical modifications, with the view of varying the recurring melody. Thus we have the simple sign of two points, 'ז קָטֹן‎ or 'ז סְתָם‎, with a simpler melody; and a double sign, made up of the two points and the upright line named above,—a double Zaqeph [37],—with a fuller, stronger tone. This form of the accent is known as 'ז גָּדוֹל‎. (We must not, however, be misled by the names, and suppose that 'ז גָּדוֹל‎ represents a *greater pausal* accent than 'ז קָטֹן‎ (see e. g. Gen. ii. 9[b]). The difference is simply musical [38].) The rules—which have never yet been clearly made out—for the employment of the one or other of these accents will follow in due course; as also the explanation of the other musical modifications to which Zaqeph's word is subject.

6. טִפְחָא‎ means 'handbreadth.' The name refers, as I conjecture, to the 'outspread hand,' the manual sign employed for this accent. (Unfortunately but few of these signs have been described to us by those who knew them.) Another name, in equally common use, is טַרְחָא‎, 'laboring, toiling,' which can only mean a 'slow, heavy' melody, *lento*. Ṭarcha, as immediately preceding the cadence at Athnach and Silluq, may well have been of this character. Before Silluq it had also the special name (an intimation that the melody varied slightly from that before Athnach) דְּחִי‎, 'thrust back,' in allusion to the backward inclination of the sign [39], in contrast to Silluq.

7. רְבִיעַ‎, an Aramaic word,='resting.' The name may refer to the *pause*, or the character of the *melody*, 'resting,' 'sustained' (see

---

[36] But it was quite unnecessary, and fails in many old Codd., as Add. 21161; De R. 10, 226; K. 154. Comp. Jequthiel's note to Gen. xix. 16.

[37] So we have a double Géresh and a double Mer'kha.

[38] Comp. Man. du Lect., p. 96: הזוקף נחלק לשנים פעם יקרא זקף קטון ופעם יקרא זקף גדול וזה לפי נעימות המלה.

[39] As in the list at the end of Bomb. I (copied in Ginsb. Mas. i. p. 658). So Mây'la, which has the same inclination, is called דְּחוּיָה‎. In Pet. 123 we have the Arabic name رَاجِع‎, 'thrusting back' the sign.

טעמי אמ״ת, p. 15)[40]. The shape of the accent, as laid down by grammarians[41], and *found in all Codd.*, is an ordinary *point*, like Chôlem or Chîreq. I mention this, because some scholars still cling to the notion that R. had its name from its *square* shape (רְבִיעַ=רְבִיעַ). But this form, where found in printed texts, has been simply due to the same mistaken notion on the part of the editors.

8. זַרְקָא or צִנּוֹרִי. Jewish writers on the accents derive the name זרקא from זרק, 'to sprinkle, scatter.' It may be taken to refer to the character of the melody, which is further symbolized by the *form* of the accent[42]. Comp. Villoteau, p. 838 : 'Les sons semblent *se répandre et s'étendre, en tournoyant.*' The form would then represent what is called in music 'a turn.' Originally it was so ⌐, whence the name צִנּוֹרִי, 'hook-like[43].' This form is still common in Codd. But as there was not always room for this upright sign between the lines, it was made recumbent, and delineated with a free hand assumed the shape which appears in our printed texts.

Zarqa was made *postpositive* for the sake of conformity with its position in the three Books ; and as it is in these Books seldom *repeated*, when the word is Mil'el (lest it should be confounded with Ṣinnorîth), so punctators rarely repeat it in the twenty-one Books.

9. פַּשְׁטָא or פֶּשֶׁט, 'extending,' 'stretching out in length.' The name may be most simply explained, as referring to the melody, 'indique qu'on doit *étendre et prolonger* la voix *sur le même ton*' (Villoteau, p. 840). So the Orientals chant this accent. The sign is properly a straight line inclined to the left, made *postpositive*, to distinguish it from Azla, with the same form.

When Pashṭa would come on a monosyllable, or a dissyllable which is Mil'el, and no servus precedes, it is changed into יְתִיב[44],—an accent of

---

[40] Here and there in lists (e. g. in Chayyug, p. 129) the name רביעי is found. This change of the original name, if not a corruption, may have been due to the (incorrect) notion that R. marks the *fourth* pausal division of the verse after Silluq, Athnach, and Zaqeph.

[41] As, for instance, by Aben-Ezra (צחות, p. 1), צורת החולם נקודה למעלה בסוף המלה, שלא יתערב עם הנקודה הנקראת רביע.

[42] On further consideration, this explanation appears to me more probable than that which I proposed in טעמי אמ״ת, p. 16.

[43] For צִינוֹרָא, 'hook,' comp. Levy, Neuhebr. W. B.—Menachem ben Salomo (in his work אבן בוחן) describes Zarqa כעין אגמון, this word being understood by Rabb. writers in the sense of 'hook,' and in Or. 2349 I found : زرقا وهو شكل مثل صِنّارَة, 'is in the form of a hook.'

[44] A fine musical distinction, not without parallel, as we shall see further on.

But it is surprising that the *same* signs should have been chosen for Azla and M'huppach, the servi of Pashṭa, as for Pashṭa itself and Y'thîbh. As might have been expected, no little confusion has been the result. Pashṭa has been confounded in texts with Azla, and M'huppach with Y'thîbh.

the same *disjunctive* value, but differing in form and melody; thus מִי becomes מֵי (Gen. iii. 11), אֵלֶּה, אֵלֶּה (vi. 9). This new accent was made *prepositive*, in order to distinguish it from the conjunctive accent M'huppach with the same form, e. g. אֵלֶּה and אֵלֶּה, נַעַר and נַעַר[45]. Its own *disjunctive* character was indicated by the name given it, יְתִיב, 'resting, pause.'

(Different schools did not, however, all agree in the above nomenclature. Some grammarians make יְתִיב the generic name, and understand by it generally Pashta, distinguishing when necessary between יְתִיב פַּשְׁטָא and יְתִיב מַהְפַּךְ. With others the distinction is between מִלְמַעְלָה 'י and מִלְמַטָּה 'י, or between יְתִיב *simplex*, and מוּקְדָּם 'י[46].— Y'thîbh is also known as שׁוֹפָר יְתִיב[47]. Chayyug̒ (p. 129) speaks of it as שׁוֹפָר הָפוּךְ אֲשֶׁר הוּא מוּכְרָת, i.e. 'which is disjoined.' Rashi (on Deut. xi. 30) has the name מַשְׁפֵּל, 'making low,' and Pet. 123 כָּאָרְכָה, perhaps 'enveloping,' because standing outside the vowel.)

10. תְּבִיר or תַּבְרָא (=Heb. שֶׁבֶר). The name is derived from the melody, which was a *broken* note, a series of broken tones in one measure (as it is sung in the present day). Hence T'bhîr is described as מַשְׁבִּיר הַתֵּיבָה (Man. du Lect., p. 72). The *form*—as made up of R'bhîa and Mer'kha—represents it as an intermediate accent, neither so strong as the former, nor so weak as the latter (R'bhîa, T'bhîr, Mer'kha, is the frequent order in the full melody preceding Ṭiphcha).

11. גֶּרֶשׁ, גְּרִישׁ, *expulsio*. This accent was one of the highest notes (see p. 13), and required a strong 'expulsion' of the voice to produce it. It was also known as טָרֵף, מַרְפָּא, being a *trill* like Pazer[48]. Another very common name is טֶרֶם, טְרִים, 'bar[49],' derived from the

---

[45] It may be noted that, where there is no vowel under the first letter, M'huppach is (in carefully pointed Codd.) placed under the *middle* of the letter, Y'thîbh more to the *right*, e. g. פָּל and פָּל, קָדַשׁ and קָדַשׁ.

Moses the punctator tells us (דרכי הנקוד, p. 27) that Y'thîbh was also distinguished by being *smaller* in size, which is false (as any Codex will shew). Equally so is his statement that the melody was the *same* as that of Pashṭa, for then there would have been no change in the sign.

[46] For these different names, see Mishp. hat., 32ª, 35ᵇ; Man. du Lect., pp. 77, 94.

[47] Mishp. hat., 37ª.

[48] See note 35 and Dikd. hat., p. 17 note. In De R. 1262, Géresh and Pazer are both described as מרעישות, 'making (the voice) tremble.'

[49] See Fleischer's note in Levy's Neuhebr. W. B., ii. p. 211. So Ab'ul-walîd, Lexicon, p. 113, uses تُرْس for Heb. בריח. Chayyug̒ (p. 128) has the form תרים, which is more correct, in view of the derivation.

form (properly a straight line) and indicating the *disjunctive* character of this accent. So we use 'bar' of a dividing line in music.

גֶּרֶשׁ and גֵּרְשַׁ֞יִם, 'Double Géresh,' (called ג' קטן and ג' גדול respectively in Ox. 2512, p. 18), differed musically, and in the rules for their employment. Their *disjunctive* value is the same.

12. פָּזֵר, פָּזְרָא, derives its name from its melody, מגביה וחוזר ובלשון מתפזר (Dikd. hat., p. 18). It was a *trill*, but of a more pronounced character than Géresh. Like Géresh it occurs with a twofold melody and two different signs, known as Great and Little Pazer. The original sign of the former, still preserved in many Codd., was no doubt פָּזֵר גָּד֞וֹל, in which we may see a representation of the manual sign used for this accent, '*two fingers turned upwards*' (Man. du Lect., p. 108). Sometimes in Codd. Little Pazer differs only in being *smaller*, but generally there is a slight alteration in the form as well, thus : פֹּ֞ר, פֹּ֜ר. The original meaning of the sign was after a time lost sight of, and many variations of form were introduced.

By a poor figure of speech Great Pazer was commonly known as קַרְנֵי פָרָה, 'cow-horns;' in Man. du Lect., p. 91, it is likened to the *antennae* of the locust, כקרני חגבים; and in Pet. 123 it is مِقْرَاض, 'a pair of scissors.' This accent, from its rare occurrence (it is found only sixteen times), attracted the attention of the punctators, who amused themselves with giving it various ornamental forms, one of which is that which appears in printed texts and is made to resemble two T'lishas,—a misleading representation, for Pazer had no connection (as far as we know) with T'lisha. The Mas. parva to Ezek. xlviii. 21, which describes Great Pazer with its servus Galgal as אופן ועגלה, 'wheel and waggon,' was doubtless due to this form.

Little Pazer—sometimes called סָתָם 'פ—is the ordinary Pazer of our texts, and is of very frequent occurrence.

13. תַּלְשָׁ֔א or תְּלִישָׁ֔א. Like Géresh and Pazer, a musical term (from the root תְּלַשׁ, 'to pluck out, draw out with effort') indicating that this accent 'drew out' the voice with a marked effort and impulse. (It was one of the highest notes, p. 13.) The sign is properly a small circle [50], which seems to have been intended to symbolize the melody [51]. From this circular form was derived another name, תַּרְסָא, 'shield [52].'

---

[50] دَائِرَة صَغِيرَة, Ox. 2512, and so it is marked in Cod. Bab. and Yemen Codd.

[51] Comp. Villoteau, p. 842, who after giving the melody as he had heard it in the East, adds : 'Il faut arracher la voix avec force du fond de la poitrine, et étendre les sons, en faisant *un petit circuit*.'

[52] תרסא = תרים, but I have found no other example of this form. The name תרים was avoided, as being too like to טרים, No. 11. For 'round as a shield,' comp. Dozy, s.v. ترس.

T'lísha had, like Géresh and Pazer, with which it is so often associated, a twofold melody, distinguished as תְּלִישָׁא גְדוֹלָה and תְּלִישָׁא קְטַנָּה ;
but here the weaker melody is a *conjunctive*. The sign of the former
is *prepositive* and sometimes called in consequence ת' יָמִין, that of the
latter *postpositive*, ת' שְׂמֹאל. Grammarians tell us that they were so
placed, that they might not be confounded with the circular sign –͡– ,
marked over words which are the object of a Massoretic note [53]. For
the same reason punctators rarely *repeat* the sign.

14. לְגַרְמֵיהּ ׀, i. e. מוּנַח לְגַרְמֵיהּ [54]. The name L'garmeh means 'for
or by itself, independent' = disjunctive, and was chosen to designate
a particular *disjunctive* melody—which must originally have resembled Munach—in contrast to the *conjunctive* Munach, with or
without Paseq following. With Paseq, the signs are the same.
How the one was distinguished from the other in practice we shall
see further on. But it was clearly a mistake to employ the *same
signs* for two distinct accentual values,—a mistake that has been
avoided in the Babylonian system. (Such mistakes are sure to lead
to confusion, and the present instance forms no exception, as any one
who has consulted the Paseq-lists will have observed.)

The melody of L. must have been 'drawn out' in comparison with
that of the simple Munach, as we gather from the name נֶגֶד, נֶגְדָּא,
protractio, assigned to this accent in Dikd. hat., p. 17 (see Baer's note),
and elsewhere.

II. 1. Of the CONJUNCTIVES, the most important, owing to their
frequent occurrence, are those belonging to the Shophar-class, so
named as the sign was meant to represent the שׁוֹפָר, 'trumpet,' which
is still employed by the Jews in their religious observances. This
musical instrument, the only one in use since the destruction of the
second temple, could hardly have been passed over, in choosing the
signs and names for the musical notes.

Early writers on the accents distinguish as follows :—

a. שׁוֹפָר מְיַשֵּׁב or שׁוֹפָר מוּנַח [55], representing a 'sustained' note.
(The name Munach does not refer, as is generally supposed, to the
position under the word, but to the melody.)

---

[53] Man. du Lect., p. 92.

[54] We must not call it פסק לגרמיה, as Qimchi does (עט סופר, p. ל), and above all
not מונח לפני לגרמיה, as in the printed Mas. to Ex. xxx. 13 (although Frensdorff
has copied without scruple): לפני is a clerical error. Parallel to our Munach
L., are the Azla L. and M'huppach L. of the three Books.

[55] The name מיושב is regularly used in Man. du Lect. for Munach (it is also
found in Chayyug, p. 128), and is thus explained, p. 87 : לשון מיושב שהמלה תצא
בו בנעימה מיושבת לא למעלה ולא למטה. Corresponding names in עט סופר,
p. ל, and Ox. 2512, p. 18, are ש' מַעֲמָד and ש' עוֹמֵד. The Arabic name is
ش' נַחַת = שׁוֹפָר وَضْع.

b. שׁ׳ נָשׂוֹא (נָשׂוֹאִי) or שׁ׳ מוּרָם, שׁוֹפָר עִלּוּי, had, as its names imply, an 'ascending' tone [56].

c. שׁוֹפָר מְכַרְבֵּל or שׁ׳ כַּרְבְּלָא, an *ornamental* note, whence its name, in reference to 1 Chr. xv. 27 and Dan. iii. 21. Its only use was to vary the melody before Zaqeph. The musical character was a 'broken' note (answering to the שׁ׳ שָׁבוּר of the three Books), as the names שׁ׳ מְנַעֲנֵעַ and שׁ׳ קַלְקֵל (so pointed) shew. That it was also a 'descending' note appears from another name, שׁ׳ נָחִית [57].

The שׁוֹפָר therefore, according to its position before this or that disjunctive accent, had a 'sustained,' an 'ascending' or a 'descending' melody; and thus (speaking roughly) one may say that the three Shophars are explained. Precise rules are laid down for their respective employment, which will be referred to hereafter.

But why (it has been asked) three such different melodies with *one and the same sign?* I think I can explain. These three Shophar-intonations were meant to correspond to the three notes (or trumpet-calls) appointed to be sounded on the Shophar upon the great Festival of the New Year [58]. Not that the musical value was the same. But the *threefold* distinction in the one case suggested the same distinction for the other. We have the *Shophar with three notes* in both cases.

The *single sign* employed, however, gradually led to the obliteration of the distinction so carefully laid down; and though a variety of names (including some of those given above) came into use, they had a common signification, and pointed to *one* accent (instead of to three) [59]. Such names are שׁ׳ הוֹלֵךְ, שׁ׳ יָשָׁר, שׁ׳ גָּדוֹל κατ᾽ ἐξοχήν, שׁוֹפָר עִלּוּי, מוּנָח (these three last names in contrast to שׁ׳ מְהֻפָּךְ), and lastly—most inappropriate of all—גַּלְגַּל [60]. As the musical division has no meaning

---

[56] For these names, see Mishp. hat., 6ᵇ; Man. du Lect., p. 87; Chayyug, p. 128; and עט סופר, p. לב. (Here for נשוא the editor has carelessly printed, twice over, בשוא!) The Arabic name is شّ׳ رَفْع.

[57] For the above names, see Mishp. hat., 11 and 13; Man. du Lect., pp. 103, 108; Chayyug, l.c., and עט סופר, l.c. (קַלְקֵל is Infinitive-form of קִלְקֵל, Ezek. xxi. 26). The Arabic name was borrowed from the Hebrew. Ben-Bil. (Ox. MS.) says of this accent that it was chanted בהכרעה והנעה, 'with an emphatic agitation' (of the voice).

[58] Viz. תקיעה, יבבות (or שברים), and תרועה. See Mishna at the end of ראש השנה. The New Year is the only occasion on which the Shophar is so used, and to the present day much is made of this part of the Festival ceremonies.

[59] And so in the chanting of the present day, there is but *one* melody in use.

[60] One or other of these names will be found in the list printed in Ginsb. Mas., i. p. 658, in עט סופר, p. ל, in the several Zarqa-lists, &c. But how are we to explain the strange name גַּלְגַּל, 'wheel,' found in some texts of the Italian Zarqa-list (whence Norzi has borrowed it, e.g. in his note to Gen. i. 3)? A form of

for us, we too may be content with one name and may accept that which has become established by long use, viz. Munach, although the proper signification of the term no longer applies.

d. שׁוֹפָר הָפוּךְ, מְהֻפָּךְ or מַהְפָּךְ, so named from its form. It was an 'inverted' Shophar [61]. As compared with Munach its use was limited, for it occurs only before Pashṭa. Its musical value is described (Dikd. hat., p. 19) יורד ועולה וגם מתעלה; so that we might also term it מְהֻפָּךְ in regard to its melody [62].

2. מֵירְכָא), מַאֲרִיךְ or מַאֲרְכָא מֵירְכָא (מֵרְכָא). These names are all from the same root ארך, (מֵירְכָא like מֵימְרָא and מֵיכְלָא), and indicate the accent as 'prolonging' the modulation. It had a *long* tone [63], which was at the same time, as the Massora and all writers on the accents describe it, a *descending* tone [64]. In MSS. it is generally represented as a *straight* line, turned more or less to the left, but in some made perpendicular.

[It may be noted that the term מאריך is often used in the Massora and elsewhere not only for the accent Mer'kha, but for Gaya=Métheg as well. And even the *signs* are not always kept distinct in Codd. Hence an excuse may be found for our printed texts, which constantly mark the (euphonic) Métheg at the end of a word as *Mer'kha*, פַּדֶּנָה (Gen. xxviii. 5) for פַּדֶּנָה; וַתֹּשַׁע (Is. lxiii. 5) for וַתֹּשַׁע, &c. Another occasional use of מאריך in the Massora is to indicate the *opposite to*

Munach occurs occasionally in Codd. with the angle rounded off ⌐, and it must have appeared to some punctator—one of the class, whose restless ingenuity was wholly occupied with such trifles—that here was an opening for a new name, after the analogy of Galgal, No. 6. The name has, however (as far as I have noticed), been adopted only by Norzi.

If we find any of the names above given, loosely used in the Massora (MS. or printed), we must not suppose that the genuine Massora sanctioned them. Both copyists and editors have introduced the modern names familiar to them.

[61] עומד בקרן הפוך (Man. du Lect., p. 73). Comp. the נון הפוכה, Mas. to Num. xi. 1.

[62] By Chayyug, p. 127, this accent is called מקיף, fully שׁופר הפוך מקף (Ox. 2512, p. 18). The meaning is 'conjunctive' (comp. Dikd. hat., § 30, and Ginsb. Mas. מ, § 235), in opposition to the disjunctive Y'thibh with the same form. An extraordinary name occurs in Pet. 123, הליל צגיר, i. e. هِلال صَغِير, 'small new moon.' *Mutatis mutandis*, the explanation is the same as for Gilgal above.

[63] מחוברת לאחותה בארוכה (Dikd. hat., p. 19), 'joined to its partner with a *long* tone.' And so Ben-Bil. (Ox. MS.) ונקראת מירכא שמאריכה המלה. Another explanation is '*long-stroke*' in contrast to Shophar, but the other meanings of the term (given above) shew that this explanation is not the true one.

[64] Comp. Mas. to Num. xxxvi. 3 (נָחַת); Dikd. hat., § 21; Mishp. hat., p. 16; Man. du Lect., p. 97 below, &c. Hence in Pet. 123, the double name of مَاڵ, 'lengthening,' and خَابَة, 'descending.'

Maqqeph, thus: עַל ח' מאריכין בטעם בספרא (Mas. to Lev. i. 11), i. e.
'eight instances in Lev. lengthen out the particle עַל with an *accent*'
(instead of contracting it with Maqqeph). Comp. Mas. parva to Esth.
ii. 5. As these instances affect the accentuation, it seemed necessary
to allude to them.]

Mer'kha appears in a few instances *doubled*, and is termed מֵירְכָא
כְּפוּלָה, or תְּרֵין חוּטְרִין, 'two rods or strokes.' As the servus of T'bhîr
always precedes, this Double Mer'kha was regarded as a reduced or
impoverished T'bhîr, whence the fanciful name given to it of הַמִּסְכֵּן,
pauper, tenuis [65]. Qimchi (Mikhlol 89ª) goes so far as to say that its
melody was like T'bhîr's. But his authority on such a point is not of
much weight.

3. דַּרְגָּא is also termed שַׁלְשֶׁלֶת and שִׁישְׁלָא (ﻟﺴﻤ) [66]. These latter
names seem to indicate a certain relationship with the disjunctive
Shalshéleth. And in some old Codd., as De R. 10 and K. 154, the sign
for Darga is precisely the *same* as that for Shalshéleth, as also it is
described in Dikd. hat., p. 19, and Man. du Lect., p. 76. But the
Shalshéleth-sign stands, as we have seen, p. 17, for *a trill*. Such
then would seem to have been the musical value of Darga. The name
דרגא had also probably this meaning. Comp. ﺩﺭﺝ, *he chanted, or sang,
in a trilling or quavering manner* (Lane). Of course, the trill or
quaver must have been feeble, in comparison with that of Shalshéleth [67].
The sign in common use, and the modern melody of a descending
scale running through the octave, represent דַּרְגָּא in its ordinary
meaning of *scala*.

4. אַזְלָא, אָזֵל, i. e. 'going on,' not pausing in the melody, = conjunctive
(in contrast to Pashta, disjunctive, with the same sign) [68]. Other names for
this accent are מַקֵּל, 'rod,' 'stroke' (comp. l. 7 above), and אֶשֶׁל, 'cord,' 'line.'
When associated with Géresh, it is frequently termed קַדְמָא, Géresh
then, by a strange confusion of terms, being known as אַזְלָא [69]; or the
two are described by the Massoretic formula אָזֵל וְאָתֵי. The melody is
an *ascending* one, לעולם עולה (Dikd. hat., p. 19).

---

[65] Dikd. hat., p. 18. Baer indeed explains the term of *Silluq*. But this is a
mistake; for Ox. 2512, p. 15ᵇ, expressly names the Double Mer'kha in תֵּעְשֵׂה
(Ex. v. 15) מסכן. The description also, given in Dikd. hat., l. c., exactly suits
this accent.

[66] Chayyug, p. 128 below; Man. du Lect., p. 76; Dikd. hat., § 19. The ignorant
Qalonymos gives a further name שופר גלגל, which is quite false (the name
belongs to another accent, see p. 23). Yet he is followed by El. Levita, Heidenheim, Ewald, and others.

[67] It ought also to have a corresponding name, ש' קְמַנָּה, as in De R. 1262.

[68] So David ben Abraham (10th century) in his Dictionary (Journal Asiatique,
1862, p. 77 note) uses הוֹלֵך, 'joined on,' as opposed to מוּכְרֶת, 'separated.'

[69] קַדְמָא וְאַזְלָא, as it were 'the leader and the goer on' with the melody. The

5. תְּלִישָׁא קְטַנָּה [70]. See Remarks under תְּלִישָׁא above, p. 22. The melody of Little T'lisha must have been similar to that of Great T'lisha, although of course feebler. Ben-Naphtali apparently treated this accent as a *disjunctive* (comp. חלופי הנקוד to Gen. xix. 17 and Baer's note), and so the modern Ashkenazic Jews give a certain *pausal* value to Little T'lisha, as in chanting וַיֵּסֶר בַּיּוֹם הַהוּא אֶת־הַתְּיָשִׁים (Gen. xxx. 35). Bad taste indeed!

6. גַּלְגַּל, 'wheel.' Although this accent occurs only sixteen times (always immediately before Great Pazer) punctators exercised their ingenuity in devising for it a number of names and even forms. Its original circular form may be gathered from the name 'wheel.' Under this form it was also called עֲגוּלָה, 'round,' and תְּלִישָׁא קְטַנָּה or ת' זְעֵירָה [71], being like a small T'lisha. With the circle incomplete [72], it became יָרֵחַ בֶּן יוֹמוֹ [73], 'the moon a day old.' Other forms of Galgal, beside that found in printed texts, are ⌣ and a small Têth, answering to similar forms, on a larger scale, of Great Pazer. The original melody probably resembled that of Little T'lisha.

7. נְטוּיָה, מְאַיְלָא, or דְּחוּיָה [74]. Names given to Tiphcha, when in the same word with Athnach or Silluq. (It occurs only fifteen or sixteen times [75].) The character of Tiphcha was changed, hence a new name was given to it. But somewhat of the melody of Tiphcha must have been retained in the chanting, for we find the same subordinate accents as before Tiphcha,—and Zaqeph preceding, which requires for

---

expression is found in Chayyug, p. 127, in the printed Mas. (e. g. to Ex. iv. 11), in the Italian Zarqa-list, &c., and is commonly used by the Jews in the present day. The two accents may come together in the *same* word, and are then called in Pet. 123 طَارِفْتَيِن, as if they were both Géresh! see p. 20.

[70] In the list, Chayyug, p. 128, this accent is actually called תלישא רבא ! to distinguish it from Galgal, which is there termed תלישא זעירא (see No. 6 above). What we call Great T'lisha has the simple name תלשא. One sees there is no end to the vagaries of schools and punctators in these trivial matters!

[71] As in Chayyug, p. 128; Man. du Lect., p. 76 below; Ox. 2512, p. 10.

[72] So the Massoretic circle and the Arabic Gezm are sometimes complete, sometimes incomplete in MSS.

[73] As in Mas. magna to Ezek. xlviii. 21, the Zarqa-lists, &c. In Pet. 123 this name is changed to هِلَال كَبِير, 'the great new moon,' because Galgal had to be contrasted with M'huppach, 'the small new moon' (see note 62).

[74] For these several names, see Mishp. hat., p. 6ᵇ; Dikd. hat., p. 19 and note; Chayyug, p. 128; and Man. du Lect., p. 73.

These names are also given to an accent of the same form (but different character) in the three Books, see טעמי אמ״ת, p. 19.

[75] Properly speaking, it does not belong to our list (of Conjunctives). I have however inserted it, as all Rabbinical writers on the accents, and even the Massora, number it among the משרתים (*servi*).

the melody Ṭiphcha following. The name מאילא (the one now in common use) must have been first employed by the grammarians, who wrote in Arabic, for it is مَآئِلَة, i. e. 'inclined [76].' The Hebrew names have the same signification. In Dikd. hat., p. 17, the name is מתחה, 'extending,' scil. the melody of the word in which it occurs.

(The term מאילא is also found in a rare Mas. printed in Bomb. 2 at Gen. xxx. 16 and elsewhere. It is there used for the *Mer'kha* preceding *Zarqa*. But such a use is opposed to the testimony of early writers on the accents, who expressly state that Mây'la occurs *only* before Athnach and Silluq. The Mas., in this form, is undoubtedly false [77].)

Were we able to trace the development of the graphical representation of the accentual melodies, we should probably find that it was, at first, confined to Athnach and Soph Pasuq [78]; and that it was only *gradually* that the other signs, of which we have just treated, came into use.

The first step towards a musical arrangement of the text was the breaking it up into a number of 'sections,' פְּסוּקִים—verses, as we call them—of varying length, according as the sense or the requirements of the cantillation suggested. Each section or verse was then treated as an independent whole; and, whatever its connection in sense with the verse preceding or the verse following, had its musical division assigned to it, quite irrespectively of them [79]. These verses we must accept, as (with rare exceptions) common to all texts [80]. Their number is counted and fixed by the Massora for each Book.

---

[76] Comp. the use of the word, as it is found in Ox. 2512, p. 10, in the description of Mer'kha: هو عصا تحت الكلمة مَآئِل الى اليسار.

[77] It may perhaps be traced to a *single* MS. For Moses the punctator (דרכי הנקוד, p. 27), after quoting it at length, adds זה נמצא בספר אספמיא אחד. This quotation seems then to have passed into other works, as Simson's חבור הקונים, and was copied *verbatim* by Jacob ben-Chayyim in the Mas. to Gen. xxx. 16. Perhaps the original form of the Mas. was י"ח מילין מאריכין בין אולא לודקא וגו'.

[78] Many extant Codd. do not (as is well known) go beyond this simple division.

[79] Hence it is often called in the Talmud קְרָא (e. g. Qiddushin 30ᵃ) and מִקְרָא (Yoma 52ᵃ), properly 'portion to be read' (chanted), 'lection.'

[80] It was not always so. For a long time there were considerable differences between the various schools, a reminiscence of which is found in the *Pisqas*

The verses, like all the other divisions, were marked off for the *cantillation* [81]. They necessarily vary in length; but the general rule is to avoid *too short* or *too long* verses. Hence a short period is often attached to a longer one preceding or following (Gen. i. 10; v. 1; xxxvii. 2; xxxix. 6), and two short periods are constantly brought together into one verse (i. 5, 8; xlvii. 31). On the other hand, when the period runs on to any length, it is broken up into two or more verses. So the protasis may be separated from the apodosis (Ex. ix. 2, 3; Deut. xxx. 17, 18); a compound subject or object kept apart from the verb (Num. xxxi. 22; Neh. x. 29); a speech extended through any number of verses (Gen. xii. 1–3; xxiv. 34–49); details of every kind marked off in groups—often small, for distinctness of enunciation—(Gen. x. 11–18; Ex. xxxv. 10–19; Deut. xi. 2–6; Jer. xxv. 17–26; &c.) The division, it must be allowed, shews freedom enough, as when we find the apodosis in the same verse with the *last part* of the protasis (Gen. xxiv. 44; 2 Sam. xi. 21; 1 Ki. x. 5; Ezek. xviii. 9); or a shorter period in the same verse with the *last part* of a long period preceding (Gen. i. 18; xiv. 20; l. 17; Ex. xii. 27; Jer. xi. 5; li. 64). In such cases, the division which seemed most convenient for the cantillation was adopted. The musical principle admitted,—and due allowance made for divisions, designed to emphasize, or otherwise give effect to the reading,—we shall not often have occasion to find fault with the verses as marked off. The above remarks refer particularly to the *prose* portions of the text. For the *poetical*, the parallelism of the members sufficed generally to fix the limits of the verse.

The rules for the division of the *verse itself* must now engage our attention.

---

marked in our text (for the list of which see Baer's note on Hos. i. 2). These Pisqas, always coming after Athnach, indicate that some authorities made *two* verses, where our Massoretic text has only *one*. The latest treatise on the differences named is by Graetz in the Monatschrift für Geschichte und Wissenschaft des Judenthums, 1885, p. 97 ff. But the learned professor has not succeeded in throwing any fresh light on a very obscure and perplexing subject.

[81] The verses, once fixed, would furnish suitable portions for separate reading, when a translation of the text was to be given at the same time. So in the Mishna, Megilla iv. 4, the translator is directed to render verse by verse in the reading of the Tora. But I cannot consider (with Vitringa and Hupfeld) that the verses owed their origin to the necessity of providing for the translation *small divisions in the sense* which the congregation could easily follow. The Mishna, l. c., appointed *three* verses of the Prophets to be read together, before the translation was given.

CHAPTER III.

THE DICHOTOMY. GENERAL.

EVERY verse, however short, was divided, for the purpose of chanting, into *two* parts. This is what Christian writers on the accents have termed the DICHOTOMY of the verse. The accent employed to mark the division is generally Athnach, but in some cases other accents are allowable, or are even necessary from the influence of musical laws.

The further division was on the same principle. Each half-verse constituted by the main dichotomy—if of sufficient length—was divided by a *minor* dichotomy. And the parts thus formed were subjected to the same process, which was continued, as long as the condition just named, of there being a sufficient number of words in the clause, was fulfilled. We thus arrive at the law of the CONTINUOUS DICHOTOMY, the simple principle that regulates the division of the verse. It is sufficient at present to lay down the general law. The conditions for its application cannot be stated as simply as for the three Books. It will depend on the particular accent, whose clause has to be divided, whether three or even more words can stand without the dichotomy. But the law must be accepted. It constitutes one of the marked and distinguishing features of the system of Hebrew accentuation [1].

We naturally ask, what was the purpose designed by this remarkable process of division and minute sub-division? No doubt it served to mark the logical and syntactical interpunction. But the logical use will account only very partially for its introduction; and even for the syntactical, it was not needed to anything like the extent to which it was applied. Some

---

[1] Jewish writers on the accents had no more idea of this law than they had of many of the chief grammatical rules. Its discovery is due to the unwearied diligence, with which the study of the accents was pursued by Christian scholars of the 17th century.

other explanation therefore is necessary. And there can be no question that the object aimed at, was that which is the essential characteristic of the accentuation,—*musical effect*. The result of the continuous dichotomy was a succession of pausal melodies (more or fewer) fixed by rule, which, with the conjunctive melodies dependent on them, gave the cantillation of the verse. It was a peculiar system, but one that must have answered its purpose. Certainly it secured fulness and variety for the melody. How far it corresponded to our modern notions of a melodious result, we have no sufficient means of determining, inasmuch as we are but imperfectly acquainted with the musical value of the accents, and not at all with the changes which they doubtless underwent, according to their relative position.

As for the *origin* of the system, it seems to me that it may have been as follows. We may well suppose that a musical recitation was early employed for the *poetical* parts of the Tora, as the שִׁירוֹת, Ex. xv and Deut. xxxii. Such parts would, from their very character, be the first to claim it. We may further consider that the musical divisions as we now have them were first established for these pieces. For how does the matter stand with them? The dichotomy — resulting from *parallelismus membrorum*—is the reigning principle of division, and shews itself not only in the bisection of the verse, but often in that of the subordinate parts as well. This *formal* dichotomy necessarily supplied (as far as it went) the basis for the *musical*, and from its constant recurrence seems to have suggested to the originators of the accentual system a guiding principle for the musical division *in general*. We note that in the poetical pieces, it did not need frequent application. It is not often that the sub-division is carried beyond the *second* minor dichotomy. The continuous dichotomy shews itself therefore here in a simple form.

When now it was determined to introduce a musical recitation for the *prose* parts, there was, according to the above hypothesis, a model already provided. True, in these parts there is, generally speaking, no *formal* dichotomy to serve as a basis for the *musical*. But this could form no objection, for there are even in the poetical pieces verses that read as simple prose, e. g. Ex. xv. 18, Deut. xxxii. 19, and yet have the dichotomy applied to them. The model then was accepted, and the principle of the continuous dichotomy adopted for the prose reading. Here, owing to the long verses often marked off, its application became more extended and much more complicated.

One drawback was involved in its adoption. Two or more *equal* pauses, in succession, cannot be represented as such. *Subordination* (variously carried out) necessarily takes place[2]. No doubt the accentuators would have been often glad to mark the equal pauses by accents of equal disjunctive value, if the law which they had laid down for themselves would have permitted it, as in Gen. xlix. 31 ; Josh. vii. 14[b]; Is. iii. 24 ; lxvi. 3 ; &c. In certain cases, indeed, the same accent is *repeated* in the division of the clause ; but, from the very nature of the continuous dichotomy, *it loses in disjunctive value* each time of repetition. Instances are Zaqeph repeated (often more than once) in Silluq's clause, R'bhîa in Zaqeph's clause, &c.

The question how the *position* of the dichotomy (main or minor) was fixed, has been already answered. It is found, where the main *logical* pause of the clause, or the rules for *syntactical* division require it. But, as has been pointed out, pp. 3, 4, there are many notable exceptions. I would here only once more remind the reader that we have to do with a system of *public recitation*, the main object of which (like that of all effective delivery) was to bring out and impress upon the minds of the hearers the full meaning of the Sacred Text. And I would add that unless we are prepared to recognise the utmost freedom in the application of the dichotomy, we shall never be able to explain to ourselves the accentual division. In the higher style, where *parallelism* is found, the same freedom necessarily prevails.

I purpose, in the present chapter, to consider certain *general* principles of division, which will, in my opinion, account for the most noticeable instances of deviation from rule, just referred

---

[2] So *abiit, evasit, erupit*, could not, when turned into (accented) Hebrew, be separated by *equal pauses*. Comp. : וַיֵּלֶךְ וַיִּבְרַח וַיִּמָּלֵט (1 Sam. xix. 12).

ii *b*. On the other hand, with the dichotomy on the *fourth* word, Athnach is generally—in something like ten cases out of eleven—employed.

This is the case, whether the subordinate pause before Silluq fall on the first, second, or third word. In the great majority of cases it falls on the second word,—we notice again the *rhythmical* effect,—and is made by R'bhîa mugrash. See Ps. iv. 4; ix. 5; x. 9, 13; xiii. 4, 5; &c.

The advantage of admitting Olév'yored into the fourth place is, as before, that it allows an *emphasis* (of melody and sense) to be thrown into the words following—by the employment of Athnach and R'bhîa mugrash [19]—above what is possible, when Athnach occupies the fourth place, and only R'bhîa mugrash can follow; see Ps. ix. 15; xviii. 13; xxxii. 10; lxii. 5; lxix. 4; &c. At the same time in the short clause, —of only four words—which here follows the dichotomy, it was not thought necessary to introduce this more emphatic accentuation often. To us it is a drawback that it is so frequently effaced, e.g. in Ps. i. 2, by the law of transformation.

iii *a*. When the dichotomy falls on the *third* word Athnach maintains its position.

See Ps. i. 5, 6; ii. 3, 7, 9, 10, 12; &c. [20]

iii *b*. So also, on the *second* word, as in Ps. ii. 1, 2, 4, 5, 6, &c. Only here, under certain circumstances, Athnach must be transformed into R'bhîa mugrash [21], e. g.

עוּרָה כְבוֹדִי עוּרָה הַנֵּבֶל וְכִנּוֹר אָעִירָה שָּׁחַר׃ (Ps. lvii. 9).

iii *c*. On the word immediately preceding Silluq, Athnach is always transformed into R'bhîa mugrash.

Such cases are however, in the original text, of rare occurrence. To the poet himself a certain measure of rhythmical equilibrium must have seemed necessary. We have noticed above the tendency to rhythmical effect even in the minor sections of the verse. We need not therefore be surprised to find that in only a

---

[19] There are only two passages in our texts, Ps. iv. 7 and lv. 23, where there is not room for these two accents after Olév'yored. And here D'chî and Athnach, if there had been no transformation, would have come instead. As before, I pass over lxviii. 20, with סֶלָה as last word.

[20] So in Ps. cxxx. 1, שִׁיר הַמַּעֲלוֹת is marked with Athnach, whereas in all the other 'Songs of Degrees' it has Olév'yored.

[21] See chapter on Transformation.

few instances—notwithstanding the large number of *short* verses—
does the main pause fall on the word *immediately preceding* Silluq[22]. Beside the passages already given in p. 29—in which the
dichotomy has been moved back by the accentuators,—I have
noted only Ps. xxxiv. 8; xxxv. 24; cxix. 52; cxxxvii. 9; and
Prov. viii. 33[23]. In these cases, it did not seem possible to them
to change the position of the dichotomy; it consequently remains
on the word before Silluq, marked by R'bhîa mugrash.

The first verses indeed of a few Psalms, if we remove the additions
prefixed to the original text, have the dichotomy immediately before
Silluq, e. g. : הָרִיעוּ לֵאלֹהִים כָּל־הָאָרֶץ (Ps. lxvi. 1). But I have no doubt
that these short clauses, consisting of only *three* words, belong properly
to the verses following : (1) because verses of only three words *do not
occur elsewhere* in the text proper[24]; and (2) because in one case, Ps.
lxxxvii. 1, we should be reduced to a verse of *two* words. The other
instances are xviii. 2; c. 1; cix. 1; cxxx. 1; and cxlvi. 1.

The dichotomy has been further introduced in the word preceding
Silluq in the following cases :

(1) The last verses in Pss. civ–cvi, cxiii, cxv–cxvii, cxxxv, and
cxlvi–cl, which all end with הַלְלוּיָהּ (doubtless a liturgical addition
to the original text).

(2) The verses heading the speeches in Job, like

וַיַּעַן אֱלִיפַז הַתֵּימָנִי וַיֹּאמַר : (iv. 1)[25].

And (3) the superscriptions of some Pss. containing only three words,
e. g. : מִזְמוֹר לְדָוִד לְהַזְכִּיר (xxxviii. 1), and so in lx, lxix, lxxxi, lxxxiii,
and cviii. In these cases, R'bhîa mugrash has been transformed,
according to rule, but in : שִׁיר מִזְמוֹר לִבְנֵי־קֹרַח (xlviii. 1) it must be
retained, with most Codd. and with Ben-Bil. 10. 10, although in opposition to the *Masora magna* to Ps. lxxxiii. 1.

Lastly, after what has been said above, we should not expect
to find the chief logical (or syntactical) pause on the *first* word of
the verse. Indeed, so few are these cases, that no provision was

---

[22] In the prose system it is otherwise, see Gen. i. 3, 7; v. 5; &c.

[23] Ps. lxxvi. 5 and Prov. viii. 23 I propose to correct, by dropping the Maqqeph
between the two last words, and introducing a conjunctive accent instead. This
pointing I have found in some Codd. (Comp. lxxx. 11[b] and Job v. 10[a].) Others
move back the dichotomy a word.

[24] In the prose text we have such verses, e. g. Gen. xxvi. 6; xliii. 1; but not in the
poetical. Verses with *two* words occur only in the Decalogue (Ex. xx. 13–15).

[25] Most Codd. and edd. point these verses with *R'bhîa simplex*, by a common
mistake, see chapter on R'bhîa mugrash at end.

שְׁמְךָ יַעֲקֹב, to intimate that the patriarch, though he had a new name given him, was not (like Abraham) to lose the old one. The words are made emphatic: '*Thy name is, and shall be, Jacob!*'[9] In 2 Chr. ii. 13 the accentuators have abandoned the obvious accentuation, in order that they might emphasize the lesson that a son is bound to follow his father's occupation and to support his mother, when left a widow![10] Such instances are however rare. That a few occur is not surprising, when we bear in mind the influence that Haggadic teaching has always exercised among the Jews.

III. *a.* It is on the same principle that the introductory part of the verse, although logically requiring the main accent (Athnach) after it, is constantly passed over, that this accent may be introduced where the weight of meaning of the passage seems to lie[11]. Observe the division in the following instances:

'There I will meet with thee, and I will speak with thee, from above the mercy-seat, from between the two cherubim which are upon the ark of the testimony, | all that I will command thee to the children of Israel' (Ex. xxv. 22).

'And Moses wrote all the words of Jehovah; and rose up early in the morning, and builded an altar under the mount, | and twelve pillars, according to the twelve tribes of Israel' (Ex. xxiv. 4). [The accentuation draws attention to the altar and the twelve representative pillars. They were to be noted from their connection with the Covenant, the ratification of which is the grand subject of the narrative.]

'Yet it pleased Jehovah to bruise him,—He hath put him to grief: when Thou shalt make his soul an offering for sin, he shall see his seed, he shall prolong his days, | and the pleasure of Jehovah shall prosper in his hand' (Is. liii. 10). [It is on the *glorious results* of the sufferings of 'the servant of Jehovah' that the accentuation dwells.]

'And he said, Naked came I out of my mother's womb, and naked shall I return thither: Jehovah gave, and Jehovah hath taken away; | blessed be the name of Jehovah' (Job i. 21).

And so even in short and simple sentences like the following:

'And Abraham stretched forth his hand, and took the knife | to slay his son' (Gen. xxii. 10).

'Then these men assembled, and found Daniel | making petition and supplication before his God' (Dan. vi. 12).

---

[9] Comp. Berakhoth 13ᵃ. So R. El'azar in the Midrash (Ox. 2338) insists, ויאמר אלהים שמך יעקב שמך יעקב מכל מקום.

[10] See Qimchi on the passage.

[11] Hence often where הִנֵּה precedes the second clause, e. g. in Lev. xiii. 5, &c.; Num. xvii. 7; 1 Sam. xx. 2; xxx. 16; 2 Ki. vi. 25; Ezek. x. 1; Amos vii. 7.

Where the reader sees at once that the pause comes in just where it is most telling.

This free mode of division, adopted for the sake of effect and impressiveness in the reading, is not to be regarded as exceptional, but is found everywhere. It is, however, so different from our own ideas of interpunction, that I append some other examples, which the student may examine for himself: Gen. xxxiv. 7; Ex. iii. 12; xii. 23; Num. xx. 13; Deut. iii. 11; 1 Sam. xiv. 27; 2 Sam. xii. 4; Is. xxvii. 13; Jer. ii. 23; Ezek. xxxix. 13; Qoh. vii. 2; ix. 12 [12].

The above are all instances of division by Athnach; but of course the same principle applies to the division of the half-verse or any section of the same, e. g. Is. xxxvii. 9^b; Jer. xxvi. 12^b; Mal. iii. 3^a.

β. Particularly noteworthy is the way in which the words that introduce a speech—or anything similar, as a command, decree, oath, covenant, &c. — are treated. They constantly occupy a *subordinate position*, as far as the accents are concerned. The clause containing *the speech itself, the command*, &c., is counted the more important, and receives the main accentuation. In short, the division is made (as above) just as if the introductory words were absent, e. g. [13]

'And God said, Let there be a firmament in the midst of the waters, | and let it divide the waters from the waters' (Gen. i. 6).

'And Jehovah said to him, Therefore whosoever slayeth Cain, | vengeance shall be taken sevenfold' (iv. 15).

'And Moses said to the children of Israel, See, Jehovah hath called by name | Bezalel, the son of Uri, &c.' (Ex. xxxv. 30).

'The Lord Jehovah hath sworn by His holiness, that lo! the days shall come

---

[12] He may also compare Gen. vi. 9; xi. 10; xxxvii. 2; where we do not find Athnach with the superscriptions, as we should have expected, but the clause following is divided, just as if the superscriptions were absent.

[13] There is no real difficulty here; we divide often in the same way: 'And they said, Nay; but we will abide in the street all night' (Gen. xix. 2). 'And Lot said unto them, Oh, not so, my lord: behold now, thy servant &c.' (xix. 18, 19). Only the accentuators go farther than we do, subordinating the words in question to a syntactical, as well as logical, division (see examples in text).

upon you, | that they shall take you away with hooks, and your residue with fish-hooks' (Amos iv. 2).

'And he commanded to destroy | all the wise men of Babylon' (Dan. ii. 12).

'Thou, O king, hast made a decree, that every man that shall hear the sound of the cornet, ... and all kinds of music, | shall fall down and worship the golden image' (iii. 10).

Such cases occur in every page.

γ. What is next to be noticed is that α and β may be combined, or β may be repeated; in other words, we may have a *compound* procœmium consisting of two (or even more) members, each of which will be subordinated, directly or indirectly, to the same main division of the speech, &c., marked by Athnach or some other leading accent. The position of this accent is indicated, as before, in the following examples:

'And Jacob awaked out of his sleep, and said, Surely Jehovah is in this place; | and I knew it not' (Gen. xxviii. 16)[14].

'And he told it to his father and to his brethren; and his father rebuked him, and said unto him, What is this dream that thou hast dreamed? | Shall I and thy mother and thy brethren indeed come to bow down ourselves to thee to the earth?' (xxxvii. 10).

'Go and say to Hezekiah, Thus saith Jehovah, the God of David thy father, I have heard thy prayer, I have seen thy tears: | behold, I will add unto thy days fifteen years' (Is. xxxviii. 5)[14].

'From the uttermost part of the earth have we heard songs, "Glory for the righteous!" But I said, I pine away, I pine away, woe is me! | the treacherous dealers have dealt treacherously; yea, the treacherous dealers have dealt very treacherously' (xxiv. 16).

'And she conceived again, and bare a daughter. And He said unto him, Call her name Lo-ruchamah: | for I will no more have mercy on the house of Israel, that I should in any wise pardon them' (Hos. i. 6).

Other examples are Gen. i. 28; viii. 21; xxi. 17; xlvii. 29; Ex. x. 3; xxxii. 13; 2 Ki. i. 6; v. 15; Is. xlvii. 8; lix. 21; Jer. xlii. 20.

The student, when he has become familiar with the rules for the accentuation, may examine these examples for himself. He will observe that the several procœmial members are *variously subordinated*,

---

[14] Our interpunction is here the same. And so in Gen. xxxvii. 32; 2 Sam. iv. 8; Is. vi. 7; xlvii. 8; lxii. 11; Jer. xxxviii. 25; Job i. 16; and many other passages. (See the Revised Version.)

sometimes the first to the second, sometimes all to Athnach, &c. The accentuators chose the musical pauses, which seemed to them suitable, nor is there generally any cause to find fault with their selection.

δ. Lastly, among proœmial expressions are to be reckoned וְהָיָה and וַיְהִי, in the sense of 'coming to pass,' which are usually subordinated by the accents to the first word or words of the clause which they introduce: יַהַרְגֵנִי | וְהָיָה כָל־מֹצְאִי (Gen. iv. 14); יִהְיֶה־לְּךָ לְפֶה | וְהָיָה הוּא (Ex. iv. 16; comp. Gen. xxiv. 15); אֶת־דִּבְרֵי שְׁלֹמֹה | וַיְהִי כִּשְׁמֹעַ חִירָם (1 Ki. v. 21); שָׁנָה | וַיְהִי בִשְׁלֹשִׁים וָשֶׁבַע (2 Ki. xxv. 27). The merely *formal* character of these introductory words suffices to account for their subordinate position.

IV. In contrast to the *proœmium*, are the cases where an *appendage* is made to the clause, without affecting the division of the same. (Here the proper logical divison would have been immediately *before* the appendage.) Such cases are not so numerous as the proœmial instances. They may be divided into three classes:

a. Those in which there is a close connection in *sense* between the concluding member of the clause and the appendage. Thus in Gen. i. 16, וְאֵת הַכּוֹכָבִים is not preceded by Athnach, but is joined on by the accents to the part of the clause describing the 'lesser light,' because the stars were appointed *with the moon* to lighten up the night[15]. In iii. 19 the accentual division is: 'In the sweat of thy face shalt thou eat bread, | till thou return unto the ground, for out of *it* thou wast taken;' and in iv. 25: 'God hath appointed me another seed | in place of Abel, because Cain *slew him*.' Comp. xxxiv. 7 end; xlix. 10; Lev. xiii. 6 end; Deut. xvi. 3ᵇ; Judg. vi. 21ᵇ (see Bertheau); 1 Ki. xx. 12ᵇ; Is. xxxviii. 16; lv. 5; lxvi. 13; 1 Chr. xvi. 33 (as Ps. xcvi. 13).

β. The second class embraces certain recurrent phrases, which

[15] Comp. Jer. xxxi. 35: 'Thus saith Jehovah, who giveth the sun for a light by day, and the ordinances *of the moon and stars for a light by night.*'

are occasionally attached to the end of the verse, without affecting the regular division preceding, as אָמַר יְהֹוָה, נְאֻם יְהֹוָה and cognate expressions, Is. i. 20; xvii. 6; Jer. xlviii. 43; Ezek. v. 15; xv. 8; xxx. 12; Amos i. 15; &c. So אֲנִי יְהֹוָה, Lev. xix. 10; xxi. 12; xxii. 2, 3; xxvi. 45; and יְהֹוָה שְׁמוֹ, Jer. xxxi. 35; xxxiii. 2; Amos v. 8; ix. 6.

γ. The third class relates to the peculiar division often found before לֵאמֹר, e. g. וַיְצַו יְהֹוָה אֱלֹהִים | עַל־הָאָדָם לֵאמֹר (Gen. ii. 16); בַּיּוֹם הַהוּא כָּרַת יְהֹוָה אֶת־אַבְרָם | בְּרִית לֵאמֹר (xv. 18); וַיֻּכּוּ שֹׁטְרֵי בְּנֵי יִשְׂרָאֵל | אֲשֶׁר־שָׂמוּ עֲלֵהֶם נֹגְשֵׂי פַרְעֹה (Ex. v. 14); וַיְהִי דְבַר־יְהֹוָה אֶל־יִרְמְיָהוּ שֵׁנִית | וְהוּא לֵאמֹר עוֹדֶנּוּ עָצוּר בַּחֲצַר הַמַּטָּרָה לֵאמֹר (Jer. xxxiii. 1). In these examples the clauses have been divided, just as if לֵאמֹר were not present, with the consequence that לֵאמֹר and the word (or words) between it and the main dichotomy preceding are brought together in a very awkward way. And so in numberless other passages. The object of the division seems to have been purely *musical*, to introduce more variety into the chanting than would have been possible if the division had been always on the word immediately preceding לֵאמֹר, and to secure a fuller melody for *long* sentences (e. g. 2 Sam. vii. 7; Jer. xliv. 15). From the frequent occurrence of לֵאמֹר with Athnach and Silluq, it is here that the monotony would have been most felt; and here the above division is most common. With the other accents, it is frequently neglected [16].

V. It is important to notice the influence which *parallelism* has on the division of the verse. This main ornament of the Hebrew style [17] characterizes all the poetical and (to a great

---

[16] Thus in Genesis, it occurs only twice (xlii. 37; xlv. 16), as far as I have observed, out of some thirty examples.

[17] But not confined to Hebrew, for it is found equally in old Egyptian and Assyrian compositions.

extent) the prophetical parts of the twenty-one Books. It is also found in the simply narrative portions, for a poetic colouring often shews itself even there. The most conspicuous instances are where it is marked by the main dichotomy, but it appears hardly less frequently in the minor divisions of the verse.

For the different kinds of parallelism, I may be allowed to refer to my remarks in ת״מא ימעט, pp. 24–28.

The most common form in which it appears is that of *partial* parallelism,—with or without addition, thus:

a. Without addition, e. g.

'In blessing I will bless thee, and in multiplying I will multiply thy seed as the stars of heaven, | and as the sand which is upon the sea-shore' (Gen. xxii. 17).

'Your new moons and your appointed feasts my soul hateth; they are a burden upon me, | I am weary of bearing them' (Is. i. 14).

'Like as many were astonished at thee,—his visage was so marred more than man, | and his form more than the sons of men' (lii. 14).

'They are waxen fat, they shine: yea, they overpass the deeds of wickedness; they plead not the cause, the cause of the fatherless, that they should prosper; | and the right of the needy do they not judge' (Jer. v. 28) [18].

In these and similar cases, the main idea of the verse (or clause) is first given, and then follows an echo (as it were) of the *last* part of the same. The logical division is disregarded. No less is this the case, in many of the instances of parallelism

β. With addition, e. g.

'But the multitude of thy foes shall be like small dust, | and the multitude of the terrible ones as chaff that passeth away: and it shall be at an instant suddenly' (Is. xxix. 5).

'For Jehovah is our judge, Jehovah is our lawgiver, | Jehovah is our king; He will save us' (xxxiii. 22).

'I will bring the blind by a way that they know not; in paths that they know not will I lead them: | I will make darkness light before them, and crooked places straight. These are the things which I will do and not forbear' (xlii. 16).

'Sing, O barren, thou that hast not borne; | break forth into singing and cry aloud, thou that hast not travailed with child: for more are the children of the desolate than the children of the married wife, saith Jehovah' (liv. 1).

---

[18] For the sake of beginners, I add a few more examples: Gen. xlix. 27; Is. xxx. 10; xli. 20; Jer. i. 10 (antithetic); Hos. vi. 1; Amos v. 11; ix. 14; Nah. iii. 7.

'Go up to Lebanon, and cry; and lift up thy voice in Bashan; | and cry from Abarim: for all thy lovers are destroyed' (Jer. xxii. 20) [19].

I have noted a few instances of what has been termed *progressive* parallelism, e. g.

'Therefore the abundance they have gotten | and their store—over the poplar-brook shall they carry them' (Is. xv. 7).

'The meadows by the Nile, by the brink of the Nile, | and all that is sown by the Nile,—shall become dry, be driven away, and be no more' (xix. 7).

'A thousand at the rebuke of one, | at the rebuke of five,—shall ye flee' (xxx. 17).

'Yea, from of old men have not heard, nor perceived by the ear, | eye hath not seen,—a God beside Thee, who worketh &c.' (lxiv. 3).

This kind of parallelism is more common in the three Books.

VI. In cases of *specification*, we often find the proper logical or syntactical division—particularly the latter—neglected, and the main musical pause introduced *between the details* or *particulars given*. Distinctness of enunciation, and emphasis (where necessary), were thus secured. The pause was introduced where it seemed likely to be most effective. Thus the *logical* division is disregarded:

'And Moses said, With our young and with our old will we go, | with our sons and with our daughters, with our flocks and with our herds will we go; for we must hold a feast unto Jehovah' (Ex. x. 9).

'I have sent among you the pestilence after the manner of Egypt; I have slain with the sword your young men, and given your horses into captivity, | and I have made the stink of your camp to come up even into your nostrils: yet have ye not returned unto Me, saith Jehovah' (Amos iv. 10) [20].

Comp. Gen. xlii. 36[b]; Lev. xxii. 13[a]; Is. xliv. 12; Jer. xlii. 14; Ezek. xiv. 7 (not 4); Amos vi. 2; Ob. 11.

Syntactical clauses are treated in the same way, and subject, object, &c. are cut in two—or members that belong together, separated—by the dichotomy. (A logical pause may occur in the verse or not.)

---

[19] I give a few additional examples: Is. ii. 12; v. 29; viii. 10; x. 15; xiii. 4; lii. 1; lvii. 6; Ezek. xvi. 45; Joel i. 12.

[20] It is interesting to compare with this verse, vv. 6, 8, 9, 11, all with the same refrain. The details in these verses are not so numerous, hence the division is *regular*.

'In the selfsame day entered Noah, and Shem and Ham and Japheth the sons of Noah, | and Noah's wife, and the three wives of his sons with them, into the ark' (Gen. vii. 13).

'And Isaac was forty years old, when he took Rebekah, the daughter of Bethuel the Aramean of Paddan-aram, | the sister of Laban the Aramean, to be his wife' (xxv. 20).

'And every man, with whom was found blue and purple and scarlet, and fine linen, and goats' hair, | and rams' skins dyed red, and sealskins, brought them' (Ex. xxxv. 23).

'And ye shall offer a burnt-offering unto Jehovah, two young bullocks and one ram, | and seven he-lambs of the first year; they shall be unto you without blemish' (Num. xxviii. 19; comp. 11ᵇ).

'And I will set a sign among them, and I will send such as escape of them unto the nations,—to Tarshish, Pul and Lud that draw the bow, to Tubal and Javan, | to the isles afar off, that have not heard My fame, neither have seen My glory,— and they shall declare My glory among the nations' (Is. lxvi. 19).

Perhaps the most notable instances of this mode of division are the following:

'And Jehovah said unto Moses, Speak unto Aaron thy brother, that he come not at all times *into the holy place within the veil,* | *before the mercy-seat which is upon the ark,* that he die not; for I will appear in the cloud upon the mercy-seat' (Lev. xvi. 2). [Specification with emphasis [21].]

'And thou shalt say in thy heart, Who hath borne me these? seeing I was bereaved and barren, | an exile and outcast; and these, who hath brought them up? Behold, I was left alone; these, where were they?' (Is. xlix. 21). [The grouping of the words, though forced, is not without effect.]

Comp. Gen. xxxiv. 28; Ex. xxvii. 19; Deut. xi. 6; Josh. vi. 21; 2 Ki. x. 5ᵃ; Jer. xli. 3; Ezek. xxvii. 27; Esth. ix. 26; Ezra iv. 17 [22].

---

[21] It appears to me a mistake to suppose, with Luzzatto, Malbim, and Geiger (whom Dillmann follows), that the Athnach here rests on a fanciful interpretation given in the name of R. Jehuda, Menachoth 27ᵇ. Had this interpretation indeed represented the traditional and generally accepted view of the passage, we might have allowed that the accentuation had been influenced by it. But, so far from this being the case, it was *opposed* to the recognised teaching (note רבנן סברו וגו' l. c.). Nor is it found in the Versions or in any Rabbinical Commentary. In short, there is nothing to shew that it was anything more than the extravagant conceit of a single Rabbi, who perhaps imagined that he had the accentuation on his side. (Geiger, Jüdische Zeitschrift, ii. p. 30, has certainly not succeeded in establishing his point that R. Jehuda's view was that held by the *Pharisees*.)

[22] Gen. xii. 8 and Is. ix. 8 seem to belong under this head. In the former passage, the details are so accented as to draw special attention to the *place* which Abraham chose for pitching his tent and solemnizing the worship of Jehovah. In the latter, it is the *last* of the details that is marked off, but that is an important one.

It is not often that this prominent division occurs, where only *two* objects are specified, or *two* particulars given :

'The bread of his God, both of the most holy, | and of the holy, shall he eat' (Lev. xxi. 22).

'And the holy oblation | and the sanctuary of the house shall be in its midst' (Ezek. xlviii. 21ᵇ).

'For three transgressions of Damascus | and for four, I will not turn it away' (Amos i. 3 ; comp. 6, 9, &c.).

(Such instances answer to the progressive parallelism of p. 40.) See further, Gen. vi. 9ª (two adjectives); Deut. ix. 28 ; 1 Ki. vii. 7ª, 36ª ; Ezek. xlv. 11 ; Qoh. iii. 17ᵇ ; 1 Chr. vi. 34 ; xxix. 4.

Other modes of dealing with specification present no difficulty. The several details are usually marked with accents in regular *crescendo* order,—a *climax ascendens*,—or are formed into pairs or groups, which are treated in the same way. For examples, see Gen. xii. 5 ; xv. 9; Josh. xi. 16 ; Is. iii. 24 ; lxvi. 3 ; Qoh. ix. 11ª: and comp. the rules for the division of the verbal clause, p. 49.

Where specification runs on in *successive verses*, the same principle of distinct enunciation is observable. For instance, when strings of names occur, we constantly find them broken up into *short* verses. See Gen. x. 15 ff. ; Is. iii. 18 ff. ; Ezra vii. 1 ff. ; 1 Chr. viii. 14 ff. ; &c.

VII. The *parenthesis* may be indicated in various ways.

It may occupy a separate verse (or verses), as in Deut. ii. 10–12 ; iii. 9, 11 ; Jer. xxxix. 1, 2.

Or it may occur in the *middle* or at the *end* of the verse, when the rule is to mark it off with the accent *next greater than that which precedes it* (with Athnach or Silluq after Zaqeph, with Zaqeph or Ṭiphcha after R'bhîa, &c.). The principle of the rule is evident [23].

'If they sin against Thee' [R'bhîa],—'for there is no man that sinneth not' [Zaqeph],—'and Thou be angry with them, &c.' (1 Ki. viii. 46).

'Now Pashchur the son of Immer the priest heard' [Zaqeph],—'and he was chief officer in the house of Jehovah' [Athnach],—'Jeremiah prophesying these things' (Jer. xx. 1).

---

[23] It is very rarely indeed that this rule fails. Ex. xxx. 13ᵇ is an unimportant exception. In Ezek. xxxiii. 33 the accentuators perhaps supplied יאמרו, as the LXX ἐροῦσιν. A strange mistake occurs in 1 Ki. xi. 26. For צרוּעֶה point צרועה, with Ox. 1, 7, 10, &c.

So the scruples of the accentuators led them to mark a parenthesis in the well-known passage:

'And the lamp of God was not yet gone out' [Zaqeph],—'and Samuel was asleep [24]' [Athnach]—'in the temple of Jehovah' (1 Sam. iii. 3).

For other examples, see Gen. xix. 20[b]; Deut. iii. 19; 2 Sam. xiv. 26; xxi. 2; Jer. xli. 9; Amos vi. 14; 2 Chr. xxxii. 9.

The above are the usual modes of marking the parenthesis. Variations are infrequent. Sometimes the clause is broken up into parts, each of which is treated successively as above, e. g.

'Like as many were astonished at thee' [Zaqeph],—'his visage was so marred more than man' [Athnach], 'and his form more than the sons of men' [Silluq],—'so &c.' (Is. lii. 14, 15).

'And the sons of Reuben, the first-born of Israel' [Zarqa],—'for he was the first-born' [S'gôlta]; 'but forasmuch as he defiled his father's couch, his birth-right was given unto the sons of Joseph' [Athnach]; 'and the genealogy is not to be reckoned after the birthright' [Silluq] (1 Chr. v. 1). The parenthesis in this case, from its length and many details, passes on into the next verse.

Comp. 1 Ki. xii. 2 (2 Chr. x. 2); Esth. ii. 12; 1 Chr. viii. 13.

Sometimes again, where verses are closely connected in sense and construction,—as 1 Ki. xviii. 3, 4; 2 Ki. ix. 14, 15; 2 Chr. v. 11, 12,—the parenthesis occupies the last half of one verse, and is then continued in the next [25]; or it may occur even at the *beginning* of the verse, as in 1 Ki. viii. 42; ix. 11 (but this is unusual).

In the course of the present chapter, the most frequent and most important cases of irregular division have been considered. My aim has been, by the comparison of a sufficient number of examples, to shew that a *principle* underlies the deviation in each case. An explanation thus determined can hardly (I venture to think) be called in question.

---

[24] Rabb. Comm. supply בִּמְקוֹמוֹ (see verse 2), or something similar, after שֹׁכֵב.

[25] There is nothing peculiar in this, for other constructions are treated in the same way, in the verse-division. It must, however, be allowed that the arrangement in Judg. xx. 27, 28 is awkward in the extreme.

CHAPTER IV.

ON SYNTACTICAL DICHOTOMY.

THE most frequent, although for us the least important, instances of the application of the dichotomy come under this head. In almost every verse—owing to the minute subdivisions which the continuous dichotomy introduces—we meet with cases where the *syntactical* relation of the words to one another, and to the whole clause of which they form a part, alone decides its position. And it is not always easy to see on what principle the dichotomy in such cases is made. It is therefore necessary to consider somewhat at length what *the relation is between syntax and the accentual division*.

We should not expect the dichotomy to intervene where only *two* words come together, either as forming an independent clause, or as simply left together in the course of the accentual division. Occasionally indeed (as we shall see) under the influence of musical laws, or in cases where a distinct or emphatic enunciation was desired, separation takes place even here. But the rule is *to keep two words united*. Concepts therefore—as subject and predicate, adverb and verb,—which are kept apart in longer clauses, are here constantly brought together, thus : יְהֹוָה הוֹדִיעַנִי ; (Is. xxxiii. 22) יְהֹוָה מַלְכֵּנוּ (Jer. xi. 18) ; עַל־מִשְׁמַרְתִּי אֶעֱמֹדָה (Ezek. xii. 12) ; בַּעֲלָטָה וַיֵּצֵא (Hab. ii. 1). And as words united by Maqqeph are regarded (for accentual purposes) as constituting a single word, we meet with such combinations as וְהָיָה־אִישׁ כְּמַחֲבֵא־רוּחַ (Is. xxxii. 2) ; תִּפְתַּח־אֶרֶץ וְיִפְרוּ־יֶשַׁע (xlv. 8).

But in sentences consisting of three or more words, the dichotomy is more or less regularly introduced. Here the first step is to notice which of the component parts of a grammatical clause—subject, object, verb, &c.—precedes [1].

---

[1] In this chapter, where it is necessary to distinguish the main from a minor dichotomy, I mark the former by d 1, and the latter by d 2, d 3, &c.

I. The SUBJECT may precede, and—from its independent position [2]—is generally marked off by the main dichotomy: וְאַבְרָהָם | הָיוֹ יִהְיֶה | הָיְתָה תֹהוּ וָבֹהוּ | וְהָאָרֶץ (Gen. i. 2); הָאִשָּׁה אֲשֶׁר נָתַתָּה עִמָּדִי | הִיא | לְגוֹי גָּדוֹל וְעָצוּם (xviii. 18); נָתְנָה־לִּי מִן־הָעֵץ וָאֹכֵל (iii. 12). The subject may be common to two clauses, as in וְצֹאנִי | מִרְמַס רַגְלֵיכֶם תִּרְעֶינָה | וּמִרְפַּשׂ^{d2} רַגְלֵיכֶם תִּשְׁתֶּינָה (Ezek. xxxiv. 19).

The usual exceptions come under the following heads:

1. The *personal* and *other pronouns* are not always considered important enough to stand by themselves, thus: אֲנִי אַגִּיד | צִדְקָתֵךְ (Is. lvii. 12); comp. הוּא (Gen. ii. 11); אַתָּה (vi. 21); זֶה (v. 1); אֵלֶּה (xxxvi. 14); אֲשֶׁר (xiv. 20); מִי (Num. xxiii. 10); &c.[3]

The same may be said of the indefinite אִישׁ, אָדָם, 'one, any one' (Qoh. vi. 2; ix. 15^b), and the distributive אִישׁ, 'each, every one' (Lev. xix. 3).

2. When the clause, which the subject introduces, consists of two parts, the first syntactically complete in itself, the second a supplemental appendage (a *Zusatz*, to use a German term, which exactly expresses the construction), consisting generally of a preposition with its government or an adverbial expression, the main dichotomy may be placed at the end of the first part [4]. The subject will then either have no disjunctive accent, or be marked with a minor dichotomy. The following examples will explain what I mean: וְשָׂרָה שֹׁמַעַת | פֶּתַח הָאֹהֶל (Gen. xviii. 10); הָאֵל מָעוּזִּי | חָיִל | יְהוָה יִמְלֹךְ | לְעֹלָם וָעֶד (Ex. xv. 18); וּמָתְנָיו חֲגֻרִים | בְּכֶתֶם אוּפָז (Dan. x. 5). Or the minor dichotomy appears: וְהַנָּחָשׁ | הָיָה עָרוּם^{d1} | מִכֹּל חַיַּת הַשָּׂדֶה^{d2} (Gen. iii. 1); וַיהוָה^{d2} | בֵּרַךְ אֶת־אֲדֹנִי^{d1} | מְאֹד (xxiv. 35). Such cases are very common [5].

Instances of a *double* Zusatz are found, as in וְאַנְשֵׁי סְדֹם | רָעִים^{d2} וְחַטָּאִים | לַיהוָה^{d1} מְאֹד (Gen. xiii. 13), and 2 Chr. xxix. 34^b, but are rare.

---

[2] See Gesenius' Gr., § 144.

[3] Of course, in such cases, the minor dichotomy is due, if the length of the part of the clause before the main dichotomy requires it, e. g. אָנֹכִי | יוֹצֵר עֲלֵיכֶם^{d1} רָעָה^{d2} (Jer. xviii. 11).

[4] The *Zusatz* answers to the supplemental clause in the logical division, p. 32.

[5] It being understood that the division is quite optional. Hence Codd. frequently vary. Thus we have וְרוּחַ יְהֹוָה and וְרוּחַ יְהֹוָה (1 Sam. xvi. 14); וְהַשָּׂטָן and וְהַשָּׂטָן (Zech. iii. 2); הָרָצִים and הָרָצִים (Esth. iii. 15). Even the same verse sometimes shews a different division, as Gen. xxxi. 25^b; Josh. vi. 9.

3. Sometimes, notwithstanding the position of the subject at the head of the clause, the main tone or emphasis lies—or was considered by the accentuators to lie—further on in the clause. In such cases they did not hesitate to transfer the main dichotomy accordingly,—the subject being marked, where necessary, by a *minor* dichotomy,—e. g.

יְהֹוָה ׀ הִפְנִיעַ בּוֹ ׀ (2 Ki. x. 10); ׀ יְהֹוָה עָשָׂה ׀ אֵת אֲשֶׁר דִּבֶּר בְּיַד עֲבְדוֹ אֵלָיְהוּ

הָאֱמִים ׀ אֵת עֲוֹן כֻּלָּנוּ (Is. liii. 6); כִּי הַחַיִּים ׀ יוֹדְעִים ׀ שֶׁיָּמֻתוּ (Qoh. ix. 5);

וְצַדִּיק בֶּאֱמוּנָתוֹ ׀ יִחְיֶה (Hab. ii. 4). לְפָנִים ׀ יָשְׁבוּ בָה (Deut. ii. 10);

Comp. Gen. xix. 24; Num. xv. 13; Josh. ix. 3; 1 Sam. v. 1; Is. iii. 1; viii. 7; lxiv. 3[b][7].

4. Lastly, we cannot but expect to find the subject occupying an inferior position, when its verb governs a clause introduced by כִּי (אֲשֶׁר) or an Infinitive with לְ. Such clauses are often of considerable length, and it would manifestly have been awkward in the extreme to mark off always the subject at the commencement. The rule, therefore, is to make the main dichotomy immediately precede these clauses (just as we, in reading, make a slight pause before them), e. g. יְהֹוָה ׀ צִוָּה

וְאָבִיו וְאִמּוֹ ׀ לֹא יָדֵעוּ ׀ (Josh. xvii. 4); אֶת־מֹשֶׁה ׀ לָתֶת־לָנוּ נַחֲלָה בְּתוֹךְ אַחֵינוּ

כִּי מֵיְהֹוָה הִיא (Judg. xiv. 4). (Corresponding instances with the *object*, II, or an *adverbial expression*, III, at the head of the clause, are, I believe, very rare. I mention, therefore, here the only ones I have noted: 1 Ki. xvii. 4[b]; 2 Chr. xxviii. 10, 13.)

II. The OBJECT may precede, and as its position at the head of the clause implies a distinct emphasis, it is marked off by the main dichotomy: אַךְ־בָּשָׂר ׀ בְּנַפְשׁוֹ דָמוֹ לֹא תֹאכֵלוּ (Gen. ix. 4);

---

[6] Much has been written on the accentuation of this passage. Unquestionably it may stand as in our texts, comp. Ezek. xiv. 14[b]; Dan. ii. 25[a]. But it is to be noted that the great majority of Codd. (I have not noticed a single exception) *point regularly* וְצַדִּיק ׀ בֶּאֱמוּנָתוֹ יִחְיֶה.

[7] That variations occur in Codd. is no more than we should expect. Thus, we have עַמִּי and עַמִּי (Jer. viii. 7); וְעַרְמֹנִים and וְעַרְמֹנִים (Ezek. xxxi. 8); מַלְכָּא and מַלְכָּא (Dan. v. 12); וַיְהֹוָה and וִיהֹוָה (2 Chr. xviii. 22), with a different tone or emphasis according to the taste of the punctators. In a few unimportant instances the division is quite arbitrary. Thus in Gen. x. 8, 13, 15, 24 *bis*, the subject is regularly marked off before יָלַד; then in verse 26 comes an instance to the contrary, וְיָקְטָן יָלַד ׀ אֶת־אַלְמוֹדָד. Comp. 1 Chr. iv. 2, where there is a change in the *same* verse, (in verse 8 point וְקוֹץ with Codd.) We have here such a variation of tone as a reader in the present day might adopt, without assigning to it any particular meaning. (So when the object or an adv. expression precedes, Neh. iii. 6; Gen. x. 25.)

הֵמֵת לְיָרָבְעָם בָּעִיר | יֹאכְלוּ | צָחֹק (xxi. 6); עָשָׂה לִי אֱלֹהִים
הַכְּלָבִים (1 Ki. xiv. 11).

The exceptions follow the same lines as with the subject, but are
far fewer in number. The accentuators rightly felt that the emphatic
position of the *object* was to be as little disturbed as possible.

1. Thus under the head of the *pronouns*, I have noted only זֶה (אֵלֶּה),
מָה, and אֲשֶׁר, without the dichotomy: זֶה יִתְּנוּ | כָּל־הָעֹבֵר עַל־הַפְּקֻדִים
(Ex. xxx. 13); אֵלֶּה עָשָׂה | בְּנָיָהוּ בֶּן־יְהוֹיָדָע (2 Sam. xxiii. 22); | מָה אֲדֹנִי
מְדַבֵּר אֶל־עַבְדּוֹ (Josh. v. 14); אֲשֶׁר־בָּרָא אֱלֹהִים (Gen. ii. 3); and with
the minor dichotomy אֲשֶׁר יְהוָה אֱלֹהֶיךָ נֹתֵן לְךָ (Deut. xix. 10).

2. The *Zusatz*, however, is freely used, on the same principle as
with the subject: וְאֶת־דָּמוֹ יִשְׁפֹּךְ | אֶל־יְסוֹד מִזְבַּח הָעֹלָה (Lev. iv. 25);
וְאֶת־גֻּלְגָּלְתּוֹ תָקְעוּ | בֵּית דָּגוֹן (Ezek. xxxiii. 7); צֹפֶה נְתַתִּיךָ | לְבֵית יִשְׂרָאֵל
(1 Chr. x. 10); or with the minor dichotomy on the object: כִּי־אֹתוֹ אָהַב
אֲבִיהֶם | מִכָּל־אֶחָיו (Gen. xxxvii. 4); דָּבָר שָׁלַח אֲדֹנָי | בְּיַעֲקֹב (Is. ix. 7).

3. In only a few other cases has the emphasis, due on the object,
been *moved further on* in the clause, e.g. אִשָּׁה אֶל־אֲחֹתָהּ | לֹא תִקָּח
(Lev. xviii. 18); חָטְאוּ יִשָּׂא | הָאִישׁ הַהוּא (Num. ix. 13); שְׁעָרֵרֻת
כִּי־עֲנָבִים בְּפִיהֶם | הֵמָּה עֹשִׂים (Ezek. xxxiii. 31); יַיִן לֹא־יִשְׁתּוּ | כָּל־כֹּהֵן (xliv. 21). In Jer. ix. 7ᵇ; x. 13ᵇ
(li. 16) texts vary.

III. ADVERBS, and PREPOSITIONS with their government, at
the beginning of the clause, are also generally marked off by the
main dichotomy, e.g. וּלְאָדָם | לֹא־מָצָא עֵזֶר כְּנֶגְדּוֹ (Gen. ii. 20);
מֵהָעוֹף לְמִינֵהוּ (Jer. vi. 26); פִּתְאֹם | יָבֹא הַשֹּׁדֵד עָלֵינוּ
וּמִן־הַבְּהֵמָה לְמִינָהּ מִכֹּל רֶמֶשׂ הָאֲדָמָה לְמִינֵהוּ | שְׁנַיִם מִכֹּל
יָבֹאוּ אֵלֶיךָ לְהַחֲיוֹת (Gen. vi. 20).

The exceptions run for the most part parallel to those with the
subject and object.

1. Prepositions with *pronominal suffix*, or with the independent
pronouns, often occupy an inferior position: מֵהֶם תִּקְנוּ | עֶבֶד וְאָמָה
(Lev. xxv. 44); מֵאֲשֶׁר יִשְׁאֲבוּן | הַנְּעָרִים (Ruth ii. 9); [8] | אַחֲרָיו הֶחֱזִיק
נְחֶמְיָה בֶן־עַזְבּוּק (Neh. iii. 16); אַחֲרֵי מִי יָצָא | מֶלֶךְ יִשְׂרָאֵל (1 Sam. xxiv. 15);

---

[8] So עַל־יָדוֹ, עַל־יָדָם, verses 2, 4, &c., 'beside him (them).'

עָמּוֹ | הָרֵאוּבֵנִי וְהַגָּדִי | לָקְחוּ נַחֲלָתָם אֶת־יִשְׂרָאֵל (Judg. vi. 15); בַּמֶּה אוֹשִׁיעַ | אֶת־יִשְׂרָאֵל (Josh. xiii. 8).

2. Instances with the *Zusatz* are common enough: | בְּעִצָּבוֹן תֹּאכְלֶנָּה וּלְאַבְרָם הֵיטִיב | בַּעֲבוּרָהּ (Gen. iii. 17); כֹּל יְמֵי חַיֶּיךָ (xii. 16). And with the minor dichotomy, לַמּוֹעֵד | אָשׁוּב אֵלֶיךָ | כָּעֵת חַיָּה (xviii. 14). The double Zusatz is found in Lev. xxiv. 4, לִפְנֵי יְהוָה תָּמִיד, and Deut. xxix. 14, עִמָּנוּ הַיּוֹם.

3. As with the subject and object, the main dichotomy is at times *moved forward* in the clause to where the chief stress or emphasis seems to rest, e.g. בְּרֵאשִׁית | בָּרָא אֱלֹהִים | אֵת הַשָּׁמַיִם וְאֵת הָאָרֶץ (Gen. i. 1); וּפִתְאֹם יָבוֹא אֶל־ | אֵת שֶׁפֶט יִשְׂרָאֵל | יַכּוּ עַל־הַלְּחִי | בַּשֵּׁבֶט (Mic. iv. 14); הֵיכָלוֹ | הָאָדוֹן | אֲשֶׁר־אַתֶּם מְבַקְשִׁים (Mal. iii. 1).

4. Sometimes *two* adverbial expressions are found together at the head of the clause,—answering to the double Zusatz at the close,— e.g. עַל־שֻׁלְחַן הַמֶּלֶךְ תָּמִיד (2 Sam. ix. 13); לְפָנִים בְּיִשְׂרָאֵל (1 Sam. ix. 9); בַּיּוֹם הַשְּׁבִיעִי כְּטוֹב לֵב־הַמֶּלֶךְ בַּיָּיִן (Esth. i. 10). Comp. Cant. iii. 1; Dan. ii. 19; iii. 8; 1 Chr. xii. 37.

5. Lastly, the rule for the dichotomy is often relaxed in the case of the common and less important adverbs, as עַל־כֵּן, לָכֵן, אוּלַי, אָז, אַף, גַּם, אֵיךְ, מַדּוּעַ, עוֹד, עַתָּה, שָׁם, אַחֲרֵיכֶן, &c. Such cases are very common, see אוּלַי in Gen. xviii. 24; אַחֲרֵיכֶן, xxiii. 19, &c.[9] To them may be added the frequently recurring adverbial expressions, בָּעֵת הַהִיא, בַּיּוֹם הַהוּא (Is. ii. 20; xxxix. 1, &c.), and בְּיָמָיו (2 Ki. xxiv. 1).

IV. The VOCATIVE, at the beginning of the clause, is generally marked off by the dichotomy: אֲדֹנָי יְהוִה | בַּמָּה אֵדַע כִּי אִירָשֶׁנָּה (Gen. xv. 8). But when a *long* clause follows, it is almost necessarily subordinated to a part of the same, as in Gen. xviii. 3; Deut. iii. 24; Ezek. xliv. 5; 1 Chr. xxix. 16; &c.

[If it be asked, how, when we have marked off the subject, object, &c., we are to proceed with the division of the rest of the clause, the answer is very simple. We start *de novo* with the members remaining, always supposing there are at least three words left to be divided. If the subject is succeeded by the

---

[9] In these minor matters Codd. often vary. Sometimes the Massora fixes the accentuation, as Gersháyim in לָךְ (Jer. vii. 32); and T'bhîr in וְעַתָּה (Mic. iv. 11).

object, or the object by the subject, &c., we have simply to
proceed as before, and mark off this second member by a *minor*
dichotomy, e. g. הֵמָּה ⸣d1 בָּנַיִךְ וּבְנוֹתַיִךְ ⸣d2 יִקָּחוּ (Ezek. xxiii. 25);
כָּלָה וְנֶחֱרָצָה ⸣d1 דְּבַר אֵלֶיךָ ⸣d2 הַנָּבִיא ⸣d1 דָּבָר גָּדוֹל (2 Ki. v. 13);
אֲדֹנָי יְהוִה צְבָאוֹת ⸣d3 עֹשֶׂה ⸣d2 בְּקֶרֶב כָּל־הָאָרֶץ (Is. x. 23, where
the three last words are treated as a verbal clause); עַל מְאוּרַת
צִפְעוֹנִי ⸣d1 גָּמוּל ⸣d2 יָדוֹ הָדָה (xi. 8); and so on. But in most cases
the verb succeeds, and we then divide according to Rule V,
immediately following.]

V. With the VERB[10], the division is quite different. Here
the weight of the clause lies at the *end;* and the *last member*
is first separated by the dichotomy, then the second from the
end, and so on till we reach the verb: הוֹצִיא יְהוָה ⸣d3 אֶת־בְּנֵי
יִשְׂרָאֵל ⸣d1 מֵאֶרֶץ מִצְרַיִם ⸣d2 עַל־צִבְאֹתָם ⸣d4 וַיִּקֶן אֶת־ (Ex. xii. 51);
חֶלְקַת הַשָּׂדֶה ⸣d3 אֲשֶׁר נָטָה־שָׁם אָהֳלוֹ ⸣d2 מִיַּד בְּנֵי־חֲמוֹר אֲבִי
שְׁכֶם ⸣d1 בְּמֵאָה קְשִׂיטָה (Gen. xxxiii. 19)[11].

The student may find for himself examples in every page.

Variations from this simple rule are the following:

1. The several parts of a compound member are constantly
treated by the accentuation as *separate* members, e. g. וְנָתַתִּי לְךָ ⸣d4 וּלְזַרְעֲךָ
אַחֲרֶיךָ ⸣d3 אֵת אֶרֶץ מְגֻרֶיךָ ⸣d2 אֵת כָּל־אֶרֶץ כְּנַעַן ⸣d1 לַאֲחֻזַּת עוֹלָם (Gen. xvii. 8);
כֹּה־אָמַר יְהוָה ⸣d2 אֱלֹהֵי צְבָאוֹת ⸣d1 אֲדֹנָי (Amos v. 16).

Or else they are grouped in various ways: וַיִּתֶּן־לוֹ צֹאן וּבָקָר ⸣d2 וְכֶסֶף ⸣d3
וְזָהָב ⸣d1 וַעֲבָדִם וּשְׁפָחֹת וּגְמַלִּים וַחֲמֹרִים (Gen. xxiv. 35); וַיִּקְרָא שְׁמוֹ ⸣d3 פֶּלֶא
יוֹעֵץ ⸣d2 אֵל גִּבּוֹר ⸣d1 אֲבִי־עַד שַׂר־שָׁלוֹם (Is. ix. 5).

---

[10] Participles, infinitives, and verbal adjectives come, so far as they have verbal
government, under the category of the verb.

With הֵן (הִנֵּה), עוֹד, אֵין, יֵשׁ, the verbal idea is often *implied* (see Gesenius'
Gr., § 100. 5), Gen. xxii. 13; xxiv. 23; xxviii. 17; xxxi. 14.

[11] The vocative is generally made a *separate* member, e. g. in Judg. v. 31;
Mic. vi. 8; but sometimes not, when the suffix of the 2nd pers. precedes, as in Is.
viii. 8; x. 22; or even *follows*, Is. xiv. 31; Mic. ii. 12.

2. On the other hand, adverbial expressions or prepositions with
their government—homogeneous members, be it observed—are some-
times *kept together* by the accentuation [12], e. g. | אִשָּׁה אֵלִבְרָהָם | וַתִּתֵּן אֹתָהּ
וַיִּקְרָא | מַלְאַךְ יְהֹוָה | אֶל־אַבְרָהָם | שֵׁנִית מִן־הַשָּׁמַיִם | לֹו לְאִשָּׁה (Gen. xvi. 3);
(xxii. 15);   וַיַּעַל אֵלִיָּהוּ | בַּסְעָרָה הַשָּׁמָיִם (2 Ki. ii. 11;   comp. ver. 1).
Other examples are Ex. ii. 5; xxv. 30; Lev. xiv. 27 (not 16); Num.
xiv. 37; Josh. xxi. 8; Is. xl. 2 end; Jer. xxxvi. 10; Qoh. ii. 15;
1 Chr. xxiii. 31.

3. Some *anomalous* cases occur, which may almost all be explained
by the desire to *emphasize* the part of the clause, to which the dichotomy has, contrary to rule, been transferred. It is enough to trace the
principle which guided the accentuators. We are not bound always to
agree with them.

(*a*) Thus, when the verb which introduces the clause, receives its
nearer definition through another verb, governing an accusative,
adverbial expression, &c., and this accusative or adverbial expression
is placed *before* the verb on which it depends, they considered that a
certain emphasis was intended, and pointed accordingly: אֲשֶׁר לֹא־נִסְּתָה
הַמַּעֲמִיקִים מֵיְהֹוָה | לַסְתִּר עֵצָה | הַגֵּן עַל־הָאָרֶץ (Deut. xxviii. 56);   כִּי־רַגְלָה
(Is. xxix. 15);   [13] הֲלֹוא־שָׁמַעְתָּ לְמֵרָחֹוק | אֹותָהּ עָשִׂיתִי (xxxvii. 26);   וְלֹא־אָבוּ
הָלֹוךְ | בִּדְרָכָיו (xlii. 24);   לָא־חָשְׁחִין אֲנַחְנָא עַל־דְּנָה | פִּתְגָם | לַהֲתָבוּתָךְ (Dan.
iii. 16);   לָא־כָהֲלִין פְּשַׁר־מִלְּתָא | לְהַחֲוָיָה (v. 15; comp. vv. 8, 16 [14], and
iv. 15). And so in 2 Sam. xv. 20; xxi. 4; Qoh. viii. 3; Esth. ii. 9; Dan.
vi. 5; Ezra iv. 22; 2 Chr. xxxi. 7, 10.

(*β*) In the following passages the accentuators have placed the
dichotomy even at the *status constructus* [15], as a measure of emphasis
seemed to be due there: [16] הָאֱמֹרִי | מַמְרֵא בְּאֵלֹנֵי שֹׁכֵן וְהוּא (Gen. xiv. 13);

[12] Particularly at the *end* of the clause, like the double Zusatz at the end of
the nominal clause. It is but rarely (as far as I have observed) that the expressions referred to come together in the *middle* of the clause, as in 1 Ki. xi. 36;
2 Ki. xvii. 13; Is. xxix. 4.

[13] Here Luzzatto and Delitzsch have both misapprehended the accentuation,
which, it must be allowed, is ambiguous.

[14] The change Baer makes (see his note) is therefore quite unnecessary.

[15] Such a free division is not without parallel in our own chanting, as in the
Te Deum: 'Heaven and earth are full of the majesty | of Thy glory,' of which
we might make a verbal clause in Heb., with the dichotomy at the st. const.:

מָלְאוּ הַשָּׁמַיִם וְהָאָרֶץ הֹוד | כְּבֹודֶךָ

[16] That Abraham should be dwelling at *such* a place was a circumstance worthy
of observation! The Midrash has something to say on the point.

(Ex. וְעָשׂוּ אֲרוֹן | עֲצֵי שִׁטִּים (xl. 3); וַיִּתֵּן אֹתָם בְּמִשְׁמַר | בֵּית שַׂר הַטַּבָּחִים [17]
xxv. 10; similar vv. 13, 31; xxxvi. 31; xxxvii. 4; xxxix. 25).
The further instances I have noticed are Ex. xxxii. 22; Num. vi. 5ᵇ;
Deut. xiv. 6; xxxiii. 24ᵇ; Judg. iv. 5; Is. xxviii. 4; Jer. xix. 1; Esth.
vi. 1 [18].

(γ) A few other isolated cases shew divergence. Thus we have
וַיִּטַּע יְהֹוָה אֱלֹהִים | גַּן בְּעֵדֶן (Gen. ii. 8), to avoid the awkward
junction of אֱלֹהִים גַּן | בְּעֵדֶן. In Gen. xxx. 7, 10, 12 the maids of *Leah*
and *Rachel* are carefully distinguished. In Num. xxvii. 16 אִישׁ is
kept apart from the Divine titles. In 1 Sam. xxv. 8ᵇ; 1 Ki. i. 45;
Jer. xxxiv. 6; xxxviii. 11; Ezek. xxvi. 7; Nah. ii. 1ᵇ; Cant. vii. 7;
Lam. iii. 50; and 2 Chr. xxvi. 15, it is not difficult to see that
a certain emphasis was designed, and is, in most cases, appropriate
enough. They are none of them passages of any importance.

The above are the only exceptions I have observed. Others may,
perhaps, be found. Against them are to be set the thousands of instances, in which the *rule for the division of the verbal clause is
carried out.*

VI. In nominal sentences, when *the predicate precedes*, the
division is the same as with the verb, e. g. טוֹב |ᵈ² תִּתִּי אֹתָהּ
רִאשׁוֹן הוּא |ᵈ² לָךְ |ᵈ¹ מִתִּתִּי אֹתָהּ לְאִישׁ אַחֵר (Gen. xxix. 19);
כִּי־קָרוֹב אֵלֶיךָ |ᵈ¹ הַדָּבָר |ᵈ² לָכֶם |ᵈ¹ לְחָדְשֵׁי הַשָּׁנָה (Ex. xii. 2);
מְאֹד (Deut. xxx. 14).

Only when הָיָה follows, the dichotomy comes not on it, but
on the predicate (which is indeed in the accusative): עֶבֶד
כִּי אָהֵב | הָיָה חִירָם לְדָוִד (Gen. ix. 25); עֲבָדִים | יִהְיֶה לְאֶחָיו
(1 Ki. v. 15).

_____

[17] The place is to be noted. All Joseph's future history depends on their having
been sent *there!* Once introduced, this division is repeated in verse 7 and xli. 10.
We might be tempted to point בְּמִשְׁמָר with Qāmeṣ, as in xlii. 17, and then all
would be regular; but this would be contrary to the Massora, which requires
Pathach, בְּמִשְׁמַר ג' פתחין.

[18] One might be inclined to explain some of these cases by a reference to
rhythm, or equilibrium in the section of the clause, but such explanations will
not apply, for the simple reason that in other similar instances, and those the
great majority, these influences do not make themselves felt, but the division is
according to the *rule* for the verbal clause. See Gen. iii. 24ᵇ; Judg. viii. 5ᵇ;
1 Ki. xi. 27ᵇ; Jer. xxxviii. 6; 1 Chr. xvi. 10ᵇ; &c.

An occasional exception is indeed found, as in | הָיוֹת הָאָדָם ‏ ^{d2}| לֹא־טוֹב ‏^{d1}
לְבַדּוֹ (Gen. ii. 18); בֶּן־שֶׁבַע שָׁנִים | יְהוֹאָשׁ בְּמָלְכוֹ (2 Ki. xii. 1; and
similar passages); עֲבָדְךָ אָנִי | ^{d2}‏ (Lev. xxv. 10); יוֹבֵל הִיא | תִּהְיֶה לָכֶם
אֶהְיֶה | הַפֶּלֶךְ ‏^{d1} (2 Sam. xv. 34); and נָכוֹן יִהְיֶה | הַר בֵּית־יְהוָֹה (Is. ii. 2);
the explanations of which will readily suggest themselves. In Jer.
iv. 27ᵃ, texts vary.

VII. Lastly, the CONJUNCTIONS, as אֲשֶׁר, אוֹ, אִם, אַף, גַּם,
אִין, בַּל, לֹא, פֶּן, עַד, לְמַעַן, לוּ, כִּי, יַעַן, the NEGATIVES, as
עַל כִּי, כִּי אִם, בִּלְתִּי, בְּלִי, and forms compounded from them, as
עַד־בִּלְתִּי, אִם לֹא, כִּי לֹא, &c., need not detain us. They are,
from their character, generally *joined*, either by a conjunctive
accent or Maqqeph, to the word following. It is unnecessary to
give examples, as they may be found in every page.

But, sometimes on musical grounds, sometimes with a view to
emphasis, even these unimportant words, which have so little claim
to an independent position, are found marked with a pausal accent,
thus: אִם (Gen. iv. 7); אֲשֶׁר (xi. 7); גַּם (xxxii. 21); כִּי (ii. 17; and
often); יַעַן (Is. vii. 5; and often); לֹא (Gen. ii. 25); אַל־נָא (xviii. 30);
אִם־לֹא (Ezek. xxxiv. 8; Baer rightly); לֹא כִּי (1 Ki. xi. 22; and
often); but לֹא כִּי (iii. 22, 23; Is. xxx. 16); &c. These two last
examples shew that the punctators are not always consistent, even
where we should expect them to be so. And so in Codd. there is, in
these trifling points, frequent variation, thus in לֹא־קָרָעְתָּ שָׁמַיִם (Is.
lxiii. 19) some have לֹא, others לוֹא; in Mic. vi. 5 we find לְמַעַן and
לְמַעַן, &c. Sometimes the Massora comes in and *fixes* the accentuation,
as כִּי כ״ג בט׳; וְאִם ב׳ בט׳; יַעַן ג׳ בטעם; &c.

The INTERJECTIONS are used in the same way, e. g. הֵן, הִנֵּה
(Gen. iii. 22; xxvii. 42ᵇ)[19]; הוֹי (Is. xvii. 12; xviii. 1); הָבָה
(Ex. i. 10).

Thus far we have had to do with the division of the *clause* into its
several members, but there is a further point that requires consideration, and that is, the division, in certain cases, of the *members themselves*. Every member of a clause—subject, object, &c.—will be either

---

[19] רְאֵה and רְאוּ, as in Gen. xxvii. 27; Ex. xxxv. 30; Deut. i. 8; ii. 31, may
take the place of הִנֵּה.

simple, consisting of one word, or *compound*, consisting of two or more words. And such compound members introduce a new element into the dichotomy of the verse, about which it is necessary to say a few words.

1. Two Nouns in *apposition* are generally kept together by the accentuation, as אֶת־חַוָּה אִשְׁתּוֹ, הַמֶּלֶךְ דָּוִד, יְהֹוָה אֱלֹהִים (Gen. iv. 1), &c.

But where emphasis or distinctness of enunciation seems to require it, the dichotomy—and even the main dichotomy of the clause—may come between, e. g. שָׁלוֹם הִנְנִי נֹתֵן לוֹ אֶת־בְּרִיתִי | הִנְנִי (Num. xxv. 12); נָתַן יְהֹוָה אֶת־אֹיְבֵיכֶם | בְּיֶדְכֶם d1 | אֶת־מוֹאָב d2 | מֵבִיא אֶת־עַבְדִּי | צֶמַח (Zech. iii. 8); (Judg. iii. 28). And so the emphatic pronoun may be separated from the noun, הוּא | וְעָבַד הַלֵּוִי (Num. xviii. 23).

The cases, in which more than two nouns come in apposition, or instead of the noun we have a nominal expression consisting of several words, present no difficulty. The subdivision of such expressions will be according to the general rules for the dichotomy, see Gen. xxiii. 16; Num. xvi. 2; 1 Ki. xi. 36ᵇ; Amos v. 16.

2. So two Nouns, *in the same construction and joined by* וֹ, are constantly kept together by the accentuation, as וּבַלַּיְלָה בַּיּוֹם (Gen. i. 18); עָפָר וָאֵפֶר (xviii. 27); גָּדוֹל וְכָבֵד (l. 10), &c.

But for the reasons above given, they may be separated by the dichotomy, e. g. וּדְבַשׁ | חָלָב זָבַת אֶרֶץ, וָבֹהוּ | הָיְתָה תֹהוּ (i. 2); (Ex. iii. 8); וַיִּזְעַק חֶרֶב לַיהֹוָה | וּלְגִדְעוֹן (Judg. vii. 20); לֹא־אוּכַל אָוֶן | וַעֲצָרָה (Is. i. 13); שֵׁשׁ־אַמּוֹת בָּאַמָּה | וָטֹפַח (Ezek. xl. 5). וְזַעֲקָה גְדוֹלָה | וּמָרָה (Esth. iv. 1);

Examples, where several nouns come together, or where the nominal expression consists of several words (see remark above), are Deut. xxix. 7; Is. xxvii. 1; xxx. 30; xxxvii. 12 [20].

3. The substantive may be *qualified* in various ways, either by another substantive in apposition, or by an adjective, relative or adverbial expression following. In these several cases (as we have seen with the apposition [21]), the substantive may be *separated* from the qualifying expression by the main (or a minor) dichotomy. Somewhat more of weight generally attaches to the latter in consequence. Thus

(a) Substantive and adjective: וַיַּהֲפֹךְ יְהֹוָה רוּחַ־יָם | חָזָק מְאֹד (Ex. x. 19); וָאֶרְאֶה אֶת־אֲדֹנָי יֹשֵׁב d1 | אֲשֶׁר־יִשְׁכַּב אֶת־אִשָּׁה d2 | וְאִישׁ (Lev. xx. 18); וְאֵיךְ תָּשִׁיב אֶת־פְּנֵי פַחַת אַחַד עַבְדֵי אֲדֹנִי | עַל־כִּסֵּא | רָם וְנִשָּׂא (Is. vi. 1); הַקְּטַנִּים (xxxvi. 9). And so the demonstrative זֶה (אֵלֶּה) often stands

---

[20] Sometimes the nouns appear ἀσυνδέτως, as עֵץ (Gen. i. 11, not 12).

[21] In reality, the adjective and relative are to be regarded as *in apposition*, see Ewald, §§ 293 a, 364 c; Stade, § 176; and even the adv. expression, when we can supply אשר before it (see note 23), is equally *in apposition*.

outside the rest of the clause: הַזֶּה | הַנִּכְבָּד וְהַנּוֹרָא אֶת־הַשֵּׁם לְיִרְאָה
(Deut. xxviii. 58); הַזֹּאת | הַטּוֹבָה אֶת־הָאָרֶץ לְךָ נֹתֵן אֱלֹהֶיךָ יְהֹוָה (ix. 6);
הָאֵלֶּה | הָרְשָׁעִים הָאֲנָשִׁים אָהֳלֵי מֵעַל נָא סוּרוּ (Num. xvi. 26).

(β) *Substantive and relative.* Here it is not so much the *separation*
of the relative clause from the substantive, to which attention has to
be drawn (for in our own interpunction such separation is common
enough), as the character of the dichotomy,—the *main*, where we look for
a minor,—e. g. אֲשֶׁר־נִשְׁבַּע | אֶת־הָאָרֶץ וִירִשְׁתֶּם וּבָאתֶם | וּרְבִיתֶם תִּחְיוּן לְמַעַן
לַאֲבֹתֵיכֶם יְהֹוָה לָלֶכֶת | לְהַכְעִסֵנִי עָשׂוּ אֲשֶׁר רָעָתָם מִפְּנֵי (Deut. viii. 1);
וַאֲבֹתֵיכֶם אַתֶּם הֵמָּה יְדָעוּם לֹא אֲשֶׁר | אֲחֵרִים לֵאלֹהִים לַעֲבֹד לְקַטֵּר (Jer. xliv. 3).
For the relative, we may have the participle : הַמִּתְהַפֶּכֶת | הַחֶרֶב לַהַט אֵת
וְצַלְמֵי עַפֹּלֵיכֶם צַלְמֵי וַעֲשִׂיתֶם (Gen. iii. 24); רֹאִי | לַחַי בְּאֵר (xxiv. 62);
אֶת־הָאָרֶץ הַמַּשְׁחִיתִם | עָכְבְּרֵיכֶם (1 Sam. vi. 5).

Often the relative conjunction is *understood:* בְּאֵשׁ בְּיַעֲקֹב וַיִּבְעַר
מִבּוֹר אֲסִירַיִךְ שִׁלַּחְתִּי בְּרִיתֵךְ בְּדַם גַּם־אַתְּ (Lam. ii. 3); | אָכְלָה סָבִיב לֶהָבָה
בּוֹ מַיִם אֵין (Zech. ix. 11).

Obs. Sometimes, for emphasis' sake, the dichotomy appears in the
middle of the relative clause, e.g. בֶּן־אָמוֹץ יְשַׁעְיָהוּ | חָזָה אֲשֶׁר הַדָּבָר
(Is. ii. 1. The weight of the clause does not rest on הדבר, but on
the *contents* of the same, *a vision of Isaiah*[22]); לֹא | בְּרַגְלָיו (אשר) אֹרַח
יָבוֹא (xli. 3, בְּרַגְלָיו emphatic); שָׁם אַנְשֵׁי־חַיִל כִּי | יָדַע אֲשֶׁר הַמָּקוֹם (2 Sam.
xi. 16, 'the place where he *knew*' &c.). Comp. Deut. i. 31, 39; xi. 2,
7; xxviii. 69; xxxiii. 1; Judg. xviii. 10ᵇ; xx. 15ᵇ.

(γ) Adverbs, and prepositions with their government, are constantly
employed to qualify a noun (subst. or adj.), and are joined to it by the
accents; but frequently they appear with the dichotomy preceding,
e. g. לָרָשׁ | כֶּעָפָר וַיְשִׂמֵם (2 Ki. xiii. 7); מֵרָחוֹק לַגּוֹיִם וְנָשָׂא־נֵס (Is. v. 26;
comp. Joel iv. 12); מִיַּעַר | אַרְיֵה הִכָּם עַל־כֵּן (Jer. v. 6); בְּעֵינַי | הָרַע (vii. 30); לָרֹב מְאֹד | חַיִל בְּיָדָם נָתַן | וַיהֹוָה (2 Chr. xxiv. 24).
Comp. יִשְׂרָאֵל לְמַלְכֵי (1 Ki. xiv. 19) and לֶאֱלִישָׁע (2 Ki. v. 9)[23]. An
extreme case is בְּעֵדָה | וְכָל־הַנְּשִׂאִים אַהֲרֹן אֵלָיו וַיָּשֻׁבוּ (Ex. xxxiv. 31).

---

[22] The first verses of Hos., Joel, Mic., Hab., and Zeph. are similarly divided.
(Comp. Jer. li. 59.) On the other hand, in בֶּן־אָמוֹץ יְשַׁעְיָהוּ חָזָה אֲשֶׁר | בָּבֶל מַשָּׂא
(Is. xiii. 1), the weight of the clause comes on the *first* words.

[23] We may often in such expressions supply אשר. Comp. Lev. iv. 7 and 18
(לִפְנֵי); Num. xxvi. 63ᵇ and xxxi. 12ᵇ (עַל); 1 Sam. xxvi. 1ᵇ and 3 (do.); Is. xxxvi.
2ᵇ and 2 Ki. xviii. 17ᵇ (בְּ); where it fails in the first, but is given in the second
of the verses quoted.

4. The connection between a noun in *status constructus* and the genitive following is closer than that in any of the cases already considered, yet even here, under certain circumstances, the dichotomy intervenes,—as when the word in st. constr. is followed by *two or more* others, which together express the genitive relation, e. g. | עֵץ אָבִי | יֵשֵׁב אֹהֶל וּמִקְנֶה | הַדַּעַת טוֹב וָרָע (Gen. ii. 9); | דְּמֵי אָחִיד | קוֹל (iv. 10); בְּיוֹם | חָבַשׁ (Num. ix. 18); כָּל־יְמֵי | אֲשֶׁר יִשְׁכֹּן הֶעָנָן עַל־הַמִּשְׁכָּן (iv. 20); יְהוָה אֶת־שֶׁבֶר עַמּוֹ (Is. xxx. 26)[24].

When several nouns follow one another in st. constr., they are marked off (as far as is necessary) in succession : אֶת־יְמֵי שְׁנֵי חַיֵּי אֲבֹתַי (Gen. xlvii. 9); אֶת־רוּחַ בֹּל שְׁאֵרִית הָעָם (Hag. i. 14); קוֹל שָׁאוֹן מַמְלְכוֹת גּוֹיִם (Is. xiii. 4).

The following variations occur : (*a*) In the case last-named, the dichotomy sometimes comes after the *second* noun, particularly when the two first nouns form together a *compound* idea, e. g. | עֲטֶרֶת גֵּאוּת שִׁכֹּרֵי אֶפְרָיִם (Is. xxviii. 1); בְּכִי תַחֲנוּנֵי | בְּנֵי יִשְׂרָאֵל (Jer. iii. 21); אֹהֶל מוֹעֵד | הָאֱלֹהִים (2 Chr. i. 3)[25]. In Is. xxi. 17 *five* nouns are brought together in st. constr., and the dichotomy comes, suitably enough, after the *third* : שְׁאָר מִסְפַּר־קֶשֶׁת | גִּבּוֹרֵי בְנֵי־קֵדָר.

(β) The small and frequently recurring words אֵת and בֹּל, regarded as in st. constr., are often marked off by the dichotomy (Gen. i. 25; ii. 20). So also the prepositions, as אַחַר, אַחֲרֵי (v. 4; xv. 1); בֵּין (xiii. 7); עַד (xii. 6); עַל (viii. 4); עִם (xxxi. 32); לִפְנֵי (xli. 46); בַּעֲבוּר (xxvi. 24); &c. But these words are all more commonly joined by Maqqeph or a conjunctive accent to the word following, or are marked by a minor dichotomy, (see text passim) according to the taste of the punctators. (Codd. in consequence vary greatly. Where some place R'bhîa or Zaqeph, others have Maqqeph, &c.)

Other small words of frequent occurrence, treated in the same way, are בֵּן and בַּת (Gen. vii. 6; xvii. 17); אָב (xvii. 5[b]); בֵּית (1 Ki. x. 21); דְּבַר (Deut. xxii. 24); יוֹם (Gen. ii. 4; Is. lviii. 5); יְמֵי (Deut. xxxiv. 8[b]; Judg. xviii. 31); עֵת (Mic. v. 2); and יַד (Jer. xxii. 25).

5. Correlative expressions, formed by כְּ—כְּ, בְּ—וּב, בֵּין—וּבֵין, &c., are sometimes kept together and sometimes separated by the accents.

---

[24] The relative דִּי, which often expresses the genitive relation in Chaldee, leads to another division. See Dan. vi. 17, 25; Ezra iv. 15; v. 13, 16; vii. 21[b]. In reality this particle is in *apposition* (comp. Philippi, Status constructus, p. 114), and the division is to be explained accordingly.

[25] Gen. l. 17; Ex. xxviii. 11; Num. iii. 36; 2 Sam. xxiii. 20[b]; Is. x. 12[b]; xxviii. 1[b], 16[b]; 1 Chr. xxiii. 28[b], may be compared. Sometimes *emphasis* may have influenced the division, as in Is. xxxvi. 9.

Equilibrium of the parts of the clause will generally decide. Thus we have וַיַּבְדֵּל אֱלֹהִים | בֵּין הָאוֹר וּבֵין הַחֹשֶׁךְ (Gen. i. 4), but וַיַּבְדֵּל בֵּין הַמַּיִם אֲשֶׁר מִתַּחַת לָרָקִיעַ | וּבֵין הַמַּיִם אֲשֶׁר מֵעַל לָרָקִיעַ (ver. 7). Verses 6, 14, 18 are like the former, but xiii. 7; xx. 1, like the latter. (In Num. xvii. 13 texts vary.) And so בְּדָוִד וּבַקִּיר are joined in 1 Sam. xix. 10, but separated in xviii. 11. In Gen. xviii. 25 we have וְהָיָה כַצַּדִּיק | כָרָשָׁע, but necessarily כַּקָּטֹן כַּגָּדֹל | תִּשְׁמָעוּן (Deut. i. 17).

It is the same with the contrasted prepositions מִן—אֶל, מִן—עַד, מִן—לְ, which are, according to the taste of the punctators, kept together, as in Gen. xiii. 3; xv. 18; Ex. xxviii. 28; or separated, as in Gen. xxv. 18; Num. xxxiii. 49; Jos. xiii. 5.

6. The VERB.—(a) Two verbs, in the same construction, are joined by the accents: אֶת־מִי | דָאַגְתְּ וַיִּקֹּד וַיִּשְׁתַּחוּ | לְאַפָּיו (Num. xxii. 31); וַתִּירָאִי (Is. lvii. 11).

Yet, not unfrequently, particularly if emphasis is to be marked, the dichotomy comes between: הֲלֹא יִמְצְאוּ | יְחַלְּקוּ שָׁלָל (Judg. v. 30); אֶת־קִבַּעַת כּוֹס הַתַּרְעֵלָה שָׁתִית | מָצִית אֶת־מִי חֶרְפָּתֶךָ | וְנִדַּפְתָּ (Is. xxxvii. 23); (li. 17). Comp. Is. lxii. 7; Jer. vi. 27[b]; vii. 29[b]; Jon. iii. 9; and with three verbs, Is. xxxvii. 37; Esth. iii. 13.

(β) The *inf. abs.* is generally joined to the *verb. fin.*, as in הַרְבָּה אַרְבֶּה | עִצְּבוֹנֵךְ (Gen. iii. 16); הָשֵׁב תְּשִׁיבֶנּוּ | לוֹ (Ex. xxiii. 4).

(γ) When two verbs are connected to form one idea[26], this connection is constantly marked by the accents: וַתֹּסֶף לָלֶדֶת | אֶת־אָחִיו (Gen. iv. 2); שׁוּב קַח־לְךָ | מְגִלָּה אַחֶרֶת (Jer. xxxvi. 28); לֹא־אָבוּ שְׁמוֹעַ | תּוֹרַת יְהֹוָה (Is. xxx. 9); &c. תְּדַבְּרוּ | גְבֹהָה (1 Sam. ii. 3); Or the first verb receives the *minor* dichotomy: אַתָּה הַחִלּוֹתָ[d2] | לְהַרְאוֹת אֶת־עַבְדְּךָ[d1] | אֶת־גָּדְלְךָ (Deut. iii. 24).

We may also note the cases where the first verb is merely *introductory* to the other, which is the main verb of the clause, e. g. בֹּא וּרְאֵה | אֶת־הַתּוֹעֵבוֹת לֶךְ־נָא רְאֵה | אֶת־שְׁלוֹם אַחֶיךָ (Gen. xxxvii. 14); (Ezek. viii. 9); שְׁלַח הָעֵז | אֶת־מִקְנֶךָ (Ex. ix. 19); וְיֵצֵא הָעָם הָרָעוֹת וְלִקְטוּ | דְּבַר־יוֹם בְּיוֹמוֹ (xvi. 4). And so יֵרַד (Gen. xviii. 21); עָמַד (Num. ix. 8); קָרַב (Deut. v. 24); סָבַב (Cant. ii. 17); קָם (Jer. i. 17); שָׁמַע (Deut. xxxiv. 9; Jer. xxxv. 10); and many other verbs[27].

---

[26] In the sense laid down in Ges. Gr., § 142.

[27] Of the verbs used in this way בָּא and הָלַךְ are particularly common. These verbs sometimes *follow* the main verb in a complemental sense, and are still joined to it by the accents: אֶתְיַעֲצוּן בְּתֵיכֶם | קְחוּ וָלֵכוּ (Gen. xlii. 33). Comp. Ex. xvii. 5; Deut. xii. 26; 1 Sam. xxx. 22.

In conclusion, I have once more to draw attention to the peculiar use of the ZUSATZ. We have already had many instances of this construction. It remains only to mention that, like the apposition, relative, &c., it often belongs syntactically only to the *last part* of the clause, or division of the verse, preceding. Note how we divide sometimes, in chanting, in the same way :

'As it was in the beginning, is now, and ever shall be | world without end.'

Examples are :

'And they heard the voice of Jehovah God, walking in the garden | at the cool of the day' (Gen. iii. 8).

'And he shall dip them and the living bird in the blood of the bird that was killed | over the running water' (Lev. xiv. 6).

'And they took his land in possession, and the land of Og king of Bashan, the two kings of the Amorites, which were beyond Jordan | toward the sun-rising' (Deut. iv. 47, comp. 49).

'Wilt thou keep silence, and afflict us | very sore?' (Is. lxiv. 11).

Comp. Gen. xxii. 4; xxxviii. 12^b; xlix. 29^b; Lev. xxvii. 18^a; Deut. xi. 28^b; Is. lxi. 10^b; Mic. ii. 8; Ezra vi. 21 [28].

Of course, we may have one Zusatz duly marked off, and then another following :

'These are the commandments and the judgments, which Jehovah commanded, by the hand of Moses, $^{d\,2}$| unto the children of Israel, $^{d\,1}$| in the plains of Moab by the Jordan of Jericho' (Num. xxxvi. 13).

What is irregular is the *double Zusatz,* e. g.

'These are the statutes, ... which Jehovah made between Him and the children of Israel, | in Mount Sinai, by the hand of Moses' (Lev. xxvi. 46) [29].

It is observable that the relative, or a term in apposition, may take the place of one member of the double Zusatz. (This is possible, inasmuch as the relative, apposition, and Zusatz appear under the *same conditions,* at the end of the clause.) Comp. Deut. iv. 40^b, with the Zusatz כל־הימים, and xxviii. 52^a with בכל־ארצך, both after the relative. In this way Is. ii. 20^b may be explained, without having recourse to the Rabbinical rendering to account for the accentuation. A somewhat similar case is Gen. i. 11 : 'Fruit-tree bearing fruit after its kind, | in which is the seed thereof, upon the earth,' where על־הארץ

---

[28] Sometimes it is the second accusative, which we express by a preposition, that serves as Zusatz, as in Gen. xlix. 25, after בְּרֶךְ; and Num. xxii. 18 after מְלֹא.

[29] So virtually Is. lxiii. 13 : 'Who led them through the depths, | like the horse on the plain, without stumbling.' And so Gen. xiii. 10^b may be explained.

does not refer to the relative clause [30], but to the clause preceding the dichotomy.—An instance of Zusatz + Apposition is found in Deut. xxvi. 15[b].

Having completed the examination of the principles on which the division—logical and syntactical—proceeds, we are now prepared to enter on the analysis of the verse and its component parts. It will (I think) be found that we have already mastered the chief difficulties of our investigation. Henceforth our main task will be to *observe the accents,* that are employed to mark the necessary divisions. The rules above laid down will be applied at every step, and I shall not consider it necessary to draw the reader's attention to their particular application, but shall take it for granted that he has made himself familiar with them in a general way, so as to be able readily to refer to them for the explanation of any particular case. Beside the above rules, we shall find that musical and rhythmical laws have to be taken into account.

Perhaps before I leave this, the preparatory part of my work, it may be well to remind the student that the accents employed to mark the various divisions of the verse, have no *fixed* interpunctional value. We could not say that one answers *per se* to our comma, another to our semicolon, and so on; for they simply note *musical* divisions, which are bound to appear whatever the logical or grammatical construction of the verse may be. Hence Athnach, for instance, may represent at one time the fullest logical, and at another the feeblest syntactical pause; and hence too the same clause will be marked by quite different accents, as it varies its position in the verse. (See e. g. Jos. vii. 14[b]; 1 Ki. vii. 21[b].) The point which the student must bear in mind is that the interpunctional value of the accents is *relative,* not absolute.

---

[30] At least, no one (I presume) will accept Dillmann's explanation: *In welcher sein Same* [ist zur Fortpflanzung!] *auf der Erde.*

Corrigenda [31]

(in accordance with the rules laid down in this chapter).

1. The *casus absolutus* (p. 45) must be marked off in

נָבִיא פַּח יָקוֹשׁ עַל־כָּל־דְּרָכָיו (Hos. ix. 8), with Ox. 1, 5, 6, 7, &c. 'As for the prophet—the snare of the fowler is on all his ways.'

2. The accentual arrangement of the *verbal clause* (p. 49) has to be corrected in the following passages:

תִּהְיֶה זֹאת אוֹת (Jos. iv. 6), with Par. 9; Hm. 3. T'bhîr is evidently due at זֹאת.

הֲבָא־עוֹד הֲלֹם אִישׁ (1 Sam. x. 22), with Ox. 16; Erf. 1, 2, 3.

וַתִּהְיֶיןָ נַם־שְׁתֵּיהֶן לוֹ לְנָשִׁים: (xxv. 43), with Ox. 16, 72, 75, &c. T'bhîr is again out of place in our texts.

וַתְּהִי־שָׁם הַמַּגֵּפָה גְדוֹלָה (2 Sam. xviii. 7), with Add. 11657; Ber. 2. Géresh is properly due (as we shall afterwards see) at הַמַּגֵּפָה, but has been transformed.

לֹא בָא־כֵן עֲצֵי אַלְמֻגִּים (1 Ki. x. 12), with Ox. 1, 6, 8, &c.

וַיָּשֶׁב אֶת־הַצֵּל בַּמַּעֲלוֹת אֲשֶׁר יָרְדָה בְמַעֲלוֹת אָחָז אֲחֹרַנִּית (2 Ki. xx. 11), with Or. 2091; Par. 30; Ber. 32; and so Is. xxxviii. 8. The pointing of our texts, הַצֵּל, makes the shadow to have already gone down backwards, *before* the sign was performed!

הוֹלֵךְ גּוֹלָה מִירוּשָׁלַם בָּבֶלָה: (xxiv. 15), with Ox. 1, 7, 10, &c.

וְהִצַּתִּי אֶת־הָעִיר הַזֹּאת בָּאֵשׁ (Jer. xxxii. 29), with Ox. 1, 5, 6, &c.

וְעָטָה ׀ אֶת־אֶרֶץ מִצְרַיִם כַּאֲשֶׁר־יַעֲטֶה הָרֹעֶה אֶת־בִּגְדוֹ (xliii. 12). R'bhîa is absolutely necessary here, and is supplied by Add. 15252; Par. 30; Ber. 32; De R. 942.

לָשֵׂאת מַעֲשַׂר הַחֹמֶר הַבַּת (Ezek. xlv. 11), with Ox. 2421; Harl. 5498; Or. 2091; Vi. 2, &c.

וָאֹמַר אֶל־הַמַּלְאָךְ הַדֹּבֵר בִּי (Zech. ii. 2), with Ox. 1, 4, 9, &c.

וַיִּבְחַר יְהוָה אֱלֹהֵי־יִשְׂרָאֵל בִּי מִכֹּל בֵּית־אָבִי (1 Chr. xxviii. 4), Harl. 1528; Hm. 16; and De R. 384, have rightly Munach, instead of the Pazer of our texts. Here the dichotomy due before בִּי ought properly to have been marked with Paseq.

---

[31] I have not thought it necessary to give the minor accentual variations in the Codd. quoted, where the principle of division is the same.

3. With the *nominal predicate* (p. 51) at the head of the clause, we must point in the following passages thus :

שֶׁמֶן מִשְׁחַת־קֹדֶשׁ יִהְיֶה זֶה לִי (Ex. xxx. 31), with Ox. 6, 18, 20, &c.

וְעָמֹק אֵין־מַרְאֶהָ מִן־הָעוֹר (Lev. xiii. 4), with Ox. 18 ; Add. 4709 ; Erf. 1.

כִּי־אִישׁ גָּדוֹל הוּא מְאֹד׃ (2 Sam. xix. 33), with Ox. 68, 76.

4. The accentuation in the case of a few *compound members* (p. 53 ff.) needs correcting, as follows :

בַּעַל הַחֲלֹמוֹת הַלָּזֶה (Gen. xxxvii. 19), with Ox. 2436 ; Par. 4.

וּפָרְשׂוּ בֶגֶד כְּלִיל תְּכֵלֶת (Num. iv. 6), with K. 251 ; De R. 2. Comp. Ex. xxviii. 31.

כִּמֵי הַמָּרִים הַמְאָרְרִים (v. 19), with Add. 15252 ; De R. 384. Comp. ver. 18 end.

רָאשׁ אֲמוֹת בֵּית־אָב (xxv. 15), with Ox. 3, 6, 8 ; Erff. 1–4.

הַנַּעַר הַמַּחֲזִיק בְּיָדוֹ (Judg. xvi. 26), with all Codd.

אֶבֶן־שְׁלֵמָה מַסָּע (1 Ki. vi. 7), with all Codd.

עַתָּה־זֶה (1 Ki. xvii. 24), with Ox. 76 ; Ber. 2 ; and עַתָּה זֶה (2 Ki. v. 22), with K. 187 ; De R. 440. The two adverbs cannot be separated as in our texts.

אֵת כָּל־הָרָעָה אֲשֶׁר עָשָׂה יִשְׁמָעֵאל בֶּן־נְתַנְיָה׃ (Jer. xli. 11), with Ox. 5, 72, &c.

דֶּרֶךְ הֵנָּה פְנֵיהֶם (Jer. l. 5), with Ox. 13, 72. See also Rashi and Qimchi.

בַּאֲשֶׁר לְמִי (Jon. i. 8), with Ox. 4, 7 ; like בְּשֶׁלְמִי, ver. 7.

כְּנֹבְרִים בּוֹסִים בְּטִיט חוּצוֹת (Zech. x. 5), with Ox. 4, 6, 7, &c.

[32] וִימֵי הַפּוּרִים הָאֵלֶּה (Esth. ix. 28), with Ox. 51 ; Harl. 5506.

וְרַבִּים מִיְּשֵׁנֵי אַדְמַת־עָפָר (Dan. xii. 2), with Ox. 1, 5, 7.

In these trifling matters, I have been often satisfied, when I have found *two* Codd. supporting the obviously necessary correction. The instances shew how even the best editors have failed to master, or at least to observe, the simplest rules of the accentuation.

Other similar instances will doubtless be found, which have escaped my notice, and which will all have to be corrected in the same way, unless (as is sometimes the case) they should admit of explanation, from the application of some special rule.

---

[32] הָאֵלֶּה qualifies not הַפּוּרִים, as in texts, but יָמִים, see the first words of the verse.

CHAPTER V.

SILLUQ.

SILLUQ's clause is to be considered as embracing the *whole* verse [1].

The verse itself is of varying length. It may contain only *two* words. But such cases are exceedingly rare. The only examples are Gen. xlvi. 23; Ex. xx. 13–15 (Deut. v. 17); and Num. xxvi. 11. Here Ṭiphcha appears as *musical foretone* to Silluq in the first word, e. g. לֹא תִרְצָֽח׃.

Where *three* or *more* words occur in the verse, we have, first of all, to observe the rules for the *main division* of the same. The following cases will occur:

I. The main dichotomy—fixed by the rules we have already laid down—may come on the *first* word before Silluq, and will be marked by Ṭiphcha or Athnach.

1. Ṭiphcha is by far the more common (perhaps for the sake of the musical foretone), whether the verse be long or short, e. g.

וַיְהִי בָאַרְבַּע (Gen. ii. 1); וַיְכֻלּוּ הַשָּׁמַיִם וְהָאָרֶץ וְכָל־צְבָאָם

עָשְׂרֵה שָׁנָה לַמֶּלֶךְ חִזְקִיָּהוּ עָלָה סַנְחֵרִיב מֶלֶךְ־אַשּׁוּר עַל

כָּל־עָרֵי יְהוּדָה הַבְּצֻרוֹת וַיִּתְפְּשֵׂם (Is. xxxvi. 1) [2].

With *only three* words in the verse,—as in Gen. xxvi. 6; Ex. xxviii. 13 [3]; Num. vi. 24,—Ṭiphcha is always used.

2. Athnach occurs occasionally, and more particularly in cases

---

[1] So Pasûqa's clause is treated in Syriac. Comp. Bar-Zu'bî (ed. Martin), p. 4.

[2] Other examples of long verses with Ṭiphcha are Num. ix. 1; Deut. v. 23; vi. 22; Jos. xiii. 16; Jer. viii. 1; xiii. 13; xxix. 2; lii. 18; Ezek. xli. 17; Neh. v. 17; 1 Chr. xxviii. 1; 2 Chr. xx. 22; xxiv. 9; xxxiv. 20.

Ṭiphcha, as the main divider of the verse, constantly *lengthens* the short vowel, as Athnach would have done: פֶּסַח (Num. ix. 2); יְרוּשָׁלָ͏ם (Jer. viii. 1; xiii. 13); אֶפְרָיִם (Hos. iv. 17); חָיִל (1 Chr. xxviii. 1).

[3] The Massora to this passage cites fourteen such verses in the Tora, ten of which come under this head.

of a *marked logical pause,* e. g. וַיֹּ֣אמֶר אֱלֹהִים֒ יְהִי־א֖וֹר וַֽיְהִי־אֽוֹר
(Gen. i. 3); וַתָּבֹ֙אנָה֙ אֶל־קִרְבֶּ֔נָה וְלֹ֣א נוֹדַ֗ע כִּי־בָ֙אוּ֙ אֶל־קִרְבֶּ֔נָה
וּמַרְאֵיהֶ֣ן רַ֔ע כַּאֲשֶׁ֖ר בַּתְּחִלָּ֑ה וָאִיקָֽץ (xli. 21). Comp. v. 5;
xlii. 20; Ex. xxiii. 23; Num. x. 28; Ezek. vii. 21; Hag. ii. 5.
Such instances, with Athnach on the first word, are the only
ones in which the foretone fails before Silluq.

II. With the main dichotomy on the *second* word before
Silluq, the same accents are employed to mark it. But Athnach
is here the more common (the foretone Ṭiphcha following on the
first word). Examples are, with Ṭiphcha : וַֽיְהִי־עֶ֖רֶב וַֽיְהִי־בֹ֑קֶר
יוֹם שְׁלִישִֽׁי (Gen. i. 13); יְהֹוָ֥ה יִמְלֹ֖ךְ לְעֹלָ֥ם וָעֶֽד (Ex. xv. 18);
שִׁמְע֣וּ אֶת־הַדָּבָ֗ר אֲשֶׁ֨ר דִּבֶּ֧ר יְהֹוָ֛ה עֲלֵיכֶ֖ם בֵּ֥ית יִשְׂרָאֵ֑ל (Jer.
x. 1); and with Athnach : וַיִּתֵּ֥ן אֹתָ֛ם אֱלֹהִ֖ים בִּרְקִ֣יעַ הַשָּׁמָ֑יִם
וּבַחֹ֤דֶשׁ הַשֵּׁנִי֙ בְּשִׁבְעָ֣ה וְעֶשְׂרִ֔ים לְהָאִ֖יר עַל־הָאָֽרֶץ (Gen. i. 17);
יֹ֥ום לַחֹ֖דֶשׁ יָבְשָׁ֥ה הָאָֽרֶץ (viii. 14).

We have to notice a further variation. When Silluq's word,
or the word preceding it, is *long* [4], Zaqeph is admissible instead
of Ṭiphcha, and is indeed generally preferred, for the sake of
the rhythmical cadence at the close of the verse (Ṭiphcha, as
before, marking the foretone on the first word), e. g. וַיִּשְׁתַּ֖חוּ
וַיִּשְׁמַ֥ע מֹשֶׁ֖ה וַיִּיטַֽב; אַבְרָהָ֔ם לִפְנֵ֥י עַם־הָאָֽרֶץ (Gen. xxiii. 12);

---

[4] A *long* word is technically one that has two or more vowels before the tone-
syllable, or if only one vowel, that vowel must be *long,* followed by Métheg and
Sh'va. In the latter case, the Sh'va may be *mobile,* as in קִֽטְל֣וּ, אָֽהֲבָ֔ה, or
quiescens, as in בָּֽתִּ֑ים, בֵּֽיתָאֵ֑ל.

With *two short* words following, Ṭiphcha is bound to appear. See the list of
names of the spies, Num. xiii. 4 ff., where the only instance in which Ṭiphcha
stands is of this kind, ver. 8. Or comp. I Chr. xi. 27–47, where vv. 35 and 42
alone have Ṭiphcha and for the same reason. Some few exceptions indeed
occur, as לִקְר֗וֹ לְנֶ֖פֶשׁ תִּדְרְשֶֽׁנּוּ (Lam. iii. 25); and (where Zaqeph marks a minor
dichotomy) in Ex. xxxiii. 1; Is. xlviii. 4; lxii. 6; Ezra vi. 12. But these are only
the exceptions that prove the rule; for the rule is carried out in hundreds, if not
thousands, of instances. Jer. v. 30 is pointed with Athnach in Ox. 1, 7.

בְּעֵינָיו (Lev. x. 20); אַחֲרֵי־כֵן פָּתַח אִיּוֹב אֶת־פִּיהוּ וַיְקַלֵּל
אֶת־יוֹמוֹ (Job iii. 1). Tiphcha, however, not unfrequently
retains its place, as in בַּיהוָה יִצְדְּקוּ וְיִתְהַלְלוּ כָּל־זֶרַע יִשְׂרָאֵל
(Is. xlv. 25).

As under I, when the verse consists of *only three* words,
Ṭiphcha (Zaqeph) can alone be employed. See Gen. xliii. 1;
Lev. xi. 14; Num. i. 6, 9; Is. ii. 18.

How entirely *optional*, in other cases, the use of Ṭiphcha (Zaqeph)
or Athnach was, may be seen from a comparison of 2 Sam. xxii. 2 ff.
and 1 Chr. xvi. 8 ff. We have here the prose accentuation applied
to certain Psalms (2 Sam. xxii gives us Ps. xviii, and 1 Chr. xvi parts
of Pss. cv, xcvi, and cvi). Now these Psalms are similar in their
build, consisting mainly of short verses, with from five to seven
words in each. Yet we find that wherever the choice lay between
Ṭiphcha (Zaqeph) on the one hand and Athnach on the other—as
when the main dichotomy is on the second word (the case before us),
or on the third and fourth (see III following)—the accentuators
invariably decided in 2 Sam. xxii for the latter (Athnach), and in
1 Chr. xvi as invariably for the former. Comp. e. g. 2 Sam. xxii. 4,
23, 47, with 1 Chr. xvi. 9, 11, 31. The matter is not without interest,
although no one, as far as I am aware, has taken any notice of it.
For we have here a manifest attempt (as far as it goes) to provide
different modes of chanting for different Psalms. And what is more,
it can hardly be doubted that we have in 2 Sam. xxii and 1 Chr. xvi
the *original* melodies of certain Psalms as they were chanted *before*
the poetical accentuation was introduced (see טעמי אמ״ת, pp. 8, 9) [5].

III. With the main dichotomy on the *third* or *fourth* word,
either Athnach or Zaqeph [6] may be employed to mark it, but the
former is much the more common,—particularly on the *fourth*

---

[5] The musical division carried out in 2 Sam. xxii is found (with little or no
variation) in other poetical pieces, such as Gen. xlix; Ex. xv; Deut. xxxii and
xxxiii; &c. Lam. iii and v (with their short verses) are alone divided as
1 Chr. xvi. But it is interesting to notice that the Oriental text had this division
for the whole of Job (see a specimen prefixed to Baer's edition), and without
doubt for Proverbs also, and at least a part of the Psalms.

[6] Zaqeph occurs mostly in *short* verses, and is particularly common in the few
words that *head an address*, as Ex. xii. 1; xx. 1; xxi. 1; Lev. xiii. 1; xv. 1; Is.
vii. 10; viii. 5; Jer. vii. 1; and in *lists of names, numbers*, &c., as Josh. xii. 9–24;
Ruth iv. 18–22; Ezra ii. 3 ff.; 1 Chr. xi. 27–47; xxv. 10–31. Sometimes texts vary,
as in 2 Sam. i. 27; xxiii. 39; where Athnach is better. In 1 Chr. xviii. 12, many
Codd. have Zaqeph.

word. The farther back the main division is removed from Silluq, the greater is the tendency to employ Athnach to mark it. We can understand that, by this weightier accent, the balance of the melody was better marked and sustained. So with the main dichotomy on the *fifth* word and further, Athnach *alone* can be employed [7]. For examples under this head, see below.

The accents that mark the *main dichotomy* of the verse have now been determined. The verse has been divided into (what we may call) its two halves; and the next question is how the accentual division of each of these halves is to be carried out. With the first we are not at present concerned. It is under the government of Ṭiphcha, Zaqeph, or Athnach; and the rules for its division cannot be settled, till we come to treat of these accents respectively. But the last half is still under Silluq's control, and its subdivision must now engage our attention.

When the main dichotomy comes on the first or second word before Silluq (I and II), it is clear that no further division is possible. But when it comes on the third or any further word (III), such division is not only possible but necessary.

For Silluq's clause is subject, in all its parts, to the strict rule of the dichotomy, viz. that wherever three or more words come together, the dichotomy is to be introduced. Now under III, there will be at least three, and there may be many more words, in the last half of the verse. The *minor dichotomy* therefore cannot fail. Its musical notation will be necessarily Ṭiphcha, if it come on the first word, and Ṭiphcha (Zaqeph) on the second.

---

[7] The rule that Athnach *alone can stand on the fifth word and further*, is strictly carried out. Hence the Zaqeph in Qoh. iii. 3, 4, 6–8, is changed into Athnach in vv. 2 and 5. I have noted only two trifling exceptions to the rule, in Ezra ii. 35 (repeated Neh. vii. 38) and Neh. vii. 17, where, for uniformity with the headings in the long list before and after, Zaqeph has been retained. Other exceptions in our texts must be corrected, as Zaqeph on the *fifth* word, Cant. vi. 12 (where עַמִּי־נָדִיב must be written as one word, see Baer's note), and 1 Chr. xxiii. 12 (point קְהָת, with Ox. 5, 9, 11). Zaqeph occurs on the *sixth* word in 1 Chr. vii. 13 (corr. נַפְתְּלִי, with Ox. 4, 5, 9) and 2 Chr. i. 18 (point שְׁלֹמֹה, with ditto); and on the *seventh* word in Is. xl. 5 (corr. יְהוָה, with Baer).

On the third word or further it will be Zaqeph. In this last
case a further subdivision will be necessary.

The following examples of the various cases that arise will
make these remarks clear[8]:

I. *a.* With Athnach, as main divider of the verse, on the *third* or
fourth word: וַיִּקְרָא יְהוָה אֱלֹהִים אֶל־הָאָדָם וַיֹּאמֶר לוֹ אַיֶּכָּה
(Gen. iii. 9); וַיֹּאמְרוּ הַכְזוֹנָה יַעֲשֶׂה אֶת־אֲחוֹתֵנוּ (xxxiv. 31);
וַיְצַו יְהוָה אֱלֹהִים עַל־הָאָדָם לֵאמֹר מִכֹּל עֵץ־הַגָּן אָכֹל תֹּאכֵל
(ii. 16); וְעַתָּה יוֹשֵׁב יְרוּשָׁלַ͏ִם וְאִישׁ יְהוּדָה שִׁפְטוּ־נָא בֵּינִי
וּבֵין כַּרְמִי (Is. v. 3). The last is the only case in which a
second minor dichotomy is due.

β. With Zaqeph, in place of Athnach, on the third or fourth
word: יִשָּׂא יְהוָה פָּנָיו אֵלֶיךָ וְיָשֵׂם לְךָ שָׁלוֹם (Num. vi. 26);
אַךְ־ דּוֹר הֹלֵךְ וְדוֹר בָּא וְהָאָרֶץ לְעוֹלָם עֹמָדֶת (Qoh. i. 4);
לֹא יָדַעְתִּי נַפְשִׁי בָּשָׂר בְּנַפְשׁוֹ דָמוֹ לֹא תֹאכֵלוּ (Gen. ix. 4);
בֵּהּ בְּלֵילְיָא קְטִיל (Cant. vi. 12); שָׂמַתְנִי מַרְכְּבוֹת עַמִּי־נָדִיב
(Cant. vi. 12); בֵּלְאשַׁצַּר מַלְכָּא כַשְׂדָּאָה (Dan. v. 30).

·In the two last instances, Zaqeph has been *repeated*, to mark the
minor dichotomy. Such cases are, however, not common, and occur
only in the later Books. Athnach with Zaqeph following was preferred to two Zaqephs.

II. With Athnach, as main divider of the verse, on the *fifth
word or further.*

1. Here, as above, there may be only *one* minor dichotomy,—
marked by Ṭiphcha on the first word, or Ṭiphcha (Zaqeph) on
the second: וַיְהִי מִקֵּץ יָמִים וַיָּבֵא קַיִן מִפְּרִי הָאֲדָמָה מִנְחָה
לַיהוָה (Gen. iv. 3); וַיַּעַשׂ נֹחַ כְּכֹל אֲשֶׁר צִוָּה אֹתוֹ אֱלֹהִים כֵּן
(Gen. iv. 3);

---

[8] The student will notice in the examples given the logical and syntactical
grounds for marking off the several dichotomies. He will observe that Zaqeph is
often *repeated*, and will see that, from the very principle of the dichotomy, the
first Zaqeph must have a greater disjunctive value than the second, the second
than the third, &c.

וְאֶל־קַיִן וְאֶל־מִנְחָתוֹ לֹא שָׁעָה וַיִּחַר לְקַיִן מְאֹד (vi. 22); עָשָׂה וַיִּפְּלוּ פָנָיו (iv. 5).

2. There may be *two* minor dichotomies, the first of which will be marked by Zaqeph, the second as under 1 : אִמְרִי־נָא אֲחֹתִי אָתְּ לְמַעַן יִיטַב־לִי בַעֲבוּרֵךְ וְחָיְתָה נַפְשִׁי בִּגְלָלֵךְ (xv. 8); וַיֹּאמֶר אֲדֹנָי יֱהֹוִה בַּמָּה אֵדַע כִּי אִירָשֶׁנָּה (xii. 13); חָזוּת קָשָׁה הֻגַּד־לִי הַבּוֹגֵד ׀ בּוֹגֵד וְהַשּׁוֹדֵד ׀ שׁוֹדֵד עֲלִי עֵילָם צוּרִי מָדַי כָּל־אַנְחָתָה הִשְׁבַּתִּי (Is. xxi. 2).

3. There may be *three* minor dichotomies, the first two of which will be marked by Zaqeph, the third as under 1 : וְהָאָדָם יָדַע אֶת־חַוָּה אִשְׁתּוֹ וַתַּהַר וַתֵּלֶד אֶת־קַיִן וַתֹּאמֶר קָנִיתִי וַתֹּסֶף לָלֶדֶת אֶת־אָחִיו אֶת־הָבֶל (Gen. iv. 1); אִישׁ אֶת־יְהוָֹה וְאִם כֹּה (iv. 2); וַיְהִי־הֶבֶל רֹעֵה צֹאן וְקַיִן הָיָה עֹבֵד אֲדָמָה יֹאמַר לֹא חָפַצְתִּי בָּךְ הִנְנִי יַעֲשֶׂה־לִּי כַּאֲשֶׁר טוֹב בְּעֵינָיו (2 Sam. xv. 26).

4. *Four* minor dichotomies are also frequent enough, the three first marked by Zaqeph, the fourth as under 1 : וַיֹּאמֶר דָּוִיד לִשְׁלֹמֹה בְנִי אֲנִי הָיָה עִם־לְבָבִי לִבְנוֹת בַּיִת לְשֵׁם יְהוָֹה אֱלֹהָי (1 Chr. xxii. 7). Comp. Gen. iii. 1 ; xxvii. 42 ; xliv. 16 ; Deut. xv. 4 ; 1 Ki. xvi. 34 ; Is. xxiv. 2 ; Ezek. xxvii. 3.

5. Of *five* minor dichotomies I have found only two certain instances in our texts, 2 Sam. xvii. 9 and 2 Ki. i. 3 [9].

We have now completed the analysis of Silluq's clause, and have traced the application of the law of the *continuous dichotomy*, on which the whole fabric of the accentuation rests. Scholars

---

[9] Ben-Bil. (Mishp. hat. 9ᵃ), and other writers on the accents, do not allow even these instances.—Four Zaqephs are found in Judg. xiii. 8 ; but here we have an early misprint (Bomb. 2), which has been preserved in our texts: שָׁלַחְתָּ is impossible after Gersháyim, and must be changed to שָׁלָחְתָּ (R'bhîa).—In 2 Ki. xvii. 34 most Codd. I have examined (Ox. 1, 5, 7, 8, &c.) have עֹשִׂים (R'bhîa).

still hesitate about accepting this law. But it is hoped that no one, who has carefully examined the examples above given, will any longer doubt its operation. It remains to be seen whether it will equally explain the phenomena that occur with the other accents.

SERVUS OF SILLUQ

is always Mer'kha. Silluq has never more than one servus.

In five passages [10] the Palestinian authorities have introduced Ṭiphcha (in place of Métheg) into the *same word* with Silluq : לְהֵחַלּוֹ (Lev. xxi. 4); לְדֹרֹתֵיכֶם (Num. xv. 21); [11] וְקִוֵּיתִי־לוֹ (Is. viii. 17); מִמִּצְוֺתֵיהֶם (Hos. xi. 6); and וְהָאֶשְׁתָּאֻלִי (1 Chr. ii. 53). As the notions that led them to mark these few words with an anomalous accentuation have not been handed down to us, conjectures on the subject seem to me useless.—It is to be noted that in the first four cases Athnach immediately precedes, in the last Zaqeph.

Grammarians call the accent here a *servus*, and give it the name מָאיְלָא (see p. 26).

Corrigenda.

Zaqeph fails, or has been wrongly introduced, in the following passages (which must be corrected, as we should correct cases of false interpunction in a modern text):

וְקָמוּ נְדָרֶיהָ וֶאֱסָרֶהָ אֲשֶׁר־אָסְרָה עַל־נַפְשָׁהּ יָקֻמוּ (Num. xxx. 8), as in vv. 5 and 12. And so Ox. 13 and Harl. 1528 point.

וְלוֹ־תִהְיֶה לְאִשָּׁה תַּחַת אֲשֶׁר עִנָּהּ לֹא־יוּכַל שַׁלְּחָהּ כָּל־יָמָיו (Deut. xxii. 29), with Ox. 3, 8; Erf. 1, 3.

קוּם בָּרָק וּשֲׁבֵה שֶׁבְיְךָ בֶּן־אֲבִינֹעַם (Judg. v. 12), with Ox. 16, 36, 2437; Harl. 5706.

וַיְנַתֵּק אֶת־הַיְתָרִים כַּאֲשֶׁר יִנָּתֵק פְּתִיל־הַנְּעֹרֶת בַּהֲרִיחוֹ אֵשׁ וְלֹא נוֹדַע כֹּחוֹ (Judg. xvi. 9), with Ox. 6, 7, 15; Erf. 3.

כְּשׁוּב הַכֹּל הָאִישׁ אֲשֶׁר־אַתָּה מְבַקֵּשׁ כָּל־הָעָם יִהְיֶה שָׁלוֹם (2 Sam. xvii. 3), with Ox. 1, 13, 68, 72.

וַיְקַנְאוּ אֹתוֹ מִכֹּל אֲשֶׁר עָשׂוּ אֲבֹתָם בְּחַטֹּאתָם אֲשֶׁר חָטָאוּ (1 Ki. xiv. 22), with all Ox. Codd. I have examined, and others.

---

[10] Enumerated in the Mas. to Lev. xxi. 4.

[11] Cod. Bab. has לוֹ וְקִוֵּיתִי (no doubt the Oriental pointing), and this is correct. Maqqeph is out of place here. In Hos. xi. 6 the Palestinian accentuation has found its way into this text, as is not unfrequently the case.

וּנְתַתִּים לְזַעֲוָה לְכֹל מַמְלְכוֹת הָאָרֶץ לְאָלָה וּלְשַׁמָּה וְלִשְׁרֵקָה וּלְחֶרְפָּה בְּכָל־הַגּוֹיִם אֲשֶׁר־הִדַּחְתִּים שָׁם (Jer. xxix. 18), Zaqeph for R'bhîa on הָאָרֶץ, with Ox. 13, 72; Harl. 5498, 5722; &c.[12]

אָמַר יְהֹוָה אֱלֹהֵי־צְבָאוֹת שְׁמוֹ (Amos v. 27), with Ox. 17; Vi. 5; the only two Codd. I have found that point according to the sense.

עוֹר בְּעַד־עוֹר וְכֹל אֲשֶׁר לָאִישׁ יִתֵּן בְּעַד נַפְשׁוֹ (Job ii. 4), with Ox. 4, 5, 19; Bomb. 1; &c.

הִנָּם כְּתוּבִים עַל דִּבְרֵי חוֹזָי (2 Chr. xxxiii. 19). R'bhîa, as in texts, is impossible.

Further, nothing is more common in Codd. and printed texts than the interchange of Ṭiphcha and Mer'kha before Silluq. These accents must be brought into their proper places in the following instances:

בֵּית אֵל בְּרִית (Judg. ix. 46, 'the house of El-berîth'), with Ox. 6, 7, 8, &c.; not as in texts, בֵּית אֵל בְּרִית, a mispunctuation, which has led in some Codd. to the writing of בֵּיתְאֵל as one word!

וַיֹּאמֶר יוֹנָתָן וְשָׁאוּל וְהָעָם יָצָאוּ (1 Sam. xiv. 41), with all Ox. Codd. The pointing of our texts makes nonsense.

וְעֵינֶיךָ עַל־רָמִים תַּשְׁפִּיל (2 Sam. xxii. 28), with Ox. 1, 5, 6, 7.

אַתָּה וּשְׁאָר יָשׁוּב בְּנֶךָ (Is. vii. 3), with Ox. 12, 17, 78.

וְקִיר עֵרָה מָגֵן (xxii. 6), with Ox. 1, 4, 9, 12; Cod. Bab.; &c.

וּכְכַרְמֶל בַּיָּם יָבוֹא (Jer. xlvi. 18), with Ox. 7, 19, 2436; Hm. 10; &c.

נָתַן שְׁאוֹן קוֹלָם (li. 55), with Ox. 9, 70, 2324; Cod. Bab.; &c.

אֶת־יְהֹוָה עָזְבוּ לִשְׁמֹר (Hos. iv. 10), with Ox. 17, 75, 76, 78; Bomb. 1; &c.

חֲמִשָּׁה רָאשִׁים כֻּלָּם (1 Chr. vii. 3), with Ox. 4, 7, 11; Erf. 3; &c. 'Five; all of them chief men.'

Baer has already corrected Gen. xxii. 1; Is. xxviii. 17; xxix. 4; Ezek. iii. 14; viii. 3; &c. On the same principle as the correction in Ezek. viii. 3, we must point in ver. 5, סֵמֶל וַקִּנְאָה הַזֶּה בַּבִּאָה:.

---

[12] But Harl. 5498 is the only one that has the subordinate accents right.

CHAPTER VI.

ATHNACH.

THE rules for Athnach's clause are so similar to those for Silluq's, that there is but one point that will detain us, in considering them.

Athnach may stand *alone*, at the beginning of the verse, e. g. וַיֹּאמְרוּ (Gen. xxxiv. 31); וְצֹאנִי (Ezek. xxxiv. 19).

When there are only *two* words in the clause, Ṭiphcha must appear as foretone to Athnach: וַיְגָרֶשׁ אֶת־הָאָדָם (Gen. iii. 24).

When there are *three* or *more* words:

I. The main dichotomy, if on the *first* word before Athnach, is marked by Ṭiphcha: וַיֹּאמֶר אֱלֹהִים יְהִי־אוֹר (i. 3); וַיִּבֶן יְהֹוָה אֱלֹהִים ׀ אֶת־הַצֵּלָע אֲשֶׁר־לָקַח מִן־הָאָדָם לְאִשָּׁה (ii. 22).

II. If on the *second* word, also by Ṭiphcha: וַיִּתֵּן אֹתָם אֱלֹהִים בִּרְקִיעַ הַשָּׁמָיִם (i. 17); וַיהֹוָה פָּקַד אֶת־שָׂרָה כַּאֲשֶׁר אָמָר (xxi. 1); for which Zaqeph may be substituted, under the same conditions as before Silluq (p. 62)[1]: יִקָּווּ הַמַּיִם מִתַּחַת הַשָּׁמַיִם וְתֵרָאֶה הַיַּבָּשָׁה (i. 9); וְהָיוּ לִמְאוֹרֹת בִּרְקִיעַ אֶל־מָקוֹם אֶחָד (i. 15); וַיַּרְא אֵלָיו יְהֹוָה בְּאֵלֹנֵי הַשָּׁמַיִם לְהָאִיר עַל־הָאָרֶץ מַמְרֵא (xviii. 1).

III. If on the *third* word, by Zaqeph—the minor dichotomy being marked as before Silluq (p.65),—e.g. וַיַּעַשׂ אֱלֹהִים אֶת־שְׁנֵי הַמְּאֹרֹת הַגְּדֹלִים (i. 16); וְהָאָרֶץ הָיְתָה תֹהוּ וָבֹהוּ וְחֹשֶׁךְ עַל־פְּנֵי תְהוֹם (i. 2); וְאֶעֶשְׂךָ לְגוֹי גָּדוֹל וַאֲבָרֶכְךָ וַאֲגַדְּלָה שְׁמֶךָ (xii. 2).

---

[1] Ṭiphcha may indeed remain with one or both of the words following *long*, as in Gen. ii. 6; iv. 16; vii. 9. But with *both words short*, Zaqeph is of unusual occurrence. Among the few instances I have noted are Gen. xxv. 3; xxxvi. 32; Is. xxxvii. 27; Hos. ii. 18. Comp. p. 62, note.

Exceptions. In a few instances, where the first and second words are both monosyllables, *Tiphcha* marks the main dichotomy on the third word: וַיִּרָא שַׂר־הָאוֹפִים כִּי טוֹב פָּתָר (Gen. xl. 16); and so in Ex. iii. 4; xii. 39; Num. xxii. 36; 1 Sam. xxviii. 13; 1 Ki. xxi. 16; Is. xlviii. 11; lx. 1; Amos iii. 8 [2]. Here, for the first time, as far as we have gone, the strict rule for the dichotomy gives way.

IV. If on the *fourth* word or *further*, by Zaqeph or S'gôlta,—the former being more common when the main dichotomy is *near to* Athnach, the latter when it is *farther removed from* Athnach. The minor dichotomies are marked as after Athnach in Silluq's clause (pp. 65, 66).

1. Examples of *one* minor dichotomy are: וַיֹּאמֶר אֱלֹהִים חֲזוֹן יְשַׁעְיָהוּ בֶן־אָמוֹץ אֲשֶׁר (Gen. i. 6); יְהִי רָקִיעַ בְּתוֹךְ הַמָּיִם וַיְבָרֶךְ אֹתָם אֱלֹהִים (Is. i. 1); חָזָה עַל־יְהוּדָה וִירוּשָׁלָ͏ִם וַיֹּאמֶר לָהֶם אֱלֹהִים פְּרוּ וּרְבוּ וּמִלְאוּ אֶת־הָאָרֶץ וְכִבְשֻׁהָ (Gen. i. 28).

2. Examples of *two* and *three* minor dichotomies are: וַתִּפָּלַחְנָה וַיֵּצֵא אֶת־אֲשֶׁר (iii. 7); עֵינֵי שְׁנֵיהֶם וַיֵּדְעוּ כִּי עֵירֻמִּם הֵם עַל־בֵּיתוֹ לֵאמֹר מִלֵּא אֶת־אֲמִתְחַת הָאֲנָשִׁים אֹכֶל כַּאֲשֶׁר וַיֵּרָא יְהֹוָה אֶל־אַבְרָם וַיֹּאמֶר לְזַרְעֲךָ (xliv. 1); יוּכְלוּן שְׂאֵת וַיַּעַשׂ אֱלֹהִים אֶת־הָרָקִיעַ (xii. 7); אֶתֵּן אֶת־הָאָרֶץ הַזֹּאת וַיַּבְדֵּל בֵּין הַמַּיִם אֲשֶׁר מִתַּחַת לָרָקִיעַ וּבֵין הַמַּיִם אֲשֶׁר מֵעַל לָרָקִיעַ (i. 7).

With S'gôlta there are a few instances of *four* minor dichotomies, as in Num. xvi. 28; Jer. lii. 30; and two of *five*, 2 Ki. i. 6; Ezek. xlviii. 10 [3].

Exceptions. A few, like those given above, occur, in which Tiphcha marks the last minor dichotomy on the *third* word, e. g. וַיֹּאמֶר אֵלַי בֶּן־אָדָם הֲרֹאֶה אַתָּה מֶה הֵם עֹשִׂים (Ezek. viii. 6); and so in 1 Sam. xvii. 39; 2 Sam. xii. 19; 1 Ki. ii. 37; 2 Ki. i. 4; xi. 1; Is. liv. 4; lix. 16.

---

[2] Codd. however vary, often joining these small words with Maqqeph.

[3] In 2 Chr. viii. 13, *Zaqeph* has four minor dichotomies following, but many Codd. (Ox. 4, 5, 9, 11, &c.) point here R'bhía instead of the first Zaqeph. I have not noticed any other instance.

On the relation of S'gôlta to Athnach.

It has been up to the present day a moot point, whether S'gôlta is to be regarded as a main disjunctive, coordinate with Athnach, or as a subordinate in Athnach's clause. The following considerations will shew, I believe, beyond doubt, that the latter is the case:

1. Under the law of the continuous dichotomy, two *coordinate* accents are impossible. S'gôlta must be either a greater, or a less disjunctive than Athnach. But who will say that it is a *greater ?*

2. *The Massora treats it as Zaqeph.* Thus the Mas. magna to Is. xiv. 9 gives a list of fourteen passages, which have אֶ֫רֶץ with Zaqeph and Qāmeṣ[4]. But if we examine these passages, we find that two (Is. li. 13 and Jer. xxxi. 8) are pointed not with Zaqeph, but *S'gôlta*. Again in the Mas. magna to Neh. ix. 6 we are told that לְבַדֶּ֑ךָ occurs three times with Zaqeph, yet in this very passage it has not Zaqeph but *S'gôlta*[5]. In chap. viii I shall have occasion to quote another Massora, in which Shalshéleth (the name given to S'gôlta, when on the first word of the verse) is also spoken of as Zaqeph. It is strange that these Massoras have never been turned to account, or even noticed, by any writer on the accents (Jewish or Christian). Either the Massoretic text must be shewn to be corrupt in the several rubrics quoted[6], or we must allow that the early Massoretes, by putting S'gôlta under the general category of Zaqeph, regarded it as *subordinated to Athnach*, in just the same way as Zaqeph is.

3. S'gôlta frequently stands where Zaqeph might with equal propriety have stood. Hence the two are found to *interchange* in Codd. Take, for instance, Dan. iii. 15 (where we have one of the longest Athnach-clauses in the whole text). Here some Codd. point with S'gôlta, others with Zaqeph; and so little disturbance does the substitution occasion that the whole long series of subordinate accents

---

[4] One instance is Ps. xliv. 4 with R'bhîa (Great). Properly the Palestinian Massoretes, when they introduced their system for the three Books, ought to have dropped this example from their list. But they did not venture to alter the old Massora, and left their readers to understand that Great R'bhîa before 'Olev'-yored is the same as Zaqeph before Athnach. We may take it for granted that the original accentuation was

כִּי לֹא בְחַרְבָּם֩ יִרְשׁוּ־אָ֗רֶץ וּזְרוֹעָם֙ לֹא־הוֹשִׁ֣יעָה לָּ֔מוֹ וגו'

[5] Ginsb. Mas., נ, § 622 c, may also be compared, where שְׁכָב (1 Sam. iii. 9) comes in a similar list.

[6] I am aware that the word קְפוּין fails in some MSS. for the first two of the Massoras quoted, but it is found in others, and among them some of the oldest (as Cod. Bab. and Add. 21161). *Its absence is easily accounted for.* The third Mas. did not admit (as we shall see) of being so readily altered by punctators and copyists.

preceding passes over from the one to the other without a break, save
that the Zarqa immediately preceding S'gôlta, has to be changed to
Pashta before Zaqeph. We learn from this example (see also p. 86)
that the rules for the division of Zaqeph's and S'gôlta's clauses are
the same, a further proof of the relationship between these two accents.

4. The chief logical pause in the verse, when S'gôlta and Athnach
occur together, is regularly marked by Athnach, shewing that S'gôlta
was regarded as *subordinated* to it, e. g.

'And he blessed them that day, saying [*S'gôlta*], In thee shall Israel bless,
saying, God make thee as Ephraim and as Manasseh [Athnach]. And he set
Ephraim before Manasseh' (Gen. xlviii. 20).

'At that time Jehovah spake by Isaiah, the son of Amoz, saying [*S'gôlta*], Go
and loose the sackcloth from off thy loins, and put thy shoe from off thy foot
[Athnach]. And he did so, going naked and barefoot' (Is. xx. 2).

Comp. Gen. i. 7; xxiv. 7; xxxvi. 6; l. 5; Ex. xx. 24; Lev. xxii.
13; Num. iv. 15; Deut. ix. 4; 2 Ki. xxiii. 4; Jer. xxviii. 11.

S'gôlta may indeed sometimes *appear* to be independent of Athnach,
but all such cases admit of ready explanation from the rules laid down
in chaps. iii and iv, for the logical and syntactical division of the verse.
Many of the examples there given are instances of S'gôlta.

5. It is surprising that those who insist on S'gôlta's being *par
dignitate* with Athnach, have not noticed the lack of *pausal forms*
with it. It has them indeed occasionally, but *in the proportion in
which Zaqeph, not Athnach, has them.* Comp. סַף with סָף (Ex. xii.
22); פֶּרַח with פָּרַח (xxv. 33); יְרוּשָׁלַ֖ם (2 Sam. xx. 3) with יְרוּשָׁלָ֑ם
(v. 14); &c.

Other reasons might be adduced. I take it, however, for granted
that they are unnecessary.

But if we are to accept S'gôlta as a substitute for, and representative
of Zaqeph, it may be asked: What is the difference between the two?
and why could not Zaqeph always have stood, where we now have
S'gôlta? The difference is simply *musical*. The *melody* of S'gôlta
was quite distinct from that of Zaqeph; and its introduction into
Athnach's clause is an indication of that love for *musical variety*,
which is one of the marked characteristics of the accentual system.
It has a Zaqeph *parvus* and a Zaqeph *magnus* (differing only musically),
and S'gôlta was a Zaqeph *major* or *maximus*, with a fuller and
weightier melody, which served better to mark and emphasize the
main pause in the longer clauses in which it usually occurs.

We are thus led to consider the musical laws which regulate the
appearance of S'gôlta. It can come only *once* in the verse, and then
always marks the place of the main dichotomy in Athnach's clause.
It may, therefore, have Zaqeph after, but never before it. Its proper
place is *at a distance* from Athnach. For the ninth word, and

further, it is almost exclusively employed[7]. It is found, indeed, nearer to Athnach, but the nearer it comes, the less frequent—in comparison with Zaqeph—is its occurrence, till on the fifth word (where Zaqeph is as common as possible) it occurs but seldom, and on the fourth but twice[8]. These musical phenomena we can register, but not explain. We see only that here, as elsewhere, the accentuators allowed themselves the utmost liberty within the limits assigned by the melody.

SERVI OF ATHNACH.

One servus is 'Illûy[9], or as we term it Munach; which is repeated, in the few passages in which there are two servi.

In יְדִידְיָהּ (2 Sam. xii. 25) and שֶׁעְמְהָם (1 Chr. v. 20), both compound words, the servus has taken the place of Métheg in the same word with Athnach[10].

In ten or eleven passages the Palestinian[11] accentuation has introduced Ṭiphcha into the same word with Athnach. They are: וַיֵּצֵא־נֹחַ (Gen. viii. 18); בְּשָׁבֻעֹתֵיכֶם (Num. xxviii. 26); וּבָאתְ־שָׁמָּה (2 Ki. ix. 2); מַאְפֵּלְיָה (Jer. ii. 31); קְפַדָה־בָא (Ezek. vii. 25); לְאוֹפַנִּים (x. 13); וּבָאוּ־שָׁמָּה (xi. 18); וַתֹּאמַרְנָה־לָּהּ (Ru. i. 10); לְכִלָּא־בֵהּ (Dan. iv. 9, 18); וַיֵּשְׁבוּ־בָהּ (2 Chr. xx. 8). See Mas. magna to 2 Chr. xx. 8. It is there stated that there was a difference of opinion (פלוגתא) about Ezek. x. 13. Hence many authorities (Jequthiel on Num. xxviii. 26; Qimchi on Ezek. xi. 18; Man. du Lect., p. 103; &c.) number only ten.

It is vain to attempt to assign reasons for the anomalous accentuation in the above passages[12]. See the remark under Silluq, p. 67.

Grammarians make the accent here a *servus*, and name it מָאְיְלָא (see p. 26); but that it is really Ṭiphcha is clear from its having the servus of Ṭiphcha in Jer. ii. 31 (where most Codd. give also the subordinate disjunctive T'bhîr, אָם), and from Zaqeph immediately preceding in Num. xxviii. 26.

---

[7] Zaqeph occurs but rarely on the ninth word, and still more rarely (some five or six times) on the tenth. Beyond the tenth word it is not found, except in a few corrupt passages, which I have corrected. On the eighth word Zaqeph and S'gôlta are about equally common, but on the seventh, and still more on the sixth word, the preponderance of Zaqeph is very marked.

[8] Deut. iii. 19 and 1 Chr. vi. 62.   [9] Mishp. hat. 12.

[10] Baer has rightly dropped the servus in Hos. vii. 15.

[11] Cod. Bab. (which represents the Oriental punctuation) has no trace of this accentuation. In Jer. ii. 31 it has Munach instead; and in Ezek. vii. 25; xi. 18, Maqqeph fails.

[12] To mark still more the anomaly in Dan. iv. 9, 18, some few punctators and Ben-Bil. (Mishp. hat. 11) have given the previous word the impossible accent Azla, and so Baer has edited. But the great majority of Codd. point regularly with Mer'kha, as in Jer. ii. 31.

Corrigenda.

In a few verses Athnach has been wrongly placed. It is clear that we must point:

וּלְרוּחַ מִשְׁפָּט לַיּוֹשֵׁב עַל־הַמִּשְׁפָּט (Is. xxviii. 6), with Add. 4708; K. 533; De R. 196; Hm. 9.

וּמַכָּתִי אֲנוּשָׁה מֵאֲנָה הֵרָפֵא (Jer. xv. 18), with Ox. 7; Vi. 5; K. 182; Hm. 16.

אִם־יִמָּלְאוּ הֶעָבִים גֶּשֶׁם עַל־הָאָרֶץ יָרִיקוּ וְאִם־יִפּוֹל עֵץ בַּדָּרוֹם וְאִם בַּצָּפוֹן מְקוֹם שֶׁיִּפּוֹל הָעֵץ שָׁם יְהוּא: (Qoh. xi. 3). But I have found only one Codex, De R. 10 (old), which accents correctly.

Zaqeph fails, or has been falsely introduced, in some passages, which must be corrected as follows:

וְלֹא־יִמְכְּרוּ מִמֶּנּוּ וְלֹא יָמֵר וְלֹא יַעֲבִיר רֵאשִׁית הָאָרֶץ (Ezek. xlviii. 14), with Ox. 9, 12, 69; Erf. 1; &c.[13]

כִּי־מִי אֲשֶׁר־יְחֻבַּר אֶל כָּל־הַחַיִּים יֵשׁ בִּטָּחוֹן (Qoh. ix. 4). So the old Codex., De R. 10 (see above), rightly points.

וַתִּגְנֹב אֹתוֹ מִתּוֹךְ בְּנֵי־הַמֶּלֶךְ הַמּוּמָתִים (2 Chr. xxii. 11). See 2 Ki. xi. 2. אֹתוֹ can never stand.

וַיְנַתְּצוּ לְפָנָיו אֵת מִזְבְּחוֹת הַבְּעָלִים (xxxiv. 4). The correction is equally necessary, with Ox. 1, 7, 9, &c.

The only objection to וַיֹּאמֶר (Gen. xxvii. 36; 1 Sam. xx. 29) is that Zaqeph is too far removed from Athnach. This the Massoretes saw, and appointed Pazer instead (Mas. to 2 Sam. xxiii. 17). For the same reason we must point וַיִּקְבְּצוּ הַמִּצְפָּתָה (1 Sam. vii. 6), with all Codd. that I have examined.

Early misprints, carefully preserved by subsequent editors, are אִיתַי בֶּן־רִיבַי מִגִּבְעַת בְּנֵי בִנְיָמִן (1 Sam. xi. 5); וַיֹּאמֶר שָׁאוּל מַה־לָּעָם כִּי יִבְכּוּ (1 Chr. xi. 31); מִן־בְּנֵי שִׁמְעוֹן גִּבּוֹרֵי חַיִל לַצָּבָא (xii. 25). One would have thought that the veriest tyro in the accentuation would have seen that Zaqeph alone can stand in these cases.

Many mistakes have been already corrected in Baer's texts, e. g. Gen. i. 11; Is. xxviii. 21; Esth. vii. 8.

---

[13] So it is better to point לֹא יַחֲלִיפֶנּוּ (Lev. xxvii. 10), with Erf. 1, 2, 4; Jequthiel, &c.

CHAPTER VII.

ZAQEPH

appears under two forms, Great and Little Zaqeph (p. 18). Great Zaqeph always stands *alone*.

In the present chapter we have to determine the rules for the division of Little Zaqeph's clause, which I shall call simply Zaqeph.

There may be *two* words (and no more) in Zaqeph's clause.

The rule for the foretone, as it shews itself before the leading accents, Silluq, Athnach, and S'gôlta, begins here to give way. It is only when Zaqeph's word is *long*[1], that the foretone Pashṭa[2] appears; otherwise, the servus (Munach) is employed. Contrast, for instance: וַיֹּאמֶר אַבְרָהָם (Gen. xxi. 24) and וַיֹּאמֶר אַבְרָם (xv. 3); וְרִבְקָה שֹׁמַעַת (xxvii. 5) and וְרִבְקָה אָמְרָה (6); בְּזֹאת תֵּדַע (Ex. vii. 17) and בֹּאת תִּדְעוּן (Num. xvi. 28); וָאֶבְחַר בִּירוּשָׁלַ‍ם (2 Chr. vi. 6ª) and וָאֶבְחַר בְּדָוִיד (6ᵇ). The musical principle that underlies these variations is not difficult to apprehend.

The rule for Munach is strictly carried out[3]; whereas that for Pashṭa is occasionally relaxed. Small words — particles, pronouns, and nouns in st. constr. — are sometimes found with Munach, instead of Pashṭa, as הוּא (Gen. ii. 13); לֹא (iii. 1); מִי (vii. 10); כִּי (xxi. 16; and often); בְּנֵי (Num. i. 28, 42; &c.); זֶה (Jer. xxxviii. 21); וָקוֹל (Ezek. xxvi. 13); אֲשֶׁר (2 Chr. xxx. 7); &c. Even longer words of frequent occurrence are joined in the same way, as וַיְחִי (Gen. v. 15); לְמַטֶּה (Num. xiii. 7, 9, 14; &c.); וְאַתָּה בֶן־אָדָם (Ezek. xxi. 19; xxxiii. 7[4]; &c.). But

---

[1] The technical meaning of a *long* word has been already explained, p. 62 note.

[2] It is understood that, when speaking of Pashṭa, I include Y'thîbh.

[3] The few exceptional cases in our texts may be all corrected by the testimony of Codd.: אֲדֹנָי (Is. lxiii. 3); וְאֶדְרְכֵם בְּאַפִּי (Gen. xxxvi. 2); וְאָהֳלִיבָמָה בַּת־עֲנָה (Is. lxiii. 3); הֶעָשִׂיתִי שְׁמִי (x. 8); וַיָּבֹאוּ פְלִשְׁתִּים (1 Chr. i. 43); בֶּלַע בֶּן־בְּעוֹר (Dan. v. 8); עֲלָיִן (xxv. 17). Baer has already corrected Is. xl. 6; lxvi. 24; Ezek. ix. 10; Hab. iii. 8. Other instances I have not noticed.

[4] See the Mas. parva to this passage, which fixes Munach.

all such forms occur also regularly pointed. So that here a certain license was allowed, and the punctators were at liberty in these unimportant matters to decide for themselves[5].

It is *only* when there are *two* words (and no more) in Zaqeph's clause that the above rules apply.

When there are more than two words, the following cases will occur :

I. The main dichotomy may come on the *first* word before Zaqeph, and will always be marked by Pashṭa[6], e. g. וַיִּקְרָא אֱלֹהִים ׀ לָאוֹר יוֹם (Gen. i. 5); הֲלוֹא אִם־תֵּיטִיב שְׂאֵת (iv. 7). See text passim.

II. The main dichotomy may come on the *second* word before Zaqeph,

1. And will still be most frequently marked by Pashṭa (with servus following): וַיַּרְא אֱלֹהִים אֶת־כָּל־אֲשֶׁר עָשָׂה (i. 31); לָמָּה חָרָה לָךְ (iv. 6); וְנָהָר יֹצֵא מֵעֵדֶן וַיִּקַּח בֶּן־בָּקָר (ii. 10); רַךְ וָטוֹב וַיִּתֵּן אֶל־הַנַּעַר (xviii. 7).

2. But R'bhîa is admissible (and is common enough), *if one of the following words be long*[7]. (Pashṭa will then appear on the intermediate word.) E. g. וַיַּעַשׂ אֱלֹהִים אֶת־חַיַּת הָאָרֶץ (i. 25); שְׁלֹשׁ מֵאוֹת אַמָּה אָרְכָּהּ לְמִינָהּ וְאֶת־הַבְּהֵמָה לְמִינָהּ

---

[5] But this license in small matters is no justification for the mistakes of our texts in such passages as Lev. viii. 27; xiv. 52; Jos. xxi. 16; 1 Sam. x. 18ᵇ; 2 Sam. xvii. 5; 2 Ki. i. 3ᵇ; Jer. xvii. 3; xxii. 23; Esth. ix. 25; Dan. i. 13; 1 Chr. xxiii. 19; xxv. 11, 13, 16; 2 Chr. xxviii. 3ᵇ; xxxiv. 14; all of which must be corrected with the concurrence of Codd.

[6] In Jer. xxvii. 9 we have in all our texts R'bhîa! Point the second וְאֶל with Pashṭa (so all Ox. Codd.) in accordance with II. 2. In Joel iv. 7 מְעֵינָם must have (with correct texts) Zaqeph instead of R'bhîa.

[7] The condition that Zaqeph's word, or that preceding, must be *long*, for R'bhîa to appear, is carefully observed. Hence we may have R'bhîa in אִם־יִשְׁמְרוּ בָנֶיךָ אֶת־דַּרְכָּם לָלֶכֶת בְּתוֹרָתִי (2 Chr. vi. 16), because Zaqeph's word is long; but in אִם־יִשְׁמְרוּ בָנֶיךָ אֶת־דַּרְכָּם לָלֶכֶת לְפָנַי (1 Ki. viii. 25), where both words are *short*, Pashṭa alone can be used. I have noticed only one exception : אֲשֶׁר אָמַרְתִּי אֶתֵּן לְזַרְעֲכֶם (Ex. xxxii. 13), comp. p. 62 note. In Lev. xxvi. 25 I point נֹקֶם, with Erf. 1, 3; Ox. 6, 16; and in Num. xxi. 6 אֵת, with Jequthiel, Norzi, &c.

הַתֵּבָה (vi. 15); וַיֵּשְׁכֵּם אַבְרָהָם בַּבֹּקֶר וַיַּחֲבֹשׁ אֶת־חֲמֹרוֹ
(xxii. 3); וַיֹּאמֶר הִשָּׁבְעָה לִּי (xlvii. 31).

We have here simply *musical variation*. Hence we may have the
same expression pointed either way, with the full rhythmical cadence
or not, è. g. אָבִי הִכְבִּיד אֶת־עֻלְּכֶם (2 Chr. x. 14) and אָבִי הִכְבִּיד אֶת־עֻלְכֶם
(1 Ki. xii. 14). This varying rhythmical cadence (though no one has
observed the fact) runs through a great part of the accentual system.
It is found with all the leading accents. We have already traced it
before Athnach and Silluq; and shall notice it afterwards before S'gôlta
and Tiphcha. (With R'bhia and the minor disjunctives it fails.)

III. The main dichotomy may come on the *third* word from
Zaqeph.

1. R'bhia is usually employed and is very common. (Of course,
Pashta must follow on the first or second word.) וְהָאָרֶץ הָיְתָה
תֹהוּ וָבֹהוּ (Gen. i. 2); וַיִּקְרָא הָאָדָם שֵׁמוֹת לְכָל־הַבְּהֵמָה
וְהִשְׁמִיעַ יְהוָה אֶת־הוֹד קוֹלוֹ וְנַחַת (ii. 20); וּלְעוֹף הַשָּׁמַיִם
זְרוֹעוֹ יַרְאֶה (Is. xxx. 30).

2. Pashta is comparatively rare (although more frequent than
Tiphcha on the third word before Athnach). Here the strict rule
for the dichotomy again gives way: הָאִשָּׁה אֲשֶׁר נָתַתָּה עִמָּדִי
(Gen. iii. 12); וַיְדַבֵּר יְהוָה אֶל־מֹשֶׁה לֵךְ עֲלֵה מִזֶּה (Ex. xxxiii.
1); לָכֵן הִנֵּה יָמִים בָּאִים (Jer. li. 47)[8]. In the same way, it is
only occasionally that Pashta marks a *minor* dichotomy on the
third word, under the heads following.

IV. But, when the main dichotomy comes on the *fourth*
word or further, it is always marked by R'bhia. Here several
cases arise:

1. There may be only *one* minor dichotomy, occurring on the
first, second, or third word, and necessarily marked by Pashta[9]:

---

[8] The two words following Pashta are generally such as might be, and in Codd.
often are, joined by Maqqeph. In four cases out of five, the first of them is אֲשֶׁר.
It is to be observed that two servi cannot stand before Zaqeph, *without Pashta*
preceding. Hence correct Ezek. xvi. 23 לָךְ אוֹי אוֹי (with Ox. 1, 13; Erf. 3).

[9] Unless R'bhia takes the place of Pashta on the second word, in accordance
with II. 2, e. g. Judg. xiv. 19.

וַיֹּאמֶר אֱלֹהִים יִקָּווּ הַמַּיִם מִתַּחַת הַשָּׁמַיִם אֶל־מָקוֹם אֶחָד

וְלֹא הָיִיתָ כְּעַבְדִּי דָוִד אֲשֶׁר שָׁמַר מִצְוֹתַי וַאֲשֶׁר (Gen. i. 9);

וַיְדַבְּרוּ אֵלָיו אֵת ;(1 Ki. xiv. 8) הָלַךְ אַחֲרַי בְּכָל־לְבָבוֹ

כָּל־דִּבְרֵי יוֹסֵף אֲשֶׁר דִּבֶּר אֲלֵהֶם (Gen. xlv. 27).

2. There may be *two* or *more* minor dichotomies, requiring to be marked between R'bhîa and Zaqeph. Such cases necessitate the *repetition* of R'bhîa—just as Zaqeph itself is *repeated*, for the like purpose, before Silluq and Athnach—and that as often as is needful, till we come to the last dichotomy, accented as above. Thus we have *two* R'bhîas in אָנָה ׀ אֲנַחְנוּ עֹלִים אַחֵינוּ הֵמַסּוּ

אֶת־לְבָבֵנוּ לֵאמֹר עַם גָּדוֹל וָרָם מִמֶּנּוּ ;(Deut. i. 28) וַנִּסַּע

מֶחֹרֵב וַנֵּלֶךְ אֵת כָּל־הַמִּדְבָּר הַגָּדוֹל וְהַנּוֹרָא הַהוּא אֲשֶׁר

וַיֹּאמֶר יַעַן אֲשֶׁר עָבְרוּ הַגּוֹי ;(i. 19) רְאִיתֶם דֶּרֶךְ הַר הָאֱמֹרִי

הַזֶּה אֶת־בְּרִיתִי אֲשֶׁר צִוִּיתִי אֶת־אֲבוֹתָם (Judg. ii. 20); and *three* R'bhîas in 1 Ki. iii. 11 and 1 Chr. xiii. 2.

But this rule undergoes modification. It is a musical law that when R'bhîa is to be repeated, *there must be three words or more* (i. e. a sufficient melody) *between the two R'bhîas*[10]. Where this is not the case, the second R'bhîa is *transformed*, and Pashṭa

---

[10] The rule is simple enough, and should not have given so much trouble to accentuologists. Luzzatto (Torath emeth, p. 63 ff.) sets to work to *count the syllables* between the two R'bhîas. But this is mere trifling, and leads to no result; as he himself would have found out, if he had examined a sufficient number of examples. The fact is, there is here, as elsewhere, common ground, on which the two accents meet. Thus, whilst in the great majority of cases, where only *three* words intervene, Pashṭa takes the place of R'bhîa, in some twenty instances R'bhîa maintains its position (see Lev. xxii. 3; Deut. i. 28; iv. 9, 19; xvii. 8; Jer. iv. 30; &c.). On the other hand, R'bhîa is far more common where *four* words come between, and Pashṭa appears only in Deut. iii. 21; 2 Sam. ix. 7; Jer. xxiv. 8ᵇ; xxxviii. 12; 2 Chr. i. 11. When there are *less than three* words, Pashṭa alone can be employed. Hence Judg. xv. 14 must be corrected by introducing the Munach-melody אֲשֶׁר (with Ox. and Erff. Codd.); and Pashṭa must come for R'bhîa in Jer. xix. 13ᵇ and 2 Chr. xxx. 6ᵇ. When there are *more than four* words, R'bhîa must stand. 1 Ki. xiv. 21 (2 Chr. xii. 13) therefore needs

put in its stead. Thus, with two R'bhîas due: בַּיּוֹם הַזֶּה

נִבְקְעוּ֙ כָּל־מַעְיְנוֹת֙ תְּהוֹם רַבָּה (Gen. vii. 11, not נִבְקָעוּ֔);

וַיֹּ֨אמֶר אֵלָ֤יו הָֽאֱלֹהִים֙ בַּֽחֲלֹ֔ם גַּ֣ם אָֽנֹכִ֤י יָדַ֨עְתִּי֙ כִּ֤י בְתָם־לְבָֽבְךָ֒

עָשִׂ֣יתָ זֹּ֗את (xx. 6, not יָדַ֔עְתִּי). Comp. iii. 22; xxx. 15ᵇ; Is. i.

7ᵇ; iii. 16, 24; Jer. xx. 3ᵇ; Ezek. x. 1; &c. Examples of this
transformation are (as we should expect) much more numerous
than those in which R'bhîa remains.

Three R'bhîas are often due, but in only two passages (given
above) do they all stand. Either the two first are found, the
third being changed to Pashṭa: וַיַּעֲל֣וּ אֵלֶ֗יהָ סַרְנֵ֤י פְלִשְׁתִּים֙

וַיֹּ֨אמְרוּ לָ֜הּ פַּתִּ֣י אוֹת֗וֹ וּרְאִי֙ בַּמֶּה֙ כֹּח֣וֹ גָד֔וֹל (Judg. xvi. 5);

וַתִּבָּקַ֣ע הָעִ֗יר וְכָל־אַנְשֵׁ֤י הַמִּלְחָמָה֙ יִבְרְח֗וּ וַיֵּצְא֤וּ מֵהָעִיר֙ לַ֔יְלָה

דֶּ֣רֶךְ שַׁ֗עַר בֵּ֤ין הַחֹֽמֹתַ֨יִם֙ אֲשֶׁר֙ עַל־גַּ֣ן הַמֶּ֔לֶךְ (Jer. lii. 7). Or,
the *second* R'bhîa is changed into Pashṭa, the *third* always
maintaining its position [11], e. g. וַיָּ֨עַן יִצְחָ֤ק וַיֹּ֨אמֶר֙ לְעֵשָׂ֔ו הֵ֣ן

correction, and we must either point שָׁם (Ox. 7, 68), or מִכָּל־ with Maqqeph (Ox.
13, 16, 72, &c.).

Does any one ask: What is the difference between counting the words and
counting the syllables? I answer: A certain number of *words* means a certain
melody, which makes all the difference in the world.

[11] We come then to the curious result that Pashṭa (as the representative of the
R'bhîa, which it has displaced) is a *greater disjunctive* than the R'bhîa which
follows. Had the *second* and *third* R'bhîas been *both* changed into Pashṭa, we
should have had, with the foretone to Silluq, *three* Pashṭas following one
another, which would doubtless have been unmusical. (This concurrence is
condemned by all Jewish writers on the accents.) Hence the first of three
Pashṭas in 1 Ki. viii. 25 (2 Chr. vi. 16) must be corrected to Azla, לְעַבְדְּךָ.
Y'thîbh and two Pashṭas are as bad. Correct יַעַן (2 Ki. x. 30) and לְכָל־עַמָּא
(Ezra vii. 25).

Two Pashṭas often come together. But then the first is always due to transformation, and R'bhîa *must precede*. Observe how וַיָּבֹ֨אוּ֙ וַיַּֽעַמְד֔וּ בִּתְעָלַ֖ת הַבְּרֵכָ֣ה
הָעֶלְיוֹנָ֗ה (2 Ki. xviii. 17) becomes changed into וַיַּֽעֲמֹ֗ד בִּתְעָלַ֛ת (Is. xxxvi. 2),
when וַיָּבֹאוּ is dropped. Hence such careless mistakes as occur in Cant. i. 16
(point הִנְּךָ with Azla); Ezra vi. 8ᵇ (point מַלְכָּא); 1 Chr. vi. 17 (לִפְנֵי with Azla);
1 Chr. xxi. 17ᵇ (אֱלֹהַי); 23 (וַיֹּאמֶר with Azla); 2 Chr. vi. 13ᵇ (עָלָיו); and xvi. 12
(שְׁלוֹשִׁים), must be at once corrected.

(Gen. גְּבִיר שַׂמְתִּיו לָךְ וְאֶת־כָּל־אֶחָיו נָתַתִּי לוֹ לַעֲבָדִים
xxvii. 37); וַיִּקָּהֵל הָעָם עַל־אַהֲרֹן וַיֹּאמְרוּ אֵלָיו קוּם ׀ עֲשֵׂה־לָנוּ
עַמִּי זְכָר־נָא (Ex. xxxii. 1); אֱלֹהִים אֲשֶׁר יֵלְכוּ לְפָנֵינוּ
מַה־יָּעַץ בָּלָק מֶלֶךְ מוֹאָב[12] (Mic. vi. 5)[13].

There are but three examples, where R'bhîa is due *four* times,
viz. 2 Sam. xiv. 7; 1 Ki. ii. 24; 1 Chr. xiii. 2; and only one,
with R'bhîa due *five* times, Ezra vii. 25.

SERVI OF ZAQEPH.

Great Zaqeph has no servus.

Little Zaqeph may have *one* or *two* servi, both of which will be
Munachs (as we term them). Properly, as all careful writers on the
accents lay down [14], the servus, when there is only *one*, is M'kharbel
(p. 23), if it comes on the *first* letter of the word, as רֶגַע; and 'Illûy, if
it comes on any other letter, as וְרֶגַע. With *two* servi, the first is
always M'kharbel, the second 'Illûy.

RULES FOR MUNACH AND M'THÎGA IN THE SAME WORD WITH LITTLE ZAQEPH; AND FOR GREAT ZAQEPH [15].

We have once more to deal with musical variations (see p. 18).

1. If Zaqeph stands without its servus (Munach) in the previous
word, this servus may take the place of Métheg [16] in the same word

---

[12] In this example note how the R'bhîas and Pashṭas come from syntactical
division in *successive* words. So also in 1 Sam. v. 8; Zech. iv. 12; &c.

[13] Of the many examples that come under this head, fully a third are falsely
pointed in our texts. See Corrigenda. In 1 Chr. v. 21, the first R'bhîa, on
which the whole chain of the accentuation depends, has been changed to T'lîsha!
and yet none of our modern editors has thought of correcting.

[14] See e. g. Ben-Bil. Mishp. hat. 13.

[15] For these rules, I have found nothing satisfactory in any treatise on the
Accents. Heidenheim, in Mishp. hat. 13, 14, is inaccurate and incomplete. His
texts shew that he had no clear ideas on the subject.

[16] It is understood, the *light* Métheg, for the heavy Métheg (Ga'ya) does not
admit of such substitution. Hence Munach cannot come in לְוָרְעֶךָם (Ex. xxxii. 13)
or אֶת־הַלְוִיִּם (Num. viii. 6). On the distinction between the two Méthegs, and
the rules for their employment, see Baer in Merx' Archiv, i. pp. 57 ff. and 194 ff.,
or Ges., Heb. Gr., § 16. 2.

with Zaqeph, only not on the *first letter* [17], e. g. אֶל־הָאִשָּׁה (Gen. iii. 1,
but הָאִשָּׁה, ver. 13); וַיֵּדְעוּ (iii. 7); וַיֹּאמְרוּ (xviii. 5); וְנִחַלְתָּךְ (Deut.
ix. 26); מִנַּאֲקָתָם (Judg. ii. 18); בַּל־יִחְיוּ (Is. xxvi. 14) [18].

EXCEPTIONS. Forms like וַיַּעַשׂ (Deut. xxxiv. 9), and וּנְחִטָּא (Is.
lxiv. 4), retain the Métheg [19]. (It would seem that the short vowels,
Pathach and S'gôl, so near to the tone, have not strength enough for
the accent.) On the other hand, in מִמָּחֳרָת (Gen. xix. 34, and often);
אֶל־נָעֳמִי (Ruth iv. 14), owing to the notion of Jewish grammarians
that the Qāmeṣ is long [20], Munach appears.

When the foretone Pashṭa comes in the word immediately preceding,
no further musical change is introduced, but when Zaqeph's word
stands *alone*, and Munach (according to the rule just given) is not
admissible, one or other of the following changes takes place:

2. If there is a closed syllable in the word, separated by one or
more others—or, at least, by vocal Sh'va—from the tone-syllable, an
emphatic intonation (a *high* tone, as the position of its sign above the
word implies) was introduced, serving as a forebeat (*Vorschlag*) to
Zaqeph, in the absence of the foretone. It was known as מְתִיגָה [21], being
like an upper Métheg (comp. the use of the term in the accentuation

---

[17] See Chayyûǵ, p. 127, l. 28, and Qimchi, עט סופר, p. לב, l. 16. The musical
reader may perhaps see the reason for this restriction. Ordinary texts indeed
often place the servus under the *first* letter, and even the Mas. parva is wrong at
2 Ki. ii. 11, אֵלִיָּהוּ ב' במעם.

[18] Our texts, of course, need constant correction. They omit the Munach
where it is due, introduce it when it stands already in the previous word, &c.
Even the Massoretes have not always been as correct as we should have expected.
Thus, at מִבֵּיתְאֵל (Gen. xxxv. 16) we have the rubric: ג' במעם שופר, when there
are really *six* instances that require to be so pointed, viz. Gen. xxxv. 16; Jos.
viii. 17; 1 Ki. xii. 32 (*bis*); xiii. 4; Am. vii. 13. (In the last passage, Baer's
correction cannot stand. It is against the syntactical division and Codd.) And
again, in the Mas. finalis, p. 17, הבתי'ם ג' בתרי מעמי, to the three examples given
we must add a fourth, 2 Chr. xxxiv. 11.

[19] This punctuation for the derivatives of עָשָׂה is fixed by the Mas. fin., p. 51
(comp. Dikd. hat., § 35). Analogy decides for the kindred forms. Codd. and
printed texts have, however, constantly Munach in such forms. Hence has arisen
a false Mas. given at Num. xxvi. 44 (more fully by Jequthiel at ver. 17), which
assigns the following accentuation to לְבַעֲמָן, ver. 40.

[20] See Preface to Baer's edition of Job, p. vi.

[21] Mishp. hat. 13[b]. It would further appear that it was in reality a kind of
Métheg (i. e. heavy Métheg = Ga'ya), the difference being that it gave a more
marked *musical* expression to the syllable than Ga'ya would have done (Ben-Naphtali has Ga'ya. We thus see that it is only in syllables that admit of Ga'ya, that

of the three Books, טעמי אמ״ת, p. 70). Properly, like Munach, it is *non-initial*, yet the tendency is to place it (on musical grounds) as near to the beginning of the word as possible, and under certain conditions it is found on the *first* letter. The following examples exhibit it in its ordinary position : וְאַבְרָהָם (Gen. xviii. 18) ; וְהִתְקַדִּשְׁתֶּם (Lev. xx. 7) ; וְכָל־יִשְׂרָאֵל (Deut. xiii. 12) ; הַנִּסְתָּרֹת (xxix. 28) ; וְאֶתְנָה (Gen. xxxiv. 12) ; שְׁמָר־לְךָ (Ex. xxxiv. 11) [22].

Initial M'thiga is due to *transposition :*

(*a*) In forms like אֶת־נַדְלְךָ (Deut. iii. 24) ; וַיְפַסְּחוּ (1 Ki. xviii. 26) ; וַיִּשְׁמְעוּ (Ezra iv. 1), &c., M'thiga is transposed to the first syllable, to cancel the Ga‘ya (לבטול הגעיא as Jewish grammarians express it [23]) which is due there [24]. Ga‘ya and M'thiga, from the similarity of their character (see note 21), could not come together.

(*β*) But Ben-Asher and his school went further. If Ga‘ya was only *admissible* in certain forms, on the first syllable, they equally transposed to it the M'thiga, which we should have expected to find on the second syllable. So I explain such cases as וּבְחַטָּאתוֹ (1 Ki. xv. 34) ; וּפְקַדְתָּם (Is. xv. 7) ; וּדְבַרִיהֹוָה (2 Ki. xx. 4) ; and אֶל־הַמָּקוֹם (Gen. xix. 27) ; מִן־הַשָּׂדֶה (Lev. xxv. 12) ; אֶת־הַדְּבָרִים (Ex. xxxiv. 1) [25]. It is only in the above forms that I have found this transposition.

---

this sign can appear). The musical value we learn from Ben-Bil.'s statement, l. c., that M'thiga comes before Zaqeph, לתיקון הנגינה, 'for the right ordering of the melody;' and in the present day it has a distinct melody assigned to it in the chanting (although whether it is correctly rendered is another question). The old grammarians had however no idea of any musical relationship between it and Pashṭa or Azla, which it resembles in form.

The sign has a variety of names. The most common is מקל, 'stroke.' Grammarians, who wrote in Arabic, term it قَـمْـزَة (see טעמי אמ״ת, p. 112, and Ginsb. iii. p. 51) from هَمَز, *impulit*, in reference to the impulse of the voice in the intonation. Hence doubtless the name דרבן, 'goad,' = مِهْمَز (Man. du Lect., p. 77 infra). Qimchi (עט סופר, p. לב) calls it מראה מקום, 'indicator,' and by a name taken from the form, פשט קמן, 'little Pashṭa.' The name in modern use, Qadma = Azla, is similarly derived and equally incorrect.

[22] It will not be expected that I should point out the mistakes of our texts. The matter is not of sufficient importance. Even Baer is not always consistent.

[23] See e. g. Mishp. hat. 14ᵃ supra.

[24] That this is Ben-Asher's pointing may be seen from the חלופים to Lev. xxv. 37; Deut. iii. 24. On the rule for Ga‘ya in the examples given, see Merx' Archiv, i. p. 197.

[25] Comp. Ben-Asher's pointing in the חלופים to Deut. x. 2. That Ga‘ya is admissible, although irregular, in such cases, may be seen from examples cited in Mishp. hat. 58ᵃ, and by Baer in Merx' Archiv, i. p. 201. Ben-Naphtali has it always.

3. When Zaqeph stands *alone, and neither Munach nor M'thîga is admissible* (according to rules 1 and 2) *in its word*, it takes the form and melody of GREAT ZAQEPH, e. g. וָעֵץ (Gen. ii. 9); וַיֹּאמֶר (iii. 10); וַיְחִי־שֵׁת (v. 6); וַאֲבִימֶלֶךְ (xx. 4); הַכְּזוֹנָה (xxxiv. 31); וְיָדַעְתֶּם (Ex. xvi. 6); וַיַּעֲבֹר (Gen. xxxii. 23); בְּבִצְעוֹ (1 Ki. xv. 30); וְלַעֲשׂוֹת (2 Chr. vii. 17); מֵאַחֲרֵי (xxxiv. 33).

Punctators and editors (even the best) exhibit the utmost confusion in the employment of this accent, pointing the *same form*, and frequently even the *same word*, sometimes with Little, sometimes with Great Zaqeph! And yet the rule above given is simple enough. It will be necessary therefore to correct such instances as [26] וּלְהַבְדִּיל (Gen. i. 18); וַיְעַקֹב (xxxi. 47); הָאֶזְרָח (Lev. xvi. 29); אֶל־תַּעֲלוֹ (Num. xiv. 42); וַיַּעֲנוּ (Josh. i. 16); וַיַּעֲשׂוּ (2 Sam. xxi. 14); וּכְנִצָּה (Is. i. 30); לְמַעֲנִי (xxxvii. 35); וַיְמַהֲרוּ (lix. 7); וְרָאִיתָ וְקָרָאתָ (Jer. li. 61); אַל־יִרְעוּ (Jon. iii. 7); in all of which, and other similar examples, *Great Zaqeph must appear.*

Corrigenda in Zaqeph's clause.

1. Where three R'bhîas are due, and the second has been transformed to Pashṭa, punctators—misled by the usual consecution of R'bhîa, Pashṭa, and Zaqeph—have frequently changed the third R'bhîa into Zaqeph, and this false accentuation has passed into our texts. Thus R'bhîa must be restored to its rights[27] in הַתּוֹרָה (Josh. i. 7), with Ox. 1, 5, 7, 8;—הָאָרֶץ (Judg. ii. 1), Ox. 10, 2322, 2323, 2328;—נָשָׂא (1 Sam. x. 3), Ox. 1, 5, 6, 8;—וְנַעַבְרָה (xiv. 6), Ox. 1, 5, 6, 8;—עוֹד (xxviii. 15), Ox. 5, 6, 10, 15;—וַיֹּאמֶר (2 Sam. xv. 2), Ox. 12, 92, 2322;—בַּיִת (1 Ki. v. 17), Ox. 6, 7, 10; Bomb. 2;—עֹמְדִים (xii. 6; 2 Chr. x. 6), Ox. 5, 6,

---

[26] וּלְהַבְדִּיל is found in Ox. 5, 21, 35; Harl. 1528; Or. 1379; Add. 4709; &c. I give ample MS. authority here, because this is the example which has misled writers on the accents from Qimchi's time (עט סופר, p. לב) downwards. Finding the word falsely accented in their texts, and contrasting it with לְהַבְדִּיל, ver. 14, they jumped to the conclusion that Métheg was the cause of Little Zaqeph, *without considering the numberless instances in which Métheg (even when it occurs twice in the word) exercises no such influence.*

[27] As the accentuation is wrong in only *one word*, I have not thought it worth while to quote the passages at length. The student will doubtless look them up for himself, and observe how the sense requires the correction in each case. The testimony of more Codd. might have been given had it been necessary.

7, 8 ;—הָעֲלֹתָה (1 Ki. xvii. 19), Ox. 7 ; Par. 30, 89 ; K.182 ;—אֵלָיו (xxi. 4),
Ox. 1, 6, 13, 15 ;—הָאֲנָשִׁים (2 Ki. x. 24), Ox. 1, 76, 2322, 2323 ;—עֹמֵד
(1 Chr. xxi. 16), Ox. 4, 9, 11 ; Erf. 3 ;—עֻזִּיָהוּ (2 Chr. xxvi. 18), Ox. 4,
9, 12, 15 ;—לִדְרֹשׁ (xxxii. 31), Ox. 1, 9, 11 ; Erf. 3 ;—and לְמַהֵר (xxxiv.
3), Ox. 4, 5, 9, 11. Baer has already corrected Gen. i. 11 ; xvii. 19 ;
Ezek. xliii. 7 ; xlvii. 8 ; Qoh. ix. 9 ; Esth. vii. 8 ; Dan. vii. 19 [28].

The same mistake shews itself, but not so frequently, in the change
of *Pashṭa* into Zaqeph, with R'bhîa and Pashṭa preceding. So we
must correct צְרוּעָה (1 Ki. xi. 26), with Ox. 1, 7, 10 ; Erf. 2 ;—וּבֵין
הַמֶּלֶךְ (2 Ki. xi. 17), Ox. 5, 8, 10, 12 ;—and מִכָּל־חַטֹּאתָו (Ezek. xviii. 21),
Ox. 1, 7 ; Erf. 2, 3.

2. Another frequent source of error is the confusion between Azla
and Pashṭa in Zaqeph's clause [29]. The student need never scruple to
put the one for the other, where a change is necessary, e. g. בָּהָר (Deut.
xxxii. 50); אָבִי (1 Ki. xii. 11); נָקֵל (Is. xlix. 6); וְלִבִּי (Qoh. vii. 25).
Compare the corrections, p. 79, note 11.

3. The blunders of Van der Hooght's text, copied without scruple
by Theile, Hahn, and J. D'Allemand (whose texts are unfortunately in
common use with students), are often under this head most provoking.
Thus Zaqeph is substituted for Gersháyim, and vice versa! מִן־הַיֹּום
(Num. xv. 23) for מִן־הַיֹּום ; and see other instances in Is. xii. 4 ; Ezek.
xxiii. 43 ; xxiv. 27 ; xl. 49 ; Neh. v. 9 ; 2 Chr. xvi. 1 ; xxxv. 15. In
Josh. xi. 8, Gersháyim is *repeated* (the second time for R'bhîa)! In
Judg. xiii. 8b and 2 Chr. xxv. 23b, it divides Zaqeph's (for R'bhîa's)
clause! And in Jer. i. 1b, Ṭiphcha (instead of Pashṭa) is made to
divide Zaqeph's clause! These are specimens of the egregious
mistakes which, once introduced into a text regarded as standard, have
been preserved with religious care by subsequent editors, who
have not taken the trouble of consulting the far more correct and
reliable text (founded on a careful collation of MSS.), brought out
soon after Van der Hooght's, by a much more competent scholar,
J. H. Michaelis.

---

[28] Luzzatto pointed out the errors in most of the above passages, Torath emeth,
p. 63 ff.; but was not able always to adduce MS. authority for his emendations.
No other writer on the accents—Spitzner, Ewald, &c.—had been at the pains of
tracing out and drawing attention to these manifest mistakes.

[29] So Ginsburg, in his edition of the Massora, constantly confounds them.

CHAPTER VIII.

S'GÔLTA.

THIS accent must, on musical grounds, be always preceded by its foretone, Zarqa[1].

It cannot therefore stand on the *first* word of the verse. When due there (according to the notions of the accentuators), it gives place to Shalshéleth (p. 17). Yet there are only seven words, in which this substitution takes place : וַיִּתְמַהְמָהּ ׀ (Gen. xix. 16); וַיֹּאמַר ׀ (xxiv. 12); וַיְמָאֵן ׀ (xxxix. 8); וַיִּשְׁחָט ׀ (Lev. viii. 23); וָאֹמַר־לָהּ ׀ (Ezra v. 15)[2]; וַיֹּאמַר ׀ (Am. i. 2); וְנִבְהָלוּ ׀ (Is. xiii. 8).

Why, one naturally asks, a special sign for just these few (mostly unimportant) instances? There was no *necessity* for its introduction at all. For if we examine the passages, and compare the rules (p. 73) for the interchange of S'gôlta and Zaqeph, we shall see that *Zaqeph might have stood in every case.* When, instead of employing Zaqeph, the accentuators chose to introduce a new accent, it must have been because they designed to attach a *special meaning* to the passages in question,—to which they sought to draw attention by a peculiar melody and a peculiar sign[3]. That meaning has, however, as in other similar cases, been lost. Not that the loss is a serious one. For we may be sure that we should have had some fanciful Midrash explanation, which we can well afford to dispense with[4].

---

[1] It is also invariably followed by Athnach,—another proof (if further proof were needed) of its *dependence* on Athnach. In Job i. 8 and Ezra vii. 13 Athnach is wanting; but here S'gôlta has been wrongly placed, and must be changed into Athnach (see Baer's notes).

[2] See Mas. to Lev. viii. 23.

[3] No other explanation seems possible. For note the strange selection! *Three* out of the seven words are forms of אמר, and how often does this verb stand at the beginning of the verse! Note too that *emphatic* words in this position,—as וְקִדַּשְׁתּוֹ (Lev. xxi. 8); וְהַקְּלָלָה (Deut. xi. 28),—which, if a special accent was to be employed, had a claim to be marked by it, are passed over! There seems also something fanciful in the very *number* of the passages selected, four from the Tora, two from the Prophets, and one from the K'thubhim,—making up the sacred number seven!

[4] Such as is given in the Midrash לקח טוב on Gen. xxxix. 8: וַיְמָאֵן מיאון; אחד מיאון הרבה פעמים, דכתיב בפסק ובשלשלת; or such as I found assigned to Jehuda Ḥasîd in Zalman the punctator's treatise on the accents (Par. 5), where, speaking of Shalshéleth, he says: בכל מקום שהיא בא מדבר הענין ממלאך בפירוש או במדרש, בשמו רבינו יהודה הסיר, i. e. there is a reference to an angel (!) either direct or implied.

I have only one point of interest to mention in connection with this accent. The Mas. to Lev. viii. 15 runs thus[5]: י״א זוגין מן תרין בעגין קדמא רביע תני׳ זקף וסי׳ הַסּוֹבֵב (Gen. ii. 11) הַסּוֹבֵב (ii. 13) וַיִּשְׁחָט (Lev. viii. 15) וּכו׳ (viii. 23) וַיִּשְׁחָט (i. e. eleven groups of two words each in the same section, the first with R'bhîa, the second with Zaqeph, &c.). N.B. The Shalshéleth in Lev. viii. 23 is here put under the general category of *Zaqeph*. We see then that the Massoretes well understood, not only that S'gôlta is the representative of Zaqeph, but that Shalshéleth, which takes the place of S'gôlta, is equally so[6]. I have already (p. 71) drawn attention to the importance of this rubric. How is it that no writer on the accents has taken notice of it?

When there are only *two* words in S'gôlta's clause, Zarqa necessarily comes on the first, וַיֹּאמֶר הָאָדָם (Gen. ii. 23).

When the clause consists of *three* or *more* words, the following cases will occur. (Here we have only to substitute Zarqa for Pashṭa, and we have a mere repetition of the rules already laid down for the division of Zaqeph's clause):

I. The main dichotomy may be on the *first* word. before S'gôlta, and will then be always marked by Zarqa: וַיַּעַשׂ וְהִגֵּה יְהֹוָה נִצָּב עָלָיו וַיֹּאמַר אֱלֹהִים אֶת־הָרָקִיעַ (Gen. i. 7); (xxviii. 13).

II. The main dichotomy may come on the *second* word,

1. And will be still generally marked by Zarqa, e. g. הַנֹּפְלִים וָאֹכַל פְּרִי בְהֶמְתְּךָ וּפְרִי־ (Gen. vi. 4); הָיוּ בָאָרֶץ בַּיָּמִים הָהֵם אַדְמָתְךָ עַד הִשָּׁמְדָךְ (Deut. xxviii. 51).

2. But R'bhîa is admissible *if one, or both, of the following words be long* (Zarqa then coming on the first word), e. g. הַמַּלְאָךְ הַגֹּאֵל אֹתִי מִכָּל־רָע יְבָרֵךְ אֶת־הַנְּעָרִים (Gen. xlviii. 16); הַשֹּׁלֵחַ בַּיָּם צִירִים וּבִכְלֵי־גֹמֶא עַל־פְּנֵי־מָיִם (Is. xviii. 2). See also Ex. xxxvi. 2; Num. xxi. 5; xxiii. 3; Deut. i. 41; iv. 39; Jer. iii. 25; xviii. 21; xxxi. 8, 9.

---

[5] Comp. אכלה ואכלה, § 227.

[6] Ginsburg, ט, § 234, copying from a false text (when correct texts without number were available), or himself introducing an unwarrantable correction, has pointed וַיִּשְׁחָט, in direct opposition to the Mas. he gives directly after, § 236! Even were Zaqeph due, it must be Great Zaqeph.

III. The main dichotomy may be on the *third* word.

1. R'bhîa is usually employed to mark it, and is very common (Zarqa following on the first or second word): הַעִידֹ֫תִי בָכֶ֔ם (Deut. iv. 26); הַיֹּום אֶת־הַשָּׁמַיִם וְאֶת־הָאָ֫רֶץ כִּי־אָבֹד תֹּאבֵדוּן֮ מַהֵר֒ (Is. liii. 12). לָכֵ֞ן אֲחַלֶּק־לֹ֣ו בָרַבִּ֗ים וְאֶת־עֲצוּמִים֮ יְחַלֵּ֣ק שָׁלָל֒

2. Zarqa occurs (like Pashṭa before Zaqeph), but is comparatively rare, כִּי לָ֥א מוּעָף֮ לַאֲשֶׁ֣ר מוּצָ֣ק לָ֒הּ (Is. viii. 23); see Gen. iii. 14; Ex. xxviii. 27; Deut. xii. 1; Am. ix. 14; Neh. ix. 32.

So it is only occasionally that Zarqa marks the *minor* dichotomy on the third word, under the following heads.

IV. When the main dichotomy is on the *fourth* word or *further*, it is always marked by R'bhîa [7].

1. The minor dichotomy may be on the first, second, or third word, and is necessarily marked by Zarqa, e. g. זָכֹ֣ור אֶת־יֹ֧ום הַשַּׁבָּ֣ת לְקַדְּשֹׁ֑ו שֵׁ֤שֶׁת יָמִים֙ תַּעֲבֹד֮ וְעָשִׂ֣יתָ כָּֽל־מְלַאכְתֶּ֒ךָ (Ex. xx. 8, 9); יֹ֗ום אֲשֶׁ֨ר עָמַ֜דְתָּ לִפְנֵ֨י יְהוָ֤ה אֱלֹהֶ֨יךָ֙ בְּחֹרֵ֔ב (Deut. iv. 10); וַיֹּ֣אמְר֔וּ מָ֚ה הָֽאָשָׁם֙ אֲשֶׁ֣ר נָשִׁ֣יב לֹ֔ו (1 Sam. vi. 4).

2. There may be *two* minor dichotomies. Here R'bhîa has to be *repeated* (as before Zaqeph), e. g. וַיֹּ֣אמֶר הַכֹּהֵ֗ן חֶ֤רֶב גָּלְיָ֣ת הַפְּלִשְׁתִּ֞י אֲשֶׁר־הִכִּ֣יתָ ׀ בְּעֵ֣מֶק הָאֵלָ֗ה הִנֵּה־הִ֨יא לוּטָ֤ה בַשִּׂמְלָה֙ אַחֲרֵ֣י הָאֵפֹ֔וד (1 Sam. xxi. 10); and so in Ex. xx. 3–5[8]; Deut. v. 7–9[8]; 1 Ki. ix. 9; Dan. iii. 15; v. 23; 2 Chr. vii. 22.—Or, Pashṭa comes instead of the second R'bhîa (under the same conditions as with Zaqeph, pp. 78, 79): וַיֹּ֣אמֶר הָעָ֞ם אֶל־שָׁא֗וּל הַיֹֽונָתָ֤ן ׀ (1 Sam. xiv. 45). Comp. Deut. xii. 18; Josh. xviii. 14; 2 Sam. iii. 8; 1 Ki. xii. 10; xviii. 21.

---

[7] Marked falsely with Zaqeph in our texts, 1 Sam. xi. 11; 2 Chr. xiv. 7.

[8] According to טעם העליון. Ex. xx. 2 and Deut. v. 6 must not be included in S'gôlta's clause, but pointed with the *single* accentuation (as in many Codd. and by Heidenheim in his edition of הקורא עין). The dichotomy marked with Zaqeph, as in our texts, is impossible.

Where, however, Pashṭa would come *close* to Zarqa—i. e. adjoining it, or with only one word between—it is changed into Zarqa (of course only on musical grounds), and Zarqa appears *repeated*[9]: וַיְהִי ׀ בַּחֲצִי

וַיָּקׇם דָּוִד וַיָּבֹא (Ex. xii. 29); הַלַּיְלָה וַיהֹוָה הִכָּה כׇל־בְּכוֹר בְּאֶרֶץ מִצְרַיִם

אֶל־הַמָּקוֹם אֲשֶׁר חׇנָה־שָׁם שָׁאוּל (1 Sam. xxvi. 5). Comp. Gen. xlii. 21; 2 Ki. i. 6; vii. 13; Is. xx. 2; xlv. 14; Jer. xxi. 4; Job i. 5; &c.[10]

3. There is only one passage in which *three* minor dichotomies occur[11], and for this isolated case a peculiar accentuation was fixed,—*three* Zarqas follow one another: וַיְדַבֵּר אֵלָיו כֹּה־אָמַר

יְהֹוָה יַעַן אֲשֶׁר־שָׁלַחְתָּ מַלְאָכִים לִדְרֹשׁ בְּבַעַל זְבוּב אֱלֹהֵי

עֶקְרוֹן (2 Ki. i. 16). The regular accentuation would have been

מַלְאָכִים לִדְרֹשׁ, as in similar cases under Zaqeph. Verse 6 might have been accented in the same way.

SERVI OF S'GÔLTA.

S'gôlta may have (like Zaqeph) one or two servi, both 'Illûys (Mishp. hat. 32), or, as we term them, Munachs. See examples above.

Corrigenda.

It has been already mentioned that in Job i. 8, and Ezra vii. 13, S'gôlta must be changed into Athnach. For the former passage, *all Codd.* (as far as I have observed) are right; for the latter, *not a single one !*[12] Even Ben-Asher's famous Codex at Aleppo is wrong.

S'gôlta stands on the wrong word in Josh. x. 28 and 2 Chr. vii. 5. Point the former וַיַּכֶּהָ לְפִי־חֶרֶב וְאֶת־מַלְכָּהּ הֶחֱרִם אוֹתָם וגו׳, with almost all Codd.; and the latter וַיִּזְבַּח הַמֶּלֶךְ שְׁלֹמֹה אֶת־זֶבַח הַבָּקָר וגו׳, with Ox. 1, 4, 9; Erf. 1, 3; &c.

---

[9] Comp. the change of Great R'bhia into Ṣinnor (Zarqa), under similar circumstances, in the accentuation of the three Books, p. 56.—But Zarqa cannot be repeated, unless R'bhia precedes. Hence בֹם (1 Sam. ii. 15) must be changed into בֹּם or בֶּם, with various Codd., although Ben-Bil. (Mishp. hat. 7ᵇ) supports it. On Is. xlv. 1, see Notes at end.

[10] In Lev. xvii. 5; Josh. xxii. 5; 2 Chr. xxiii. 18, Maqqeph has fallen out after אֲשֶׁר, and in 2 Chr. xxxv. 24 after עַל. In 2 Ki. iv. 13 we must point R'bhia for the first Zarqa, וַיֹּאמֶר לוֹ אֱמׇר־נָא אֵלֶיהָ (so Ox. 31, 68; De R. 2).

[11] With Zaqeph (as we have seen) there are many such instances. The reason of the difference is that Zaqeph constantly divides Athnach's clause *near* to Athnach, whereas S'gôlta's proper place is *at a distance* from Athnach, with a shorter clause between it and the beginning of the verse.

[12] Baer indeed names one Codex, but the Athnach there is due to a second, and apparently quite modern, hand.

CHAPTER IX.

TIPHCHA.

TIPHCHA's word often stands alone, as בְּרֵאשִׁית (Gen. i. 1).

When there are *two* words (and no more) in the clause, the servus will precede, as וַיְהִי־עֶרֶב וַיְהִי־בֹקֶר (i. 5); יְהִי רָקִיעַ (i. 6); but T'bhîr is sometimes found, when Tiphcha's word is *long*, e. g. 1 Ki. ii. 46; Jer. xxxiv. 5. (Comp. p. 75; but there is no *rule* here, as in the case of Zaqeph.)

When there are *three* or *more* words in the clause, we find, *mutatis mutandis*, the rules for the division of Zaqeph's clause again carried out:

I. The main dichotomy may come on the *first* word before Tiphcha, and will then be regularly marked by T'bhîr, e. g. וַיַּרְא אֱלֹהִים אֶת־הָאוֹר יְהֹוָה אֱלֹהִים ' (Gen. i. 4); תַּרְדֵּמָה עַל־הָאָדָם (ii. 21).

II. The main dichotomy may come on the *second* word,

1. And will still be generally marked by T'bhîr, e. g. וָאִירָא אִם־אֶמְצָא בִסְדֹם חֲמִשִּׁים צַדִּיקִם (iii. 10); כִּי־עֵירֹם אָנֹכִי וַיִּבֶן יְהֹוָה אֱלֹהִים ' אֶת־הַצֵּלָע אֲשֶׁר־לָקַח מִן־הָאָדָם (xviii. 26); (ii. 22).

2. But R'bhîa is admissible—as before Zaqeph—*if one of the following words be long.* (The intermediate word will then be always marked with T'bhîr[1].) Thus: יֹאכַל גּוֹיִם צָרָיו וַיַּחְתְּרוּ הָאֲנָשִׁים לְהָשִׁיב (Num. xxiv. 8); וְעַצְמֹתֵיהֶם יְגָרֵם וַיִּסְעוּ בְנֵי־יִשְׂרָאֵל וַיָּבֹאוּ אֶל־עָרֵיהֶם אֶל־הַיַּבָּשָׁה (Jon. i. 13); (Josh. ix. 17).

---

[1] Texts must therefore be corrected in Ex. xxx. 7; Lev. iv. 4; &c. In Job i. 1, I point with Ox. 4, 5, 7, 9, &c., אִישׁ הָיָה בְאֶרֶץ־עוּץ (see Norzi).

III. When the main dichotomy comes on the *third* word, or
further, it is always marked by R'bhîa. Here the several
cases we have had before repeat themselves:

1. There may be *only one* minor dichotomy, which is due on
the first or second word. This dichotomy will be marked with
T'bhîr: וַיִּשְׁלֶם לָבָן בַּבֹּקֶר וַיְנַשֵּׁק לְבָנָיו וְלִבְנוֹתָיו (Gen. xxxii.
1); וַהֲקִמֹתִי אֶת־בְּרִיתִי בֵּינִי וּבֵינֶךָ וּבֵין זַרְעֲךָ אַחֲרֶיךָ לְדֹרֹתָם
(xvii. 7); כִּי לֹא אֱלֹהִים הֵמָּה כִּי אִם־מַעֲשֵׂה יְדֵי־אָדָם עֵץ
וָאָבֶן (Is. xxxvii. 19).

2. There may be *more than one* minor dichotomy. All such
cases necessitate the *repetition* of R'bhîa; the same rule being
followed as before Zaqeph and S'gôlta, that the second R'bhîa be
changed into Pashṭa, unless at least three words intervene[2].
T'bhîr will still mark the last of the minor dichotomies on the
first or second word.

Thus R'bhîa is *repeated* in Jer. xxviii. 14: כִּי כֹה־אָמַר יְהוָֹה
צְבָאוֹת אֱלֹהֵי יִשְׂרָאֵל עֹל בַּרְזֶל נָתַתִּי עַל־צַוַּאר כָּל־הַגּוֹיִם
הָאֵלֶּה לַעֲבֹד אֶת־נְבֻכַדְנֶאצַּר מֶלֶךְ־בָּבֶל. And so in Josh.
xiii. 30; Jer. xxix. 14; Ezek. xiii. 18; Qoh. v. 17; and a few
other instances.

On the other hand, it is changed into Pashṭa, in Is. xxxvi. 1:
וַיְהִי בְּאַרְבַּע עֶשְׂרֵה שָׁנָה לַמֶּלֶךְ חִזְקִיָּהוּ עָלָה סַנְחֵרִיב
מֶלֶךְ־אַשּׁוּר עַל כָּל־עָרֵי יְהוּדָה הַבְּצֻרוֹת. Comp. Deut. xx.
20[b]; xxviii. 14; Josh. x. 11; 2 Chr. xvi. 9; &c.

Pashṭa cannot, however, (on musical grounds), stand in close
proximity to T'bhîr. There must be at least *two* words between[3].

---

[2] Even with three words intervening there is, as far as I have observed, only
one instance of R'bhîa, Jer. xxix. 14. Comp. p. 78 note.

[3] In Num. vii. 87; Judg. xvi. 23; and 2 Chr. xviii. 23 there is only *one* word
between. The Maqqeph before T'bhir must be dropped, with various Codd.—
Once, Deut. xxvi. 2, the transformation takes place *with two words intervening*.
But here, Ox. 21, 51; Add. 9404 have rightly Pashṭa, instead of the first T'bhir.
In 1 Ki. v. 20 there is a misprint. For בְּנֵי read בְּנֵי. In xxi. 16 we may point
לָרֶדֶת with Ox. 1, 5, 6, 8, &c.

If this is not the case, Pashṭa is itself changed into T'bhîr, and the latter accent appears *repeated*[4]. (The case is exactly parallel to the change of Pashṭa into Zarqa, in S'gôlta's clause, see p. 88.) E. g. וַהֹּאמֶר בְּרָב רִכְבִּי (Num. xiv. 40); הִנֶּֽנּוּ וְעָלִינוּ אֶל־הַמָּקוֹם אֲשֶׁר־אָמַר יְהֹוָה אֲנִי עָלִיתִי מְרוֹם הָרִים (Is. xxxvii. 24). Such instances are sufficiently numerous. Comp. Gen. viii. 17; Ex. iii. 1; Deut. iii. 27; iv. 38; vi. 10; viii. 2; 1 Sam. xx. 21; xxi. 3; &c.

3. In a few passages, *three* R'bhîas are due, but the second—owing to there not being in any case a sufficient interval between it and the first—is always changed to Pashṭa, e.g. וַיִּנָּחֶם יְהוּדָה וַיַּעַל עַל־גֹּזֲזֵי צֹאנוֹ הוּא וְחִירָה רֵעֵהוּ הָעֲדֻלָּמִי (Gen. xxxviii. 12). The other examples are Ex. xxxvi. 3; Josh. vii. 19[5]; 1 Sam. xxvii. 5[5]; 2 Ki. v. 13[5]; xxiii. 12[5]; Jer. li. 64[5]; Dan. ii. 47; Ezra vi. 12; 1 Chr. xxvi. 26.

SERVI OF ṬIPHCHA.

I. *One* servus is always Mer'kha, וַיֹּאמֶר אֱלֹהִים (Gen. i. 3). In eight instances Mer'kha appears, in Palestinian texts, in the *same word* with Tiphcha[6]: בְּכָל־מוֹשְׁבֹתֵיכֶם (Lev. xxiii. 21); כָּל־הֶחָרוּתֶיהָ (2 Ki. xv. 16); מִכָּל־תּוֹעֲבֹתֵיכֶם (Jer. viii. 18); וּמִכָּל־גִּלּוּלֵיכֶם (Ezek. xxxvi. 25); מַבְלִינִיתִי (xliv. 6); שֶׁהֵם (Cant. vi. 5); וּנְבִזְבְּיָתָךְ (Dan. v. 17); לְמַבְּרָאשׁוֹנָה (1 Chr. xv. 13). In most of the above cases, the object seems to have been to provide a fuller melody for the *long* words, by the substitution of an accent for Métheg[7]. In שֶׁהֵם the servus marks the first syllable as properly distinct, comp. שֶׁהֵם (Lam. iv. 9); שֹׁאֵף (Ps. cxlvi. 3).

II. The following (fourteen) are the only instances in which Tiphcha has *two* servi[8],—the first Darga and the second Double Mer'kha: וַיָּבֹא לוֹ יַיִן (Gen. xxvii. 25); לָמָּה תַעֲשֶׂה כֹּה (Ex. v. 15); אֲשֶׁר הֲלוֹא טוֹב לָנוּ (Num. xiv. 3); וַיִּקְרָא לָהּ נֹבַח (xxxii. לֹא צִוָּה (Lev. x. 1);

---

[4] It is clear that the change in question can only take place *when R'bhîa precedes*. Hence texts are incorrect in Josh. xx. 4 (point וְדֻבַּר), and Baer in his note to Qoh. vi. 2.

[5] See Corrigenda. Even Ben-Bil. (Mishp. hat. 35) is quite wrong, in the list he gives of these passages.

[6] These instances are fixed by the Mas. to Lev. xxiii. 21.

[7] But the Oriental text (to judge from Cod. Bab.) made no change. At Jer. viii. 18, the Massora and sign are Palestinian (see Strack's note).

[8] See the Mas. to Num. xxxii. 42 and Dikd. hat., § 22.

42); אֲשֶׁר לֹא הִגִּיד (1 Ki. x. 3 ; 2 Chr. ix. 2); וַיְחַגֵּנוּ אֵלֶּה נְכַח־אֵלֶּה (1 Ki.
xx. 29); הֲלוֹא (Ezek. xiv. 4); וַיְהִי רִיב וּמָדוֹן (Hab. i. 3); נְעֵנֵיתִי לוֹ בָא
38); זֶה אוּד (Zech. iii. 2); וְרִי לֹא יָדַע (Ezra vii. 25); וַיְהִי לֵב לָעָם (Neh. iii.
38); וַיָּנַח לוֹ אֱלֹהָיו (2 Chr. xx. 30).

The double Mer'kha here, as the servus Darga shews, is a weakened
form of T'bhîr[9], though what reasons led to its introduction it is vain
to conjecture. The fancies that influenced the Palestinian accentuators
have not been handed down to us. It is clear that in every case T'bhîr
might have stood, or Maqqeph been employed. The Oriental system
(see Cod. Bab.) rightly rejected this irregular and unmeaning accentuation.

Corrigenda.

In Ṭiphcha's clause—as in Zaqeph's (p. 83)—we find instances of
Zaqeph where R'bhîa should have stood. Thus we must point :

כָּבוֹד (Josh. vii. 19), with Ox. 1, 5, 6, 7; Bomb. 2 ;—וַיֹּאמֶר לוֹ (Judg.
xiii. 11), Ox. 10, 15, 83, 84 ; Bomb. 2 ;—מָקוֹם (1 Sam. xxvii. 5), Ox.
6, 7, 8, 15; Bomb. 2 ;—הַשְּׁלְחָן (1 Ki. vii. 48), all Codd. that I have
examined ;—גָּדוֹל (2 Ki. v. 13), Ox. 1, 5, 7, 8 ; Bomb. 2 ;—אֲשֶׁר־עָשָׂה
מְנַשֶּׁה (xxiii. 12), Ox. 7, 8, 10, 2323 ;—[10] הַכְּלִי (Jer. xviii. 4), Ox. 1, 9 ;
Erf. 1, 2 ;— הֲרֵעָה (li. 64), Ox. 5, 2323, 2324, 2331. If the student
will examine these passages for himself, he will see how necessary the
correction is in each case.

Obs.—It is hoped that the rules for marking the dichotomy
in the clauses thus far considered have appeared to the reader
precise and clear. We have had a first group of accents—with
similar rules—formed by Silluq and Athnach ; and a second,
consisting of Zaqeph, S'gôlta, and Ṭiphcha. We pass on now
to the third group, embracing R'bhîa, Pashṭa, T'bhîr, and Zarqa.
A leading characteristic of this group is the *much greater variety*
in the accents employed for the necessary dichotomical divisions.
We shall in consequence have to notice many merely *musical*
variations. With this group, the formal rules for the dichotomy
come to an end.

---

[9] Comp. p. 25. Hence in our texts, R'bhîa stands in Ezek. xiv. 4[b], in accordance
with III. 1. But it is better to point with Zaqeph, as Ox. 6, 12, 13, 14, &c., do.

[10] In the same clause read בַּחֹמֶר for בַּחֹמֶר (see Norzi).

CHAPTER X.

R'BHÎA.

R'BHÎA's word stands often *alone*, as : וְהָאָ֗רֶץ (Gen. i. 2).

When there are *two* words (and no more) in the clause, the servus is commonly employed, as in וַיֹּ֣אמֶר אֱלֹהִ֔ים (i. 9); פְּר֣וּ וּרְב֔וּ (i. 22); but if R'bhîa's word is *long*, Géresh (i. e. Ger-sháyim)[1] may appear: וְהִשְׁמַדְתִּ֞י אֶת־בָּמֹֽתֵיכֶ֗ם (Lev. xxvi. 30).

The other examples are Gen. x. 14 (1 Chr. i. 12); Lev. xviii. 17; Deut. xxxiv. 11; Ezek. xiii. 21; xxvii. 29; 2 Chr. iv. 20. The accentuators have chosen instances, in which Gersháyim's word is long as well.

On L'garmeh, with two words in the clause, see chap. XIII.

When there are *three* or *more* words in the clause, the following cases will occur:

I. The main dichotomy may be on the *first* word before R'bhîa, and is usually marked by *Géresh :* וַיֹּ֨אמֶר לָהֶ֜ם אֱלֹהִ֗ים (Gen. i. 28); וַיַּ֣עַשׂ אֱלֹהִ֡ים אֶת־חַיַּ֣ת הָאָרֶץ֩ לְמִינָ֨הּ (i. 25); וַיַּ֨עַן אֶחָ֣ד מֵהַנְּעָרִ֮ים וַיֹּ֗אמֶר (1 Sam. xvi. 18).

With only *three* words in the clause, a servus may come: אֲנִ֥י עָנִ֖יתִי וַאֲשׁוּרֶ֑נּוּ (Hos. xiv. 9); וַיֹּ֧אמֶר ל֣וֹ יְהוָ֗ה (Gen. iv. 15).

This variation in the melody seems due to the *lighter* character of R'bhîa. With such an accent, the absence of the cadence, due from the dichotomy, would not be so much felt. We have indeed already seen—under Zaqeph, S'gôlta, and even Athnach—that with only *three* words, there was not the same necessity for marking the dichotomy. But these cases differed from ours in that some compensation was made for the failure of the cadence by the presence of the minor Disjunctive—Pashṭa, Zarqa, and Ṭiphcha, respectively—in the *third* word. With the still lighter accents, that have yet to be considered, the cadence regularly fails.

What is here fixed for the *main* dichotomy, holds equally good for the *minor*. The same remark applies to the rules that follow.

---

[1] It is understood that when, in this and the following chapters, I speak of Géresh, I include Gersháyim.

II. The main dichotomy may be on the *second* word, and is still marked by Géresh: אַשְׁרֶיךָ יִשְׂרָאֵל מִי כָמוֹךָ (Deut. xxxiii. 29); וַיַּעַל לוֹט מִצּוֹעַר וַיֵּשֶׁב בָּהָר (Gen. xix. 30).

When there are only *three* words in the clause, L'garmeh may take the place of Géresh, thus affording a variety in the melody[2]. It is particularly common with small words, as כִּי, אֶת, אֲשֶׁר, כֹּל; but is not confined to them, e. g. יְהֹוָה ׀ אֱלֹהֵי הַשָּׁמַיִם (Gen. xxiv. 7); הָרִאשֹׁנוֹת ׀ מָה הֵנָּה (Is. xli. 22).

In three passages, where both R'bhía's word and that preceding are *long*, we find the fuller melody of Great T'lísha followed by Géresh: כָּל־קָרְבָּנָם לְכָל־מִנְחָתָם וּלְכָל־חַטָּאתָם (Num. xviii. 9); and so in Deut. xxv. 19 (minor dichotomy) and Jer. xxix. 14. The case is parallel to what we have observed under Athnach, Zaqeph, &c. But the cadence is too heavy for R'bhía and generally fails.

III. The main dichotomy may be on the *third* word. Here the melody varies between Géresh and Great T'lísha.

1. Géresh, followed by L'garmeh, when the minor dichotomy is on the second word, or by two servi (see above), when it is on the first, e. g. חָלִלָה לְּךָ מֵעֲשֹׂת ׀ כַּדָּבָר הַזֶּה (Gen. xviii. 25); וַיֹּאמֶר יְהוּדָה לְתָמָר כַּלָּתוֹ שְׁבִי אַלְמָנָה בֵית־אָבִיךְ (Gen. xxxviii. 11). Comp. i. 29; xxvi. 18; xxix. 2; l. 24[b]; Ex. iv. 18[3].

2. Great T'lísha, with Géresh to mark the minor dichotomy on the first or second word, e. g. וְאָמַרְתָּ אֵלָיו הִשָּׁמֵר וְהַשְׁקֵט (Is. vii. 4); וַיֹּאמֶר אֵלָיו חַי־יְהֹוָה כִּי־יָשָׁר אַתָּה אַל־תִּירָא (1 Sam. xxix. 6). Comp. 2 Sam. vii. 8; Jer. xxvi. 19; xxxiv. 3[b]; Ezra ix. 12.

Pazer is found in the place of T'lisha, in וַאֲמַרְתֶּם זֶבַח־פֶּסַח הוּא לַיהֹוָה (Ex. xii. 27), and in Jer. xxxix. 16[4].

---

[2] In Ex. xxvi. 2, 8 and xxxvi. 9, 15, these accents interchange in the *same* expression. Comp. also Num. xvi. 17, 18.

[3] Drop L'garmeh in Josh. i. 4; Ezek. xvii. 9, with Codd.

[4] Both here, and in the instances given IV. 2, Pazer is out of order, for it is properly followed by Great or Little T'lisha.

IV. The main dichotomy may be on the *fourth* word. Géresh, Great T'lîsha, and Pazer are all employed to mark it.

1. Géresh, with L'garmeh (occasionally repeated) to mark the minor dichotomy (or dichotomies) between it and R'bhîa, e. g.

וֵאלֹהֵי אֲבִיכֶם אֶמֶשׁ ׀ אָמַר אֵלַי לֵאמֹר (Gen. xxxi. 29);

וַיִּשְׂאוּ בְנֵי־יִשְׂרָאֵל אֶת־עֵינֵיהֶם וְהִנֵּה מִצְרַיִם ׀ נֹסֵעַ אַחֲרֵיהֶם
(Ex. xiv. 10); אֱמֹר אֲלֵיהֶם חַי־אָנִי ׀ נְאֻם ׀ אֲדֹנָי ׀ יֱהוִֹה (Ezek.
xxxiii. 11). Comp. Lev. xiii. 52; Josh. xxiv. 13; Jer. xxix. 32;
xliv. 26[b]; xlvi. 28[b]; Jon. i. 3[b].

L'garmeh is not, however, available to mark the minor dichotomy, when due on the *first* word [5]. Hence we have R'bhîa with *three* servi in וַיֵּשֶׁב מֵאַחֲרָיו וַיִּקַּח אֶת־צֶמֶד הַבָּקָר וַיִּזְבָּחֵהוּ (1 Ki. xix. 21), and in 2 Sam. xxi. 2[b]; 2 Ki. xx. 3 (Is. xxxviii. 3); Qoh. iv. 8[6]. But this accentuation is so anomalous, that I do not hesitate to correct it in the few passages in which it occurs, although it is found in most Codd., and recognised by the grammarians. See Corrigenda.

2. Great T'lîsha, with Géresh for the minor dichotomy, and occasionally L'garmeh as well, where a second minor dichotomy has to be marked: אַבֵּד תְּאַבְּדוּן אֶת־כָּל־הַמְּקֹמוֹת אֲשֶׁר
עָבְדוּ־שָׁם הַגּוֹיִם (Deut. xii. 2); וַיִּשְׁלַח אַבְשָׁלוֹם אֶת־אֲחִיתֹפֶל
פַּרְשֶׁגֶן אִגַּרְתָּא דִּי־שְׁלַח תַּתְּנַי ׀ (2 Sam. xv. 12); הַגִּילֹנִי יוֹעֵץ דָּוִד
פֶּחַת עֲבַר־נַהֲרָה (Ezra v. 6). It is unnecessary to give further examples. We have here merely a musical variation of the cases under 1.

We note that Géresh cannot be employed to mark the minor dichotomy on the *first* word, because we should then have the two T'lîshas brought together, which is contrary to (musical) rule. A change in the accentuation becomes here necessary, see 3 below.

In a few instances, Pazer takes the place of Great T'lîsha, under

---

[5] L'garmeh on the first word is reserved for a particular purpose, see chapter on L'garmeh, p. 119.

[6] There are two other instances where Géresh marks a *minor* dichotomy, Num. iv. 14 and Is. v. 25.

this head, e. g. וַיִּשְׁמְעוּ כִּי־פָקַד יְהֹוָה אֶת־בְּנֵי יִשְׂרָאֵל (Ex. iv. 31). The others are Gen. xxxii. 33; Deut. xxii. 6; 1 Sam. xx. 2; Jer. xxviii. 14; xxxviii. 7; Esth. vii. 9; Dan. v. 23; Ezra vi. 9 (minor dichotomy).

3. From the love of musical variation exhibited in the divisions just considered, we might have expected to find Pazer employed to mark the main dichotomy, with Great T'lisha and Géresh for the minor dichotomies, as in וְשָׁם הָיוּ לְפָנִים נְתֻנִים אֶת־הַמִּנְחָה הַלְּבוֹנָה וְהַכֵּלִים (Neh. xiii. 5). But such instances are quite uncommon[7]. The proper use of Pazer on the fourth word is to provide the means of marking the minor dichotomy on the *first* word, which means fail, as we have seen, under 1 and 2. The accent employed is always Géresh, e. g. וַיֹּאמֶר הֲכִי קָרָא שְׁמוֹ יַעֲקֹב (Gen. xxvii. 36); וַיִּשְׁלַח דָּוִד אֶת־יוֹאָב וְאֶת־עֲבָדָיו עִמּוֹ (2 Sam. xi. 1); הָלֹךְ וְקָרָאתָ בְאָזְנֵי יְרוּשָׁלַ͏ִם וְאֶת־כָּל־יִשְׂרָאֵל לֵאמֹר (Jer. ii. 2); and so often.

V. With the main dichotomy on the *fifth* word or further, Pazer becomes the regular dividing accent.

The following are the only variations I have noticed:

Great T'lisha may appear on the fifth word, with Géresh to mark the minor dichotomy on the third or fourth word, e. g. וַיֹּאמֶר שָׁאוּל הַשְּׁמִיעוּ אֶל־בָּבֶל צַר־לִי מְאֹד וּפְלִשְׁתִּים נִלְחָמִים בִּי (1 Sam. xxviii. 15); כִּי בִמְקוֹם אֲשֶׁר יִהְיֶה־שָּׁם רַבִּים כָּל־דֹּרְכֵי קֶשֶׁת חֲנוּ עָלֶיהָ סָבִיב (Jer. l. 29); אֲדֹנִי הַמֶּלֶךְ (2 Sam. xv. 21).

Other variations are uncommon. Great T'lisha occurs on the sixth word in Lev. xiii. 59; Deut. xiii. 6; Josh. xix. 47[8]; 1 Sam. xvii. 25; comp. Ezra iii. 8b;—and Géresh on the fifth word in 1 Ki. xiv. 21; xvi. 7; Qoh. vi. 2. None of these variations occasion any difficulty.

Otherwise, Pazer is the accent employed,—*repeated* according to the requirements of the dichotomy, or for the sake of distinct

---

[7] The other examples are Is. lxvi. 20; Ezek. xliv. 25; 1 Chr. v. 24; vii. 2. In three of these, Pazer marks a minor dichotomy.

[8] Point here וַיִּפְגּוּ־אוֹתָהּ, with Maqqeph (Ox. 8, Erf. 2, Bomb. 1). Otherwise we should have the one solitary example of Great T'lisha on the *seventh* word.

enunciation of details. The division of the portion of the clause between the last Pazer and R'bhîa will be according to the rules laid down above, which are (as has been stated) equally applicable to the minor as to the main dichotomy.

Examples of *one* Pazer are common, e. g. וְהֶעָרִים יַהֲרֹסוּ
וְכָל־חֶלְקָה טוֹבָה יַשְׁלִיכוּ אִישׁ־אַבְנוֹ וּמִלְאוּהָ (2 Ki. iii. 25);
וּבָאוּ וְנָתְנוּ אִישׁ כִּסְאוֹ פֶּתַח ׀ שַׁעֲרֵי יְרוּשָׁלַ͏ִם (Jer. i. 15); and
Ex. vii. 19; 1 Ki. xvi. 7; Jer. xiii. 13; xxxv. 14; &c.

Two Pazers are also met with occasionally, as in וַיֹּאמֶר אַבְנֵר
אֶל־דָּוִד אָקוּמָה ׀ וְאֵלְכָה וְאֶקְבְּצָה אֶל־אֲדֹנִי הַמֶּלֶךְ אֶת־כָּל־
יִשְׂרָאֵל (2 Sam. iii. 21); וּשְׁבָה אֶל־גְּדַלְיָה בֶן־אֲחִיקָם בֶּן־שָׁפָן
אֲשֶׁר הִפְקִיד מֶלֶךְ־בָּבֶל בְּעָרֵי יְהוּדָה (Jer. xl. 5); and Deut.
v. 8; 2 Sam. xxiv. 13[b]; Jer. xvii. 25; 2 Chr. xxiv. 5.

Three Pazers are found in Dan. iii. 15; 1 Chr. v. 24; xxv. 3, 4;—*four* in Josh. viii. 33; Dan. iii. 3; v. 12;—and *five* in 1 Chr. xvi. 5.

These eight instances are all I have noticed, in which Pashṭa is repeated more than once in R'bhîa's clause. In no case was the repetition necessary, for the accentuation might have been easily arranged otherwise. I confess, it looks to me as if there were something fanciful in the introduction of these instances, for (if I am not mistaken) there is the same number, *eight,* of similar instances in Pashṭa's and T'bhîr's clauses [9].

SERVI OF R'BHÎA.

I. *One* servus is always Munach, וַיֹּאמֶר אֱלֹהִים (Gen. i. 9).
In five cases [10] it is found in the *same word* with R'bhîa: [11] אַל־תֵּעָצְבוּ

---

[9] In Syriac the same accent is constantly *repeated* any number of times to mark successive details (see Bar-Hebræus, Phillips' ed., p. 43). Here we have a *rule,* which the few examples that occur of Pazer repeated for the same purpose do not justify us in laying down for the Hebrew.

[10] Fixed by the Massora to Gen. xlv. 5. In our texts it occurs falsely in 2 Ki. xxi. 7; Ezek. xiii. 21; xxxv. 12; xxxvi. 11.

[11] The idea seems to have been to draw attention to the distinction between this form and אַל־תֵּעָצֵבוּ (Neh. viii. 10). Care was to be taken to read here tēāṣ'vû, not tēāṣēvû.

(Gen. xlv. 5); [12] וְאֶסְעָרֵם (Zech. vii. 14); אָנָּא (Ex. xxxii. 31); אֵילוֹ (Qoh. iv. 10); and בֵּלְטְשַׁאצַּר (Dan. i. 7). We can understand its introduction in the three last cases, the object being to indicate a *compound word*.

II. With *two* servi, the first is Darga and the second Munach, e. g. וְהִנֵּה רִבְקָה יֹצֵאת (Gen. xxiv. 15) [13].

III. For *three* servi, we have Munach, Darga, and Munach. The few instances that occur are probably all to be corrected. See below.

Corrigenda.

The following are the cases of Géresh on the fourth word with servi following, referred to p. 95, which I propose to correct as follows:

וְנָתְנוּ עָלָיו אֶת־כָּל־כֵּלָיו אֲשֶׁר יְשָׁרְתוּ־עָלָיו בָּהֶם (Num. iv. 14), with Ox. 3, 6, 10; Erf. 1, 4.

וְהַגִּבְעֹנִים לֹא־מִבְּנֵי יִשְׂרָאֵל הֵמָּה (2 Sam. xxi. 2), with Ox. 1, 7, 13, 16, &c.

וַיֵּשֶׁב מֵאַחֲרָיו וַיִּקַּח אֶת־צֶמֶד־הַבָּקָר וַיִּזְבָּחֵהוּ (1 Ki. xix. 21), with Ox. 76; K. 403; De R. 305. Other Codd., as Ox. 32; Harl. 1528; Add. 4709; Or. 2091; De R. 226, have Zaqeph instead of R'bhia, when the pointing of the clause will be וַיֵּשֶׁב מֵאַחֲרָיו וַיִּקַּח אֶת־צֶמֶד הַבָּקָר וַיִּזְבָּחֵהוּ.

זְכָר־נָא אֵת אֲשֶׁר הִתְהַלַּכְתִּי לְפָנֶיךָ (2 Ki. xx. 3; Is. xxxviii. 3), with Ox. 7, 13, 75; Jabl., &c.

חָרָה אַף־יְהֹוָה בְּעַמּוֹ וַיֵּט־יָדוֹ עָלָיו וַיַּכֵּהוּ (Is. v. 25), with Ox. 5, 9, 13, 17, 75.

יֵשׁ אֶחָד וְאֵין שֵׁנִי גַּם־בֵּן וָאָח אֵין־לוֹ (Qoh. iv. 8), with Ox. 1, 4, 6; Erf. 2, 3.

---

[12] Perhaps to mark the peculiar grammatical form.

[13] Codd. have here constantly two Munachs—an error against which Ben-Bil. expressly warns in Mishp. hat. 26—and so our texts in Josh. xiv. 6; Jer. xxx. 11; Dan. iii. 15, &c.

CHAPTER XI.

PASHṬA, T'BHÎR, AND ZARQA.

THESE three accents may be taken together, as the rules for the division of the clauses governed by them are identical.

Our investigation is further much simplified in that these rules are adopted, with little change, from those for R'bhîa's clause. The same accents (with the exception of L'garmeh, which is rarely employed) are in use to mark the necessary divisions.

It is to be noted that we are now approaching the limits of the musical division. The tendency to employ a *lighter melody* is, in consequence, observable. This tendency, which began to shew itself under R'bhîa, becomes more marked in the clauses we are about to consider; and still more so with the accents, to be examined in the next chapter, which close the musical scale.

We proceed to the analysis of the clauses governed by Pashṭa [1], T'bhîr, and Zarqa.

When there are *two* words (and no more) in the clause, the first is marked with a servus, as וְהָיוּ לִמְאוֹרֹת (Gen. i. 15); וַיַּעַשׂ אֱלֹהִים (i. 4); וַיַּרְא אֱלֹהִים (i. 7).

Géresh is however admissible, when the latter of the two words is *long* and the interval between the tone-syllables considerable, as in וְעָשָׂה אֶת־חַטָּאתְךָ (Lev. ix. 7); וְיִשְׁמְרוּ אֶת־כָּל־צוּרָתוֹ (Ezek. xliii. 11). But the punctators seldom availed themselves of this variation. I have noticed it, besides, only in Ex. xxxviii. 23; 2 Sam. iii. 25; Jer. xxx. 16; Ezek. xi. 18; xliv. 4; and Dan. i. 12 [2]. (Comp. the few similar examples before R'bhîa, p. 93. The number seems to be the same, viz. *eight*.)

When there are *three* or more words in the clause, we have to consider, as before, the various cases that may occur:

---

[1] Pashṭa appears, as we have seen, p. 19, under two forms, Pashṭa proper and Y'thîbh; but, as the latter *always stands alone*, it does not come under consideration in the rules that follow. For this accent, see p. 106.

[2] Baer's pointing וַיַּעַן הָאִישׁ (Zech. i. 10) cannot stand, any more than וּכְחַכֵּי־אִישׁ גְּדוּדִים (Hos. vi. 9), with R'bhîa.

I. The main dichotomy may be due on the word immediately preceding. Here we should expect it to be marked (as before R'bhîa) by Géresh. But this is rarely the case. Generally, *transformation takes place, the servi of Géresh remaining.* In other words, the rhythmical cadence at the close of the clause is, with these lighter accents, purposely omitted, e. g. הָעֵד הֵעִד בָּ֫נוּ (Gen. xliii. 3); הָאִישׁ לֵאמֹר וַיֵּדַ֣ אֹתָם מֶ֫לֶךְ בָּבֶל וַיְמִיתֵם (2 Ki. xxv. 21); הַעִדֹ֫תִי בָכֶ֫ם הַיֹּום (Deut. xxx. 19).

That the dichotomy is *due*, in all such cases, in the first word, is clear not only from the rules for the same, but from the comparison of such identical expressions as 2 Ki. xxi. 3[b] (R'bhîa) and 2 Chr. xxxiii. 3[b] (Pashṭa); 1 Ki. xxii. 35 (Tiphcha) and 2 Chr. xviii. 34 (T'bhîr); and Josh. viii. 18 (R'bhîa) and xi. 6 (Zarqa). Indeed, in the next chapter we shall find this dichotomy, although in abeyance, exercising an influence on the accents preceding.

It is only when the closing word of the clause is *long* (see above) that Géresh appears, e. g. וַיְהִ֣י אִישׁ אֲנִי שִׁלַּח אֶת־כָּל־מַגֵּפֹתַי (Ex. ix. 14); אֶחָד מִן־הָרָמָתַיִם (1 Sam. i. 1); וַיְדַבֵּר אֶל־קֹרַח וְאֶל־כָּל־עֲדָתֹו (Num. xvi. 5). But even here it more generally fails[3].

II. The main dichotomy may be due on the *second* word,

1. And is commonly marked (as before R'bhîa) with Géresh, e. g. וַיָּבֹא קַיִן מִפְּרִי (Gen. i. 9); יִקָּו֣וּ הַמַּ֫יִם מִתַּ֫חַת ∙ הַשָּׁמַ֫יִם הָאֲדָמָה (iv. 3); וְהִנֵּה יְהֹוָה נִצָּב עָלָיו (xxviii. 13).

2. But where the clause contains only *three* words, we often find the lighter melody of a *servus*, e. g. דִּרְשׁוּ מֵעַל־סֵפֶר יְהֹוָה (Is. xxxiv. 16); וּמָשׁ חֲצִי הָהָר (Zech. xiv. 4); נִגַּשׂ וְהוּא נַעֲנֶה (Is. liii. 7)[4].

3. Less frequent than 1 or 2, but not uncommon, is the musical variation of Great T'lîsha. Here Géresh should properly

---

[3] The other examples I have noticed are: before Pashṭa, Ex. xxxi. 6; xxxviii. 17; 1 Sam. xv. 18; Is. xxv. 6; Jer. xix. 13[b] (corr.);—before T'bhîr, Gen. xxxvi. 18; Num. xxxiii. 2; Josh. iii. 17; 1 Ki. i. 10;—and before Zarqa, 2 Chr. xviii. 5.

[4] Codd., as we might expect, often vary. Thus we have וַיַּעַן and וַיַּעַן (Zech. iv. 6); וְיָצָא and וְיָצָא (xiv. 2); כְּהָנֶיךָ and כְּהָנֶיךָ (2 Chr. vi. 41); &c.

come on the first word (see the examples under R'bhîa), but has been, according to rule, transformed [5] : פֶּן־יֶחֱרֶה אַף־יְהֹוָה
אֱלֹהֶיךָ (Deut. vi. 15); וַיַּעֲבֹר יְהוֹשֻׁעַ וְכָל־יִשְׂרָאֵל עִמּוֹ (Josh. x. 29); שָׁמַעְתִּי אֶת־תְּפִלָּתְךָ וְאֶת־תְּחִנָּתְךָ (1 Ki. ix. 3) [6].

In five passages, Gen. v. 29; Lev. x. 4; 2 Ki. xvii. 13; Ezek. xlviii. 10; Zeph. ii. 15 (see Mas. to Gen. v. 29), Géresh and T'lisha are found together in the same word,—an intimation that ancient authorities *differed* as to the chanting. The later Massoretes, unable to decide which was right, directed that *both* accents should be chanted (הקורא יטעים הגרש קדם התלישא), Géresh first, as being the more common. And this chanting is observed in the present day.

It is to be noticed that the rules already laid down and those which follow, apply equally to the *minor* dichotomy, when the main dichotomy divides the clause earlier than in the several cases given.

III. With the main dichotomy on the *third* word, Géresh and Great T'lîsha—more rarely Pazer—are employed to mark it (as also with R'bhîa).

1. But Great T'lîsha becomes now the more common,—the minor dichotomy, if due on the second word, being marked by Géresh [7]; or, if on the first word, by Géresh transformed [8]; e. g. with Pashṭa : וַיָּשֻׁבוּ וַיָּבֹאוּ אֶל־עֵין מִשְׁפָּט (Gen. xiv. 7); לְמַעַן תֵּדְעוּ וְתַאֲמִינוּ לִי וְתָבִינוּ (Is. xliii. 10).

---

[5] Moreover—according to the analogy of Zaqeph on the second word before Athnach or Silluq, R'bhîa on the second word before Zaqeph, &c.—one or other of the words following T'lisha should be *long*. But the *necessity* for this condition fails, with the transformation of Géresh and the consequent disappearance of the full rhythmical cadence. Hence we find two short words in 1 Sam. xxx. 12; Is. xxix. 4, before Pashṭa; Jon. ii. 3, before T'bhîr; and Deut. iii. 19, before Zarqa.

[6] The careless mistakes in 2 Ki. xvi. 7 and Neh. ix. 37[b] must be corrected and Azla put for Great T'lîsha, with Codd.

[7] It is not often that Géresh fails when due in the second word; yet after the analogy of II. 2, a servus may come, as in Num. xix. 10 and Josh. ii. 3, before Pashṭa;—Gen. xlii. 30 and Deut. xxii. 29, before T'bhîr;—and Num. xxx. 9; Josh. xxiii. 16, before Zarqa.

[8] In two instances, Lev. v. 12 and Num. xiv. 29, where Pashṭa's word is *long*, Géresh remains.

For T'bhîr, see Gen. xix. 20 ; Jer. xiii. 9 ;—for Zarqa, Gen. xix. 19 ; Josh. x. 24[9].

The (musical) variations under this head are—

(a) The fanciful transposition of T'lisha and Géresh[10], e.g. וְאִם־חֶּרְאָה עוֹד בַּבֶּגֶד אֹו־בַשְׁתִי אֹו־בָעֵרֶב (Lev. xiii. 57). The other examples are 2 Chr. xxxv. 12, with Pashṭa ;—Gen. xiii. 1 ; Deut. xxvi. 12 ; Josh. xxiii. 4 ; Am. viii. 13 ; Ezra v. 3, with T'bhîr ;—and Neh. iii. 15, with Zarqa.

(β) The substitution of Pazer for Great T'lisha, Géresh remaining, as in עַל־כֵּן אֶבְכֶּה בִּבְכִי יַעְזֵר (Is. xvi. 9). Comp. Dan. ii. 28 ; 1 Chr. xxvii. 25 ; 2 Chr. iii. 3, before Pashṭa ;—Gen. x. 13 (1 Chr. i. 11) ; 1 Sam. xxx. 14 ; 2 Ki. viii. 29 (2 Chr. xxii. 6) ; Qoh. viii. 11[b] ; 1 Chr. xxiv. 4, before T'bhîr ;—and 2 Chr. xxxv. 7, before Zarqa. (In Neh. xii. 36 ; xiii. 15, Pazer marks a minor dichotomy[11].)

2. Examples of Géresh are : וַיֹּאמֶר לֹו אֱלֹהִים אֲנִי אֵל שַׁדַּי (Gen. xxxv. 11) ; וַתִּקַּח רִצְפָּה בַת־אַיָּה אֶת־הַשַּׂק וַתַּטֵּהוּ לָהּ אֶל־הַצּוּר (2 Sam. xxi. 10). Comp. for T'bhîr, Gen. xxxiv. 13 ; Lev. xiii. 37 ; and for Zarqa, Ex. xxix. 21 ; 1 Ki. iii. 6. (For the instances in which the minor dichotomy is due on the *first* word, comp. R'bhîa, III. 1[12].)

3. Pazer also, followed by Great T'lisha to mark the minor dichotomy on the second word, is quite regular, e. g. וּבָאוּ עָלַיִךְ וַיְצַו הַמֶּלֶךְ אֶת־יֹואָב וְאֶת־הַצֵּן רֶכֶב וְגַלְגַּל (Ezek. xxiii. 24) ; אֲבִישַׁי וְאֶת־אִתַּי (2 Sam. xviii. 5). So before T'bhîr, Num. xxix. 18 ; Josh. ii. 1[b] ; and before Zarqa, Gen. xxxvi. 6 ; Jer. xxxvi. 14. Such examples are, however, much less frequent than those under 1 and 2.

---

[9] For the rest of the chapter, I think it sufficient to give in full the examples with Pashṭa, as those with T'bhîr and Zarqa present no difference.

[10] Of course their relative disjunctive value becomes changed, with the change of position.

[11] Pazer is out of order in these instances, because it is properly followed by Great or Little T'lisha.

[12] Neh. v. 18 must be corrected שׁוֹר אֶחָד צֹאן שֵׁשׁ־בְּרֻרֹות וְצִפֳּרִים, as the minor dichotomy is on the first word. Harl. 5506 and Par. 102 have Munach for Great T'lisha.

IV. With the main dichotomy on the *fourth* word, Great T'lîsha and Pazer are employed to mark it. Géresh is seldom available.

1. Great T'lîsha, when the minor dichotomy (marked with Géresh) is on the second or third word, e. g. וְאָמַרְתָּ אֲלֵיהֶם לֹא וְהִבִּיתֶם (Jer. xvii. 20); שִׁמְעוּ דְבַר־יְהוָֹה מַלְכֵי יְהוּדָה וְחָרָה אַפִּי בוֹ בַיּוֹם־ אֶת־יוֹשְׁבֵי יָבֵשׁ גִּלְעָד (Judg. xxi. 10); הַהוּא וַעֲזַבְתִּים וְהִסְתַּרְתִּי פָנַי מֵהֶם (Deut. xxxi. 17). For T'bhîr, comp. Num. xviii. 7; Is. lxvi. 19; and for Zarqa, Deut. xxxi. 21; Jer. xlix. 19.

The variations under this head are as before:

(*a*) The transposition of T'lîsha and Géresh, in וַתּוֹצֵא הָאָרֶץ דֶּשֶׁא עֵשֶׂב מַזְרִיעַ זֶרַע (Gen. i. 12); and Lev. iv. 7; 1 Ki. xvi. 21; Ezek. iii. 15; Dan. ix. 26; Ezra viii. 17[b]; all before Pashṭa[13].

(β) The substitution of Pazer for T'lîsha, Géresh remaining, in Lev. xiii. 58; Josh. xviii. 28, before Pashṭa;—and in Num. xviii. 17; Jer. xxxviii. 25; xliv. 18; Esth. i. 17; 2 Chr. xx. 26, before T'bhîr[14].

2. Pazer also may come, followed by Great T'lîsha, to mark the minor dichotomy on the second or third word, e. g. הַסִּפִּים אַף כִּי־ וְהַחַלּוֹנִים הָאֲטֻמוֹת וְהָאַתִּיקִים ׀ סָבִיב (Ezek. xli. 16); אַרְבַּעַת שְׁפָטַי ׀ הָרָעִים חֶרֶב וְרָעָב וְחַיָּה רָעָה (xiv. 21); וַיֹּאמֶר קַח־נָא אֶת־בִּנְךָ אֶת־יְחִידְךָ אֲשֶׁר־אָהַבְתָּ (Gen. xxii. 2). Comp. Josh. vi. 23; 2 Ki. xvi. 10; Ezek. xxxvii. 25; and for T'bhîr's clause, Gen. vii. 2; xlv. 23; 2 Sam. iii. 29. I have noticed no example in Zarqa's clause.

But Pazer's proper function in the fourth word is to mark the main dichotomy, when the minor dichotomy—represented by Géresh transformed[15]—is due on the *first* word. (Great T'lîsha

---

[13] The minor dichotomies are so pointed in Pashṭa's clause, 1 Sam. xvii. 51; and in T'bhîr's, Gen. xxi. 14.

[14] In 1 Ki. xix. 11, where Pazer marks a minor dichotomy, Géresh must come on the second word, with many Codd.

[15] In Lev. xx. 4, where Pashṭa's word is *long*, Géresh is found; and so in 1 Ki. x. 5, with Pazer on the fifth word. Contrast the division in R'bhia's clause, where Géresh *always stands*.

cannot be used, because it would come immediately before Little
T'lîsha,—a juxtaposition which, as we have seen, is not allowed.)
E. g. וְאַתָּה אַל־תִּירָא֟ עַבְדִּי יַעֲקֹב נְאֻם־יְהוָֹה֟ (Jer. xxx. 10);
וַיֹּאמֶר אֶת־אֱלֹהַי֟ אֲשֶׁר־עָשִׂיתִי לָקַחְתֶּם וְאֶת־הַכֹּהֵן (Judg.
xviii. 24); and so in Gen. xlviii. 15; Ex. v. 14; &c., before
Pashṭa; and in 2 Ki. xxiii. 29; Is. liv. 17; &c., before T'bhîr [16].
Here again examples with Zarqa fail.

EXCEPTIONS.—Géresh cannot properly appear on the *fourth* word,
except by transposition (see 1. *a* above) or by the introduction of
L'garmeh [17] to mark the minor dichotomy. Such instances, therefore,
as כִּי־אָמַר עַבְדְּךָ֡ אֶחְבְּשָׁה־לִּ֟י הַחֲמוֹר וְאֶרְכַּב עָלֶיהָ (2 Sam. xix. 27), must
either be regarded as exceptional and altogether anomalous, or we
must be prepared to correct them (like the similar instances in R'bhîa's
clause, p. 98) with the help of Codd. The latter is (I doubt not) the
proper course. For instance, in the passage just given, I propose to
point אֶחְבְּשָׁה־לִּ֟י הַחֲמוֹר, with Add. 15451; Harl. 5722; De R. 554, &c.
By the simple insertion of Maqqeph between the first word and T'bhîr
in Josh. xxi. 11, and between the second and third words in Judg. xx.
34 and 1 Ki. v. 25, these passages are reduced to order. In Jer. xxxviii.
16 I have found Pazer—and in Num. iii. 39; 1 Sam. xviii. 5; 2 Sam.
xiv. 30; and 2 Chr. ix. 25, R'bhîa—for Géresh. These are the only
passages which (as far as I have observed) need correction. I have not
thought it necessary to cite, for the several instances, the authority
on which the correction is made. It is enough that the student should
understand that the anomaly which they exhibit admits of being
removed, and that so the rules above laid down are confirmed. It is
only from this latter point of view that the emendations made are of
any consequence [18].

V. With the main dichotomy on the *fifth* word or further,
Pazer is (as in R'bhîa's clause) the regular dividing accent.

---

[16] In the lists Ezek. xliii. 11; Dan. iii. 2; Neh. xi. 7; and 2 Chr. xvii. 8, Pazer
(marking a minor dichotomy) comes on the *third* word, because of two servi in the
first.

[17] Lev. x. 6; xxi. 10; and Ruth i. 2, are the only examples of this division.

[18] There are besides, the passages in which Géresh marks a *minor* dichotomy,
and which must be corrected in the same way. Thus Maqqeph will come between
the first word and T'bhîr in 1 Ki. ix. 11; between the first and second words in
Deut. xx. 14 and 2 Sam. xviii. 29 (where לְשֻׁלֹחַ must at the same time have its
accent changed to Azla); and between the second and third words in Josh. xxi. 6
and Dan. x. 11. Pazer will take the place of Géresh in 1 Sam. xvii. 23, and Great
T'lîsha that of Little T'lîsha in Esth. vi. 13.

As before R'bhîa, Great T'lîsha may stand on the fifth word, with Géresh to mark the minor dichotomy on the third word, e. g. וַיִּתְקַבְּצוּ אֵלָיו כָּל־אִישׁ מָצוֹק וְכָל־אִישׁ אֲשֶׁר־לוֹ נֹשֶׁא (1 Sam. xxii. 2). Comp. for Pashṭa, Ex. ii. 14; 1 Ki. xiv. 21;—for T'bhîr, Num. ix. 1; Is. xxxvi. 22;—and for Zarqa, Zech. xiv. 4; Ezra v. 17[19].

Géresh cannot come on the fifth word,—as L'garmeh altogether fails for the minor dichotomy,—except indeed, as in Deut. xvii. 5, through *transposition*. Three passages need in consequence correction, Ex. v. 8; 2 Ki. v. 1[20]; and 2 Chr. xxii. 11[b]; in all of which I point with various Codd., Great for Little T'lîsha.

In all other instances Pazer is employed,—*repeated* if necessary, according to the requirements of the dichotomy, or for the sake of distinct enunciation of details.

Examples of *one* Pazer are common enough: גַּם כָּל־הָאָדָם אֲשֶׁר נָתַן־לוֹ הָאֱלֹהִים עֹשֶׁר וּנְכָסִים וְהִשְׁלִיטוֹ לֶאֱכֹל מִמֶּנּוּ (Qoh. v. 18); וַיִּירְשׁוּ בָּתִּים מְלֵאִים־כָּל־טוּב בֹּרוֹת חֲצוּבִים כְּרָמִים וְזֵיתִים (Neh. ix. 25); וְאַתָּה הֻפְקַד אֶת־הַלְוִיִּם עַל־מִשְׁכַּן הָעֵדֻת וְעַל כָּל־כֵּלָיו (Num. i. 50). Other examples in Pashṭa's clause are 2 Ki. ix. 26; Esth. iii. 13; 2 Chr. xxxv. 18[b];— in T'bhîr's, 1 Sam. xvii. 40; 1 Ki. ix. 26; Ezek. xxii. 30;—and in Zarqa's, 2 Ki. xxiii. 4; Ezek. xlviii. 21; 2 Chr. xxxii. 15.

Two Pazers are also not uncommon, e. g. עַתָּה הִנֵּה בָטַחְתָּ וַיְמַהֲרוּ לְךָ עַל־מִשְׁעֶנֶת הַקָּנֶה הָרָצוּץ הַזֶּה (2 Ki. xviii. 21); וַיֻּשְׁלְכֵמוּ וַיֵּצְאוּ אַנְשֵׁי־הָעִיר לִקְרַאת־יִשְׂרָאֵל לַמִּלְחָמָה הוּא וְכָל־עַמּוֹ (Josh. viii. 14). Comp. for Pashṭa, Ezek. xxi. 3; Dan. iii. 5; Neh. i. 6;—and for T'bhîr, Num. ix. 5; 1 Chr. xii. 40; 2 Chr. xxiii. 1. Two Pazers are not found in Zarqa's clause.

---

[19] Deut. xx. 14; Josh. xxi. 6; 1 Ki. ix. 11; and Dan. x. 11;—as corrected, see previous note,—come under this head. In 1 Sam. xvii. 51 Great T'lîsha appears on the sixth word; but it is better to point with R'bhîa instead (so Ox. 16; Add. 9398, 11657). We thus avoid having Great T'lîsha both before and after Géresh.

[20] In this passage, a double change is necessary. No doubt Great T'lîsha in the first word is to be made Little T'lîsha, with Ox. 7, 13, 20, 24, &c., וְנַעֲמָן. The two T'lîshas constantly interchange in Codd.

Three Pazers are found in Dan. iii. 7; Ezra viii. 16; Neh. viii. 4; xi. 7; xii. 41; xiii. 15; 1 Chr. iii. 24; xxviii. 1;—*four* in Josh. vii. 24; Ezek. xliii. 11; Dan. iii. 2; 1 Chr. xv. 24;—*five* in Neh. xii. 36; 2 Chr. xvii. 8;—*six* in Neh. viii. 7;—and *eight* in 1 Chr. xv. 18.

Eight of these sixteen examples are in Pashṭa's clause, and eight in T'bhîr's. They are mostly instances where details have to be given of names, &c. In all, the multiplication of the Pazers might have been avoided, if the accentuators had been so minded. Comp. the remark under R'bhîa, p. 97. The examples (it will be observed) occur almost all in the later Books.

ON Y'THÎBH IN THE PLACE OF PASHṬA.

The substitution is entirely on musical grounds. In the chanting of Pashṭa's word, an *anacrusis* or *appoggiatura* was needed, which it was not possible to introduce, when the tone came on the *first letter* and no servus preceded[21]. In such cases the melody of Pashṭa underwent a change, represented by Y'thîbh (see p. 19), e. g. אַף כִּי־אָמַר אֱלֹהִים (Gen. iii. 1); אֵלֶּה תּוֹלְדֹת נֹחַ (vi. 9).—When the servus preceded, as in וְהָאָרֶץ הָיְתָה תֹהוּ (i. 2); וַיִּקַּח מִשָּׁם אֶבֶן (1 Sam. xvii. 49), the *appoggiatura* (or a substitute for it) was provided.

As the sign for M'huppakh is the same as that for Y'thîbh, there would be occasionally uncertainty as to which accent was intended. The cases are those in which the word, requiring the one or other of these accents, comes between R'bhîa and the Pashṭa which serves as foretone to Zaqeph. Here M'huppakh is, of course, as common as possible. But Y'thîbh is sometimes due, as the representative of R'bhîa repeated (according to the rule, p. 78, 2), e. g. וַיֹּאמֶר יְהֹוָה אֵלַי שֶׁקֶר הַנְּבִיאִים נִבְּאִים בִּשְׁמִי (Jer. xiv. 14), where, however, many Codd. (and our texts) point M'huppakh. To obviate confusion in these cases, and others which might arise from the ignorance or carelessness of punctators[22], the Massoretes drew up a list of the

---

[21] According to Ben-Asher, vocal Sh'va sufficed for the auxiliary note, שְׁתַּיִם חֻגְּרוֹת אִישׁ (Ezek. i. 11); but not apparently in Ben-Naphtali's view, who pointed שְׁתַּיִם with Y'thîbh. (This punctuation is found in our texts, Ezek. xli. 24.)

[22] As 2 Ki. x. 30, corrected p. 79, note 11.

passages in which, according to their judgment, the word immediately preceding Pashṭa was to be pointed with *Y'thîbh* [23], viz. אָז (Lev. v. 2); אֵת (Deut. i. 4; Is. v. 24); כָּל (Is. xxx. 32; Ezra ix. 4); שֶׁקֶר (Jer. xiv. 14); אִישׁ (xvi. 12; xxii. 30); and דִּי (Dan. ii. 10; vii. 27; Ezra vi. 8). In all other cases, M'huppakh was to be chanted [24].

SERVI OF PASHṬA, T'BHÎR, AND ZARQA [25].

The chief difference is in the servi immediately preceding these accents. The other servi—when there are two or more—follow the same general rules.

I. ONE SERVUS.

1. **Pashṭa** has sometimes M'huppakh, sometimes Mer'kha.

a. M'huppakh, when one or more syllables intervene between the servus and the tone-syllable of Pashṭa's word (vocal Sh'va and furtive Pathach being allowed to count as syllables), e. g. הִנֵּה־נָא הוֹאַלְתִּי (Gen. xviii. 31); שְׁלֹשׁ סְאִים (xviii. 6); לִשְׁלֹחַ יָד (Esth. iii. 6).

In a few forms, compounded with שֶׁ, M'huppakh appears in the *same word* with Pashṭa, שֶׁאֲהֲבָה (Cant. i. 7). Comp. i. 12; iii. 4; Qoh. i. 7; vii. 10 [26]. The object is to indicate a compound word [27].

β. Mer'kha, when no syllable intervenes, e. g. הָיְתָה תֹהוּ (Gen. i. 2); יָדַע שׁוֹר (Is. i. 3). But if Paseq comes between the words, M'huppakh will stand, יוֹם ׀ יוֹם (Is. lviii. 2) [28].

---

[23] טעמא לאחור (Mas. to Dan. ii. 10), i. e. 'with the accent put backwards,' in reference to the position of Y'thîbh.

[24] So far the list answers a certain purpose. But in itself it is a poor one, and has been but little regarded by punctators or editors. In only three instances is Y'thîbh really required.

[25] These servi, owing to the fine musical distinctions and the many exceptions, give more trouble than all the other servi put together. The Orientals and Ben-Naphtali had more simple rules.

As before, I cannot undertake to enumerate the many errors of our texts. The student, as he comes across them, may correct them according to the following rules, which are firmly established.

[26] See Norzi on Cant. i. 7.

[27] So the Mas. requires M'huppakh in אֲסַרְחַדּוֹן (Ezra iv. 2), a compound of two words, which are kept distinct in ordinary texts.

[28] As Baer has rightly pointed. And so we must correct Jer. xii. 5 and 1 Chr. viii. 38 (ix. 44 is right). The Mas. to Deut. viii. 15 (which gives the instances where Paseq comes between two nouns, the first of which has M'huppakh and the second Pashṭa) is very defective. Beside the above instances, Ezek. xlvii. 16 and Ruth iv. 11 are wanting.

2. **T'bhîr** has sometimes Darga, sometimes Mer'kha.

a. Darga, when two or more syllables intervene between the servus and T'bhîr (vocal Sh'va generally and furtive Pathach counting as above), e.g. וַיִּקְרָא הָאָדָם (Gen. iii. 20); כִּי־נַחֵשׁ יְנַחֵשׁ (xliv. 15); וְכִי תִזְבְּחוּ (Lev. xix. 5); נָתַתִּי לָךְ (Gen. xlviii. 22); מַדּוּעַ קִוֵּיתִי (Is. v. 4).

β. Mer'kha, when only one syllable, or none at all, intervenes: נַעֲשֶׂה אָדָם (Gen. i. 26); וְהָיָה לָךְ (vi. 21); ✻ וַיִּבֶן נֹחַ (viii. 20); וַיִּקְרָא שָׁם (xiii. 4) [29].

Exceptions.—The simple vocal Sh'va which follows a vowel, whether short or long, was not counted of sufficient length to constitute a syllable. Hence we find Mer'kha appointed for all such cases as אֲשֶׁר פָּקְדוּ (Gen. i. 28); הַנִּבְּאִים בִּשְׁמִי (Jer. xxiii. 25); פָּרוּ וְרָבוּ (Num. xxvi. 64); וְאִם־לֹא תֵלְכִי (Judg. iv. 8); וְשַׂמְתִּי שֹׁמְרוֹן (Mic. i. 6). The explanation seems to be that the pronunciation of the Sh'va in these cases was less distinctly heard than when it comes at the beginning of a word, or at the beginning of a syllable after silent Sh'va [30].

---

[29] The Mas. to Ex. xxi. 35 lays it down that there are thirteen exceptions in which Darga comes, where Mer'kha is due. (We must strike out the words זוּגִין מתחלפין, with which Jacob ben-Chayyim has headed the list. They make non-sense, and have come from confusion with the Mas. to Lev. xi. 12.) The list is most correctly given in Dikd. hat., § 19: הָיוּ (Gen. xviii. 18); יֵצֵּף (Ex. xxi. 35); לוֹ (Lev. vii. 33); אֲשֶׁר (Deut. xiv. 10; Is. xix. 25); בֵּין (Josh. viii. 9, 12); מֵאוֹת (1 Sam. xxx. 17); יָרַע (2 Sam. xx. 6); כְּשֹׁד (Hos. x. 14); תִּמְצָא (Qoh. ix. 10); הַפַּךְ (2 Chr. xviii. 33); לֹא (xxx. 3). It is clear to my mind that we have in these exceptions (and those which follow) merely the errors of some model Codex, for the *same words in the same connection* are at one time pointed according to rule, at another against it. Comp. Lev. xi. 12 (אֲשֶׁר) with Deut. xiv. 10, and 1 Ki. xxii. 34 (הַפַּךְ) with 2 Chr. xviii. 33.

[30] Heidenheim (Mishp. hat. 27ᵇ) and Baer (Dikd. hat., p. 13 note) maintain indeed the Sh'va in the above cases—even when the vowel is long—to be *quiescent;* and cite Ben-Asher, Chayyug̃, Aben-Ezra, and others as of the same view. But that these early grammarians were only driven to adopt their view from the supposed exigencies of the accentuation is clear from the punctuation of certain MSS. lately brought from Yemen,—provided with a peculiar system of superlinear vocalization, not yet familiar to scholars,—*which invariably mark the Sh'va after a long vowel as vocal.* (See, e.g. Pl. LIV of the Palæographical Society's publications, Oriental series, and the accompanying description.) The sign used is a bar over the letter, thus—I drop the peculiar vocalization— אֲשֶׁר יָצְאוּ (Num. xxxiii. 1, in the Plate), the Mer'kha, it will be observed, still retained. We thus see that there were Jewish authorities, which did not accept Ben-Asher's view, just as Qimchi (Mikhlol, 152ᵇ) emancipated himself from the error of his predecessors.

But when Paseq follows, Darga always stands: הַמּוֹל ׀ יִמּוֹל (Gen. xvii. 13); מִיּוֹם ׀ לְיוֹם (Esth. iii. 7); &c.

Obs.—Mer'kha, if no other servus precedes, is sometimes found in the *same word* with T'bhîr. The rule is as follows :—When a *long* vowel, with Métheg and simple Sh'va following, immediately precedes T'bhîr, Mer'kha takes the place of the Métheg, e. g. יָדְךָ (Deut. xiii. 10); אֶת־יֹשְׁבֵי (xiii. 16); בְּבִירְתָּא (Ezra vi. 2); וָאֵצֵא (2 Chr. i. 10)[31]. But when a vowel or half-vowel (compound Sh'va) intervenes, Métheg remains, as in אָהֳלִיבָמָה (Gen. xxxvi. 18); וְרָחֲצוּ (Ex. xxx. 19)[32].

Ben-Naphtali and the Orientals (as may be seen in Cod. Bab.) did not follow this rule, which really seems to have no *raison d'être*. Indeed, although adopted by grammarians, it was but little observed in practice.

3. **Zarqa** has Munach (properly 'Illuy), e. g. וַיְבָרֶךְ אֹתָם (Gen. i. 28); וַיִּקְרְבוּ יְמֵי־יִשְׂרָאֵל (xlvii. 29)[33]; אָשֵׁמִים ׀ אֲנַחְנוּ (xlii. 21).

II. Two servi. The first will be Munach, if on the *first letter*,— if on any other, Azla[34]; the second will be according to Rule I.

---

[31] Ben-Bil. (MS.) lays down the rule in the following terms : התביר אם שרתו משרת אחד בתיבתו לא יהיה כי אם מרכא, ואשר מזקיקו להיות עמו מרכא בתיבתו לשרתו הם ב׳ תנאים, האחד הוא שיהיה קודם האות שתחתיו התביר אות שתחתיו שבא או שוכן או מניע, והשני הוא שיהיה קודם האות שתחתיו שבא אחד מן ג׳ המלכים אה או אי, כגון וַיֵּצֵא, יִשְׂתָּרֵג, הָתְבּוֹנְנוּ, בר מן אחד שיש עם אות המרכא נקודה מלמטה, והוא בְּבִירְתָּא דבעזרא. No one else (as far as I have seen) has given the rule correctly. Heidenheim (Mishp. hat. 26[b]) has copied the false text of Moses the punctator. The rubrics in Ginsb. Mas. מ, § 239 ff., are a complete muddle.

[32] Three exceptions are indeed named (Dikd. hat., § 20): וַתַּעֲלוּ (Ezek. xxxvi. 3); אַל־תִּלָּחֵמוּ (2 Chr. xiii. 12); עַל־הַפְּתָחִים (xxxi. 9). But doubtless Métheg and Mer'kha have been here confounded (in Codd. they are often quite alike), just as Ben-Bil. (Mishp. hat. 29[b]) and others have confounded them in אִם־תָּעִירוּ ׀ וְאִם־תְּעוֹרְרוּ (Cant. ii. 7), where Mer'kha, following Darga, is impossible.

[33] In ten passages, according to the Mas., Mer'kha comes instead of Munach: אָמֹר (Ex. vi. 6); אֵת־רֹאשׁ (xxx. 12); בֹּל (2 Sam. vii. 7; 1 Chr. xvii. 6); שׁוֹר (1 Ki. i. 19, 25); וחֵצִי (1 Chr. v. 18); וַיַּעֲלוּ (xiv. 11); נֹסְפָּה (xxi. 12); and נֵגֶד (Ruth iv. 4). See Dikd. hat., § 21 end. (There has apparently been some confusion, in the punctuation of these words, with the rule for Zarqa's servi under II. Perhaps some of my readers, who have occupied themselves with the accentuation, have occasionally made, as I have found myself making, the same mistake.) Many authorities omit either 1 Chr. xvii. 6, or 1 Ki. i. 25, thus leaving one example exceptional, and another (with the same words) regular. Comp. note 29.

[34] The principle of this variation has been explained under Y'thîbh, p. 106. Here also, when another servus (Little T'lîsha) precedes, Azla will stand even on the first letter.

1. **Pashṭa.** שָׂא נָא עֵינֶיךָ (Gen. xiii. 14); לֵיל שִׁמֻּרִים הוּא (Ex. xii. 42); יְצַו יְהוָֹה אִתְּךָ (Deut. xxviii. 8); וַיַּעֲבֵר אֱלֹהִים רוּחַ (Gen. viii. ɪ)[35].

In seven instances, Azla takes the place of Métheg in the *same word* with M'huppakh (or Mer'kha): וּבָאֲחֵיכֶם (Lev. xxv. 46); כָּל־הָעֵדָה (Num. xx. ɪ); הַמַּאֲכִלְךָ (Deut. viii. 16). Comp. Ezek. xliii. 11; Dan. iii. 2 ; Ezra vii. 24; 2 Chr. xxxv. 25 [36]. Once Munach comes [37] with the first letter, שֶׁהֵם (Lam. iv. 9).—Ben-Naphtali and the Orientals had no such instances, nor in the similar cases that follow.

2. **T'bhîr.** זֶה יִהְיֶה לְךָ (Num. xviii. 9); וְהֶבֶל הֵבִיא גַם־הוּא (Gen. iv. 4); וַיֵּחָלֵק עֲלֵיהֶם ׀ לַיְלָה (xiv. 15)[38].

In six instances, Azla takes (in some texts) the place of Métheg in the *same word* with Darga or Mer'kha[39] : וַתֹּאמְרוּ (Is. xxx. 16); עַד־ יֶעְרֶה (xxxii. 15); וָאֲמַלְּטָה (Job i. 15, 16, &c.); בֶּן־קוֹלָיָה (Neh. xi. 7); וְיֹחָנָן (1 Chr. iii. 24); וַאֲדֹנִיָּהוּ (2 Chr. xvii. 8).

3. **Zarqa.** וַיֹּאמֶר (xx. 9); שֵׁשֶׁת יָמִים תַּעֲבֹד (Ex. iv. 11); מִי שָׂם פֶּה (viii. 5)[40].

But here a curious musical change may take place. If Métheg occurs in Zarqa's word, or Paseq precedes, Mer'kha comes instead of Munach, between Azla and Zarqa, e. g. וַיָּבֹא יַעֲקֹב מִן־הַשָּׂדֶה (Gen. xxx. 16); זְבָדַנִי אֱלֹהִים ׀ אֹתִי (xxx. 20)[41]. Ben-Naphtali, and—to judge from Cod. Bab.—the Orientals, made no distinction of this kind.

---

[35] Once (Dikd. hat., § 23) Munach is said to come instead of Azla, בְּיוֹם אַרְבָּעָה עָשָׂר (Esth. ix. 15). And so our texts. But most Codd. point regularly.

[36] See Mas. to Lev. xxv. 46; and for Deut. viii. 16, Mishp. hat. 25.

[37] See Mas. parva טעמים בתרי ב׳, viz. here and Cant. vi. 5 (with Ṭiphcha).

[38] One exception is named (Dikd. hat., § 19) : כִּי אֵין לַעֲמוֹד (Ezra ix. 15) for אֵין, and so our texts. Evidently a *lapsus calami*.

[39] There is no Mas. here, and the double accentuation fails very generally for some of the instances in Codd. In support of it, see Baer's note to Is. xxxii. 15.

[40] In two passages, 2 Ki. viii. 5 and 2 Chr. vi. 32, Mer'kha is said to occur for Munach in the *first* word (Dikd. hat., p. 23). Maqqeph (which is marked in our texts) has fallen out, and then Métheg been taken for Mer'kha.

Ewald, p. 224, gives a string of passages (copied from Spitzner) in which Munach is put for Azla, when the tone is *not* on the first letter. But *they are all false examples,* and do not appear in correct texts !

[41] The exceptions under this head given by grammarians (e. g. Dikd. hat., § 21) are that (1) Mer'kha occurs four times, Deut. xix. 5 ; 2 Sam. iv. 8 ; v. 11 (1 Chr. xiv. 1), *without either Métheg or Paseq ;* (2) Munach three times, Josh. xviii. 14; Dan. vi. 13; Neh. viii. 15, *before Métheg ;* and (3) Munach twice, Gen. xxxvii. 22

In three instances, Azla takes the place of Métheg in the *same word* with Mer'kha : וְאֶל־אִֽיתָמָר֙ ׀ (Lev. x. 12); אִם־יֵצְא֣וּ בְנֽוֹת־שִׁילוֹ֙ (Judg. xxi. 21); לָאוֹצָר֖וֹת ׀ (Neh. xii. 44)[42].

III. THREE SERVI. The first is Little T'lisha, the second Azla, and the third as under II, e. g. בְּרִ֣ית מֶ֣לַח עוֹלָ֣ם הוּא֙ (Num. xviii. 19); וַיָּ֣שָׁב בַּיּ֥וֹם הַה֖וּא עֵשָׂ֛ו (Gen. xxxiii. 16); וַיֹּ֤אמֶר יְהֹוָ֣ה אֱלֹהִים֙ ׀ אֶל־הַנָּחָשׁ֙ (iii. 14).

It is to be noted that three or more servi are entirely due to the transformation of Géresh in the first word,—i. e. allowing the corrections made p. 104. Not unfrequently, Paseq is employed to mark the dichotomy due on this word.

IV. FOUR or MORE SERVI. All preceding Little T'lisha will be Munachs, e. g. וַיַּרְעֵ֣ם יְהֹוָ֣ה ׀ בְּקוֹל־גָּדוֹל֩ בַּיּ֨וֹם הַה֤וּא עַל־פְּלִשְׁתִּים֙ (1 Sam. vii. 10); הֲל֣וֹא כִבְנֵ֣י כֻשִׁיִּ֞ים אַתֶּ֥ם לִ֣י בְּהַדֹּ֧רֽ יְהֹוָ֣ה אֱלֹֽהֶיךָ֙ אֹתָ֜ם ׀ (Amos ix. 7); מִלְּפָנֶ֔יךָ (Deut. ix. 4).

T'bhir and Zarqa are not found with more than *four* servi; Pashta has *five* in Josh. xix. 51; 1 Sam. vii. 10; Ezek. xxi. 3; and 2 Chr. ii. 3; and once, 2 Ki. xviii. 14, *six*. But such long clauses as those last named are generally avoided by the employment of Pazer or Great T'lisha in subordination to the last servus, see next chap., p. 118.

---

and 2 Ki. iv. 13, *before Paseq*. But how unreliable such lists are may be seen from their all omitting Num. xxx. 15, which is fixed by a standard Massoretic rubric to Gen. xxx. 16. Even the Massora is quite wrong in a rubric, cited briefly in Mishp. hat. 16[b] and Ginsb. Mas. מ, § 229, but which I found given at length in Ox. 2325 to Deut. xix. 5: כל דאתי זרקא עם געיא במרכא בֹמֹ דאתין בלא את געיא והם במרכא וסימ', then follow the seven instances under 1 and 2, i. e. those under 2 are all *without Métheg!*

[42] See Mas. to Lev. x. 12, or Dikd. hat., p. 23.

CHAPTER XII.

GÉRESH, PAZER, AND GREAT T'LÎSHA.

I TAKE these three accents together, not only because of their frequent interchange, but because they all serve the same purpose of marking the divisions in the clauses governed by R'bhîa, Pashṭa, &c.

GÉRESH. This accent appears under two forms, Géresh proper, and Double Géresh or Gersháyim[1]. Neither admits of repetition.

Géresh is used when the tone is on the *penultimate*, e. g. וַיֹּאמֶר (Gen. xix. 2), מַדּוּעַ (Judg. xi. 7); or *when Azla precedes*, as in וַיֹּאמֶר אֱלֹהִים (Gen. vi. 13);—Gersháyim, when the tone is on the *ultimate*, and Azla does *not* precede, e. g. וַיִּשְׁמָעֵ֞ (iii. 8); עֵץ פְּרִי (i. 11); קַח־בְּיָדְךָ (Jer. xliii. 9)[2].

Géresh and Gersháyim may stand without a servus. Or Géresh may have from one to five servi[3], but Gersháyim can only have one.

1. One servus (a) is Munach, when on the *first* letter of the word, תַּחַת הַנְּחֹשֶׁת (Is. lx. 17). This is the only servus Gersháyim can take.

(β) When not on the first letter, the servus is Azla: שְׁנַיִם שְׁנַיִם (Gen. vii. 9); וַיַּקַּח תֶּרַח (xi. 31); חָלְלָה לְּךָ (xviii. 25).

2. Two servi. The first is Little T'lîsha, and the second Azla (even on the first letter): וַיֹּאמֶר אֵלָיו הָאֱלֹהִים (xx. 6); וַיֹּאמֶר לָהּ בֹּעַז (Ruth ii. 14).

3. Three or more servi. All before Little T'lîsha are Munachs. Three servi are common, four much less so, and five rare[4].

---

[1] Both were high notes,—the double stroke (we may suppose) with a *fuller* intonation than the single.

[2] Our texts have, of course, their mistakes. Thus Gersháyim is falsely placed in Josh. vi. 23; 1 Sam. xxvi. 19; 2 Ki. ix. 10; &c.

[3] It will be observed that the servi are the same, as the second, third, &c., before Pashṭa, T'bhîr, and Zarqa. The reason is that the *servi of Géresh remained*, after the transformation of Géresh in the first word before the accents named.

[4] The examples I have noted with *five* servi are Judg. xi. 17; 1 Ki. xxi. 2; Jer. iii. 1; viii. 1; xxxvi. 6; Ezek. xlvii. 18; Dan. i. 4. In Jer. viii. 1 our texts have falsely *six* servi, (see Mishp. hat. 10.)

Obs.—Azla may take the place of light Métheg[5] in the *same word* with Géresh (only of course not on the *first* letter), when no other servus precedes[6], e. g. וְנָתַתִּי (Gen. xlviii. 4); וַיֹּאמְרוּ (Ex. xvi. 15); וְהָיְתָה (Is. xxviii. 4); וּבָתִּים (Deut. vi. 11); כָּל־הֶעָרִים (Josh. xxi. 38).

Exceptions are: (*a*) Forms like וַתֶּעְבֹּר (2 Ki. xiv. 9) and כִּי־אֶעֱשֶׂה (Jer. xix. 12). Comp. the failure of Munach with the same forms in Zaqeph's word, p. 81. (*β*) When R'bhia follows[7], e. g. וַיֹּאמְרוּ הָבָה ׀ נִבְנֶה־לָּנוּ עִיר (Gen. xi. 4) and וְהָיְתָה חֶבֶל הַיָּם (Zeph. ii. 6). Yet if Great T'lisha precedes, Azla takes the place of Métheg, even before R'bhia, comp. Lev. xiv. 51; Deut. vii. 13; xxv. 19; &c.[8]

PAZER appears under two forms,—the same in disjunctive value[9],—Great and Little Pazer, see p. 21.

Little Pazer, or Pazer (as it is simply called), is of frequent occurrence, indeed is indispensable for the proper division of the clauses governed by R'bhia, Pashta, &c. It may be repeated (as we have seen) as often as is judged necessary. Once, 1 Chr. xv. 18, it occurs eight times in succession.

---

[5] Not of heavy Métheg. Hence כָּל־הַמַּחֲלָה (Ex. xv. 26). Comp. p. 80, note 16. These fine distinctions have not been noticed by accentuologists. The instances in our texts in which Azla is omitted, or falsely introduced, are hardly worth recording.

[6] The Mas. fin. 33ª names four passages,—Josh. viii. 25; 1 Ki. xii. 24; 1 Chr. xv. 18; xxviii. 11,—in which Azla stands for Métheg, *although Little T'lisha precedes*. (Great T'lisha might have stood, and then all would have been regular.)

[7] See Mas. to 1 Sam. xi. 9 and Zeph. ii. 6.

[8] Little T'lisha has always Azla after it, and as the melody of the two T'lishas must have been similar, it is not surprising to find the same tendency on the part of Great T'lisha.

[9] حكمهم واحد فى القطع (Ox. 2512). Great Pazer had no doubt a fuller and stronger *melody*, הרעמתו גדולה (De R. 1262).

It will be found that Pazer alone, or the last of a series, has generally in musical sequence Great or Little T'lisha after it. Most of the examples to the contrary have been already given in chaps. X and XI, to which are to be added Ex. xxxiv. 4; Jer. xxxviii. 12; Esth. vi. 13; and the instances in which L'garmeh takes the place of Great T'lisha (p. 118), Gen. xxviii. 9; 1 Sam. xiv. 3, 47; 2 Sam. xiii. 32; 2 Ki. xviii. 17; Jer. xl. 11; and Ezek. ix. 2. Sometimes we can correct our texts, as שְׁתֵּי (Josh. iv. 8); בְּנֵי (xxii. 9, 31); שְׁנֵי (Judg. vii. 25).

Little Pazer may stand alone, or may have from one to six servi, all of which will be Munachs[10]. One, two, and three servi are very common, four less so, and five or six quite rare[11]. Examples may be seen in Gen. i. 21; xxi. 14; xxxvi. 6; Num. iii. 4; &c.

Great Pazer, or Qarne Phara (as it is commonly called), occurs only sixteen times[12], and in every instance Little Pazer might be substituted for it. The object of its introduction seems to have been to draw attention to something which seemed to the accentuators *noteworthy* in the verse in which it occurs[13]. Thus in Num. xxxv. 5 to the *measurement* laid down (which has indeed perplexed commentators to the present day); in 2 Sam. iv. 2 to the *defective reading* (בֹּשֶׁת־אִישׁ לְ has fallen out); in Jer. xiii. 13 to the remarkable explanation of the *symbol*, verse 12 (comp. the similar example in Neh. v. 13); &c. All mere trifling! nor need we be surprised if we cannot, in some instances, trace the fancy which led to the employment of this peculiar sign. Some punctators dispensed with it altogether[14]. Unlike Little Pazer, it does not admit of repetition.

Great Pazer never stands *alone*, but is always preceded by at least two servi, the first of which is Munach, and the second Galgal. It may have as many as six servi, all of which, except the last, will be Munachs[15].

---

[10] Once the servus occurs in the *same word* with Pazer, אַלָּא (Gen. l. 17). Texts have it falsely in וְהַפִּהֲלִים (Neh. xii. 41).

[11] *Five* servi I have noticed only in 1 Ki. vi. 1, and *six* only in Jer. xxxv. 15.

[12] Fixed by the Mas. to Ezek. xlviii. 21, viz. Num. xxxv. 5; Josh. xix. 51; 2 Sam. iv. 2; 2 Ki. x. 5; Jer. xiii. 13; xxxviii. 25; Ezek. xlviii. 21; Esth. vii. 9; Ezra vi. 9; Neh. i. 6; v. 13; xiii. 5, 15; 1 Chr. xxviii. 1; 2 Chr. xxiv. 5; xxxv. 7. Eight times before R'bhîa, and eight times before Pashṭa and its sister-accents. (On the number *eight* in connection with these accents and Pazer, see p. 97.)

[13] Comp. Man. du Lect., p. 92 above: טעם אלו הפזרים הגדולים אמרו לפי שיש, i.e. בפסוקים אלה חוזק ביותר ונגבהין יותר מדאי, לכך נעשו פזרים גדולים. 'because there is in these verses a greater weight, and they are to be made more than usually prominent, for this reason Great Pazers were appointed.'

[14] So the Codex known as Sinai: ולא נקד קרני פרה בכל הסיני (Ginsb. Mas. ח, § 665).

[15] It has *five* servi in Josh. xix. 51; 1 Chr. xxviii. 1; and *six* in Ezek. xlviii. 21; Ezra vi. 9; (see Man. du Lect., p. 91.) The Mas. to Ezek. l. c. has a notice that it has twice *seven* servi. For the correction, see Baer's note on the passage.

GREAT T'LÎSHA, like Géresh and Pazer, marks the division in clauses governed by R'bhîa, Pashṭa, &c. It cannot be repeated[16]; nor can Great and Little T'lîsha come together without a disjunctive between[17].

Great T'lîsha may stand alone, or may have from one to five servi, all of which will be Munachs. One or two servi are very common, three less so, and four or five quite rare[18].

N. B. Great and Little T'lîsha, as being similar in melody, are constantly interchanged in Codd., particularly where the former is subordinated to Géresh or the servus that takes the place of Géresh, p. 116 ff. In such cases the one or the other may stand, e. g. וְיֹּאכַל or וְיֹּאכַל (Lev. vii. 18); וַיִּשְׁלַח or וַיִּשְׁלַח (2 Sam. v. 11); יְהוּא or יְהוּא (2 Ki. x. 25); שָׂמְתָּ or שָׂמְתָּ (Jer. xxxii. 20); וַיֵּצֵא or וַיֵּצֵא (xli. 6); &c. Of a different class are the mistakes in our texts[19]: אֶרֶץ (Gen. xxiii. 15); נֵזֶר (Lev. xxi. 12); יִשְׂאוּ (Josh. vi. 4); וְאֶת־עַבְדֵיכֶם (1 Sam. viii. 16); לְבָרֵךְ (1 Ki. i. 47); וַיַּשְׁכֵּם (2 Ki. vi. 15); בַּלָּאֶרֶן (2 Ki. xx. 12; Is. xxxix. 1); כָּל־הַדָּבָר (Jer. xlii. 4); מִלְחַמְתָּם (Ezek. xxxii. 27); גִּדְבְרִיָּא (Dan. iii. 3); קַרְנָא (iii. 7); פְּסַנְתֵּרִין (iii. 15); הַבָּאִים (Ezra viii. 35); סַמִּים (2 Chr. xiii. 11)[20]; with the particles also, אֲשֶׁר, כִּי, לֹא (Ex. ix. 24; 1 Sam. ii. 24; Jer. xxix. 10; Ezek. iii. 5);—all contrary to the rules for the consecution of the servi, or for the logical (syntactical) division of the clause. Doubtless, it is the frequent interchange of these two accents,

---

[16] As in ordinary texts falsely, Deut. v. 14.

[17] One example occurs, 2 Sam. xiv. 32, which is doubtless to be corrected, although supported by the testimony of Codd. and of grammarians like Ben-Bil. 9ᵃ, and his copyists, Chayyug, p. 129, and Man. du Lect., p. 82. It is a mistake, like the two Zarqas (1 Sam. ii. 15), also defended by Ben-Bil., and like S'gôlta (Ezra vii. 13), which has the support of all Codd. without exception, and yet which so conservative an editor as Baer has found it necessary to reject. The simplest correction is found in Ox. 8, Erf. 3, Bomb. 1, וְאִשְׁלְחָה אֹתָךְ אֶל־הַמֶּלֶךְ לֵאמֹר, whereby the Little T'lîsha is cancelled.

Ben-Bil. (Mishp. hat. 35ᵇ) lays down a strange rule, which Baer has adopted in his note to Gen. vii. 7, that Great T'lîsha is not allowed after Zaqeph, unless the latter has Pashṭa preceding. Such a rule, if it existed, would admit of no conceivable explanation. But it *does not exist,* see Ex. x. 14; Deut. xii. 8; 1 Ki. xvii. 20; xxii. 14; Ruth iv. 14.

[18] *Four* I have noticed only in Judg. xviii. 7; 2 Sam. viii. 10; Neh. iv. 1; vi. 1; and *five* only in Jer. xli. 1; Ezek. xlvii. 12.

[19] All of which admit of correction by the help of Codd.

[20] Correct here also וּבָעֶרֶב with Maqqeph. Texts have R'bhia!

and the loose way in which Little T'lîsha is often subordinated to Géresh, where Great T'lîsha might have stood [21], that has led to the mistaken notion that Little T'lîsha has sometimes a *disjunctive* value. Comp. p. 26, 5 [22].

The three accents we have just considered mark the *last* musical and interpunctional divisions. The consequence is that the dichotomy generally fails in their clauses, the utmost that is done to mark it being the occasional introduction of the slight pause made by Paseq : קַח מַטְּךָ וּנְטֵה־יָדְךָ עַל־מֵימֵי מִצְרַיִם (Deut. xxxi. 17); וְאָם־ (Ex. vii. 19); וְחָרָה אַפִּי בוֹ בַיּוֹם־הַהוּא וַיְדַבֵּר אַחְאָב אֶל־נָבוֹת ׀ (Mal. i. 6); אָב אָנִי אַיֵּה כְבוֹדִי אִם־יַעַבְרוּ בְנֵי־גָד (1 Ki. xxi. 2); לֵאמֹר ׀ תְּנָה־לִּי אֶת־כַּרְמְךָ וַתִּשָּׂא אֹתִי רוּחַ ׀ בֵּין־ (Num. xxxii. 29); וּבְנֵי־רְאוּבֵן ׀ אֶתְכֶם הָאָרֶץ וּבֵין־הַשָּׁמַיִם (Ezek. viii. 3).

This is particularly the case with Pazer and Great T'lîsha; but with Géresh, the established musical sequence, of which we had so many examples in the chapters treating of R'bhîa, Pashṭa, &c., has been utilized, so as to make Pazer and Great T'lîsha serve as dividers of its clause,—Great T'lîsha on the first or second word, Pazer on the third word or further [23],—e. g. וַיְמַן יְהוָֹה־אֱלֹהִים קִיקָיוֹן וַיַּעַל ׀ מֵעַל לְיוֹנָה (Jon. iv. 6; instead of וַיִּזְבְּחוּ בַיּוֹם הַהוּא זְבָחִים גְּדוֹלִים; (וַיְמַן יְהוָֹה־אֱלֹהִים קִיקָיוֹן) וְאָמַרְתָּ לֶהָרִים (Neh. xii. 43; instead of בַּיּוֹם הַהוּא); וַיִּשְׂמָחוּ וְלַגְּבָעוֹת לָאֲפִיקִים וְלַגֵּאָיוֹת כֹּה־אָמַר ׀ אֲדֹנָי יְהוִה (Ezek. xxxvi. 6; instead of וְאָמַרְתָּ לֶהָרִים וְלַגְּבָעוֹת); וַתִּסְתִּירֵהוּ יְהוֹשַׁבְעַת בַּת־הַמֶּלֶךְ יְהוֹרָם אֵשֶׁת ׀ יְהוֹיָדָע הַכֹּהֵן וגו' (2 Chr.

---

[21] See, for instance, Gen. i. 25; Judg. x. 6; 2 Sam. xv. 2; 2 Ki. xxiv. 2; Is. xxvii. 1; Jer. iii. 1; viii. 1; Ezek. ix. 6; xliv. 5; Mal. i. 6.

[22] The Mas. to 1 Sam. xii. 3 numbers eight passages, in which Little T'lîsha is followed by Paseq,—a proof, if any were needed, that it cannot really serve as a disjunctive.

[23] Pazer rarely comes on the *second* word, as in Ex. xxxiv. 4 (comp. p. 113, note 9).

xxii. 11; Pazers instead of Munachs). Comp. Gen. xvii. 8;
Num. iii. 38; xix. 13; 1 Sam. xvii. 39; 2 Sam. ix. 10; xx. 3;
1 Ki. ii. 33[b]; viii. 20[b]; Jer. xxxv. 15; Qoh. vi. 2 [24].

The distinctness and emphasis, which it might be required to
note, were thus secured for Géresh's clause; although it must
be allowed that the division fails at times where we should
have expected to find it [25].

Writers on the accents have found here a confusion, which has
much perplexed them. For, in the division of clauses governed by
R'bhîa, Pashṭa, &c., Pazer constantly marks the main dichotomy, with
Great T'lîsha following for the first, and Géresh for the second of the
minor dichotomies (Géresh therefore marking the *smallest* of the dichotomies); whereas here, in the same clauses, *Géresh marks the main
dichotomy*, and has Pazer and Great T'lîsha subordinated to it. The
explanation (as it seems to me) is that the *musical pause* in the case
of these several minor disjunctives was so *slight*, that they readily lent
themselves to this variation in their (relative) interpunctional value [26].
Something similar occurs in our own system of interpunction. The
logical pause with the *comma* is always slight; and sometimes one
comma is subordinated to another, sometimes to a colon, semicolon,
&c., farther on in the clause.

This subordination was carried out still further. Géresh (as we
have seen) does not always maintain its position. When due on
the first word before Pashṭa, T'bhîr, or Zarqa, it is almost invariably transformed to a servus (p. 100). What is observable is
that Great T'lîsha and Pazer are often found *subordinated to
this servus* (which stands for Géresh), just as if Géresh itself were

---

[24] Sometimes, when there are only *two* words in Géresh's clause, the first is, for
the sake of emphasis or distinctness, pointed with Great T'lîsha, as in Gen. vi. 19;
Ex. xxx. 31 (corrected p. 60); 1 Ki. xiii. 33; 2 Chr. iii. 2.

[25] A corresponding division in Great T'lîsha's clause, with Pazer to mark the
dichotomy, is very rare. I have noted only the following instances: Gen. viii. 22;
Lev. xx. 17; 1 Ki. vi. 1 (point מְצֻקִּ֫ים with Codd.); Esth. iii. 13; Ezra iii. 9;
2 Chr. xxxi. 2.

[26] Of course the accentuators might have adopted another course. They might
have introduced new musical notes or phrases, with corresponding signs; but this
would have complicated the system, without any appreciable advantage. Practically little or no inconvenience or confusion has resulted from the simpler course,
which they preferred to adopt, although theoretically it must be pronounced
irregular.

present [27], e. g. סוּרוּ נָא אֶל־בֵּית עַבְדְּכֶם וְלִינוּ (Gen. xix. 2);

וְשַׂמְתִּי מָקוֹם לְעַמִּי לְיִשְׂרָאֵל וּנְטַעְתִּיו (2 Sam. vii. 10; I Chr.

xvii. 9); וַתָּשֹׁבְנָה הֶעָרִים אֲשֶׁר לָקְחוּ־פְלִשְׁתִּים מֵאֵת יִשְׂרָאֵל (I Sam. vii. 14); וַיִּבָּדֵל אַהֲרֹן לְהַקְדִּישׁוֹ קֹדֶשׁ קָדָשִׁים לְיִשְׂרָאֵל

הוּא־וּבָנָיו (I Chr. xxiii. 13). Comp. for T'bhîr's clause, Ex. xxviii. 30[b]; Lev. i. 11; Deut. vi. 22; Josh. xi. 7;—and for Zarqa's, Judg. vii. 20; 2 Sam. iv. 8; Neh. viii. 17.

EXCEPTIONS.—Instead of Great T'lîsha, L'garmeh is occasionally employed to mark the division in Géresh's clause. The Mas. to Jer. iv. 19 notes eleven passages, in which this accent is subordinated to (משרת)[28] Géresh, at the second word from it, viz. Gen. xxviii. 9; I Sam. xiv. 3, 47; 2 Sam. xiii. 32; 2 Ki. xviii. 17; Jer. iv. 19; xxxviii. 11; xl. 11; Ezek. ix. 2; Hag. ii. 12; and 2 Chr. xxvi. 15. Once, Is. xxxvi. 2, it is subordinated to Géresh transformed. The accentuators must have designed by this exceptional accentuation to signalize these passages as deserving of special notice or special emphasis. The reader may be left to trace for himself these Massoretic fancies, which (it so happens) are for the most part sufficiently obvious. The most notable instance is 2 Ki. xviii. 17 [29], on which see notes at end.

---

[27] Comp. in the poetical system (טעמי אמ״ת, p. 61) L'garmeh and Pazer subordinated to the servus that stands for D'chî.

[28] The expression is hardly correct (although the term ܡܫܪܛ is similarly used in Syriac, comp. Bar-Zu'bî, ed. Martin, p. 4). Ox. 2322 and Jequthiel to Gen. xxviii. 9 have סמוך instead.

[29] Where our texts have falsely Little T'lîsha with Paseq, for L'garmeh.

CHAPTER XIII.

L'GARMEH [1].

I. L'GARMEH's proper place is in R'bhîa's clause [2].

1. It marks the dichotomy there, and admits of repetition, as we saw in the chapter on R'bhîa, §§ II, III, IV.

2. It stands in the place of Paseq, when this latter sign is due before R'bhîa [3]. Thus לֹא ' וַיֹּאמֶר (Gen. xviii. 15); ' מִיָּמִים יָמִימָה ' הַבְּכֹר ' נָדָב (1 Sam. ii. 19); אָבִי ' אָבִי (2 Ki. xiii. 14); (Num. iii. 2) are all instances of *Paseq;* but the corresponding examples, לֹא ' וַיֹּאמֶר (Josh. v. 14); יָמִימָה ' מִיָּמִים (Judg. xi. 40); אָבִי ' אָבִי (2 Ki. ii. 12); and אַמְנֹן ' הַבְּכוֹר (1 Chr. iii. 1), all *L'garmehs* [4].

The object of the change was simply musical. The rules for Paseq will shew that it could only have stood when R'bhîa's clause consists of *two* words, or has *Géresh on the second word.* But here L'garmeh was musically admissible, and was preferred to the simpler melody of Munach-Paseq.

For us indeed the change made has no meaning. For we cannot appreciate the musical distinction, and even the *signs* are, in the Palestinian system, by some strange oversight, *the same* (see p. 22).

---

[1] To prevent mistakes in the chanting, some punctators marked in the margin of their texts לג, against the instances in which L'garmeh is due (so Ox. 15, 70, 71; Add. 21161; De R. 2; &c.); and Ginsburg has thought it worth while to fill up page after page of his great work with these marginal notes. But they are *no Massora!* And what is one to say to them, when they are not even correctly given?!

[2] Comp. Ben-Bil. (Mishp. hat. 7ᵇ): כל לגרמי' שבמקרא באים לפני רביע, לבד במקומות מעוטים.

[3] The Massora and grammarians allow but one exception in favour of Paseq: כְּה־אָמַר הָאֵל ' יְהוָֹה (Is. xlii. 5). So Ox. 4 in the Mas. marg. to this passage, לית פסק, סמוך לרביע, i. e. 'the only instance of Paseq immediately followed by R'bhîa,' and so Ben-Bil. l. c. The fancy seems to have been to make this passage agree with Ps. lxxxv. 9, where Paseq with the same words must stand.

[4] A list of these L'garmehs will be found after the Paseq-list, p. 129.

II. The following are the only examples in which L'garmeh occurs, without R'bhîa following :

Before Pashṭa, Lev. x. 6; xxi. 10; Ruth i. 2 ;[5] and before Géresh (or Géresh transformed), the passages cited p. 118 [6]. In these few anomalous cases, it comes where Great T'lîsha might have stood. The grounds for the change have been indicated, l. c.

SERVI OF L'GARMEH.

L'garmeh may stand alone, or may have one or two servi.

One servus is Mer'kha, מִצְרַיִם הִנֵּה ׀ (Ex. xiv. 10).

Two servi. The first is Azla and the second Mer'kha[7] : חָסֵר וְאֵינֶנּוּ ׀ לְנַפְשׁוֹ (Qoh. vi. 2); שָׁנָה עֶשְׂרֵה וּשְׁבַע ׀ (1 Ki. xiv. 21; 2 Chr. xii. 13). These are, I believe, the only instances [8]. So there are only two passages in the three Books in which L'garmeh has *two* servi (טעמי אמ״ת, p. 94).

CHAPTER XIV.

PASEQ.

WE come to the *final* touch, applied to the system we have been so long considering. After the verse had been arranged musically, according to the rules above laid down, two or more words might be left joined by the accents, which it might nevertheless seem desirable, for the sake of effect in the reading, to separate by a slight pause. The sign Paseq—a short perpendicular line, like a bar—was placed between the words for that purpose. The meaning of the term פָּסֵק, 'cutting off,' =

---

[5] See Mas. parva to Lev. xxi. 10, and Mishp. hat. 34[b].

[6] Ben-Bil. indeed (Mishp. hat. 34[a]) makes L'garmeh come before Pazer, citing as examples Dan. iii. 2 and Neh. viii. 7. But these are instances of Paseq. (Yet Heidenheim does not correct this manifest error.)

[7] So the Massora requires, see Norzi on 2 Chr. xii. 13 and Ginsb. ם, § 230. The authorities quoted by Baer (in his note on Qoh. vi. 2) for *two Mer'khas* must therefore be rejected.

[8] The two other passages, cited in Mishp. hat. 23[b]—1 Sam. xxvii. 1 and Ezek. viii. 6—are in most Codd. pointed as in printed texts.

'separating,' indicates its function. This sign had no proper musical value, and was therefore not numbered among the accents.

There is only one exception to the general meaning of the sign, and that is when it is associated with Munach, to constitute the independent musical accent, known as L'garmeh. The inventive faculty of the accentuators was certainly here at fault.

In the case of Shalshéleth, Paseq is apparently joined to a *disjunctive* accent. In reality it has been introduced in imitation of the Great Shalshéleth of the three Books, where it has its proper meaning. Unnecessary it is, and fails in many Codd. See p. 18 above [1].

This sign was subject to certain general rules in its application ; but before proceeding to investigate these rules, we must ascertain *where it is really due* in the text.

Modern writers on the accents have been quite content to take the printed text as a guide, without being aware how incorrect it is. I have noted more than *sixty* instances in which Paseq fails in Van der Hooght's edition, to say nothing of the passages in which it is falsely introduced.—The printed lists are our only other authority for the Paseqs, but they too are not to be trusted. That given in Bomb. 2 (*Massora finalis*, letter פ) and copied in Buxtorf's Rabbinical Bible (ditto, pp. 60, 61) is disfigured by a mass of L'garmehs, has many omissions, and often marks Paseq falsely in the passages cited. Ginsburg's list, I. p. 647 ff., is equally faulty, frequently offending against the Massora itself and the readings of all respectable Codd. Baer's lists, as far as they go, are of course far more correct, but even they are not altogether reliable.

I was thus driven to draw up a list for myself, and succeeded, after some trouble, in bringing together the necessary materials. Several Codd. exist, which enumerate the Paseqs for the whole of the text, quoting the passages in which they occur [2]. Others do the same for particular Books [3]. Whilst a third class have the Paseqs marked in the margin by the abbreviation פס or פ [4]. By the comparison

---

[1] It is surprising to find Prof. Graetz, in an article on Paseq (in his Monatschrift for Sept. 1882, pp. 394–5), placing it after Pashta and T'bhír ! Other extraordinary mistakes are found in the same article.

[2] They are the Aleppo Cod. (see Preface, p. x) ; the St. Petersburg Cod. B 19ᵃ (dated A.D. 1009) ; Add. 15251 ; and Modena xxvi. By far the most correct of these is the St. Petersburg list, for a copy of which I am indebted to Dr. Harkavy.

[3] As Add. 21161, Ar. Or. 16, Or. 2628 ; Ox. 2438 ; De R. 196 ; and Simson's חבור הקונים.

[4] Add. 21161 ; Ox. 15, 70, 71 ; K. 154 ; and De R. 2. Cod. Bab. is also to some extent useful.

of these several sources, I have been able to compile what I believe
to be a correct list of the Paseqs, according to the Massora and the
ideas of the old punctators. It will be found at the end of the present
chapter, and will, of course, be adopted for the rules that follow.

I divide the Paseqs into two classes, the ordinary Paseq,
which may precede *any* disjunctive accent, and separates *two*
words that are kept together by the accents; and the extraordinary Paseq (*Paseq dichotomicum*), which is *confined to certain
accents* (named below), and appears where *three* or *more* words are
conjoined [5].

I. The ordinary Paseqs may be subdivided into

1. *Paseq distinctivum*, which comes between two words, that
are to be distinguished as to *sense*, e. g. וַיֹּאמְרוּ ׀ לֹא (Gen. xviii.
15) [6], in contrast to וַיֹּאמֶר לוֹ;—עָשׂוּ ׀ כָּלָה (xviii. 21), כָּלָה
not to be made (as the ordinary construction would make it)
accusative;—הָצוֹר ׀ חֲדַתָּה (Josh. xv. 25), to be treated as two
distinct names, like הָצוֹר ׀ רָמָה (Neh. xi. 33), and the instances in Josh. xv. 55; xix. 7; Ezek. xlvii. 16.

This Paseq is further found in a few cases of *specification*, where
attention is to be drawn to details, as נָטָף ׀ וּשְׁחֵלֶת (Ex. xxx. 34)
and אֲרָיוֹת ׀ בָּקָר (1 Ki. vii. 29) [7]. It is necessary in Neh. ii. 13 and
1 Chr. xxvii. 12 to insure correctness of reading; and in וַיִּשֶּׂם ׀ פָּנָיו
(Dan. xi. 17, 18) it seems meant as a *nota bene* to the reader to
distinguish these instances from וַיָּשֶׁב פָּנָיו (ver. 19).

2. *Paseq emphaticum*, e. g. יְהוָה ׀ יִמְלֹךְ (Ex. xv. 18); יְהוָה ׀

---

[5] We have here a proof that Paseq was the *latest* of the signs, for its
presence depends on the other (accentual) signs having been fixed. I mention
this, because some scholars (as Graetz) have supposed that its use preceded that
of the accents.

[6] Cf. Judg. xii. 5; 1 Sam. ii. 16 (Q'rî); 1 Ki. ii. 30; xi. 22. Yet וַיֹּאמְרוּ לֹא
(Gen. xix. 2; 1 Sam. viii. 19) is not so distinguished from וַיֹּאמְרוּ לוֹ (Judg.
xviii. 19; Esth. vi. 13).

[7] The other examples are Josh. viii. 33; Ezra vii. 17; Neh. xii. 44; and the
names in 1 Chr. i. 24; viii. 38 (ix. 44); and xv. 18. This Paseq, once introduced,
might evidently have been multiplied to any extent, but seems to have been
intended only in the few instances given.

אֶחָד ' חֵרַפְתָּ (Deut. vi. 4); יָמוּת ' הֲיוֹנָתָן ' הַיוֹנָתָן (1 Sam. xiv. 45); אֲדֹנָי ' (Is. xxxvii. 24); תֹּאכֵלוּ ' עַל־הַדָּם (Ezek. xxxiii. 25); יָמֵינוּ ' כַּצֵּל (1 Chr. xxix. 15).

The examples under this head are sufficiently numerous, indeed so much so, that we may regard this emphatic use as the chief object of the ordinary Paseq.

In a few cases this Paseq is introduced—to insure emphatic pronunciation—between the Divine names. The most notable instance of the kind occurs in Josh. xxii. 22; but this belongs under II. 2. The other examples are יְהוָה ' הָאָדֹן (Ex. xxiii. 17; xxxiv. 23); הָאֱלֹהִים ' יְהוָה (2 Chr. xxx. 19). הָאֵל ' יְהוָה (Is. xlii. 5);

3. *Paseq homonymicum.* Where a word is *repeated*, in the same or a similar form, Paseq not unfrequently appears between. (This use of Paseq is closely related to that last given.) E. g. אַבְרָהָם ' אַבְרָהָם (Gen. xxii. 11); אָמֵן ' אָמֵן (Num. v. 22); יִמּוֹל ' הִמּוֹל (Gen. xvii. 13); תְּשַׁקְּצֶנּוּ ' שַׁקֵּץ (Deut. vii. 26); יִשְׁמָע ' הַשֹּׁמֵעַ (Ezek. iii. 27); יִמְצָאֶנּוּ מִי עָמֹק ' עָמֹק (Qoh. vii. 24).

We must not, however, suppose that we have here to do with a *rule*. The accentuators found a certain emphasis in the expressions quoted, which they marked with Paseq, but in the majority of similar instances they omitted the sign. A particular emphasis is no doubt lacking in most cases[8], yet they might have introduced it, on their own principle, in many other passages, as גָּאָה גָּאֹה ' כִּי (Ex. xv. 1);

---

[8] Thus, we could understand the failure of Paseq, in the case of numerals, שִׁבְעָה שִׁבְעָה (Gen. vii. 2); שְׁנַיִם שְׁנַיִם (vii. 9), &c.,—of distributives generally, as אִישׁ אִישׁ (Lev. xvii. 3); עֵדֶר עֵדֶר (Gen. xxxii. 17); גּוֹי גּוֹי (2 Ki. xvii. 29); בַּבֹּקֶר בַּבֹּקֶר (Ex. xvi. 21), &c.,—and of current expressions like מְאֹד מְאֹד (Gen. vii. 19); פָּנִים אֶל־פָּנִים (Gen. xxxii. 31), עַיִן בְּעַיִן (Deut. xix. 21); מְעַט מְעַט (Ex. xxiii. 30); &c. But instances like these account only very partially for the omission of the sign. For instance, it rarely comes between the inf. abs. and the finite verb, מוֹת תָּמוּת, &c.; although the very object of this construction is to give strength and emphasis to the expression. Sometimes perhaps we may account for its absence, by supposing that the words were meant to be pronounced with animation and rapidity, as סוּרוּ סוּרוּ (Is. li 11); סֹלּוּ־סֹלּוּ (lvii. 14).

שַׁבַּת שַׁבָּתוֹן (xxxi. 15); רָזִי־לִי רָזִי־לִי (Is. xxiv. 16); הַמּוֹנִים הַמּוֹנִים (Joel iv. 14); &c. They have been very particular in placing it (twenty-six times) wherever סָבִיב ׀ סָבִיב occurs in Ezekiel (viii. 10; xxxvii. 2; xl. 5; &c.), so that more than one third of the examples they give consists of these instances. On the other hand they intentionally omitted it in מֹשֶׁה מֹשֶׁה (Ex. iii. 4), and the Midrash gives the reason: 'With Moses the prophetic gift *never ceased*' (לֹא פָסֵק)[9]!

4. *Paseq euphonicum* is introduced, in a few cases, for the sake of distinct pronunciation, *when one word ends and the next begins with the same letter:* גַּן ׀ נָעוּל (Cant. iv. 12); אֲנָשִׁים ׀ מְעַט (Neh. ii. 12); בַּרְזֶל ׀ לָרֹב (1 Chr. xxii. 3); and once with cognate letters, נָחָשׁ ׀ שָׂרָף (Deut. viii. 15)[10].

The other instances are Judg. i. 7; 1 Chr. ii. 25; xxii. 5; xxix. 11; 2 Chr. xx. 1; xxxiv. 12. But this small number of examples shews that *the failure of Paseq is the rule*[11], as in בַּשָּׁמַיִם מִמַּעַל (Deut. iv. 39; Josh. ii. 11); עֵשֶׂב בְּשָׂדֶךָ (Deut. xi. 15); שָׁמַע עַבְדְּךָ (1 Sam. xxiii. 11); לֹא־תֹאכַל לֶחֶם (1 Ki. xiii. 17); &c. The student may find for himself as many examples as he pleases.

N.B. כִּי ׀ יָרֵא (Gen. xviii. 15) does not come under this head, for כִּי is constantly followed by Yôd, e.g. כִּי יָרֵא (xix. 30); nor יְהֹוָה הֵלִילוּ ׀ וְזַעֲקוּ (Jer. יְהֹוָה ׀ יִמְלֹךְ (Ex. xv. 18); (אֲדֹנָי) ׀ יָרֵא (xxii. 14); xlviii. 20). These are all instances of *Paseq emphaticum*.

II. The extraordinary Paseq—or *Paseq dichotomicum*, as it will be more convenient to call it—was due to the circumstance that the accentual system failed to provide the necessary signs for marking the dichotomy, in clauses governed by certain of the minor disjunctive accents. Paseq was then (occasionally) employed in place of the missing disjunctive sign. Thus—

---

[9] See Midrash rabba on Exodus, sect. 2, towards end (quoted by Levy, Neuhebr. W.B., s.v. פסק), or Norzi ad loc.

[10] In Berakhoth 15ᵇ below, the careful pronunciation of such words is insisted on; but no hint is given that Paseq sometimes comes between, to insure it.— This sign was, of course, unknown in the Talmudic time.

[11] The notion that the separation by Paseq takes place, when other letters, as two different labials, or (as Graetz supposes) Mem and Aleph (!), come together, is thus clearly shewn to have no foundation.—If the *same* letters are generally not separated by Paseq, a fortiori *dissimilar* ones would not be.

(1) On the *first* word before Pashṭa, T'bhîr, and Zarqa (see p. 100): וַיִּקְרָא אֱלֹהִים ׀ לָאוֹר (Gen. i. 5; comp. וַיִּקְרָא אֱלֹהִים לָרָקִיעַ, verse 8, with the dichotomy *marked* by T'bhîr); בְּהַדְף יְהוָֹה אֱלֹהֶיךָ אֹתָם ׀ (xviii. 15); וַתְּכַחֵשׁ שָׂרָה ׀ לֵאמֹר מִלְּפָנֶיךָ (Deut. ix. 4).

In a few instances, this Paseq represents a *minor* dichotomy as well: Josh. xix. 51; Judg. xx. 25; 1 Sam. xxiv. 11 (comp. xxvi. 23); Jer. li. 37; 1 Chr. xxi. 15.—In 2 Ki. xviii. 14 it occurs thrice.

(2) On *any word* before Géresh, Pazer, or Great T'lîsha, because these accents have regularly no subordinate disjunctive. For the same reason, Paseq is not unfrequently *repeated*. E. g. וַיְדַבֵּר אַחְאָב אֶל־נָבוֹת ׀ לֵאמֹר ׀ תְּנָה־לִּי אֶת־כַּרְמְךָ (1 Ki. xxi. 2); הֲתָבוֹא לְךָ שֶׁבַע־שָׁנִים ׀ רָעָב ׀ בְּאַרְצֶךָ (2 Sam. xxiv. 13); בְּהָנִיחַ יְהוָה אֱלֹהֶיךָ ׀ לְךָ (Deut. xxv. 19).

EXCEPTIONS.—Before the other disjunctive accents, Silluq, Athnach, Zaqeph, &c., there was no necessity for Paseq, as a subordinate disjunctive was always available to mark the dichotomy [12]. The only exception is in the case of S'gôlta, in the following passages: Gen. xxvi. 28; Ex. xxxv. 35; Deut. ix. 21; 1 Sam. xi. 7; Jer. xliv. 25; 1 Chr. xxi. 12. Here Paseq takes the place of *Zarqa*,—another proof to my mind of its late introduction, for its appearance is doubtless due to the false notion, which prevailed at least from Ben-Asher's time downwards, that S'gôlta is to be regarded as a kind of appendage to Zarqa (see p. 17). Like Zarqa therefore it might have Paseq before it.

In deciding whether the dichotomy should be marked or not, the accentuators were guided by the same general principles as in the use of the ordinary Paseq. (It is only under the first head that a necessary difference exists, and that an extension must be given to the meaning of the term used.) Thus we have:

1. *Paseq distinctivum*, marking details, indicating a slight logical pause, easing the reading of a long syntactical clause, &c. Comp. the examples given above, and Gen. i. 21 (Ezek. xlvii. 9);

---

[12] Comp. קָדוֹשׁ (Is. vi. 3) and עֲבָדַי (lxv. 13 *bis*).

Ex. xx. 4; 1 Sam. vii. 14; 1 Ki. xiii. 11; Jer. xxxv. 15; Ezek. xlv. 1; Ezra vi. 9; Neh. viii. 17, &c.[13]

It is particularly employed to separate the Divine Name (in any of its forms) from the word following. In such cases the Divine Name *directly precedes* one of the accents we are considering[14]. With any of the other disjunctive accents, it would in such a position be necessarily marked off by the dichotomy.—A half of the examples of *Paseq distinctivum* are of this class. Comp. Gen. i. 5, 10, 27; ii. 21, 22; iii. 14; &c.

2. *Paseq emphaticum*, in Deut. xvi. 16; 1 Sam. xii. 3; Jer. xii. 5; xlix. 37; Ezek. xiv. 21; xxxvi. 5; &c.

But care must be taken to note the context. Graetz has asked, Why has וַיִּתֵּן לָהֶם ׀ אֲבִיהֶם in 2 Chr. xxi. 3 Paseq, and in Job xlii. 15 no Paseq? Answer, Because of the marked contrast in the former passage between the first and second halves of the verse—a contrast which fails in the latter.

3. *Paseq homonymicum*, in the following (eight) instances: Num. xvii. 28; Josh. viii. 33; 2 Sam. xiv. 26; Jer. xv. 12; Ezek. xlvii. 12 and xlviii. 21 (not xlv. 7); 2 Chr. xxi. 19; xxx. 10.

4. *Paseq euphonicum*, in Ex. xx. 4 (second example); Num. xxxii. 33; Is. vi. 2; lxv. 13; Jer. li. 37 (*bis*); Hos. ix. 1; 2 Chr. xxxv. 18; &c.

5. *Paseq euphemisticum*. The object of this Paseq was to separate the Divine Name from a word, which it seemed unseemly to associate with it. We found no example of this Paseq between *two* words, and the only instances of it in our present division are: אֲשֶׁר בָּרָא אֱלֹהִים ׀ אָדָם (Deut. iv. 32); רוּחַ

---

[13] This Paseq is (as stated) used with more freedom than when only two words have to be taken into account. Thus it appears, at first sight, strange that וַיַּשְׁכֵּם אַבְרָהָם ׀ בַּבֹּקֶר (Gen. xxi. 14) should be marked with Paseq (Moses' rising, Ex. xxxiv. 4, is not so signalized). The explanation seems to be that just before, xix. 27, and just after, xxii. 3, this expression has the dichotomy, and so it is introduced here. In 2 Ki. xxv. 4, the pause made by the Paseq may indicate the missing verb, יִבְרְחוּ (Jer. lii. 7). In Gen. xxxvii. 22 and 2 Ki. iv. 13 the anomalous *servus* (p. 110, note 41) may intimate that some punctators dispensed with the Paseq, which certainly appears *de trop*.

[14] When it is the *second* word, e. g. Gen. i. 25; Deut. ix. 4; Is. viii. 7, Paseq almost always fails.

רָעָה ׀ אֱלֹהִים (1 Sam. xviii. 10; xix. 9) and שָׂטָן ׀ יְהוָה וַיָּקֶם
(1 Ki. xi. 14)[15]. This Paseq is more common in the three Books.

But, as in the case of the ordinary Paseq, the *failure* of the sign is
more conspicuous than its presence. It is constantly wanting where it
might have marked a necessary *distinction*, or *emphasis;* and where
two like words, or like letters coming together require it[16]. Writers
on the accents, from Ben-Asher to Ewald, have not troubled themselves at all about this strange lack of consistency in the use of Paseq,
although it stands in such marked contrast to the precision in the
employment of the accentual signs. This circumstance seems again to
point to a (comparatively) late introduction of the sign.—The same
want of system is seen in the three Books, comp. טעמי אמ״ת, p. 97.

LIST OF PASEQS[17].

(In making use of this list, the student must be careful to distinguish
the *L'garmehs* of the text, see pp. 119, 120.)

Gen. (29) i. 5, 10, 21, 27; ii. 21, 22; iii. 14; xii. 17; xiv. 15 (עֲלֵיהֶם ׀);
xvii. 13; xviii. 15 (*ter*, כִּי ׀ יִרְאֶה), 21; xxi. 14, 17; xxii. 11, 14;
xxvi. 28; xxx. 8, 20; xxxvii. 22; xxxix. 10; xlii. 13, 21, 22; xliii.
11; xlvi. 2 (*bis*).

Ex. (14) xiii. 18 (אֱלֹהִים ׀); xiv. 21; xv. 18; xvi. 5; xvii. 6, 15; xx.
4 (*bis*); xxiii. 17; xxx. 34; xxxiv. 6 (*bis*), 23; xxxv. 35.

Lev. (8) v. 12; x. 3, 6, 12; xi. 32, 35; xiii. 45; xxiii. 20.

Num. (22)[18] iii. 2, 38 (אֹהֶל־מוֹעֵד ׀); v. 22; vi. 20, 25, 26; ix. 10; xi.
25, 26 (*bis*); xv. 31; xvi. 7 (*bis*); xvii. 21, 28; xxi. 1; xxii. 20;
xxx. 13 (אֹתָם ׀); xxxii. 29, 33; xxxv. 16.

Deut. (22) iii. 20; iv. 32; v. 8 (*bis*, as in Ex. xx. 4); vi. 4, 22; vii.
1, 26 (*bis*); viii. 15; ix. 4, 21; xvi. 16; xvii. 8; xxii. 6; xxv. 19;
xxvii. 9; xxviii. 12, 20, 25, 68; xxix. 12 (הַיּוֹם ׀).

---

[15] Some punctators on this principle mark אַתָּה אֱלֹהִים ׀ נְשִׂיא (Gen. xxiii. 6).
So De R. 7, 266; Bomb. 1 and 2. See Norzi and Ginsb. iii. p. 54.

[16] So also after the Divine Name, as in Gen. iv. 15[b]; viii. 1[b]; xi. 8; Ex. xxxiii.
11; Is. liv. 17[b]; 1 Chr. xxviii. 4; &c. Sometimes individual punctators introduce
the Paseq in such instances.

[17] I have put in brackets the Paseqs (61) that fail in Van der Hooght's text.

The *totals* of the Paseqs for the several Books I have taken from the St. Pet.
Cod. Other lists supply the same partially. These numbers supply a useful
means of control, so that it is rarely necessary to take account of the variations
that occur in Codd.

[18] The lists give 22 as the total, but furnish only 21. I have no doubt that the
missing example is וַיָּמָת נָדָב וַאֲבִיהוּא ׀ לִפְנֵי יְהוָה (iii. 4). Paseq is found here in
many Codd., Ox. 19, 22, 23, 26, &c., also in Bomb. 1; and is marked in the
margin פס, in Erf. 1; De R. 2, 7.

Josh. (22) i. 15; ii. 19 (בֵיתֶךָ ׀); viii. 33 (*ter*); xi. 20; xiv. 10 (יְהֹוָה ׀ אוֹתִי); xv. 7, 25, 55; xix. 7 (עֵץ ׀), 11, 51 (*ter*); xxii. 22 (*quater*), 31 (הַיּוֹם ׀), 32; xxiv. 32.

Judg. (9) i. 7; ii. 18; xi. 17 (*bis*, אֱדוֹם ׀); xii. 5 (וַיֹּאמֶר ׀ לֹא); xviii. 2; xx. 25 (*bis*, לִקְרָאתָם ׀), 35.

1 Sam. (32)[19] i. 3 (מִיָּמִים ׀ יָמִימָה); ii. 16, 19; iii. 9 (לֵךְ ׀), 10; v. 9 (יַד־יְהֹוָה ׀); vii. 14; ix. 10, 16, 24 (הָעָם ׀); xi. 7; xii. 3; xiv. 3 (כֹּהֵן ׀ יְהֹוָה), 36 (פְלִשְׁתִּים ׀), 45 (הֲיוֹנָתָן ׀), 47; xvii. 40; xviii. 10 (*ter*); xix. 9; xx. 12, 21 (קָחֶנּוּ ׀); xxiv. 11 (*bis*); xxv. 14, 25, 31, 36; xxvi. 7, 23; xxviii. 12 (אֶל־שָׁאוּל ׀).

2 Sam. (11) ii. 1; iii. 12, 21; vii. 24; xiv. 26, 32; xx. 3; xxiv. 3, 13 (*bis*), 16.

1 Ki. (25)[19] i. 36, 45 (הַנָּבִיא ׀); ii. 30; vii. 24, 25 (*bis*, פָּנִים ׀ יָמָּה), 29, 35 (עָגֹל ׀); viii. 65; xi. 14, 22, 36; xii. 16 (*bis*, אֶת־הַמֶּלֶךְ ׀), 32 (*bis*); xiii. 4, 11; xviii. 12; xix. 7; xx. 25, 30; xxi. 2 (*bis*, לֵאמֹר ׀); xxii. 8.

2 Ki. (17) iii. 16; iv. 13, 19; vii. 1; x. 5, 6; xii. 22; xiii. 14; xviii. 14 (*ter*); xix. 4, 16, 23 (חֵרַפְתָּ ׀); xxiv. 2; xxv. 4, 17.

Is. (27)[20] iii. 7; iv. 5; v. 19; vi. 2 (עֹמְדִים ׀), 3; x. 14; xi. 11 (אֲדֹנָי ׀); xxi. 2 (*bis*); xxii. 13; xxiv. 3 (*bis*); xxv. 7; xxvi. 3; xxxi. 4; xxxvii. 4, 17, 24; xl. 28; xlii. 5; lvii. 19; lviii. 2 (יוֹם ׀ יוֹם)[21]; lxiii. 7; lxv. 13; lxvi. 19, 20 (*bis*).

Jer. (30) i. 13; iv. 1, 19[22]; vi. 11, 14; vii. 9; viii. 11; ix. 2; xi. 5; xii. 5; xv. 12; xvii. 25; xxi. 7; xxiii. 6; xxxi. 40; xxxii. 44; xxxiii. 16; xxxiv. 1; xxxv. 15 (*bis*); xli. 10; xliv. 25; xlviii. 20; xlix. 24 (וְרָמְטוּ ׀), 37; l. 14, 29; li. 2, 37 (*bis*, בָּבֶל ׀).

Ezek. (24)[23] iii. 27 (*bis*); vii. 11 (הֲחָמָס ׀); viii. 3; xiv. 21; xxi. 3; xxvi. 16; xxxiii. 25 (עַל־הַדָּם ׀); xxxiv. 8; xxxv. 12; xxxvi. 5; xxxix. 11; xli. 16; xlv. 1; xlvii. 9, 12 (*bis*), 16, 17; xlviii. 1 (חֶתְלֹן ׀), 21 (*ter*), 35. And, as the Massora adds, כל סָבִיב ׀ סָבִיב דכותהון.

Minor Prophets (8). Hos. ix. 1 (יִשְׂרָאֵל ׀), 4 (לַיהֹוָה ׀); Zeph. iii. 15; Hag. i. 12; ii. 4, 20; Zech. xi. 12; xiv. 2[24].

---

[19] The number fixed by the St. Pet. list for Samuel is 43; and for Kings, 42.

[20] By a *lapsus calami* on the part of the copyist, the St. Pet. Cod. gives the total as 13!

[21] This example fails in all lists, although fixed by the Mas. to Gen. xxxix. 10.

[22] The second מֵעַי ׀ is with Paseq; the first with L'garmeh, p. 118.

[23] There has been again a mistake on the part of the copyist of the St. Pet. Cod., for while he gives the total as 23, the list contains 24.

[24] Baer gives besides Zech. iii. 2; iv. 7, on the authority of the Mas. parva Erf. ms. But this Codex is elsewhere wrong, in fixing the Paseqs, e. g. in 1 Sam. viii. 19; 2 Ki. iii. 25. Some few texts indeed also give these examples in Zech., but they are not found in any list.

Five Megillôth. Cant. (**8**) i. 13, 14 ('הַכֹּפֶר); ii. 7, 13 ('וְהַגְּפָנִים); iii. 5, 11 ('צֹאנָה); iv. 12ᵃ; viii. 4;—Ruth iv. 11;—Lam. (**8**) i. 15, 16; ii. 1, 5, 6, 7 ('אֲדֹנָי), 8; v. 21;—Qoh. (**2**) i. 6; vii. 24;—Esth. (**14**) iii. 7; ix. 7–9, 27 (*bis*, 'הַיְּהוּדִים); x. 1 ('אֲחַשְׁרֵשׁ).

Dan. (**9**) iii. 2; iv. 20; v. 12 ('מְפַשַּׁר), 23; ix. 18, 19 (*bis*); xi. 17, 18 ('וְיָשֵׂם).

Ezra (**5**)²⁴ vi. 9 (*ter*, 'בְּיוֹם 'יוֹם); vii. 17 ('תּוֹרִין); x. 9.

Neh. (**12**) ii. 12, 13; viii. 6, 7 (*bis*), 9, 17 ('הַשְּׁבִי), 18; xi. 33 ('חָצוֹר); xii. 44 ('לָאוֹצָרוֹת); xiii. 15 (*bis*).

1 Chr. (**28**)²⁵ i. 24 ('שֵׁם); ii. 25; viii. 38; ix. 20, 44; xii. 18, 20, 40; xiii. 6; xv. 18; xvii. 22; xxi. 3 ('עַל־עַמּוֹ), 12 (*bis*), 15 (*bis*); xxii. 3, 5; xxiv. 6; xxvii. 1 (*bis*)²⁶, 12 ('לַבֵּן 'יָמִין); xxviii. 1 ('וּמִקְנֶה); xxix. 2, 11, 15 ('כַּצֵּל), 21, 23.

2 Chr. (**29**) i. 11 ('אֱלֹהִים); ii. 9; iv. 3, 4 (*bis*, 'פֹּנִים 'יָמָּה); x. 16; xii. 6, 7; xiii. 12; xvi. 8 ('לְחַיִל); xviii. 7; xix. 10; xx. 1, 8, 22; xxi. 3, 18, 19; xxiv. 11 ('לְיוֹם); xxvi. 17; xxx. 10, 19, 21; xxxiii. 14; xxxiv. 12; xxxv. 18, 21 (*bis*), 25.

I add a list of the L'garmehs, which take the place of Paseq before R'bhîa (p. 119)²⁷. The rules for their occurrence will be the same as those for the *ordinary* Paseq, given above²⁸.

Gen. iii. 15; xvii. 14; xxiii. 6; xxix. 9ᵇ; xlv. 5; Ex. xxx. 13; Num. vii. 13ᵇ, 19ᵇ, &c.; x. 29, 35ᵇ; xx. 21; Deut. i. 33ᵇ; v. 4, 22ᵇ; xxxii. 39; Josh. v. 14; ix. 12; Judg. xi. 40; xvi. 2; xviii. 7ᵇ; xx. 28²⁹, 31ᵇ; xxi. 19, 22²⁹; 1 Sam. ix. 9, 12ᵇ; xvi. 5, 7ᵇ; xx. 25; xxvi. 16ᵇ; 2 Sam. xii. 23; xv. 20, 30²⁹; 1 Ki. vi. 29; vii. 23ᵇ; xix. 4ᵇ; 2 Ki. ii. 12; v. 22; xvii. 36; xxv. 16; Is. ix. 16; xix. 16ᵇ; xxi. 8ᵇ; xxii. 2, 11; xlix. 21ᵇ; Jer. xx. 4; l. 34; lii. 20; Ezek. xxiv. 17; xxxv. 12; Zech. i. 8²⁹; vi. 15²⁹; xiv. 12ᵇ; Cant. iv. 14; viii. 14; Ruth i. 13; iii. 3, 13; Qoh. ix. 3; Dan. iv. 15ᵇ; Neh. ii. 12; 1 Chr. iii. 1ᵇ; xxviii. 10; 2 Chr. iv. 2ᵇ; xxi. 19.

---

²⁴ The number for Ezra and Neh. varies between 15 and 17. Some lists (as St. Pet., Aleppo, and Modena) reject the first example in Neh. viii. 7; and all omit xii. 44, although the Mas. to Lev. x. 12 requires it. Note what Ben-Asher says (Dikd. hat., p. 23), וּמִקְצָת הַסּוֹפְרִים הָרִאשׁוֹנִים קוֹרִים לָאוֹצָרוֹת לַתְּרוּמוֹת. And so the old Codd. Add. 21161 and Erf. 3 point.

²⁵ The number fixed in the St. Pet. list for Chronicles is 57.

²⁶ The lists omit the second Paseq of Van der Hooght's text.

²⁷ Perhaps some additional instances may be found, which I have overlooked. I have purposely omitted Josh. xv. 18 (comp. Judg. i. 14); Is. vii. 25 (although marked in Baer's text); Dan. xi. 6 (with various Codd.); and 2 Chr. xviii. 3 (do.).

²⁸ Attention may be drawn to Judg. xvi. 2; 1 Sam. xvi. 7; and 2 Chr. xxi. 19, where L'garmeh seems to indicate the defective grammatical construction, as Paseq in 2 Ki. xxv. 2.

²⁹ Many texts omit.

APPENDIX I.

(A.V. stands for Authorized Version; R.V. for Revised Version; and Prob. for *Probebibel*, the German revision of Luther's translation.)

Gen. xx. 13. וַיְהִי כַּאֲשֶׁר הִתְעוּ אֹתִי אֱלֹהִים מִבֵּית אָבִי וגו׳. The R'bhîa here—the greatest disjunctive in S'gôlta's clause—is due to the over-scrupulousness of the early accentuators, who shrank from associating the Sacred Name with a Verb signifying 'to cause to *err!*' What monstrous interpretations were the result may be seen in Targ. Onq. and Sopherim iv. 6 [1]. The proper accentuation is וַיְהִי כַּאֲשֶׁר־הִתְעוּ אֹתִי ׀ אֱלֹהִים מִבֵּית אָבִי, found, more or less correctly given, in various Codd. [2]

xxxv. 22. We have here a *double* accentuation,—the one with Silluq at יִשְׂרָאֵל., answering to the number of verses (154) in the Parasha and further indicated by פ (פתוחה) following,—the other with Athnach at ישראל, adopted by the Occidentals, that Reuben's abominable act might be slurred over in the chanting as rapidly as possible [3]. The Orientals kept to the single accentuation with *two* verses (see Baer's Five Megillôth, p. v, and Ginsb. Mas. i. p. 592), which must have been the original.

Ex. xx. 3–17 and Deut. v. 7–18. The Orientals and Occidentals differed also in the pointing of the Decalogue. The former had the single accentuation (known as טעם העליון) according to the command-ments [4]. This was no doubt the original, for the verses of the Parasha in each case are reckoned accordingly (72 and 118). On the other

---

[1] The Jerus. Talm. (Megilla 13ᵃ) and Jerus. Targ. try to get over the fancied difficulty by treating אֱלֹהִים as חֹל (*profanus*); but this explanation did not meet with acceptance, as the accents shew. Some commentators indeed adopted it and sought to accommodate it to the recognised accentuation, by taking אֱלֹהִים מִבֵּית אָבִי as 'the (false) gods of my father's house!' So Bekhor Shor, and the author of the old Commentary known as ג״י (quoted in פענח רזא *ad loc.*).

[2] Ox. 1, 5, 34, 2437; Add. 15250, Harl. 1528; Berl. 4; Leipz. 1.

[3] On the same ground the Mishna (Megilla 25ᵃ) directs: נקרא ולא מתרגם, 'to be read without Targum.'

[4] See Pinsker, Einleitung, p. 48 ff.

hand, the Palestinians introduced a second division (טעם התחתון), breaking up the longer verses (3–6, 8–11), and bringing together the shorter ones (13–16); with the view of easing and equalizing the reading [5].

xxv. 34 (xxxvii. 20). One of the five passages in the Tora, named in the Talmud (Yoma 52[a]) and Mas. to Deut. xxxi. 16, as אֵין לָהֶם [6] הַכְרֵעַ, 'about (the accentual division of) which no decision had been arrived at.' The question was whether מְשֻׁקָּדִים is to be taken with what precedes, or what follows (see Rashi). The LXX translate one way, the Targums another. The Massoretic text agrees with the latter.

xxxii. 1[b]. זֶה ׀ מֹשֶׁה הָאִישׁ. The traditional construction supposes a transposition, 'This man Moses.' See LXX, Vulg., Pesh.—Similarly הַמָּקוֹם comes after the nom. pr., Ezra viii. 17.

xxxiii. 19. וְקָרָאתִי בְשֵׁם יְהֹוָה. According to the accents, 'And I will proclaim Jehovah by name.' Comp. xxxiv. 6 and R. V. xxxiv. 5 marg.

Num. xxxvi. 5. כֵּן, with Zaqeph (although no Codex so); comp. xxvii. 7. כֵּן is made by the accents a particle, as in verse 10[b]: so the LXX οὕτως. In the same way כִּי, Is. iii. 24[b], is treated in most texts as a particle.

Deut. v. 19. קוֹל גָּדוֹל וְלֹא יָסָף, kept together by the accents, in accordance with the strange rendering found in the Talmud (Sota 10[b], Sanhedrin 17[a]), Targums, and Pesh., 'With a loud voice, that did not cease,' i.e. without intermission [7]. See Rashi.

xxvi. 5. אֲרַמִּי אֹבֵד אָבִי cannot be rendered, according to the accents, 'An Aramæan, ready to perish, was my father,' for that would require the Pashṭa at אֹבֵד; but must be taken to mean, with Targ., Midrash [8], Vulg., and Rashi, 'An Aramæan (Laban) sought to destroy my father.' Aben-Ezra, Rashbam, Qimchi, and modern scholars generally, reject the accentuation. Yet Heidenheim, in his commentary מודע לבינה, defends it, and Baer (in a letter to me) agrees!

---

[5] But this division seems not to have come into general use. At least, the public reading has long been according to the longer verses.

The terms עליון and תחתון have reference to the position of the accents,—the longer verses shewing a large proportion of accents placed *above* the words, whereas in the shorter verses the accents *below* the words greatly preponderate. Comp. the expressions טעמא מלעיל and מלרע in the Mas. to Gen. xxiii. 3.

[6] A technical phrase not understood by Hupfeld, Stud. u. Krit., 1837, p. 852, or Dillmann, Herzog's Encycl. ii. p. 392.

[7] יסף taken in the sense of אסף (Niphal). The same meaning was assigned to the word in Gen. xxxviii. 26 and Num. xi. 25.

[8] Siphre and לקח טוב.

xxxii. 5. שִׁחֵת לוֹ לֹא. Accents must remain, as both Targums,
LXX, and Pesh. shew. We must then translate, 'They corrupted
(injured) *Him* not.' Jerome, Aben-Ezra, and of course moderns,
rightly break loose from the accents.

Josh. iv. 3. הָכֵן שְׁתֵּים־עֶשְׂרֵה אֲבָנִים. Kept together by the accents.
The inf. constr. (fixed by Mas. *ad loc.*) must not be confounded—as
by Targ., Qim., R. V., &c.—with inf. abs. הָכֵן (iii. 17), and joined,
contrary to the accents, with the words preceding. Comp. Knobel
and Keil.

vi. 10^b. Accents support Driver's view, Heb. Tenses, p. 161, Obs.
Parallel is 2 Sam. x. 5^b (1 Chr. xix. 5).

Judg. vi. 24. Some Codd.—as Ox. 13, 2324; Harl. 5773; Erf.
2—and the Soncino ed., point וַיִּקְרָא־לוֹ יְהוָה שָׁלוֹם, and this is no
doubt correct[9]; except that, according to the Paseq rules, we ought to
have יְהוָה ׀ שָׁלוֹם, comp. Ex. xvii. 15; Ezek. xlviii. 35.

xii. 4^b. According to the accents (note the two Zaqephs) we must
render:

      'Fugitives of Ephraim are ye!
Gilead (his place) is in the midst of Ephraim, in the midst of Manasseh.'

Comp. Ewald, Gesch. ii. p. 455.

xiv. 15 end. The accentuation requires us to take הֲלֹא as הֲלֹם,
'hither.' So Targ. and Tanchum. If the punctators had regarded
הֲלֹא as interrogative, they must have pointed: הֲלֹא לָנוּ קְרָאתֶם הַיְרִשֵׁנוּ.
Some few Codd. (see De R. Var. Lect.) *read* הֲלֹם, but this is contrary
to the Mas. (Frensdorff, p. 251)[10].

xv. 19^b. עַל־כֵּן ׀ קָרָא שְׁמָהּ עֵין הַקּוֹרֵא אֲשֶׁר בַּלֶּחִי. A false accentuation, due to a false rendering,—to be traced in LXX, Vulg., and
Pesh.,—which takes לֶחִי here, as in the early part of the verse, in the
sense of 'jaw-bone.'

xvi. 28^b. וְאִנָּקְמָה נְקַם־אַחַת מִשְּׁתֵי עֵינַי מִפְּלִשְׁתִּים.—אַחַת is made by
the accents emphatic; Samson asks for vengeance for *one* of his eyes.
The reward for the other was to be in the world to come! This
explanation—although not accepted by Targ., LXX, Vulg., and many
modern scholars—is found in Talmud[11], Midrash[11], Rashi, Qim., and

---

[9] This too is what is meant in Midrash rabba on Leviticus, Par. 9.

[10] There is an interesting marginal note in the old Reuchlin Cod. of the
Prophets (K. 154): פליג׳ בקריות של סוראי הלם כתיב וקרי הלא, לנהרדעי כת׳
הלא וק׳ הלם. The Schools at Sura and Neharda'a belonged to the general
category of Orientals (מדנחאי).

[11] See Jerusalem Talmud, Sota, cap. 1, § 8; and Midrash rabba on Numbers,
Par. 9.

adopted by our best modern commentator, Bertheau. It seems indeed the only possible one, with the text as it is.

2 Sam. v. 6[b]. The accentuation is in accordance with Targ., LXX, and Vulg., which make the subj. of the second לֵאמֹר 'the blind and the lame,' who are represented as making themselves responsible for the safety of the city against David's attacks.

xi. 25 end. The message sent is the important part of the verse. Hence it commands the main division (comp. p. 35 β). וַחֲזָקֵהוּ, as of minor importance, is joined on to the latter part of the speech.

xv. 34. Note the mispunctuation of our texts, וְאִם־הָעִיר תָּשׁוּב וְאָמַרְתָּ לְאַבְשָׁלוֹם עַבְדְּךָ אֲנִי הַמֶּלֶךְ אֶהְיֶה וגו', which can only mean: 'And thou shalt say to Absalom thy servant: I will be the king, &c.'! Correct עַבְדְּךָ אֲנִי הַמֶּלֶךְ, with Ox. 1, 10, 12, 13, &c.

xx. 18 end. וְכֵן הֵתַמּוּ, made by accents a part of the מָשָׁל, 'And so they will certainly attain their end.' Perf. of assurance, like הֲסִירְךָ, v. 6 (see above). If the accentuators had meant to express the meaning adopted by Vulg., Qim., and moderns, they must have pointed לֵאמֹר with R'bhia instead of Zaqeph.

1 Ki. vi. 1. The emphasis is thrown on the *second* of the dates named. (Just so in Ezek. xl. 1.) But point מִצְרַיִם, Great T'lisha, with Ox. 7, 76, 2326; Harl. 5710; &c.

xviii. 42[b], 46. The accents dwell on the pictorial features. Hence the division is not as with us.

2 Ki. iii. 25. עַד־הִשְׁאִיר אֲבָנֶיהָ בַּקִּיר חֲרָשֶׂת. The false accentuation here is due to the mistaken notion, found in Targ., Verss., Rashi, &c., that חֲרָשֶׂת is an *appellative:* 'They left the stones thereof in the wall' (broken to pieces, like) 'a mass of sherds.' Even the vocalization, קִיר with the article, seems occasioned by this strange explanation. Qimchi was apparently the first to see that קִיר חֲרֶשֶׂת is *nom. pr.*, as in Is. xvi. 7.

x. 15. וַיֹּאמֶר יְהוֹנָדָב יֵשׁ וָיֵשׁ. Rabb. comm., one and all, take יֵשׁ וָיֵשׁ together. Their explanation is כפל לחזק. With the rendering usually adopted—found in LXX and Vulg.—the accents must have been quite otherwise.

xviii. 17. וַיִּשְׁלַח מֶלֶךְ־אַשּׁוּר אֶת־תַּרְתָּן וְאֶת־רַב־סָרִיס וְאֶת־רַב־שָׁקֵה מִן־לָכִישׁ. Why the irregular L'garmeh (p. 118) in Géresh's clause? Because the accentuators designed a special warning for the reader. Only Rab-shakeh's name was to be associated with Lachish. Tartan and Rab-saris, as they are not named in Is. xxxvi. 2, were supposed to have come later, at the head of the second embassy (xix. 9). But that was sent from Libnah, *not from Lachish* (xix. 8)[12]. Their names

---

[12] Comp. Seder 'Olam, cap. 23, quoted by Rashi and Qimchi.

therefore were carefully separated from Lachish by the special disjunctive L'garmeh, whilst Rab-shakeh's was joined to it in the regular way. A notable specimen of Massoretic exegesis, the connection of which with the accentuation seems to have escaped every one's notice.

Is. i. 5. Targ., Abu'l-walîd (*Opuscules*, p. cv), and Aben-Ezra join עוֹד with the words following, and this pointing is found in some Codd.,—as Bab.; Ox. 23, 78,—עַל־מֶה תֻכּוּ עוֹד תּוֹסִיפוּ סָרָה. But unquestionably the *textus rec.* is right.

i. 9. Here also כִּמְעַט כִּסְדֹם הָיִינוּ are taken together, in Berakhoth 19ᵃ, and by Targ., Abu'l-walîd (l. c.), Rashi, and even Cheyne,—against the better sense, the unvarying accentuation, and the Massora (כִּמְעַט בְּ).

i. 13. קְטֹרֶת תּוֹעֵבָה הִיא לִי, 'incense of abomination is it to me.' So Targ., Rashi, Ewald, &c. The disregard of the accents, found in LXX, Vulg., and some Rabb. comm., shews itself also in A. V. and R. V.

v. 24. Cod. Bab. has וְחָשַׁשׁ לְהָבָה יִרְפֶּה, making לְהָבָה *acc. loci.* Even with our pointing, it may be so rendered, see p. 46, 3. It is quite unnecessary, with Ewald, Hitzig, and Ges. Lex., to translate *foenum flammae,* i. e. *flagrans.*

viii. 14ᵇ. No commentator, ancient or modern, seems to have noticed that the accentuation here is untenable. It has been due to a false interpretation, found in Targ. and Rashi, which takes לְפַח וּלְמוֹקֵשׁ as *in apposition* to לִשְׁנֵי בָתֵּי יִשְׂרָאֵל, 'To the two houses of Israel, who set themselves as a gin and a snare' &c. If we would pay any regard to the sense, we must point: וּלְאֶבֶן נֶגֶף וּלְצוּר מִכְשׁוֹל לִשְׁנֵי בָתֵּי יִשְׂרָאֵל.

viii. 23. The marked emphasis resting on the words וְהָאַחֲרוֹן הִכְבִּיד has led to the main pause of the verse being placed there. What follows, דֶּרֶךְ הַיָּם וגו', may be treated as Zusatz (see p. 57), 'by the way of the sea, &c.' Comp. Ewald. It is not necessary to suppose, with Luzzatto, that the Athnach is due to the Haggadic paraphrase of Targ.

ix. 5ᵇ. וַיִּקְרָא שְׁמוֹ פֶּלֶא יוֹעֵץ, an abnormal accentuation,—the object being to mark not only the Name, but in a special and emphatic manner the *separation* of פֶּלֶא from יוֹעֵץ, 'Wonder,—Counsellor¹³.'

---

¹³ Which Cheyne and others have not seen; or, if they have, ought, in all fairness, to have pointed out.

May I (without offence) remark that one learned professor after another has got out of his depth in trying to explain the accentual and grammatical peculiarities of the few words quoted? (1) Caspari (Micha, p. 223) makes of the Pashṭa a Qadma,

The regular accent for this purpose would have been פֶּלָא ׀. (On the general division of the half-verse, see p. 49, 1.)

xvii. 5. כְּאֹסֵף קָצִיר קָמָה. Most commentators neglect the accents, which however are duly regarded in LXX and Pesh.; קָצִיר being taken in the same sense as in verse 11.

xix. 9. שְׂרִיקוֹת, adjective outside the rest of the clause, see p. 53, 3 a. Not to be rendered as Delitzsch proposes.

xx. 4. The Athnach fixes the limit to the comparison made with Isaiah, for certainly he did not go חֲשׂוּף שֵׁת.

xxiii. 7ᵇ. According to the accents must be translated : ʻWhose feet were wont to carry her, from days of old, from her first beginning, to sojourn afar off.' The version of Rabbinical commentators and most moderns would require : מִימֵי־קֶדֶם קַדְמָתָהּ.

xxv. 1. יְהֹוָה אֱלֹהַי אַתָּה. ʻJehovah, my God art Thou !' Emphasis.

xxviii. 28. The R.V. pays attention to the accentuation. Not so the bulk of modern commentators.

xxix. 16ᵃ. Not understood,—as ancient Verss. and Jewish comm. down to Luzzatto shew. Hence the false accentuation : כְּחֹמֶר הַיֹּצֵר.

xxx. 7ᵇ. In Ox. 4, 74, 78; Add. 11657, we have the pointing רַהַב הֵם שָׁבֶת, which suits the rendering : ʻRahab! they are a sitting still.'

xxx. 21. Accents make the last words *a part of the speech.* So Targ., LXX, Vulg., Pesh., and Qim., against Aben-Ezra and moderns.

xxx. 32. No commentator (as far as I have observed) has seen that for the ordinary rendering to stand, we must have R'bhia at מוּסָדָה ; but this we cannot introduce, because the Massora (see p. 107) has fixed Y'thibh for כָּל. Vulg. and Prob. pay regard to the accentuation.

xxxiii. 23. A case of parallelism with addition (p. 39). Jewish commentators refer the whole verse to Assyria. Had they referred,

---

and will give a reason for it ! (2) Delitzsch proposes an impossible accentuation, וַיִּקְרָא שְׁמוֹ פֶּלֶא יוֹעֵץ אֵל גִּבּוֹר וגו׳, Géresh before and after Tʻlisha ! (3) Kautzsch (Ges. Gr., § 93, Anm. 1. D), disregarding the accentuation—as though vowels and accents were not from the same source—would have us believe on the authority of Dikd. hat., § 36, that פֶלֶא is in *st. constr.;* yet if he had looked on a few pages to § 72 of the same work, he would have found this notion plainly contradicted, as indeed it must have been sooner or later, for it is in direct opposition to the Mas. to Lev. xxii. 23. One would not have expected to find an antiquated error, due to the first groping after grammatical rules, revived by a German professor in the present day !

with many modern commentators, the first part of the verse to Jerusalem and the second to Assyria, Athnach could not have failed at נֵס. As it is, the helpless hulk falls a ready prey.

xxxvi. 2. See note, 2 Ki. xviii. 17.

xxxviii. 13ᵃ. How are we to account for the accentuation? Gesenius and those who have followed him, down to Cheyne, say: 'From the exigencies of rhythm,'—a notion which Jewish writers would have passed by as שִׁבּוּשׁ. With the rendering which these scholars propose we should have had שִׁוִּיתִי עַד־בֹּקֶר כָּאֲרִי וגו'; comp. xl. 3 and a hundred other passages. The accents are no doubt to be traced to the same source as the false version of Targum: 'I roared as a lion, till the morning.' Comp. also Sa'adia[14].

xlv. 1. According to Rashi on Megilla 12ᵃ, the anomalous accentuation (Zarqa without S'gôlta following[15]) was meant to draw attention to the traditional דרש, found in the text of the Talmud, l. c.: 'Was then Cyrus משיח? Nay! the Holy One said to the Messiah, I complain to thee concerning Cyrus, &c.'[16] Such crotchets of Jewish learning we may well put on one side, and point regularly (with our ordinary text and many Codd.) לְכֹ֫ורֶשׁ. Only then we shall require R'bhîa, instead of the first Zarqa[17], כֹּה־אָמַר יְהֹוָה לִמְשִׁיחֹו לְכֹ֫ורֶשׁ.

xlv. 24ᵇ. An alternative punctuation is found in Ox. 2421; Add. 21161; Hm. 9: עָדָיו יָבֹוא וְיֵבֹ֫שׁוּ, which is an improvement, but contrary to the Mas. Lev. xi. 34. With the ordinary pointing, וְיֵבֹשׁוּ must be taken as = בַּכְּלִמָּה, ver. 16ᵇ.

lvi. 9. The ridiculous accentuation of this verse can only be rendered in one way. See Rashi, Qimchi, &c.

lxvi. 5ᵇ. For the meaning of the accents, see Rashi, Aben-Ezra, or Rosenmüller.—The Vulg. and most moderns (see e.g. Delitzsch) rightly disregard them.

lxvi. 12. Strange that no commentator before Luzzatto should

---

[14] Sa'adia's text is to be read: وساويت الاسد فى زيّاره الى الغَداة, 'And I was like the lion in his roaring, until the morning.' So Or. 1474, 2211. No sense can be made of the Ox. text, as edited by Paulus.

[15] Cf. Baer's text and the Mas. parva found in many Codd. (Ox. 69, 2323; Erf. 1, &c.) זרקא בלא סגולה ל, or זרקא אחר רביע ל.

[16] So Sa'adia: كذى قال الله لـلسيـح عن (regarding) كورش. The title משיח, applied to no other heathen king, was counted too great a one for Cyrus. Hence some other interpretation had to be found; and Cyrus' name, in comparison, slurred over.

[17] With Harl. 5498, Add. 9398, 9399; Par. 4, &c.

have found any difficulty in the accentuation [18]: 'Behold, I extend to her, as a peaceful river and as an overflowing stream, the glory of the Gentiles,' &c.   Did the accentuators miss the art. in כְּנָהָר and consider that something else was intended than by the בַּנָּהָר שְׁלוֹמָהּ of xlviii. 18 ?

Jer. xxxii. 9[b]. שִׁבְעָה שְׁקָלִים וַעֲשָׂרָה הַכָּסֶף.   On the division here, which has completely baffled commentators, see Rule, p. 42 above.

Ezek. i. 11. וּפְנֵיהֶם וְכַנְפֵיהֶם פְּרֻדוֹת מִלְמָעְלָה,—another instance of the Rule just quoted.

iii. 20. הוּא יָמוּת to be made, as accents indicate, a relative clause. (So Abendana, Ewald, Hitzig, and Prob.)   In b the logical division is neglected, that the emphasis may come on the first words : '*Because thou hast not warned him, in his iniquity he shall die.*'

iv. 6.   Punctators sometimes shew the same differences of opinion as commentators.   In this verse, Ox. 17 ; Harl. 5498 ; and Par. 4, have Athnach at אַרְבָּעִים יוֹם.   And so in vii. 13[b], Ox. 17, 69, and Bab. have בַּעֲוֹנוֹ or בַּעֲוֹנוֹ;—in xv. 2 Bab. has מִכָּל־עֵץ הַזְּמוֹרָה, with LXX, Vulg., and Ewald ;—in xviii. 30[b], Ox. 1, 6, 7; Erf. 1, 3, have וְלֹא־יִהְיֶה לָכֶם לְמִכְשׁוֹל עָוֹן; and in xxxi. 15 most Codd. have הֶאֱבַלְתִּי. Such examples might be greatly multiplied.

vi. 10. וְיָדְעוּ כִּי־אֲנִי יְהוָה וגו'.   Note the emphasis thrown by Athnach on the Divine Name.   'And they shall know that *I Jehovah* have not spoken in vain,' &c.   If the student has any doubt on the point, let him turn to such parallel passages as xxii. 22[b]; xxxv. 12 ; xxxvii. 14[b]; Num. xiv. 14 ; Jer. ii. 19.

xxi. 3[b].   Render, 'Behold, I kindle in thee a fire, and it shall devour in thee every green tree and every dry tree, without being quenched[19],— inflaming flame (that it will be).'   The last words are in apposition to the latent subject in אָכְלָה, and come in, as such, with marked effect, at the close of the clause.   Comp. Jer. ii. 23[b].   The ordinary rendering would require Zaqeph, or at least R'bhia, on יָבֵשׁ.

xxv. 9[b].   Accents, 'the glory of the land of Beth-jeshimoth,' &c., and so Pesh. renders; but this cannot be correct.   Yet I have not found צְבִי אֶרֶץ, which is what we require, in any Codex.

xl. 1.   The stress is laid on the *second* of the dates named (comp. above, 1 Ki. vi. 1).   The destruction of the old city is emphasized, in contrast to the revelation of the new one, in the verse following.

xliv. 22[b].   On the Zaqeph in אַלְמָנָה see Comm.

---

[18] It is traceable in LXX, Vulg., Arab. (Polygl.), and Cod. Ambros. (Syr.), but not in Targ., Pesh., or Rabb. Comm.

[19] Driver, Heb. Tenses, § 162.

Mic. ii. 4[b]. לְשׁוֹבֵב שָׂדֵינוּ יְחַלֵּק. Accents evidently treat שׁוֹבֵב as inf., with LXX, Rashi, Qim., and even some modern authorities. For the rendering usually adopted, 'rebellious, reprobate,' we need Ṭiphcha on לְשׁוֹבֵב, and this is found in some Codd., as Ox. 6, 7; Add. 4708, Or. 1474.

iv. 10[b]. וּבָאתָ עַד־בָּבֶל שָׁם תִּנָּצֵלִי. We expect Zaqeph at בָּבֶל (comp. modern interpunction). But a fine antithesis is established by the accentuation: 'Thou shalt come to Babylon, there to be *delivered.*' Babylon was the last place in the world where deliverance could have been anticipated.

Hab. i. 3. וַיְהִי רִיב וּמָדוֹן יִשָּׂא. Almost all modern commentators neglect the accentuation, although this is one of the passages in which the Massoretes have been very particular in fixing it (see p. 92). רִיב וּמָדוֹן make a common subject to יִשָּׂא (Ges. Heb. Gr., § 148. 2).

ii. 18. The Athnach simply represents a pause for effect, such as we might make in reading the verse. Rabbinical commentators, however, see in it the main logical pause, and begin the second half of the verse by repeating מָה הוֹעִיל, 'What profit is there in all these, that &c. ?'

iii. 3, 9, 13. The extraordinary rendering assigned to סֶלָה, = לְעוֹלָם, in Talm., Targ., &c., suffices to account for the false accentuation, most conspicuous in verse 9.

Hag. ii. 16. מִהְיוֹתָם, 'Since they (those days) were,' *subordinated,* as בִּימֵי, &c., p. 48, 5.

Cant. viii. 6[b]. Most Codd. have רִשְׁפֵּי as our texts (see Rashi on the accentuation). But the modern rendering, 'Its flashes are flashes of fire, a flame of Jah,' is much more effective, and has also the support of Codd., Ox. 6, 2437; Add. 15282, Harl. 5506, &c., thus: רְשָׁפֶיהָ רִשְׁפֵּי אֵשׁ שַׁלְהֶבֶתְיָה.

Qoh. ii. 3[b]. Almost all modern commentators silently transfer Athnach to בְּסִכְלוּת. The accentuation on the other hand will give the meaning: 'And my heart was to guide me in wisdom, and was (at the same time) to lay hold on folly [20].' This rendering, with its oxymoron of *insipiens sapientia,* is far more telling than the tame construction adopted, as more regular, by moderns.

ii. 16. The weight of meaning comes on the first clause. Hence the Athnach.

viii. 10[a]. The A. V., with the old Verss. and Rabb. comm. generally, respects the accents; but R. V. and most moderns follow Aben-Ezra, and quite disregard them.

---

[20] On the inf. with לְ, as continuing the part. construction, see Driver, Heb. Tenses, § 206.

viii. 11. ‫אֲשֶׁר אֵין־נַעֲשָׂה פִתְגָם מַעֲשֵׂה הָרָעָה מְהֵרָה וגו׳‬. Ewald and Hengstenberg try to do justice to the accentuation; but, with the rendering usually adopted by both ancients and moderns, we must point, ‫אֲשֶׁר אֵין־נַעֲשָׂה פִתְגָם מַעֲשֵׂה הָרָעָה מְהֵרָה‬, with Ox. 20, 36; Add. 9399, Or. 2696; De R. 10; (comp. similar examples, p. 51 above)[21].

ix. 10. Codd., e. g. Ox. 13, 17, 26, 34, give us the option of joining ‫בְּכֹחֲךָ עֲשֵׂה‬, 'do it with thy might,' as Targ., LXX, Vulg., A. V., R. V., &c.

xi. 8. The last words, ‫כָּל־שֶׁבָּא הָבֶל‬, are properly logically distinct, but have been joined on to the clause preceding, from their supposed close connection with it in sense: 'Let him remember the days of darkness, that they will be many, (that) all that cometh (after the present life) is vanity.'

Esth. ix. 31. The Athnach is better transferred to ‫הַמַּלְכָּה‬, as Targ., Vulg., and Rabb. comm. render. See also Bertheau. This pointing is found in Add. 4709 and Hm. 19.

1 Chr. vi. 46[a]. There is a fatal omission here, which Jewish commentators do not fail to notice, and which the accents are meant to indicate: ‫מִמִּשְׁפַּחַת הַמַּטֶּה‬ is supposed to stand for ‫מִמִּשְׁפַּחַת מַטֵּה אֶפְרַיִם‬ (comp. Josh. xxi. 5)[22].

ix. 17[b]. ‫וַאֲחִיהֶם‬ is contrary both to the Mas. (which requires ‫וַאֲחִיהֶם‬)[23] and the accentuation. Yet no commentator makes any remark. Vulg. *frater eorum* and Pesh. are right. The reading ‫וַאֲחִיהֶם‬ has necessarily led to the pointing of our texts, which we must correct with Codd., ‫וַאֲחִיהֶם שַׁלּוּם הָרֹאשׁ‬.

2 Chr. xxiv. 14. Translators and commentators follow LXX and Vulg. in the rendering of ‫הָעֲלוֹת‬, but the latter have not a syllable to say about this rendering being contrary to the accents. The accents indeed represent the uniform Jewish tradition that an instrument or vessel of some kind is meant[24]. A tradition of this kind introduced into the Massoretic text deserves at least notice.

---

[21] Luzzatto (Kerem Chemed ix. 7) saw that this pointing was necessary, but found no MS. to support it. Delitzsch, in his remark on the accentuation, has not seen that the Zaqeph extends its influence to Athnach, which makes his explanation inadmissible.

[22] It is considered that ‫וּמִמַּטֵּה־דָן‬ (Josh. l. c.) may be dispensed with, because Dan is not named—but included in Ephraim—vers. 51–54.

[23] See Frensdorff, p. 9, and ‫אכלה ואכלה‬, § 17.

[24] The word is derived by Abu'l-walîd (Lex. s. v.) from the Hiphil form. The notion—found in Pseudo-Rashi, and marg. of A. V. and R. V.—that it is the pl. of ‫עֱלִי‬ (Prov. xxvii. 22), 'pestles,' cannot be entertained, for the article is out of place here, and the meaning quite inappropriate.

2 Chr. xxx. 18, 19. Not only LXX, Vulg., and Pesh., but Jewish tradition from very early times, as in the Middôth of R. Eli'ezer, § 11 [25], made these verses run into one another. By the abrupt break in the middle of the prayer, the Massoretes seem to have designed (*more suo*, when employing an anomalous accentuation) to draw special attention to the prayer itself,—a. prayer without a parallel, the meaning of which extended far beyond the occasion that called it forth.

The following notes relate to passages of less importance :

Josh. ii. 5. R'bhia has been falsely introduced. Point וַיְהִי הַשַּׁעַר לִסְגּוֹר בַּחֹשֶׁךְ, with Ox. 2436 ; Harl. 5683, 5773, Or. 2091; &c.: 'And the gate was about to close at dusk.'

Judg. iv. 21[b]. וְהוּא־נִרְדָּם וַיָּעַף וַיָּמֹת, with Ox. 19 ; Add. 4709, 9398, Or. 2696 ; &c. Comp. p. 33, note. For the Qāmes in נִרְדָּם, see Norzi.

1 Ki. vii. 6[b]. Better וְעַמֻּדִים וְעָב עַל־פְּנֵיהֶם, with Ox. 13 ; Hm. 3, 11 ; as Vulg. and Thenius render.

vii. 36[b]. If we are to make any sense, we must point כְּמַעַר־אִישׁ וְלֹיוֹת סָבִיב, with Ox. 1, 72, 2329 ; Harl. 5722 ; &c.—a double Zusatz, see R. V. The words were not understood by Jewish scholars, who derive מער from the post-biblical עָרָה (Piel), 'to join.' Hence the false accentuation of our texts.

2 Ki. xxii. 14 (2 Chr. xxxiv. 22). Point חֻלְדָּה הַנְּבִיאָה אֵשֶׁת שַׁלֻּם בֶּן־תִּקְוָה בֶּן־חַרְחַס שֹׁמֵר הַבְּגָדִים, with Vi. 5; K. 172. Printed texts and Codd. generally make Charchas, not Shallum, 'keeper of the robes.'

Is. xxviii. 16[b]. אֶבֶן בֹּחַן פִּנַּת יִקְרַת מוּסָד מוּסָּד, with Ox. 1, 9, 69 ; Erf. 2 ; &c. R'bhia is necessary for the sense.

xxxv. 1[b]. Better וְתָגֵל עֲרָבָה וְתִפְרַח כַּחֲבַצָּלֶת, with Bab.; Ox. 13 ; Erf. 1, 3.

xl. 13. Here also it is better to accent מִי־תִכֵּן אֶת־רוּחַ יְהֹוָה, with Bab.; Ox. 5, 82 ; Erf. 2 ; &c.; and so avoid the mistake of Targ., Sa'adia, and Qim., who render: 'Who hath prepared the spirit? Jehovah.'

---

[25] The tradition was followed by Sa'adia, Qim., Pseudo-Rashi, and the author of the Comm. on Chron. edited by Kirchheim. If we except the doubtful paraphrase of the Targum, Aben-Ezra (e. g. in Ṣachoth, p. 73[b]) was the first to propose an independent construction for ver. 18, by supplying אלה after בער. He owns that he stands alone. And he hardly found a follower till Gesenius in his Thesaurus, p. 706, proposed the same explanation.

Jer. li. 58. Again the better pointing is חֹמוֹת בָּבֶל הָרְחָבָה עַרְעֵר תִּתְעַרְעָר, with Ox. 70, 72, 76; Erf. 1; &c.: 'The broad wall of Babel shall be razed to the ground.' Comp. Ewald, § 318[a].

Ezek. xlv. 21[b]. חַג שְׁבֻעוֹת יָמִים מַצּוֹת יֵאָכֵל. Note the st. constr. in חַג.

Amos vi. 6. The accentuation of our texts הַשֹּׁתִים בְּמִזְרְקֵי יַיִן corresponds to Targ., and the notion of Rabb. comm. (see Baur's note) that the st. constr. stands here for st. abs.! But Bab.; Ox. 70, 76; Erf. 3; &c., point regularly הַשֹּׁתִים בְּמִזְרְקֵי־יַיִן.

Cant. i. 3. Point שֶׁמֶן תּוּרַק שְׁמֶךָ. So Ox. 15, 19, 51; Erf. 1, 2, 4; and the Verss.

Qoh. i. 5[b]. Targ., Verss., Rashi, Aben-Ezra, all render as if they had before them וְאֶל־מְקוֹמוֹ שׁוֹאֵף, which is beyond doubt the true accentuation, and is found in Ox. 12, 26; Add. 4709, 21160; &c.

Dan. ix. 25. R'bhía and Géresh must clearly change places, thus: וְתֵדַע וְתַשְׂכֵּל מִן־מֹצָא דָבָר לְהָשִׁיב וגו'. Ox. 97; Add. 15250; De R. 518, have R'bhía, but only Ox. 97, Géresh right.

Ezra x. 14. The same correction is necessary: יַעֲמְדוּ־נָא שָׂרֵינוּ לְכָל־הַקָּהָל וְכָל־אֲשֶׁר בְּעָרֵינוּ הַהֹשִׁיב וגו'. But here Codd. are all wrong. Only Par. 31; De R. 737; and Hm. 16, have R'bhía right.

I Chr. iii. 17. Jewish tradition, LXX, Vulg., and A.V. make אַסִּר a *nom. proprium*. We must then point וּבְנֵי יְכָנְיָה אַסִּר, with Ox. 6, 71, 72; Add. 9399; &c.

iv. 19. A similar correction is needed here: וּבְנֵי אֵשֶׁת הוֹדִיָּה אֲחוֹת נַחַם אֲבִי קְעִילָה הַגַּרְמִי. But this I have found only in De R. 552 (old) and 775.

2 Chr. iv. 9[b]. For the sense it is necessary to point: וּדְלָתוֹת לָעֲזָרָה, with Harl. 1528, Add. 15252; Ber. 32.

NOTE.—My readers may perhaps have noticed in the foregoing remarks that the Targum, and no less Rabbinical commentaries, do not always agree with the accentuation. We see that from early times a certain liberty was claimed in rendering and expounding the text. The accents, although respected and generally followed, were not regarded—notwithstanding particular assertions, as those of Aben-Ezra, to the contrary[26]—as of final authority. With respect to the Targums, we may bear in mind that the most important ones are of *Oriental* origin, which circumstance may account for some at least of the variations.

---

[26] Comp. Luzzatto, Prolegomeni, p. 187 ff.

APPENDIX II.

ON THE SUPERLINEAR [SO-CALLED BABYLONIAN] SYSTEM OF ACCENTUATION.

The researches of a Qaraite Jew, Abraham Firkowitsch, in the synagogues of the Crimea, brought to light, about fifty years ago, some Hebrew MSS. marked with a peculiar system of punctuation, previously quite unknown to scholars[1]. The characteristic of this system, as regards the position of the signs, is that they are almost all *above* the words (i. e. above the line from which the words depend). To the term '*superlinear*' therefore as describing it, no exception can be taken; whereas 'Babylonian,' as we shall afterwards see, is a misnomer.

The accentual notation found in these MSS. (as compared with the Palestinian) is as follows :

1. Silluq remains unchanged . . . . . . דָּבָר׃

2. Athnach is the same, but is placed *above* the word . דָּבָר

3. S'gôlta is represented by a mutilated Shîn, the initial of שְׁרֵי (p. 17) . . . . דָּבָר

---

[1] For a description of the MSS. containing this punctuation, see Cat. of Heb. MSS. in the Imperial Library at St. Petersburg, Nos. 132, 133, and B 3. (Ox. 64 is a fragment of 132, although not so described in the Ox. Cat.) Of the three MSS. named by far the most important is B 3, which contains in a state of perfect preservation the whole of the later Prophets. It was photo-lithographed in 1876, at the expense of the late Emperor of Russia, and so placed at the service of scholars. The text of this Codex—known as *Codex Babylonicus*—is all we need to form a correct idea of the system we are about to consider. I may, however, add that there is in the St. Petersburg Library a fourth MS., not yet catalogued (but labelled as Tschufut-Kale 8ᵃ), containing Job xxxv. 10 to end of the book. (A specimen of some verses of this Codex is prefixed to Baer's edition of Job.) Till these MSS. were discovered, the only notice of the existence of a superlinear system of punctuation was contained in the following epigraph to a MS. of the Pent. with Targ. in De Rossi's Library (dated 1311), no. 12 : תרגום זה נעתק מספר מסּר אשר הובא מארץ בבל והיה מנוקד למעלה בנקוד ארץ אשור, והסכו ר' נתן נרבי מכיר בר' מנחם מאנקונא בר' שמואל בר' מכיר ממדינת אוייירי בר' שלמה הוא אשר גדע קרן המתלוצץ בארץ מגנצא בשם המבורך בר' מנחם בר' צדוק הנקרן, והגיהו ונסחו לנקוד סבוני. (comp. Zunz, Zur Geschichte u. Literatur, p. 110).

Shalshéleth has the figure of a hanging 'chain' (p. 17),
followed by the sign for S'gôlta [2] .   .   .   .   דְּבָ֓ר

4. Great and Little Zaqeph are not distinguished. The
sign is the initial letter of זָקֵף [3] .   .   .   .   דְּבָ֔ר

5. Ṭiphcha before Athnach is Athnach inverted .   .   דְּבָ֖ר
Ṭiphcha before Silluq is the Palestinian sign, or the
initial of דְּחִי (p. 18) [4] .   .   .   .   .   .   דְּבָ֖ר

6. R'bhîa is represented by the initial of חָזֵר [5]   .   .   דְּבָ֗ר

7. Zarqa. The initial letter could not be used, because
it was appropriated to Zaqeph. So apparently the
name צִנּוֹרִי (p. 19) was taken, and the *second* letter
chosen as the sign [6] .   .   .   .   .   .   דְּבָ֮ר

8. Pashṭa and Y'thîbh are not distinguished. The common
sign is the initial of יְתִיב (p. 20). For the peculiar
form of the sign, see (in Cod. Bab.) Is. xix. 25 marg.   דְּבָ֚ר
Where Pashṭa is repeated, a simpler form is given to
the second sign, and it is made recumbent .   .   דְּבָ֚ר

9. T'bhîr, represented by the initial letter .   .   .   דְּבָ֛ר

10. Géresh and Gersháyim have one sign, the initial of
טֶרֶס (p. 20) .   .   .   .   דְּבָ֜ר

11. L'garmeh. The sign is the initial of נֶגֶד (p. 22) .   דְּבָ֓ר
Pazer and Great T'lîsha fail.

---

[2] This accent is described in the Mas. to Is. xiii. 8 as זרקא מסלסלא,—which
should rather have been שרי מסלסלא. But Zarqa, according to the fancy of the
later Massoretes, threw S'gôlta into the shade (see p. 17).

[3] In Cod. Bab. (Mas. to Jer. xiv. 18) we find the strange name אוקומי, 'set
upright,' used for Zaqeph. Comp. Ginsb. Mas. iii. p. 364, § 19.

[4] In the text of Job this sign is regularly used; in Cod. Bab. but very rarely,
except in the first page, Is. i. 4, 8, 9, &c.

[5] This name for R'bhîa occurs in a list at the end of Sepher Hariqma, p. 239,
and in a manuscript list before me. Certainly no name could be more appropriate,
for the frequent 'recurrence' of this accent is a main characteristic of the system.
In Or. 1473, I found the initial of רביע used, דְּבָ֗ר.

[6] So in the Mas. magna to Num. i. 20, the סימן for the names of five out of
the twelve tribes is either the *second* or the *third* letter; and in Arabic, the sign
for ﺔَﻤْﺸَﻜ is خ, the *third* letter.—The Dagesh in the case before us was
retained, to distinguish the sign from that used for L'garmeh, no. 11.

The *servi* employed—Munach, M'huppakh, Mer'kha, Darga, Azla, and Little T'lîsha—are the same as in the Palestinian system.

The originators of this system seem to have taken note of the weak points of (what I must assume for the present was) the older system, and to have applied a suitable correction. Thus the sign for L'garmeh cannot now be mistaken for Munach-Paseq; and Pashṭa can no longer be confounded with Azla, nor Y'thîbh with M'huppakh. *Simplicity* was also evidently aimed at by the employment of a *single* sign respectively for Zaqeph, Pashṭa, and Géresh; and by dispensing with the unmeaning accent, Great Pazer (and Galgal). But it was a mistake to reject Little Pazer and Great T'lisha, which are (generally speaking) needed for the division of the clauses in which they occur. R'bhîa, which takes their place in this system, does not answer the purpose.

Before proceeding to the special rules for this system of accentuation, there is a question *in limine*, that requires to be answered. Was this superlinear accentuation, with its equally peculiar vocalization, *identical with the Oriental mode of punctuation?* Such (as far as I have noticed) is the view of all scholars, who have expressed an opinion on the subject. But this is a mistake, which, though excusable, is none the less a serious one. The notation in use among the Orientals (מדנחאי) was beyond question the same as that of the Occidentals (מערבאי), differing only occasionally in its application. How otherwise are we to explain the Oriental reading of [7] וַתֵּעְגַּב סגול (Ezek. xxiii. 5)? The superlinear system *has no S'gôl*, and writes this word (as Cod. Bab. shews) וֹתֵעְגֹּב (וַתֵּעְגֹּב). We learn from this example that the Massoretes, in giving the חלופי מדנחאי, quoted a text constructed on the same system as the Palestinian. Can indeed (I would ask) a single Massoretic rubric be found, which *alludes to the peculiarities of the superlinear system?* and yet the differences of this system are far more important than most of those which are given under the name of the Orientals. The system was in short for the Palestinian Massoretes non-existent.—Moreover, what Gaon, what grammarian (Rabbinical or Qaraite), what Jewish writer, of the East or West, can be named who mentions *a different mode of punctuation* as in use among the Orientals[8]? Has their silence no meaning?

---

[7] See Baer's edition of Ezekiel, p. 110, and Ginsb. Mas. i. p. 596, and iii. p. 32.

[8] Where reference is made, as it often is, by Jewish authorities, to the חלופין between the two great Schools of the East and West, it is in such terms as we might apply to the remains that have come down to us. I have given two instances, p. 6, note 14, and here is a third, clearer still, as late as the 12th century, from the חלוק הקראים והרבנים of Elia ben-Abraham (quoted by Pinsker, Liqq. Qad., p. 102): ועוד ראו חלופי מערבאי ומדנחאי בתורה, זה אומר בכה וזה אומר בכה, מה שילמוד זה חסר ילמוד זה מלא, ומה שילמוד זה מלא ילמוד זה

Especially important is this negative testimony as furnished by
Sa'adia's writings. Here was a Gaon, at the head of one of the chief
Oriental Academies—a scholar, who was in the habit of going into
the minutest details of any subject which he handled—(who lived too
after the date of the introduction of the system we are considering [9]),
and yet who knows positively nothing of any Oriental differences
answering to the differences of the superlinear punctuation. For
instance, in chap. ii. § 2 of his commentary on Jeṣîra [10], he enumerates
the seven vowels, including S'gôl, and in iv. § 3 he lays down the
vocalization of the article in הֶהָרִים, as with S'gôl, and of the final
guttural in forms like לִשְׁמֹעַ, as with Pathach; yet does not add
(as according to modern scholars he ought to have done) that the
Orientals had no S'gôl, and that they pointed הַהָרִים with Pathach
and לִשְׁמַע without Pathach. What is observable is that in the very
section last quoted he mentions *other* differences of pronunciation
between the Orientals and Occidentals.—The conclusion is that the
Oriental system of vocalization had no such distinguishing peculiarities
as the superlinear, in other words was identical with the Palestinian;
and what is true of the vocalization, must have held equally good
for the accentuation [11].

חסר, מה שילמוד זה תיבה אחת ילמוד זה שתי תיבות, מה שילמוד זה במסורת

במשרת) ילמד זה בטעם, וכן מסורת הרבה אחד למערבאי ואחד למדנחאי. (lege). I may
add the undesigned testimony of R. Petachiah, who visited Bagdad, circa 1180, and
who refers to the נקוד in use among the Jews of that region (Benisch's ed., p. 15),
but makes no allusion to any different notation, which yet, had it existed, must
have struck him, a Western Jew, as something very remarkable and deserving of
being chronicled in his narrative.—Moreover, copies of MSS. have been brought
from China, and published by the 'Society for promoting Christianity among the
Jews,' which, from the epigraphs, are clearly of *Persian* origin, but which have
the ordinary punctuation. We may conclude that in Persia, as in other parts of
the East, this was the prevalent system.

[9] Cod. Bab. was written in the year 916, and Sa'adia was called to Sura (when
thirty-six years of age) in 928.

[10] I quote from the Ox. Cod.

[11] We now see the unfortunate mistake that has been made in naming this
newly discovered system *Babylonian* (= Oriental). The mistake is not, however,
altogether of modern origin. For it is but fair to state that this system is
recognised as 'Oriental' in some of the Tschufut-Kale Bible Codd. (48, 87, 103,
116), e. g. Cod. 87, 1 Sam. xxv. 3, Mas. קרין בֻּלֹבֹּי כֹת כלבו נ לֹמדֹ; and 2 Sam. xiii. 21,

למערב והסלך דוד שׁׁלֹע אֶת כל-הדבְרִים האֵלֹה כֹת וכן קֹ Mas.

ולמדנח שֵׁׁׁלֹע כל-הֹדֹבֹרֹים הֹאֹּלֹה כֹת וכן קֹ

and Cod. 116, Ps. cxxxvii. 5, אֶשְׁכָּחֵךְ, note, קֹ אֹשׁבֹּחֹכֹי כֹת אֹשכחדך למדנח. (I am
indebted for these extracts to Prof. Strack of Berlin, who very kindly placed at
my disposal the notes he had taken from the various Tschufut-Kale MSS.) The

In what light then are we to regard this superlinear punctuation? It stands outside the system common to the Oriental and Occidental Schools, and would seem to have been an attempt to simplify and introduce regularity into the older system. The influence of the Arabic is evident in the vocalization, and perhaps also in the accentuation, where *initial letters* represent the accents, just as in Arabic they stand for Teshdîd, Medda, &c.

Such an attempt, even if more successful than it actually was, could hardly have been looked on with favour by the heads of Schools in the East, and by other scholars, who may have become acquainted with it; for it must have seemed to them very like a tampering with sacred things,—the punctuation being referred at least to the authority of Ezra. Hence we may explain their silence with regard to it. The inventors of the system themselves shrank from applying their new-fangled signs to the Sacred Name יהוה (אדני), which is either marked with the older Qāmeṣ-sign יְהוָה (as in 132, 133), or not marked at all (as in Cod. Bab. and Tschufut-Kale 8ª)[12]. A proof of the inferior esteem in which this system was held is that in Yemen, where it was in use in a modified and much simpler form, the Sacred text, when associated with Targum or Forms of prayer, has generally the Palestinian signs, and only the latter the superlinear[13].

That this system is of *Oriental origin* may indeed be taken for granted from its exhibiting, as in Cod. Bab., the readings peculiar to the Orientals. It was *an* Oriental, but not *the* Oriental, system.

The relation in which it stood to the Palestinian (which was one and the same with the Oriental) is indicated by the vowels and accents of this last-named system being constantly found in the MSS. with superlinear punctuation. This phenomenon receives its ready explanation, if we suppose the superlinear punctuation to have been an offshoot from the Oriental,—in which case it naturally remained under the influence of the system from which it was derived, and by which it must have been always overshadowed. I shall aim, in the following remarks, at shewing that the relation thus indicated really

---

writers of these notices were doubtless in the same position as modern scholars. They had no other texts with Oriental readings, and naturally concluded that the texts which contained such readings, exhibited also the Oriental mode of punctuation.—It is different with the name 'Assyrian,' adopted by some scholars, on the authority of the epigraph, quoted in note 1. But can we trust the unsupported testimony of a single copyist? Is it likely that an Italian Jew, of the 14th century, should have known the *origin* of this system, when scribes living in the East were ignorant of it? The statements contained in the epigraphs to Jewish texts have always to be received *cum grano*.

[12] Later punctators indeed, as those of the Yemen Codd. of the 14th and 15th centuries in the British Museum, were less particular.

[13] A specimen of Bible text with Targum is given in Pl. XCI of the Palæographical Society's Publications (Oriental Series). Oxford Scholars may also compare the Siddurs (1145 and 2498) in the Bodleian Library.

existed. Of course I shall confine myself to the accentuation; but we may rest satisfied that if so important a part of the punctuation was *derived*, the whole system was no less so.

It is time now to turn to *the peculiarities* of this system (as far as the accents are concerned). And of these by far the most striking is *the frequent recurrence of R'bhîa*, in season and out of season. This accent is found subordinated not only to S'gôlta, Zaqeph, and Tiphcha (as in our system), but to all the disjunctives in turn (except L'garmeh), even to Géresh and a second R'bhîa! Indeed the originators of this system went out of their way to bring in this favourite accent, as may be seen in Is. x. 24; Jer. xiii. 11; xxxvi. 6; &c. In the case of the other disjunctives, the variations from the Palestinian usage (mistakes having been corrected) are unimportant. Géresh and L'garmeh are found more freely used (with the exception that L'garmeh is not repeated) before R'bhîa; L'garmeh and Paseq frequently interchange, &c. But these are minor matters. The *general conformity* of the two texts—when allowance has been made for the abnormal use of R'bhîa [14]—has not been sufficiently noticed by scholars [15]. But the key found, all is perfectly simple.

---

[14] Thus, with this allowance made, all the main rules for the sequence of the accents given in the previous pages—as for the position of Athnach in the verse; the substitution of Zaqeph for Tiphcha before Silluq or Athnach, pp. 62 and 69; the subordination of S'gôlta and Zaqeph to Athnach, p. 70; of R'bhîa and Pashṭa to Zaqeph, p. 77 f.; &c.—are carried out.

[15] Who, for instance, would suppose, from reading Pinsker's 'Einleitung in das Babylonisch-Hebräische Punctationssystem,' that there was this general conformity? Prof. Strack indeed remarks (Zeitsch. für Luth. Theol. 1877, p. 31): 'Die Accente werden im *Codex Babylonicus* nach ziemlich denselben Regeln gesetzt, welche für unsere Bibelhandschriften gelten. Man hat nur wenige Besonderheiten des babylonischen Systems stetz im Gedächtniss zu behalten, um im Stande zu sein, die meisten tiberianisch interpungirten Verse umzuaccentuiren.' But though he mentions, in the note, that R'bhîa takes the place of a second Zaqeph, and may occur as many as seven times in the same half-verse, he has failed to see that the singular rules for the introduction of R'bhîa are the main cause of the peculiarities to which he refers. He was, however, on the right track in adding (p. 32): 'Dies ist ein neuer Beweis dafür, dass das babylonische System sich nicht selbständig gebildet hat.' It is a pity that the learned Professor did not pursue his investigations further. But he was doubtless hampered by the notion held by him, in common with other scholars (see his article on the Massora, Herzog's Encyclop. ix. p. 393), that the Babylonian system of punctuation was one and the same with the superlinear,—a notion which he has supplemented by the hypothesis (l. c.): 'Dass ursprünglich warscheinlich nur *ein* System existirte, welchem das übliche, tiberiensische, in bezug auf Stellung und Form der Zeichen näher gestanden haben dürfte als das babylonische.' I give these views of Dr. S., though only partially agreeing with my own, because he is the only scholar, beside Pinsker, who has carefully considered the subject of the superlinear accentuation.

The following rules will shew how it is that R'bhîa is of such frequent occurrence:

1. Pazer and Great T'lisha are wanting; and Géresh is confined to R'bhîa's clause, and even there is not admitted if L'garmeh follows. And *instead of these accents*—i. e. of Pazer and Great T'lisha; of Géresh in the clauses of Pashṭa, Zarqa, and T'bhîr; and of Géresh in R'bhîa's clause, when L'garmeh follows—*R'bhîa is used;* or if two of them come together, R'bhîa, preceded by Géresh (or less frequently L'garmeh), may be employed. It is these changes that occasion the most frequent variations in the accentuation.

2. The repetition of Zaqeph is not allowed. If due a second' or third time (according to our texts), *R'bhîa appears instead.*

3. *R'bhîa is not transformed* (as in the Palestinian system, see p. 90, 2) in Ṭiphcha's clause.

The result of the above variations is that many clauses are *over-burdened with R'bhîas.* The question suggests itself, Could such a system have ever been practically in use for chanting?

Let us next notice how these rules are carried out; and we shall see clearly that we have to do with a *derived*—not, as is generally supposed, an original and independent—system.

a. Of course, when R'bhîa takes the place of Pazer, Great T'lisha, or Géresh, the servi (if any) should be made to conform to the change of accent. But what do we find? *The original servi* (as I shall call them) *constantly left standing.* Thus, those of Pazer, כִּי־כֹה אָמַר־יְהוָה ׀ אֵלַי (Is. xxxi. 4); of T'lisha, וְשִׁבְעִים־אִישׁ מִזִּקְנֵי בֵית־יִשְׂרָאֵל (Ezek. viii. 11); and more conspicuously of Géresh, יוֹצִיאוּ אֶת־עַצְמוֹת מַלְכֵי־יְהוּדָה וְאֶת־ עַצְמוֹת־שָׂרָיו וְאֶת־עַצְמוֹת הַכֹּהֲנִים (Jer. viii. 1). And yet R'bhîa, when standing in its own right, has its servi in agreement with the Palestinian system, as in Is. v. 25; xi. 2; xxx. 6; &c.

β. So when Géresh stands for Pazer, Great T'lisha, or Pashṭa, *the servi of these accents remain,* e. g. of Pazer, אִם־לֹא יָעֵן הֱיוֹת־צֹאנִי ׀ לָבַז (Ezek. xxxiv. 8); of T'lisha, כִּי כַאֲשֶׁר הַשָּׁמַיִם הַחֳדָשִׁים (Is. lxvi. 22); of Pashṭa, לֹא־יִשָּׂא גוֹי אֶל־גּוֹי (Is. ii. 4). But Géresh, when originally due, has its regular and well-known servi, as may be seen everywhere in the text, e. g. Jer. iii. 1 (five servi) [16].

γ. The rule for the transformation of a second and third Zaqeph is regularly carried out [17]. Thus, כַּקּוֹנֶה כַּמּוֹכֵר כַּמַּלְוֶה כַּלֹּוֶה כַּנֹּשֶׁה כַּאֲשֶׁר נֹשֶׁא becomes כַּקּוֹנֶה כַּמּוֹכֵר כַּמַּלְוֶה כַּלֹּוֶה כַּנֹּשֶׁה כַּאֲשֶׁר נֹשֶׁא בוֹ׃ (Is. xxiv. 2).

---

[16] Note in connection with Géresh, וַיִּקַּח עֶבֶד־מֶלֶךְ אֶת־הָאֲנָשִׁים (Jer. xxxviii. 11), where וַיִּקַּח has evidently been taken from the Palestinian text, without any recognition of the value of L'garmeh (p. 118).

[17] The original accentuation sometimes shews itself through the disguise that has been thrown over it, as in Jer. xxviii. 11; xxxi. 23; xliv. 2; Ezek. xxiv. 27;

Here also we see that we have to do with a *derived* system; for where
Zaqeph (with two words in its clause) has Pashṭa preceding, as in the
example just quoted, R'bhîa takes Géresh before it, but where Zaqeph
has a servus, as מִמְּדִבָּר בָּא (Is. xxi. 1), R'bhîa retains the servus. Now
for Zaqeph there is a fixed rule, see p. 75; but there is no corresponding rule for R'bhîa in this system[18].

Observe also what confusion is the result of this transformation of
Zaqeph. There may be a R'bhîa subordinated to it,—as in Is. lxii. 4;
Jer. iii. 16; Ezek. xx. 28[b],—but instead of this R'bhîa being transformed to Géresh (or L'garmeh), as the sense requires, when R'bhîa
has taken the place of Zaqeph, it is allowed to remain! In short, as
with the servi above, the transformation has been only half carried
out.

δ. This system accepts the principle of the transformation of R'bhîa
in Zaqeph's clause; for where Pashṭa stands in our text, according to
the rule pp. 78–9, it has also Pashṭa[19]. In the few instances also in
Cod. Bab.,—Is. xx. 2; xlv. 14; Jer. xxi. 4; xxxvi. 32,—in which a
second R'bhîa is due before S'gôlta, transformation has taken place,
although not to Zarqa, as in our texts (see p. 88), but to L'garmeh.
[The query is, whether Zarqa was not originally intended; comp. the
similarity of the two signs, p. 143.] So far the Palestinian practice
has been followed. But the inconsistency that runs through the whole
system again shews itself. The rule for the transformation of R'bhîa
has not, and could not have, been carried out *generally*, or the main
characteristic of the system (p. 147) would have disappeared. Hence
two or more R'bhîas in immediate sequence are as common as can be.
Even in Ṭiphcha's clause the second R'bhîa stands, e.g. וַתֹּאמֶר בְרַב
רִכְבִּי אֲנִי עָלִיתִי מְרוֹם הָרִים (Is. xxxvii. 24), where we have רכב׳ (see the
rule and examples, p. 91). In Ezek. xl. 42 we find R'bhîa transformed
in the first half of the verse before Zaqeph, but *not* transformed in the
second half before Ṭiphcha.

It is unnecessary to go into further details. We may conclude, with
absolute certainty, from the instances cited, that the Palestinian punctuation was before the originators of this superlinear system[20]. Their

---

and Deut. ix. 5[b] (Ox. 64), where, through an oversight, the second Zaqeph *has been
left standing*. In Jer. xix. 15; xxv. 30; xxxv. 17, the second Zaqeph has been
transformed, but *not the third*.

[18] Another indication is that where our text has קָמֵץ בֻּזְקָף, and the Zaqeph is
changed into R'bhîa, Qāmeṣ still remains, as in Jer. ii.19; Ezek. vii.12; Hos. iii.4.

[19] Or, by some strange mistake,—as in Is. xxxviii. 3; Jer. v. 19[b]; xliii. 10,—
T'bhîr. That Pashṭa, however, is the proper sign is clear from the servus M'huppach preceding.

[20] I believe that it would be equally easy to shew that the superlinear *vocalization*, which, as a system, is far more complete and coherent, still presupposes the
Palestinian as a basis.

attempt, however, to modify and improve upon it must, as far at least as the accents are concerned, be pronounced a failure, and for us quite worthless. Inconsequent and contradictory, this new system is a mere travesty of the Palestinian. Even the simplicity apparently aimed at by the constant introduction of R'bhia leads only to confusion, by destroying the fine lines of distinction established for the sense by the older system.—I do not, of course, mean to deny the proper value attaching to Codd. with this peculiar notation, which consists in their furnishing Oriental readings, *quantum valeant*, not to be found else-where,—among which are accentual variations that are sometimes not without interest.

I have already mentioned that the superlinear system is found in a modified and much simpler form in MSS. that have been lately brought from Yemen. But these MSS. will not detain us. The *accentuation*, so far as it is superlinear [21], is in all cases *very incomplete*. Some-times it is confined to Silluq and Athnach [22]. At others, Zaqeph is found as well (often with a strange admixture of Palestinian signs) [23]. It need hardly be added that I have found these MSS. of no service to me in my investigations.

One point, which has escaped the notice of scholars, I may mention in conclusion. These Yemen MSS. do not exhibit the Oriental readings. We have in them the *Palestinian* text, with a superlinear punctuation.

---

[21] In Or. 1467, 2363, we find the confusing arrangement of the Palestinian accentuation with the superlinear vocalization. See Pl. LIV of the Palæo-graphical Society's Publications, Oriental Series (Or. 1467 is, however, incorrectly described there as of Babylonian or Persian origin).

[22] As in Or. 1469, 2373, 2374.

[23] In Or. 2366, 2368, 2703, 2704.

INDEX I. SUBJECTS.

(The numbers refer to the pages; n stands for note.)

INDEX II. HEBREW TECHNICAL TERMS.

INDEX III. SCRIPTURE PASSAGES.

THE END.